Philosophy and Contemporary Issues

Seven:
Art and
Society

Philosophy and Contemporary Issues

THIRD EDITION

John R. Burr
Milton Goldinger

University of Wisconsin — Oshkosh

Macmillan Publishing Co., Inc
NEW YORK
Collier Macmillan Publishers
LONDON

Macmillan Publishing Co., Inc.
866 Third Avenue, New York, New York 10022
Collier Macmillan Canada, Ltd.

Library of Congress Cataloging in Publication Data

Burr, John Roy   comp.
  Philosophy and contemporary issues.

  Includes bibliographies.
    1. Philosophy, Modern—20th century—Collected works.
2. Philosophy—Collected works. I. Goldinger, Milton,
1936– joint comp. II. Title.
B804.A1B87 1980   190'.9'04   79-12668
ISBN 0-02-317240-1

Printing: 3   4   5   6   7   8   Year: 1   2   3   4   5   6

Preface to the Third Edition

The continuing and increasingly favorable response to *Philosophy and Contemporary Issues* prompts this third edition. The general aim of our book, as stated in the Preface to the First Edition, remains the same.

About a third of this new edition consists of new material. The editors have made every effort to choose selections not only for their philosophic interest but also for their clarity and readability.

We wish to thank Kenneth J. Scott, Philosophy Editor of the Macmillan Publishing Company, the many users of our book who have been kind enough to send us their comments and criticisms, the Oshkosh Public Library, the University of Wisconsin-Oshkosh Library, and Mrs. Nathalie Moore.

J. R. B.
M. G.

Preface to the Second Edition

The very favorable response to *Philosophy and Contemporary Issues* prompts this second edition. The aim of our book, as stated in the Preface to the First Edition, remains the same.

However, a significant amount of new material has been added to this second edition. Part Four, "Democracy and Society." is new, bringing the total number of parts to seven instead of the six of the first edition. At least one or more new readings have been added to each of the original six parts of the first edition. A few readings have been eliminated.

We wish to thank Kenneth J. Scott, Philosophy Editor of the Macmillan Publishing Company, the Oshkosh Public Library, the University of Wisconsin-Oshkosh Library, Mrs. Nathalie Moore, and Ms. Ann L. Youmans for their help.

J.R.B.
M.G.

Preface to the First Edition

The purpose of this anthology is to show how philosophy illuminates and in some measure helps solve some of the important problems troubling contemporary man. The editors intend it to be an introductory text. Unfortunately, many introductory texts in philosophy are flawed by one of two major defects: (1) they are too difficult for the beginning student or (2) they are too simple for the beginning student. Some introductory philosophy texts are introductory in name only because they demand of the philosophically innocent student a mastery of technical philosophical language and a knowledge of the history of philosophy one could reasonably expect only from a professional philosopher. No wonder students struggling to understand such books become convinced of the truth of the popular view that philosophy is a subject wholly unintelligible to all except a few compulsive adepts and completely irrelevant to life outside of the classroom. On the other hand, in an attempt to eliminate excessive philosophical sophistication, other introductory philosophy texts are philosophical in name only because they contain no technical philosophy. Not surprisingly, students reading such books in order to learn about philosophy as a distinct discipline find them hollow and conclude philosophy is not worth serious study.

In designing the structure of this book, in selecting the readings, in writing the introductions to the various parts, and in choosing the books to be listed in the bibliographies, the editors have striven to produce a work avoiding both defective extremes. Throughout, the guiding aim has been to make philosophy interesting and intelligible to students undertaking their first sustained study of the subject and, above all, to encourage them to engage in philosophizing themselves. To achieve this end, each part of this volume contains pro and con articles on provocative contemporary issues, which in turn raise fundamental philosophical issues. In addition to the material dealing directly with contemporary issues, each part includes other selections discussing at length and in depth some of the philosophical problems raised by the contemporary controversies. Therefore, each part forms a coherent unit of mutually relevant sections rather than a miscellaneous grouping. Every effort has been made to pick readings for their substance, their intelligibility, and their freshness for the beginning student of philosophy. Since the editors planned a single volume and not a library, not all philosophical issues, positions, movements, and methods could be included. It should also be pointed out that the readings in one part often will throw light on the material dealt with in other parts. Of course, the decisions as to what material is covered in his course and in what order it is taken up are those of the individual instructor. Nothing is implied by the order in which the parts of this book are arranged.

This introductory text in philosophy is a mutual enterprise, each editor sharing equally in the work of its production and benefiting from the comments and suggestions of his colleague.

We wish to thank Charles E. Smith, former Philosophy Editor of the Macmillan Publishing Company, the Oshkosh Public Library, the Wisconsin State University-Oshkosh Library, and Mrs. Natalie Moore for their help.

J.R.B.
M.G.

Contents

Five:
Mind and Body   293

Six:
Knowledge and Science   355

Seven:
Art and Society   461

General Introduction

Many university and college students take their academic courses as travelers visit Eufaula, Alabama; Sweetgrass, Montana; or Passadumkeag, Maine. They simply pass through and go on their way. After a short passage of time, memory fades out and the experience leaves no detectable trace. Obviously, in such cases the students have wasted their time in class and the professor has squandered his. On the contrary, if a course of study is to be worthwhile, the subject matter must be assimilated by the student. Worthwhile philosophy courses provide no counterinstances to this generalization.

This process of assimilating a subject means more than diligently and doggedly memorizing names, dates, and definitions—more than the accumulating of inert information long enough to pass examinations and then allowing it to scatter, soon to be lost. A student who truly assimilates a subject finds himself changed in significant ways at the conclusion of his philosophy course. In this respect, taking a philosophy course should be analogous to undergoing battle in war, getting married, or giving birth to a child. At least some of the beliefs, values, methods of thinking, and general attitudes of the students should be altered.

But altered in what way? The editors of this volume think the change should be from less to more intellectual independence on the part of the student. An introductory philosophy course cannot transform a neophyte into a professional philosopher, a sophomore into a profound thinker. Still, it can strengthen students' courage and skill in thinking for themselves. An introductory philosophy course can advance the enlightenment of students. Immanuel Kant, one of the great philosophers, wrote an essay entitled "What Is Enlightenment," in which he defined *Enlightenment* in the following words:

> Enlightenment is the emergence of man from the immaturity for which he is himself responsible. Immaturity is the inability to use one's understanding without the guidance of another. Man is responsible for his own immaturity, when it is caused, by lack not of understanding, but of the resolution and the courage to use it without the guidance of another. *Sapere aude!* Have the courage to use your own reason! is the slogan of the Enlightenment.

3

Of course, Kant was trying to articulate the spirit of the eighteenth-century Enlightenment. Nevertheless, such "enlightenment" is not something appropriate only to a past historical period. It must be renewed in every age, particularly in our own, which the classical scholar Gilbert Murray has dubbed an "age of lying." And we must remember that in the story it was a youngster who dared to say out loud that the Emperor was wearing no clothes. Often young people have not become hopelessly habituated to hypocrisy and intellectual conformity as have their elders. Many university or college students have not degenerated as yet to the state of the average American who reacts to new ideas much like he reacts to the onset of Asian flu and who denounces all critical thinking concerning fundamental assumptions as sheer cynicism. The youthfulness of students, in short, argues a certain plasticity, a willingness to change. At least occasionally many students, however vaguely, recognize their immaturity in Kant's sense of the term. They know they possess the understanding but need the courage and resolution to use their reason "without the guidance of another."

Students tend to distrust authority, be it political, moral, aesthetic, scientific, religious, parental, academic, or that of the adolescent herd. Chaotic visions and confused indignations afflict them. However dimly and erratically, students want "enlightenment," intellectual independence; at least the best among them in their best moments desire to be bold and skeptical, not timid and believing. Therefore, however unconsciously, they desire to philosophize, to clarify and criticize basic assumptions in all fields, to free themselves from conventional pictures of reality by constructing new ones and defending them by argument.

Philosophy has performed many different functions in the course of its long history. Certainly not the least of these in importance has been the encouragement of intellectual independence. Because of their advocacy and practice of intellectual independence, philosophers again and again have appeared dangerous to their fellows and as a consequence have been persecuted by them. The ancient Greeks invented philosophy as they did so many other cultural disciplines. The ancient Greeks also were typical of "good" citizens in all times and places for they distrusted many of their best men, considered them subversive, persecuted them, exiled them, and even executed some of them. All educated people know the fate of Socrates, who questioned the soundness of conventional morality, ironically exposing the bogus "wisdom" of politicians, priests, and prominent citizens, and casting doubt on the superior virtue of democracy. Socrates attempted to substitute the authority of reason in place of the authority of tradition, myth, and majority opinion and to quicken the torpid intellectual life of the community by his probing questions.

However, the task of intellectual vivification to which Socrates devoted himself must be undertaken anew by every generation. Contemporary "good" citizens closely resemble those of ancient Athens in their distrust of unconventional ideas and their opposition to the assertion of intellectual independence. A prominent American educator recently declared:

> There seems to be nothing in the study of chemistry that makes you feel like a superior order of being, but you study Plato and you begin to believe you're a philosopher—and a philosopher should be king. This is a dangerous trend, and it jeopardizes the democratic principles on which this country was founded.[1]

In the *Apology,* Plato represents his teacher, Socrates, defending himself against the charges of corrupting the youth and introducing strange gods by saying:

> Men of Athens, I honor and love you; but I shall obey God rather than you, and while I have life and strength I shall never cease from the practice and teaching of philosophy, exhorting anyone whom I meet and saying to him after my manner: You, my friend,—a citizen of the great and mighty and wise city of Athens,—are you not ashamed of heaping up the greatest amount of money and honor and reputation, and caring so little about wisdom and truth and the greatest improvement of the soul, which you never regard or heed at all?

This is the most fundamental contemporary issue confronting every thinking individual personally: Are you on the side of Socrates or on that of his accusers?

The argument against the development of intellectual independence claims that it will result in anarchy, destroying law and order. Socrates, on the contrary, contended that a society where reason is sovereign will be more stable and just than any other because such a rational collective life will rest on knowledge, not on ignorance, fear, fraud, and force. Socrates further seemed to hold that truth is consistent and unchanging. Therefore, to the extent that men know the truth, they will agree. Men disagree through ignorance. Hence, the ideal or "real" community, being based on full knowledge of all the truth, would be free of internal dissension and perfectly stable, having taken on the characteristics of truth. The hegemony of reason will produce the only enduring social unity and harmony, the only "real" law and order. Appeal to authorities other than reason produces only a temporary and therefore illusory simulacrum of social order and harmony. Socrates was tried and condemned to death for introducing strange gods and corrupting the youth. He was found guilty by a jury of his peers and probably rightly so. Reason is a strange god and corrupts provincial ignorance and complacency.

[1]Dr. Samuel I. Hayakawa, "The Playboy Panel: Student Revolt," *Playboy,* September 1969, p. 98. Reprinted by permission of *Playboy.*

This book of introductory readings in philosophy now in your hands has been designed in the spirit of Socrates. The readings have been selected and arranged in order to encourage the student to use his own reason. Socrates counted men and women truly his followers, not because they agreed with his conclusions but because they dared to "follow the argument wherever it may lead." The son of a father who was a stonecutter and of a mother who practiced the trade of midwife, Socrates neglected stonecutting, in which he had been trained, and in a sense adopted the vocation of his mother. Socrates called himself an intellectual midwife, helping others to give birth to the new ideas with which their minds already were pregnant. Nearly every day Socrates could be found in the busy public square of ancient Athens, where all day long he buttonholed the rich politicians, poets, generals, businessmen, actors, philosophers, and all the Rotarians and intellectuals and "beautiful people," all the shrewd old men of power and the clever young men of ambition of his time, and asked them searching questions about what they were doing, what they wanted, what they believed and why they were doing, wanting, believing it. As the great and powerful, the talented, the learned, the old, and the young passed by, Socrates asked them: What do you really want? Riches, power, happiness, knowledge? Is the Good pleasure and Evil pain? Does might really make right? What is love and what is worthy of love? Should children always obey their parents? How do you know your teacher really is wise? What can be taught and learned and what not? Can anything be taught? Who should rule the city: politicians, wealthy families, soldiers, intellectuals, artists? Do the gods really exist? Is there a life after death? Or is religion a confidence game perpetrated by clever priests? Who knows the truth: philosophers, inspired artists, men of practical experience, or drug-crazed oracles? And what is "truth"? In short, Socrates put the questions asked by intelligent, sensitive, civilized people—the questions that always occur to young people—indeed, many of the questions no doubt formulated at one time or another by you, the reader.

It has been well said that philosophy begins in the conflict of opinions. Each part of this book contains a section of readings dealing with certain contemporary issues, with some of the questions asked and discussed in the public life of America today: Can men be made happy by science? Is anyone ever responsible for his acts and deserving of punishment? Should obscene art be censored? Do we live forever or rot when we are dead? Do we need religion to lead a meaningful life? Can scientific technology solve our ecological problems, or must we look to mystical insight instead? Are men merely complex machines? Can we have a sound sexual morality? Should society promote greater equality, or should it encourage excellence?

The selections chosen for each contemporary issue clearly conflict with one another. Both affirmative and negative sides of the debate are presented on each issue, and every effort has been made by the editors to find equally powerful and persuasive statements both *pro* and *con.*

Yet whatever the issue, as men reflect and by argument are driven back to question their fundamental assumptions, as the protagonists discover they were ignorant of their own ignorance, as they realize they know least about that of which they talk most, then debate and discussion mature into philosophical inquiry. Etymologically, *philosophy* means "love of wisdom." This definition may satisfy the beginning student temporarily. However, more probing queries soon come to mind. What is love? What is wisdom? Does Jean-Paul Sartre really love wisdom? Was William James really wise? Traditionally, philosophy has been surveyed into such general fields as Ethics, Metaphysics, Logic, Epistemology, and, more recently, Aesthetics or Philosophy of Art. Library catalogues still divide philosophy in this manner. Yet this approach with its dry and abstract schematism sheds little illumination for the unskilled in philosophy. The editors judge that students will derive the most enlightenment from first encountering philosophy as a congeries of problems or issues invariably met by men when they no longer are content to reflect superficially on human life. As long as men are certain that their fundamental assumptions in morality, politics, religion, art, science, and other cultural enterprises are true and complete, they do not philosophize. If they argue, it is only over matters of detail, over the application to particular cases of commonly accepted principles. In our revolutionary era, no such complacency remains honorable for intelligent and informed people. The Contemporary Issues sections in each part of the book show men being led to question their fundamental assumptions. Grouped with the Contemporary Issues selections are readings scrutinizing some of the relevant philosophical issues all too often left implicit. One cannot sensibly discuss whether or not religion is necessary to a meaningful life until he has settled for himself the question of whether or not religion is an illusion. How can men be praised or blamed if they are not morally responsible but are complex machines? Why censor art if it produces no effect on human conduct? Why should we elect car salesmen, country lawyers, chicken farmers, real estate agents, and other such people ignorant of science to the United States Congress if all genuine knowledge comes from science? Faced with questions such as these, one may ignore them and play golf, make money, watch television—in short, act the typical middle-class citizen of the world and be content to be a fatuous, go-getting cipher. Or he may pluck up his courage and think for himself, follow his own reason, and philosophize.

Intellectual independence does not necessitate the repudiation of all tradition. Ample and venerable precedent exists for inaugurating a new enterprise with ten commandments. Here are ten commandments for beginning philosophizers written down by the late Bertrand Russell, one of the most intellectually independent men of our day:

1 Do not feel certain of anything.

2 Do not think it worthwhile to produce belief by concealing evidence, for the evidence is sure to come to light.

3 Never try to discourage thinking, for you are sure to succeed.

4 When met with opposition, even if it should be from your husband or your children, endeavour to overcome it by argument and not by authority, for a victory dependent upon authority is unreal and illusory.

5 Have no respect for the authority of others, for there are always contrary authorities to be found.

6 Do not use power to suppress opinions you think pernicious, for if you do the opinions will suppress you.

7 Do not fear to be eccentric in opinion, for every opinion now accepted was once eccentric.

8 Find more pleasure in intelligent dissents than in passive agreement, for, if you value intelligence as you should, the former implies a deeper agreement than the latter.

9 Be scrupulously truthful, even when truth is inconvenient, for it is more inconvenient when you try to conceal it.

10 Do not feel envious of the happiness of those who live in a fool's paradise, for only a fool will think that it is happiness.[2]

---

[2]Bertrand Russell, *The Independent,* June 1965, p. 4. Reprinted by permission of *The Independent.*

What Philosophy Can Be

1. Philosophy: The Guide of Life   C. J. Ducasse

Curt John Ducasse (1881–1969), born in France and educated in the United States, was a distinguished American philosopher and teacher of philosophy. His interests and writings ranged widely from philosophy of religion, metaphysics, and aesthetics to psychical research. He is the author of numerous books, including *Philosophy as a Science: Its Matter and Method; Nature, Mind, and Death;* and *A Critical Examination of the Belief in a Life After Death.*

In *The History of Phi Beta Kappa* by Oscar M. Voorhees we read that *Philosophia Biou Kubernetes,* the Greek phrase that gives the Society its name, was "formed and adopted" by John Heath, a student of Greek classics at the College of William and Mary, on whose initiative the Phi Beta Kappa Society was founded in 1776. This phrase—philosophy, or love of wisdom, the guide of life—and the Latin phrase *Societas Philosophiae,* the initials of which appear on the reverse of the Phi Beta Kappa key, express the five founders' conviction about the right role of philosophy in life.

But although taking philosophy as one's guide through life seemed to John Heath and his fellow-students an eminently wise resolve, today the perspective in which educated people view human life is different from that of 1776; and members of Phi Beta Kappa may find themselves challenged to give reasons for adopting philosophy as the guide of life in preference to religion or to science, either of which today enjoys far more general prestige than does philosophy. I propose to consider those reasons here.

Why Not Science as Guide?

At the time of the founding of Phi Beta Kappa any suggestion that man should take science rather than philosophy as his guide in the conduct of his life would have been hardly intelligible. The investigation of puzzling natural phenomena was not commonly thought to be a potential source of counsels for living. The justification, if any, for studying the mysteries of nature was held to lie only in such gratification of idle curiosity as it might yield to the few impractical persons who engaged in that study. The attitude then prevalent towards their research is well exempli-

From *The Key Reporter,* Vol. XXIII, No. 2 (January, 1958). Reprinted with the permission of *The Key Reporter* and Phi Beta Kappa.

fied by the reaction that greeted the first observations of electric current, made about 1786 by Luigi Galvani, then professor of physiology at the University of Bologna.

The story is that his wife was ill with tuberculosis; and her physician having prescribed a broth made with frogs' legs to give her strength, Galvani was getting some ready for cooking one day, sitting on his balcony. As he proceeded he suspended each pair of legs from the balcony's railing by a copper hook; and he noticed that whenever any of the legs so suspended happened to touch the iron uprights, the leg muscles contracted sharply.

This curious little fact, however, had no discernible utility, nor did it fit in with the scientific knowledge possessed in his day. Hence nobody took seriously what he reported. "I am attacked," he complained in 1792, "by two quite opposite sects—the learned and the ignorant. The ones and the others laugh at me and call me the frogs' dancing master. Yet I know that I have discovered one of the forces of nature."

Other reports of facts or theories belying what W. F. G. Swann has called "the common sense of a given epoch" have encountered a similar attitude, which has been a persistent feature of the history of science. Nevertheless science developed rapidly during the nineteenth century and has continued to do so at an even faster pace in the twentieth. The result of this has been, in the words of Sir William Dampier, that "the whole conception of the natural Universe has been changed by the recognition that man, subject to the same physical laws and processes as the world around him, cannot be considered separately from that world, and that scientific methods of observation, induction, deduction and experiment are applicable, not only to the original subject matter of pure science, but to nearly all the many and varied fields of human thought and activity."[1]

Furthermore, the fruits of pure scientific research have in many cases turned out to be applicable to the solution of concrete practical problems; and in civilized countries these practical applications have immeasurably improved the material conditions of human life. That science has put into the hands of man power undreamed of before over the processes of nature, and enabled him to utilize her forces for attainment of his purposes, is today evident to everybody, and accounts for the enormous prestige science now enjoys.

On the other hand, the fact is now becoming all too evident that the ledger of scientific progress has a debit as well as a credit side. The power that scientific knowledge brings has indeed made possible the cure or prevention of many diseases; it has provided new and highly efficient means of production, communication, and transportation; and it has given man all the convenient gadgets on which he is today so dependent. But at the same time it has complicated his life, robbed it in large measure of the joy of craftsmanship, multiplied its needs, and brought it new diseases and ghastly perils. The natural sciences and the might they have brought to man are in themselves wholly neutral as regards values; they lend them-

---

[1]Sir William Dampier, *A History of Science* (New York, Macmillan, 1936) p. 217.

selves equally to the efficient implementation of good and of evil purposes.

But whereas in the last hundred years the natural sciences have made more progress than in the preceding thousands, the soul of man, on the contrary, has during that time undergone no great change. Some customs and institutions have altered, but the passions that are the main springs of human conduct have remained much the same. Men are better informed today but probably not much more intelligent than before; their economic standard of living has risen; but when occasion offers, they exhibit a nature hardly less selfish or brutal or greedy than of old. They are not fundamentally much more self-disciplined, honest, kindly, or wise than in earlier ages. Measured in terms of spiritual maturity, the average man today is still a child. And it is in the hands of that child that the natural sciences, almost overnight, have placed powers that in their magnitude and possibilities of evil, no less than of good, are to those man had earlier as dynamite is to the strength of bare hands. Great nations have risen in the past only to fall victim to destructive forces within them. But today it is the whole of life on earth, or even the very earth itself, the continued existence of which is in danger.

Obviously, then, if man is to be saved, what he now needs is not more of the power the natural sciences bring, but more wisdom wherewith to direct the use he makes of the powers he already has.

Why Not Religion as Guide?

For such direction, and for the serenity that obedience to it brings, men have traditionally turned to religion. But to many people nowadays religion no longer carries the authority it did in earlier times.

A number of factors are responsible for this. As a result of efficient means of communication and transportation, men—and especially educated men—are better acquainted than in earlier times with the religions of mankind other than their own. A person with the wider perspective of such acquaintance sees that the dogmas of the other religions are different from, and sometimes irreconcilable with, those of his own; and yet that the needs that turn men to religion are on the whole satisfied by the other religions for their devotees as effectively as they are satisfied for him by his own.

Furthermore, he realizes that if he had been born and brought up in a different part of the world, his religion would almost automatically have been the one that happened to prevail in that particular region. And this thrusts upon him the question whether the location of a man's birthplace determines not merely which religion he *will believe,* but also its *truth or falsity.* And of course merely to ask this question is virtually to answer it, especially in an epoch when so many of the traditional religious teachings about the place of the earth in the universe, the age and history of the earth, and the origin of life and of man, have been conclusively disproved by the knowledge that science has produced in lieu of mere creeds, pious opinions, and crude cosmological or biological fancies handed down by the religious traditions.

In the light of these and similar considerations, the articles of faith of the various religions—of one's own as well as of the others—are seen to be not statements known to be true or false, but essentially *psychological tools:* instruments mankind has automatically devised for performance of certain important social and personal functions. For religious dogmas to influence the conduct, the feelings, and the attitudes of men, they need not be true but need only be firmly *believed.*

Like other tools, moreover, they can be used otherwise than in the beneficent manner that gives them worth. As we know only too well, bigoted men who were ignorant, stupid, arrogant, sadistic or perverse, and who happened to have power over their fellows, have too often interpreted the dogmas of their religion as warranting the wars, persecutions, and senseless cruelties that stain the histories of even the monotheistic, self-styled higher religions. This forces on modern man's attention the fact that the religions, like the sciences, are ambivalent and have a dark side; and hence that the teachings contained in their various sacred books or promulgated by their officials cannot be uncritically assumed to supply ready-made the wise guidance that man so direly needs. Rather, those teachings have to be carefully sifted and the wisdom or folly of each intelligently appraised.

How About Philosophy?

And this brings us back to philosophy. Does it offer a better prospect than either science or religion of furnishing man with the wisdom he needs?

In the popular opinion at least, hardly so. For philosophy is commonly reputed to be nearly the most nebulous and impractical thing there is. Yet if philosophy were really so remote from practical affairs, it would be hard to understand either the execration or the veneration in which various philosophers have at times been held. Why, for instance, should Socrates, Hypatia, and Giordano Bruno have been put to death, Plato sold into slavery, and Campanella imprisoned, for voicing the philosophical opinions they held? On the other side of the picture, why should the same Plato have sometimes been referred to as "the divine Plato," and Kant as "the immortal Kant"? Why have their writings and those of other great philosophers continued to be read and prized through the centuries?

The answer, I believe, lies in the fact that philosophy, despite the seeming idleness of some of its technicalities, really has practical import and indeed in this respect may ultimately outrank most things of more obvious utility.

The nature of the practical value peculiar to philosophy will become evident if we try to gain a clearer conception than is common of what philosophy and philosophical reflection in fact are.

Philosophical reflection is not an activity indulged in only by specialists called philosophers who allegedly live in architectural monstrosities known as ivory towers. Just as each of us at times engages casually in horticulture or medicine or carpentry without special training, so practically all of us on certain occasions spontaneously occupy ourselves with philosophical questions.

We may, for example, read in the newspapers of a child born hopelessly malformed and defective, but who, if operated upon at once, might nonetheless be kept alive. And we may read further that the physician in charge, realizing that the child's life could not be other than a grievous burden to himself, to his parents, and to society, refrained from operating and allowed the child to die. Then, in letters from readers to the editors of newspapers all over the country, controversy rages about whether the physician's action was morally right or morally wrong. And even if we do not ourselves take active part in them, we too form opinions on the question.

In such a controversy the participants do not merely state their moral appraisal of the physician's course. They also give reasons of one kind or another to support the validity of their judgment. And if these reasons are in turn challenged, each participant brings forth considerations he believes adequate to vindicate the validity of his reasons.

The reasons, and the reasons for the reasons, that are thus appealed to as grounds for endorsing or condemning the physician's action, constitute a moral philosophy, or at least a fragment of one. And the mental activity of searching for those reasons, and of then so editing them as to purge them of the inconsistencies or exaggerations or errors that opponents were able to point out, constitute philosophizing, or philosophical reflection.

In this example the issue is a moral one, and the philosophy constructed on the spur of the occasion by a participant is therefore, as far as it goes, a moral philosophy: that is, a theory of the nature of the difference between moral right and wrong, and of the nature of the situations to which appraisal in terms of morality and immorality is congruous. But similar controversies, or indeed doubts within one person's mind, arise about issues of other kinds: about the merits of certain works of art, for example, or about educational issues, or about the sufficiency of the evidence offered as basis for a given assertion, and so on. The fragmentary philosophies similarly improvised on such occasions are then a philosophy of art, a philosophy of education, or a philosophy of knowledge. And there can be no doubt that, on the occasions impelling us to engage in such reflection, a judgment shaped by the conclusions reached in that reflective manner is likely to be wiser than would be one made without it.

Practical problems of the type illustrated induce philosophical reflection automatically and cannot be solved without it if the solution is to be rational, not arbitrary. Let us call them *practical problems of appraisal*. They do not arise from ignorance or misinformation about the objective circumstances of the action or thing appraised. The disagreement concerning the moral rightness or wrongness of the physician's inaction did not arise from a difference of opinion about the possibility of the child's being cured eventually if he had lived. If this was the issue, it was then medical, not philosophical.

A divergence of appraisals is philosophical only if the conflicting judgments are of strictly the same action or thing in the same circumstances. When this is the case, the divergence of appraisals has one of two sources. One is inadequate understanding of the criterion of moral rightness or wrongness, or, as the case may be, of truth or falsity, of justice or injustice, of beauty or ugliness, of wisdom or folly, and so forth. The ordinary ingenuous understanding we all have of the meaning of such predicates is good enough to enable us to apply them without doubt or dispute in stereotyped cases. Hence in such cases problems of the type in view do not arise. If one does arise, it is because the case concerned is not a stereotyped one and therefore requires a more precise, analytical understanding of the meaning of the value-predicate employed, in order to reach a responsible, not arbitrary, appraisal. One needs to know, for example, precisely what constitutes the moral rightness or wrongness of an action.

The other possible source of divergence of appraisals is uncertainty about the congruity of appraising the action in terms of the proposed value-predicate. For example, could the act of rubbing one's chin in ordinary circumstances be, without incongruity, judged either morally right or morally wrong? What characteristics must something have in order that it may appropriately be appraised in moral terms, rather than in, perhaps, aesthetic terms?

Philosophical reflection is the only process by which divergence of appraisal arising from either of these two sources can be responsibly removed. If one engages in philosophical reflection under pressure of immediate need to solve a particular practical problem of appraisal, such reflection will inevitably be hasty and relatively uncritical. But the persons called philosophers make it their life work to reflect on the meaning of the various value-predicates and on the kind of subject that is alone congruously appraisable in terms of each. They attempt to purge such reflection of the narrowness and imprecision that are the unavoidable defects of the extempore philosophical reflection we all undertake as occasion compels. Not only does the philosopher strive to carry on his reflections in a thoroughly methodical manner; he also strives to make them comprehensive rather than particularistic. That is, his business as a philosopher is not to solve himself the many practical problems of appraisal. It is, on the one hand, to clarify, in the two directions described, the various value-concepts that enter into the formulation of the problems; and on the other, to specify the kinds of empirical knowledge that must be obtained in order to discern whether or not a given appraisal is valid in a given case. Actually to obtain that empirical knowledge is not the business of the philosopher; it is the business of the particular person who is confronted with a particular practical problem of appraisal.

Clarification of the meaning of terms, however, whether in general or in the particular case of terms of appraisal, is a semantic task. Consequently the question immediately suggests itself whether philosophical reflection, in undertaking it, is not concerning itself with mere words, and therefore, presumably, with something of no great importance.

The answer is that to speak of "mere words" is much like speaking of "mere dynamite." For although words do not in themselves control the processes of inanimate nature, they do control the thoughts, the feelings, and the acts of men—initiating and shaping them, or inhibiting them. In men's dealings with one another and in the individual's dealings with himself, words are analogous in function and in importance to the insignificant-looking switches that govern the operations of giant machines in industry.

Hence it is of the greatest moment for man to know just where the psychological wires lead from the verbal switches; for the terrible thing about words is that to a great extent they cause and shape the acts of men, whether or not they really fit the things to which men apply them, and whether or not men understand their meaning correctly. Common sayings such as "Give a dog a bad name, and you can hang him," or "Slander on, some of it always sticks," testify to this fact. Among us today, for example, to call a man a Communist is to damage his reputation even if it is not true that he is a Communist, and even if the persons who hear him so called have but the vaguest idea of what communism is. And, similarly, the most potent of the weapons Communists have employed is perversion of the meaning of words: calling "liberation" what is in fact enslavement, for example.

Thus when the words we use do not fit or are ill-understood, the feelings, the beliefs, and the courses of action they nonetheless generate cheat our aims and stultify us. This is especially true when the words concerned are value-predicates, for a man's course is shaped at innumerable points by evaluative statements. Whether he formulates these for himself or accepts them from others ready-made, they determine the basic policies, the tactics, and the strategic decisions of his life. This vast power of language is what gives outstanding practical importance to clear, analytical knowledge of just which things our substantives denote, and just what characters our adjectives predicate of the things to which we apply them.

Love of Wisdom as the Guide of Life

In conclusion let us consider briefly the term "wisdom" and note the light that philosophical analysis of its meaning throws on Phi Beta Kappa's counsel to take philosophy—that is, love of wisdom—as the guide of life.

What exactly, then, is wisdom? It consists in *knowledge of what in given circumstances would on the whole be the best thing for a person with given equipment to do.*

Thus the counsel to make love of wisdom the guide of one's life packs together four distinct recommendations, which may be separately stated.

One is that, when a person attempts to reach a wise decision about a difficult practical problem, he should inform himself as accurately and completely as is practicable about its *objective circumstances.*

Another is that, with similar care, he should take stock of *the powers at his disposal:* on the one hand, of the diverse means he happens to have, any one of which would enable him to achieve a particular end he might decide on; and on the other, of the diverse ends, any one of which he could achieve with the particular stock of means he commands.

The third recommendation is that he should then consider *the various kinds of value*—positive and negative, intrinsic and instrumental—which, for the persons who would be affected, would follow from each of the courses of action open to him in the circumstances of the case, with only the particular powers he has.

And the fourth recommendation is that, when he has thus considered as well as he can all the values at stake, he should then choose the course of action that *on the whole is best,* or *least bad:* the course that, *everything considered,* will probably yield the maximum total positive value, or the minimum total negative value.

Needless to say, this choice will in many cases be anything but easy or confident. And the person who makes it may well come eventually to judge it to have been mistaken. But this will be the judgment of the wiser person he will then have become by learning from his mistakes. At the time a decision has to be made, however, no way exists for any man to make a wiser one than by the procedure just described. For "wisdom"— so much of it as in practice happens to be obtainable by a given person at a given time—*means* what emerges out of that procedure.

Finally, under the shelter of the preceding elucidations I shall venture to state as a sharp choice what I take to be the gist of Phi Beta Kappa's advice to its initiates. And to formulate it I shall borrow the sharp words of the title of a book on a somewhat similar theme, written by an Australian journalist.

That sharp choice, so sharply worded, is *Think—or be damned!*[2]

---

[2]Brian Penton, *Think—or be damned* (Sydney, Angus and Robertson, 1944).

One:
Freedom
or
Determinism

Introduction

As currently discussed, the issue of whether man's behavior is free or determined has been generated by the development of the natural sciences since
the sixteenth century. A basic assumption of the evolving sciences was universal causation, i.e., that every event has a cause. Further, it was thought
that events occurred in orderly patterns, which could be formulated as causal
or natural laws. On the basis of these laws and knowledge of the actual
causes at work, accurate predictions would be made. In principle, any event
could be predicted; it was only the lack of knowledge of the laws or the present causes that limited prediction. The theory asserting universal causation
and total predictability traditionally has been called *determinism.*

For the determinist, human actions are events as predictable as any other
type of event. Just as the behavior of water heated to 212 degrees can be
predicted, so, in principle, can the behavior of a person given a million
dollars. The determinist would admit that, at the moment, the latter sort of
prediction cannot be made reliably because we lack the necessary exact laws
of human behavior. Someday, however, the social sciences may find such
laws, and correct predictions will become possible.

In "The Arguments for Determinism," Herman Horne, though not himself a
determinist, presents a clear, concise statement of some of the main
arguments for determinism. He states that the laws and working hypotheses
of both the natural and social sciences eliminate any role for freedom in
human conduct. He asserts that even ethics and theology may require a
deterministic conception of human behavior.

Determinism is rejected by a group of theorists holding a position called
libertarianism. Although libertarians present a number of specific criticisms
of determinism, most of these objections are concerned primarily with what
appears to be a consequence of that position. Libertarians contend that if all
actions are the result of causes (and those causes of other causes, and so
on), then no actions are ones for which anyone can be held morally
responsible. The robber sticking up a bank today does so as a result of a
series of causes which can be traced back prior to his birth. His behavior
results from such factors as his education, a lack of parental love, and the
nutritional quality of the food he ate as a child. In turn, these causes flow
from the kind of education his parents received, their lack of parental love,
and other such elements. How can the robber justifiably be held responsible

or blamed for his behavior? He could not help the way his parents treated him nor the manner in which they were educated. For the libertarian, to be considered responsible for an act is to be free to have acted otherwise; but such freedom apparently cannot exist when all human actions are the predictable outcome of various causes. In "Freedom of Choice and Human Responsibility," Corliss Lamont presents a detailed defense of libertarianism. He maintains that we have an immediate, powerful, common-sense intuition that we are free. While such an intuition could be false, it puts the burden of proving that it is so on the determinists. Also, Lamont maintains that determinism must be considered false because if it were true it would imply that all deliberation is illusory since one never can choose. To maintain that all our deliberation never results in any real choice seems, to Lamont, absurd.

Not all philosophers have been willing to accept the libertarian claim that determinism erases moral responsibility. Some, defending *soft determinism,* maintain that people can be morally responsible even though their behavior is determined. One argument soft determinists frequently use holds that a person's behavior is free if it is not the result of any compulsion. If you go to the movies because you wish to and are not pressured or coerced by anyone to do so, then your action ordinarily would be called a free one. Of course your wish is the result of numerous causes swarming in your background. Thus, we have an action which is determined and yet called "free." The soundness of this soft determinist argument depends on the cogency of the analysis of the meaning of "free." W. T. Stace defends soft determinism in his article "The Problem of Free Will."

A number of important issues have arisen as a result of different views regarding determinism. One often debated issue concerns the control of human behavior. Determinists see enormous possibilities in directing the development of man through the study of the hereditary and environmental factors influencing behavior. Many look forward to the day when the various social sciences will have formulated laws which allow us to produce happier and "better" people. The selections from B. F. Skinner's *Walden Two* give us a famous psychologist's view of an ideal society possibly resulting from a greater knowledge of human conditioning. Skinner argues that through the application of various conditioning and reinforcement techniques, we can produce people who have those psychological characteristics necessary for a productive and viable society. In the selection, he shows how children might be conditioned to have self-control and a large degree of tolerance to annoying situations. It should be kept in mind that Skinner does not desire to manipulate men otherwise free; rather, he wants to change present causal determinants for ones productive of more capable and happy human beings.

Libertarians maintain that precise laws of human behavior will always elude investigators because such behavior, being undetermined, is unpredictable.

Other philosophers think human behavior may be controllable someday, but they fear the manner in which such power might be used. In "Ignoble Utopias," Joseph Wood Krutch argues that even if a society like Walden Two were possible, it would be morally unpalatable because such a community would end in a dictatorship capable of manipulating men in any way the rulers desired. He feels that before any techniques are tried, there should first be some agreement on the goals sought. But perhaps more worrisome to Krutch is the conviction that, if conditioning procedures are successful, all human thinking as we have known it will come to an end. Unlike Thomas Huxley, whom he quotes, Krutch is appalled at the prospect that man might be turned into a robot. Skinner, who feels that Krutch is really fearful of new scientific developments, sees no virtue in ignorance. New scientific knowledge can help us better understand man and design a world that satisfies man's needs. Rejection of science would mean the end of our only hope to build a better world.

A second frequently debated problem arising from the conflict between determinists and libertarians involves the proper treatment of criminals. Many determinists argue that any punishment resting on notions of moral blame, retribution, and desert should be replaced by a treatment of criminals that recognizes their lack of responsibility. Thus, such advocates often defend changing the character of society or rehabilitating criminals rather than any sort of traditional punishment. In "Address to the Prisoners in the Cook County Jail," Clarence Darrow maintains that criminals are no more responsible for being in a jail than honest men are for being outside of one. Since certain factors in our environment cause crime, he is convinced crime would be eliminated if the environment were suitably changed. A more equitable distribution of the wealth would, he believes, eliminate men's desire to commit crimes and, so, the need for any jails.

C. S. Lewis, in his article "The Humanitarian Theory of Punishment," asserts that the criminals are responsible for their actions and, thus, deserve punishment. He opposes both those who favor replacing punishment with rehabilitation and those who would use punishment to influence people's future behavior. He believes that the methods used to rehabilitate criminals can be harsher and more inhuman than traditional penalties, and that the use of punishment merely to influence people's behavior is open to a variety of moral abuses. He champions punishment on the basis of desert because only this position avoids morally unacceptable consequences and preserves the criminal's dignity as a responsible agent.

Determinism

2. The Arguments for Determinism   Herman H. Horne

Herman Harrell Horne (1874–1946) taught philosophy and education at a number of prominent American universities, and published numerous books and articles. His best-known work, *The Democratic Philosophy of Education* (1932), was a critical analysis of John Dewey's educational theories.

In presenting these arguments our purpose is to be succinct, systematic, comprehensive, and as convincing as the case allows. To this end the arguments have been grouped under related headings, nine in all, that seemed appropriate. These arguments have not been drawn from specific determinists but represent a general condensation of the main features in the deterministic view of life. As we read, we may feel that we all might be determinists on the basis of these arguments; at least it were well for us so to feel before passing to any criticisms later. The arguments follow:

I. The Argument from Physics

This argument rests on the hypothesis of the conservation of physical energy. According to this hypothesis, the sum total of physical energy in the world is a constant, subject to transformation from one form to another, as from heat to light, but not subject either to increase or diminution. This means that any movement of any body is entirely explicable in terms of antecedent physical conditions. This means that the deeds of the human body are mechanically caused by preceding conditions of body and brain, without any reference whatsoever to the mind of the individual, to his intents and purposes. This means that the will of man is not one of the contributing causes to his action; that his action is physically determined in all respects. If a state of will, which is mental, caused an act of the body, which is physical, by so much would the physical energy of the world be increased, which is contrary to the hypothesis universally adopted by physicists. Hence, to physics, the will of man is not a *vera causa* in explaining physical movement.

Reprinted with permission of Macmillan Publishing Co., Inc. from *Free Will and Human Responsibility* by Herman H. Horne. Copyright 1912 by Macmillan Publishing Co., Inc., renewed 1940 by Herman Harrell Horne.

2. The Argument from Biology

The discussions of evolution during the latter half of the nineteenth century brought this argument to the front. The argument rests upon the hypothesis of biology that any organism is adequately explained by reference to its heredity and environment. These are the two real forces, the diagonal of whose parallelogram explains fully the movements of the organism. Any creature is a compound of capacities and reactions to stimuli. The capacities it receives from heredity, the stimuli come from the environment. The responses referable to the mentality of the animal are the effects of inherited tendencies on the one hand and of the stimuli of the environment on the other hand. The sources of explanation are deemed adequate for the lower animals; why not also for man, the higher animal?

3. The Argument from Physiology

As we pass from physics, on the one hand, to biology and physiology, on the other, from the physical to the natural sciences, it is to be observed that the natural sciences, dealing with animate matter, have borrowed their methods of explanation from the physical sciences of physics and chemistry, that deal with inanimate matter. Science today tends to reject any form of "vitalism" as a principle of explanation, "vitalism" implying that the living principle is, in some sense, a cause. This will clearly appear in the argument for determinism based on physiology.

This argument rests on the hypothesis made famous by Huxley, that man is a conscious automaton. The existence of consciousness cannot easily be denied by any man. But its efficacy is denied by this physiological theory. All the actions of man conform to the automatic type, despite their complexity, and these actions are accompanied by consciousness, which, however, is not in the chain of causal phenomena, but stands outside as an "epi-phenomenon," to use Huxley's word. The individual in his deeds is really a vast complex of reflex actions, an aggregate of physical forces balanced against each other. Man is a conscious machine whose acts, however, are in no sense attributable to his conscious purposes.

This theory that men are machines may be repellant to our feelings, but there are many reasons that make it attractive to the scientific intellect. One might object that the deeds of men are too complicated to be those of a machine undirected by consciousness, but, as Spinoza urged, we do not really know the limits of the body's actions, as any somnambulist, unguided by his waking consciousness, would illustrate. The theory, furthermore, is characterized by that simplicity, so dear to the scholastic and the scientist alike, as a sign of truth. The theory gives a continuous principle of explanation of conduct according to the theory of reflex action, without appealing to a non-physical and interrupting cause. Really, too, it is unknown just how consciousness could move a molecule in the brain, though the popular mind is ready to assert that it does. Furthermore, this view is in harmony with the theory, generally accepted by science, of the uniformity of nature, subject to no interruptions from a non-physical source. If man is a conscious automaton, an act of free will, whereby choice determined conduct, would be a miracle. But it is against all the foundations of science to allow a miracle, in the sense of the temporary suspension of the natural order. In physiology, the soul is no cause. It is very natural that the regular practitioners, brought up on strictly scientific physiology, should reject the mental healers of every type, and that on theoretical as well as practical grounds.

4. The Law of Causation

It is evident from the arguments already urged here that they each turn upon a certain use of the law of causation. We must now state the argument based upon this law. The law of causation is one which no man would care to deny; it simply and undeniably asserts that every effect has its cause. No one indeed can think otherwise. Causation, in fact, as Kant showed, is one of the ways in which we must think; it is, as he says, an *a priori* form of thought; we did not learn from experience to think causally, but rather by thinking causally we help to constitute experience. The mind does not so much experience cause as cause experience.

Upon this basis the argument for determinism proceeds as follows: Like effects have like causes, the effect is like the cause, the effect is in fact the cause transformed, as the lightning is the effect of the preceding electrical conditions. Now human action is, of course, a physical effect; hence, we must expect to find only a physical cause; hence, any non-physical, psychical cause is from the nature of the case precluded, hence, of course the human will effects nothing. The actions of a man, a dog, a tree, a stone, all are due alike to antecedent physical conditions, which alone as causes determine the effects. We no longer explain the lightning in psychical terms—as the bolts of Jove; no more should we explain a man's deeds by reference to the intention of his soul.

5. The Argument from Science's Philosophy of Nature

This argument has been somewhat anticipated in the preceding paragraph. It is but a generalization of all the four preceding arguments. A philosophy of nature is a general theory explanatory of all the occurrences of nature. Now the ideal of scientific explanation in physics, chemistry, biology, physiology, and everywhere is mechanical. Events do not happen because anybody or any will wants them to happen; they happen because they have to happen; they happen because they must. And it is the business of science to find this necessary connection between the occurrences of nature. The universe, by this hypothesis, whole and part, is governed by the action of mechanical law. The reign of law is universal. Man is a very small creature upon a small earth, which is itself a comparatively small planet in one of the smaller solar systems of an indefinitely large number of solar systems which partially fill infinite space. The universe is a physical mechanism in which law rules, and man is but a least part of this universal machine. How then can he do otherwise than he does do? A single free-will act would introduce caprice, whim, chance, into a universe whose actions are so mechanically determined that an omniscient observer of the present could predict infallibly all futurity. . . .

Suppose now we pass from the objective sciences of nature to the subjective sciences of man, to the sciences that study mental things, in order to see how determinism defends itself here in the very regions of will.

6. The Argument from Psychology

The typical subjective science is psychology. The last fifty years of the wonderful nineteenth century saw psychology, hitherto rational and introspective, invaded by the scientific methods of observation, experimentation, and explanation. Since the methods of science exclude freedom of the will, it is natural that most scientific psychologists today are, as psychologists at least, determinists. The lamented Professor James is a noted exception, but his psychology has been most criticized by his fellows just on the ground of his "unscientific" retention of freedom of the will. As illustrating the contemporary attitude toward freedom, the following somewhat contemptuous and evasive reference may be cited: "We may prate as much as we please about the freedom of the will, no one of us is wholly free from the effects of these two great influences [heredity and environment]. Meantime, each of us has all the freedom any brave, moral nature can wish, *i. e.*, the freedom to do the best he can, firm in the belief that however puny his actual accomplishment there is no better than one's best."[1] The question is not whether we are "wholly free" from these influences, but whether we are at all free.

The psychological defenders of determinism refer to "the working hypothesis of psychology," *viz.*, there is no mental state without a corresponding brain-state; that the brain-state is to be regarded as the explanation of the mental state since successive mental states have no quantitative measurable relations; that the brain-state is itself to be explained not by reference in turn to the mental state but by reference to the preceding brain-state. Thus the chain of physical causation is unbroken; it is self-explanatory; it also explains the mental series; but the mental series in turn explains nothing on the physical side. This working hypothesis does effectually exclude the conscious will from all efficaciousness. In favor of this hypothesis as a working basis for psychology, it is to be remarked that our modern knowledge of localization of brain functions, of the aphasias, of the insanities, is largely dependent upon it.

Psychology also emphasizes our ignorance respecting the real relations of mind and brain, and emphasizes our inability to imagine just how attention could change a brain-state, though just such an effect is attributed to attention in some theories of free will.

Psychology as a science of mind also has its presuppositions respecting law. If the mental region is to be understood, it also must have its laws. These laws must be without any exception, such as free will would imply. It is the business of psychology, as a science, to deny exceptions and discover laws. . . .

[1]Angell, "Psychology," 4th Ed., New York, 1908, p. 437.

One of these laws affects our present question intimately. It is the law of motive. It asserts there is no action of will without a motive and that the strongest motive determines the will. Action is always in accord with the strongest motive, and the motives are provided by the heredity or the environment, or both. How could one choose to follow the weaker of two motives?

Psychologists are better aware than others of the sense of freedom revealed to introspection. Men often feel they are free to decide in either of two ways. Such a feeling, however, the psychologists do not consider as proof of the fact of freedom. The mind often cherishes false opinions concerning matters of fact; delusions are among the commonest mental phenomena. Schopenhauer, particularly, admitted that men felt at times they were free, while he denied they were really free. A straight staff appears bent, in a clear pool, and cannot be made to appear otherwise, despite the fact of its straightness and despite our knowledge of the fact. If we had never seen it out of the pool we should probably affirm it was crooked. So most people, judging by appearances, believe in freedom because they feel they are free. There is thus a possibility of general deception respecting this belief in freedom. This possibility is appreciated if we recall some hypnotic phenomena. A man may, though awake, under the influence of post-hypnotic suggestion, give away some of his property; he may then sign a statement saying he did it of his own free will and accord; spectators know otherwise. . . .

7. The Argument from Sociology

The sociologists have rewritten the free-will question in their own way. They have taken it out of the region of the individual and put it in the region of the social. This is a most fruitful thing to do because man really lives and acts in society and not in isolation. Now, in society, the laws that control are those of imitation and suggestion. The members of a crowd are not freely deciding; they are following the leader. The leader himself is not freely deciding; he is fascinated by some idea in his mind, he has put deliberation behind. So a man's deeds are traceable to the deeds of others and to his own dominating ideas. So the science of the action of men in groups becomes possible through asserting social determinism and denying individual freedom.

A peculiarly suggestive illustration of what appears to be freedom turning out to be determinism is afforded by the application of statistical methods of study in sociology. Supposed free-will acts are really capable of prediction in the mass. One decides to get married; he says he does so of his own free will and accord; many others do the same. But the statistician can predict in advance the approximate number of marriages that will take place next year. Was it not predetermined then, in the nature of the social situations, that so many marriages would occur? How otherwise account for the prediction? And if the prediction is possible, how then were the marriages due to free will? Viewed thus in the large, free-will acts appear subject to general laws. Indeed, without such legality, such predictability, how could society make its plans and assume responsibilities? So sociology as a science speaks for determinism.

8. The Argument from Ethics

The interests of ethics, of such matters as duty, obligation, conscience, reward, and blame, are peculiarly bound up with the doctrine of freedom, in the eyes of many. Yet there is also an argument from ethics for determinism. It runs as follows: a man's character determines his acts, he is responsible, for the act is his own; he committed it because, being the man he is, he could not have done otherwise. If his act were an effect of free will, no one could count upon him, he would be an irresponsible agent. Just because he is bound by his character, he is dependable. If his acts are good, he is to be congratulated on his character, not praised overmuch; if his acts are bad, he is to be pitied for his character, not blamed overmuch. He is rewarded, not because he could have done otherwise, but as a tribute to the stability of his character and as a stimulus to continued right action. He is punished, again not because he need not have done wrong, but to help him do right next time. All our instruction, reproof, and correction of others presupposes they may be determined by such influences. Thus the whole outfit of ethical categories may be read in deterministic terms, and indeed are so read by many ethical thinkers and writers, beginning with Socrates, who held that right ideas determine right conduct. Some practical teachers say, though believing in freedom for themselves, they must believe in determinism for their pupils. At any rate the theory of conduct, which ethics attempts, is not necessarily committed to the defense of freedom. . . .

9. The Argument from Theology

. . . The argument from theology for determinism runs somewhat as follows: God is omniscient, He therefore knows what I am going to do before I do it, there is therefore nothing for me to do except what He knows I am going to do, there is consequently but one reality, not two possibilities awaiting me in the future; therefore I am not free to do otherwise than I must do when the time comes. Thus the doctrine of the foreknowledge of God is held to exclude the freedom of man's choice. But to deny that God has foreknowledge would be derogatory to His dignity. . . .

Libertarianism

3. Freedom of Choice and Human Responsibility
Corliss Lamont

Corliss Lamont (1902–) is an American philosopher whose philosophical defense of Humanism has been combined with active participation in human affairs. Secretary-Treasurer of the *Journal of Philosophy,* he is also Chairman of the National Emergency Civil Liberties Committee.

It is my thesis that a man who is convinced he possesses freedom of choice or free will has a greater sense of responsibility than a person who thinks that total determinism rules the universe and human life. Determinism in the classic sense means that the flow of history, including all human choices and actions, is completely predetermined from the beginning of time. He who believes that "whatever is, was to be" can try to escape moral responsibility for wrongdoing by claiming that he was compelled to act as he did because it was predestined by the iron laws of cause and effect.

But if free choice truly exists at the moment of choosing, men clearly have full moral responsibility in deciding between two or more genuine alternatives, and the deterministic alibi has no weight. The heart of our discussion, then, lies in the question of whether free choice or universal determinism represents the truth. I shall try to summarize briefly the main reasons that point to the existence of free will.

First, there is the immediate, powerful, common-sense intuition shared by virtually all human beings that freedom of choice is real. This intuition seems as strong to me as the sensation of pleasure or pain; and the attempt of the determinists to explain the intuition away is as artificial as the Christian Scientist claim that pain is not real. The intuition of free choice does not, of course, in itself prove that such freedom exists, but that intuition is so strong that the burden of proof is on the determinists to show that it is based on an illusion.

Second, we can defuse the determinist argument by admitting, and indeed insisting, that a great deal of determinism exists in the world. Determinism in the form of if-then causal laws governs much of the human body's functioning and much of the universe as a whole. We can be glad that the automatic system of breathing, digestion, circulation of the blood, and beating of the heart operate deterministically—until they

Reprinted from *Religious Humanism,* Vol. III, No. 3, Summer, 1969. This paper was followed by a discussion by Professors Van Meter Ames, Robert Atkins, John Herman Randall, Williard Enteman, James Gould, Milic Capek, and Sterling Lamprecht. A copy of these papers can be obtained from the Fellowship of Religious Humanists, Yellow Springs, Ohio.

get out of order. Determinism *versus* free choice is a false issue; what we always have is *relative* determinism and *relative* free choice. Free will is ever limited by the past and by the vast range of if-then laws. At the same time, human beings utilize free choice to take advantage of those deterministic laws embodied in science and man-made machines. Most of us drive cars, but it is we and not the autos that decide when and where they are to go. Determinism wisely used and controlled—which is by no means always the case—can make us freer and happier.

Third, determinism is a relative thing, not only because human free choice exists, but also because contingency or chance is an ultimate trait of the cosmos. Contingency is best seen in the intersection of mutually independent event-streams between which there was no previous causal connection. My favorite example here is the collision of the steamship *Titanic* with an iceberg off Newfoundland, in the middle of the night on April 14, 1912. It was a terrible accident, with more than 1,500 persons lost. The drifting of the iceberg down from the north and the steaming of the *Titanic* west from England clearly represented two causal streams independent of each other.

Even if a team of scientific experts had been able, *per impossible*, to trace back the two causal streams and ascertain that the catastrophe had been predestined from the moment the steamship left Southampton, that would not upset my thesis. For the space-time relation of the iceberg and the *Titanic*, as the ship started on its voyage, would have been itself a matter of contingency, since there was no relevant cause to account for that precise relation.

The pervasive presence of contingency in the world is also proved by the fact that all natural laws, as I have observed, take the form of if-then sequences or relations. The *if* factor is obviously conditional and demonstrates the continual coexistence of contingency with determinism. The actuality of contingency negates the idea of total and all-inclusive necessity operating throughout the universe. As regards human choice, contingency ensures that at the outset the alternatives one faces are indeterminate in relation to the act of choosing, which proceeds to make one of them determinate.

My fourth point is that the accepted meaning of *potentiality,* namely, that every object and event in the cosmos possesses plural possibilities of behavior, interaction, and development, knocks out the determinist thesis. From the determinist viewpoint, multiple potentialities are an illusion. If you want to take a vacation trip next summer, you will no doubt think over a number of possibilities before you make a final decision. Determinism logically implies that such deliberation is mere playacting, because you were destined all the time to choose the trip you did choose. When we relate the causal pattern to potentiality, we find that causation as mediated through free choice can have its appropriate effect in the actualization of any one of various possibilities.

Fifth, the normal processes of human thought are tied in with potentiality as I have just described it, and likewise tend to show that freedom of choice is real. Thinking constantly involves general conceptions, universals, or abstractions under which are classified many varying particulars. In the case that I discussed under my fourth point, "vacation travel" was the general conception and the different places that might be visited were the particulars, the alternatives, the potentialities, among which one could freely choose. Unless there is free choice, the function of human thought in solving problems becomes superfluous and a mask of make-believe.

Sixth, it is clarifying for the problem of free choice to realize that only the present exists, and that it is always some present activity that builds up the past, as a skier leaves a trail behind him in the snow as he weaves down a hill. Everything that exists—the whole vast aggregate of inanimate matter, the swarming profusion of earthly life, man in his every aspect—exists only as an event or events taking place at this instant moment, which is now. The past is dead and gone; it is efficacious only as it is embodied in present structures and activities.

The activity of former presents establishes the foundations upon which the immediate present operates. What happened in the past creates both limitations and potentialities, always conditioning the present. But conditioning in this sense is not the same as determining; and each day sweeps onward under its own momentum, actualizing fresh patterns of existence, maintaining other patterns and destroying still others. Thus a man choosing and acting in the present is not wholly controlled by the past, but is part of the unending forward surge of cosmic power. He is an active, initiating agent, riding the wave of the present, as it were, and deliberating among open alternatives to reach decisions regarding the many different phases of his life.

My seventh point is that the doctrine of universal and eternal determinism is seen to be self-refuting when we work out its full implications in the cases of *reductio ad absurdum* implied. If our choices and actions today were all predestined yesterday, then they were equally predestined yesteryear, at the day of our birth, and at the birth of our solar system and earth some five billion years ago. To take another instance: for determinism, the so-called *irresistible impulse* that the law recognizes in assessing crimes by the insane must hold with equal force for the actions of the sane and virtuous. In the determinist philosophy, the good man has an irresistible impulse to tell the truth, to be kind to animals, and to expose the graft in City Hall.

Eighth, in the novel dialect of determinism many words lose their normal meaning. I refer to such words as *refraining, forbearance, self-restraint,* and *regret*. If determinism turns out to be true, we shall have to scrap a great deal in existing dictionaries and do a vast amount of redefining. What meaning, for example, is to be assigned to *forbearance* when it is determined in advance that you are going to refuse that second Martini cocktail? You can truly forbear only when you refrain from doing something that it is possible for you to do. But under the determinist dispensation it is not possible for you to accept the second cocktail because fate has already dictated your "No." I am not saying that nature necessarily conforms to our linguistic usages, but human language habits that have evolved over aeons of time cannot be neglected in the analysis of free choice and determinism.

Finally, I do not think that the term *moral responsibility* can retain its traditional meaning unless freedom of choice exists. From the viewpoint of ethics, law, and criminal law, it is difficult to understand how a consistent determinist would have a sufficient sense of personal responsibility for the development of decent ethical standards. But the question remains whether there have ever been or can be any consistent determinists or whether free choice runs so deep in human nature as an innate characteristic that, as Jean-Paul Sartre suggests, "We are not free to cease being free."

Soft Determinism

4. The Problem of Free Will   W. T. Stace

Walter Terence Stace (1886–1967) was born in Britain and served in the British Civil Service in Ceylon before coming to the United States to teach at Princeton University in 1932. He has written widely acclaimed books in many areas of philosophy.

[A] great problem which the rise of scientific naturalism has created for the modern mind concerns the foundations of morality. The old religious foundations have largely crumbled away, and it may well be thought that the edifice built upon them by generations of men is in danger of collapse. A total collapse of moral behavior is, as I pointed out before, very unlikely. For a society in which this occurred could not survive. Nevertheless the danger to moral standards inherent in the virtual disappearance of their old religious foundations is not illusory.

I shall first discuss the problem of free will, for it is certain that if there is no free will there can be no morality. Morality is concerned with what men ought and ought not to do. But if a man has no freedom to choose what he will do, if whatever he does is done under compulsion, then it does not make sense to tell him that he ought not to have done what he did and that he ought to do something different. All moral precepts would in such case be meaningless. Also if he acts always under compulsion, how can he be held morally responsible for his actions? How can he, for example, be punished for what he could not help doing?

It is to be observed that those learned professors of philosophy or psychology who deny the existence of free will do so only in their professional moments and in their studies and lecture rooms. For when it comes to doing anything practical, even of the most trivial kind, they invariably behave as if they and others were free. They inquire from you at dinner whether you will choose this dish or that dish. They will ask a child why he told a lie, and will punish him for not having chosen the way of truthfulness. All of which is inconsistent with a disbelief in free will. This should cause us to suspect that the problem is not a real one; and this, I believe, is the case. The dispute is merely verbal, and is due to nothing but a confusion about the meanings of words. It is what is now fashionably called a semantic problem.

How does a verbal dispute arise? Let us consider a case which, although it is absurd in the sense that no one would ever make the mistake which is involved in it, yet illustrates the principle which we shall have to use in the solution of the problem. Suppose that someone believed that the word "man" means a certain sort of five-legged animal; in short that "five-legged animal" is the correct *definition* of man. He might then look around the world, and rightly observing that there are no five-legged animals in it, he might proceed to deny the existence of men. This preposterous conclusion would have been reached because he was using an incorrect definition of "man." All you would have to do to show him his mistake would be to give him the correct definition; or at least to show him that his definition was wrong. Both the problem and its solution would, of course, be entirely verbal. The problem of free will, and its solution, I shall maintain, is verbal in exactly the same way. The problem has been created by the fact that learned men, especially philosophers, have assumed an incorrect definition of free will, and then finding that there is nothing in the world which answers to their definition, have denied its existence. As far as logic is concerned, their conclusion is just as absurd as that of the man who denies the existence of men. The only difference is that the mistake in the latter case is obvious and crude, while the mistake which the deniers of free will have made is rather subtle and difficult to detect.

Throughout the modern period, until quite recently, it was assumed, both by the philosophers who denied free will and by those who defended it, that *determinism is inconsistent with free will.* If a man's actions were wholly determined by chains of causes stretching back into the remote past, so that they could be predicted beforehand by a mind which knew all the causes, it was assumed that they could not in that case be free. This implies that a certain definition of actions done from free will was assumed, namely that they are actions *not* wholly determined by causes or predictable beforehand. Let us shorten this by saying that free will was defined as meaning indeterminism. This is the incorrect definition which has led to the denial of free will. As soon as we see what the true definition is we shall find that the question whether the world is deterministic, as Newtonian science implied, or in a measure indeterministic, as current physics teaches, is wholly irrelevant to the problem.

Of course there is a sense in which one can define a word arbitrarily in any way one pleases. But a definition may nevertheless be called correct or incorrect. It is correct if it accords with a *common usage* of the word defined. It is incorrect if it does not. And if you give an incorrect definition, absurd and untrue results are likely to follow. For instance, there is nothing to prevent you from arbitrarily defining a man as a five-legged animal, but this is incorrect in the sense that it does not accord with the ordinary meaning of the word. Also it has the absurd result of leading to a denial of the existence of men. This shows that *common usage is the criterion for deciding whether a definition is correct or not.* And this is the principle which I shall apply to free will. I shall show that indeterminism is not what is meant by the phrase "free will" *as it is commonly used.* And I shall attempt to discover the correct definition by inquiring how the phrase is used in ordinary conversation.

Here are a few samples of how the phrase might be used in ordinary conversation. It will be noticed that they include cases in which the question whether a man acted with free will is asked in order to determine whether he was morally and legally responsible for his acts.

Jones   I once went without food for a week.
Smith   Did you do that of your own free will?
Jones   No. I did it because I was lost in a desert and could find no food.

But suppose that the man who had fasted was Mahatma Gandhi. The conversation might then have gone:

Gandhi   I once fasted for a week.
Smith   Did you do that of your own free will?
Gandhi   Yes. I did it because I wanted to compel the British Government to give India its independence.

Take another case. Suppose that I had stolen some bread, but that I was as truthful as George Washington. Then, if I were charged with the crime in court, some exchange of the following sort might take place:

Judge   Did you steal the bread of your own free will?
Stace   Yes. I stole it because I was hungry.

Or in different circumstances the conversation might run:

Judge   Did you steal of your own free will?
Stace   No. I stole because my employer threatened to beat me if I did not.

At a recent murder trial in Trenton some of the accused had signed confessions, but afterwards asserted that they had done so under police duress. The following exchange might have occurred:

Judge   Did you sign this confession of your own free will?
Prisoner   No. I signed it because the police beat me up.

Now suppose that a philosopher had been a member of the jury. We could imagine this conversation taking place in the jury room.

Foreman of the Jury   The prisoner says he signed the confession because he was beaten, and not of his own free will.
Philosopher   This is quite irrelevant to the case. There is no such thing as free will.
Foreman   Do you mean to say that it makes no difference whether he signed because his conscience made him want to tell the truth or because he was beaten?
Philosopher   None at all. Whether he was caused to sign by a beating or by some desire of his own—the desire to tell the truth, for example—in either case his signing was causally deter-

mined, and therefore in neither case did he act of his own free will. Since there is no such thing as free will, the question whether he signed of his own free will ought not to be discussed by us.

The foreman and the rest of the jury would rightly conclude that the philosopher must be making some mistake. What sort of a mistake could it be? There is only one possible answer. The philosopher must be using the phrase "free will" in some peculiar way of his own which is not the way in which men usually use it when they wish to determine a question of moral responsibility. That is, he must be using an incorrect definition of it as implying action not determined by causes.

Suppose a man left his office at noon, and were questioned about it. Then we might hear this:

Jones Did you go out of your own free will?
Smith Yes. I went out to get my lunch.

But we might hear:

Jones Did you leave your office of your own free will?
Smith No. I was forcibly removed by the police.

We have now collected a number of cases of actions which, in the ordinary usage of the English language, would be called cases in which people have acted of their own free will. We should also say in all these cases that they *chose* to act as they did. We should also say that they could have acted otherwise, if they had chosen. For instance, Mahatma Gandhi was not compelled to fast; he chose to do so. He could have eaten if he had wanted to. When Smith went out to get his lunch, he chose to do so. He could have stayed and done some more work, if he had wanted to. We have also collected a number of cases of the opposite kind. They are cases in which men were not able to exercise their free will. They had no choice. They were compelled to do as they did. The man in the desert did not fast of his own free will. He had no choice in the matter. He was compelled to fast because there was nothing for him to eat. And so with the other cases. It ought to be quite easy, by an inspection of these cases, to tell what we ordinarily mean when we say that a man did or did not exercise free will. We ought therefore to be able to extract from them the proper definition of the term. Let us put the cases in a table:

Free Acts	*Unfree Acts*
Gandhi fasting because he wanted to free India.	The man fasting in the desert because there was no food.
Stealing bread because one is hungry.	Stealing because one's employer threatened to beat one.
Signing a confession because one wanted to tell the truth.	Signing because the police beat one.
Leaving the office because one wanted one's lunch.	Leaving because forcibly removed.

It is obvious that to find the correct definition of free acts we must discover what characteristic is common to all the acts in the left-hand column, and is, at the same time, absent from all the acts in the right-hand column. This characteristic which all free acts have, and which no unfree acts have, will be the defining characteristic of free will.

Is being uncaused, or not being determined by causes, the characteristic of which we are in search? It cannot be, because although it is true that all the acts in the right-hand column have causes, such as the beating by the police or the absence of food in the desert, so also do the acts in the left-hand column. Mr. Gandhi's fasting was caused by his desire to free India, the man leaving his office by his hunger, and so on. Moreover there is no reason to doubt that these causes of the free acts were in turn caused by prior conditions, and that these were again the results of causes, and so on back indefinitely into the past. Any physiologist can tell us the causes of hunger. What caused Mr. Gandhi's tremendously powerful desire to free India is no doubt more difficult to discover. But it must have had causes. Some of them may have lain in peculiarities of his glands or brain, others in his past experiences, others in his heredity, others in his education. Defenders of free will have usually tended to deny such facts. But to do so is plainly a case of special pleading, which is unsupported by any scrap of evidence. The only reasonable view is that all human actions, both those which are freely done and those which are not, are either wholly determined by causes, or at least as much determined as other events in nature. It may be true, as the physicists tell us, that nature is not as deterministic as was once thought. But whatever degree of determinism prevails in the world, human actions appear to be as much determined as anything else. And if this is so, it cannot be the case that what distinguishes actions freely chosen from those which are not free is that the latter are determined by causes while the former are not. Therefore, being uncaused or being undetermined by causes, must be an incorrect definition of free will.

What, then, is the difference between acts which are freely done and those which are not? What is the characteristic which is present to all the acts in the left-hand column and absent from all those in the right-hand column? Is it not obvious that, although both sets of actions have causes, the causes of those in the left-hand column are *of a different kind* from the causes of those in the right-hand column? The free acts are all caused by desires, or motives, or by some sort of internal psychological states of the agent's mind. The unfree acts, on the other hand, are all caused by physical forces or physical conditions, outside the agent. Police arrest means physical force exerted from the outside; the absence of food in the desert is a physical condition of the outside world. We may therefore frame the following rough definitions. *Acts freely done are those whose immediate causes are psychological states in the agent. Acts not freely done are those whose immediate causes are states of affairs external to the agent.*

It is plain that if we define free will in this way, then free will certainly exists, and the philosopher's denial of its existence is seen to be what it is—nonsense. For it is obvious that all those actions of men which we should ordinarily attribute to the exercise of their free will, or of which we should say that they freely chose to do them, are in fact actions which have been caused by their own desires, wishes, thoughts, emotions, impulses, or other psychological states.

In applying our definition we shall find that it usually works well, but that there are some puzzling cases which it does not seem exactly to fit. These puzzles can always be solved by paying careful attention to the ways in which words are used, and remembering that they are not always used consistently. I have space for only one example. Suppose that a thug threatens to shoot you unless you give him your wallet, and suppose that you do so. Do you, in giving him your wallet, do so of your own free will or not? If we apply our definition, we find that you acted freely, since the immediate cause of the action was not an actual outside force but the fear of death, which is a psychological cause. Most people, however, would say that you did not act of your own free will but under compulsion. Does this show that our definition is wrong? I do not think so. Aristotle, who gave a solution of the problem of free will substantially the same as ours (though he did not use the term "free will") admitted that there are what he called "mixed" or borderline cases in which it is difficult to know whether we ought to call the acts free or compelled. In the case under discussion, though no actual force was used, the gun at your forehead so nearly approximated to actual force that we tend to say the case was one of compulsion. It is a borderline case.

Here is what may seem like another kind of puzzle. According to our view an action may be free though it could have been predicted beforehand with certainty. But suppose you told a lie, and it was certain beforehand that you would tell it. How could one then say, "You could have told the truth"? The answer is that it is perfectly true that you could have told the truth *if* you had wanted to. In fact you would have done so, for in that case the causes producing your action, namely your desires, would have been different, and would therefore have produced different effects. It is a delusion that predictability and free will are incompatible. This agrees with common sense. For if, knowing your character, I predict that you will act honorably, no one would say when you do act honorably, that this shows you did not do so of your own free will.

Since free will is a condition of moral responsibility, we must be sure that our theory of free will gives a sufficient basis for it. To be held morally responsible for one's actions means that one may be justly punished or rewarded, blamed or praised, for them. But it is not just to punish a man for what he cannot help doing. How can it be just to punish him for an action which it was certain beforehand that he would do? We have not attempted to decide whether, as a matter of fact, all events, including human actions, are completely determined. For that question is irrelevant to the problem of free will. But if we assume for the purposes of argument that complete determinism is true, but that we are nevertheless free, it may then be asked whether such a deterministic free will is compatible with moral responsibility. For it may seem unjust to punish a man for an action which it could have been predicted with certainty beforehand that he would do.

But that determinism is incompatible with moral responsibility is as much a delusion as that it is incompatible with free will. You do not excuse a man for doing a wrong act because, knowing his character, you felt certain beforehand that he would do it. Nor do you deprive a man of a reward or prize because, knowing his goodness or his capabilities, you felt certain beforehand that he would win in.

Volumes have been written on the justification of punishment. But so far as it affects the question of free will, the essential principles involved are quite simple. The punishment of a man for doing a wrong act is justified, either on the ground that it will correct his own character, or that it will deter other people from doing similar acts. The instrument of punishment has been in the past, and no doubt still is, often unwisely used; so that it may often have done more harm than good. But that is not relevant to our present problem. Punishment, if and when it is justified, is justified only on one or both of the grounds just mentioned. The question then is how, if we assume determinism, punishment can correct character or deter people from evil actions.

Suppose that your child develops a habit of telling lies. You give him a mild beating. Why? Because you believe that his personality is such that the usual motives for telling the truth do not cause him to do so. You therefore supply the missing cause, or motive, in the shape of pain and the fear of future pain if he repeats his untruthful behavior. And you hope that a few treatments of this kind will condition him to the habit of truth-telling, so that he will come to tell the truth without the infliction of pain. You assume that his actions are determined by causes, but that the usual causes of truth-telling do not in him produce their usual effects. You therefore supply him with an artificially injected motive, pain and fear, which you think will in the future cause him to speak truthfully.

The principle is exactly the same where you hope, by punishing one man, to deter others from wrong actions. You believe that the fear of punishment will cause those who might otherwise do evil to do well.

We act on the same principle with non-human, and even with inanimate, things, if they do not behave in the way we think they ought to behave. The rose bushes in the garden produce only small and poor blooms, whereas we want large and rich ones. We supply a cause which will produce large blooms, namely fertilizer. Our automobile does not go properly. We supply a cause which will make it go better, namely oil in the works. The punishment for the man, the fertilizer for the plant, and the oil for the car, are all justified by the same principle and in the same way. The only difference is that different kinds of things require different kinds of causes to make them do what they should. Pain may be the appropriate remedy to apply, in certain cases, to human beings, and oil to the machine. It is, of course, of no use to inject motor oil into the boy or to beat the machine.

Thus we see that moral responsibility is not only consistent with determinism, but requires it. The assumption on which punishment is based is that human behavior is causally determined. If pain could not be a cause of truth-telling there would be no justification at all for punishing lies. If human actions and volitions were uncaused, it would be useless either to punish or reward, or indeed to do anything else to correct people's bad behavior. For nothing that you could do would in any way influence them. Thus moral responsibility would entirely disappear. If there were no determinism of human beings at all, their actions would be completely unpredictable and capricious, and therefore irresponsible. And this is in itself a strong argument against the common view of philosophers that free will means being undetermined by causes.

Contemporary Issues

The Control of Men

5. Walden Two: Selections   B. F. Skinner

Burrhus Frederic Skinner (1904–), professor of psychology at Harvard University, is one of America's most prominent psychologists. He is known both for his defense of behaviorism and his experimentation with modern teaching devices.

The participants of the following discussion are Frazier, the founder of Walden Two; Castle, a philosopher who is skeptical of the society's achievements and purposes; and Professor Burris, the narrator of the discussion, who is trying objectively to evaluate Frazier's new society.

"Each of us," Frazier began, "is engaged in a pitched battle with the rest of mankind."

"A curious premise for a Utopia," said Castle. "Even a pessimist like myself takes a more hopeful view than that."

"You do, you do," said Frazier. "But let's be realistic. Each of us has interests which conflict with the interest of everybody else. That's our original sin, and it can't be helped. Now, 'everybody else' we call 'society.' It's a powerful opponent, and it always wins. Oh, here and there an individual prevails for a while and gets what he wants. Sometimes he storms the culture of a society and changes it slightly to his own advantage. But society wins in the long run, for it has the advantage of numbers and of age. Many prevail against one, and men against a baby. Society attacks early, when the individual is helpless. It enslaves him almost before he has tasted freedom. The 'ologies' will tell you how it's done. Theology calls it building a conscience or developing a spirit of selflessness. Psychology calls it the growth of the super-ego.

"Considering how long society has been at it, you'd expect a better job. But the campaigns have been badly planned and the victory has never been secure. The behavior of the individual has been shaped according to revelations of 'good conduct,' never as the result of experimental study. But why not experiment? The questions are simple enough. What's the best behavior for the individual so far as the group is concerned? And how can the individual be induced to behave in that way? Why not explore these questions in a scientific spirit?

"We could do just that in Walden Two. We had already worked out a code of conduct—subject, of course, to experimental modification. The code would keep things running smoothly if everybody lived up to it. Our job was to see that everybody did. Now, you can't get people to follow a useful code by making them into so many jacks-in-the-box. You can't foresee all future circumstances, and you can't specify adequate future conduct. You don't know what will be required. Instead you have to set up certain behavioral processes which will lead the individual to design his own 'good' conduct when the time comes. We call that sort of thing 'self-control.' But don't be misled, the control always rests in the last analysis in the hands of society.

"One of our Planners, a young man named Simmons, worked with me. It was the first time in history that the matter was approached in an experimental way. Do you question that statement, Mr. Castle?"

"I'm not sure I know what you are talking about," said Castle.

"Then let me go on. Simmons and I began by studying the great works on morals and ethics—Plato, Aristotle, Confucius, the New Testament, the Puritan divines, Machiavelli, Chesterfield, Freud—there were scores of them. We were looking for any and every method of shaping human behavior by imparting techniques of self-control. Some techniques were obvious enough, for they had marked turning points in human history. 'Love your enemies' is an example—a psychological invention for easing the lot of an oppressed people. The severest trial of oppression is the constant rage which one suffers at the thought of the oppressor. What Jesus discovered was how to avoid these inner devastations. His technique was to *practice the opposite emotion.* If a man can succeed in 'loving his enemies' and 'taking no thought for the morrow,' he will no longer be assailed by hatred of the oppressor or rage at the loss of his freedom or possessions. He may not get his freedom or possessions back, but he's less miserable. It's a difficult lesson. It comes late in our program."

"I thought you were opposed to modifying emotions and instincts until the world was ready for it," said Castle. "According to you, the principle of 'love your enemies' should have been suicidal."

"It would have been suicidal, except for an entirely unforeseen consequence. Jesus must have been quite astonished at the effect of his discovery. We are only just beginning to understand the power of love because we are just beginning to understand the weakness of force and aggression. But the science of behavior is clear about all that now. Recent discoveries in the analysis of punishment—but I am falling into one digression after another. Let me save my explanation of why the Christian virtues—and I mean merely the Christian techniques of self-control—have not disappeared from the face of the earth, with due recognition of the fact that they suffered a narrow squeak within recent memory.

"When Simmons and I had collected our techniques of control, we had to discover how to teach them. That was more difficult. Current educational practices were of little value, and religious practices scarcely any better. Promising paradise or threatening hell-fire is, we assumed, generally admitted to be unproductive. It is based upon a fundamental fraud which, when discovered, turns the individual against society and nourishes the very thing it tries to stamp out. What Jesus offered in return for loving one's enemies was heaven *on earth,* better known as peace of mind.

"We found a few suggestions worth following in the practices of the clinical psychologist. We undertook to build a tolerance for annoying experiences. The sunshine of midday is extremely painful if you come from a dark room, but take it in easy stages and you can avoid pain altogether. The analogy can be misleading, but in much the same way it's possible to build a tolerance to painful or distasteful stimuli, or to frustration, or to situations which arouse fear, anger or rage. Society and nature throw these annoyances at the individual with no regard for the development of tolerances. Some achieve tolerances, most fail. Where would the science of immunization be if it followed a schedule of accidental dosages?

"Take the principle of 'Get thee behind me, Satan,' for example," Frazier continued. "It's a special case of self-control by altering the environment. Subclass A 3, I believe. We give each child a lollipop which has been dipped in powdered sugar so that a single touch of the tongue can be detected. We tell him he may eat the lollipop later in the day, provided it hasn't already been licked. Since the child is only three or four, it is a fairly diff—"

"Three or four!" Castle exclaimed.

"All our ethical training is completed by the age of six," said Frazier quietly. "A simple principle like putting temptation out of sight would be acquired before four. But at such an early age the problem of not licking the lollipop isn't easy. Now, what would you do, Mr. Castle, in a similar situation?"

"Put the lollipop out of sight as quickly as possible."

"Exactly. I can see you've been well trained. Or perhaps you discovered the principle for yourself. We're in favor of original inquiry wherever possible, but in this case we have a more important goal and we don't hesitate to give verbal help. First of all, the children are urged to examine their own behavior while looking at the lollipops. This helps them to recognize the need for self-control. Then the lollipops are concealed, and the children are asked to notice any gain in happiness or any reduction in tension. Then a strong distraction is arranged—say, an interesting game. Later the children are reminded of the candy and encouraged to examine their reaction. The value of the distraction is generally obvious. Well, need I go on? When the experiment is repeated a day or so later, the children all run with the lollipops to their lockers and do exactly what Mr. Castle would do—a sufficient indication of the success of our training."

"I wish to report an objective observation of my reaction to your story," said Castle, controlling his voice with great precision. "I find myself revolted by this display of sadistic tyranny."

"I don't wish to deny you the exercise of an emotion which you seem to find enjoyable," said Frazier. "So let me go on. Concealing a tempting but forbidden object is a crude solution. For one thing, it's not always feasible. We want a sort of psychological concealment—covering up the candy by paying no attention. In a later experiment the children wear their lollipops like crucifixes for a few hours."

> Instead of the cross, the lollipop,
> About my neck was hung,

said Castle. . . .

"How do you build up a tolerance to an annoying situation?" I said.

"Oh, for example, by having the children 'take' a more and more painful shock, or drink cocoa with less and less sugar in it until a bitter concoction can be savored without a bitter face."

"But jealousy or envy—you can't administer them in graded doses," I said.

"And why not? Remember, we control the social environment, too, at this age. That's why we get our ethical training in early. Take this case. A group of children arrive home after a long walk tired and hungry. They're expecting supper; they find, instead, that it's time for a lesson in self-control: they must stand for five minutes in front of steaming bowls of soup.

"The assignment is accepted like a problem in arithmetic. Any groaning or complaining is a wrong answer. Instead, the children begin at once to work upon themselves to avoid any unhappiness during the delay. One of them may make a joke of it. We encourage a sense of humor as a good way of not taking an annoyance seriously. The joke won't be much, according to adult standards—perhaps the child will simply pretend to empty the bowl of soup into his upturned mouth. Another may start a song with many verses. The rest join in at once, for they've learned that it's a good way to make time pass."

Frazier glanced uneasily at Castle, who was not to be appeased.

"That also strikes you as a form of torture, Mr. Castle?" he asked.

"I'd rather be put on the rack," said Castle.

"Then you have by no means had the thorough training I supposed. You can't imagine how lightly the children take such an experience. It's a rather severe biological frustration, for the children are tired and hungry and they must stand and look at food; but it's passed off as lightly as a five-minute delay at curtain time. We regard it as a fairly elementary test. Much more difficult problems follow."

"I suspected as much," muttered Castle.

"In a later stage we forbid all social devices. No songs, no jokes—merely silence. Each child is forced back upon his own resources—a very important step."

"I should think so," I said. "And how do you know it's successful? You might produce a lot of silently resentful children. It's certainly a dangerous stage."

"It is, and we follow each child carefully. If he hasn't picked up the necessary techniques, we start back a little. A still more advanced stage"—Frazier glanced again at Castle, who stirred uneasily—"brings me to my point. When it's time to sit down to the soup, the children count off—heads and tails. Then a coin is tossed and if it comes up heads, the 'heads' sit down and eat. The 'tails' remain standing for another five minutes."

Castle groaned.

"And you call that envy?" I asked.

"Perhaps not exactly," said Frazier. "At least there's seldom any aggression against the lucky ones. The emotion, if any, is directed against Lady Luck herself, against the toss of the coin. That, in itself, is a lesson worth learning, for it's the only direction in which emotion has a surviving chance to be useful. And resentment toward things in general, while perhaps just as silly as personal aggression, is more easily controlled. Its expression is not socially objectionable." . . .

"May you not inadvertently teach your children some of the very emotions you're trying to eliminate?" I said. "What's the effect, for example, of finding the anticipation of a warm supper suddenly thwarted? Doesn't that eventually lead to feelings of uncertainty, or even anxiety?"

"It might. We had to discover how often our lessons could be safely administered. But all our schedules are worked out experimentally. We watch for undesired consequences just as any scientist watches for disrupting factors in his experiments.

"After all, it's a simple and sensible program," he went on in a tone of appeasement. "We set up a system of gradually increasing annoyances and frustrations against a background of complete serenity. An easy environment is made more and more difficult as the children acquire the capacity to adjust."

"But *why?*" said Castle. "Why these deliberate unpleasantnesses—to put it mildly? I must say I think you and your friend Simmons are really very subtle sadists."

"You've reversed your position, Mr. Castle," said Frazier in a sudden flash of anger with which I rather sympathized. Castle was calling names, and he was also being unaccountably and perhaps intentionally obtuse. "A while ago you accused me of breeding a race of softies," Frazier continued. "Now you object to toughening them up. But what you don't understand is that these potentially unhappy situations are never very annoying. Our schedules make sure of that. You wouldn't understand, however, because you're not so far advanced as our children."

Castle grew black.

"But what do your children get out of it?" he insisted, apparently trying to press some vague advantage in Frazier's anger.

"What do they get out of it!" exclaimed Frazier, his eyes flashing with a sort of helpless contempt. His lips curled and he dropped his head to look at his fingers, which were crushing a few blades of grass.

"They must get happiness and freedom and strength," I said, putting myself in a ridiculous position in attempting to make peace.

"They don't sound happy or free to me, standing in front of bowls of Forbidden Soup," said Castle, answering me parenthetically while continuing to stare at Frazier.

"If I must spell it out," Frazier began with a deep sigh, "what they get is escape from the petty emotions which eat the heart out of the unprepared. They get the satisfaction of pleasant and profitable social relations on a scale almost undreamed of in the world at large. They get immeasurably increased efficiency, because they can stick to a job without suffering the aches and pains which soon beset most of us. They get new horizons, for they are spared the emotions characteristic of frustration and failure. They get—" His eyes searched the branches of the trees. "Is that enough?" he said at last.

"And the community must gain their loyalty," I said, "when they discover the fears and jealousies and diffidences in the world at large."

"I'm glad you put it that way," said Frazier. "You might have said that they must feel superior to the miserable products of our public schools. But we're at pains to keep any feeling of superiority or contempt under control, too. Having suffered most acutely from it myself, I put the subject first on our agenda. We carefully avoid any joy in a personal triumph which means the personal failure of somebody else. We take no pleasure in the sophistical, the disputative, the dialectical." He threw a vicious glance at Castle. "We don't use the motive of domination, because we are always thinking of the whole group. We could motivate a few geniuses that way—it was certainly my own motivation—but we'd sacrifice some of the happiness of everyone else. Triumph over nature and over oneself, yes. But over others, never."

"You've taken the mainspring out of the watch," said Castle flatly.

"That's an experimental question, Mr. Castle, and you have the wrong answer." . . .

"Are your techniques really so very new?" I said hurriedly. "What about the primitive practice of submitting a boy to various tortures before granting him a place among adults? What about the disciplinary techniques of Puritanism? Or of the modern school, for that matter?"

"In one sense you're right," said Frazier. "And I think you've nicely answered Mr. Castle's tender concern for our little ones. The unhappinesses we deliberately impose are far milder than the normal unhappinesses from which we offer protection. Even at the height of our ethical training, the unhappiness is ridiculously trivial—to the well-trained child.

"But there's a world of difference in the way we use these annoyances," he continued. "For one thing, we don't punish. We never administer an unpleasantness in the hope of repressing or eliminating undesirable behavior. But there's another difference. In most cultures the child meets up with annoyances and reverses of uncontrolled magnitude. Some are imposed in the name of discipline by persons in authority. Some, like hazings, are condoned though not authorized. Others are merely accidental. No one cares to, or is able to, prevent them.

"We all know what happens. A few hardy children emerge, particularly those who have got their unhappiness in doses that could be swallowed. They become brave men. Others become sadists or masochists of varying degrees of pathology. Not having conquered a painful environment, they become preoccupied with pain and make a devious art of it. Others submit—and hope to inherit the earth. The rest—the cravens, the cowards—live in fear for the rest of their lives. And that's only a single field—the reaction to pain. I could cite a dozen parallel cases. The optimist and the pessimist, the contented and the disgruntled, the loved and the unloved, the ambitious and the discouraged—these are only the extreme products of a miserable system.

"Traditional practices are admittedly better than nothing," Frazier went on. "Spartan or Puritan—no one can question the occasional happy result. But the whole system rests upon the wasteful principle of selection. The English public school of the nineteenth century produced brave men—by setting up almost insurmountable barriers and making the most of the few who came over. But selection isn't education. Its crops of brave men will always be small, and the waste enormous. Like all primitive principles, selection serves in place of education only through a profligate use of material. Multiply extravagantly and select with rigor. It's the philosophy of the 'big litter' as an alternative to good child hygiene.

"In Walden Two we have a different objective. We make every man a brave man. They all come over the barriers. Some require more preparation than others, but they all come over. The traditional use of adversity is to select the strong. We control adversity to build strength. And we do it deliberately, no matter how sadistic Mr. Castle may think us, in order to prepare for adversities which are beyond control. Our children eventually experience the 'heartache and the thousand natural shocks that flesh is heir to.' It would be the cruelest possible practice to protect them as long as possible, especially when we *could* protect them so well.'

Frazier held out his hands in an exaggerated gesture of appeal.

"What alternative *had* we?" he said, as if he were in pain. "What else could we do? For four or five years we could provide a life in which no important need would go unsatisfied, a life practically free of anxiety or frustration or annoyance. What would *you* do? Would you let the child enjoy this paradise with no thought for the future—like an idolatrous and pampering mother? Or would you relax control of the environment and let the child meet accidental frustrations? *But what is the virtue of accident?* No, there was only one course open to us. We had to *design* a series of adversities, so that the child would develop the greatest possible self-control. Call it deliberate, if you like, and accuse us of sadism; there was no other course." . . .

"A modern, mechanized, managerial Machiavelli—that is my final estimate of you, Mr. Frazier," he [Castle] said, with the same challenging stare.

"It must be gratifying to know that one has reached a 'final estimate,'" said Frazier.

"An artist in power," Castle continued, "whose greatest art is to conceal art. The silent despot."

"Since we are dealing in 'M's,' why not sum it all up and say 'Mephistophelian'?" said Frazier, curiously reviving my fears of the preceding afternoon.

"I'm willing to do that!" said Castle. "And unless God is very sure of himself, I suspect He's by no means easy about this latest turn in the war of the angels. So far as I can see, you've blocked every path through which man was to struggle upward toward salvation. Intelligence, initiative—you have filled their places with a sort of degraded instinct, engineered compulsion. Walden Two is a marvel of efficient coordination—as efficient as an anthill!"

"Replacing intelligence with instinct—" muttered Frazier. "I had never thought of that. It's an interesting possibility. How's it done?" It was a crude maneuver. The question was a digression, intended to spoil Castle's timing and to direct our attention to practical affairs in which Frazier was more at home.

"The behavior of your members is carefully shaped in advance by a Plan," said Castle, not to be taken in, "and it's shaped to perpetuate that

Plan. Intellectually Walden Two is quite as incapable of a spontaneous change of course as the life within a beehive."

"I see what you mean," said Frazier distantly. But he returned to his strategy. "And have you discovered the machinery of my power?"

"I have, indeed. We were looking in the wrong place. There's no *current* contact between you and the members of Walden Two. You threw us off the track very skillfully on that point last night. But you were behaving as a despot when you first laid your plans—when you designed the social structure and drew up the contract between community and member, when you worked out your educational practices and your guarantees against despotism—What a joke! Don't tell me you weren't in control *then!* Burris saw the point. What about your career as organizer? *There* was leadership! And the most damnable leadership in history, because you were setting the stage for the withdrawal of yourself as a personal force, knowing full well that everything that happened would still be your doing. Hundreds—you predicted millions—of unsuspecting souls were to fall within the scope of your ambitious scheme."

Castle was driving his argument home with great excitement, but Frazier was lying in exaggerated relaxation, staring at the ceiling, his hands cupped behind his head.

"Very good, Mr. Castle," he said softly. "I gave you the clue, of course, when we parted last night."

"You did, indeed. And I've wondered why. Were you led into that fatal error by your conceit? Perhaps that's the ultimate answer to your form of despotism. No one could enjoy the power you have seized without wishing to display it from time to time."

"I've admitted neither power nor despotism. But you're quite right in saying that I've exerted an influence and in one sense will continue to exert it forever. I believe you called me a *primum mobile*—not quite correctly, as I found upon looking the term up last night. But I did plan Walden Two—not as an architect plans a building, but as a scientist plans a long-term experiment, uncertain of the conditions he will meet but knowing how he will deal with them when they arise. In a sense, Walden Two is predetermined, but not as the behavior of a beehive is determined. Intelligence, no matter how much it may be shaped and extended by our educational system, will still function as intelligence. It will be used to puzzle out solutions to problems to which a beehive would quickly succumb. What the plan does is to keep intelligence on the right track, for the good of society rather than of the intelligent individual—or for the eventual rather than the immediate good of the individual. It does this by making sure that the individual will not forget his personal stake in the welfare of society."

"But you are forestalling many possibly useful acts of intelligence which aren't encompassed by your plan. You have ruled out points of view which may be more productive. You are implying that T. E. Frazier, looking at the world from the middle of the twentieth century, understands the best course for mankind forever."

"Yes, I suppose I do."

"But that's absurd!"

"Not at all. I don't say I foresee the course man will take a hundred years hence, let alone forever, but I know which he should take now."

"How can you be sure of it? It's certainly not a question you have answered experimentally."

"I think we're in the course of answering it," said Frazier. "But that's beside the point. There's no alternative. We must take that course."

"But that's fantastic. You who are taking it are in a small minority."

Frazier sat up.

"And the majority are in a big quandary," he said. "They're not on the road at all, or they're scrambling back toward their starting point, or sidling from one side of the road to the other like so many crabs. What do you think two world wars have been about? Something as simple as boundaries or trade? Nonsense. The world is trying to adjust to a new conception of man in relation to men."

"Perhaps it's merely trying to adjust to despots whose ideas are incompatible with the real nature of man."

"Mr. Castle," said Frazier very earnestly, "let me ask you a question. I warn you, it will be the most terrifying question of your life. *What would you do if you found yourself in possession of an effective science of behavior?* Suppose you suddenly found it possible to control the behavior of men as you wished. What would you do?"

"That's an assumption?"

"Take it as one if you like. *I* take it as a fact. And apparently you accept it as a fact too. I can hardly be as despotic as you claim unless I hold the key to an extensive practical control."

"What would I do?" said Castle thoughtfully. "I think I would dump your science of behavior in the ocean."

"And deny men all the help you could otherwise give them?"

"And give them the freedom they would otherwise lose forever!"

"How could you give them freedom?"

"By refusing to control them!"

"But you would only be leaving the control in other hands."

"Whose?"

"The charlatan, the demagogue, the salesman, the ward heeler, the bully, the cheat, the educator, the priest—all who are now in possession of the techniques of behavioral engineering."

"A pretty good share of the control would remain in the hands of the individual himself."

"That's an assumption, too, and it's your only hope. It's your only possible chance to avoid the implications of a science of behavior. If man is free, then a technology of behavior is impossible. But I'm asking you to consider the other case."

"Then my answer is that your assumption is contrary to fact and any further consideration idle."

"And your accusations—?"

"—were in terms of intention, not of possible achievement."

Frazier sighed dramatically.

"It's a little late to be proving that a behavioral technology is well advanced. How can you deny it? Many of its methods and techniques are really as old as the hills. Look at their frightful misuse in the hands of the Nazis! And what about the techniques of the psychological clinic? What about education? Or religion? Or practical politics? Or advertising and salesmanship? Bring them all together and you have a sort of rule-of-thumb technology of vast power. No, Mr. Castle, the science is there for the asking. But its techniques and methods are in the wrong hands—they are used for personal aggrandizement in a competitive world or, in the case of the psychologist and educator, for futilely corrective purposes. My question is, have you the courage to take up and wield the science of behavior for the good of mankind? You answer that you would dump it in the ocean!"

"I'd want to take it out of the hands of the politicians and advertisers and salesmen, too."

"And the psychologists and educators? You see, Mr. Castle, you can't have that kind of cake. The fact is, we not only *can* control human behavior, we *must*. But who's to do it, and what's to be done?"

"So long as a trace of personal freedom survives, I'll stick to my position," said Castle, very much out of countenance.

"Isn't it time we talked about freedom?" I said. "We parted a day or so ago on an agreement to let the question of freedom ring. It's time to answer, don't you think?"

"My answer is simple enough," said Frazier. "I deny that freedom exists at all. I must deny it—or my program would be absurd. You can't have a science about a subject matter which hops capriciously about. Perhaps we can never *prove* that man isn't free; it's an assumption. But the increasing success of a science of behavior makes it more and more plausible."

"On the contrary, a simple personal experience makes it untenable," said Castle. "The experience of freedom. I *know* that I'm free."

"It must be quite consoling," said Frazier.

"And what's more—you do, too," said Castle hotly. "When you deny your own freedom for the sake of playing with a science of behavior, you're acting in plain bad faith. That's the only way I can explain it." He tried to recover himself and shrugged his shoulders. "At least you'll grant that you *feel* free."

"The 'feeling of freedom' should deceive no one," said Frazier. "Give me a concrete case."

"Well, right now," Castle said. He picked up a book of matches. "I'm free to hold or drop these matches."

"You will, of course, do one or the other," said Frazier. "Linguistically or logically there seem to be two possibilities, but I submit that there's only one in fact. The determining forces may be subtle but they are inexorable. I suggest that as an orderly person you will probably hold—ah! you drop them! Well, you see, that's all part of your behavior with respect to me. You couldn't resist the temptation to prove me wrong. It was all lawful. You had no choice. The deciding factor entered rather late, and naturally you couldn't foresee the result when you first held them up. There was no strong likelihood that you would act in either direction, and so you said you were free."

"That's entirely too glib," said Castle. "It's easy to argue lawfulness after the fact. But let's see you predict what I will do in advance. Then I'll agree there's law."

"I didn't say that behavior is always predictable, any more than the weather is always predictable. There are often too many factors to be taken into account. We can't measure them all accurately, and we couldn't perform the mathematical operations needed to make a prediction if we had the measurements. The legality is usually an assumption—but none the less important in judging the issue at hand."

"Take a case where there's no choice, then," said Castle. "Certainly a man in jail isn't free in the sense in which I am free now."

"Good! That's an excellent start. Let us classify the kinds of determiners of human behavior. One class, as you suggest, is physical restraint—handcuffs, iron bars, forcible coercion. These are ways in which we shape human behavior according to our wishes. They're crude, and they sacrifice the affection of the controllee, but they often work. Now, what other ways are there of limiting freedom?"

Frazier had adopted a professorial tone and Castle refused to answer.

"The threat of force would be one," I said.

"Right. And here again we shan't encourage any loyalty on the part of the controllee. He has perhaps a shade more of the feeling of freedom, since he can always 'choose to act and accept the consequences,' but he doesn't feel exactly free. He knows his behavior is being coerced. Now what else?"

I had no answer.

"Force or the threat of force—I see no other possibility," said Castle after a moment.

"Precisely," said Frazier.

"But certainly a large part of my behavior has no connection with force at all. There's my freedom!" said Castle.

"I wasn't agreeing that there was no other possibility—merely that *you* could see no other. Not being a good behaviorist—or a good Christian, for that matter—you have no feeling for a tremendous power of a different sort."

"What's that?"

"I shall have to be technical," said Frazier. "But only for a moment. It's what the science of behavior calls 'reinforcement theory.' The things that can happen to us fall into three classes. To some things we are indifferent. Other things we like—we want them to happen, and we take steps to make them happen again. Still other things we don't like—we don't want them to happen and we take steps to get rid of them or keep them from happening again.

"*Now,*" Frazier continued earnestly, "if it's in our power to create any of the situations which a person likes or to remove any situation he doesn't like, we can control his behavior. When he behaves as we want him to behave, we simply create a situation he likes, or remove one he doesn't like. As a result, the probability that he will behave that way again goes up, which is what we want. Technically it's called 'positive reinforcement.'

"The old school made the amazing mistake of supposing that the reverse was true, that by removing a situation a person likes or setting up one he doesn't like—in other words by punishing him—it was possible to *reduce* the probability that he would behave in a given way again. That simply doesn't hold. It has been established beyond question. What is emerging at this critical stage in the evolution of society is a behavioral and cultural technology based on positive reinforcement alone. We are gradually discovering—at an untold cost in human suffering—that in the long run punishment doesn't reduce the probability that an act will occur. We have been so preoccupied with the contrary that we always take 'force' to mean punishment. We don't say we're using force when we send ship-loads of food into a starving country, though we're displaying quite as much *power* as if we were sending troops and guns."

"I'm certainly not an advocate of force," said Castle. "But I can't agree that it's not effective."

"It's *temporarily* effective, that's the worst of it. That explains several thousand years of bloodshed. Even nature has been fooled. We 'instinc-tively' punish a person who doesn't behave as we like—we spank him if he's a child or strike him if he's a man. A nice distinction! The immediate effect of the blow teaches us to strike again. Retribution and revenge are the most natural things on earth. But in the long run the man we strike is no less likely to repeat his act."

"But he won't repeat it if we hit him hard enough." said Castle.

"He'll still *tend* to repeat it. He'll *want* to repeat it. We haven't really altered his potential behavior at all. That's the pity of it. If he doesn't repeat it in our presence, he will in the presence of someone else. Or it will be repeated in the disguise of a neurotic symptom. If we hit hard enough, we clear a little place for ourselves in the wilderness of civiliza-tion, but we make the rest of the wilderness still more terrible.

"Now, early forms of government are naturally based on punishment. It's the obvious technique when the physically strong control the weak. But we're in the throes of a great change to positive reinforcement—from a competitive society in which one man's reward is another man's punish-ment, to a cooperative society in which no one gains at the expense of anyone else.

"The change is slow and painful because the immediate, temporary effect of punishment overshadows the eventual advantage of positive reinforcement. We've all seen countless instances of the temporary effect of force, but clear evidence of the effect of not using force is rare. That's why I insist that Jesus, who was apparently the first to discover the power of refusing to punish, must have hit upon the principle by accident. He certainly had none of the experimental evidence which is available to us today, and I can't conceive that it was possible, no matter what the man's genius, to have discovered the principle from casual observation."

"A touch of revelation, perhaps?" said Castle.

"No, accident. Jesus discovered one principle because it had immedi-ate consequences, and he got another thrown in for good measure."

I began to see light.

"You mean the principle of 'love your enemies'?" I said.

"Exactly! To 'do good to those who despitefully use you' has two unrelated consequences. You gain the peace of mind we talked about the other day. Let the stronger man push you around—at least you avoid the torture of your own rage. *That's* the immediate consequence. What an astonishing discovery it must have been to find that in the long run you could *control the stronger man* in the same way!"

"It's generous of you to give so much credit to your early colleague," said Castle, "but why are we still in the throes of so much misery? Twenty centuries should have been enough for one piece of behavioral engineering."

"The conditions which made the principle difficult to discover made it difficult to teach. The history of the Christian Church doesn't reveal many cases of doing good to one's enemies. To inoffensive heathens, perhaps, but not enemies. One must look outside the field of organized religion to find the principle in practice at all. Church governments are devotees of *power*, both temporal and bogus."

"But what has all this got to do with freedom?" I said hastily.

Frazier took time to reorganize his behavior. He looked steadily toward the window, against which the rain was beating heavily.

"Now that we *know* how positive reinforcement works and why negative doesn't," he said at last, "we can be more deliberate, and hence more successful, in our cultural design. We can achieve a sort of control under which the controlled, though they are following a code much more scrupulously than was ever the case under the old system, nevertheless *feel free*. They are doing what they want to do, not what they are forced to do. That's the source of the tremendous power of positive reinforcement— there's no restraint and no revolt. By a careful cultural design, we control not the final behavior, but the *inclination* to behave—the motives, the desires, the wishes.

"The curious thing is that in that case *the question of freedom never arises*. Mr. Castle was free to drop the matchbook in the sense that nothing was preventing him. If it had been securely bound to his hand he wouldn't have been free. Nor would he have been quite free if I'd covered him with a gun and threatened to shoot him if he let it fall. The question of freedom arises when there is restraint—either physical or psychological.

"But restraint is only one sort of control, and absence of restraint isn't freedom. It's not control that's lacking when one feels 'free,' but the objectionable control of force. Mr. Castle felt free to hold or drop the matches in the sense that he felt no restraint—no threat of punishment in taking either course of action. He neglected to examine his positive reasons for holding or letting go, in spite of the fact that these were more compelling in this instance than any threat of force.

"We have no vocabulary of freedom in dealing with what we want to do," Frazier went on. "The question never arises. When men strike for freedom, they strike against jails and the police, or the threat of them— against oppression. They never strike against forces which make them want to act the way they do. Yet, it seems to be understood that governments will operate only through force or the threat of force, and that all other principles of control will be left to education, religion, and commerce. If this continues to be the case, we may as well give up. A government can never create a free people with the techniques now allotted to it.

"The question is: Can men live in freedom and peace? And the answer is: Yes, if we can build a social structure which will satisfy the needs of everyone and in which everyone will want to observe the supporting code. But so far this has been achieved only in Walden Two. Your ruthless accusations to the contrary, Mr. Castle, this is the freest place on earth. And it is free precisely because we make no use of force or the threat of force. Every bit of our research, from the nursery through the psychological management of our adult membership, is directed toward that end—to exploit every alternative to forcible control. By skillful planning, by a wise choice of techniques we *increase* the feeling of freedom.

"It's not planning which infringes upon freedom, but planning which uses force. A sense of freedom was practically unknown in the planned society of Nazi Germany, because the planners made a fantastic use of force and the threat of force.

"No, Mr. Castle, when a science of behavior has once been achieved, there's no alternative to a planned society. We can't leave mankind to an accidental or biased control. But by using the principle of positive reinforcement—carefully avoiding force or the threat of force—we can preserve a personal sense of freedom."

6. Ignoble Utopias   Joseph Wood Krutch

Joseph Wood Krutch (1893–1970) was a philosopher, essayist, and naturalist. He taught English at Columbia until the early 1950's, when he moved to the Arizona desert. *The Measure of Man* is generally considered his most important philosophical work.

Walden Two is a utopian community created by an experimental psychologist named Frazier who has learned the techniques for controlling thought with precision and who has conditioned his subjects to be happy, obedient and incapable of antisocial behavior. Universal benevolence and large tolerance of individual differences reign—not because it is assumed, as the founders of such utopias generally do assume, that they are natural to all innocent men uncorrupted by society—but because an experimental scientist, having at last mastered the "scientific ability to control men's thoughts with precision," has caused them to think benevolently and tolerantly.

An appeal to reason in contradistinction to passion, habit, or mere custom has been the usual basis of utopias from Plato to Sir Thomas More and even down to Samuel Butler. Mr. Skinner's is, on the other hand, distinctly modern in that it puts its faith in the conditioned reflex instead, and proposes to perfect mankind by making individual men incapable of anything except habit and prejudice. At Walden Two men behave in a fashion we are accustomed to call "reasonable," not because they reason, but because they do not; because "right responses" are automatic. At the very beginning of the story we are shown a flock of sheep confined to the area reserved for them by a single thread which long ago replaced the electric fence once employed to condition them not to wander. As predicted in official Communist theory, the State—represented here by electricity—has "withered away" and no actual restraint is necessary to control creatures in whom obedience has become automatic. Obviously the assumption is that what will work with sheep will work with men.

Now though men can reason, they are not exclusively reasoning creatures. None, therefore, of the classic utopias could be realized because each is based on the assumption that reason alone can be made to guide human behavior. Moreover—and what is perhaps more important—few people have ever seriously wished to be exclusively rational. The good life which most desire is a life warmed by passions and touched with that ceremonial grace which is impossible without some affectionate loyalty to traditional forms and ceremonies. Many have, nevertheless, been very willing to grant that a little more reason in the conduct of private and public affairs would not be amiss. That is why, as fantasies, the utopias of Plato and Sir Thomas More have seemed interesting, instructive, even inspiring. But who really wants, even in fancy, to be, as Walden Two would make him, more unthinking, more nearly automatic than he now is? Who, even in his imagination, would like to live in a community where, instead of thinking part of the time, one never found it possible to think at all?

Is it not meaningful to say that whereas Plato's Republic and More's Utopia are noble absurdities, Walden Two is an ignoble one; that the first two ask men to be more than human, while the second urges them to be less? When, in the present world, men behave well, that is no doubt sometimes because they are creatures of habit as well as, sometimes, because they are reasonable. But if one proposes to change Man as Professor Skinner and so many other cheerful mechanists propose, is it really so evident that he should be changed in the direction they advocate? Is he something which, in Nietzsche's phrase, "must be surpassed," or is he a creature to whom the best advice one can give is the advice to retreat—away from such reasoned behavior as he may be capable of and toward that automatism of which he is also capable.

Obviously Walden Two represents—glorified, perfected, and curiously modernized—that ideal of a "cloistered virtue" which European man has tended to find not only unsatisfactory as an ideal but almost meaningless in terms of his doubtless conflicting aspirations. Nevertheless it must be admitted that Thomas Henry Huxley, a protomodern, once admitted in an often quoted passage that "if some great power would agree to make me always think what is true and do what is right, on condition of being turned into a sort of clock and wound up every morning before I got out of bed, I should instantly close with the offer." And what a Huxley would have agreed to, prospective candidates for admission into Walden Two might also find acceptable.

Frazier himself is compelled to make a significant confession: the motives which led him to undertake his successful experiment included a certain desire to exercise power over his fellows. That is not admirable in itself and is obviously not without its dangers. But he insists that the danger will disappear with him because those who succeed to his authority and inherit his techniques will have enjoyed, as he did not, the advantages of a scientific conditioning process and that therefore such potentially antisocial impulses as his will no longer exist. In other words, though the benevolent dictator is a rare phenomenon today, the happy chance which produced this one will not have to be relied on in the future. Walden Two will automatically produce the dictators necessary to carry it on.

Nevertheless and even if the skeptical reader will grant for the sake of argument that automatic virtue represents an ideal completely satisfactory, a multitude of other doubts and fears are likely to arise in his mind. He will remember of course that Brook Farm and the rest failed promptly and decisively. Perhaps he will remember also that Russian communism achieved at least some degree of permanence only by rejecting, more and more completely, everything which in any way parallels the mildness, the gentleness, and the avoidance of all direct restraints and pressures which is characteristic of Walden Two; that the makers of Soviet policy came to denounce and repress even that somewhat paradoxical enthusiasm for the culture of a different world which was as much encouraged in the earliest days of the experiment as it is at Walden Two.

Hence, if a Walden Two is possible it obviously has become so only because—and this is a point which presumably Mr. Skinner himself wishes to emphasize—it differs in several respects from all superficially similar projects. Like the Russian experiment it assumes that, for all practical purposes, man is merely the product of society; but it also assumes a situation which did not exist when the Communist state was set up: namely one in which "the scientific ability to control men's thoughts with precision" has fully matured.

Thus if the man upon whom the experiment is performed is nothing but the limitlessly plastic product of external processes operating upon him and is, by definition, incapable of any significant autonomous activity, he is also, in this case, a creature who has fallen into the hands of an ideally competent dictator. His desires, tastes, convictions and ideals are precisely what the experimenter wants to make them. He is the repository of no potentialities which can ever develop except as they are called forth by circumstances over which he has no control. Finally, of course, his happy condition is the result of the fortunate accident which determined that the "engineer" who created him and, indirectly, will create all of his progeny, was an experimenter whose own random conditioning happened to produce, not the monster who might just as likely have been the first to seize the power that science offered, but a genuinely benevolent dictator instead.

A propos this last premise it might, in passing, be remarked as a curious fact that though scientific method abhors the accidental, the uncontrollable and the unpredicted; though Mr. Skinner's own ideal seems to be to remove forever any possible future intrusion of it into human affairs; yet the successful establishment of the first utopia depended ultimately on the decisive effect of just such an accident as will henceforth be impossible.

Critics of the assumption that technological advance is the true key to human progress have often urged that new powers are dangerous rather than beneficial unless the question of how they should be used is at least opened before the powers become available. With more than usual anxiety they might contemplate the situation in which we are now placed if it is true that only chance will answer the question by whom and in the interest of what "our approaching scientific ability to control men's thoughts with precision" is to be used. But this is only one of several desperate questions which the premises of *Walden Two* provoke. Most of them can also be related to points made by Mr. Skinner in less fanciful contexts and to one or two of them we may turn in connection with a more general consideration of problems raised if we are ready to assume that we actually do stand at the threshold of a world in which men's thoughts will be controlled scientifically and as a matter of course.

To begin with, we must, of course, abandon the old platitude, "You can't change human nature," and accept its opposite, "You can change human nature as much and in whatever direction you wish"—because "human nature" does not exist in the sense which the phrase implies. Whatever desires, tastes, preferences, and tendencies have been so general and so persistent as to create the assumption that they are innate or "natural" must be, as a matter of fact, merely the most ancient and deeply graven of the conditionings to which the human animal has been subjected. As Pascal—an odd thinker to be invoked in defense of a mechanistic and completely relativist ethic—once exclaimed in one of those terrifying speculations of which, no doubt, his own conditioning made him capable: "They say that habit is Second Nature; but perhaps Nature is only First Habit."

By eager reformers "You can't change human nature" has often been denounced as both a counsel of despair and a convenient excuse for lazy indifference in the face of the world's ills. Yet the fact or alleged fact which the phrase attempts to state has also its positive aspect. To say that human nature cannot be changed means that human nature is something in itself and there is at least the possibility that part of this something is valuable. If we say that it cannot be changed we are also saying that it cannot be completely corrupted; that it cannot be transformed into something which we would not recognize as human at all. This is what the eighteenth century allowed Pope to say for it, and as long as one holds the doctrine that the term Nature actually describes some enduring set of possibilities and values, then some limit is set, not only to human perfectibility, but also, and more encouragingly, to things which it can become or be made.

But once this view of "Nature" has been dismissed as an illusion and even what appear to be the most persistent of its traits are thought of as merely the result of conditioning, then there is no limit to the extent to

which men may become different from what they now are. There is nothing against which it may be assumed that human nature will revolt. Only
by a temporarily established convention is any kind of vice a "creature of
so frightful mien." Anything can be made to seem "natural." Cruelty,
treachery, slander and deceit might come generally to seem not frightful
but beautiful. And if it be said that the successful putting into practice of
certain recent political philosophies supports the contention of determinists that man may, indeed, be taught to believe precisely this, it must be
added that something more is also implied: namely that we must abandon—along with the conviction that human nature cannot be changed—
all the hopes expressed in such phrases as "human nature will in the end
revolt against" this or that.

Since no human nature capable of revolting against anything is now
presumed to exist, then some other experimenter—conditioned perhaps
as the son of the commandant of a Nazi labor camp—might decide to
develop a race of men who found nothing more delightful than the
infliction of suffering, and to establish for them a colony to be called Walden Three. By what standards could the dictator of Walden Two presume
to judge that his utopia was any more desirable than its new rival? He
could not appeal to God's revealed word; to the inner light of conscience;
or to that eighteenth-century stand-by, the voice of Nature. He could say
only that the accidents of his previous existence in a world where accident
still played its part in determining how an individual should be conditioned had conditioned him to prefer what he would, in full realization of
the unjustifiability of the metaphor, call "light rather than darkness." The
life in Walden Two appears to him as "good" but the adjective would, of
course, have no meaning in relation to anything outside himself.

In the light of such possibilities those who have not yet been molded
by either Walden Two or Walden Three will tend to feel that before the
"scientific ability to control men's thoughts with precision" has been fully
utilized by whoever may seize the limitless power it will confer, we had
better take a last look around—if not for that way of escape which may
not exist, then at least in order to grasp certain implications and possible
consequences as they appear to the minds of men who are still "free"—
free at least in the limited sense that they are the product of conditions
which were brought about, in part, through the presence of random factors destined to play a smaller and smaller part in determining human
personality. That second generation of dictators to whom the dictator of
Walden Two expects to pass on the control of affairs will be conditioners
who have themselves been conditioned. The circle of cause and effect will
have been closed and no man will ever again be anything which his predecessor has not consciously willed him to be.

According to the mechanist's own theories, everything which happened in the universe from its beginning down, at least until yesterday,
was the result of chance. The chemical molecule didn't "want" or "plan"
to grow more complex until it was a protein; the protein did not plan to
become protoplasm; and the amoeba did not plan to become man. As a
matter of fact, a theory very popular at the moment explains the fact that
life seems to have arisen on our earth but once in all the billions of years

of the planet's existence by saying that it could arise only as the result of a combination of circumstances so fantastically improbable that they have never occurred again. Yet though they owe to chance both their very existence and all progress from the protozoan to civilization, they are eager to take a step which would make it forever impossible for the unexpected and the unplanned to erupt again into the scheme which will pass completely under their own control.

No doubt many practical-minded people will object that such speculations as these are a waste of time. After all, they will say, even Walden Two does not exist except in fancy and no one has yet claimed that the "approaching scientific ability to control men's thoughts with precision" has already arrived. Logical dilemmas and metaphysical difficulties are cobwebs which will not entangle those who refuse to take seriously their gossamer threads. We have work to do and practical problems to solve.

But to all such it may be replied that practical problems and the metaphysical forms to which they may be reduced are not so unrelated as they may think, and that the logical extreme sometimes serves to make clear the real nature of a purely practical problem. It is true that no man has yet established a Walden Two or Walden Three, and that neither has any man yet controlled *with precision* men's thoughts. But it is also true that there has been a movement in a direction which suggests Walden Two as an ideal. Moreover, statesmen, educators and publicists have already achieved considerable success in their frankly admitted attempts to use the techniques already developed to control and condition large sections of the public and have increasingly declared their faith in the desirability and practicality of such methods in contradistinction to what used to be called education, on the one hand, and appeals to the enlightened understanding of the public, on the other. Already it has quite seriously and without any conviction of cynicism been proposed that the advertisers' principle, "say a thing often enough and it will be believed," be utilized by those who have what they regard as "correct" or "healthy" or "socially useful" ideas to sell. Every time it is proposed that schools should develop certain attitudes in their pupils or that the government should undertake propaganda along a certain line, the question of the difficult distinction between education in some old-fashioned sense and "conditioning" definitely arises.

Moreover, it is because the techniques of the social scientist and the experimental psychologists do to some extent work that some attempt must be made to understand their implications. By their methods many men may be made to do and think many things. Already in the relatively simple case of education versus "useful conditioning," the difficult distinction ceases to be difficult once a border line has been definitely crossed. Writing to George Washington not long after our particular democracy had been founded, Thomas Jefferson remarked, "It is an axiom in my mind that our liberty can never be safe but in the hands of the people themselves, and that, too, of the people with a certain degree of instruction." What would Jefferson have thought of the suggestion that "a certain degree of instruction" be interpreted to mean "a certain degree of conditioning"? Would he not have pointed out that the distinction between the two is clear and fundamental; that "conditioning" is achieved by methods which by-pass or, as it were, short-circuit those very reasoning faculties which education proposes to cultivate and exercise? And would he not have added that democracy can have no meaning or no function unless it is assumed that these faculties do lie within a realm of freedom where the sanctions of democracy arise?

Thus the whole future of mankind may well depend not only on the question whether man is entirely or only in part the product of conditionings, but also on the extent to which he is treated as though he were. Will we come ultimately to base what we call "education," in and out of schools, on the assumption that conditioning by propaganda as well as other methods is the most effective, even if it is not the only, method of influencing human beings.

To all such questions an answer in pragmatic terms has already been given at least positively enough to make it very pertinent to ask into whose hands the power already being exercised is to fall; to ask who is to decide in what direction the citizen is to be conditioned, and on the bases of what standards of value those decisions are to be made. That is simply the practical aspect of the theoretical question, "Who shall be master of Walden Two?"

In the totalitarian countries, where deterministic theories have been accepted in their most unqualified form and the techniques of control most systematically practiced, the question just posed has been answered in the simplest possible manner, and very much in the same way that it was answered at Walden Two. Power is exercised by those who seized it and, theoretically at least, this seizure was the last event which could "happen" because henceforward human destiny will be in the hands of those who are now in a position to control it. The question whether they ought to have done so and whether it is well for humanity that they did was either always meaningless or soon to become so since all the value judgments made in the future will be made by those who have been conditioned to approve what has happened to them.

One result of all this is that during the transition period while there are still survivors from the age when men's minds had not yet been controlled with precision and a conflict of wills is still possible—*i.e.,* under the conditions prevailing in the totalitarian states as they actually exist—a sharp distinction has to be made between those in possession of the power which they have seized and those who are subject to their manipulations. As a catchword the old term "classless society" may be used, but it is evident that no two classes could be more widely separated than the class of those who decide what shall be done and the class of those who are conditioned and controlled.

Obviously such a situation cannot arise either in Germany, Russia or Walden Two until the seizure of power has actually occurred and the power seized must include not only the classic essential, "the instruments of production," but also those "instruments of thought control" which seem to be assuming a more crucial importance than Marx assigned them.

No less obviously this seizure has not yet been made in the countries still called "democratic." Power may be drifting into the hands of certain groups but most of the members of these groups are not quite so completely committed as the totalitarian leaders were to the theories by which they justified their acts and are therefore not so ready to assume the dictatorship which may possibly be already within their reach. In such countries it is, therefore, still possible to consider certain questions, both practical and metaphysical, which even those still capable of considering them are forbidden to raise publicly in totalitarian states. We can still think—or at least go through those mental motions which were formerly called thinking—about the direction in which our own society seems to be moving, about certain large questions of values and ethics, even about the possibilities that under certain conditions men may not be the automata they are more and more assumed to be and that therefore their thoughts never can be controlled either completely or "with precision." Even more specifically we may ask whether totalitarianism on either the model of Soviet Russia or Walden Two is what we wish for or must inevitably accept.

It has sometimes been said that the totalitarian state is merely what democracy must in time become. Enthusiastically in the one case, reluctantly in the other, the same premises lead to the same methods and the same methods to the same results. What one proclaims definitively as dogma is the same as what the other drifts toward and this distinction is the only one which can be made, no matter where we attempt to draw it. In this view a "people's democracy" is only a "welfare state" which has fully accepted its implications. In theory as well as in practice the difference is always merely in the degree to which the logic of any position has been followed to its ultimate conclusion.

No doubt reality is much less simple. But after this large proviso has been accepted much can be said to support the contention that what we of the democracies toy with and lean toward are the same scientific hypotheses and the same philosophical notions that totalitarians proclaim as truths it is forbidden to question.

Roman Catholic doctrine makes the useful distinction between those beliefs which are *de fide* and those which are no more than *pia sententia*. The one must be accepted without dispute by all who wish to remain within the fold; the other, though part of commonly held opinion, have the weight of no authority behind them. In many cases the distinction between what the Communist state proclaims concerning the real nature of man and the proper methods of dealing with it differs from what many of our own psychologists and sociologists tend to assume only as an article of belief which has been proclaimed *de fide* differs from *pia sententia*. What we may tend to deduce from, say, the Pavlovian experiments does not differ too significantly from what an orthodox Russian scientist would say that these same experiments have proved with ultimate finality.

In what the sociologist previously quoted was pleased to call "today's thinking" man tends to appear very much what the Russian version of Marxist science would make him and those who follow such lines of thought are inevitably led to the same next step. If man is the product of the conditioning to which chance has subjected him, why should we not make him what we would like him to be?

We have, it is said, already effectively asserted our control over nature, animate and inanimate. Technology has already entered its mature phase and biology is entering it. We have mastered the atom; we have also learned how both to breed and to train animals. Since man is part of nature he also should be subject to control and no more should be necessary to make him so than easy extensions of the methods already successfully applied. We boast that we have mastered nature but that mastery can hardly be called complete until human nature is at least as completely under our control as the other phenomena of animate nature have become.

Perhaps the most general aspect of this subtle but inclusive shift of emphasis is revealed in the almost unconscious substitution of one term for another when the characteristics of a good social order are discussed. At the beginning of the democratic movement the watchword was "opportunity." Social and political evils were thought of as impediments to the free development of aspirations and abilities. But because "opportunity" as an ideal implies faith in the autonomous powers of the individual it has given way to others embodied in words which suggest in one way or another, not what men may be permitted to do for themselves, but what with benevolent intentions of course may be done to them.

The most brutally frank of such words is of course "control" but it is used most freely by those who have come frankly to accept a barely disguised totalitarian ideal. In those who wish still to pay lip service at least to some sort of faith in democracy and freedom the preferred words are "education," "adjustment" and, with a closer approach to frankness, "conditioning." But the difference is one of degree, not in the fundamental assumption which is that men should not be left to develop but must have their characters and temperaments, as well as their daily lives, somehow "planned" for them. The most benign aspect of this assumption is revealed in the desire for a "welfare state" which will assure the physical well-being of its citizens. The most sinister aspect is that more fully revealed in the speculations of the most advanced and theoretical social psychologists who have passed on, as the author of *Walden Two* has, to consider how the character, opinions and tastes of the individual may also be "planned" for him.

No doubt many of those who agree with that Dean of the Humanities to whose happy phrase we find ourselves again and again recurring would speak with the customary horror of the frankly totalitarian states which have, to date, achieved the greatest success in controlling men's thoughts with precision. They would carefully avoid such frank terms as "brain washing" which the Communists use to state clearly their intentions. But it is difficult to see what difference there is except the difference between a philosophy which is still tentative and somewhat reluctant to admit its ultimate implications and one which, facing those implications, proceeds confidently to put into practice the techniques which it has found effective. If "adjustment" is not to become "control" and "conditioning" is to shop short of "brain washing," some limits must be set which are not defined or even hinted at in such statements as those made by some psychologists.

Even those of us whose convictions permit us to doubt that men's thoughts will ever be completely controlled with absolute "precision" must realize, nevertheless, that the "scientific ability" to control them to some considerable degree has been growing and that in all probability it will grow still further. The terrifying extent to which many (if not all) the individuals in a group may be made to act and think in ways which we would once have thought inconceivable is already all too evident. Hence the question of how that power, whether it be limited or unlimited, will be used in our own society is of immediate as well as remote importance. It is no longer merely a metaphysical one.

It does no good to say that the democracy to which we assure ourselves we are committed safeguards us against the arbitrary use of that power. To say anything of the sort is merely to beg the question because an essential part of the question has to do with the reasonable doubt whether what we call democracy can survive the maturing techniques for determining in advance what "the voice of the people" will say. "Democracy," as the West defined it and in contradistinction to the new definition which totalitarianism has attempted to formulate, is meaningless except on the assumption that the individual man's thoughts and desires are to some extent uncontrollable and unpredictable. There can be no possible reason for taking a vote if the results can either be determined or even predicted in advance. In a society which assures, rightly or wrongly, that events are predictably determined, elections can be no more than those rituals with only a formal, ceremonial significance which, in Soviet Russia and Nazi Germany, they actually became.

In Walden Two this fact is tacitly recognized. Its founding dictator expects authority to "wither away" at the time of his death if not before, precisely as, in Communist theory, the dictatorship of the party will some day wither. But before withering away has occurred, the whole future history of mankind will have been set in a pattern which can never suffer any fundamental change because it must correspond to the pattern of conditionings which are self-perpetuating once they have been firmly and universally established. It is hard to see how we can accept even pragmatically the convictions and ideals of Walden Two without incurring consequences which correspond in the realm of the actual to the theoretical consequences of its theoretical premises. The question whether our own society is in the process of turning itself into some sort of Walden Two is far from being merely fantastic.

The Responsibility of Criminals

7. Address to the Prisoners in the Cook County Jail
Clarence Darrow

Clarence Seward Darrow (1857–1938) was one of America's outstanding criminal and trial lawyers. Among his famous cases were the Leopold and Loeb murder trial and the Scopes's evolution trial in Tennessee. He was an outspoken agnostic and an opponent of traditional penal practices.

Reprinted with permission of Charles H. Kerr Publishing Company from *Crime and Criminals* by Clarence Darrow, published in 1975.

If I looked at jails and crimes and prisoners in the way the ordinary person does, I should not speak on this subject to you. The reason I talk to you on the question of crime, its cause and cure, is that I really do not in the least believe in crime. There is no such thing as a crime as the word is generally understood. I do not believe there is any sort of distinction between the real moral conditions of the people in and out of jail. One is just as good as the other. The people here can no more help being here than the people outside can avoid being outside. I do not believe that people are in jail because they deserve to be. They are in jail simply because they cannot avoid it on account of circumstances which are entirely beyond their control and for which they are in no way responsible.

I suppose a great many people on the outside would say I was doing you harm if they should hear what I say to you this afternoon, but you cannot be hurt a great deal anyway, so it will not matter. Good people outside would say that I was really teaching you things that were calculated to injure society, but it's worth while now and then to hear something different from what you ordinarily get from preachers and the like. These will tell you that you should be good and then you will get rich and be happy. Of course we know that people do not get rich by being good, and that is the reason why so many of you people try to get rich some other way, only you do not understand how to do it quite as well as the fellow outside.

There are people who think that everything in this world is an accident. But really there is no such thing as an accident. A great many folks admit that many of the people in jail ought to be there, and many who are outside ought to be in. I think none of them ought to be here. There ought to be no jails; and if it were not for the fact that the people on the outside are so grasping and heartless in their dealings with the people on the inside, there would be no such institution as jails.

I do not want you to believe that I think all you people here are angels. I do not think that. You are people of all kinds, all of you doing the best you can—and that is evidently not very well. You are people of all kinds and conditions and under all circumstances. In one sense everybody is equally good and equally bad. We all do the best we can under the circumstances. But as to the exact things for which you are sent here, some of you are guilty and did the particular act because you needed the money. Some of you did it because you are in the habit of doing it, and some of you because you are born to it, and it comes to be as natural as it does, for instance, for me to be good.

Most of you probably have nothing against me, and most of you would treat me the same as any other person would, probably better than some of the people on the outside would treat me, because you think I believe in you and they know I do not believe in them. While you would not have the least thing against me in the world, you might pick my pockets. I do not think all of you would, but I think some of you would. You would not have anything against me, but that's your profession, a few of you. Some of the rest of you, if my doors were unlocked, might come in if you saw anything you wanted—not out of any malice to me, but because that is your trade. There is no doubt there are quite a number of people in this jail who would pick my pockets. And still I know this—that when I get outside pretty nearly everybody picks my pocket. There may be some of you who would hold up a man on the street, if you did not happen to have something else to do, and needed the money; but when I want to light my house or my office the gas company holds me up. They charge me one dollar for something that is worth twenty-five cents. Still all these people are good people; they are pillars of society and support the churches, and they are respectable.

When I ride on the streetcars I am held up—I pay five cents for a ride that is worth two and a half cents, simply because a body of men have bribed the city council and the legislature, so that all the rest of us have to pay tribute to them.

If I do not want to fall into the clutches of the gas trust and choose to burn oil instead of gas, then good Mr. Rockefeller holds me up, and he uses a certain portion of his money to build universities and support churches which are engaged in telling us how to be good.

Some of you are here for obtaining property under false pretenses—yet I pick up a great Sunday paper and read the advertisements of a merchant prince—"Shirtwaists for 39 cents, marked down from $3.00."

When I read the advertisements in the paper I see they are all lies. When I want to get out and find a place to stand anywhere on the face of the earth, I find that it has all been taken up long ago before I came here, and before you came here, and somebody says, "Get off, swim into the lake, fly into the air; go anywhere, but get off." That is because these people have the police and they have the jails and the judges and the lawyers and the soldiers and all the rest of them to take care of the earth and drive everybody off that comes in their way.

A great many people will tell you that all this is true, but that it does not excuse you. These facts do not excuse some fellow who reaches into my pocket and takes out a five-dollar bill. The fact that the gas company bribes the members of the legislature from year to year, and fixes the law, so that all you people are compelled to be "fleeced" whenever you deal with them; the fact that the streetcar companies and the gas companies have control of the streets; and the fact that the landlords own all the earth—this, they say, has nothing to do with you.

Let us see whether there is any connection between the crimes of the respectable classes and your presence in the jail. Many of you people are in jail because you have really committed burglary; many of you, because you have stolen something. In the meaning of the law, you have taken some other person's property. Some of you have entered a store and carried off a pair of shoes because you did not have the price. Possibly some of you have committed murder. I cannot tell what all of you did. There are a great many people here who have done some of these things who really do not know themselves why they did them. I think I know why you did them—every one of you; you did these things because you were bound to do them. It looked to you at the time as if you had a chance to do them or not, as you saw fit; but still, after all, you had no choice. There may be people here who had some money in their pockets and who still went out and got some more money in a way society forbids. Now, you may not yourselves see exactly why it was you did this thing, but if you look at the question deeply enough and carefully enough you will see that there were circumstances that drove you to do exactly the thing which you did. You could not help it any more than we outside can help taking the positions that we take. The reformers who tell you to be good and you will be happy, and the people on the outside who have property to protect—they think that the only way to do it is by building jails and locking you up in cells on weekdays and praying for you Sundays.

I think that all of this has nothing whatever to do with right conduct. I think it is very easily seen what has to do with right conduct. Some so-called criminals—and I will use this word because it is handy, it means nothing to me—I speak of the criminals who get caught as distinguished from the criminals who catch them—some of these so-called criminals are in jail for their first offenses, but nine tenths of you are in jail because you did not have a good lawyer and, of course, you did not have a good lawyer because you did not have enough money to pay a good lawyer. There is no very great danger of a rich man going to jail.

Some of you may be here for the first time. If we would open the doors and let you out, and leave the laws as they are today, some of you would be back tomorrow. This is about as good a place as you can get anyway. There are many people here who are so in the habit of coming that they would not know where else to go. There are people who are born with the tendency to break into jail every chance they get, and they cannot avoid it. You cannot figure out your life and see why it was, but still there is a reason for it; and if we were all wise and knew all the facts, we could figure it out.

In the first place, there are a good many more people who go to jail in the wintertime than in summer. Why is this? Is it because people are more wicked in winter? No, it is because the coal trust begins to get in its grip in the winter. A few gentlemen take possession of the coal, and unless the people will pay seven or eight dollars a ton for something that is worth three dollars, they will have to freeze. Then there is nothing to do but to break into jail, and so there are many more in jail in the winter than in summer. It costs more for gas in the winter because the nights are longer, and people go to jail to save gas bills. The jails are electric-lighted. You may not know it, but these economic laws are working all the time, whether we know it or do not know it.

There are more people who go to jail in hard times than in good times—few people, comparatively, go to jail except when they are hard up. They go to jail because they have no other place to go. They may not know why, but it is true all the same. People are not more wicked in hard times. That is not the reason. The fact is true all over the world that in hard times more people go to jail than in good times, and in winter more people go to jail than in summer. Of course it is pretty hard times for people who go to jail at any time. The people who go to jail are almost always poor people—people who have no other place to live, first and last. When times are hard, then you find large numbers of people who go to jail who would not otherwise be in jail.

Long ago, Mr. Buckle, who was a great philosopher and historian, collected facts, and he showed that the number of people who are arrested increased just as the price of food increased. When they put up the price of gas ten cents a thousand, I do not know who will go to jail, but I do know that a certain number of people will go. When the meat combine raises the price of beef, I do not know who is going to jail, but I know that a large number of people are bound to go. Whenever the Standard Oil Company raises the price of oil, I know that a certain number of girls who are seamstresses, and who work night after night long hours for somebody else, will be compelled to go out on the streets and ply another trade, and I know that Mr. Rockefeller and his associates are responsible and not the poor girls in the jails.

First and last, people are sent to jail because they are poor. Sometimes, as I say, you may not need money at the particular time, but you wish to have thrifty forehanded habits, and do not always wait until you are in absolute want. Some of you people are perhaps plying the trade, the profession, which is called burglary. No man in his right senses will go into a strange house in the dead of night and prowl around with a dark lantern through unfamiliar rooms and take chances of his life, if he has plenty of the good things of the world in his own home. You would not take any such chances as that. If a man had clothes in his clothes-press and beefsteak in his pantry and money in the bank, he would not navigate around nights in houses where he knows nothing about the premises whatever. It always requires experience and education for this profession, and people who fit themselves for it are no more to blame than I am for being a lawyer. A man would not hold up another man on the street if he had plenty of money in his own pocket. He might do it if he had one dollar or two dollars, but he wouldn't if he had as much money as Mr. Rockefeller has. Mr. Rockefeller has a great deal better hold-up game than that.

The more that is taken from the poor by the rich, who have the chance to take it, the more poor people there are who are compelled to resort to these means for a livelihood. They may not understand it, they may not think so at once, but after all they are driven into that line of employment.

There is a bill before the legislature of this state to punish kidnaping children with death. We have wise members of the legislature. They know the gas trust when they see it and they always see it—they can furnish light enough to be seen; and this legislature thinks it is going to stop kidnaping children by making a law punishing kidnapers of children with death. I don't believe in kidnaping children, but the legislature is all wrong. Kidnaping children is not a crime, it is a profession. It has been developed with the times. It has been developed with our modern industrial conditions. There are many ways of making money—many new ways that our ancestors knew nothing about. Our ancestors knew nothing about a billion-dollar trust; and here comes some poor fellow who has no other trade and he discovers the profession of kidnaping children.

This crime is born, not because people are bad; people don't kidnap other people's children because they want the children or because they are devilish, but because they see a chance to get some money out of it. You cannot cure this crime by passing a law punishing by death kidnapers of children. There is one way to cure it. There is one way to cure all these offenses, and that is to give the people a chance to live. There is no other way, and there never was any other way since the world began; and the world is so blind and stupid that it will not see. If every man and woman and child in the world had a chance to make a decent, fair, honest living, there would be no jails and no lawyers and no courts. There might be some persons here or there with some peculiar formation of their brain, like Rockefeller, who would do these things simply to be doing them; but they would be very, very few, and those should be sent to a hospital and treated, and not sent to jail; and they would entirely disappear in the second generation, or at least in the third generation.

I am not talking pure theory. I will just give you two or three illustrations.

The English people once punished criminals by sending them away. They would load them on a ship and export them to Australia. England was owned by lords and nobles and rich people. They owned the whole earth over there, and the other people had to stay in the streets. They could not get a decent living. They used to take their criminals and send them to Australia—I mean the class of criminals who got caught. When these criminals got over there, and nobody else had come, they had the whole continent to run over, and so they could raise sheep and furnish their own meat, which is easier than stealing it. These criminals then became decent, respectable people because they had a chance to live. They did not commit any crimes. They were just like the English people who sent them there, only better. And in the second generation the descendants of those criminals were as good and respectable a class of people as there were on the face of the earth, and then they began building churches and jails themselves.

A portion of this country was settled in the same way, landing prisoners down on the southern coast; but when they got here and had a whole continent to run over and plenty of chances to make a living, they became respectable citizens, making their own living just like any other citizen in the world. But finally the descendants of the English aristocracy who sent the people over to Australia found out they were getting rich, and so they went over to get possession of the earth as they always do, and they organized land syndicates and got control of the land and ores, and then they had just as many criminals in Australia as they did in England. It was not because the world had grown bad; it was because the earth had been taken away from the people.

Some of you people have lived in the country. It's prettier than it is here. And if you have ever lived on a farm you understand that if you put a lot of cattle in a field, when the pasture is short they will jump over the fence; but put them in a good field where there is plenty of pasture, and they will be law-abiding cattle to the end of time. The human animal is just like the rest of the animals, only a little more so. The same thing that governs in the one governs in the other.

Everybody makes his living along the lines of least resistance. A wise man who comes into a country early sees a great undeveloped land. For instance, our rich men twenty-five years ago saw that Chicago was small and knew a lot of people would come here and settle, and they readily saw that if they had all the land around here it would be worth a good deal, so they grabbed the land. You cannot be a landlord because somebody has got it all. You must find some other calling. In England and Ireland and Scotland less than five per cent own all the land there is, and the people are bound to stay there on any kind of terms the landlords give. They must live the best they can, so they develop all these various professions—burglary, picking pockets and the like.

Again, people find all sorts of ways of getting rich. These are diseases like everything else. You look at people getting rich, organizing trusts and making a million dollars, and somebody gets the disease and he starts out. He catches it just as a man catches the mumps or the measles; he is not to blame, it is in the air. You will find men speculating beyond their means, because the mania of money-getting is taking possession of them. It is simply a disease—nothing more, nothing less. You cannot avoid catching it; but the fellows who have control of the earth have the advantage of you. See what the law is: when these men get control of things, they make the laws. They do not make the laws to protect anybody; courts are not instruments of justice. When your case gets into court it will make little difference whether you are guilty or innocent, but it's better if you have a smart lawyer. And you cannot have a smart lawyer unless you have money. First and last it's a question of money. Those men who own the earth make the laws to protect what they have. They fix up a sort of fence or pen around what they have, and they fix the law so the fellow on the outside cannot get in. The laws are really organized for the protection of the men who rule the world. They were never organized or enforced to do justice. We have no system for doing justice, not the slightest in the world.

Let me illustrate: Take the poorest person in this room. If the community had provided a system of doing justice, the poorest person in this room would have as good a lawyer as the richest, would he not? When you went into court you would have just as long a trial and just as fair a trial as the richest person in Chicago. Your case would not be tried in fifteen or twenty minutes, whereas it would take fifteen days to get through with a rich man's case.

Then if you were rich and were beaten, your case would be taken to the Appellate Court. A poor man cannot take his case to the Appellate Court; he has not the price. And then to the Supreme Court. And if he were beaten there he might perhaps go to the United States Supreme Court. And he might die of old age before he got into jail. If you are poor, it's a quick job. You are almost known to be guilty, else you would not be there. Why should anyone be in the criminal court if he were not guilty? He would not be there if he could be anywhere else. The officials have no time to look after all these cases. The people who are on the outside, who are running banks and building churches and making jails, they have no time to examine 600 or 700 prisoners each year to see whether they are guilty or innocent. If the courts were organized to promote justice the people would elect somebody to defend all these criminals, somebody as smart as the prosecutor—and give him as many detectives and as many assistants to help, and pay as much money to defend you as to prosecute you. We have a very able man for state's attorney, and he has many assistants, detectives and policemen without end, and judges to hear the cases—everything handy.

Most all of our criminal code consists in offenses against property. People are sent to jail because they have committed a crime against property. It is of very little consequence whether one hundred people more or less go to jail who ought not to go—you must protect property, because in this world property is of more importance than anything else.

How is it done? These people who have property fix it so they can protect what they have. When somebody commits a crime it does not follow that he has done something that is morally wrong. The man on the outside who has committed no crime may have done something. For instance: to take all the coal in the United States and raise the price two dollars or three dollars when there is no need of it, and thus kill thousands of babies and send thousands of people to the poorhouse and tens of thousands to jail, as is done every year in the United States—this is a greater crime than all the people in our jails ever committed; but the law does not punish it. Why? Because the fellows who control the earth make the laws. If you and I had the making of the laws, the first thing we would do would be to punish the fellow who gets control of the earth. Nature put this coal in the ground for me as well as for them, and nature made the prairies up here to raise wheat for me as well as for them, and then the great railroad companies came along and fenced it up.

Most all of the crimes for which we are punished are property crimes. There are a few personal crimes, like murder—but they are very few. The crimes committed are mostly those against property. If this punishment is right the criminals must have a lot of property. How much money is there in this crowd? And yet you are all here for crimes against property. The people up and down the Lake Shore have not committed crime; still they have so much property they don't know what to do with it. It is perfectly plain why these people have not committed crimes against property; they make the laws and therefore do not need to break them. And in order for you to get some property you are obliged to break the rules of the game. I don't know but what some of you may have had a very nice chance to get rich by carrying a hod for one dollar a day, twelve hours. Instead of taking that nice, easy profession, you are a burglar. If you had been given a chance to be a banker you would rather follow that. Some of you may have had a chance to work as a switchman on a railroad where you know, according to statistics, that you cannot live and keep all your limbs more than seven years, and you can get fifty dollars or seventy-five dollars a month for taking your lives in your hands; and instead of taking that lucrative position you chose to be a sneak thief, or something like that. Some of you made that sort of choice. I don't know which I would take if I was reduced to this choice. I have an easier choice.

I will guarantee to take from this jail, or any jail in the world, five hundred men who have been the worst criminals and lawbreakers who ever got into jail, and I will go down to our lowest streets and take five hundred of the most abandoned prostitutes, and go out somewhere

where there is plenty of land, and will give them a chance to make a living, and they will be as good people as the average in the community.

There is a remedy for the sort of condition we see here. The world never finds it out, or when it does find it out it does not enforce it. You may pass a law punishing every person with death for burglary, and it will make no difference. Men will commit it just the same. In England there was a time when one hundred different offenses were punishable with death, and it made no difference. The English people strangely found out that so fast as they repealed the severe penalties and so fast as they did away with punishing men by death, crime decreased instead of increased; that the smaller the penalty the fewer the crimes.

Hanging men in our county jails does not prevent murder. It makes murderers.

And this has been the history of the world. It's easy to see how to do away with what we call crime. It is not so easy to do it. I will tell you how to do it. It can be done by giving the people a chance to live—by destroying special privileges. So long as big criminals can get the coal fields, so long as the big criminals have control of the city council and get the public streets for streetcars and gas rights—this is bound to send thousands of poor people to jail. So long as men are allowed to monopolize all the earth, and compel others to live on such terms as these men see fit to make, then you are bound to get into jail.

The only way in the world to abolish crime and criminals is to abolish the big ones and the little ones together. Make fair conditions of life. Give men a chance to live. Abolish the right of private ownership of land, abolish monopoly, make the world partners in production, partners in the good things of life. Nobody would steal if he could get something of his own some easier way. Nobody will commit burglary when he has a house full. No girl will go out on the streets when she has a comfortable place at home. The man who owns a sweatshop or a department store may not be to blame himself for the condition of his girls, but when he pays them five dollars, three dollars, and two dollars a week, I wonder where he thinks they will get the rest of their money to live. The only way to cure these conditions is by equality. There should be no jails. They do not accomplish what they pretend to accomplish. If you would wipe them out there would be no more criminals than now. They terrorize nobody. They are a blot upon any civilization, and a jail is an evidence of the lack of charity of the people on the outside who make the jails and fill them with the victims of their greed.

8. The Humanitarian Theory of Punishment   C. S. Lewis

Clive Staples Lewis (1898–1963) was professor of Medieval and Renaissance English at Cambridge University from 1954 until his death. He is most famous for his numerous books and essays that defend various aspects of Christianity.

Reprinted with the permission of the Trustees of the C. S. Lewis Estate, from *God in the Dock: Essays on Theory and Ethics,* ed. by Walter Hooper (Grand Rapids: Eerdmans, 1970).

In England we have lately had a controversy about Capital Punishment. I do not know whether a murderer is more likely to repent and make a good end on the gallows a few weeks after his trial or in the prison infirmary thirty years later. I do not know whether the fear of death is an indispensable deterrent. I need not, for the purpose of this article, decide whether it is a morally permissible deterrent. Those are questions which I propose to leave untouched. My subject is not Capital Punishment in particular, but that theory of punishment in general which the controversy showed to be almost universal among my fellow-countrymen. It may be called the Humanitarian Theory. Those who hold it think that it is mild and merciful. In this I believe that they are seriously mistaken. I believe that the "Humanity" which it claims is a dangerous illusion and disguises the possibility of cruelty and injustice without end. I urge a return to the traditional or Retributive theory not solely, nor even primarily, in the interests of society but in the interests of the criminal.

According to the Humanitarian theory, to punish a man because he deserves it, and as much as he deserves, is mere revenge, and, therefore, barbarous and immoral. It is maintained that the only legitimate motives for punishing are the desire to deter others by example or to mend the criminal. When this theory is combined, as frequently happens, with the belief that all crime is more or less pathological, the idea of mending tails off into that of healing or curing and punishment becomes therapeutic. Thus it appears at first sight that we have passed from the harsh and self-righteous notion of giving the wicked their deserts to the charitable and enlightened one of tending the psychologically sick. What could be more amiable? One little point which is taken for granted in this theory needs, however, to be made explicit. The things done to the criminal, even if they are called cures, will be just as compulsory as they were in the old days when we called them punishments. If a tendency to steal can be cured by psychotherapy, the thief will no doubt be forced to undergo the treatment. Otherwise, society cannot continue.

My contention is that this doctrine, merciful though it appears, really means that each one of us, from the moment he breaks the law, is deprived of the rights of a human being.

The reason is this. The Humanitarian theory removes from Punishment the concept of Desert. But the concept of Desert is the only connecting link between punishment and justice. It is only as deserved or undeserved that a sentence can be just or unjust. I do not here contend that the question "Is it deserved?" is the only one we can reasonably ask about a punishment. We may very properly ask whether it is likely to deter others and to reform the criminal. But neither of these two last questions is a question about justice. There is no sense in talking about a "just deterrent" or a "just cure." We demand of a deterrent not whether it is just but whether it will deter. We demand of a cure not whether it is just but whether it succeeds. Thus when we cease to consider what the criminal deserves and consider only what will cure him or deter others, we have tacitly removed him from the sphere of justice altogether; instead of a person, a subject of rights, we now have a mere object, a patient, a "case."

The distinction will become clearer if we ask who will be qualified to determine sentences when sentences are no longer held to derive their propriety from the criminal's deservings. On the old view the problem of fixing the right sentence was a moral problem. Accordingly, the judge who did it was a person trained in jurisprudence; trained, that is, in a science which deals with rights and duties, and which, in origin at least, was consciously accepting guidance from the Law of Nature, and from Scripture. We must admit that in the actual penal code of most countries at most times these high originals were so much modified by local custom, class interests, and utilitarian concessions, as to be very imperfectly recognizable. But the code was never in principle, and not always in fact, beyond the control of the conscience of the society. And when (say, in Eighteenth Century England) actual punishments conflicted too violently with the moral sense of the community, juries refused to convict and reform was finally brought about. This was possible because, so long as we are thinking in terms of Desert, the propriety of the penal code, being a moral question, is a question on which every man has the right to an opinion, not because he follows this or that profession, but because he is simply a man, a rational animal enjoying the Natural Light. But all this is changed when we drop the concept of Desert. The only two questions we may now ask about a punishment are whether it deters and whether it cures. But these are not questions on which anyone is entitled to have an opinion simply because he is a man. He is not entitled to an opinion even if, in addition to being a man, he should happen also to be a jurist, a Christian, and a moral theologian. For they are not questions about principle but about matter of fact; and for such *cuiquam in sua arte credendum.** Only the expert "penologist" (let barbarous things have barbarous names), in the light of previous experiment, can tell us what is likely to deter: only the psychotherapist can tell us what is likely to cure. It will be in vain for the rest of us, speaking simply as men, to say, "but this punishment is hideously unjust, hideously disproportionate to the criminal's deserts." The experts with perfect logic will reply, "but nobody was talking about deserts. No one was talking about *punishment* in your archaic vindictive sense of the word. Here are the statistics proving that this treatment deters. Here are the statistics proving that this other treatment cures. What is your trouble?"

The Humanitarian theory, then, removes sentences from the hands of jurists whom the public conscience is entitled to criticize and places them in the hands of technical experts whose special sciences do not even employ such categories as Rights or Justice. It might be argued that since this transference results from an abandonment of the old idea of punishment, and, therefore, of all vindictive motives, it will be safe to leave our criminals in such hands. I will not pause to comment on the simple minded view of fallen human nature which such a belief implies. Let us rather remember that the "cure" of criminals is to be compulsory; and let us then watch how the theory actually works in the mind of the Humanitarian. The immediate starting point of this article was a letter I read in

*["experts must be believed."—ed.]

one of our Leftist weeklies. The author was pleading that a certain sin, now treated by our Laws as a crime, should henceforward be treated as a disease. And he complained that under the present system the offender, after a term in gaol, was simply let out to return to his original environment where he would probably relapse. What he complained of was not the shutting up but the letting out. On his remedial view of punishment the offender should, of course, be detained until he was cured. And of course the official straighteners are the only people who can say when that is. The first result of the Humanitarian theory is, therefore, to substitute for a definite sentence (reflecting to some extent the community's moral judgment on the degree of ill-desert involved) an indefinite sentence terminable only by the word of those experts—and they are not experts in moral theology nor even in the Law of Nature—who inflict it. Which of us, if he stood in the dock, would not prefer to be tried by the old system?

It may be said that by the continued use of the word Punishment and the use of the verb "inflict" I am misrepresenting the Humanitarians. They are not punishing, not inflicting, only healing. But do not let us be deceived by a name. To be taken without consent from my home and friends; to lose my liberty; to undergo all those assaults on my personality which modern psychotherapy knows how to deliver; to be remade after some pattern of "normality" hatched in a Viennese laboratory to which I never professed allegiance; to know that this process will never end until either my captors have succeeded or I grown wise enough to cheat them with apparent success—who cares whether this is called Punishment or not? That it includes most of the elements for which any punishment is feared—shame, exile, bondage, and years eaten by the locust—is obvious. Only enormous ill-desert could justify it; but ill-desert is the very conception which the Humanitarian theory has thrown overboard.

If we turn from the curative to the deterrent justification of punishment we shall find the new theory even more alarming. When you punish a man *in terrorem,* make of him an "example" to others, you are admittedly using him as a means to an end; someone else's end. This, in itself, would be a very wicked thing to do. On the classical theory of Punishment it was of course justified on the ground that the man deserved it. That was assumed to be established before any question of "making him an example" arose. You then, as the saying is, killed two birds with one stone; in the process of giving him what he deserved you set an example to others. But take away desert and the whole morality of the punishment disappears. Why, in Heaven's name, am I to be sacrificed to the good of society in this way?—unless, of course, I deserve it.

But that is not the worst. If the justification of exemplary punishment is not to be based on desert but solely on its efficacy as a deterrent, it is not absolutely necessary that the man we punish should even have committed the crime. The deterrent effect demands that the public should draw the moral, "If we do such an act we shall suffer like that man." The punishment of a man actually guilty whom the public think innocent will not have the desired effect; the punishment of a man actually innocent will, provided the public think him guilty. But every modern State has powers which make it easy to fake a trial. When a victim is urgently needed for exemplary purposes and a guilty victim cannot be found, all the purposes of deterrence will be equally served by the punishment (call it "cure" if you prefer) of an innocent victim, provided that the public can be cheated into thinking him guilty. It is no use to ask me why I assume that our rulers will be so wicked. The punishment of an innocent, that is, and undeserving, man is wicked only if we grant the traditional view that righteous punishment means deserved punishment. Once we have abandoned that criterion, all punishments have to be justified, if at all, on other grounds that have nothing to do with desert. Where the punishment of the innocent can be justified on those grounds (and it could in some cases be justified as a deterrent) it will be no less moral than any other punishment. Any distaste for it on the part of a Humanitarian will be merely a hang-over from the Retributive theory.

It is, indeed, important to notice that my argument so far supposes no evil intentions on the part of the Humanitarian and considers only what is involved in the logic of his position. My contention is that good men (not bad men) consistently acting upon that position would act as cruelly and unjustly as the greatest tyrants. They might in some respects act even worse. Of all tyrannies a tyranny sincerely exercised for the good of its victims may be the most oppressive. It may be better to live under robber barons than under omnipotent moral busybodies. The robber baron's cruelty may sometimes sleep, his cupidity may at some point be satiated; but those who torment us for our own good will torment us without end for they do so with the approval of their own conscience. They may be more likely to go to Heaven yet at the same time likelier to make a Hell of earth. Their very kindness stings with intolerable insult. To be "cured" against one's will and cured of states which we may not regard as disease is to be put on a level with those who have not yet reached the age of reason or those who never will; to be classed with infants, imbeciles, and domestic animals. But to be punished, however severely, because we have deserved it, because we "ought to have known better," is to be treated as a human person made in God's image.

In reality, however, we must face the possibility of bad rulers armed with a Humanitarian theory of punishment. A great many popular blue prints for a Christian society are merely what the Elizabethans called "eggs in moonshine" because they assume that the whole society is Christian or that the Christians are in control. This is not so in most contemporary States. Even if it were, our rulers would still be fallen men, and, therefore, neither very wise nor very good. As it is, they will usually be unbelievers. And since wisdom and virtue are not the only or the commonest qualifications for a place in the government, they will not often be even the best unbelievers. The practical problem of Christian politics is not that of drawing up schemes for a Christian society, but that of living as innocently as we can with unbelieving fellow-subjects under unbelieving rulers who will never be perfectly wise and good and who will sometimes be very wicked and very foolish. And when they are wicked the Humanitarian theory of Punishment will put in their hands a finer instrument of tyranny than wickedness ever had before. For if crime and disease are to be regarded as the same thing, it follows that any state of mind which our masters choose to call "disease" can be treated as crime; and compulsorily cured. It will be vain to plead that states of mind which displease government need not always involve moral turpitude and do not therefore always deserve forfeiture of liberty. For our masters will not be using the concepts of Desert and Punishment but those of disease and cure. We know that one school of psychology already regards religion as a neurosis. When this particular neurosis becomes inconvenient to government what is to hinder government from proceeding to "cure" it? Such "cure" will, of course, be compulsory; but under the Humanitarian theory it will not be called by the shocking name of Persecution. No one will blame us for being Christians, no one will hate us, no one will revile us. The new Nero will approach us with the silky manners of a doctor, and though all will be in fact as compulsory as the *tunica molesta* or Smithfield or Tyburn, all will go on within the unemotional therapeutic sphere where words like "right" and "wrong" or "freedom" and "slavery" are never heard. And thus when the command is given every prominent Christian in the land may vanish overnight into Institutions for the Treatment of the Ideologically Unsound, and it will rest with the expert gaolers to say when (if ever) they are to re-emerge. But it will not be persecution. Even if the treatment is painful, even if it is life-long, even if it is fatal, that will be only a regrettable accident; the intention was purely therapeutic. Even in ordinary medicine there were painful operations and fatal operations; so in this. But because they are "treatment," not punishment, they can be criticized only by fellow-experts and on technical grounds, never by men as men and on grounds of justice.

This is why I think it essential to oppose the Humanitarian theory of Punishment, root and branch, wherever we encounter it. It carries on its front a semblance of Mercy which is wholly false. That is how it can deceive men of good will. The error began, perhaps, with Shelley's statement that the distinction between Mercy and Justice was invented in the courts of tyrants. It sounds noble, and was indeed the error of a noble mind. But the distinction is essential. The older view was that Mercy "tempered" Justice, or (on the highest level of all) that Mercy and Justice had met and kissed. The essential act of Mercy was to pardon; and pardon in its very essence involves the recognition of guilt and ill-desert in the recipient. If crime is only a disease which needs cure, not sin which deserves punishment, it cannot be pardoned. How can you pardon a man for having a gum-boil or a club foot? But the Humanitarian theory wants simply to abolish Justice and substitute Mercy for it. This means that you start being "kind" to people before you have considered their rights, and then force upon them supposed kindnesses which they in fact had a right to refuse, and finally kindnesses which no one but you will recognize as kindnesses and which the recipient will feel as abominable cruelties. You have overshot the mark. Mercy, detached from Justice, grows unmerciful. That is the important paradox. As there are plants which will flourish only in mountain soil, so it appears that Mercy will flower only when it grows in the crannies of the rock of Justice; transplanted to the marshlands of mere Humanitarianism, it becomes a man-eating weed, all the more dangerous because it is still called by the same name as the mountain variety.

But we ought long ago to have learned our lesson. We should be too old now to be deceived by those humane pretensions which have served to usher in every cruelty of the revolutionary period in which we live. These are the "precious balms" which will "break our heads."

There is a fine sentence in Bunyan: "It came burning hot into my mind, whatever he said, and however he flattered, when he got me home to his house, he would sell me for a slave." There is a fine couplet, too, in John Ball:

> Be ware ere ye be wo
> Know your friend from your foe.

One last word. You may ask why I send this to an Australian periodical. The reason is simple and perhaps worth recording; I can get no hearing for it in England.

Suggestions
for Further Reading

Anthologies

Enteman, Willard F. (ed.). *The Problem of Free Will.* New York: Scribners, 1967. A collection of important articles on various aspects of the free will-determinism controversy. Since most of the articles are easily readable, this is a good book for the beginning student to turn to for additional reading.

Hook, Sidney (ed.). *Determinism and Freedom in the Age of Modern Science.* New York: New York U.P., 1958. A collection of twenty-seven articles that analyzes the concepts of determinism and freedom and the significance of these concepts in physics, law, and ethics. Most of the articles will be difficult for the beginning student.

Individual Works

Clemens, Samuel, "What Is Man?" in *What Is Man? and Other Essays.* New York: Harper, 1917. An interesting and amusing statement of the determinist position by a famous writer.

Cranston, Maurice. *Freedom: A New Analysis.* London: Longmans, 1953. The latter half of this book is a good discussion of the main positions and a defense of libertarianism.

D'Angelo, Edward. *The Problem of Freedom and Determinism.* Columbia, Mo.: U. of Missouri, 1968. A good, clear discussion of the three major positions.

Darrow, Clarence. *Crime: Its Cause and Treatment.* New York: Crowell, 1922. A famous discussion of criminal treatment from the hard determinist viewpoint.

Lamont, Corliss, *Freedom of Choice Affirmed.* New York: Horizon, 1967. A clear statement and defense of libertarianism.

Matson, Floyd W. *The Broken Image.* New York: George Braziller, 1964. A good discussion of how the hard determinist position has affected man's image of himself. There is also an examination of Skinner and other behaviorists in this connection.

O'Connor, D. J. *Free Will*. Garden City, N.Y.: Doubleday, 1971. A careful survey of the main arguments both for and against determinism.

Schopenhauer, Arthur. "Free-Will and Fatalism" in *The Pessimist's Handbook (Parerga und Paralipomena)*. Translated by T. Bailey Saunders, edited by Hazel E. Barnes. Lincoln: U. of Nebraska, 1964. A concise and forceful defense of fatalism. Schopenhauer, a clear stylist, uses many illustrations drawn from everyday human behavior and world literature in this essay intended for the general reading public.

Taylor, Richard. *Metaphysics*. Englewood Cliffs, N.J.: Prentice-Hall, 1974 (2nd ed). Chapter Five contains a clearly written attack on hard and soft determinism and a defense of a version of libertarianism.

Dictionary of the History of Ideas: Studies of Selected Pivotal Ideas. Philip P. Weiner, editor-in-chief. New York: Scribners, 1973. Substantial and clearly written essays emphasizing the historical development of topics discussed in this part. Designed to inform the nonspecialist, each essay concludes with a select bibliography.

Encyclopedia of Philosophy. Paul Edwards, editor-in-chief. New York: Macmillan, 1967. The student will find many worthwhile articles on the subject treated in this part, and excellent bibliographies.

Two: God and Religion

Introduction

A question troubling many students is whether they should believe in religion. One reason for their hesitation simply to follow in the paths of their parents in this matter is their conviction that religion has failed to bring about a better world for mankind. Perhaps an even more important reason is that there appears to be no scientific manner by which the basic religious tenets can be established. The desire that one's beliefs be supported by science has its roots in the movement of Western civilization away from a religious view of the world to a scientific one. The great success of science has led many to the view that we should believe only those things that can be established in a proper scientific manner. Further, the advance of science has certainly tended to undermine any simplistic acceptance of religious doctrines and writings. The scientifically trained no longer accept, for example, the biblical accounts of creation and the garden of Eden as literally true. Thus, it is easy to understand why so many of today's students are dubious about accepting traditional orthodox religion. In the light of modern science it appears to be a remnant of ancient superstition that will one day be completely replaced by a scientific view of the world.

Contemporary religious thinkers generally deplore the tendency to view science and religion as competing views of the world. For them, religion and science are concerned with different issues. Science is concerned to discover the laws that are operative in the physical universe, whereas religion is concerned with issues beyond the scope of science, such as the reason for the existence of the universe, the existence of God, and the purpose of man's life. Since the issues with which religion is concerned are not within the scope of science, it is held to be inappropriate to demand that religious beliefs should be substantiated by scientific facts.

Must religious beliefs be supported by scientific evidence, or is it acceptable to believe without proof? Do the discoveries of modern science show that the views of the major religions are untenable? These are some of the questions that the philosopher seeks to answer about religion. The philosopher's interest in such questions arises out of the fact that religion gives answers to many of man's most fundamental questions about himself and his place in the world. The philosopher wants to know if the answers are true. Thus, in examining religious views, the philosopher is concerned with their accurate assessment rather than their defense or destruction. The readings in this section show that a great diversity of opinion exists among philosophers regarding the truth and value of religion. Some hold that only in a religious framework can a foundation for morality and a meaning to life be found. Others see various religious views as not only false but a great detriment to man's happiness. The student's job is to assess carefully the various positions and arguments to determine which, if any, is sound.

The basic tenet of the major Western religions is that there exists a supernatural being called "God." God is defined as being an all-good, all-knowing, all-powerful creator of the universe. God is viewed as concerned with our affairs rather than being withdrawn and aloof. For the most part, religious believers are convinced that such a God exists without inquiring into the question of scientific or rational proofs for their conviction. Yet many religious theorists believe it important to show, if possible, that the existence of God can be proven or at least shown to be probable on the basis of scientific evidence or other rational arguments. If God's existence could be proven, not only could the skeptics and atheists be converted but many who believe would feel more confident in their belief.

Numerous proofs have been offered for the existence of God. Most are of little interest to philosophers since they are clearly unsound. Typical of these widely used but unsound arguments are the argument from agreement and the argument from Scripture. *The argument from agreement* consists in attempting to show that God exists on the basis of the fact that so many people throughout the world have believed in the existence of God. It is claimed that such a widespread belief cannot be explained on any other basis than the actual existence of God. One problem with arguing in this manner is that it makes the majority opinion the basis of truth; but it is certainly well known that large majorities have been wrong. At one time there was widespread agreement that the earth was flat. Another difficulty with this argument is that the widespread belief in God can perhaps be explained as the result of superstition, wishful thinking, or fear. If so, the belief in God would not indicate his existence but the psychological characteristics or the lack of scientific knowledge of the majority of mankind. *The argument from Scripture* attempts to prove God's existence on the basis of the fact that we have some writings (Old Testament, New Testament, Koran, and so on) that tell of God. These writings are assumed to be inspired by God and therefore reliable. The obvious difficulty with attempting to prove God in this manner is that the events recorded in the writings must be proved to be accurate and such proof seems impossible to get. Those who doubt the existence of God will also be doubtful that the Bible was inspired by God and that the events given there are accurately reported.

In the readings that follow, some of the arguments that philosophers have considered more plausible are presented. The one that will probably be most familiar to the student is the *argument from design.* According to this argument the world is so intricately put together to maintain the existence of various types of life that it must have been designed by an extremely rational being. This argument is presented in a simple, straightforward manner by A. Cressy Morrison, a highly respected American scientist. Morrison argues that life could not possibly exist by chance since the probability of all the necessary factors existing in the proper relationships would be too great. Also, he claims that the fact that nature is so balanced that no species can conquer all the others indicates that some great Intelligence planned the world. The soundness of the argument is attacked by Clarence Darrow, who argues that the universe shows no clear order or design. He goes on to say that even if it did, it was apparently not designed for human life since we could easily imagine ways in which the world could have been made to provide a better habitation for human beings.

Another frequently encountered argument, *the argument from religious experience,* is presented by James Bisset Pratt. Pratt maintains that belief in God can be upheld by mystical experiences that supporters of various religions have had. The main problem that he feels stands in the way of acceptance of such experiences as evidence of God is the naturalistic explanation of them given by psychologists. It would seem that if such experiences could be accounted for as the result of unusual psychological states, then they could not be considered as evidence of God's existence. Pratt argues, however, that such psychological interpretations are not necessarily incompatible with a religious interpretation of the same phenomena. The student should consider whether Pratt has shown merely that certain experiences could be given a religious interpretation, or whether he has shown that such experiences must be given a religious interpretation and thus are good evidence of God's existence.

In "The Basis of the Moral Law," C. S. Lewis presents a version of the *moral argument* for God. He maintains that men have a sense of moral obligation, which they feel as a claim coming from outside themselves. No naturalistic account of this sense of obligation in terms of human needs or interests satisfactorily explains it. It can only be explained, Lewis argues, by assuming the existence of a lawgiver outside the universe. The crucial issue in assessing this argument is whether he is correct in denying that the sense of obligation can be given an alternative explanation.

Many of the arguments for the existence of God, including the argument from design, are discussed by Bertrand Russell. Russell maintains that none of the arguments for the existence of God are convincing. Further, he attacks all religions, not just Christianity, on several grounds. Religion, he maintains, is born of fear and a desire to have a protector. We must not give in to such feelings but must learn to stand on our own feet and conquer the world by intelligence. Further, the various organized religions have hindered progress by defending a morality that is not conducive to human happiness. To improve human institutions and allow for moral progress, the morality of the churches must be opposed.

Some philosophers have maintained that not only is God's existence unprovable but that we can show that God does not exist. The main attempt to show that an all-good, all-powerful God does not exist arises from a consideration of the evil that exists in the world. It seems undeniably true that bad or evil things happen. Hurricanes and floods destroy houses and crops, children are born crippled or deformed, and murderers and thieves plague our cities. The question that must be answered is this: Why does a God who has the power to eliminate such evils allow them to occur? If God is indifferent to or powerless to prevent such evils, then he is not the kind of good and all-powerful being that Western religions worship. Many theologians have argued that all of the things we call evils are allowed to occur by God for some good purpose. For this view to be defended, it must be shown that God could not have produced equally good results without this evil or at least with less of it.

The existence of evil and its bearing on God's existence is discussed by Baron d'Holbach and John Hick. Baron d'Holback presents a battery of arguments to show that it is impossible to reconcile the existence of an all-powerful, all-good God with the existence of evil. He maintains that God could have created a perfect world without reducing man's status in any manner. Since evil has not been prevented or distributed in a just manner, one must conclude either that God is evil or that there is no such being. John Hick argues that evil is allowed to exist because God's purpose for man in this world is not to provide him with a carefree, happy existence but to continue the process of "soul-making." To achieve full development, man must experience and learn to overcome the problems that exist in this world.

When confronted with the difficulty of proving the existence of God, many philosophers and theologians fall back on faith as the basis for religious belief. Faith is usually thought of as belief unsupported by evidence. The contention that it is acceptable to believe the claims of religion or any other topic without evidence has not gone unchallenged. In "The Ethics of Belief," W. K. Clifford argues that it is always wrong to believe anything without evidence since such a belief could either produce some harm or lead the holder to accept too readily other unsupported and potentially harmful beliefs. Our beliefs should be determined by an assessment of the evidence and probabilities involved, not by unfounded hopes and wishes. In contrast to this view of the value of faith, William James argues that belief without evidence is sometimes justified. James is careful to point out, however, that such belief is justified only in certain types of situations. He does not want to encourage the holding of unsupported beliefs in every instance where evidence is not available. Ultimately, James believes that to withhold belief on an important matter like religion just because there is insufficient evidence of God's existence would be too cautious. Since withholding belief might cut one off from God's grace, he believes that one should run the risk of error in hopes one's belief may be true. In considering James's position, the student should consider whether it rests on a conception of God as a wrathful being. Would James's argument be correct if God would not punish those who do not believe without evidence? Also, it is interesting to decide if there are any areas outside of religion where one should believe without evidence.

An issue that has received increasing attention in recent years is whether statements that cannot be shown to be true or false by sense-experience are meaningful. Discussion of this issue was given a strong impetus by the publication in 1936 of *Language, Truth and Logic* by A. J. Ayer, who argued that a variety of statements, including ones about God, were meaningless because they were unverifiable. In "Has 'God' a Meaning?" Bernard Williams rejects Ayer's extreme stand on this issue, but he believes that religious statements are either meaningless or expressible in non-religious terms.

In his response to Williams, Bishop Robinson grants that statements about God are meaningless insofar as they are held to refer to an invisible being who exists outside of and apart from our experience. Robinson does not believe that religious statements refer to such a being, but that they affirm that there is a love and a purpose to which personal relationships are the highest response. Even if Bishop Robinson can make his interpretation of religious statements sufficiently comprehensible to rebut Williams' criticisms, it must be decided whether his interpretation would satisfy the traditional believers who view God as a spiritual being with the ability to affect human welfare.

Does God Exist?

9. Seven Reasons Why a Scientist Believes in God
A. Cressy Morrison

A. Cressy Morrison (1884–1951) was an astronomer and president of the New York
Academy of Sciences, 1938–39. He wrote a number of books on scientific topics, as
well as *Man Does Not Stand Alone,* from which the following article was
condensed.

We are still in the dawn of the scientific age and every increase of light
reveals more brightly the handiwork of an intelligent Creator. In the 90
years since Darwin we have made stupendous discoveries; with a spirit of
scientific humility and of faith grounded in knowledge we are approaching even nearer to an awareness of God.

For myself, I count seven reasons for my faith:

First: *By unwavering mathematical law we can prove that our universe was
designed and executed by a great engineering Intelligence.*

Suppose you put ten pennies, marked from one to ten, into your
pocket and give them a good shuffle. Now try to take them out in
sequence from one to ten, putting back the coin each time and shaking
them all again. Mathematically we know that your chance of first drawing
number one is one to ten; of drawing one and two in succession, one to
100; of drawing one, two and three in succession, one in a thousand, and
so on; your chance of drawing them all, from number one to number ten
in succession, would reach the unbelievable figure of one chance in ten
billion.

By the same reasoning, so many exacting conditions are necessary for
life on the earth that they could not possibly exist in proper relationship
by chance. The earth rotates on its axis one thousand miles an hour; if it
turned at one hundred miles an hour, our days and nights would be ten
times as long as now, and the hot sun would then burn up our vegetation
each long day while in the long night any surviving sprout would freeze.

Again, the sun, source of our life, has a surface temperature of 12,000
degrees Fahrenheit, and our earth is just far enough away so that this
"eternal fire" warms us *just enough and not too much!* If the sun gave off
only one half its present radiation, we would freeze and if it gave half as
much more, we would roast.

The slant of the earth, tilted at an angle of 23 degrees, gives us our
seasons; if it had not been so tilted, vapors from the ocean would move

north and south, piling up for us continents of ice. If our moon was, say, only 50 thousand miles away instead of its actual distance, our tides would be so enormous that twice a day all continents would be submerged; even the mountains would soon be eroded away. If the crust of the earth had been only ten feet thicker, there would be no oxygen, without which animal life must die. Had the ocean been a few feet deeper, carbon dioxide and oxygen would have been absorbed and no vegetable life could exist. Or if our atmosphere had been much thinner, some of the meteors, now burned in space by the millions every day, would be striking all parts of the earth, setting fires everywhere.

Because of these and a host of other examples, there is not one chance in millions that life on our planet is an accident.

Second: *The resourcefulness of life to accomplish its purpose is a manifestation of all-pervading Intelligence.*

What life itself is, no man has fathomed. It has neither weight nor dimensions; but it does have force; a growing root will crack a rock. Life has conquered water, land and air, mastering the elements, compelling them to dissolve and reform their combinations.

Life, the sculptor, shapes all living things; an artist, it designs every leaf of every tree, and colors every flower. Life is a musician and has taught each bird to sing it love songs, the insects to call each other in the music of their multitudinous sounds. Life is a sublime chemist, giving taste to fruits and spices, and perfume to the rose, changing water and carbonic acid into sugar and wood, and, in so doing, releasing oxygen that animals may have the breath of life.

Behold an almost invisible drop of protoplasm, transparent, jellylike, capable of motion, drawing energy from the sun. This single cell, this transparent mistlike droplet, holds within itself the germ of life, and has the power to distribute this life to every living thing, great and small. The powers of this droplet are greater than our vegetation and animals and people, for all life came from it. Nature did not create life; fire-blistered rocks and a saltless sea could not meet the necessary requirements.

Who, then, has put it here?

Third: *Animal wisdom speaks irresistibly of a good Creator who infused instinct into otherwise helpless little creatures.*

The young salmon spends years at sea, then comes back to his own river, and travels up the very side of the river into which flows the tributary where he was born. What brings him back so precisely? If you transfer him to another tributary he will know at once that he is off his course and he will fight his way down and back to the main stream and then turn up against the current to finish his destiny accurately.

Even more difficult to solve is the mystery of eels. These amazing creatures migrate at maturity from all ponds and rivers everywhere—those from Europe across thousands of miles of ocean—all bound for the same abysmal deeps near Bermuda. There they breed and die. The little ones, with no apparent means of knowing anything except that they are in a wilderness of water, nevertheless start back and find their way not only to the very shore from which their parents came but thence to the rivers, lakes or little ponds—so that each body of water is always populated with eels. No American eel has ever been caught in Europe, no European eel in American waters. Nature has even delayed the maturity of the European eel by a year or more to make up for its longer journey. Where does the directing impulse originate?

A wasp will overpower a grasshopper, dig a hole in the earth, sting the grasshopper in exactly the right place so that he does not die but becomes unconscious and lives on as a form of preserved meat. Then the wasp will lay her eggs handily so that her children when they hatch can nibble without killing the insect on which they feed; to them dead meat would be fatal. The mother then flies away and dies; she never sees her young. Surely the wasp must have done all this right the first time and every time, else there would be no wasps. Such mysterious techniques cannot be explained by adaptation; they were bestowed.

Fourth: *Man has something more than animal instinct—the power of reason.*

No other animal has ever left a record of its ability to count ten, or even to understand the meaning of ten. Where instinct is like a single note of a flute, beautiful but limited, the human brain contains all the notes of all the instruments in the orchestra. No need to belabor this fourth point; thanks to human reason we can contemplate the possibility that we are what we are only because we have received a spark of Universal Intelligence.

Fifth: *Provision for all living is revealed in phenomena which we know today but which Darwin did not know—such as the wonders of genes.*

So unspeakably tiny are these genes that, if all of them responsible for all living people in the world could be put in one place, there would be less than a thimbleful. Yet these ultramicroscopic genes and their companions, the chromosomes, inhabit every living cell and are the absolute keys to all human, animal, and vegetable characteristics. A thimble is a small place in which to put all the individual characteristics of two billions of human beings. However, the facts are beyond question. Well, then— how do genes lock up all the normal heredity of a multitude of ancestors and preserve the psychology of each in such an infinitely small space?

Here evolution really begins—at the cell, the entity which holds and carries the genes. How a few million atoms, locked up as an ultramicroscopic gene, can absolutely rule all life on earth is an example of profound cunning and provision that could emanate only from a Creative Intelligence; no other hypothesis will serve.

Sixth: *By the economy of nature, we are forced to realize that only infinite wisdom could have foreseen and prepared with such astute husbandry.*

Many years ago a species of cactus was planted in Australia as a protective fence. Having no insect enemies in Australia the cactus soon began a prodigious growth; the alarming abundance persisted until the plants covered an area as long and wide as England, crowding inhabitants out of towns and villages, and destroying their farms. Seeking a defense, the entomologists scoured the world; finally they turned up an insect which lived exclusively on cactus, and would eat nothing else. It would breed freely, too; and it had no enemies in Australia. So animal soon conquered vegetable and today the cactus pest has retreated, and with it all but a small protective residue of the insects, enough to hold the cactus in check forever.

Such checks and balances have been universally provided. Why have not fast-breeding insects dominated the earth? Because they have no lungs such as man possesses; they breathe through tubes. But when insects grow large, their tubes do not grow in ratio to the increasing size of the body. Hence there never has been an insect of great size; this limitation on growth has held them all in check. If this physical check had not been provided, man could not exist. Imagine meeting a hornet as big as a lion!

Seventh: *The fact that man can conceive the idea of God is in itself a unique proof.*

The conception of God rises from a divine faculty of man, unshared with the rest of our world—the faculty we call imagination. By its power, man and man alone can find the evidence of things unseen. The vista that power opens up is unbounded; indeed, as man's perfected imagination becomes a spiritual reality, he may discern in all the evidences of design and purpose the great truth that heaven is wherever and whatever; that God is everywhere and in everything but nowhere so close as in our hearts.

It is scientifically as well as imaginatively true, as the Psalmist said: *The heavens declare the glory of God and the firmament showeth His handiwork.*

10. The Delusion of Design and Purpose   Clarence Darrow

Seldom do the believers in mysticism fail to talk about the evidence of purpose and design shown in the universe itself. This idea runs back at least one hundred and five years, to Paley's "Natural Theology." There was a time when this book was a part of the regular course in all schools of higher learning, which then included theology; but the book is now more likely to be found in museums.

Paley points out that if a man travelling over the heath should find a watch and commence examining it he would soon discover in the watch itself abundant evidence of purpose and design. He would observe the wheels that fit into each other and turn the hour hand and the minute hand, the crystal made to fit over the face, etc., etc.

What the hypothetical man would observe and conclude would depend on the man. Most men that we know would think that the watch showed a design to accomplish a certain purpose, and therefore must have had a maker. They would reach that conclusion because they are familiar with tools and their use by man. But, suppose the watch had been picked up by a bushman or some other savage or an ape? None of them would draw an inference, for the article would be new to them. Supposing, instead of a man, a coyote or wolf came upon the watch, turned it over and examined it, would the animal read or sense any design? Most assuredly not. Suppose the civilized man should pick up an unfamiliar object, a stone, or a piece of quartz; he might view it and examine it, but it would never enter his head that it was designed, and yet on close inspection and careful study the stone or quartz is just as marvellous as the watch.

Paley passes from the watch to the human structure and shows how the mouth and teeth are adjusted to prepare the food for man's digestion, and how his stomach is formed to digest it; how the eye and ear were made to carry sensations to the brain, etc. Many of the clergy say the same thing to-day, in spite of the fact that the organs of man were never made for any such purpose. In fact, man never was made. He was evolved from the lowest form of life. His ancestors in the sea slowly threw its jellylike structure around something that nourished it and absorbed it. Slowly through ages of continued development and change and mutations the present man was evolved, and with him the more perfect and adaptable and specialized structure, with which he sees and hears and takes his food, and digests it and assimilates it to his structure. The stomach was not made first, and then food created for its use. The food came first, and certain forms of life slowly developed an organ that would absorb food to be utilized in the process of growth. By degrees, through the survival of the construction most fitted for life, the stomach and digestive apparatus for men and other animals gradually grew and unfolded in endless time.

To discover that certain forms and formations are adjusted for certain action has nothing to do with design. None of these developments are perfect, or anywhere near so. All of them, including the eye, are botchwork that any good mechanic would be ashamed to make. All of them need constant readjustment, are always out of order, and are entirely too complicated for dependable work. They are not made for any purpose; they simply grew out of needs and adaptations; in other words, they happened. Just as God must have happened, if he exists at all.

Turning from Paley and his wornout watch to the universe and the physical world in general, is there any more evidence here? First, the "design and order" sharks ought to tell what they mean by their terms, and how they find out what they think they understand. To say that a certain scheme or process shows order or system, one must have some norm or pattern by which to determine whether the matter concerned shows any design or order. We have a norm, a pattern, and that is the universe itself, from which we fashion our ideas. We have observed this universe and its operation and we call it order. To say that the universe is patterned on order is to say that the universe is patterned on the universe. It can mean nothing else.

The earth revolves around the sun in a long curve not far from a circle. Does that show order? Let us suppose that instead of going in a circle it formed a rectangle. Would this not have been accepted as order? Suppose it were a triangle, or any other figure. Suppose it took a toothlike course, would that, then, be considered order? As a matter of fact, the earth does not go regularly in the same path around the sun; it is drawn out into the universe with the whole solar system, and never travels the same course twice. The solar system really has an isolated place in space. The sun furnishes light and heat to nine different planets, of which the earth is one of the smallest and most insignificant. The earth has one satellite, the moon. Saturn and Jupiter have eight moons each, and, besides that, Saturn has a ring that looks very beautiful from here, running all around the planet. We do know that all the planets of the solar system, and the sun as well, are made of the same stuff. It is most likely that every moving thing in the universe has the same constituents as the earth. What is the plan that gave Jupiter eight moons, while only one was lavished upon the earth, supposed to be the special masterpiece of the Almighty, and for whose benefit all the hosts of the heavens were made? Jupiter is three hundred and seventeen times the weight of the earth, and it takes four years for it to go around the sun. Perhaps the universe was made for inhabitants that will one day live on Jupiter.

It is senseless to talk about order and system and design in the universe. Sir James Jeans' book published in 1931, "The Stars in Their Course," tells us his theory of the origin of our solar system, which is of more interest to us than the Milky Way. The theory of Jeans, and most of the other astronomers, is that there was a time when all the planets of the solar system were a part of the sun, and that some wandering star in its course across the heavens entered the sphere of the sun and dragged after it the planets and moons that make up the solar system by the power of gravitation. This is the planetismal theory, postulated by Professors Chamberlain and Moulton, of the University of Chicago. These mighty chunks of matter drawn from the sun rushed on through space at a terrific speed, and each was caught by gravitation and revolved around the sun. Their distance from the sun depended largely upon their size before gravitation held them in its grasp.

There is nothing in the solar system that could be called design and order. It came from a catastrophe of whose immensity no one could even dream. Religionists have pointed to the ability of an astronomer to fix the time of an eclipse as evidence of system. There are only a few heavenly bodies involved in an eclipse of the sun or moon, from the standpoint of the earth. The motions and positions of all these bodies are well known, and from this the passage of another heavenly planet or the moon between the earth and the sun can be easily determined. It matters not whether the date of an eclipse is far-off or near-by, the method is the same. To an astronomer the computation is as simple as the question propounded to the first-grade pupil: "If John had three apples and James gave him two more, how many apples would John then have?"

We know that gravitation caught the various planets at a certain point as they sped across space, and that these accidents of colliding bodies are very rare; the reason is that regardless of what seems to be the distance between the stars, they are so far apart that it is almost impossible for them ever to meet. To quote from Jeans': "For the most part, each voyage is in splendid isolation, like a ship on the ocean. In a scale model in which the stars are ships, the average ship will be well over a million miles from its neighbor."

Still, catastrophes have occurred and do occur. Our solar system was probably born from one. The moon was thrown from the earth by some pull of gravitation. The heavens are replete with dark planets, and parts of planets, and meteors hurrying through space. Now and then one drops onto the earth, and is preserved in some park or museum; so that in various parts of the world numerous specimens exist. If there was any purpose in the creation of the universe, or any part of it, what was it? Would any mortal dare to guess?

Our solar system is one of the smallest of the endless systems of which we have any knowledge. Our earth is eight thousand miles in diameter. The star, Betelgeuse, is so large that it would fill all the space occupied in the heavens in the whole orbit made by the earth going around the sun. There are many stars known to be much larger than Betelgeuse. The diameter of this sun is thirty-seven thousand times that of our little earth, for which all the universe is supposed to have been made, and whose inhabitants are endowed with everlasting life.

When the telescope is turned toward the heavens we learn another story. Leaving the sparsely settled section of eternity in which we live forever, and going out into the real main universe, we find worlds on worlds, systems upon systems, and nebula after nebula. No one can possibly imagine the dimensions of endless space. The great Nebula M. 31 in Andromeda is so far away from the earth that it takes light nine hundred thousand millions of years to reach our planet. The nebula itself is so vast that it takes fifty thousand years for light to cross it. To make it still more simple I have taken the pains to figure the distance of this nebula from our important planet, called the earth, which boasts of a diameter of eight thousand miles. This nebula is 5,279,126,400,000,000,000 miles away from us, if my computations are right. I would not positively guarantee the correctness of the answer, but I think it is all right, although I did it by hand. I have gone over the figures three times, and got a different result each time, so I think the answer can be pretty well depended upon. I cannot help feeling sorry for the residents of Nebula M. 31 in Andromeda, when I think what a great deprivation they must suffer through living so far away from our glorious planet, which Mark Twain named "the wart," but which theology has placed at the centre of the universe and as the sole concern of gods and men.

What lies beyond Andromeda? No one can answer that question. And still there is every reason to believe that other worlds and systems and nebulae reach out into stellar space, without end. It is obvious that no one can form a conception of the extent of space or the infinite number of suns and planets with which the limitless sky is strewn. No one can vision a beginning or an end. If it were possible for any fertile mind to imagine a conception of the end of space, then we should wonder what lies beyond that limit. We cannot attain the slightest comprehension of the extent of our pigmy solar system, much less any of the greater ones. The planet which is the farthest from our sun is Pluto, one of the smallest in our system. The diameter of Pluto's orbit around the sun is only about 7,360,000,000 miles. This may be taken as the extent of our solar system. This can be compared with the distance to the nebula in Andromeda, which I hesitate to record again, showing the trifling importance of our whole solar system in so much of the universe as we can scan.

When the new telescope is completed and mounted on the top of Mount Wilson, it is hoped that we can produce figures of distance that are real figures.

Among the endless number of stars that whirl in the vastnesses of illimitable space, how many millions of billions of planets are likely to be in existence? How many of these may possibly have as much special and historical importance as the tiny globe to which we so frantically cling? To find that number, go and count the grains of sand on all the coasts of all the waters of the earth, and then think of the catastrophe that would result to the coasts of one grain were shattered or lost.

In spite of the countless numbers of bodies moving about in limitless space, and the distances between them so great that they seldom clash, still they do sometimes clash. What is our solar system in comparison with the great nebula out there in the beginning, or end, or middle stretch of real space? Compared with that part of the heavens the density of the stellar population of our solar system is like the prairies of Kansas compared with the city of New York. Can anything be inferred about the origin or arrangement of all this, so far as man can tell, except that it is the outcome of the merest, wildest chance?

But let us try to clear the cobwebs from our brains, and the dizziness from our stomachs, and come back to earth, as it were. Let us talk of something where we can deal with what at least approaches facts. Does the earth show design, and order, and system, and purpose? Again, it would be well for the designers to tell what the scheme really is. If the plan is so clear as to justify the belief in a master designer, then it must be plain that the believers should be able to give the world some idea of the purpose of it all. Knowing winks and Delphic utterances and cryptic insin-uations are not enough. Was the earth ever designed for the home of man? Sir James Jeans, in his admirable book on astronomy, shows us in no uncertain way that it evidently was not; that the human race has made the most of a bad environment and a most unfortunate habitation. Strange that the highpriests of superstition should so convulsively clutch Jeans and Eddington; neither one believes in a future life of the individ-ual; neither one believes in the God of the theologians; neither believes in a special revelation, although Jeans does manage to say that Venus is the planet that the religionists thought was the star that led the camels over the desert to the stable where Jesus was born. Is this science or religion?— this bit of hearsay.

Even had this planet been meant for life, it plainly was not meant for human life. Three-fourths of the surface is covered with water, which would show that if it was ever designed for life it was designed for fishes and not for men. But what about the dry land? Two-thirds of this is not fitted for human beings. Both the polar zones are too cold for the abode of man. The equatorial regions are too hot. Vast deserts are spread out in various sections, and impassable and invincible mountain ranges make human habitation and the production of food impossible over immense areas. The earth is small enough, to begin with; the great seas, the wide useless stretches of land and the hostile climates have shrunk the livable portion almost to the vanishing point, and it is continually shrinking day by day. The human race is here because it is here, and it clings to the soil because there is nowhere else to go.

Even a human being of very limited capacity could think of countless ways in which the earth could be improved as the home of man, and from the earliest time the race has been using all sorts of efforts and resources to make it more suitable for its abode. Admitting that the earth is a fit place for life, and certainly every place in the universe where life exists is fitted for life, then what sort of life was this planet designed to support? There are some millions of different species of animals on this earth, and one-half of these are insects. In numbers, and perhaps in other ways, man is in a great minority. If the land of the earth was made for life, it seems as if it was intended for insect life, which can exist almost anywhere. If no other available place can be found they can live by the million on man, and inside of him. They generally succeed in destroying his life, and, if they have a chance, wind up by eating his body.

Aside from the insects, all sorts of life infest the earth and sea and air. In large portions of the earth man can make no headway against the rank growths of jungles and the teeming millions of animals that are seeking his death. He may escape the larger and most important of these only to be imperilled and probably eaten by the microbes, which seem instinctively to have their own idea of the worth and purpose of man's existence. If it were of any importance, we might view man from the standpoint of the microbe and consider his utility as the microbe's "mealticket." Can any one find any reason for claiming that the earth was meant for man, any more than for any other form of life that is spawned from land and sea and air?

But, how well is the earth itself adapted to human life? Even in the best parts of this world, speaking from the standpoint of man, one-fourth of the time it is too cold and another fourth of the seasons it is too hot, leaving little time for the comfort and pleasure of the worthiest product of the universe, or, that small fraction of it that we have some limited knowledge about.

Passing up the manifold difficulties that confront man and his brief life and career upon this mundane sphere, let us look at the world itself. It is a very wobbly place. Every year, upon the surface of this globe, and in the seas that cover such a major part of it, there are ten thousand earthquakes, ranging from light shocks to the total destruction of large areas of territory and the annihilation of great numbers of human lives. Were these, too, designed? Then, there is no such meaning as is usually applied to the word "design." What "design" was there in the earthquake that destroyed Lisbon in 1755? The entire city was blotted out, together with the destruction of thirty thousand to forty thousand human beings. This earthquake occurred on a Sunday which was also a saint's day, and a large number were killed in a cathedral, which was also destroyed. And yet people talk about design and purpose and order and system as though they knew the meaning of the words.

Let us look at the earth as it exists to-day. It is not the same earth that came into some sort of separate existence millions of years ago. It has not only experienced vast and comparatively sudden changes, like the throwing up of mountain ranges in the cooling and contracting processes, but other changes not so sudden and acute have worked their way through ages of time, and changes are still going on all the time all over the earth.

New lands keep rising, others sinking away. Volcanoes are sending out millions of tons of matter each year, new islands are rising above the surface of the sea, while other islands are lowered beneath the waves. Continents are divided by internal forces and the ruthless powers of the sea.

Great Britain was cut off from the mainland not so very long ago, according to geological time. The shores of America and Africa were once connected, as seems evident from looking at the maps, and countless other geological shiftings have happened all over the surface and inside the earth, so that the world was no more made as it is now than was man created as we find him to-day. The destruction of the island of Martinique, the Mont Pelée disaster, the earthquake of San Francisco, are all within the memory of many now living. Active volcanoes are continuously pouring solid matter into the waters and slowly or rapidly building up new land where once was only sea.

The various archipelagoes are instances of this formation of fairly recent times. The Allegheny Mountains were once thirty thousand feet high. The crevices of their rocks have been penetrated by rain, split by frost and ice, pulverized by friction, and every minute are moving off toward the Gulf of Mexico. This range of mountains, which once reached an altitude of thirty thousand feet at the highest point, now has its highest peak but six thousand feet above the sea. These mountains have been worn down day after day, and the Ohio and Tennessee and Mississippi Rivers, carrying off the sediment, are building up the delta on the Louisiana coast. The earth and its seas were never made; they are in constant flux, moved by cold and heat and rain, and with no design or purpose that can be fathomed by the wit of man.

The delta of the Nile has through the long ages been carried down in mud and sand and silt from two thousand miles away and deposited in the open sea; and this is also called design by those who look for things they wish to find.

Nature brings hordes of insects that settle over the land and destroy the farmers' crops. Who are the objects of the glorious design: the farmers who so patiently and laboriously raise the crops or the grasshoppers that devour them? It must be the insects, because the farmers hold prayer meetings and implore their God to kill the bugs, but the pests go on with their deadly work unmolested. Man prates glibly about design, but Nature furnishes not a single example or fact as proof. Perhaps the microbe who bores a hole into the vitals of man and brings him down to his death may believe in a Providence and a design. How else could he live so royally on the vitals of one of the lords of creation?

All that we know is that we were born on this little grain of sand we call the earth. We know that it is one of the smallest bits of matter that floats in the great shoreless sea of space, and we have every reason to believe that it is as inconsequential in every other respect. On board the same craft, sailing the same seas, are all sorts of living things, fighting each other, and us, that each may survive. Most of these specimens are living on the carcasses of the dead. The strongest instinct of most of our crew is to stay here and live. The strongest in intellect and prowess live the longest. Nature, in all her manifestations, is at war with life, and sooner or later will doubtless have her way. No one can give a reason for any or all of the manifestations which we call life. We are like a body of shipwrecked sailors clutching to a raft and desperately engaged in holding on.

Men have built faith from hopes. They have struggled and fought in despair. They have frantically clung to life because of the will to live. The best that we can do is to be kindly and helpful toward our friends and fellow passengers who are clinging to the same speck of dirt while we are drifting side by side to our common doom.

11. Religious Knowledge and Mystical Experience
James Bisset Pratt

James Bisset Pratt (1875–1944) was a prominent American philosopher, who wrote widely on the philosophy of religion and metaphysics.

In spite of innumerable differences between the experiences of individual Christians, the general sense of some kind of divine presence . . . is common to a surprisingly large number. For that matter, it is very like the mystical experiences found in some of the non-Christian religions. Naturally it has been differently nurtured and differently expressed in the various religious cultures within which it has arisen. It has had a prominent place in the faith and worship of every Christian generation. In our time it has received, and is receiving, unusual stress. This for two reasons. One is the interest which our time feels in psychology, and the interest which our psychologists have come to feel in religion. The other reason is of a theological sort. As we have seen, various influences have united, during the last half-century, to diminish the prestige of the historical arguments for the existence of God and to reduce almost to the vanishing point the old confidence in the literal inspiration of the Scriptures. As a result the defenders of the Christian belief have evacuated one position after another, and many of them are today concentrating their strength within the fortifications of what they sometimes call the "inner experience."

At the close of the last century the psychologists awoke to the fact that religion was interesting, and began to take the lead in studying it. The first results of this serious work of psychologists upon religion were heartening in the extreme. The theologians were assured by their technical colleagues of the reality and the depth of the religious life. The next step to be taken by the psychologists was not quite so reassuring, namely, the description and analysis of the experience. The third step was frankly disquieting, though inevitable—the attempt, namely, not only to describe but to explain. Once more it seemed that the Ark of the Lord had fallen into the hands of the Philistines. For if the religious experience could be explained, set within the nexus of scientific law, it seemed to be in effect explained away; not indeed denied, but put in a position where it could no longer be used as an empirical argument for the existence of God.

In view of this situation the attempt has been made to take back the religious experience from psychology to theology, so to speak, by insisting that theology is an empirical science and that "God" is as objective a fact as are the objects of the physical sciences. Thus it is said that in the experience of moral regeneration and in the mystics' apprehension of the Divine, God is directly presented as a scientific fact and not merely as a hypothesis for the explanation of other facts. In other words, that the religious experience is an experience of God and that this proposition is neither a philosophical hypothesis nor a matter of faith and hope, but a plain fact of science.

In making up our minds as to the tenability of this view we should first ask ourselves what we mean by a fact of science. As was pointed out in a previous paragraph, a little reflection will show that a scientific fact, as distinguished from a private and individual experience, must have the characteristics of being repeatable and verifiable. The experiences of the isolated individual may be as real as you like, but they cannot possess the social authority of a scientific fact unless they are describable in terms capable of communication to all rational beings and verifiable by all properly equipped observers. The question now is: Can God, even in the vaguest sense, as a Source of Power not identical with our empirical selves, be truly said to be a directly experienced fact in this scientific sense? Is He a verifiable object in the sense of being directly presented to the experience of all normal or standardized and properly equipped observers? For my part, I cannot honestly answer this question in the affirmative. The experience of moral regeneration through religious influence may give us reasons to infer the influence of a Power not ourselves; but God, if reached in this way, would be an inference (as logical as you like, but still an inference, a hypothesis) and not an empirical fact. The mystical experience is on a different footing from moral regeneration, for it purports to be an immediate apprehension of the Divine as a directly felt object. But while it is conceivable that God for the mystic may be no hypothesis but a fact, can we honestly say He is even here a *scientific* fact? I judge we cannot. For a scientific fact, let me repeat, must be verifiable by all standardized observers with suitable training. And very few would maintain that the God of the mystics is verifiable in this fashion; and certainly He is, at all events, very far from having been thus scientifically verified. The man who doubts the existence of X-rays can be put in a position where he can perceive them; but there is no laboratory in which the mystics' God can be exhibited to the nonmystical. Nor is it an answer to assert that the mystics' God is verifiable by anyone with the proper psychical make-up; for while this is doubtless true, it really is merely a tautologous assertion to the effect that all mystics can perceive what all mystics can perceive. As much could be said of the hallucinatory objects commonly seen under the influence of nitrous oxide. And as a fact, those most eloquent in their assertions that only a few can apprehend God in the mystic fashion are just the mystics themselves. If not all, at any rate a very large portion of them assert that no amount of training, no amount of effort will enable one to attain to the mystic apprehension. It is like the wind which bloweth where it listeth. What need we any further witness? With mystics and non-mystics agreeing almost universally that God as an object of direct appre-hension is not verifiable, it would seem to follow inevitably that God is not a scientific fact and that therefore theology cannot be regarded as an empirical science.

Hence we are back again with the religious experience in the hands of the psychologists, and faced with the question: Has the psychological description and explanation of this experience made it valueless in the attempt to give a spiritual interpretation to the universe? Students of the psychology of religion are often tempted to say that it is valueless; and it is, I think, their scientific duty to point out all that can be said to justify this negative interpretation. To put the psychologist's position in sum-mary fashion, one may maintain that since the religious experience is experience, the interpretation of it belongs solely to psychology; and that the question whether the religious experience proves the existence and presence of God is an empirical and scientific question, and one with which, therefore, not the theologian but only the psychologist is qualified to deal. If now the religious experience can be explained in purely natur-alistic fashion, it is said, we are not warranted in looking for any divine explanation or in using it as evidence for the existence of God. Can the religious experience be so explained?

With this problem in mind the psychologist proceeds to an elaborate description and analysis of the religious—and especially of the mystical—consciousness; and he comes to the conclusion that the religious experi-ence is essentially of the same sort as nonreligious experience, having the same character and the same causation. Thus there would seem to be nothing in it to indicate that the mystic or the religious person has come in touch with God in any peculiar sense. It is in content and character on a par with nonreligious experience. What *appears* to be more is a matter not of actual experience but of interpretation. It may be the philosopher can show that all experience points to God, or somehow implies the Abso-lute; but the psychologist is very doubtful whether the religious or mysti-cal experience implies God any more directly or obviously or in any other way than the most commonplace experience of sense perception.

The psychologist, moreover, has another argument against what I might call the religious interpretation of the religious experience. Not only does psychological analysis show that the religious experience is like other experience in quality; it also shows that its occurrence, its rise, inten-sity, and decline may be explained by the same general psychological laws that account for the various changes in the nonreligious consciousness. This, to be sure, is not yet fully proved. The situation is complex; many factors, some of them quite obscure, are involved, and no one could seri-ously claim that all the factors of the religious experience are known. But many of them are known, and it is the necessary hypothesis of psychology that the unknown factors must be of the same general type as the known ones. This position of the psychologist is, in a sense, a matter of faith rather than of demonstration, but it is for him a necessary faith; for unless he make the postulate that psychological laws can explain all the facts of human psychosis, he would have to give up his claim that psychology is a complete science.

A good deal has been done to substantiate the first of the two arguments referred to above, by which psychology throws a doubt on the significance of mysticism: a large part of religious experience turns out on analysis to be of the same sort as nonreligious experience. Even the more striking phenomena of ecstasy can largely be paralleled by the effects of drugs and of Yoga training. Personally I am not convinced that the peculiar joy of religion, or what Otto calls numinous feeling, is really to be paralleled outside of religion. And so far as I can judge, the central thing in the religious experience—the sense of immediate contact with some being other than, though possibly inclusive of, oneself—is strictly unique. This sense of presence differentiates the religious experience pretty sharply from the various forms of drug ecstasy, and also from the usual results of Yoga. I think it is safe to say that when Yoga brings an intuition of the Absolute as present and directly known, some other factor is at work besides the Yoga methods. In other words, the sort of experience brought about by controllable physical and psychological means lacks the one characteristic that is essential to the religious experience.

It may indeed be argued that what has been added in this experience is easily explained by the rationalizing interpretation of the mystic, on the basis of his already accepted belief in the supernatural. We must distinguish, it is frequently and properly pointed out, between what the mystic actually experiences and his interpretation of it. No one will doubt that he has the sensations which he reports; but interpretation is not the product of psychological introspection but of philosophical theory. It does not grow out of the experience, or at any rate, not out of it alone. As Professor J. M. Moore points out, "our categories and established modes of reaction are present before any particular experience, and condition the form which the experience takes. The relation of experience and interpretation is reciprocal and complex rather than being a simple one-way relation of dependence."[1]

There is much truth in this criticism of mystic pronouncements. When the Salvation Army lassie tells us she has seen Christ, when Suzo asserts that he has communed with the Madonna, when the Hindu Vaishnavite recounts his immediate apprehension of Sri Krishna, very few of us will doubt that rationalistic interpretation has been busy, and that what we are given is not a description of actually experienced fact, but an interpretation of some simpler experience, formulated on the plan of some familiar creed. There is a line, however, beyond which this distinction of immediate sense data and interpretation cannot profitably and truthfully be carried. For the simplest elements of actual adult experience are seldom if ever sensations, but what John Laird significantly calls "sign facts."[2] A pure sensation is something that few of us who have passed infancy any longer experience. Our simplest forms of perceptual activity are drenched

---

[1] J. M. Moore, *Theories of Religious Experience,* p. 187.
[2] See John Laird, *A Study of Realism,* chaps, ii, v.

with meaning. The immediately given is already significant; it is never a mere sense datum, but a sense datum that means more than it is. And this is as true of the religious man's sense of presence as of any other form of experience. What he tells us of the further nature of the being he experiences is doubtless a matter of interpretation, but his immediate awareness that he is in the presence of an Other is hardly to be analyzed further without altering it into something very different from what it really is. This awareness of an Other, stripped of its creedal interpretation, differs, so the mystic asserts, *toto coelo* from a mere belief. It comes with all the immediacy of sense perception. It has, of course, sensuous elements, as every percept has; but to identify it with any collection of mere sense data is to mutilate it beyond recognition. It is, in short, if we may trust the mystics' introspective description (not their interpretation), a sign fact.

In saying this I have not forgotten Professor Leuba's artificial production of the sense of presence in the laboratory.[3] But it is well to remind ourselves in passing that Professor Leuba did not produce the *religious* sense of presence in his laboratory. His experiments were not dealing with that directly. What his experiments showed was that a sense of presence in general may be induced without anyone actually being present. The subject, that is, may be fooled. In short, like other forms of cognitive experience, the sense of presence may be illusory. But surely we did not need experimental evidence to show us this. Occasionally any of us may be mistaken about the presence of a human fellow. We may suppose ourselves not alone in the room and discover that we are. When in doubt about the matter we put the thing to a test, using various methods to find out. The fact that sometimes we are mistaken does not prove to us that we are always mistaken. Each case must stand on its own merits and be judged by its own evidence. As a fact, the cases of mistake are so small a fraction of the total, and the cases in which we are correct form so large a majority, that in normal human experience this sense of another's presence carries with it a strong a priori probability of its own validity.

Now there is no doubt that the mystic may be mistaken like other people. As Professor James pointed out, his emotion of conviction as to the validity of his experience of presence may be authoritative for him, but it is not for anyone else. It is quite possible that various causes, known or unknown, may have united to delude him. His own certainty is no guarantee of the truth of his assertion. But the fact that he *may be* mistaken does not prove that he *is* mistaken. The fact—if it be a fact—that he is *sometimes* mistaken does not prove that he is *always* mistaken. Here as elsewhere each case must be judged on its merits. Nor can we say that there is so much uncertainty about the cause of this experience that the assertion of the religious man is entirely negligible. The matter is not left as if nothing had happened. Certainly the mystic's evidence is not as good as the ordinary evidence of eye and ear, for we have a means of testing the validity of these instruments of knowledge, and in the vast majority of cases they prove trustworthy. The mystic's assertion does not carry with it the same weight of a priori probability as does the more common convic-

[3]See Leuba, *The Psychology of Religious Mysticism,* pp. 283–286.

tion that someone we do not see is in the room with us. But the assertion of the mystic is not entirely worthless as evidence. It at least sets us a problem of further investigation; and if such investigation can produce no complete explanation for the mystic's experience, the experience must be set down at least tentatively as having a certain minimal evidential value in favor of the truth of the mystic's assertion. The strength of this evidence will be increased with every demonstration that the religious sense of presence, its joy and its other by-products, are different in quality from the corresponding experiences of the nonreligious life.

The claim to evidential validity on the part of the religious sense of presence is the more difficult wholly to deny because of the immense number of witnesses that might be called upon to give confirmatory testimony. A student of the history of religions can hardly fail to be struck with the ubiquity of this experience. The way it springs up, spontaneously and independently in remotely separated lands, among peoples of unrelated races, in nearly all the ages and in all the religions with which we are acquainted, is at least an impressive fact. Indeed, one might argue that if any evidential value whatever is to be granted the religious experience, one will have to go on and grant it a good deal, because of the cumulative nature of its testimony.

Whether it has any evidential value is, of course, just the question we are discussing. It will be recalled that there are two principal arguments for the naturalistic interpretation of the religious experience. The one based on the similarity between religious and nonreligious experiences we have discussed. The other argument—which indeed is so closely related to the first as to be hardly separable except for purposes of exposition—consists in pointing out that the same psychological laws obtain among religious facts as those which govern the whole mental life of man. In other words, it is the aim of this argument to show that the various experiences of the religious life follow laws of definite and regular sequence, and are therefore susceptible of purely psychological explanation. Since they can be explained psychologically, the argument continues, they need no other explanation, and hence cannot be used as evidence for anything beyond the human mind with its human contents and its human ways of working.

As I have already pointed out, psychology has not yet been fully successful in making out these laws of regular sequence between religious phenomena and various psychophysical conditions; they represent rather a program and ideal than an actual achievement. Much successful work toward this ideal has been done and more may be expected. The psychologist, I think, is justified in making a working hypothesis of this ideal of complete psychological explanation for all mental facts. In a sense it is a necessary hypothesis, for his claim that psychology is at least potentially a science capable of giving complete explanation and prediction depends upon it. Unfortunately many psychologists often forget that this hypothesis is as yet only a hypothesis and is very far indeed from having been empirically verified. The truth is, we cannot as yet explain all the facts of human experience and of mental activity by psychological laws. To assert in the present state of our ignorance that we can because we must—which means because we want to—is not science but dogma and the will to make believe.

It is, however, perfectly conceivable that some day all the activities of the human mind, including the religious experience, will be explicable in psychological fashion; in other words, that we shall be able to show how, say, the mystical experience follows invariably upon certain definable conditions, and that by going through certain psychophysical processes one may induce it. This possibility opens up a rather interesting logical question. For if this situation should ever be reached, how would it, and how should it be interpreted? The interpretation that would be given it by most psychologists is obvious enough: they would say that the religious experience was thereby shown to be, like any other conscious state, producible by certain definite conditions, and therefore no more significant of objective reality than dreams or hypnosis. But there would be an equally obvious interpretation open to the mystics. It will be recalled that in our discussion of the claims of theology to rank as an empirical science, I argued that this was not admissible because the mystic fact is not a scientific fact; and that it is not a scientific fact because it is not verifiable by all normal or standardized human beings—that is to say, not reproducible at will within the field of awareness. But on the hypothesis we have now set up of the future perfecting of psychology, the mystic experience is to be reproducible at will. We can therefore picture the mystics, or their philosophical defenders, turning the tables on the psychologists by saying: you told us our apprehension of the Divine was not a scientific fact because not verifiable in the sense of being reproducible. Now, thanks to your kind of researches, it is reproducible and verifiable. Is not our apprehension of the Divine, therefore, a fact, and a scientific fact? Is it not a scientific fact in the same sense as your apprehension of brain cells; and immeasurably more scientific than the physicist's apprehension of the invisible electrons? Instead of interpreting it as you do dreams and illusions, should you not rather, on your own showing, interpret it as you do veridical perception?

The situation is sufficiently bewildering. Plainly it will hardly do to argue: mysticism is illusory because its cognitive states are *not* reproducible; and with the next breath to argue, mysticism is illusory because its cognitive states *are* reproducible. To do that would be to blow hot and cold, to play fast and loose with nature. Either the religious experience is reproducible, given certain conditions, or it is not; and from both these opposites we can hardly draw the same conclusion. If it is incumbent upon us to give the devil his due, surely it is only fair to give the Lord a chance!

How, then, should we construe this rather puzzling situation? A good deal, I think, would depend on the actual details of the actual facts which, by hypothesis, psychology shall one day discover. If, for example, it were found that the religious experience, in all its fullness and with its cognizable quality, could be reproduced by a dose of some newly discovered drug, and that it never arose except under psychophysical conditions which were, in the last analysis, identical with those induced by this drug; it would then follow—that the new-found drug was an excellent means for bringing about the psychophysical conditions requisite for the religious experience! It would prove nothing more; and it would still be open to anyone who wished to do so to assert that these identical psychophysical conditions might be produced by the direct action of God. It is unlikely, however, that many would make such as assertion; and probably not only the psychologists but most of us would agree that the religious experience was a symptom of certain physical conditions but without further objective or cosmic significance. We may, however, picture other results from the scientific investigation of the religious consciousness and its "causes." We may well imagine that psychology might discover that the religious experience followed regularly upon a long process of purifying the heart and concentrating the mind, by proper means, upon the thought of the Divine. Now if this were true, if it were a verifiable scientific fact that the experience of the Divine Presence, the immediate and undoubtable sense of the numinous at hand, sufficiently different from every other sort of experience to be distinguishable and recognizable, and having the same compelling objectivity that visual and tactual experiences possess—if this form of cognitive consciousness, I say, were found to follow invariably upon a definable process of heart purification and mind concentration, how should we interpret the logic of the situation?

I think it is perfectly plain that there would be two answers. The conscientious psychologist *as psychologist* would say: The religious consciousness is now fully explained in psychological terms. I leave to the philosopher the explanation of the cosmos, but I have shown that no reference to anything supernatural, to anything outside of human nature, is needed to explain the sense of divine presence and its various by-products. It follows regularly upon definable and predictable psychophysical conditions by laws of regular and invariable sequence. On the other hand, the mystic would say: the direct apprehension of God is now become a verifiable fact. If you doubt my word, put yourself through the long course of mental and spiritual training which the psychologist and I can plan out for you, and you shall see for yourself. If any man will follow the religious life in the light of modern science, he shall know of the doctrine. For it is God who will be working in you, God who will be revealing Himself to you, who can now be *counted on* to reveal Himself to you, through the working of the laws of the human mind which He Himself made. The religious experience is now a scientific fact, and is to be explained by the actual presence of the Divine before the eyes of the soul.

Of these two interpretations which would be correct? By hypothesis all the relevant facts would be in, and further empirical evidence would be unnecessary. The question would be purely a matter of logic. Plainly it would be exceedingly difficult to prove either of the rival interpretations wrong. And I want to suggest that they might *both* be right.

For what, after all, is a psychological explanation? It consists (in logical outline) in tracing laws of regular sequence between the psychosis to be explained and certain definable conditions, either within the psychophysical mechanism of the subject or within so much of the environment as natural science is able to define, understand, and for experimental purposes, control. Psychological explanation is therefore a form of description and generalization. It does not pretend to point out ultimate or original causes. Psychology is not interested in ultimate or original causes. Its explanation is complete if it has constructed a formula of sequence among scientific, i.e., verifiable facts, and on the basis of this sequence is able without failure to predict the psychosis in question on the appearance of the facts with which the formula connects it. Now there is nothing in the actuality of this kind of an explanation inconsistent with the religious interpretation of the situation. The mystic is not interested in denying the validity of the psychologist's explanation, but he is interested in something more. To him explanation means something different from a generalized description of regular sequences. He is interested in ultimate and original causes. And provided we are willing to relieve the concept of the Divine from the attribute of arbitrariness, there is nothing to prevent our supposing that the steady action of the Divine upon the soul is the ultimate cause of the religious experience, and that what the psychologist describes is the regular process by which the soul may be exposed to this Divine influence. The white radiance of eternity, we may suppose, steadily beats upon us, but only in certain conditions of body and mind can we become sensitive to its light. If this were so, it would be quite within the province of psychology to describe exactly and completely what these conditions are, and on the basis of them to predict and "explain" the rise of the religious experience. To do so, and to do it without any reference to the ultimate source of the inflowing Light, would be to give a complete and exhaustive psychological explanation. Yet it would be equally true that religious experience was exactly what the religious man insists that it is— an immediate awareness of a Divine Other.

By making these suggestions I do not mean that God is to be taken as filling the gaps which science leaves, nor that He is to be proved by miraculous interventions. As I have said, it is quite likely that all religious experience will some day be found to have its scientific explanation—in the sense I have indicated. The Unity of the World is not destroyed. God must be conceived as existing in and expressing Himself through all reality. Yet owing to the finiteness of our human nature and our very limited and partial insight, it may be true—and I think it is true—that most of us apprehend the universal Divine more readily and clearly in some parts of our experience than in others. To the angel's vision God may be "as full, as perfect, in a hair as hart." Yet so long as man remains a little lower than the angels it is probable that he will realize God more fully and perfectly in the religious experience than anywhere else. My aim in this chapter has been, not to attack science nor to defend a view of supernatural divine interventions, but to show that something may be said for the faith of the religious man that, in what he knows as his most religious moments, it is God with whom he comes in touch. Later on he may learn that he is in touch with God always and everywhere; but it is in the mystic experience that he first and most fully *recognizes* God.

Possibly we can make a little plainer to ourselves the contribution make by mysticism to the religious view of the world if we put to ourselves one further question. Let us suppose that in all the world's history there had been no mystics, and no suggestion in any mind of an immediate apprehension of the Divine. Would not, I ask, a religious view of the world under those circumstances have been much less probable, much harder to believe, than it is today? Would not many people, would not most people, on hearing a religious philosophy propounded, have asked the question: "Why, if there be a Divine, has it never come in touch with any human mind?" In other words, if there be a God, would you not naturally expect mystics? The facts of mysticism makes the existence of God considerably more probable.

Thus, I believe, a psychological study of the mystical states combined with a philosophical interpretation of the nature of science may make a distinct contribution to the religious view of reality. But if this is to be done, religion, I trust, will make fewer demands of a specific nature than it has been accustomed to make as to the interpretation of the Divine. It will be content to *believe* in God without *defining* Him. More in particular, it will lay less stress than formerly upon the anthropomorphic and excessively personal aspects of the Divine. It will have nothing to say of specific answer to prayer or of Divine interventions. And in place of the dogmatic view of the older theology, it will adopt a more empirical attitude toward the universe, and while less eager to tell who and what God is, it will be more ready to learn.

We come back, then, after our long discussion, to the question: Is the religious experience such as to furnish any relevant empirical evidence on the ultimate religious problems of our time? The answer would seem to be emphatically in the affirmative. A chastened theology may appeal to the facts of the religious life with a certain justifiable confidence. The testimony of the religious consciousness through thirty centuries is not without cosmic significance.

12. The Basis of the Moral Law   C. S. Lewis

I now go back to what I said . . . that there were two odd things about the human race. First, that they were haunted by the idea of a sort of behaviour they ought to practice, what you might call fair play, or decency, or morality, or the Law of Nature. Second, that they did not in fact do so. Now some of you may wonder why I called this odd. It may seem to you the most natural thing in the world. In particular, you may have thought I was rather hard on the human race. After all, you may say, what I call breaking the Law of Right and Wrong or of Nature, only means that people are not perfect. And why on earth should I expect them to be? That would be a good answer if what I was trying to do was to fix the exact amount of blame which is due to us for not behaving as we expect others to behave. But that is not my job at all. I am not concerned at present with blame; I am trying to find out truth. And from that point of view the very idea of something being imperfect, of its not being what it ought to be, has certain consequences.

If you take a thing like a stone or a tree, it is what it is and there seems no sense in saying it ought to have been otherwise. Of course you may say a stone is "the wrong shape" if you want to use it for a rockery, or that a tree is a bad tree because it does not give you as much shade as you expected. But all you mean is that the stone or tree does not happen to be convenient for some purpose of your own. You are not, except as a joke, blaming them for that. You really know, that, given the weather and the soil, the tree could not have been any different. What we, from our point of view, call a "bad" tree is obeying the laws of its nature just as much as a "good" one.

Now have you noticed what follows? It follows that what we usually call the laws of nature—the way weather works on a tree for example—may not really be *laws* in the strict sense, but only in a manner of speaking. When you say that falling stones always obey the law of gravitation, is not this much the same as saying that the law only means "what stones always do"? You do not really think that when a stone is let go, it suddenly remembers that it is under orders to fall to the ground. You only mean that, in fact, it does fall. In other words, you cannot be sure that there is anything over and above the facts themselves, any law about what ought to happen, as distinct from what does happen. The laws of nature, as applied to stones or trees, may only mean "what Nature, in fact, does." But if you turn to the Law of Human Nature, the Law of Decent Behaviour, it is a different matter. That law certainly does not mean "what human beings, in fact, do"; for as I said before, many of them do not obey this law at all, and none of them obey it completely. The law of gravity tells you what stones do if you drop them; but the Law of Human Nature tells you what human beings ought to do and do not. In other words, when you are dealing with humans, something else comes in above and beyond the actual facts. You have the facts (how men do behave) and you also have something else (how they ought to behave). In the rest of the universe there need not be anything but the facts. Electrons and molecules behave in a certain way, and certain results follow, and that may be the whole story. But men behave in a certain way and that is not the whole story, for all the time you know that they ought to behave differently.

Now this is really so peculiar that one is tempted to try to explain it away. For instance, we might try to make out that when you say a man ought not to act as he does, you only mean the same as when you say that a stone is the wrong shape; namely, that what he is doing happens to be inconvenient to you. But that is simply untrue. A man occupying the corner seat in the train because he got there first, and a man who slipped into it while my back was turned and removed my bag, are both equally inconvenient. But I blame the second man and do not blame the first. I am not angry—except perhaps for a moment before I come to my senses—with a man who trips me up by accident; I am angry with a man who tries to trip me up even if he does not succeed. Yet the first has hurt me and the second has not. Sometimes the behaviour which I call bad is not inconvenient to me at all, but the very opposite. In war, each side may find a traitor on the other side very useful. But though they use him and pay him they regard him as human vermin. So you cannot say that what we call decent behaviour in others is simply the behaviour that happens to be useful to us. And as for decent behaviour in ourselves, I suppose it is pretty obvious that it does not mean the behaviour that pays. It means things like being content with thirty shillings when you might have got three pounds, doing school work honestly when it would be easy to cheat, leaving a girl alone when you would like to make love to her, staying in dangerous places when you could go somewhere safer, keeping promises you would rather not keep, and telling the truth even when it makes you look a fool.

Some people say that though decent conduct does not mean what pays each particular person at a particular moment, still, it means what pays the human race as a whole; and that consequently there is no mystery about it. Human beings, after all, have some sense; they see that you cannot have real safety or happiness except in a society where every one plays fair, and it is because they see this that they try to behave decently. Now, of course, it is perfectly true that safety and happiness can only come from individuals, classes, and nations being honest and fair and kind to each other. It is one of the most important truths in the world. But as an explanation of why we feel as we do about Right and Wrong it just misses the point. If we ask: "Why ought I to be unselfish?" and you reply "Because it is good for society," we may then ask, "Why should I care what's good for society except when it happens to pay *me* personally?" and then you will have to say, "Because you ought to be unselfish"—which simply brings us back to where we started. You are saying what is true, but you are not getting any further. If a man asked what was the point of playing football, it would not be much good saying "in order to score goals," for trying to score goals is the game itself, not the reason for the game, and you would really only be saying that football was football—which is true, but not worth saying. In the same way, if a man asks what is the point of behaving decently, it is no good replying, "in order to benefit society," for trying to benefit society, in other words being unselfish (for "society" after all only means "other people"), is one of the things decent behaviour consists in; all you are really saying is that decent behaviour is decent behaviour. You would have said just as much if you had stopped at the statement, "Men ought to be unselfish."

And that is where I do stop. Men ought to be unselfish, ought to be fair. Not that men are unselfish, nor that they like being unselfish, but that they ought to be. The Moral Law, or Law of Human Nature, is not simply a fact about human behaviour in the same way as the Law of Gravitation is, or may be, simply a fact about how heavy objects behave. On the other hand, it is not a mere fancy, for we cannot get rid of the idea, and most of the things we say and think about men would be reduced to nonsense if we did. And it is not simply a statement about how we should like men to behave for our own convenience; for the behaviour we call bad or unfair is not exactly the same as the behaviour we find inconvenient, and may even be the opposite. Consequently, this Rule of Right and Wrong, or Law of Human Nature, or whatever you call it, must somehow or other be a real thing—a thing that is really there, not made up by ourselves. And yet it is not a fact in the ordinary sense, in the same way as our actual behaviour is a fact. It begins to look as if we shall have to admit that there is more than one kind of reality; that, in this particular case, there is something above and beyond the ordinary facts of men's behaviour, and yet quite definitely real—a real law, which none of us made, but which we find pressing on us.

Let us sum up what we have reached so far. In the case of stones and trees and things of that sort, what we call the Laws of Nature may not be anything except a way of speaking. When you say that nature is governed by certain laws, this may only mean that nature does, in fact, behave in a certain way. The so-called laws may not be anything real—anything above and beyond the actual facts which we observe. But in the case of Man, we saw that this will not do. The Law of Human Nature, or of Right and Wrong, must be something above and beyond the actual facts of human behaviour. In this case, besides the actual facts, you have something else— a real law which we did not invent and which we know we ought to obey.

I now want to consider what this tells us about the universe we live in. Ever since men were able to think, they have been wondering what this universe really is and how it came to be there. And, very roughly, two views have been held. First, there is what is called the materialist view. People who take that view think that matter and space just happen to exist, and always have existed, nobody knows why; and that the matter, behaving in certain fixed ways, has just happened, by a sort of fluke, to produce creatures like ourselves who are able to think. By one chance in a thousand something hit our sun and made it produce the planets; and by another thousandth chance the chemicals necessary for life, and the right temperature, occurred on one of these planets, and so some of the matter on this earth came alive; and then, by a very long series of chances, the living creatures developed into things like us. The other view is the religious view. According to it, what is behind the universe is more like a mind than it is like anything else we know. That is to say, it is conscious, and has purposes, and prefers one thing to another. And on this view it made the universe, partly for purposes we do not know, but partly, at any rate, in order to produce creatures like itself—I mean, like itself to the extent of having minds. Please do not think that one of these views was held a long time ago and that the other has gradually taken its place. Wherever there have been thinking men both views turn up. And note this too. You cannot find out which view is the right one by science in the ordinary sense. Science works by experiments. It watches how things behave. Every scientific statement in the long run, however complicated it looks, really means something like, "I pointed the telescope to such and such a part of the sky at 2:20 A.M. on January 15th and saw so-and-so," or, "I put some of this stuff in a pot and heated it to such-and-such a temperature and it did so-and-so." Do not think I am saying anything against science: I am only saying what its job is. And the more scientific a man is, the more (I believe) he would agree with me that this is the job of science—and a very useful and necessary job it is too. But why anything comes to be there at all, and whether there is anything behind the things science observes—something of a different kind—this is not a scientific question. If there is "Something Behind," then either it will have to remain altogether unknown to men or else make itself known in some different way. The statement that there is any such thing, and the statement that there is no such thing, are neither of them statements that science can make. And real scientists do not usually make them. It is usually the journalists and popular novelists who have picked up a few odds and ends of half-baked science from textbooks who go in for them. After all, it is really a matter of common sense. Supposing science ever became complete so that it knew every single thing in the whole universe. Is it not plain that the questions, "Why is there a universe?" "Why does it go on as it does?" "Has it any meaning?" would remain just as they were?

Now the position would be quite hopeless but for this. There is one thing, and only one, in the whole universe which we know more about than we could learn from external observation. That one thing is Man. We do not merely observe men, we *are* men. In this case we have, so to speak, inside information; we are in the know. And because of that, we know that men find themselves under a moral law, which they did not make, and cannot quite forget even when they try, and which they know they ought to obey. Notice the following point. Anyone studying Man from the outside as we study electricity or cabbages, not knowing our language and consequently not able to get any inside knowledge from us, but merely observing what we did, would never get the slightest evidence that we had this moral law. How could he? for his observations would only show what we did, and the moral law is about what we ought to do. In the same way, if there were anything above or behind the observed facts in the case of stones or the weather, we, by studying them from outside, could never hope to discover it.

The position of the question, then, is like this. We want to know whether the universe simply happens to be what it is for no reason or whether there is a power behind it that makes it what it is. Since that power, if it exists, would be not one of the observed facts but a reality which makes them, no mere observation of the facts can find it. There is only one case in which we can know whether there is anything more, namely our own case. And in that one case we find there is. Or put it the other way round. If there was a controlling power outside the universe, it could not show itself to us as one of the facts inside the universe—no more than the architect of a house could actually be a wall or staircase or fireplace in that house. The only way in which we could expect it to show itself would be inside ourselves as an influence or a command trying to get us to behave in a certain way. And that is just what we do find inside ourselves. Surely this ought to arouse our suspicions? In the only case where you can expect to get an answer, the answer turns out to be Yes; and in the other cases, where you do not get an answer, you see why you do not. Suppose someone asked me, when I see a man in a blue uniform going down the street leaving little paper packets at each house, why I suppose that they contain letters? I should reply, "Because whenever he leaves a similar little packet for me I find it does contain a letter." And if he then objected, "But you've never seen all these letters which you think the other people are getting," I should say, "Of course not, and I shouldn't expect to, because they're not addressed to me. I'm explaining the packets I'm not allowed to open by the ones I am allowed to open." It is the same about this question. The only packet I am allowed to open is Man. When I do, especially when I open that particular man called Myself, I find that I do not exist on my own, that I am under a law; that somebody or something wants me to behave in a certain way. I do not, of course, think that if I could get inside a stone or a tree I should find exactly the same thing, just as I do not think all the other people in the street get the same letters as I do. I should expect, for instance, to find that the stone had to obey the law of gravity—that whereas the sender of the letters merely tells me to obey the law of my human nature, He compels the stone to obey the laws of its stony nature. But I should expect to find that there was, so to speak, a sender of letters in both cases, a Power behind the facts, A Director, a Guide.

Do not think I am going faster than I really am. I am not yet within a hundred miles of the God of Christian theology. All I have got to is a Something which is directing the universe, and which appears in me as a law urging me to do right and making me feel responsible and uncomfortable when I do wrong. I think we have to assume it is more like a mind than it is like anything else we know—because after all the only other thing we know is matter and you can hardly imagine a bit of matter giving instructions. But, of course, it need not be very like a mind, still less like a person. . . .

13. Why I Am Not a Christian   Bertrand Russell

Bertrand Russell (1872–1970) was one of the most prominent philosophers of the twentieth century. He is the author of numerous books on a wide variety of philosophical and social issues. He is known to the general public for his outspoken stands on religion, marriage, the banning of the nuclear bomb. In 1950 he was awarded the Nobel Prize for Literature.

As your Chairman has told you, the subject about which I am going to speak to you tonight is "Why I Am Not a Christian." Perhaps it would be as well, first of all, to try to make out what one means by the word *Christian.* It is used these days in a very loose sense by a great many people. Some people mean no more by it than a person who attempts to live a good life. In that sense I suppose there would be Christians in all sects and creeds; but I do not think that that is the proper sense of the word, if only because it would imply that all the people who are not Christians— all the Buddhists, Confucians, Mohammedans, and so on—are not trying to live a good life. I do not mean by a Christian any person who tries to live decently according to his lights. I think that you must have a certain amount of definite belief before you have a right to call yourself a Christian. The word does not have quite such a full-blooded meaning now as it had in the times of St. Augustine and St. Thomas Aquinas. In those days, if a man said that he was a Christian it was known what he meant. You accepted a whole collection of creeds which were set out with great precision, and every single syllable of those creeds you believed with the whole strength of your convictions.

What Is a Christian?

Nowadays it is not quite that. We have to be a little more vague in our meaning of Christianity. I think, however, that there are two different items which are quite essential to anybody calling himself a Christian. The first is one of a dogmatic nature—namely, that you must believe in God and immortality. If you do not believe in those two things, I do not think that you can properly call yourself a Christian. Then, further than that, as the name implies, you must have some kind of belief about Christ. The Mohammedans, for instance, also believe in God and in immortality, and yet they would not call themselves Christians. I think you must have at the very lowest the belief that Christ was, if not divine, at least the best and wisest of men. If you are not going to believe that much about Christ, I do not think you have any right to call yourself a Christian. Of course, there is another sense, which you find in *Whitaker's Almanack* and in geography books, where the population of the world is said to be divided into Christians, Mohammedans, Buddhists, fetish worshipers, and so on; and in that sense we are all Christians. The geography books count us all in, but that is a purely geographical sense, which I suppose we can ignore. Therefore I take it that when I tell you why I am not a Christian I have to tell you two different things: first, why I do not believe in God and in immortality; and secondly, why I do not think that Christ was the best and wisest of men, although I grant him a very high degree of moral goodness.

But for the successful efforts of unbelievers in the past, I could not take so elastic a definition of Christianity as that. As I said before, in olden days it had a much more full-blooded sense. For instance, it included the belief in hell. Belief in eternal hell-fire was an essential item of Christian belief until pretty recent times. In this country, as you know, it ceased to be an essential item because of a decision of the Privy Council, and from that decision the Archbishop of Canterbury and the Archbishop of York dissented; but in this country our religion is settled by Act of Parliament, and therefore the Privy Council was able to override their Graces and hell was no longer necessary to a Christian. Consequently I shall not insist that a Christian must believe in hell.

The Existence of God

To come to this question of the existence of God: it is a large and serious question, and if I were to attempt to deal with it in any adequate manner I should have to keep you here until Kingdom Come, so that you will have to excuse me if I deal with it in a somewhat summary fashion.

You know, of course, that the Catholic Church has laid it down as a dogma that the existence of God can be proved by the unaided reason. That is a somewhat curious dogma, but it is one of their dogmas. They had to introduce it because at one time the freethinkers adopted the habit of saying that there were such and such arguments which mere reason might urge against the existence of God, but of course they knew as a matter of faith that God did exist. The arguments and the reasons were set out at great length, and the Catholic Church felt that they must stop it. Therefore they laid it down that the existence of God can be proved by the unaided reason and they have had to set up what they considered were arguments to prove it. There are, of course, a number of them, but I shall take only a few.

The First-Cause Argument

Perhaps the simplest and easiest to understand is the argument of the First Cause. (It is maintained that everything we see in this world has a cause, and as you go back in the chain of causes further and further you must come to a First Cause, and to that First Cause you give the name of God.) That argument, I suppose, does not carry very much weight nowadays, because, in the first place, cause is not quite what it used to be. The philosophers and the men of science have got going on cause, and it has not anything like the vitality it used to have; but, apart from that, you can see that the argument that there must be a First Cause is one that cannot have any validity. I may say that when I was a young man and was debating these questions very seriously in my mind, I for a long time accepted the argument of the First Cause, until one day, at the age of eighteen, I read John Stuart Mill's Autobiography, and I there found this sentence: "My father taught me that the question 'Who made me?' cannot be answered, since it immediately suggests the further question 'Who made God?'" That very simple sentence showed me, as I still think, the fallacy in the argument of the First Cause. If everything must have a cause, then God must have a cause. If there can be anything without a cause, it may just as well be the world as God, so that there cannot be any validity in that argument. It is exactly of the same nature as the Hindu's view, that the world rested upon an elephant and the elephant rested upon a tortoise; and when they said, "How about the tortoise?" the Indian said, "Suppose we change the subject." The argument is really no better than that. There is no reason why the world could not have come into being without a cause; nor, on the other hand, is there any reason why it should not have always existed. There is no reason to suppose that the world had a beginning at all. The idea that things must have a beginning is really due to the poverty of our imagination. Therefore, perhaps, I need not waste any more time upon the argument about the First Cause.

The Natural-Law Argument

Then there is a very common argument from natural law. That was a favorite argument all through the eighteenth century, especially under the influence of Sir Isaac Newton and his cosmogony. People observed the planets going around the sun according to the law of gravitation, and they thought that God had given a behest to these planets to move in that particular fashion, and that was why they did so. That was, of course, a convenient and simple explanation that saved them the trouble of looking any further for explanations of the law of gravitation. Nowadays we explain the law of gravitation in a somewhat complicated fashion that Einstein has introduced. I do not propose to give you a lecture on the law of gravitation, as interpreted by Einstein, because that again would take some time; at any rate, you no longer have the sort of natural law that you had in the Newtonian system, where, for some reason that nobody could understand, nature behaved in a uniform fashion. We now find that a great many things we thought were natural laws are really human conventions. You know that even in the remotest depths of stellar space there are still three feet to a yard. That is, no doubt, a very remarkable fact, but you would hardly call it a law of nature. And a great many things that have been regarded as laws of nature are of that kind. On the other hand, where you can get down to any knowledge of what atoms actually do, you will find they are much less subject to law than people thought, and that the laws at which you arrive are statistical averages of just the sort that would emerge from chance. There is, as we all know, a law that if you throw dice you will get double sixes only about once in thirty-six times, and we do not regard that as evidence that the fall of the dice is regulated by design; on the contrary, if the double sixes came every time we should think that there was design. The laws of nature are of that sort as regards a great many of them. They are statistical averages such as would emerge from the laws of chance; and that makes this whole business of natural law much less impressive than it formerly was. Quite apart from that, which represents the momentary state of science that may change tomorrow, the whole idea that natural laws imply a lawgiver is due to a confusion between natural and human laws. Human laws are behests commanding you to behave a certain way, in which way you may choose to behave, or you may choose not to behave; but natural laws are a description of how things do in fact behave, and being a mere description of what they in fact do, you cannot argue that there must be somebody who told them to do that, because even supposing that there were, you are then faced with the question "Why did God issue just those natural laws and no others?" If you say that he did it simply from his own good pleasure, and without any reason, you then find that there is something which is not subject to law, and so your train of natural law is interrupted. If you say, as more orthodox theologians do, that in all the laws which God issues he had a reason for giving those laws rather than others—the reason, of course, being to create the best universe, although you would never think it to look at it—if there were a reason for the laws which God gave, then God himself was subject to law, and therefore you do not get any advantage by introducing God as an intermediary. You have really a law outside and anterior to the divine edicts, and God does not serve your purpose, because he is not the ultimate lawgiver. In short, this whole argument about natural law no longer has anything like the strength that it used to have. I am traveling on in time in my review of the arguments. The arguments that are used for the existence of God change their character as time goes on. They were at first hard intellectual arguments embodying certain quite definite fallacies. As we come to modern times they become less respectable intellectually and more and more affected by a kind of moralizing vagueness.

The Argument from Design

The next step in this process brings us to the argument from design. You all know the argument from design: everything in the world is made just so that we can manage to live in the world, and if the world was ever so little different, we could not manage to live in it. That is the argument from design. It sometimes takes a rather curious form; for instance, it is argued that rabbits have white tails in order to be easy to shoot. I do not know how rabbits would view that application. It is an easy argument to parody. You all know Voltaire's remark, that obviously the nose was designed to be such as to fit spectacles. That sort of parody has turned out to be not nearly so wide of the mark as it might have seemed in the eighteenth century, because since the time of Darwin we understand much better why living creatures are adapted to their environment. It is not that their environment was made to be suitable to them but that they grew to be suitable to it, and that is the basis of adaptation. There is no evidence of design about it.

When you come to look into this argument from design, it is a most astonishing thing that people can believe that this world, with all the things that are in it, with all its defects, should be the best that omnipotence and omniscience have been able to produce in millions of years. I really cannot believe it. Do you think that, if you were granted omnipotence and omniscience and millions of years in which to perfect your world, you could produce nothing better than the Ku Klux Klan or the Fascists? Moreover, if you accept the ordinary laws of science, you have to suppose that human life and life in general on this planet will die out in due course: it is a stage in the decay of the solar system; at a certain stage of decay you get the sort of conditions of temperature and so forth which are suitable to protoplasm, and there is life for a short time in the life of the whole solar system. You see in the moon the sort of thing to which the earth is tending—something dead, cold, and lifeless.

I am told that that sort of view is depressing, and people will sometimes tell you that if they believed that, they would not be able to go on living. Do not believe it; it is all nonsense. Nobody really worries much about what is going to happen millions of years hence. Even if they think they are worrying much about that, they are really deceiving themselves. They are worried about something much more mundane, or it may merely be a bad digestion; but nobody is really seriously rendered unhappy by the thought of something that is going to happen to this world millions and millions of years hence. Therefore, although it is of course a gloomy view to suppose that life will die out—at least I suppose we may say so, although sometimes when I contemplate the things that people do with their lives I think it is almost a consolation—it is not such as to render life miserable. It merely makes you turn your attention to other things.

The Moral Arguments for Deity

Now we reach one stage further in what I shall call the intellectual descent that the Theists have made in their argumentations, and we come to what are called the moral arguments for the existence of God. You all know, of course, that there used to be in the old days three intellectual arguments for the existence of God, all of which were disposed of by Immanuel Kant in the *Critique of Pure Reason;* but no sooner had he disposed of those arguments than he invented a new one, a moral argument, and that quite convinced him. He was like many people: in intellectual matters he was skeptical, but in moral matters he believed implicitly in the maxims that he had imbibed at his mother's knee. That illustrates what the psychoanalysts so much emphasize—the immensely stronger hold upon us that our early associations have than those of later times.

Kant, as I say, invented a new moral argument for the existence of God, and that in varying forms was extremely popular during the nineteenth century. It has all sorts of forms. One form is to say that there would be no right or wrong unless God existed. I am not for the moment concerned with whether there is a difference between right and wrong, or whether there is not: that is another question. The point I am concerned with is that, if you are quite sure there is a difference between right and wrong, you are then in this situation: Is that difference due to God's fiat or is it not? If it is due to God's fiat, then for God himself there is no difference between right and wrong, and it is no longer a significant statement to say that God is good. If you are going to say, as theologians do, that God is good, you must then say that right and wrong have some meaning which is independent of God's fiat, because God's fiats are good and not bad independently of the mere fact that he made them. If you are going to say that, you will then have to say that it is not only through God that right and wrong came into being, but that they are in their essence logically anterior to God. You could, of course, if you liked, say that there was a superior deity who gave orders to the God who made this world, or could take up the line that some of the gnostics took up—a line which I often thought was a very plausible one—that as a matter of fact this world that we know was made by the devil at a moment when God was not looking. There is a good deal to be said for that, and I am not concerned to refute it.

The Argument for the Remedying of Injustice

Then there is another very curious form of moral argument, which is this: they say that the existence of God is required in order to bring justice into the world. In the part of this universe that we know there is great injustice, and often the good suffer, and often the wicked prosper, and one hardly knows which of those is the more annoying; but if you are going to have justice in the universe as a whole you have to suppose a future life to redress the balance of life here on earth. So they say that there must be a God, and there must be heaven and hell in order that in the long run there may be justice. That is a very curious argument. If you looked at the matter from a scientific point of view, you would say, "After all, I know only this world. I do not know about the rest of the universe, but so far as one can argue at all on probabilities one would say that probably this world is a fair sample, and if there is injustice here the odds are that there is injustice elsewhere also." Supposing you got a crate of oranges that you opened, and you found all the top layer of oranges bad, you would not argue, "The underneath ones must be good, so as to redress the balance." You would say, "Probably the whole lot is a bad consignment"; and that is really what a scientific person would argue about the universe. He would say, "Here we find in this world a great deal of injustice, and so far as that goes that is a reason for supposing that justice does not rule in the world; and therefore so far as it goes it affords a moral argument against deity and not in favor of one." Of course I know that the sort of intellectual arguments that I have been talking to you about are not what really moves people. What really moves people to believe in God is not any intellectual argument at all. Most people believe in God because they have been taught from early infancy to do it, and that is the main reason.

Then I think that the next most powerful reason is the wish for safety, a sort of feeling that there is a big brother who will look after you. That plays a very profound part in influencing people's desire for a belief in God.

The Character of Christ

I now want to say a few words upon a topic which I often think is not quite sufficiently dealt with by Rationalists, and that is the question whether Christ was the best and the wisest of men. It is generally taken for granted that we should all agree that that was so. I do not myself. I think that there are a good many points upon which I agree with Christ a great deal more than the professing Christians do. I do not know that I could go with Him all the way, but I could go with Him much further than most professing Christians can. You will remember that He said, "Resist not evil: but whosoever shall smite thee on thy right cheek, turn to him the other also." That is not a new precept or a new principle. It was used by Lao-tse and Buddha some 500 or 600 years before Christ, but it is not a principle which as a matter of fact Christians accept. I have no doubt that the present Prime Minister,[1] for instance, is a most sincere Christian, but I should not advise any of you to go and smite him on one cheek. I think you might find that he thought this text was intended in a figurative sense.

Then there is another point which I consider excellent. You will remember that Christ said, "Judge not lest ye be judged." That principle

[1]Stanley Baldwin.

I do not think you would find was popular in the law courts of Christian countries. I have known in my time quite a number of judges who were very earnest Christians, and none of them felt that they were acting contrary to Christian principles in what they did. Then Christ says, "Give to him that asketh of thee, and from him that would borrow of thee turn not thou away." That is a very good principle. Your Chairman has reminded you that we are not here to talk politics, but I cannot help observing that the last general election was fought on the question of how desirable it was to turn away from him that would borrow of thee, so that one must assume that the Liberals and Conservatives of this country are composed of people who do not agree with the teaching of Christ, because they certainly did very emphatically turn away on that occasion.

Then there is one other maxim of Christ which I think has a great deal in it, but I do not find that it is very popular among some of our Christian friends. He says, "If thou wilt be perfect, go and sell that which thou hast, and give to the poor." That is a very excellent maxim, but as I say, it is not much practiced. All these, I think, are good maxims, although they are a little difficult to live up to. I do not profess to live up to them myself; but then, after all, it is not quite the same thing as for a Christian.

Defects in Christ's Teaching

Having granted the excellence of these maxims, I come to certain points in which I do not believe that one can grant either the superlative wisdom or the superlative goodness of Christ as depicted in the Gospels; and here I may say that one is not concerned with the historical question. Historically it is quite doubtful whether Christ ever existed at all, and if He did we do not know anything about Him, so that I am not concerned with the historical question, which is a very difficult one. I am concerned with Christ as He appears in the Gospels, taking the Gospel narrative as it stands, and there one does find some things that do not seem to be very wise. For one thing, He certainly thought that His second coming would occur in clouds of glory before the death of all the people who were living at that time. There are a great many texts that prove that. He says, for instance, "Ye shall not have gone over the cities of Israel till the Son of Man be come." Then He says, "There are some standing here which shall not taste death till the Son of Man comes into His kingdom"; and there are a lot of places where it is quite clear that He believed that His second coming would happen during the lifetime of many then living. That was the belief of His earlier followers, and it was the basis of a good deal of His moral teaching. When He said, "Take no thought for the morrow," and things of that sort, it was very largely because He thought that the second coming was going to be very soon, and that all ordinary mundane affairs did not count. I have, as a matter of fact, known some Christians who did believe that the second coming was imminent. I knew a person who frightened his congregation terribly by telling them that the second coming was very imminent indeed, but they were much consoled when they found that he was planting trees in his garden. The early Christians did really believe it, and they did abstain from such things as planting trees in their gardens, because they did accept from Christ the belief that the second coming was imminent. In that respect, clearly He was not so wise as some other people have been, and He was certainly not superlatively wise.

The Moral Problem

Then you come to moral questions. There is one very serious defect to my mind in Christ's moral character, and that is that He believed in hell. I do not myself feel that any person who is really profoundly humane can believe in everlasting punishment. Christ certainly as depicted in the Gospels did believe in everlasting punishment, and one does find repeatedly a vindictive fury against those people who would not listen to His preaching—an attitude which is not uncommon with preachers, but which does somewhat detract from superlative excellence. You do not, for instance, find that attitude in Socrates. You find him quite bland and urbane toward the people who would not listen to him; and it is, to my mind, far more worthy of a sage to take that line than to take the line of indignation. You probably all remember the sort of things that Socrates was saying when he was dying, and the sort of things that he generally did say to people who did not agree with him.

You will find that in the Gospels Christ said, "Ye serpents, ye generation of vipers, how can ye escape the damnation of hell." That was said to people who did not like His preaching. It is not really to my mind quite the best tone, and there are a great many of these things about hell. There is, of course, the familiar text about the sin against the Holy Ghost: "Whosoever speaketh against the Holy Ghost it shall not be forgiven him neither in this World nor in the world to come." That text has caused an unspeakable amount of misery in the world, for all sorts of people have imagined that they have committed the sin against the Holy Ghost, and thought that it would not be forgiven them either in this world or in the world to come. I really do not think that a person with a proper degree of kindliness in his nature would have put fears and terrors of that sort into the world.

Then Christ says, "The Son of Man shall send forth His angels, and they shall gather out of His kingdom all things that offend, and them which do iniquity, and shall cast them into a furnace of fire; there shall be wailing and gnashing of teeth"; and He goes on about the wailing and gnashing of teeth. It comes in one verse after another, and it is quite manifest to the reader that there is a certain pleasure in contemplating wailing and gnashing of teeth, or else it would not occur so often. Then you all, of course, remember about the sheep and the goats; how at the second coming He is going to divide the sheep from the goats, and He is going to say to the goats, "Depart from me, ye cursed, into everlasting fire." He continues, "And these shall go away into everlasting fire." Then He says again, "If thy hand offend thee, cut it off; it is better for thee to enter into life maimed, than having two hands to go into hell, into the fire that never shall be quenched; where the worm dieth not and the fire is not quenched." He repeats that again and again also. I must say that I think all this doctrine, that hell-fire is a punishment for sin, is a doctrine of cruelty. It is a doctrine that put cruelty into the world and gave the world generations of cruel torture; and the Christ of the Gospels, if you could take Him as His chroniclers represent Him, would certainly have to be considered partly responsible for that.

There are other things of less importance. There is the instance of the Gadarene swine, where it certainly was not very kind to the pigs to put the devils into them and make them rush down the hill to the sea. You must remember that He was omnipotent, and He could have made the devils simply go away; but He chose to send them into the pigs. Then there is the curious story of the fig tree, which always rather puzzled me. You remember what happened about the fig tree. "He was hungry; and seeing a fig tree afar off having leaves, He came if haply He might find anything thereon; and when He came to it He found nothing but leaves, for the time of figs was not yet. And Jesus answered and said unto it: 'No man eat fruit of thee hereafter for ever' . . . and Peter . . . saith unto Him: 'Master, behold the fig tree which thou cursedst is withered away.'" This is a very curious story, because it was not the right time of year for figs, and you really could not blame the tree. I cannot myself feel that either in the matter of wisdom or in the matter of virtue Christ stands quite as high as some other people known to history. I think I should put Buddha and Socrates above Him in those respects.

The Emotional Factor

As I said before, I do not think that the real reason why people accept religion has anything to do with argumentation. They accept religion on emotional grounds. One is often told that it is a very wrong thing to attack religion, because religion makes men virtuous. So I am told; I have not noticed it. You know, of course, the parody of that argument in Samuel Butler's book, *Erewhon Revisited*. You will remember that in *Erewhon* there is a certain Higgs who arrives in a remote country, and after spending some time there he escapes from that country in a balloon. Twenty years later he comes back to that country and finds a new religion in which he is worshiped under the name of the "Sun Child," and it is said that he ascended into heaven. He finds that the Feast of the Ascension is about to be celebrated, and he hears Professors Hanky and Panky say to each other that they never set eyes on the man Higgs, and they hope they never will; but they are the high priests of the religion of the Sun Child. He is very indignant, and he comes up to them, and he says, "I am going to expose all this humbug and tell the people of Erewhon that it was only I, the man Higgs, and I went up in a balloon." He was told, "You must not do that, because all the morals of this country are bound round this myth, and if they once know that you did not ascend into heaven they will all become wicked"; and so he is persuaded of that and he goes quietly away.

That is the idea—that we should all be wicked if we did not hold to the Christian religion. It seems to me that the people who have held to it have been for the most part extremely wicked. You find this curious fact, that the more intense has been the religion of any period and the more profound has been the dogmatic belief, the greater has been the cruelty and the worse has been the state of affairs. In the so-called ages of faith, when men really did believe the Christian religion in all its completeness, there was the Inquisition, with its tortures; there were millions of unfortunate women burned as witches; and there was every kind of cruelty practiced upon all sorts of people in the name of religion.

You find as you look around the world that every single bit of progress in humane feeling, every improvement in the criminal law, every step toward the diminution of war, every step toward better treatment of the colored races, or every mitigation of slavery, every moral progress that there has been in the world, has been consistently opposed by the organized churches of the world. I say quite deliberately that the Christian religion, as organized in its churches, has been and still is the principal enemy of moral progress in the world.

How the Churches Have Retarded Progress

You may think that I am going too far when I say that that is still so. I do not think that I am. Take one fact. You will bear with me if I mention it. It is not a pleasant fact, but the churches compel one to mention facts that are not pleasant. Supposing that in this world that we live in today an inexperienced girl is married to a syphilitic man; in that case the Catholic Church says, "This is an indissoluble sacrament. You must endure celibacy or stay together. And if you stay together, you must not use birth control to prevent the birth of syphilitic children." Nobody whose natural sympathies have not been warped by dogma, or whose moral nature was not absolutely dead to all sense of suffering, could maintain that it is right and proper that that state of things should continue.

That is only an example. There are a great many ways in which, at the present moment, the church, by its insistence upon what it chooses to call morality, inflicts upon all sorts of people undeserved and unnecessary suffering. And of course, as we know, it is in its major part an opponent still of progress and of improvement in all the ways that diminish suffering in the world, because it has chosen to label as morality a certain narrow set of rules of conduct which have nothing to do with human happiness; and when you say that this or that ought to be done because it would make for human happiness, they think that has nothing to do with the matter at all. "What has human happiness to do with morals? The object of morals is not to make people happy."

Fear, the Foundation of Religion

Religion is based, I think, primarily and mainly upon fear. It is partly the terror of the unknown and partly, as I have said, the wish to feel that you have a kind of elder brother who will stand by you in all our troubles and disputes. Fear is the basis of the whole thing—fear of the mysterious, fear of defeat, fear of death. Fear is the parent of cruelty, and therefore it is no wonder if cruelty and religion have gone hand in hand. It is because fear is at the basis of those two things. In this world we can now begin a little to understand things, and a little to master them by help of science, which has forced its way step by step against the Christian religion, against the churches, and against the opposition of all the old precepts. Science can help us to get over this craven fear in which mankind has lived for so many generations. Science can teach us, and I think our own hearts can teach us, no longer to look around for imaginary supports, no longer to invent allies in the sky, but rather to look to our own efforts here below to make this world a fit place to live in, instead of the sort of place that the churches in all these centuries have made it.

What We Must Do

We want to stand upon our own feet and look fair and square at the world—its good facts, its bad facts, its beauties, and its ugliness; see the world as it is and be not afraid of it. Conquer the world by intelligence and not merely by being slavishly subdued by the terror that comes from it. The whole conception of God is a conception derived from the ancient Oriental despotisms. It is a conception quite unworthy of free men. When you hear people in church debasing themselves and saying that they are miserable sinners, and all the rest of it, it seems contemptible and not worthy of self-respecting human beings. We ought to stand up and look the world frankly in the face. We ought to make the best we can of the world, and if it is not so good as we wish, after all it will still be better than what these others have made of it in all these ages. A good world needs knowledge, kindliness, and courage; it does not need a regretful hankering after the past or a fettering of the free intelligence by the words uttered long ago by ignorant men. It needs a fearless outlook and a free intelligence. It needs hope for the future, not looking back all the time toward a past that is dead, which we trust will be far surpassed by the future that our intelligence can create.

The Problem of Evil

14. God Is the Cause of Unnecessary Evil
Baron d'Holbach

Baron Paul Henri d'Holbach (1723–1789) was a prominent French philosopher during the Enlightenment, who is best remembered as a defender of materialism and opponent of religion. The selections by him in this text were published in a book whose announced author was Jean Meslier, a pseudonym Holbach adopted to avoid persecution for his atheistic views.

THIS PRETENDED PROVIDENCE IS LESS OCCUPIED IN
CONSERVING THAN IN DISTURBING THE WORLD—
MORE AN ENEMY THAN A FRIEND OF MAN.

Do we see, then, that Divine Providence manifests itself in a sensible manner in the conservation of its admirable works, for which we honor it? If it is Divine Providence which governs the world, we find it as much occupied in destroying as in creating; in exterminating as in producing. Does it not at every instant cause thousands of those same men to perish, to whose preservation and well-being it is supposed to give its continual attention? Every moment it loses sight of its beloved creatures; sometimes it tears down their dwellings; sometimes it destroys their harvests, inundates their fields, devastates by a drouth, arms all nature against man, sets man against man, and finishes by causing him to expire in pain. Is this what you call preserving a universe? If we attempted to consider without prejudice the equivocal conduct of Providence relative to mankind and to all sentient beings, we should find that very far from resembling a tender and careful mother, it rather resembles those unnatural mothers who, forgetting the unfortunate fruits of their illicit amours, abandon their children as soon as they are born; and who, pleased to have conceived them, expose them without mercy to the caprices of fate.

The Hottentots—wiser in this particular than other nations, who treat them as barbarians—refuse, it is said, to adore God, because if He sometimes does good, He as often does harm. Is not this reasoning more just and more conformed to experience than that of so many men who persist in seeing in their God but kindness, wisdom, and foresight; and who refuse to see that the countless evils, of which the world is the theater, must come from the same Hand which they kiss with transport?

NO! THE WORLD IS NOT GOVERNED BY AN
INTELLIGENT BEING.

The logic of common sense teaches us that we should judge a cause

From *Superstition In All Ages* by Jean Meslier. Published by Peter Eckler in 1890.

but by its effects. A cause can not be reputed as constantly good, except when it constantly produces good, useful, and agreeable effects. A cause which produces good at one time, and evil at another, is a cause which is sometimes good and sometimes bad. But the logic of Theology destroys all this. According to it, the phenomena of nature, or the effects which we see in this world, prove to us the existence of an infinitely good Cause, and this Cause is God. Although this world is full of evils, although disorder reigns here very often, although men groan every moment under the fate which oppresses them, we ought to be convinced that these effects are due to a benevolent and immutable Cause; and many people believe it, or pretend to believe it!

Everything which takes place in the world proves to us in the clearest way that it is not governed by an intelligent being. We can judge of the intelligence of a being but by the means which he employs to accomplish his proposed design. The aim of God, it is said, is the happiness of our race; however, the same necessity regulates the fate of all sentient beings—which are born to suffer much, to enjoy little, and to die. Man's cup is full of joy and of bitterness; everywhere good is side by side with evil; order is replaced by disorder; generation is followed by destruction. If you tell me that the designs of God are mysteries, and that His views are impossible to understand, I will answer, that in this case it is impossible for me to judge whether God is intelligent. . . .

EVIL AND GOOD ARE THE NECESSARY EFFECTS OF
NATURAL CAUSES. WHAT IS A GOD WHO CAN CHANGE
NOTHING?

The universe is but what it can be; all sentient beings enjoy and suffer here: that is to say, they are moved sometimes in an agreeable way, and at other times in a disagreeable way. These effects are necessary; they result from causes that act according to their inherent tendencies. These effects necessarily please or displease me, according to my own nature. This same nature compels me to avoid, to remove, and to combat the one, and to seek, to desire, and to procure the other. In a world where everything is from necessity, a God who remedies nothing, and allows things to follow their own course, is He anything else but destiny or necessity personified? It is a deaf God who can effect no change on the general laws to which He is subjected Himself. What do I care for the infinite power of a being who can do but a very few things to please me? Where is the infinite kindness of a being who is indifferent to my happiness? What good to me is the favor of a being who, able to bestow upon me infinite good, does not even give me a finite one?

THE VANITY OF THEOLOGICAL CONSOLATIONS IN
THE TROUBLES OF THIS LIFE. THE HOPE OF A
HEAVEN, OF A FUTURE LIFE, IS BUT IMAGINARY.

When we ask why, under a good God, so many are wretched, we are reminded that the present world is but a pass-way, designed to conduct man to a happier sphere; we are assured that our sojourn on the earth, where we live, is for trial; they silence us by saying that God would not impart to His creatures either the indifference to the sufferings of others, or the infinite happiness which He reserved for Himself alone. How can we be satisfied with these answers? . . .

If God is as well-disposed as they assure us He is, could He not at least, without bestowing an infinite happiness upon men, communicate to them that degree of happiness of which finite beings are susceptible? In order to be happy, do we need an Infinite or Divine happiness?

If God has not been able to render men happier than they are here below, what will become of the hope of a Paradise, where it is pretended that the elect or chosen few will rejoice forever in ineffable happiness? If God could not or would not remove evil from the earth (the only sojourning place we know of), what reason could we have to presume that He can or will remove it from another world, of which we know nothing? More than two thousand years ago, according to Lactance, the wise epicure said: "Either God wants to prevent evil, and can not, or He can and will not; or He neither can nor will, or He will and can. If He wants to, without the power, His is impotent; if He can, and will not, He is guilty of malice which we can not attribute to Him; if He neither can nor will, He is both impotent and wicked, and consequently can not be God; if He wishes to and can, whence then comes evil, or why does He not prevent it?" For more than two thousand years honest minds have waited for a rational solution of these difficulties; and our theologians teach us that they will not be revealed to us until the future life. . . .

IN VAIN DOES THEOLOGY EXERT ITSELF TO ACQUIT
GOD OF MAN'S DEFECTS. EITHER THIS GOD IS NOT
FREE, OR HE IS MORE WICKED THAN GOOD.

The world, it will be said, has all the perfection of which it was susceptible; by the very reason that the world was not the God who made it, it was necessary that it should have great qualities and great defects. But we will answer, that the world necessarily having great defects, it would have been better suited to the nature of a good God not to create a world which He could not render completely happy. If God, who was, according to you, supremely happy before the world was created, had continued to be supremely happy in the created world, why did He not remain in peace? Why must man suffer? Why must man exist? What is his existence to God? Nothing or something. If his existence is not useful or necessary to God, why did He not leave him in nothingness? If man's existence is necessary to His glory, He then needed man, He lacked something before this man existed! . . .

IT IS ABSURD TO SAY THAT EVIL DOES NOT COME
FROM GOD.

God is the author of all; still we are assured that evil does not come from God. Whence, then, does it come? From men? But who has made men? It is God: then that evil comes from God. If He had not made men as they are, moral evil or sin would not exist in the world. We must blame God, then, that man is so perverse. If man has the power to do wrong or to offend God, we must conclude that God wishes to be offended; that God, who has created man, resolved that evil should be done by him:

without this, man would be an effect contrary to the cause from which he derives his being.

THE FORESIGHT ATTRIBUTED TO GOD, WOULD GIVE TO GUILTY MEN WHOM HE PUNISHES, THE RIGHT TO COMPLAIN OF HIS CRUELTY.

The faculty of foresight, or the ability to know in advance all which is to happen in the world, is attributed to God. But this foresight can scarcely belong to His glory, nor spare Him the reproaches which men could legitimately heap upon Him. If God had the foresight of the future, did He not foresee the fall of His creatures whom He had destined to happiness? If He resolved in His decrees to allow this fall, there is no doubt that He desired it to take place: otherwise it would not have happened. If the Divine foresight of the sin of His creatures had been necessary or forced, it might be supposed that God was compelled by His justice to punish the guilty; but God, enjoying the faculty of foresight and the power to predestinate everything, would it not depend upon Himself not to impose upon men these cruel laws? Or, at least, could He not have dispensed with creating beings whom He might be compelled to punish and to render unhappy by a subsequent decree? What does it matter whether God destined men to happiness or to misery by a previous decree, the effect of His foresight, or by a subsequent decree, the effect of His justice. Does the arrangement of these decrees change the fate of the miserable? Would they not have the right to complain of a God who, having the power of leaving them in oblivion, brought them forth, although He foresaw very well that His justice would force Him sooner or later to punish them?

ABSURDITY OF THE THEOLOGICAL FABLES UPON ORIGINAL SIN AND UPON SATAN.

Man, say you, issuing from the hands of God, was pure, innocent, and good; but his nature became corrupted in consequence of sin. If man could sin, when just leaving the hands of God, his nature was then not perfect! Why did God permit him to sin, and his nature to become corrupt? Why did God allow him to be seduced, knowing well that he would be too weak to resist the tempter? Why did God create a Satan, a malicious spirit, a tempter? Why did not God, who was so desirous of doing good to mankind, why did He not annihilate, once for all, so many evil genii whose nature rendered them enemies of our happiness? Or rather, why did God create evil spirits, whose victories and terrible influences upon the human race He must have foreseen? Finally, by what fatality, in all the religions of the world, has the evil principle such a marked advantage over the good principle or over Divinity? . . .

IF GOD COULD NOT RENDER HUMAN NATURE SINLESS, HE HAS NO RIGHT TO PUNISH MAN.

Man's nature, it is said, must necessarily become corrupt. God could not endow him with sinlessness, which is an inalienable portion of Divine perfection. But if God could not render him sinless, why did He take the trouble of creating man, whose nature was to become corrupt, and which, consequently, had to offend God? On the other side, if God Himself was not able to render human nature sinless, what right had He to punish men for not being sinless? It is but by the right of might. But the right of the strongest is violence; and violence is not suited to the most Just of Beings. God would be supremely unjust if He punished men for not having a portion of the Divine perfections, or for not being able to be Gods like Himself.

Could not God have at least endowed men with that sort of perfection of which their nature is susceptible? If some men are good or render themselves agreeable to their God, why did not this God bestow the same favor or give the same dispositions to all beings of our kind? Why does the number of wicked exceed so greatly the number of good people? Why, for every friend, does God find ten thousand enemies in a world which depended upon Him alone to people with honest men? If it is true that God intends to form in heaven a court of saints, of chosen ones, or of men who have lived in this world according to His views, would He not have had a court more numerous, more brilliant, and more honorable to Him, if it were composed of all the men to whom, in creating them, He could have granted the degree of goodness necessary to obtain eternal happiness? Finally, were it not easier not to take man from nothingness than to create him full of defects, rebellious to his Creator, perpetually exposed to lose himself by a fatal abuse of his liberty? Instead of creating men, a perfect God ought to have created only docile and submissive angels. The angels, it is said, are free; a few among them have sinned; but all of them have not sinned; all have not abused their liberty by revolting against their Master. Could not God have created only angels of the good kind? If God could create angels who have not sinned, could He not create men sinless, or those who would never abuse their liberty by doing evil. If the chosen ones are incapable of sinning in heaven, could not God have made sinless men upon the earth?

IT IS ABSURD TO SAY THAT GOD'S CONDUCT MUST BE A MYSTERY TO MAN, AND THAT HE HAS NO RIGHT TO EXAMINE AND JUDGE IT.

We are told that the enormous distance which separates God from men, makes God's conduct necessarily a mystery for us, and that we have no right to interrogate our Master. Is this statement satisfactory? But according to you, when my eternal happiness is involved, have I not the right to examine God's own conduct? It is but with the hope of happiness that men submit to the empire of a God. A despot to whom men are subjected but through fear, a master whom they can not interrogate, a totally inaccessible sovereign, can not merit the homage of intelligent beings. If God's conduct is a mystery to me, it is not made for me. Man can not adore, admire, respect, or imitate a conduct of which everything is impossible to conceive, or of which he can not form any but revolting ideas; unless it is pretended that he should worship all the things of which he is forced to be ignorant, and then all that he does not understand becomes admirable. . . .

IT IS ABSURD TO CALL HIM A GOD OF JUSTICE AND GOODNESS, WHO INFLICTS EVIL INDISCRIMINATELY

ON THE GOOD AND THE WICKED, UPON THE
INNOCENT AND THE GUILTY: IT IS IDLE TO DEMAND
THAT THE UNFORTUNATE SHOULD CONSOLE
THEMSELVES FOR THEIR MISFORTUNES, IN THE VERY
ARMS OF THE ONE WHO ALONE IS THE AUTHOR OF
THEM.

Physical evil commonly passes as the punishment of sin. Calamities, diseases, famines, wars, earthquakes, are the means which God employs to chastise perverse men. Therefore, they have no difficulty in attributing these evils to the severity of a just and good God. However, do we not see these plagues fall indiscriminately upon the good and the wicked, upon the impious and the pious, upon the innocent and the guilty? How can we be made to admire, in this proceeding, the justice and the goodness of a being, the idea of whom appears so consoling to the unfortunate? Doubtless the brain of these unfortunate ones has been disturbed by their misfortunes, since they forget that God is the arbiter of things, the sole dispenser of the events of this world. In this case ought they not to blame Him for the evils for which they would find consolation in His arms? Unfortunate father! you console yourself in the bosom of Providence for the loss of a cherished child or of a wife, who made your happiness! Alas! do you not see that your God has killed them? Your God has rendered you miserable; and you want Him to console you for the fearful blows He has inflicted upon you.

The fantastic and supernatural notions of theology have succeeded so thoroughly in overcoming the simplest, the clearest, the most natural ideas of the human spirit, that the pious, incapable of accusing God of malice, accustom themselves to look upon these sad afflictions as indubitable proofs of celestial goodness. Are they in affliction, they are told to believe that God loves them, that God visits them, that God wishes to try them. Thus it is that religion changes evil into good! Some one has said profanely, but with reason: "If the good God treats thus those whom He loves, I beseech Him very earnestly not to think of me." Men must have formed very sinister and very cruel ideas of their God whom they call so good, in order to persuade themselves that the most frightful calamities and the most painful afflictions are signs of His favor! Would a wicked Genii or a Devil be more ingenious in tormenting his enemies, than sometimes is this God of goodness, who is so often occupied with inflicting His chastisements upon His dearest friends?

A GOD WHO PUNISHES THE FAULTS WHICH HE COULD
HAVE PREVENTED, IS A FOOL, WHO ADDS INJUSTICE
TO FOOLISHNESS.

What would we say of a father who, we are assured, watches without relaxation over the welfare of his feeble and unforeseeing children, and who however, would leave them at liberty to go astray in the midst of rocks, precipices, and waters; who would prevent them but rarely from following their disordered appetites; who would permit them to handle, without precaution, deadly arms, at the risk of wounding themselves severely? What would we think of this same father, if, instead of blaming himself for the harm which would have happened to his poor children, he should punish them for their faults in the most cruel way? We would say, with reason, that this father is a fool, who joins injustice to foolishness. A God who punishes the faults which He could have prevented, is a being who lacks wisdom, goodness, and equity. A God of foresight would prevent evil, and in this way would be saved the trouble of punishing it. A good God would not punish weaknesses which He knows to be inherent in human nature. A just God, if He has made man, would not punish him for not being strong enough to resist his desires. To punish weakness, is the most unjust tyranny. Is it not calumniating a just God, to say that He punishes men for their faults, even in the present life? How would He punish beings whom He alone could correct, and who, as long as they had not received grace, can not act otherwise than they do? . . .

THE REPARATION OF THE INIQUITIES AND THE
MISERIES OF THIS WORLD IN ANOTHER WORLD, IS AN
IDLE CONJECTURE AND AN ABSURD SUPPOSITION.

When we complain of the evils of which this world is the theater, we are referred to another world; we are told that there God will repair all the iniquities and the miseries which He permits for a time here below. However, if leaving His eternal justice to sleep for a time, God could consent to evil during the period of the existence of our globe, what assurance have we that during the existence of another globe, Divine justice will not likewise sleep during the misfortunes of its inhabitants? They console us in our troubles by saying, that God is patient, and that His justice, although often very slow, is not the less certain. But do you not see, that patience can not be suited to a being just, immutable, and omnipotent? Can God tolerate injustice for an instant? To temporize with an evil that one knows of, evinces either uncertainty, weakness, or collusion; to tolerate evil which one has the power to prevent, is to consent that evil should be committed.

15. The Problem of Evil   John Hick

John Hick (1922–   ) is lecturer in Divinity at Cambridge University in England. He is the author of several books on the philosophy of religion.

To many, the most powerful positive objection to belief in God is the fact of evil. Probably for most agnostics it is the appalling depth and extent of human suffering, more than anything else, that makes the idea of a loving Creator seem to implausible and disposes them toward one or another of the various naturalistic theories of religion.

As a challenge to theism, the problem of evil has traditionally been posed in the form of a dilemma: if God is perfectly loving, he must wish to abolish evil; and if he is all-powerful, he must be able to abolish evil.

John Hick, *Philosophy of Religion,* © 1963, pp. 40–46. Reprinted by permission of Prentice-Hall, Inc., Englewood Cliffs, New Jersey.

But evil exists exists; therefore God cannot be both omnipotent and perfectly loving.

Certain solutions, which at once suggest themselves, have to be ruled out so far as the Judaic-Christian faith is concerned.

To say, for example (with contemporary Christian Science), that evil is an illusion of the human mind, is impossible within a religion based upon the stark realism of the Bible. Its pages faithfully reflect the characteristic mixture of good and evil in human experience. They record every kind of sorrow and suffering, every mode of man's inhumanity to man and of his painfully insecure existence in the world. There is no attempt to regard evil as anything but dark, menacingly ugly, heart-rending, and crushing. In the Christian scriptures, the climax of this history of evil is the crucifixion of Jesus, which is presented not only as a case of utterly unjust suffering, but as the violent and murderous rejection of God's Messiah. There can be no doubt, then, that for biblical faith, evil is unambiguously evil, and stands in direct opposition to God's will.

Again, to solve the problem of evil by means of the theory (sponsored for example, by the Boston "Personalist" School) of a finite deity who does the best he can with a material, intractable and coeternal with himself, is to have abandoned the basic premise of Hebrew-Christian monotheism; for the theory amounts to rejecting belief in the infinity and sovereignty of God.

Indeed, any theory which would avoid the problem of the origin of evil by depicting it as an ultimate constituent of the universe, coordinate with good, has been repudiated in advance by the classic Christian teaching, first developed by Augustine, that evil represents the going wrong of something which in itself is good. Augustine holds firmly to the Hebrew-Christian conviction that the universe is *good*—that is to say, it is the creation of a good God for a good purpose. He completely rejects the ancient prejudice, widespread in his day, that matter is evil. There are, according to Augustine, higher and lower, greater and lesser goods in immense abundance and variety; but everything which has being is good in its own way and degree, except in so far as it may have become spoiled or corrupted. Evil—whether it be an evil will, an instance of pain, or some disorder or decay in nature—has not been set there by God, but represents the distortion of something that is inherently valuable. Whatever exists is, as such, and in its proper place, good; evil is essentially parasitic upon good, being disorder and perversion in a fundamentally good creation. This understanding of evil as something negative means that it is not willed and created by God; but it does not mean (as some have supposed) that evil is unreal and can be disregarded. On the contrary, the first effect of this doctrine is to accentuate even more the question of the origin of evil.

Theodicy,[1] as many modern Christian thinkers see it, is a modest enterprise, negative rather than positive in its conclusions. It does not claim to explain, nor to explain away, every instance of evil in human experience, but only to point to certain considerations which prevent the

---

[1]The word "theodicy," from the Greek *theos* (God) and *dike* (righteous), means the justification of God's goodness in the face of the fact of evil.

fact of evil (largely incomprehensible though it remains) from constituting a final and insuperable bar to rational belief in God.

In indicating these considerations it will be useful to follow the traditional division of the subject. There is the problem of *moral evil* or wickedness: why does an all-good and all-powerful God permit this? And there is the problem of the *non-moral evil* of suffering or pain, both physical and mental: why has an all-good and all-powerful God created a world in which this occurs?

Christian thought has always considered moral evil in its relation to human freedom and responsibility. To be a person is to be a finite center of freedom, a (relatively) free and self-directing agent responsible for one's own decisions. This involves being free to act wrongly as well as to act rightly. The idea of a person who can be infallibly guaranteed always to act rightly is self-contradictory. There can be no guarantee in advance that a genuinely free moral agent will never choose amiss. Consequently, the possibility of wrongdoing or sin is logically inseparable from the creation of finite persons, and to say that God should not have created beings who might sin amounts to saying that he should not have created people.

This thesis has been challenged in some recent philosophical discussions of the problem of evil, in which it is claimed that no contradiction is involved in saying that God might have made people who would be genuinely free and who could yet be guaranteed always to act rightly. A quote from one of these discussions follows:

> If there is no logical impossibility in a man's freely choosing the good on one, or on several occasions, there cannot be a logical impossibility in his freely choosing the good on every occasion. God was not, then, faced with a choice between making innocent automata and making beings who, in acting freely, would sometimes go wrong: there was open to him the obviously better possibility of making beings who would act freely but always go right. Clearly, his failure to avail himself of this possibility is inconsistent with his being both omnipotent and wholly good.[2]

A reply to this argument is suggested in another recent contribution to the discussion.[3] If by a free action we mean an action which is not externally compelled but which flows from the nature of the agent as he reacts to the circumstances in which he finds himself, there is, indeed, no contradiction between our being free and our actions being "caused" (by our own nature) and therefore being in principle predictable. There is a contradiction, however, in saying that God is the cause of our acting as we do but that we are free beings in relation to God. There is, in other words, a contradiction in saying that God has made us so that we shall of necessity act in a certain way, and that we are genuinely independent persons in relation to him. If all our thoughts and actions are divinely predestined, however free and morally responsible we may seem to be to ourselves, we cannot be free and morally responsible in the sight of God, but must instead be his helpless puppets. Such "freedom" is like that of a patient acting out a series of post-hypnotic suggestions: he appears, even to him-

---

[2] J. L. Mackie, "Evil and Omnipotence," *Mind* (April 1955), 209.
[3] Flew, in *New Essays in Philosophical Theology*.

self, to be free, but his volitions have actually been pre-determined by another will, that of the hypnotist, in relation to whom the patient is not a free agent.

A different objector might raise the question of whether or not we deny God's omnipotence if we admit that he is unable to create persons who are free from the risks inherent in personal freedom. The answer that has always been given is that to create such beings is logically impossible. It is no limitation upon God's power that he cannot accomplish the logically impossible, since there is nothing here to accomplish, but only a meaningless conjunction of words—in this case "person who is not a person." God is able to create beings of any and every conceivable kind; but creatures who lack moral freedom, however superior they might be to human beings in other respects, would not be what we mean by persons. They would constitute a different form of life which God might have brought into existence instead of persons. When we ask why God did not create such beings in place of persons, the traditional answer is that only persons could, in any meaningful sense, become "children of God," capable of entering into a personal relationship with their Creator by a free and uncompelled response to his love.

When we turn from the possibility of moral evil as a correlate of man's personal freedom to its actuality, we face something which must remain inexplicable even when it can be seen to be possible. For we can never provide a complete causal explanation of a free act; if we could, it would not be a free act. The origin of moral evil lies forever concealed within the mystery of human freedom.

The necessary connection between moral freedom and the possibility, now actualized, of sin throws light upon a great deal of the suffering which afflicts mankind. For an enormous amount of human pain arises either from the inhumanity or the culpable incompetence of mankind. This includes such major scourges as poverty, oppression and persecution, war, and all the injustice, indignity, and inequity which occur even in the most advanced societies. These evils are manifestations of human sin. Even disease is fostered to an extent, the limits of which have not yet been determined by psychosomatic medicine, by moral and emotional factors seated both in the individual and in his social environment. To the extent that all of these evils stem from human failures and wrong decisions, their possibility is inherent in the creation of free persons inhabiting a world which presents them with real choices which are followed by real consequences.

We may now turn more directly to the problem of suffering. Even though the major bulk of actual human pain is traceable to man's misused freedom as a sole or part cause, there remain other sources of pain which are entirely independent of the human will, for example, earthquake, hurricane, storm, flood, drought, and blight. In practice it is often impossible to trace a boundary between the suffering which results from human wickedness and folly and that which falls upon mankind from without. Both kinds of suffering are inextricably mingled together in human experience. For our present purpose, however, it is important to note that the latter category does exist and that it seems to be built into the very structure of our world. In response to it, theodicy, if it is wisely conducted, follows a negative path. It is not possible to show positively that each item of human pain serves the divine purpose of good; but, on the other hand, it does seem possible to show that the divine purpose as it is understood in Judaism and Christianity could not be forwarded in a world which was designed as a permanent hedonistic paradise.

An essential premise of this argument concerns the divine purpose in creating the world. The skeptic's assumption is that man is to be viewed as a completed creation and that God's purpose in making the world was to provide a suitable dwelling-place for this fully-formed creature. Since God is good and loving, the environment which he has created for human life to inhabit is naturally as pleasant and comfortable as possible. The problem is essentially similar to that of a man who builds a cage for some pet animal. Since our world, in fact, contains sources of hardship, inconvenience, and danger of innumerable kinds, the conclusion follows that this world cannot have been created by a perfectly benevolent and all-powerful deity.

Christianity, however, has never supposed that God's purpose in the creation of the world was to construct a paradise whose inhabitants would experience a maximum of pleasure and a minimum of pain. The world is seen, instead, as a place of "soul-making" in which free beings, grappling with the tasks and challenges of their existence in a common environment, may become "children of God" and "heirs of eternal life." A way of thinking theologically of God's continuing creative purpose for man was suggested by some of the early Hellenistic Fathers of the Christian Church, especially Irenaeus. Following hints from St. Paul, Irenaeus taught that man has been made as a person in the image of God but has not yet been brought as a free and responsible agent into the finite likeness of God, which is revealed in Christ. Our world, with all its rough edges, is the sphere in which this second and harder stage of the creative process is taking place.

This conception of the world (whether or not set in Irenaeus' theological framework) can be supported by the method of negative theodicy. Suppose, contrary to fact, that this world were a paradise from which all possibility of pain and suffering were excluded. The consequences would be very far-reaching. For example, no one could ever injure anyone else: the murderer's knife would turn to paper or his bullets to thin air; the bank safe, robbed of a million dollars, would miraculously become filled with another million dollars (without this device, on however large a scale, proving inflationary); fraud, deceit, conspiracy, and treason would somehow always leave the fabric of society undamaged. Again, no one would ever be injured by accident: the mountain-climber, steeplejack, or playing child falling from a height would float unharmed to the ground; the reckless driver would never meet with disaster. There would be no need to work, since no harm could result from avoiding work; there would be no call to be concerned for others in time of need or danger, for in such a world there could be no real needs or dangers.

To make possible this continual series of individual adjustments, nature would have to work by "special providences" instead of running according to general laws which men must learn to respect on penalty of pain or death. The laws of nature would have to be extremely flexible: sometimes gravity would operate, sometimes not; sometimes an object would be hard and solid, sometimes soft. There could be no sciences, for there would be no enduring world structure to investigate. In eliminating the problems and hardships of an objective environment, with its own laws, life would become like a dream in which, delightfully but aimlessly, we would float and drift at ease.

One can at least begin to imagine such a world. It is evident that our present ethical concepts would have no meaning in it. If, for example, the notion of harming someone is an essential element in the concept of a wrong action, in our hedonistic paradise there could be no wrong actions—nor any right actions in distinction from wrong. Courage and fortitude would have no point in an environment in which there is, by definition, no danger of difficulty. Generosity, kindness, the *agape* aspect of love, prudence, unselfishness, and all other ethical notions which presuppose life in a stable environment, could not even be formed. Consequently, such a world, however well it might promote pleasure, would be very ill adapted for the development of the moral qualities of human personality. In relation to this purpose it would be the worst of all possible worlds.

It would seem, then, that an environment intended to make possible the growth in free beings of the finest characteristics of personal life, must have a good deal in common with our present world. It must operate according to general and dependable laws; and it must involve real dangers, difficulties, problems, obstacles, and possibilities of pain, failure, sorrow, frustration, and defeat. If it did not contain the particular trials and perils which—subtracting man's own very considerable contribution—our world contains, it would have to contain others instead.

To realize this is not, by any means, to be in possession of a detailed theodicy. It is to understand that this world, with all its "heartaches and the thousand natural shocks that flesh is heir to," an environment so manifestly not designed for the maximization of human pleasure and the minimization of human pain, may be rather well adapted to the quite different purpose of "soul-making."

Contemporary Issues

Should We Believe in God Without Evidence?

16. The Ethics of Belief   W. K. Clifford

William Kingdon Clifford (1845–1879) was a prominent English mathematician and philosopher who made important contributions to the theory of knowledge and the philosophy of science.

A shipowner was about to send to sea an emigrant ship. He knew that she was old, and not over-well built at the first; that she had seen many seas and climes, and often had needed repairs. Doubts had been suggested to him that possibly she was not seaworthy. These doubts preyed upon his mind and made him unhappy; he thought that perhaps he ought to have her thoroughly overhauled and refitted, even though this should put him to great expense. Before the ship sailed, however, he succeeded in overcoming these melancholy reflections. He said to himself that she had gone safely through so many voyages and weathered so many storms that it was idle to suppose she would not come safely home from this trip also. He would put his trust in Providence, which could hardly fail to protect all these unhappy families that were leaving their fatherland to seek for better times elsewhere. He would dismiss from his mind all ungenerous suspicions about the honesty of builders and contractors. In such ways he acquired a sincere and comfortable conviction that his vessel was thoroughly safe and seaworthy; he watched her departure with a light heart, and benevolent wishes for the success of the exiles in their strange new home that was to be; and he got his insurance money when she went down in midocean and told no tales.

What shall we say of him? Surely this, that he was verily guilty of the death of those men. It is admitted that he did sincerely believe in the soundness of his ship; but the sincerity of his conviction can in no wise help him, because *he had no right to believe on such evidence as was before him.* He had acquired his belief not by honestly earning it in patient investigation, but by stifling his doubts. And although in the end he may have felt so sure about it that he could not think otherwise, yet inasmuch as he had knowingly and willingly worked himself into that frame of mind, he must be held responsible for it.

Let us alter the case a little, and suppose that the ship was not unsound after all; that she made her voyage safely, and many others after it. Will that diminish the guilt of her owner? Not one jot. When an action is once done, it is right or wrong forever; no accidental failure of its good or evil fruits can possibly alter that. The man would not have been innocent, he

Reprinted from *Lectures and Essays* by William K. Clifford, Macmillan & Co., London, 1879.

would only have been not found out. The question of right or wrong has to do with the origin of his belief, not the matter of it; not what it was, but how he got it; not whether it turned out to be true or false, but whether he had a right to believe on such evidence as was before him.

There was once an island in which some of the inhabitants professed a religion teaching neither the doctrine of original sin nor that of eternal punishment. A suspicion got abroad that the professors of this religion had made use of unfair means to get their doctrines taught to children. They were accused of wresting the laws of their country in such a way as to remove children from the care of their natural and legal guardians; and even of stealing them away and keeping them concealed from their friends and relations. A certain number of men formed themselves into a society for the purpose of agitating the public about this matter. They published grave accusations against individual citizens of the highest position and character, and did all in their power to injure those citizens in the exercise of their professions. So great was the noise they made, that a Commission was appointed to investigate the facts; but after the Commission had carefully inquired into all the evidence that could be got, it appeared that the accused were innocent. Not only had they been accused on insufficient evidence, but the evidence of their innocence was such as the agitators might easily have obtained, if they had attempted a fair inquiry. After these disclosures the inhabitants of that country looked upon the members of the agitating society, not only as persons whose judgment was to be distrusted, but also as no longer to be counted honorable men. For although they had sincerely and conscientiously believed in the charges they had made, *yet they had no right to believe on such evidence as was before them.* Their sincere convictions, instead of being honestly earned by patient inquiring, were stolen by listening to the voice of prejudice and passion.

Let us vary this case also, and suppose, other things remaining as before, that a still more accurate investigation proved the accused to have been really guilty. Would this make any difference in the guilt of the accusers? Clearly not; the question is not whether their belief was true or false, but whether they entertained it on wrong grounds. They would no doubt say, "Now you see that we were right after all; next time perhaps you will believe us." And they might be believed, but they would not thereby become honorable men. They would not be innocent, they would only be not found out. Every one of them, if he chose to examine himself *in foro conscientiae,* would know that he had acquired and nourished a belief, when he had no right to believe on such evidence as was before him; and therein he would know that he had done a wrong thing.

It may be said, however, that in both of these supposed cases it is not the belief which is judged to be wrong, but the action following upon it. The shipowner might say, "I am perfectly certain that my ship is sound, but still I feel it my duty to have her examined, before trusting the lives of so many people to her." And it might be said to the agitator, "However convinced you were of the justice of your cause and the truth of your convictions, you ought not to have made a public attack upon any man's character until you had examined the evidence on both sides with the utmost patience and care."

In the first place, let us admit that, so far as it goes, this view of the case is right and necessary; right, because even when a man's belief is so fixed that he cannot think otherwise, he still has a choice in regard to the action suggested by it, and so cannot escape the duty of investigating on the ground of the strength of his convictions; and necessary, because those who are not yet capable of controlling their feelings and thoughts must have a plain rule dealing with overt acts.

But this being premised as necessary, it becomes clear that it is not sufficient, and that our previous judgment is required to supplement it. For it is not possible so to sever the belief from the action it suggests as to condemn the one without condemning the other. No man holding a strong belief on one side of a question, or even wishing to hold a belief on one side, can investigate it with such fairness and completeness as if he were really in doubt and unbiased; so that the existence of a belief not founded on fair inquiry unfits a man for the performance of this necessary duty.

Nor is that truly a belief at all which has not some influence upon the actions of him who holds it. He who truly believes that which prompts him to an action has looked upon the action to lust after it, he has committed it already in his heart. If a belief is not realized immediately in open deeds, it is stored up for the guidance of the future. It goes to make a part of that aggregate of beliefs which is the link between sensation and action at every moment of all our lives, and which is so organized and compacted together that no part of it can be isolated from the rest, but every new addition modifies the structure of the whole. No real belief, however trifling and fragmentary it may seem, is ever truly insignificant; it prepares us to receive more of its like, confirms those which resembled it before, and weakens others; and so gradually it lays a stealthy train in our inmost thoughts, which may some day explode into overt action, and leave its stamp upon our character forever.

And no one man's belief is in any case a private matter which concerns himself alone. Our lives are guided by that general conception of the course of things which has been created by society for social purposes. Our words, our phrases, our forms and processes and modes of thought, are common property, fashioned and perfected from age to age; an heirloom which every succeeding generation inherits as a precious deposit and a sacred trust to be handed on to the next one, not unchanged but enlarged and purified, with some clear marks of its proper handiwork. Into this, for good or ill, is woven every belief of every man who has speech of his fellows. An awful privilege, and an awful responsibility, that we should help to create the world in which posterity will live.

In the two supposed cases which have been considered, it has been judged wrong to believe on insufficient evidence, or to nourish belief by suppressing doubts and avoiding investigation. The reason of this judgment is not far to seek: it is that in both these cases the belief held by one man was of great importance to other men. But for as much as no belief held by one man, however seemingly trivial the belief, and however obscure the believer, is ever actually insignificant or without its effect on the fate of mankind, we have no choice but to extend our judgment to all cases of belief whatever. Belief, that sacred faculty which prompts the

decisions of our will, and knits into harmonious working all the compacted energies of our being, is ours not for ourselves, but for humanity.
It is rightly used on truths which have been established by long experience
and waiting toil, and which have stood in the fierce light of free and fearless questioning. Then it helps to bind men together, and to strengthen
and direct their common action. It is desecrated when given to unproved
and unquestioned statements, for the solace and private pleasure of the
believer; to add a tinsel splendor to the plain straight road of our life and
display a bright mirage beyond it; or even to drown the common sorrows
of our kind by a self-deception which allows them not only to cast down,
but also to degrade us. Whoso would deserve well of his fellows in this
matter will guard the purity of his belief with a very fanaticism of jealous
care, lest at any time it should rest on an unworthy object, and catch a
stain which can never be wiped away.

It is not only the leader of men, statesman, philosopher, or poet, that
owes this bounden duty to mankind. Every rustic who delivers in the village alehouse his slow, infrequent sentences, may help to kill or keep alive
the fatal superstitions which clog his race. Every hard-worked wife of an
artisan may transmit to her children beliefs which shall knit society
together, or rend it in pieces. No simplicity of mind, no obscurity of sta-
tion, can escape the universal duty of questioning all that we believe.

It is true that this duty is a hard one, and the doubt which comes out
of it is often a very bitter thing. It leaves us bare and powerless where we
thought that we were safe and strong. To know all about anything is to
know how to deal with it under all circumstances. We feel much happier
and more secure when we think we know precisely what to do, no matter
what happens, than when we have lost our way and do not know where to
turn. And if we have supposed ourselves to know all about anything, and
to be capable of doing what is fit in regard to it, we naturally do not like
to find that we are really ignorant and powerless, that we have to begin
again at the beginning, and try to learn what the thing is and how it is to
be dealt with—if indeed anything can be learned about it. It is the sense
of power attached to a sense of knowledge that makes men desirous of
believing, and afraid of doubting.

This sense of power is the highest and best of pleasures when the belief
on which it is founded is a true belief, and has been fairly earned by
investigation. For then we may justly feel that it is common property, and
holds good for others as well as for ourselves. Then we may be glad, not
that *I* have learned secrets by which I am safer and stronger, but that *we
men* have got mastery over more of the world; and we shall be strong, not
for ourselves, but in the name of Man and in his strength. But if the belief
has been accepted on insufficient evidence, the pleasure is a stolen one.
Not only does it deceive ourselves by giving us a sense of power which we
do not really possess, but it is sinful, because it is stolen in defiance of our
duty to mankind. That duty is to guard ourselves from such beliefs as
from a pestilence, which may shortly master our own body and then
spread to the rest of the town. What would be thought of one who, for
the sake of a sweet fruit, should deliberately run the risk of bringing a
plague upon his family and his neighbors?

And, as in other such cases, it is not the risk only which has to be considered; for a bad action is always bad at the time when it is done, no matter what happens afterwards. Every time we let ourselves believe for unworthy reasons, we weaken our powers of self-control, of doubting, of judicially and fairly weighing evidence. We all suffer severely enough from the maintenance and support of false beliefs and the fatally wrong actions which they lead to, and the evil born when one such belief is entertained is great and wide. But a greater and wider evil arises when the credulous character is maintained and supported, when a habit of believing for unworthy reasons is fostered and made permanent. If I steal money from any person, there may be no harm done by the mere transfer of possession; he may not feel the loss, or it may prevent him from using the money badly. But I cannot help doing this great wrong towards Man, that I make myself dishonest. What hurts society is not that it should lose its property, but that it should become a den of thieves; for then it must cease to be society. This is why we ought not to do evil that good may come; for at any rate this great evil has come, that we have done evil and are made wicked thereby. In like manner, if I let myself believe anything on insufficient evidence, there may be no great harm done by the mere belief; it may be true after all, or I may never have occasion to exhibit it in outward acts. But I cannot help doing this great wrong toward Man, that I make myself credulous. The danger to society is not merely that it should believe wrong things, though that is great enough; but that it should become credulous, and lose the habit of testing things and inquiring into them; for then it must sink back into savagery.

The harm which is done by credulity in a man is not confined to the fostering of a credulous character in others, and consequent support of false beliefs. Habitual want of care about what I believe leads to habitual want of care in others about the truth of what is told to me. Men speak the truth to one another when each reveres the truth in his own mind and in the other's mind; but how shall my friend revere the truth in my mind when I myself am careless about it, when I believe things because I want to believe them, and because they are comforting and pleasant? Will he not learn to cry, "Peace," to me, when there is no peace? By such a course I shall surround myself with a thick atmosphere of falsehood and fraud, and in that I must live. It may matter little to me, in my cloud-castle of sweet illusions and darling lies; but it matters much to Man that I have made my neighbors ready to deceive. The credulous man is father to the liar and the cheat; he lives in the bosom of this his family, and it is no marvel if he should become even as they are. So closely are our duties knit together, that whoso shall keep the whole law, and yet offend in one point, he is guilty of all.

To sum up: it is wrong always, everywhere, and for anyone, to believe anything upon insufficient evidence.

If a man, holding a belief which he was taught in childhood or persuaded of afterwards, keeps down and pushes away any doubts which arise about it in his mind, purposely avoids the reading of books and the company of men that call in question or discuss it, and regards as impious those questions which cannot easily be asked without disturbing it—the life of that man is one long sin against mankind.

If this judgment seems harsh when applied to those simple souls who have never known better, who have been brought up from the cradle with a horror of doubt, and taught that their eternal welfare depends on what they believe, then it leads to the very serious question, Who hath made Israel to sin? . . .

Inquiry into the evidence of a doctrine is not to be made once for all, and then taken as finally settled. It is never lawful to stifle a doubt; for either it can be honestly answered by means of the inquiry already made, or else it proves that the inquiry was not complete.

"But," says one, "I am a busy man; I have no time for the long course of study which would be necessary to make me in any degree a competent judge of certain questions, or even able to understand the nature of the arguments." Then he should have no time to believe. . . .

17. The Will to Believe   William James

William James (1842–1910) is considered one of America's greatest philosophers. He attended Harvard Medical School and later taught anatomy and physiology at Harvard. Later his interests were primarily in the fields of psychology and philosophy. He is considered one of the main developers of pragmatism.

. . . I have long defended to my own students the lawfulness of voluntarily adopted faith; but as soon as they have got well imbued with the logical spirit, they have as a rule refused to admit my contention to be lawful philosophically, even though in point of fact they were personally all the time chock-full of some faith or other themselves. I am all the while, however, so profoundly convinced that my own position is correct, that your invitation has seemed to me a good occasion to make my statements more clear. Perhaps your minds will be more open than those with which I have hitherto had to deal. I will be as little technical as I can, though I must begin by setting up some technical distinctions that will help us in the end.

Let us give the name of *hypothesis* to anything that may be proposed to our belief; and just as the electricians speak of live and dead wires, let us speak of any hypothesis as either *live* or *dead*. A live hypothesis is one which appeals as a real possibility to him to whom it is proposed. If I ask you to believe in the Mahdi, the notion makes no electric connection with your nature,—it refuses to scintillate with any credibility at all. As an hypothesis it is completely dead. To an Arab, however (even if he be not one of the Mahdi's followers), the hypothesis is among the mind's possibilities: it is alive. This shows that deadness and liveness in an hypothesis are not intrinsic properties, but relations to the individual thinker. They

Reprinted from *The Will to Believe and Other Essays in Popular Philosophy* by William James. Published by Longmans, Green (New York, 1896).

are measured by his willingness to act. The maximum of liveness in an hypothesis means willingness to act irrevocably. Practically, that means belief; but there is some believing tendency wherever there is willingness to act at all.

Next, let us call the decision between two hypotheses an *option*. Options may be of several kinds. They may be—1, *living* or *dead;* 2, *forced* or *avoidable;* 3, *momentous* or *trivial;* and for our purposes we may call an option a *genuine* option when it is of the forced, living, and momentous kind.

1. A living option is one in which both hypotheses are live ones. If I say to you: "Be a theosophist or be a Mohammedan," it is probably a dead option, because for you neither hypothesis is likely to be alive. But if I say: "Be an agnostic or be a Christian," it is otherwise: trained as you are, each hypothesis makes some appeal, however small, to your belief.

2. Next, if I say to you: "Choose between going out with your umbrella or without it," I do not offer you a genuine opinion, for it is not forced. You can easily avoid it by not going out at all. Similarly, if I say, "Either love me or hate me," "Either call my theory true or call it false," your option is avoidable. You may remain indifferent to me, neither loving nor hating, and you may decline to offer any judgment as to my theory. But if I say, "Either accept this truth or go without it," I put on you a forced option, for there is no standing place outside of the alternative. Every dilemma based on a complete logical disjunction, with no possibility of not choosing, is an option of this forced kind.

3. Finally, if I were Dr. Nansen and proposed to you to join my North Pole expedition, your option would be momentous; for this would probably be your only similar opportunity, and your choice now would either exclude you from the North Pole sort of immortality altogether or put at least the chance of it into your hands. He who refuses to embrace a unique opportunity loses the prize as surely as if he tried and failed. *Per contra,* the option is trivial when the opportunity is not unique, when the stake is insignificant, or when the decision is reversible if it later prove unwise. Such trivial options abound in the scientific life. A chemist finds an hypothesis live enough to spend a year in its verification: he believes in it to that extent. But if his experiments prove inconclusive either way, he is quit for his loss of time, no vital harm being done.

It will facilitate our discussion if we keep all these distinctions well in mind. . . .

The thesis I defend is, briefly stated, this: *Our passional nature not only lawfully may, but must, decide an option between propositions, whenever it is a genuine option that cannot by its nature be decided on intellectual grounds; for to say, under such circumstances, "Do not decide, but leave the question open," is itself a passional decision,—just like deciding yes or no,—and is attended with the same risk of losing the truth.* . . .

Wherever the option between losing truth and gaining it is not momentous, we can throw the chance of *gaining truth* away, and at any rate save ourselves from any chance of *believing falsehood,* by not making up our minds at all till objective evidence has come. In scientific questions, this is almost always the case; and even in human affairs in general, the need of acting is seldom so urgent that a false belief to act on is better than no belief at all. Law courts, indeed, have to decide on the best evidence attainable for the moment, because a judge's duty is to make law as well as to ascertain it, and (as a learned judge once said to me) few cases are worth spending much time over: the great thing is to have them decided on *any* acceptable principle, and got out of the way. But in our dealings with objective nature we obviously are recorders, not makers, of the truth; and decisions for the mere sake of deciding promptly and getting on to the next business would be wholly out of place. Throughout the breadth of physical nature facts are what they are quite independently of us, and seldom is there any such hurry about them that the risks of being duped by believing a premature theory need be faced. The questions here are always trivial options, the hypotheses are hardly living (at any rate not living for us spectators), the choice between believing truth or falsehood is seldom forced. The attitude of sceptical balance is therefore the absolutely wise one if we would escape mistakes. What difference, indeed, does it make to most of us whether we have or have not a theory of the Röntgen rays, whether we believe or not in mind-stuff, or have a conviction about the causality of conscious states? It makes no difference. Such options are not forced on us. On every account it is better not to make them, but still keep weighing reasons *pro et contra* with an indifferent hand.

I speak, of course, here of the purely judging mind. For purposes of discovery such indifferences is to be less highly recommended, and science would be far less advanced than she is if the passionate desires of individuals to get their own faiths confirmed had been kept out of the game. . . . On the other hand, if you want an absolute duffer in an investigation, you must, after all, take the man who has no interest whatever in its results: he is the warranted incapable, the positive fool. The most useful investigator, because the most sensitive observer, is always he whose eager interest in one side of the question is balanced by an equally keen nervousness lest he become deceived. Science has organized this nervousness into a regular *technique,* her so-called method of verification; and she has fallen so deeply in love with the method that one may even say she has ceased to care for truth by itself at all. It is only truth as technically verified that interests her. The truth of truths might come in merely affirmative form, and she would decline to touch it. Such truth as that, she might repeat with Clifford, would be stolen in defiance of her duty to mankind. Human passions, however, are stronger than technical rules. "Le coeur a ses raisons," as Pascal says, "que la raison ne connaît pas";* and however indifferent to all but the bare rules of the game the umpire, the abstract intellect, may be, the concrete players who furnish him the materials to judge of are usually, each one of them, in love with some pet 'live hypothesis' of his own. Let us agree, however, that wherever there is no forced option, the dispassionately judicial intellect with no pet hypothesis, saving us, as it does, from dupery at any rate, ought to be our ideal.

The question next arises: Are there not somewhere forced options in

---

*[The heart has its reasons that reason does not know.—ed.]

our speculative questions, and can we (as men who may be interested at least as much in positively gaining truth as in merely escaping dupery) always wait with impunity till the coercive evidence shall have arrived? It seems *a priori* improbable that the truth should be so nicely adjusted to our needs and powers as that. In the great boarding-house of nature, the cakes and the butter and the syrup seldom come out so even and leave the plates so clean. Indeed, we should view them with scientific suspicion if they did.

Moral questions immediately present themselves as questions whose solution cannot wait for sensible proof. A moral question is a question not of what sensibly exists, but of what is good, or would be good if it did exist. Science can tell us what exists; but to compare the *worths,* both of what exists and of what does not exist, we must consult not science, but what Pascal calls our heart. Science herself consults her heart when she lays it down that the infinite ascertainment of fact and correction of false belief are the supreme goods for man. Challenge the statement, and science can only repeat it oracularly, or else prove it by showing that such ascertainment and correction bring man all sorts of other goods which man's heart in turn declares. The question of having moral beliefs at all or not having them is decided by our will. Are our moral preferences true or false, or are they only odd biological phenomena, making things good or bad for *us,* but in themselves indifferent? How can your pure intellect decide? If your heart does not *want* a world of moral reality, your head will assuredly never make you believe in one. Mephistophelian scepticism, indeed, will satisfy the head's play-instincts much better than any rigorous idealism can. Some men (even at the student age) are so naturally cool-hearted that the moralistic hypothesis never has for them any pungent life, and in their supercilious presence the hot young moralist always feels strangely ill at ease. The appearance of knowingness is on their side, of *naiveté* and gullibility on his. Yet, in the inarticulate heart of him, he clings to it that he is not a dupe, and that there is a realm in which (as Emerson says) all their wit and intellectual superiority is no better than the cunning of a fox. Moral scepticism can no more be refuted or proved by logic than intellectual scepticism can. When we stick to it that there *is* truth (be it of either kind), we do so with our whole nature, and resolve to stand or fall by the results. The sceptic with his whole nature adopts the doubting attitude; but which of us is the wiser, Omniscience only knows.

Turn now from these wide questions of good to a certain class of questions of fact, questions concerning personal relations, states of mind between one man and another. *Do you like me or not?*—for example. Whether you do or not depends, in countless instances, on whether I meet you half-way, am willing to assume that you must like me, and show you trust and expectation. The previous faith on my part in your liking's existence is in such cases what makes your liking come. But if I stand aloof, and refuse to budge an inch until I have objective evidence, until you shall have done something apt, as the absolutists say, *ad extorquendum assensum meum,* ten to one your liking never comes. How many women's hearts are vanquished by the mere sanguine insistence of some man that they *must* love him! he will not consent to the hypothesis that they cannot. The desire for a certain kind of truth here brings about that special truth's existence; and so it is in innumerable cases of other sorts. Who gains promotions, boons, appointments, but the man in whose life they are seen to play the part of live hypotheses, who discounts them, sacrifices other things for their sake before they have come, and takes risks for them in advance? His faith acts on the powers above him as a claim, and creates its own verification.

A social organism of any sort whatever, large or small, is what it is because each member proceeds to his own duty with a trust that the other members will simultaneously do theirs. Wherever a desired result is achieved by the co-operation of many independent persons, its existence as a fact is a pure consequence of the precursive faith in one another of those immediately concerned. A government, an army, a commercial system, a ship, a college, an athletic team, all exist on this condition, without which not only is nothing achieved, but nothing is even attempted. A whole train of passengers (individually brave enough) will be looted by a few highwaymen, simply because the latter can count on one another, while each passenger fears that if he makes a movement of resistance, he will be shot before any one else backs him up. If we believed that the whole car-full would rise at once with us, we should each severally rise, and train-robbing would never even be attempted. There are, then, cases where a fact cannot come at all unless a preliminary faith exists in its coming. *And where faith in a fact can help create the fact,* that would be an insane logic which should say that faith running ahead of scientific evidence is the 'lowest kind of immorality' into which a thinking being can fall. Yet such is the logic by which our scientific absolutists pretend to regulate our lives!

In truths dependent on our personal action, then, faith based on desire is certainly a lawful and possibly an indispensable thing.

But now, it will be said, these are all childish human cases, and have nothing to do with great cosmical matters, like the question of religious faith. Let us then pass on to that. Religions differ so much in their accidents that in discussing the religious question we must make it very generic and broad. What then do we now mean by the religious hypothesis? Science says things are; morality says some things are better than other things; and religion says essentially two things.

First, she says that the best things are the more eternal things, the overlapping things, the things in the universe that throw the last stone, so to speak, and say the final word. "Perfection is eternal,"—this phrase of Charles Secrétan seems a good way of putting his first affirmation of religion, an affirmation which obviously cannot yet be verified scientifically at all.

The second affirmation of religion is that we are better off even now if we believe her first affirmation to be true.

Now, let us consider what the logical elements of this situation are *in case the religious hypothesis in both its branches be really true.* (Of course, we must admit that possibility at the outset. If we are to discuss the question at all, it must involve a living option. If for any of you religion be a hypothesis that cannot, by any living possibility be true, then you need go no farther. I speak to the 'saving remnant' alone.) So proceeding, we see, first, that religion offers itself as a *momentous* option. We are supposed to gain, even now, by our belief, and to lose by our nonbelief, a certain vital good. Secondly, religion is a *forced* option, so far as that good goes. We cannot escape the issue by remaining sceptical and waiting for more light, because, although we do avoid error in that way *if religion be untrue,* we lose the good, *if it be true,* just as certainly as if we positively chose to disbelieve. It is as if a man should hesitate indefinitely to ask a certain woman to marry him because he was not perfectly sure that she would prove an angel after he brought her home. Would he not cut himself off from that particular angel-possibility as decisively as if he went and married some one else? Scepticism, then, is not avoidance of option; it is option of a certain particular kind of risk. *Better risk loss of truth than chance of error,*—that is your faith-vetoer's exact position. He is actively playing his stake as much as the believer is; he is backing the field against the religious hypothesis, just as the believer is backing the religious hypothesis against the field. To preach scepticism to us as a duty until 'sufficient evidence' for religion be found, is tantamount therefore to telling us, when in presence of the religious hypothesis, that to yield to our fear of its being error is wiser and better than to yield to our hope that it may be true. It is not intellect against all passions, then; it is only intellect with one passion laying down its law. And by what, forsooth, is the supreme wisdom of this passion warranted? Dupery for dupery, what proof is there that dupery through hope is so much worse than dupery through fear? I, for one, can see no proof; and I simply refuse obedience to the scientist's command to imitate his kind of option, in a case where my own stake is important enough to give me the right to choose my own form of risk. If religion be true and the evidence for it be still insufficient, I do not wish, by putting your extinguisher upon my nature (which feels to me as if it had after all some business in this matter), to forfeit my sole chance in life of getting upon the winning side,—that chance depending, of course, on my willingness to run the risk of acting as if my passional need of taking the world religiously might be prophetic and right.

All this is on the supposition that it really may be prophetic and right, and that, even to us who are discussing the matter, religion is a live hypothesis which may be true. Now, to most of us religion comes in a still further way that makes a veto on our active faith even more illogical. The more perfect and more eternal aspect of the universe is represented in our religions as having personal form. The universe is no longer a mere *It* to us, but a *Thou,* if we are religious; and any relation that may be possible from person to person might be possible here. For instance, although in one sense we are passive portions of the universe, in another we show a curious autonomy, as if we were small active centres on our own account. We feel, too, as if the appeal of religion to us were made to our own active good-will, as if evidence might be forever withheld from us unless we met the hypothesis half-way. To take a trivial illustration: just as a man who in a company of gentlemen made no advances, asked a warrant for every concession, and believed no one's word without proof, would cut himself off by such churlishness from all the social rewards that a more trusting spirit would earn,—so here, one who should shut himself up in snarling logicality and try to make the gods extort his recognition willy-nilly, or not get it at all, might cut himself off forever from his only opportunity of making the gods' acquaintance. This feeling, forced on us we know not whence, that by obstinately believing that there are gods (although not to do so would be so easy both for our logic and our life) we are doing the universe the deepest service we can, seems part of the living essence of the religious hypothesis. If the hypothesis *were* true in all its parts, including this one, then pure intellectualism, with its veto on our making willing advances, would be an absurdity; and some participation of our sympathetic nature would be logically required. I, therefore, for one, cannot see my way to accepting the agnostic rules for truth-seeking, or wilfully agree to keep my willing nature out of the game. I cannot do so for this plain reason, that *a rule of thinking which would absolutely prevent me from acknowledging certain kinds of truth if those kinds of truth were really there, would be an irrational rule.* That for me is the long and short of the formal logic of the situation, no matter what the kinds of truth might materially be.

I confess I do not see how this logic can be escaped. But sad experience makes me fear that some of you may still shrink from radically saying with me, *in abstracto,* that we have the right to believe at our own risk any hypothesis that is live enough to tempt our will. I suspect, however, that if this is so, it is because you have got away from the abstract logical point of view altogether, and are thinking (perhaps without realizing it) of some particular religious hypothesis which for you is dead. The freedom to 'believe what we will' you apply to the case of some patent superstition; and the faith you think of is the faith defined by the schoolboy when he said, "Faith is when you believe something that you know ain't true." I can only repeat that this is misapprehension. *In concreto,* the freedom to believe can only cover living options which the intellect of the individual cannot by itself resolve; and living options never seem absurdities to him who has them to consider. When I look at the religious question as it really puts itself to concrete men, and when I think of all the possibilities which both practically and theoretically it involves, then this command that we shall put a stopper on our heart, instincts, and courage, and *wait*—acting of course meanwhile more or less as if religion were *not* true—till dooms-day, or till such time as our intellect and senses working together may have raked in evidence enough,—this command, I say, seems to me the queerest idol ever manufactured in the philosophic cave. Were we scholastic absolutists, there might be more excuse. If we had an infallible intellect with its objective certitudes, we might feel ourselves disloyal to such a perfect organ of knowledge in not trusting to it exclusively, in not waiting for its releasing word. But if we are empiricists, if we believe that no bell in us tolls to let us know for certain when truth is in our grasp, then it seems a piece of idle fantasticality to preach so solemnly our duty of waiting for the bell. Indeed we *may* wait if we will,—I hope you do not think that I am denying that,—but if we do so, we do so at our peril as much as if we believed. In either case we *act*, taking our life in our hands. No one of us ought to issue vetoes to the other, nor should we bandy words of abuse. We ought, on the contrary, delicately and profoundly to respect one another's mental freedom: then only shall we being about the intellectual republic; then only shall we have that spirit of inner tolerance without which all our outer tolerance is soulless, and which is empiricism's glory; then only shall we live and let live, in speculative as well as in practical things. . . .

Are Statements About God Meaningless?

18. Has "God" a Meaning?   Bernard Williams

Bernard Williams (1929–   ) is Professor of Philosophy at Cambridge University in England. He has published numerous important books and articles on ethics and other philosophical subjects.

People are often tempted to think of questions about meaning as though they were all on the level of the most trivial disagreements about the use of a particular word, the sort of disagreements that are rightly called "merely verbal": exemplified, for instance, in the fact that Americans use the word "suspenders" to refer to what we call "braces." Obviously, no sane person would waste time arguing about which was the right word to use, or what the word "suspenders" *really* meant. But most questions about meaning are not nearly as superficial as this, and in issues of metaphysics or religion we cannot proceed in this way.

Philosophers have become extremely conscious of the fact that it is possible to use language in an impressive and profound-seeming way, without what one says having any meaning at all, or at least—and this is an important point—without its having the sort of meaning that the speaker would like it to have.

Some speaker may think that he is making an important statement about the nature of the universe, or of history, or something, and it may turn out, when he is pressed, that no meaning has been given to his sayings which is determinate enough for him to be making any recognizable claim at all. In particular, this will be so if there is nothing definite to distinguish what is involved in this man's claim from what would be involved in denying that claim. There has to be a difference between what things are like if it is true and what things are like if it isn't. If there is really no difference between what things are like if a certain claim is true, and what they are like if it is not true, we can say that that claim has no content at all.

One very simple example, from the field of religious belief: and I should say at once that I don't think that to criticize the sort of view I am

Reprinted from *Question* No. 1 (Pemberton Publishing Co., Ltd.: London, 1968).

going to mention is, in itself, to criticize any serious form of religious belief, since few serious religious believers would believe anything as simple as this. But there have been people who have thought that God's purposes were positively manifested in natural disasters such as eruptions and earthquakes; for instance, by the punishment of wicked persons overwhelmed by these catastrophes. It is pointed out that the same catastrophes tend rather indiscriminately to involve also innocent persons, such as small children; or presumably virtuous persons, such as members of religious orders. The simple believer then replies that this manifests God's purpose in another way, since it is good that the innocent and virtuous should go to Heaven.

He is then asked, presumably, why other innocent and virtuous persons are not given this benefit to go to Heaven quickly, but left to suffer on earth to a hearty old age; and many of the wicked, indeed, seem to do quite well and are not despatched. Something is then said to the effect that it is also good that the virtuous should have life on earth, and that the punishment of the wicked be delayed for a while, and so on. And after all this we see that absolutely anything that happened to the virtuous, the wicked, or the in-between will count equally well; natural calamities directed by God turn out to be utterly indistinguishable in principle from natural calamities not directed by anyone; and the content of the claim that the happening of such incidents reveals any sort of Divine purpose dissolves in thin air.

As I said before, I don't think the very naïve view I've just mentioned would be held by serious religious believers; in fact, I believe it would be condemned by them, as superstitious. The fact that this superstitious view turned out to be vacuous and have no content would be held by many sceptical philosophers to be the case, in a more sophisticated way, as regards the central tenets of a religion such as Christianity. One form of this more general sort of philosophical criticism was advanced by the "logical positivists."

Logical positivism started in the early years of this century, and was developed principally in Vienna in the twenties. It became known in this country through a very remarkable book by Professor A. J. Ayer, called *Language, Truth and Logic,* which was published in 1936. The positivists held that there were only two sorts of statements that genuinely have meaning. One sort were statements which were true merely because of the definitions of the terms used in them: a boring example is "all bachelors are unmarried." These need not bother us. The other sort of meaningful statement consisted of those that could be shown to be true or shown to be false by some possible sense-experience: for instance, by some possible scientific experiment or observation. All other remarks not of these two types were considered by the positivists to be meaningless. This doctrine obviously dealt pretty hard with statements of religion, which certainly don't seem to be typically verifiable by science.

Many philosophers now would agree that a principal criticism of logical positivism was the very narrow view it took of something's being meaningful. It is obviously wrong just to lump together as meaningless everything that fails the positivist test; pieces of poetry, commands, expressions of wishes, and lots of other pieces of ordinary meaningful language fail the test and yet have meaning. The positivist challenge has helped to make philosophers more conscious of different sorts of meaning. While this is so, I do not think that the positivist position, in an essential respect, is just to be dismissed. For even if it overlooked a lot of kinds of meaning, it seems to me at least roughly right about one central sort of meaning: the sort of meaning which belongs to statements which one can claim to be true or false. This point can be made in terms of belief: that to believe is to believe *something,* and if there is anything that one believes, one ought to be able to say in some way—if not in the very narrow terms of sense-experience—what the difference is between what one believes being true and what one believes not being true. In the case of religious statements, in particular statements about God, the important question, to my mind, is not whether they have a meaning, or no meaning: the important question is, what sort of meaning they have.

And this is a question which affects whether one wants to go on making such statements or not.

There is no doubt that some people at some times have given a meaning to the statement that God exists, and to other statements about God, which came very near to making those statements into a sort of supplement to science: God came in where science left off. This is the God which the Bishop of Woolwich called in his book, *Honest to God,* "the God of the gaps"—the gaps, that is to say, in science. Taken in this way, statements about God were certainly not empty or vacuous in the sort of way I have been talking about before. They made a fairly definite claim: that certain phenomena, such as the adaptation of animals to their environment, or, again, the existence of living things, did not admit of a scientific explanation. These negative claims that certain sorts of scientific explanation were impossible were certainly not empty; the trouble was that they have turned out to be false, since such scientific explanations are forthcoming and there is every sign that they will go on being forthcoming. So if that was the sort of thing meant by religious statements, if that was the sort of meaning they had, they would have to be written off as a hopeful bet against science, which science won.

At this point, some modern theologian may come along, and say something like this: "I agree that the attempts to make God fill in holes in science is hopeless: the existence of God is not a hypothesis, supplementary to science, and never should have been regarded as such." I also think the theologian may justly add that these sorts of arguments do a disservice to religion by making God into an abstract or scientific object, instead of something of living concern to people. "Christianity is about people caring; it essentially involves taking a serious attitude to the world, to personal relationships, to society. When someone says he is a Christian, and that he believes in God, it is such an attitude that he declares. His statements of his religion are not meaningless: they have just this meaning, that the speaker declares such an attitude to life."

This modern theologian I have made up is at best a composite figure; he is probably a caricature. But the tone is familiar. And my reply to him is this. "If that is what Christian remarks mean, and only that, then people should stop making them. The Christian vocabulary is unnecessary; if you want to say 'I care about personal relationships.' we have a very good English sentence for saying that, which does not mention God—namely the sentence, 'I care about personal relationships.' What is worse, the Christian vocabulary is, for the purpose you give it, actively misleading. For it is quite obvious that historically the calims of Christianity have not just been ways of expressing certain attitudes to the world and to other people: they have been taken to be, if true, very important truths which *give reasons* for having those attitudes towards personal relationships, and so on. To represent the words of Christianity as merely expressing these essentially secular attitudes is in fact to have given the thing up, while retaining the vocabulary."

It may be objected that I am engaged in the old sceptics' game of insisting that Christianity be represented in the most conservative and implausible forms so that I go on disbelieving it. I hope that that is not what I am doing. What I am rather trying to do is to insist that if Christianity is to be Christianity at all there has to be something to be believed or disbelieved, and that this has to be something over and above a mere belief about the secular order.

Christianity is a religion which is very historically articulate; one knows a good deal about what has been believed at different stages of its development. It is also a religion which is tied to certain texts, in particular, of course, the Bible, and of course to a particular figure, Christ, about whom one is told something in those texts. Given this, it seems to me possible to identify certain beliefs which must be held if it is Christianity that is being believed at all. I will suggest just one—very unambitiously and, one would hope, platitudinously. This is that God is transcendent to human affairs and to human attitudes in a sense which has the following consequence (though it is supposed to mean more as well): that God would exist whether human beings and their attitudes existed or not—even if there were no human beings or human aspirations, there would still be a God.

To believe this is certainly not enough to constitute one's being a Christian, as I understand it. A Christian has, for instance, to go on to say something very special about Christ (and not just that Christ was a better moral teacher than Socrates). But I shall leave the rest, and concentrate on this one point: that to believe what I just very roughly spelled out is at least *necessary* to having Christian beliefs. And I think it is worth asking oneself very carefully when confronted with some reinterpretation of Christian doctrine whether it passes this test: that is represents God as a being who would be there even if no human beings, or indeed other finite conscious beings, were there. If it does not, then I suspect you no longer have any form of Christianity, but probably some form of religious Humanism.

All this is still about meaning. I said the problem was about *what* Christian and other religious statements are said to mean. There is a limit to what they can be made to mean; when their meaning has changed too much, in particular when it is identified too closely with a meaning which refers *only* to human life, there is no point in going on making them in the religious form. Sometimes of course—perhaps one must say, very often—it is not at all easy to discover whether this has happened or not: clouds of ambiguity stand in the way. In this connection I think we should look extremely closely at a famous passage from Paul Tillich's *The Shaking of the Foundations* (pp. 63f) quoted in *Honest to God,* which seems to suggest that to deny that God exists is to deny that life has depth. Tillich wrote: "The Name of this infinite and inexhaustible depth and ground of all being is *God.* That depth is what the word *God* means. And if that word has not much meaning for you, translate it, and speak of the depths of your life, of the source of your being, of your ultimate concern, of what you take seriously without any reservation. Perhaps, in order to do so, you must forget everything traditional that you hare learned about God, perhaps even the word itself. For if you know that God means depth, you know much about him. You cannot then call yourself an atheist or unbeliever, for you cannot think or say: Life has not depth. Life is shallow. Being itself is surface only. If you could say this in complete seriousness, you would be an atheist; but otherwise you are not. He who knows about depth knows about God." This raises many questions. In the sense in which "life has depth" is a statement which only superficial people are going to reject—can it really be enough to represent what "God exists" is supposed to mean? When people said that God exists were they really saying just that life has depth?

Is Tillich really saying that believing in God is just the *same* as not being superficial? If not, what more? What sort of thing does his pervasive phrase, "the ground of our being," mean? Is the "ground of our being" something that would be there even if we were not? Or is the "ground of our being" something more like our deepest aspirations, which presumably would not be there if we were not?

I do not think that "God," or statements containing that word, have no meaning. I think they can have all sorts of meanings. On some, they are very difficult to interpret indeed. On others, they seem to me to make claims which can be at least well enough identified to be seen to be substantial; in those meanings, which are various, the claims seem to me personally, I must say, to be false. But at least there is something to be false, and something to be disbelieved. In yet other meanings that are given to them, they say nothing, or too little, or something of the wrong sort—representing, for instance, merely some human aspiration. Then there is nothing to be false, nothing to disbelieve. But when that is so, there is nothing to be true, nothing to believe, either.

19. Has "God" a Meaning?   J. A. T. Robinson

Rt. Rev. John Arthur Thomas Robinson (1919–   ) is an English theologian and teacher at Cambridge University. He has published many widely-read books which offer an interpretation of the meaning and significance of religion.

Reprinted with permission of Bishop Robinson from *Question* No. 1 (Pemberton Publishing Co., Ltd: London, 1968).

I would like to begin by saying outright that the word *God* does not have *a* meaning, in the usual sense in which we use that phrase. For instance, if we ask what is the meaning of the word *dog* (which is simply the same three letters the other way round), what we mean is: "How does the dictionary define it?" or "What other word would you put in its place?" In fact, if you look up the word *dog* in the *Concise Oxford Dictionary* you will realize how difficult it is to define even a dog. "Quadruped of many breeds, wild and domesticated" would be just as good a definition of "cat." If you can't put a dog into words you are hardly likely to put God into words.

The reality "God." if it is really to be *God* and not just an idol we can get our hands or our minds round, is by definition indefinable. What the *word* does is not to define God but to *point* to a mystery at the heart of our experience. It is saying that there is something which cannot be expressed, and yet which cannot be eliminated. The function of the word "God" is primarily to draw attention to this element, this dimension, if you like, in experience, which cannot be reduced to anything else.

In one sense, any word will do for this; and it may help to begin with a tradition that doesn't use the word "God," which has for us become so loaded. In the sixth century B.C. (about the time of the prophet Jeremiah) there lived one of the greatest Chinese philosophers, Lao Tzu. He was the founder of what we now call Taoism, so called because for him the word *Tao* stood for this mystery at the center of reality. It is certainly not the same as the Christian "God," but in many ways it performs the same function. It means, literally, "the Way," and perhaps its nearest equivalent in Biblical terms is "Wisdom" or "the Word." Thus he says, "All things originate from *Tao,* conform to *Tao,* and to *Tao* they at last return." And the point from which he starts is this: "The *Tao* that can be talked about is not the Eternal *Tao.* The name that can be named is not the Eternal Name." If you think you can put your finger on it or get it wrapped up in words, you haven't got it: "He who speaks does not know. He who knows does not speak." And he uses the famous metaphor of the wheel. The usefulness of a wheel entirely depends on the hole in the middle. What the word *Tao* does, or the word "God," is not to fill in that hole, so that you can now say what is in the middle, but precisely to keep guard over it—to insist that no amount of talk about the rim or the spokes tells you everything.

I don't think that's *all* there is to be said about God—otherwise he would simply be a meaningless blank. I shall come back to the content, to the colour, which the Christian and other traditions give to this word. But I would insist that it's a word that doesn't have *a* meaning which you can define. It's a way of witnessing to the belief that at the heart of our experienced relationships there is a mystery that can't be translated without remainder simply into language about man and the world (or, in other words, the spokes of the wheel).

But the trouble is precisely that the word "God" *has* come for most of us to have *a* meaning, a definition, which we can't dissociate from it. In fact, ironically, the *Concise Oxford Dictionary* is much more precise in its definition of "god" than it is of "dog!" "God," it says, with a small *g,* is a "superhuman being worshipped as having power over nature and human fortunes," and, with a big *G,* 'Supreme Being, Creator and Ruler of the universe." Do you see what's happened? God has become a substantial, supernatural Being, and talk about "God" is description of this Being. "Do you believe in God?" comes to mean "Do you believe that such a Being exists?" and whether the word "God" has meaning is made to turn on whether it is possible to make meaningful statements, not about our experience, but about an entity quite "out of this world."

Something very definite has been put in the hole. According to this interpretation, God-language must refer to this superhuman Being: it can have no other reference. And this is the point at which a good many modern theologians, myself included, would want to put in an objection. They would argue something like this.

The description of God as a supernatural Being or heavenly Person is one way of trying to make real and vivid to the human imagination the mysterious reality in experience over which the word stands guard. But it is not by any means a necessary way, and it is not what the word "God" *means.*

Let us stand back again for a moment and look at a tradition other than our own. The ancient Greeks, everyone would agree, had many profound religious insights, which are given classic expression in their tragedies. Many of these we can still enter into and make our own. What we cannot do is to take seriously the way in which they found it helpful to represent these religious realities, namely, by projecting them as gods and goddesses living on top of Mount Olympus or anywhere else. For them it made the realities more vivid, more "human," more related to everyday life. For us it simply makes them remote and ridiculous.

In the same way, Christians in the past have found that it made evil and the shadow-side of life more real by picturing it as personified in a Devil. But today, so far from bringing the reality of evil closer to human experience, as it did for medieval man, this merely makes it remote and ridiculous. The last way now to get people to take the depth of evil seriously would be to press them to believe in the existence of a supernatural figure called the Devil.

So with God. I believe strongly in the reality for which the word stands. But I do not think that the seriousness with which I take this reality depends *at all* on whether a Being exists up there, out there, or anywhere else. For this is no longer a way of representing it that is natural to most men and women today. The pity is that the word "God" has become so completely identified with this particular image or projection that both those who want to preserve the image (and there is absolutely nothing wrong with it if it serves) *and* those who want to deny the reality it stands for join in saying that the word "God" means this Being *or means nothing.* If you don't accept this identification, then you are accused of being disloyal, dishonest, or merely confused. But I want to protest vigorously against being put in this position by conservative Christians and by Humanists alike.

For me the word "God" refers to something very meaningful, though I would be the first to recognize that the *word* may now be burdened with so many associations as to be more trouble than it's worth. I should be content to sit loose to it. It was St. Thomas Aquinas, perhaps the greatest theologian ever, who said, "Wise people do not worry about names." And if we could get by without the word "God" I shouldn't shed any tears. But I doubt if we can. We need something to guard that hole, and I see no other single word to replace it. However, it's the reality that I'm concerned with, not the word. What is that reality?

Traditionally, language about God has described, as I have said, an invisible spiritual Being existing in himself quite outside of and apart from our experience. If this is the reference of the language, then I would agree with those modern philosophers who question whether we can ever make any meaningful statements about God. For is there any way of verifying them, anything in our experience that could count for or against their truth? We might just as well be making statements about celestial mermaids.

In reaction, some present-day theologians have swung to the opposite extreme and said that God-language is essentially a way of indicating what *we* hold to be of ultimate significance. It doesn't tell us about anything outside us, but it tells us a great deal about us. It describes, as it were, what we should be prepared to go to the stake for, our life's commitment. To say, for instance, that Jesus is God is to say that for us he is of final or decisive significance.

Now, I would agree that this is an important part of what is involved in using God-language. It *is* a way of expressing ultimate concern. If it didn't include this, if it didn't engage our whole being, then it wouldn't be about what is most real at all. This is a valid protest, because so much talk about "God" is in fact about something or someone who only comes in, as it were, as a sort of long-stop. It's not really talk about *God* at all.

On the other hand, I would agree with Professor Williams that if God-statements are *only* statements about man, only ways of saying, for instance, with whatever accent of finality, "I care about personal relationships," then there's no reason why you should have to use the word "God." And those who argue like this would mostly draw the conclusion that you *don't* have to. You can; but, if you prefer, you can express the same thing in other language. If this just means that you needn't be tied to the word "God," fair enough. But if it means that language about God can be translated into language about man without remainder, then I would agree that you've really given up talking about the reality for which the word "God" has traditionally stood.

For this reality has always been seen as that to which any human commitment and concern is simply *response*. "God" refers not to the commitment but to something that hits you, meets you, surrounds you, with a grace and a claim from which you cannot finally get away. Consider these typical religious statements:

Thus saith the Lord.
Abba, Father.
Herein is love not that we loved God, but that he first loved us.
Thou mastering me God! Giver of breath and bread. . . . Over again I feel
thy finger and find thee.

These are not simply statements about human attitudes; they are responses to *how things are seen to be,* to that in which human life is grounded—viewed not simply as an impersonal regularity but as claiming one in freedom and responsibility, not simply as an "It" but as a "Thou." It is *this,* as the ultimate truth about reality, that God-language is affirming. Or, rather to be accurate, it is this that God-language is affirming as it is used in the Judaeo-Christian tradition. For while the Bible certainly agrees that God cannot be defined, and shows great reluctance even in using his name, it is equally clear that God is no blank. He makes himself known; and, above all, the grace and the claim of the "Thou" "come through" supremely in Jesus the Christ.

To sum up, as I see it, language about God describes not a Being outside our experience, nor simply human attitudes, but what we respond to as ultimately and unconditionally real. Affirming, for instance, that "God is love" is staking one's whole being on the fact that this is the final truth about the nature of things. Of course, believing in God doesn't just mean supposing that life has depth (though I agree that the quotation from Tillich to which Professor Williams referred is open to that interpretation). Of course, to take another point he raised, God's reality doesn't depend on us and our aspirations—rather, our being is grounded in his. Let me try to make this clear by using an analogy—which is always dangerous.

What makes us *persons* doesn't depend simply on our genes and the rest of our biological inheritance. It depends on the fact that from the moment of birth we find ourselves in a relationship to other persons, beginning with mother-love, in which we are drawn out, not merely to reaction and response, but to freedom and responsibility. What the believer is saying is that such a relationship, such a love, is the element in which all things live and move and have their being. It is what draws the whole process of evolution onwards and upwards to its fulfillment in mind and spirit. This is the reality to which he can but stumblingly point by using this (in itself) meaningless monosyllable "God."

Finally, I should like to come back to the *difference* between what the Christian is affirming by the personal name "God" and what the Taoist means by *Tao.* In many ways, as I said, the two words perform a similar function. But what the Taoist sees at the still center of everything is a Way, a certain norm or law of life. What the Christian responds to is a grace that meets and claims him in love. It is this difference that is indicated by speaking of God as "personal."

But we should be careful here. This does *not* mean that the Christian necessarily thinks of God, as I said before, as *a* supernatural Person. He *may* picture or project the reality in this way in order to make it easier to imagine—as men have personified the Devil. But though in the past it has helped to personify God as a sort of super-Man, I am very doubtful whether it helps today. It just makes him incredible. What the Christian is affirming by using the word "God" is something about the *relationship* in which he finds himself to be held. In human terms, it is less misleading to describe it in personal language than in impersonal. For instance, the kind of security which he finds in God is more like that of a parent's love than that of an immovable lump of stone. In fact, the Bible uses both images: God is a Rock, and God is a Father. But the point is that *both* are equally metaphors. He *is* not either. There is not a super-Person out there any more than a super-Rock.

But the idea of a Person behind phenomena, an invisible Man who manipulates everything, "allowing" this and "sending" that, dies very hard. Hence the idea left in so many minds to which Professor Bernard Williams referred, and which he admitted would be condemned by serious believers, namely, that to speak of "God" means claiming to trace a hidden purpose in why particular things happen or do not happen to particular people. By sufficiently ingenious reckoning, as he said, you can make absolutely anything, good, bad, or indifferent, demonstrate the hand of God: "natural calamities directed by God turn out to be utterly indistinguishable . . . from such calamities not directed by anyone." Statements about "God" being "at work" in this or that event become utterly vacuous and meaningless.

But because vast numbers of people *do* think that this is what believers mean by a personal God at work, let me say as strongly as I can that I reject it totally. Not only is it meaningless. It is immoral. If God were a planner, manipulating, or at least privy to, the Aberfan disaster, why didn't he evacuate the children first, as any human planner would?

But this is not what I mean or I hope any mature Christian means by providence. He doesn't see an invisible Hand deliberately pulling strings. What he does say is that in everything, however purposeless (and there is no purpose or intention in the slipping of a coal tip, unless it be human negligence), that in everything, however loveless, there is a purpose and a love to be met and responded to from which *nothing*, not even death, can separate us. There is a reality deeper than tragedy which can *give* meaning even to that which in itself is meaningless.

Someone has said that the question of God is the question of whether man is alone in the universe or not. This is misleading, I think, if it implies that everything turns on whether there is some other invisible Person, like man, somewhere around. But it is right if by that is meant that the question of God is the question whether persons and personal relationships are simply on their own, up against it, in a fundamentally alien universe. For to believe in God is to affirm that at the heart of things, as the most real thing in the world, is a love and a purpose to which persons and personal relationships are, so far, the highest *response*. This is the way the grain of the universe runs.

This I do not believe to be a meaningless statement—though it is, of course, an act of trust. It is not just a statement of my commitment—"the promise to pay" is not on my side alone. It is an affirmation about how things are, defined and vindicated, for me, in what I see in Christ, including all that has led up to him and all that has flowed from him.

Suggestions for Further Reading

Anthologies

Brody, Baruch A. *Readings in the Philosophy of Religion.* Englewood Cliffs, N.J.: Prentice-Hall, 1974. A comprehensive collection emphasizing contemporary essays in the recent, analytical tradition.

Flew, Anthony and MacIntyre, Alasdair (eds.). *New Essays in Philosophical Theology.* London: SCM Press, 1955. A collection of important writings on various aspects of the philosophy of religion. Many of these articles will be difficult for the beginning student.

Hick, John (ed.). *The Existence of God.* New York: Macmillan, 1964. A good collection of classical and contemporary writings on the major arguments for the existence of God.

Kaufmann, Walter (ed.). *Religion from Tolstoy to Camus.* New York: Harper, 1961. A collection of some of the most important writings on the philosophy of religion.

Pike, Nelson (ed.). *God and Evil.* Englewood Cliffs, N.J.: Prentice-Hall, 1964. A collection of opposing views and arguments about the problem of evil. There is a good bibliography for the student who wishes to read further on this topic.

Yandell, Keith E. *God, Man, and Religion.* New York: McGraw-Hill, 1973. A collection of essays that deals with areas of primary concern to contemporary philosophers and theologians.

Individual Works

Collins, John. *God in Modern Philosophy.* Chicago: Regnery, 1959. A survey of many of the major issues in the philosophy of religion from a Catholic point of view.

Du No üy, Lecompte. *Human Destiny.* New York: Longmans, 1947. A version of the argument from design. Du No üy argues that the facts of biology cannot be adequately explained unless the existence of a Designer is accepted.

Hick, John. *Philosophy of Religion.* Englewood Cliffs, N.J.: Prentice-Hall, 1965. An excellent brief introduction to the philosophy of religion. The student will find this a valuable guide in organizing the issues raised by the readings in his text.

Hume, David. *Dialogues on Natural Religion,* edited by Norman Kemp Smith. Indianapolis: Bobbs, 1947. A classic discussion of the argument from design. The beginning student will find this difficult but very rewarding.

Matson, Wallace I. *The Existence of God.* Ithaca, N.Y.: Cornell U.P., 1965. An excellent, detailed analysis of the major arguments for the existence of God.

Paley, William. *Natural Theology: Selections,* edited by Frederick Ferré. Indianapolis: Bobbs, 1963. The classic statement of the argument from design.

Purtill, Richard L. *Thinking About Religion.* Englewood Cliffs, N.J.: Prentice-Hall, 1978. A clear, entertainingly written introduction to the main issues in the philosophy of religion.

Scriven, Michael. *Primary Philosophy.* New York: McGraw-Hill, 1966. Chapter Four presents an interesting and detailed defense of atheism.

Dictionary of the History of Ideas: Studies of Selected Pivotal Ideas. Philip P. Weiner, editor-in-chief. New York: Scribners, 1973. Substantial and clearly written essays emphasizing the historical development of topics discussed in this part. Designed to inform the nonspecialist, each essay concludes with a select bibliography.

Encyclopedia of Philosophy. Paul Edwards, editor-in-chief. New York: Macmillan, 1967. The beginning student will find many worthwhile articles on the subjects treated in this part, and excellent bibliographies.

Three: Morality and Society

Introduction

Just about everyone seeks to distinguish right behavior from wrong and to determine what is worthwhile in life. In our society we frequently encounter discussions about the morality of the death penalty, the decline in current moral values, and the injustice done to minority groups. Also, at times, we are faced with personal moral decisions: Should we lie to get out of an unpleasant situation? Should we fight in a war if we think it unjust? Should we cheat on our income tax if we are sure we will not get caught? It is these kinds of questions that produce philosophical speculations about the basis of morality and the good life.

Although the philosopher is concerned with the kinds of moral problems we face in daily life, he believes that his primary concern should be given to a number of very basic problems that must be answered before it is possible to give a reasoned answer to any other moral issues. *Ethics* is that branch of philosophy that is concerned with finding answers to these basic problems. Some of the problems most often discussed in the study of ethics are: Is there a basis for deciding whether any act is right? How can we prove or disprove that there is such a basis? What kinds of things are most worth attaining? When does a person deserve to be praised or blamed? In answering these kinds of questions, the philosopher does not merely give his opinion or list a variety of opinions on the subject but rather attempts to find reasons that will show that a certain answer is correct. The student, if he is to get much out of the readings, must pay close attention to reasons that are offered and attempt to decide which philosopher, if any, has proven his case.

Many students approach ethics with the belief that there is little to be gained from the investigation because they believe that moral standards or principles are merely products of the society in which one lives. They believe that the moral views of people in other societies, no matter how much they differ from one's own, are correct for the people in those societies. Such a view is called *relativism*.

Two kinds of relativism, sociological and ethical, must be distinguished and defined before the topic can be clearly discussed. *Sociological relativism* is the name given to the factual claim that societies sometimes have different ultimate principles. An ultimate principle is one that is used as a basis for defending all other moral judgments and principles. It seems evident that societies do have different moral principles regarding a variety of matters such as marriage, raising the young, and the treatment of women. The crucial point, however, is whether societies that obviously differ in their moral practices also differ on their view of the correct ultimate principle. The observed differences may not indicate differences in ultimate principles but merely the necessity of different behavior to satisfy the same principle. For example, a society with insufficient food to feed everyone might kill the elderly when they are no longer productive in order to save the young. A society with abundant means to care for the elderly would probably consider killing them abhorrent. Yet if the latter society were suddenly to find its means reduced to that of the former, it might well consider the killing of the elderly as a necessity because, like the first society, it too wants to ensure survival of the group.

The belief in sociological relativism has been of great significance because for many it justifies ethical relativism. *Ethical relativism* is the view that there are different but equally correct ultimate principles. This position is opposed to that of *ethical absolutism,* a theory that holds that there is only one correct ultimate principle or set of principles. The conflict between the ethical absolutist and relativist is of crucial importance. If the relativist is right, it would be necessary to give up the criticism of other societies, and possibly each individual's ultimate moral principles, although one still could criticize the application of these principles.

W. T. Stace presents the arguments for and against both ethical relativism and absolutism. He shows that sociological relativism, even if true, would not require a belief in ethical relativism; for the absolutist could claim that those ultimate moral principles contrary to the "true" one were merely mistaken. Further, Stace argues that the consequences of ethical relativism are unacceptable and that absolutism, despite the difficulty of establishing the correct moral principle, is preferable.

Philosophers have presented a number of theories concerning the correct ultimate moral principles. Three of the most prominent views are *egoism, utilitarianism,* and *formalism.* The main tenet of *egoism* is that self-interest is the only proper standard of conduct. Egoists deny that they ever have a moral duty to sacrifice their own interests for the interests of others. Egoists may frequently act generously or charitably, but this is only because they find such acts to be in their own long-term interests. Many egoists defend their position by claiming that everyone is motivated solely by self-interest, and, thus, it would be pointless to urge people to act in a nonegoistic manner. In "The Morality Trap," Harry Browne presents a forceful statement of the egoist position. For him, a person should always strive to produce the best consequences for himself. To achieve this result, two traps must be avoided—the morality trap and the unselfishness trap. The morality trap is the belief that there is some nonegoistic basis (such as God's will or the good of society) on which one should base moral judgments. The unselfishness trap is the belief that one's own happiness should be sacrificed for the happiness of others. If these two traps are avoided, one is on the road to self-fulfillment and personal happiness.

Utilitarianism is a moral theory that holds that right acts are acts producing the greatest happiness. In deciding which acts are right, a utilitarian considers the consequences of all the acts open to him and performs the one that would produce the best consequences for everybody concerned. Although many would agree that this is generally a proper procedure, sometimes there is dissatisfaction with some kinds of acts that might turn out to be right on this basis. For example, if it would produce the best results for all concerned, then it would be right to lie, steal, and even murder. Jeremy Bentham presents a clear statement of the utilitarian position and attempts to work out some of the details required for its implementation. He maintains that in assessing the consequences of various possible acts, we should be concerned with the amounts of pleasure and pain produced and perform only those acts resulting in the most pleasure or the least pain. Bentham believed that the only thing ultimately worthwhile in life is pleasure. Such a view that the good is pleasure is called *hedonism.* The student should realize, however, that a utilitarian need not be a hedonist. He could believe that many things besides pleasure, such as intellectual growth, beauty, and integrity, are worthwhile and that these should be considered in assessing possible actions.

Unlike egoists and utilitarians, some moral theorists maintain that the rightness or wrongness of actions is not determined by the consequences produced by the actions. Such a view is called *formalism* in ethical theory. The kinds of ultimate principles that formalists have held have varied widely. One formalist principle that has had great appeal is the golden rule, "Do unto others as you would have others do unto you." R. M. MacIver defends this rule as the only one that can bring agreement out of the conflicting moral viewpoints because it lays down a procedure to follow in determining proper behavior rather than stating final goals and values. A problem for the student in considering MacIver's view is to decide on what basis the golden rule is being defended. Is MacIver appealing to the utility of accepting it or is there some other basis of appeal?

An issue much debated at present is what obligation, if any, people in affluent countries have to the poor throughout the world. The practical significance of this issue increases steadily as the world's population outstrips food and other resources. In "Lifeboat Ethics: The Case Against Helping the Poor," Garrett Hardin argues that so long as there is no world government to institute rational control of the world's resources, each nation should protect its citizens against encroachments on their resources by others. Unbridled altruism by countries with surpluses will lead to eventual worldwide disaster. In "Famine, Affluence, and Morality," Peter Singer takes a quite different stand on helping the world's poor. He contends that, on utilitarian grounds, sacrifices are required insofar as they produce more total good than harm. Thus, people in affluent countries may be required to give up most of their luxuries to help the poor. The reader must decide whether there are reasons, other than egoistic ones, for refusing to lower our own standard of living to help the needy in other countries.

A recurring area of controversy in democratic countries concerns the relation that should exist between law and morality. Should there be laws that require people to act in the way that the majority of society thinks moral, or should the laws deal only with certain very important matters, such as the protection of rights and defense of one's person against physical harm? Should there be laws that prevent store-owners from opening on Sunday or laws against the possession of pornographic literature? Many people, perhaps a majority, think that suicide and sexual intercourse outside of marriage are immoral. Should there be laws against them?

Sir Patrick Devlin, a prominent English judge, considers this problem in the light of a recommendation by a government committee to eliminate any laws against homosexuality among consenting adults. He believes that such a change in the law would weaken public morality and thereby add to those pressures that could lead to the disintegration of the society. For him, "the suppression of vice is as much the law's business as the suppression of subversive activities." H. L. A. Hart opposes this view. Although he agrees that a stable society needs some moral cohesion, he doubts that every moral matter is of equal importance to society. Surely society will not disintegrate if some activities of which it disapproves are left open to the individual. Hart fears that Sir Patrick Devlin's approach to the problem might result in giving legal sanction to the public's moral whims no matter how irrational they may be.

Are Ethical Values Relative?

20. Ethical Relativism   W. T. Stace

Any ethical position which denies that there is a single moral standard which is equally applicable to all men at all times may fairly be called a species of ethical relativity. There is not, the relativist asserts, merely one moral law, one code, one standard. There are many moral laws, codes, standards. What morality ordains in one place or age may be quite different from what morality ordains in another place or age. The moral code of Chinamen is quite different from that of Europeans, that of African savages quite different from both. Any morality, therefore, is relative to the age, the place, and the circumstances in which it is found. It is in no sense absolute.

This does not mean merely—as one might at first sight be inclined to suppose—that the very same kind of action which is *thought* right in one country and period may be *thought* wrong in another. This would be a mere platitude, the truth of which everyone would have to admit. Even the absolutist would admit this—would even wish to emphasize it—since he is well aware that different people have different sets of moral ideas, and his whole point is that some of these sets of ideas are false. What the relativist means to assert is, not this platitude, but that the very same kind of action which *is* right in one country and period may *be* wrong in another. And this, far from being a platitude, is a very startling assertion.

It is very important to grasp thoroughly the difference between the two ideas. For there is reason to think that many minds tend to find ethical relativity attractive because they fail to keep them clearly apart. It is so very obvious that moral ideas differ from country to country and from age to age. And it is so very easy, if you are mentally lazy, to suppose that to say this means the same as to say that no universal moral standard exists,—or in other words that it implies ethical relativity. We fail to see that the word "standard" is used in two different senses. It is perfectly true that, in one sense, there are many variable moral standards. We speak of judging a man by the standard of his time. And this implies that different times have different standards. And this, of course, is quite true. But when the word "standard" is used in this sense it means simply the set of moral ideas current during the period in question. It means what people *think* right, whether as a matter of fact it *is* right or not. On the other hand when the absolutust asserts that there exists a single universal moral "standard," he is not using the word in this sense at all. He means by "standard" what *is* right as distinct from what people merely think right. His point is that although what people think right varies in different countries and periods, yet what actually is right is everywhere and always the same. And it follows that when the ethical relativist disputes the position of the absolutist and denies that any universal moral standard exists he too means by "standard" what actually is right. But it is exceedingly easy, if we are not careful, to slip loosely from using the word in the first sense to using it in the second sense; and to suppose that the variability of moral beliefs is the same thing as the variability of what really is moral. And unless we keep the two senses of the word "standard" distinct, we are likely to think the creed of ethical relativity much more plausible than it actually is.

The genuine relativist, then, does not merely mean that Chinamen may think right what Frenchmen think wrong. He means that what *is* wrong for the Frenchman may *be* right for the Chinaman. And if one enquires how, in those circumstances, one is to know what actually is right in China or in France, the answer comes quite glibly. What is right in China is the same as what people think right in China; and what is right in France is the same as what people think right in France. So that, if you want to know what is moral in any particular country or age all you have to do is to ascertain what are the moral ideas current in that age or country. Those ideas are, *for that age or country,* right. Thus what is morally right is identified with what is thought to be morally right, and the distinction which we made above between these two is simply denied. To put the same thing in another way, it is denied that there can be or ought to be any distinction between the two senses of the word "standard." There is only one kind of standard of right and wrong, namely, the moral ideas current in any particular age or country.

Moral right *means* what people think morally right. It has no other meaning. What Frenchmen think right is, therefore, right *for Frenchmen.* And evidently one must conclude—though I am not aware that relativists are anxious to draw one's attention to such unsavoury but yet absolutely necessary conclusions from their creed—that cannibalism is right for people who believe in it, that human sacrifice is right for those races which practice it, and that burning widows alive was right for Hindus until the British stepped in and compelled the Hindus to behave immorally by allowing their widows to remain alive.

When it is said that, according to the ethical relativist, what is thought right in any social group is right for that group, one must be careful not to misinterpret this. The relativist does not, of course, mean that there actually is an objective moral standard in France and a different objective standard in England, and that French and British opinions respectively give us correct information about these different standards. His point is rather that there are no objectively true moral standards at all. There is no single universal objective standard. Nor are there a variety of local objective standards. All standards are subjective. People's subjective feelings about morality are the only standards which exist.

To sum up. The ethical relativist consistently denies, it would seem, whatever the ethical absolutust asserts. For the absolutist there is a single universal moral standard. For the relativist there is no such standard. There are only local, ephemeral, and variable standards. For the absolutist there are two senses of the word "standard." Standards in the sense of sets of current moral ideas are relative and changeable. But the standard in the sense of what is actually morally right is absolute and unchanging. For the relativist no such distinction can be made. There is only one meaning of the word standard, namely, that which refers to local and variable sets of moral ideas. Or if it is insisted that the word must be allowed two meanings, then the relativist will say that there is at any rate no actual example of a standard in the absolute sense, and that the word as thus used is an empty name to which nothing in reality corresponds; so that the distinction between the two meanings becomes empty and useless. Finally—though this is merely saying the same thing in another way—the absolutist makes a distinction between what actually is right and what is thought right. The relativist rejects this distinction and identifies what is moral with what is thought by certain human beings or groups of human beings. . . .

I shall now proceed to consider, first, the main arguments which can be urged in favour of ethical relativity; and secondly, the arguments which can be urged against it. . . . The first is that which relies upon the actual varieties of moral "standards" found in the world. It was easy enough to believe in a single absolute morality in older times when there was no anthropology, when all humanity was divided clearly into two groups, Christian peoples and the "heathen." Christian peoples knew and possessed the one true morality. The rest were savages whose moral ideas could be ignored. But all this is changed. Greater knowledge has brought greater tolerance. We can no longer exalt our own morality as alone true, while dismissing all other moralities as false or inferior. The investigations of anthropologists have shown that there exist side by side in the world a bewildering variety of moral codes. On this topic endless volumes have been written, masses of evidence piled up. Anthropologists have ransacked the Melanesian Islands, the jungles of New Guinea, the steppes of Siberia, the deserts of Australia, the forests of central Africa, and have brought back with them countless examples of weird, extravagant, and fantastic "moral" customs with which to confound us. We learn that all kinds of horrible practices are, in this, that, or the other place, regarded as essential to virtue. We find that there is nothing, or next to nothing, which has always and everywhere been regarded as morally good by all men. Where then is our universal morality? Can we, in face of all this evidence, deny that it is nothing but an empty dream?

This argument, taken by itself, is a very weak one. It relies upon a single set of facts—the variable moral customs of the world. But this variability of moral ideas is admitted by both parties to the dispute, and is capable of ready explanation upon the hypothesis of either party. The relativist says that the facts are to be explained by the non-existence of any absolute moral standard. The absolutist says that they are to be explained by human ignorance of what the absolute moral standard is. And he can truly point out that men have differed widely in their opinions about all manner of topics including the subject-matters of the physical sciences—just as much as they differ about morals. And if the various different opinions which men have held about the shape of the earth do not prove that it has no one real shape, neither do the various opinions which they have held about morality prove that there is no one true morality.

Thus the facts can be explained equally plausibly on either hypothesis.

There is nothing in the facts themselves which compels us to prefer the relativistic hypothesis to that of the absolutist. And therefore the argument fails to prove the relativist conclusion. If that conclusion is to be established, it must be by means of other considerations.

This is the essential point. But I will add some supplementary remarks. The work of the anthropologists, upon which ethical relativists seem to rely so heavily, has as a matter of fact added absolutely nothing *in principle* to what has always been known about the variability of moral ideas. Educated people have known all along that the Greeks tolerated sodomy, which in modern times has been regarded in some countries as an abominable crime; that the Hindus thought it a sacred duty to burn their widows; that trickery, now thought despicable, was once believed to be a virtue; that terrible torture was thought by our own ancestors only a few centuries ago to be a justifiable weapon of justice; that it was only yesterday that western peoples came to believe that slavery is immoral. Even the ancients knew very well that moral customs and ideas vary—witness the writings of Herodotus. Thus the principle of the variability of moral ideas was well understood long before modern anthropology was ever heard of. Anthropology has added nothing to the knowledge of this principle except a mass of new and extreme examples of it drawn from very remote sources. But to multiply examples of a principle already well known and universally admitted adds nothing to the argument which is built upon that principle. The discoveries of the anthropologists have no doubt been of the highest importance in their own sphere. But in my considered opinion they have thrown no new light upon the special problems of the moral philosopher.

Although the multiplication of examples has no logical bearing on the argument, it does have an immense *psychological* effect upon people's minds. These masses of anthropological learning are impressive. They are propounded in the sacred name of "science." If they are quoted in support of ethical relativity—as they often are—people *think* that they must prove something important. They bewilder and over-awe the simple-minded, batter down their resistance, make them ready to receive humbly the doctrine of ethical relativity from those who have acquired a reputation by their immense learning and their claims to be "scientific." Perhaps this is why so much ado is made by ethical relativists regarding the anthropological evidence. But we must refuse to be impressed. We must discount all this mass of evidence about the extraordinary moral customs of remote peoples. Once we have admitted—as everyone who is instructed must have admitted these last two thousand years without any anthropology at all—the principle that moral ideas vary, all this new evidence adds nothing to the argument. And the argument itself proves nothing for the reasons already given. . . .

The second argument in favour of ethical relativity is also a very strong one. And it does not suffer from the disadvantage that it is dependent upon the acceptance of any particular philosophy such as radical empiricism. It makes its appeal to considerations of a quite general character. It consists in alleging that no one has ever been able to discover upon what foundation an absolute morality could rest, or from what source a universally binding moral code could derive its authority.

If, for example, it is an absolute and unalterable moral rule that all men ought to be unselfish, from whence does this *command* issue? For a command it certainly is, phrase it how you please. There is no difference in meaning between the sentence "You ought to be unselfish" and the sentence "Be unselfish." Now a command implies a commander. An obligation implies some authority which obliges. Who is this commander, what this authority? Thus the vastly difficult question is raised of *the basis of moral obligation*. Now the argument of the relativist would be that it is impossible to find any basis for a universally binding moral law; but that it is quite easy to discover a basis for morality if moral codes are admitted to be variable, ephemeral, and relative to time, place, and circumstance.

In this book I am assuming that it is no longer possible to solve this difficulty by saying naïvely that the universal moral law is based upon the uniform commands of God to all men. There will be many, no doubt, who will dispute this. But I am not writing for them. I am writing for those who feel the necessity of finding for morality a basis independent of particular religious dogmas. And I shall therefore make no attempt to argue the matter.

The problem which the absolutist has to face, then, is this. The religious basis of the one absolute morality having disappeared, can there be found for it any other, any secular, basis? If not, then it would seem that we cannot any longer believe in absolutism. We shall have to fall back upon belief in a variety of perhaps mutually inconsistent moral codes operating over restricted areas and limited periods. No one of these will be better, or more true, than any other. Each will be good and true for those living in those areas and periods. We shall have to fall back, in a word, on ethical relativity.

For there is no great difficulty in discovering the foundations of morality, or rather of moralities, if we adopt the relativistic hypothesis. Even if we cannot be quite certain *precisely* what these foundations are—and relativists themselves are not entirely agreed about them—we can at least see in a general way the *sort* of foundations they must have. We can see that the question on this basis is not in principle impossible of answer—although the details may be obscure; while, if we adopt the absolutist hypothesis—so the argument runs—no kind of answer is conceivable at all. . . .

This argument is undoubtedly very strong. It *is* absolutely essential to solve the problem of the basis of moral obligation if we are to believe in any kind of moral standards other than those provided by mere custom or by irrational emotions. It is idle to talk about a universal morality unless we can point to the source of its authority—or at least to do so is to indulge in a faith which is without rational ground. To cherish a blind faith in morality may be, for the average man whose business is primarily to live aright and not to theorize, sufficient. Perhaps it is his wisest course. But it will not do for the philosopher. His function, or at least one of his functions, is precisely to discover the rational grounds of our everyday beliefs—if they have any. Philosophically and intellectually, then, we cannot accept belief in a universally binding morality unless we can discover upon what foundation its obligatory character rests.

But in spite of the strength of the argument thus posed in favour of ethical relativity, it is not impregnable. For it leaves open one loop-hole. It is always possible that some theory, not yet examined, may provide a basis for a universal moral obligation. The argument rests upon the negative proposition that *there is no theory which can provide a basis for a universal morality.* But it is notoriously difficult to prove a negative. How can you prove that there are no green swans? All you can show is that none have been found so far. And then it is always possible that one will be found tomorrow. . . .

It is time that we turned our attention from the case in favour of ethical relativity to the case against it. Now the case against it consists, to a very large extent, in urging that, if taken seriously and pressed to its logical conclusion, ethical relativity can only end in destroying the conception of morality altogether, in undermining its practical efficacy, in rendering meaningless many almost universally accepted truths about human affairs, in robbing human beings of any incentive to strive for a better world, in taking the life-blood out of every ideal and every aspiration which has ever ennobled the life of man. . . .

First of all, then, ethical relativity, in asserting that the moral standards of particular social groups are the only standards which exist, renders meaningless all propositions which attempt to compare these standards with one another in respect to their moral worth. And this is a very serious matter indeed. We are accustomed to think that the moral ideas of one nation or social group may be "higher" or "lower" than those of another. We believe, for example, that Christian ethical ideals are nobler than those of the savage races of central Africa. Probably most of us would think that the Chinese moral standards are higher than those of the inhabitants of New Guinea. In short we habitually compare one civilization with another and judge the sets of ethical ideas to be found in them to be some better, some worse. The fact that such judgments are very difficult to make with any justice, and that they are frequently made on very superficial and prejudiced grounds, has no bearing on the question now at issue. The question is whether such judgments have any *meaning.* We habitually assume that they have.

But on the basis of ethical relativity they can have none whatever. For the relativist must hold that there is no *common* standard which can be applied to the various civilizations judged. Any such comparison of moral standards implies the existence of some superior standard which is applicable to both. And the existence of any such standard is precisely what the relativist denies. According to him the Christian standard is applicable only to Christians, the Chinese standard only to Chinese, the New Guinea standard only to the inhabitants of New Guinea.

What is true of comparisons between the moral standards of different races will also be true of comparisons between those of different ages. It is not unusual to ask such questions as whether the standard of our own day is superior to that which existed among our ancestors five hundred years ago. And when we remember that our ancestors employed slaves, practiced barbaric physical tortures, and burnt people alive, we may be inclined to think that it is. At any rate we assume that the question is one which has meaning and is capable of rational discussion. But if the ethical relativist is right, whatever we assert on this subject must be totally meaningless. For here again there is no common standard which could form the basis of any such judgments.

This in its turn implies that the whole notion of moral *progress* is a sheer delusion. Progress means an advance from lower to higher, from worse to better. But on the basis of ethical relativity it has no meaning to say that the standards of this age are better (or worse) than those of a previous age. For there is no common standard by which both can be measured. Thus it is nonsense to say that the morality of the New Testament is higher than that of the Old. And Jesus Christ, if he imagined that he was introducing into the world a higher ethical standard than existed before his time, was merely deluded. . . .

I come now to a second point. Up to the present I have allowed it to be taken tacitly for granted that, though judgments comparing different races and ages in respect of the worth of their moral codes are impossible for the ethical relativist, yet judgments of comparison between individuals living within the same social group would be quite possible. For individuals living within the same social group would presumably be subject to the same moral code, that of their group, and this would therefore constitute, as between these individuals, a common standard by which they could both be measured. We have not here, as we had in the other case, the difficulty of the absence of any common standard of comparison. It should therefore be possible for the ethical relativist to say quite meaningfully that President Lincoln was a better man than some criminal or moral imbecile of his own time and country, or that Jesus was a better man than Judas Iscariot.

But is even this minimum of moral judgment really possible on relativist grounds? It seems to me that it is not. For when once the whole of humanity is abandoned as the area covered by a single moral standard, what smaller areas are to be adopted as the *loci* of different standards? Where are we to draw the lines of demarcation? We can split up humanity, perhaps,—though the procedure will be very arbitrary—into races, races into nations, nations into tribes, tribes into families, families into individuals. Where are we going to draw the *moral* boundaries? Does the *locus* of a particular moral standard reside in a race, a nation, a tribe, a family, or an individual? Perhaps the blessed phrase "social group" will be dragged in to save the situation. Each such group, we shall be told, has its own moral code which is, for it, right. But what *is* a "group"? Can any one define it or give its boundaries? This is the seat of that ambiguity in the theory of ethical relativity to which reference was made on an earlier page.

The difficulty is not, as might be thought, merely an academic difficulty of logical definition. If that were all, I should not press the point. But the ambiguity has practical consequences which are disastrous for morality. No one is likely to say that moral codes are confined within the arbitrary limits of the geographical divisions of countries. Nor are the notions of race, nation, or political state likely to help us. To bring out the essentially practical character of the difficulty let us put it in the form of concrete questions. Does the American nation constitute a "group" having a single moral standard? Or does the standard of what I ought to do change continuously as I cross the continent in a railway train? Do different States of the Union have different moral codes? Perhaps every town and village has its own peculiar standard. This may at first sight seem reasonable enough. "In Rome do as Rome does" may seem as good a rule in morals as it is in etiquette. But can we stop there? Within the village are numerous cliques each having its own set of ideas. Why should not each of these claim to be bound only by its own special and peculiar moral standards? And if it comes to that, why should not the gangsters of Chicago claim to constitute a group having its own morality, so that its murders and debaucheries must be viewed as "right" by the only standard which can legitimately be applied to it? And if it be answered that the nation will not tolerate this, that may be so. But this is to put the foundation of right simply in the superior force of the majority. In that case whoever is stronger will be right, however monstrous his ideas and actions. And if we cannot deny to any set of people the right to have its own morality, is it not clear that, in the end, we cannot even deny this right to the individual? Every individual man and woman can put up, on this view, an irrefutable claim to be judged by no standard except his or her own.

If these arguments are valid, the ethical relativist cannot really maintain that there is anywhere to be found a moral standard binding upon anybody against his will. And he cannot maintain that, even within the social group, there is a common standard as between individuals. And if that is so, then even judgments to the effect that one man is morally better than another become meaningless. All moral valuation thus vanishes. There is nothing to prevent each man from being a rule unto himself. The result will be moral chaos and the collapse of all effective standards. . . .

But even if we assume that the difficulty about defining moral groups has been surmounted, a further difficulty presents itself. Suppose that we have now definitely decided what are the exact boundaries of the social group within which a moral standard is to be operative. And we will assume—as is invariably done by relativists themselves—that this group is to be some actually existing social community such as a tribe or nation. How are we to know, even then, what actually *is* the moral standard within that group? How is anyone to know? How is even a member of the group to know? For there are certain to be within the group—at least this will be true among advanced peoples—wide differences of opinion as to what is right, what wrong. Whose opinion, then, is to be taken as representing *the* moral standard of the group? Either we must take the opinion of the majority within the group, or the opinion of some minority. If we rely upon the ideas of the majority, the results will be disastrous. Wherever there is found among a people a small band of select spirits, or perhaps one man, working for the establishment of higher and nobler ideals than those commonly accepted by the group, we shall be compelled to hold that, for that people at that time, the majority are right, and that the reformers are wrong and are preaching what is immoral. We shall have to maintain, for example, that Jesus was preaching immoral doctrines to the Jews. Moral goodness will have to be equated always with the mediocre and sometimes with the definitely base and ignoble. If on the other hand we said that the moral standard of the group is to be identified with the moral opinions of some minority, then what minority is this to be? We cannot answer that it is to be the minority composed of the best and most enlightened individuals of the group. This would involve us in a palpably vicious circle. For by what standard are these individuals to be judged the best and the most enlightened? There is no principle by which we could select the right minority. And therefore we should have to consider every minority as good as every other. And this means that we should have no logical right whatever to resist the claim of the gangsters of Chicago—if such a claim were made—that their practices represent the highest standards of American morality. It means in the end that every individual is to be bound by no standard save his own.

The ethical relativists are great empiricists. *What* is the actually moral standard of any group can only be discovered, they tell us, by an examination on the ground of the moral opinions and customs of that group. But will they tell us how they propose to decide, when they get to the ground, which of the many moral opinions they are sure to find there is *the* right one in that group? To some extent they will be able to do this for the Melanesian Islanders—from whom apparently all lessons in the nature of morality are in future to be taken. But it is certain that they cannot do it for advanced peoples whose members have learnt to think for themselves and to entertain among themselves a wide variety of opinions. They cannot do it unless they accept the calamitous view that the ethical opinion of the majority is always right. We are left therefore once more with the conclusion that, even within a particular social group, anybody's moral opinion is as good as anybody else's, and that every man is entitled to be judged by his own standards.

Finally, not only is ethical relativity disastrous in its consequences for moral theory. It cannot be doubted that it must tend to be equally disastrous in its impact upon practical conduct. If men come really to believe that one moral standard is as good as another, they will conclude that their own moral standard has nothing special to recommend it. They might as well then slip down to some lower and easier standard. It is true that, for a time, it may be possible to hold one view in theory and to act practically upon another. But ideas, even philosophical ideas, are not so ineffectual that they can remain for ever idle in the upper chambers of the intellect. In the end they seep down to the level of practice. They get themselves acted on.

How Should We Behave

21. The Morality Trap   Harry Browne

Harry Browne (1933–   ) is an ardent supporter of free enterprise and the author of several books on finance and investment.

I. The Morality Trap

The Morality Trap is the belief that you must obey a moral code created by someone else.

This trap is a variation of the Identity Trap in that it leads you to try to be something other than yourself. It's an easy trap to get caught in and an easy way to lose your freedom.

Morality is a powerful word. Perhaps even more powerful is the word *immoral.* In an attempt to avoid being labeled *immoral,* many people allow themselves to be manipulated by others.

WHAT IS MORALITY?   At the same time, the concept of morality is very vague. What is it? Where does it come from? What purpose does it serve? How is it determined?

My dictionary defines *morality* as "Moral quality or character; rightness or wrongness, as of an action." Well then, let's refer to the definition of *moral,* which is: "Related to, serving to teach, or in accordance with, the principles of right and wrong."

Now we're getting somewhere; all we need is a definition of *right.* And I suppose you can guess what *that* is: "In accordance with justice, law, morality, etc."[1]

Unfortunately, this definitional merry-go-round is typical of the common understanding of morality. You should do something because it's "right"—but *by what standard?*

It seems to me that there are three different kinds of morality. I call them *personal, universal,* and *absolute.* By looking at each of them, I think we can get a clearer idea of what morality is and how it can be useful in helping you to achieve your freedom.

PERSONAL MORALITY.   We've seen that you act in ways that you hope will bring the best consequences to you. And the "best consequences" are those that bring you happiness.

[1] *Webster's New World Dictionary of the American Language,* 1966 edition: World Publishing Company, New York.

You always have to consider the consequences of your actions; they're the point of anything you do. However, any given act will undoubtedly cause *many* consequences. You may see that a particular action will produce a consequence you want, but you might also be aware that it could produce other consequences that you don't want. . . .

Since you're always seeking numerous different goals, you try to foresee the ways in which something immediately desirable might get in the way of other things that are ultimately more desirable. You try to consider more than just what's immediately in front of you. You're placing things in a broader context.

Obviously, you can't expect to foresee *all* the consequences of a given act, but you can try to see all the significant ones. In some cases, such as the bank-robbing example, there are obvious consequences that immediately rule out a proposed course of action.

In other cases, more subtle possibilities will be recognized after a few minutes' thought. But there will also be cases in which you won't be aware of the specific consequences until *after* you've acted and begun to experience them.

CODE OF CONDUCT.   Because you can't foresee all the specific consequences of what you do, there's a need to have some generalized rules available that can help keep you out of situations that could be troublesome. Those rules can be valuable if they do two things: (1) steer you away from potential disasters; and (2) remind you of the things you must do to satisfy your most important long-term desires.

The basic question is: "How can I get something I want without hurting my chances for other things that are more important to me?"

It is this generalized, long-term attitude that underlies an individual's basic code of conduct. And when we speak of morality, I can't think of any other sensible reason to be concerned about the subject. Its purpose is to keep you aimed in the direction you most want to go.

Personal morality is an attempt to consider all the relevant consequences of your actions.

"Relevant" means those consequences that will affect *you.* How your actions affect others is only important insofar as that, in turn, affects you.

A personal morality is basic to your overall view of how you'll find happiness. It's so important that a later chapter will be devoted entirely to questions that can help you form such a morality for yourself.

And it's important that you form it yourself. No one else (including me) is qualified to tell you how to live. A realistic morality has to consider many personal factors: your emotional nature, abilities, strengths, weaknesses, and, most important, your goals.

Your code of conduct has to be consistent with your goals so that you don't do anything that would make those goals unattainable. A code devised by someone else will necessarily be based upon the goals *he* believes possible and desirable.

To be useful, a morality shouldn't include rules for every possible situation. It shouldn't be concerned with minor questions involving only immediate consequences. It's devised to prevent big problems for you and to keep you aimed toward the ultimate goals that mean the most to you. Moral questions are concerned only with matters that involve large consequences.

There's a difference, for instance, between investing three dollars in a movie that might prove to be a dud and investing your life savings in a risky business venture. There's also a difference between tasting a different food that's commonly eaten (such as snails) and sampling toadstools in the forest. The first might cause a stomachache; the second could poison you.

A useful morality will prevent you from doing things that might take years to correct, while keeping you aimed in the direction of the things that are most important to you.

And since such matters are an outgrowth of your own personal values, it's obvious that no one else can create your morality for you.

A *personal morality* is the attempt to consider all the relevant consequences of your actions. This is only one of three common types of moralities, however.

UNIVERSAL MORALITY.   The second type is a morality that is meant to apply to everyone in the world. A *universal morality* is one that's supposed to bring happiness to anyone who uses it.

When you're exposed to the ideas of someone who has apparently done well with his own life, it's easy to conclude that he has all the final answers. His reasoning makes sense to you; he has results to show for his ideas. What further proof could you need to demonstrate that he knows how to live?

He probably *does* know how to live—*his* life. It would be foolish not to consider the ideas such a person offers. But it would also be foolish to expect that, as intelligent as he may be, he could have answers that apply to every life in the world.

His ideas have worked for him because he's been wise enough to develop ideas that are consistent with his own nature. He hasn't tried to live by the standards created by others; he's found his own. And that's vitally important.

You must do the same thing, too—if you want your code of conduct to work that well for you. Your rules have to consider everything that's unique about you—your emotions, your aptitudes, your weak points, your hopes and fears. . . .

A universal morality is a code of conduct that is presumed to bring happiness to anyone who uses it. I don't believe there can be such a thing. The differences between individuals are far too great to allow for anything but the most general kinds of rules.

ABSOLUTE MORALITY.   There's a third kind of morality. The first two are attempts to help you achieve happiness—one self-directed and the other coming from someone else. The third type is the opposite of this. An *absolute morality* is a set of rules to which an individual is expected to *surrender* his own happiness.

There are two main characteristics of an absolute morality:

1. It presumably comes from *an authority outside of the individual.* It comes from someone or somewhere more important than the individual himself.

2. It proposes that the individual should be "moral" *regardless of the consequences to himself.* In other words, doing what is "right" is more important than one's own happiness.

These two characteristics intertwine, so we'll consider them together.

Absolute morality is the most common type of morality, and it can be pretty intimidating. You can be made to appear "selfish," "whim-worshipping," "egotistic," "hedonistic," or "ruthless," if you merely assert that your own happiness is the most important thing in your life.

But what could be more important than your happiness? It's said that an authoritarian moral code is necessary to protect society. But who is society? Isn't it just a large group of people, each of whom have differing ideas concerning how one should live?

And if an individual is required to give up his own happiness, of what value is society to him?

It's also suggested that God commanded that we live by certain rules. But who can be sure he knows exactly when and how and what God said and what he meant? And even if that could be established once and for all, what would be the consequences to the individual if he acted otherwise? How do we know?

And if the code did come from God, it still had to be handled by human beings on its way to you. Whatever the absolute morality may be, you're relying upon someone else to vouch for its authority.

Suppose you use a holy book as your guide. I haven't yet seen one that doesn't have some apparent contradictions regarding conduct in it. Those contradictions may disappear with the proper interpretation; but who provides the interpretation? You'll do it yourself or you'll select someone to provide it for you. In either case, *you* have become the authority by making the choice.

There's no way someone else can become your authority; ultimately the decision will be yours in choosing the morality you'll live by—even if you choose to cite someone else (you've chosen) as the authority for your acts.

And there's no way you can ignore the consequences to yourself; a human being naturally acts in terms of consequences.

What happens, however, is that other people introduce consequences that they hope will influence you. They say that your "immoral" acts will: "prevent you from going to heaven"—or "cause other people to disapprove of you"—or "destroy society and cause chaos, and it will all be your fault."

Once again, however, it will be *you* deciding for yourself whether any of these consequences will result and whether any of them are important to you.

The absolute morality fails on its two important characteristics. Even if you choose to believe there's a higher authority, you are the authority who chooses what it is and what it is telling you to do. And since you'll always be considering consequences, even if you try to fix it so that you aren't, it's important to deliberately recognize the consequences and decide which ones are important to you. . . .

THE TRAP.   The Morality Trap is the belief that you must obey a moral code created by someone else. If you're acting in ways you hope will satisfy someone else's concept of what is moral, chances are you're using an ill-suited code of conduct—one that won't lead you to what you want and that may trap you in commitments and complications that can only cause you unhappiness. So in terms of the trap, *what* you do isn't as significant as *why* you do it.

You're in the trap if you hand a very important dollar to a beggar because "it's wrong to be selfish." Or if you continue to deal respectfully with someone who's made trouble for you because "to forgive is divine."

You're in the trap if you allow yourself to be drafted because "you have a duty to your country." Or if you prohibit drinking in your home because "it would weaken the moral fiber of society." Or if you send your children to Sunday school even though you aren't religious, because "you should give them a moral upbringing."

You might have very good reasons for any of these actions. But if you do them *only* in obedience to moral clichés, you're in the Morality Trap. . . .

YOUR MORALITY.   You are responsible for what happens to you (even if someone else offers to accept that responsibility), because you're the one who'll experience the consequences of your acts.

You are the one who decides what is right and what is wrong—no matter what meaning others may attach to those words. You don't have to obey blindly the dictates that you grew up with or that you hear around you now. Everything can be challenged, *should* be challenged, examined to determine it's relevance to you and what you want.

As you examine the teachings of others, you may find that some of it is very appropriate to you, but much of it may be meaningless or even harmful. The important thing is to carefully reappraise any moral precept that has been guiding your actions.

As you examine each of the rules you've been living by, ask yourself:

—Is this rule something that *others* have devised on behalf of "society" to restrain individuals? Or have *I* devised it in order to make my life better for myself?

—Am I acting by an old, just-happens-to-be-there morality? Or is it something I've personally determined from the knowledge of who I am and what I want?

—Are the rewards and punishments attached to the rules vague and intangible? Or do the rules point to specific happiness I can achieve or unhappiness I can avoid?

—Is it a morality I've accepted because "someone undoubtedly knows the reason for it"? Or is it one I've created because *I* know the reason for it?

—Is it a morality that's currently "in style" and accepted by all those around me? Or is it a morality specifically tailored to *my* style?

—Is it a morality that's aimed *at* me and *against* my self-interest? Or is it a morality that's *for* me and comes *from* me?

All the answers must come from you—not from a book or a lecture or a sermon. To assume that someone once wrote down the final answers for your morality is to assume that the writer stopped growing the day he wrote the code. Don't treat him unfairly by thinking that he couldn't have discovered more and increased his own understanding after he'd written the code. And don't forget that what he wrote was based upon what *he* saw.

No matter how you approach the matter, *you* are the sovereign authority who makes the final decisions. The more you realize that, the more your decisions will fit realistically with your own life. . . .

II. The Unselfishness Trap

The Unselfishness Trap is the belief that you must put the happiness of others ahead of your own.

Unselfishness is a very popular ideal, one that's been honored throughout recorded history. Wherever you turn, you find encouragement to put the happiness of others ahead of your own—to do what's best for the world, not for yourself.

If the ideal is sound, there must be something unworthy in seeking to live your life as you want to live it.

So perhaps we should look more closely at the subject—to see if the ideal *is* sound. For if you attempt to be free, we can assume that someone's going to consider that to be selfish.

We saw in Chapter 2 that each person always acts in ways he believes will make him feel good or will remove discomfort from his life. Because everyone is different from everyone else, each individual goes about it in his own way.

One man devotes his life to helping the poor. Another one lies and steals. Still another person tries to create better products and services for which he hopes to be paid handsomely. One woman devotes herself to her husband and children. Another one seeks a career as a singer.

In every case, the ultimate motivation has been the same. Each person is doing what *he* believes will assure his happiness. What varies between them is the *means* each has chosen to gain his happiness.

We could divide them into two groups labeled "selfish" and "unselfish," but I don't think that would prove anything. For the thief and the humanitarian each have the same motive—to do what he believes will make him feel good.

In fact, we can't avoid a very significant conclusion: *Everyone is selfish.* Selfishness isn't really an issue, because everyone selfishly seeks his own happiness.

What we need to examine, however, are the means various people choose to achieve their happiness. Unfortunately, some people oversimplify the matter by assuming that there are only two basic means: sacrifice yourself for others or make them sacrifice for you. Happily, there's a third way that can produce better consequences than either of those two.

A BETTER WORLD?   Let's look first at the ideal of living for the benefit of others. It's often said that it would be a better world if everyone were unselfish. But would it be?

If it were somehow possible for everyone to give up his own happiness, what would be the result? Let's carry it to its logical conclusion and see what we find.

To visualize it, let's imagine that happiness is symbolized by a big red rubber ball. I have the ball in my hands—meaning that I hold the ability to be happy. But since I'm not going to be selfish, I quickly pass the ball to you. I've given up my happiness for you.

What will you do? Since you're not selfish either, you won't keep the ball; you'll quickly pass it on to your next-door neighbor. But he doesn't want to be selfish either, so he passes it to his wife, who likewise gives it to her children.

The children have been taught the virtue of unselfishness, so they pass it to playmates, who pass it to parents, who pass it to neighbors, and on and on and on.

I think we can stop the analogy at this point and ask what's been accomplished by all this effort. Who's better off for these demonstrations of pure unselfishness?

How would it be a better world if everyone acted that way? Whom would we be unselfish for? There would have to be a selfish person who would receive, accept, and enjoy the benefits of our unselfishness for there to be any purpose to it. But that selfish person (the object of our generosity) would be living by lower standards than we do.

For a more practical example, what is achieved by the parent who "sacrifices" himself for his children, who in turn are expected to sacrifice themselves for *their* children, etc.? The unselfishness concept is a merry-go-round that has no ultimate purpose. No one's self-interest is enhanced by the continual relaying of gifts from one person to another to another.

Perhaps most people have never carried the concept of unselfishness to this logical conclusion. If they did, they might reconsider their pleas for an unselfish world.

NEGATIVE CHOICES.   But, unfortunately, the pleas continue, and they're a very real part of your life. In seeking your own freedom and happiness, you have to deal with those who tell you that you shouldn't put yourself first. That creates a situation in which you're pressured to act negatively—to put aside your plans and desires in order to avoid the condemnation of others.

As I've said before, one of the characteristics of a free man is that he's usually choosing positively—deciding which of several alternatives would make him the happiest; while the average person, most of the time, is choosing which of two or three alternatives will cause him the least discomfort.

When the reason for your actions is to avoid being called "selfish" you're making a negative decision and thereby restricting the possibilities for your own happiness.

You're in the Unselfishness Trap if you regretfully pay for your aunt's surgery with the money you'd saved for a new car, or if you sadly give up the vacation you'd looked forward to in order to help a sick neighbor.

You're in the trap if you feel you're *required* to give part of your income to the poor, or if you think that your country, community, or family has first claim on your time, energy, or money.

You're in the Unselfishness Trap any time you make negative choices that are designed to avoid being called "selfish."

It isn't that no one else is important. You might have a self-interest in someone's well-being, and giving a gift can be a gratifying expression of the affection you feel for him. But you're in the trap if you do such things in order to appear unselfish.

HELPING OTHERS.   There *is* an understandable urge to give to those who are important and close to you. However, that leads many people to think that indiscriminate giving is the key to one's own happiness. They say that the way to be happy is to make others happy; get your glow by basking in the glow you've created for someone else.

It's important to identify that as a personal opinion. If someone says that giving is the key to happiness, isn't he saying that's the key to *his* happiness?

I think we can carry the question further, however, and determine how efficient such a policy might be. The suggestion to be a giver presupposes that you're able to judge what will make someone else happy. And experience has taught me to be a bit humble about assuming what makes others happy.

My landlady once brought me a piece of her freshly baked cake because she wanted to do me a favor. Unfortunately, it happened to be a kind of cake that was distasteful to me. I won't try to describe the various ways I tried to get the cake plate back to her without being confronted with a request for my judgment of her cake. It's sufficient to say that her well-intentioned favor interfered with my own plans.

And now, whenever I'm sure I know what someone else "needs," I remember that incident and back off a little. There's no way that one person can read the mind of another to know all his plans, goals, and tastes.

You may know a great deal about the desires of your intimate friends. But *indiscriminate* gift-giving and favor-doing is usually a waste of resources—or, worse, it can upset the well-laid plans of the receiver.

When you give to someone else, you might provide something he values—but probably not the think he considers most important. If you expend those resources for *yourself,* you automatically devote them to what you consider to be most important. The time or money you've spent will most likely create more happiness that way.

If your purpose is to make someone happy, you're more apt to succeed if you make yourself the object. You'll never know another person more than a fraction as well as you can know yourself.

Do you want to make someone happy? Go to it—use your talents and your insight and benevolence to bestow riches of happiness upon the one person you understand well enough to do it efficiently—yourself. I guarantee that you'll get more genuine appreciation from yourself than from anyone else.

Give to you.

Support your local self.

ALTERNATIVES. As I indicated earlier in this chapter, it's too often assumed that there are only two alternatives: (1) sacrifice your interests for the benefit of others; or (2) make others sacrifice their interests for you. If nothing else were possible, it would indeed be a grim world.

Fortunately, there's more to the world than that. Because desires vary from person to person, it's possible to create exchanges between individuals in which both parties benefit.

For example, if you buy a house, you do so because you'd rather have the house than the money involved. But the seller's desire is different— he'd rather have the money than the house. When the sale is completed, each of you has received something of greater value than what you gave up—otherwise you wouldn't have entered the exchange. Who, then, has had to sacrifice for the other?

In the same way, your daily life is made up of dozens of such exchanges—small and large transactions in which each party gets something he values more than what he gives up. The exchange doesn't have to involve money; you may be spending time, attention, or effort in exchange for something you value.

Mutually beneficial relationships are possible when desires are compatible. Sometimes the desires are the same—like going to a movie together. Sometimes the desires are different—like trading your money for someone's house. In either case, it's the *compatibility* of the desires that makes the exchange possible.

No sacrifice is necessary when desires are compatible. So it makes sense to seek out people with whom you can have mutually beneficial relationships.

Often the "unselfishness" issue arises only because two people with nothing in common are trying to get along together—such as a man who likes bowling and hates opera married to a woman whose tastes are the opposite. If they're to do things together, one must "sacrifice" his pleasure for the other. So each might try to encourage the other to be "unselfish."

If they were compatible, the issue wouldn't arise because each would be pleasing the other by doing what was in his own self-interest.

An efficiently selfish person *is* sensitive to the needs and desires of others. But he doesn't consider those desires to be demands upon him. Rather, he sees them as *opportunities*—potential exchanges that might be beneficial to him. He identifies desires in others so that he can decide if exchanges with them will help him get what he wants.

He doesn't sacrifice himself for others, nor does he expect others to be sacrificed for him. He takes the third alternative—he finds relationships that are mutually beneficial so that no sacrifice is required.

PLEASE YOURSELF. Everyone is selfish; everyone is doing what he believes will make himself happier. The recognition of that can take most of the sting out of accusations that you're being "selfish." Why should you feel guilty for seeking your own happiness when that's what everyone else is doing, too?

The demand that you be unselfish can be motivated by any number of reasons: that you'd help create a better world, that you have a moral obligation to be unselfish, that you give up your happiness to the selfishness of someone else, or that the person demanding it has just never thought it out.

Whatever the reason, you're not likely to convince such a person to stop his demands. But it will create much less pressure on you if you realize that it's *his* selfish reason. And you can eliminate the problem entirely by looking for more compatible companions.

To find constant, profound happiness requires that you be free to seek the gratification of your own desires. It means making positive choices.

If you slip into the Unselfishness Trap, you'll spend a good part of your time making negative choices—trying to avoid the censure of those who tell you not to think of yourself. You won't have time to be free.

If someone finds happiness by doing "good works" for others, let him. That doesn't mean that's the best way for you to find happiness.

And when someone accuses you of being selfish, just remember that he's only upset because you aren't doing what *he* selfishly wants you to do.

22. Utilitarianism   Jeremy Bentham

Jeremy Bentham (1748–1832), the English philosopher and political theorist, developed the utilitarian theory as a basis for political and legal reform.

Of the Principle of Utility

I. Nature has placed mankind under the governance of two sovereign masters, *pain* and *pleasure*. It is for them alone to point out what we ought to do, as well as to determine what we shall do. On the one hand the standard of right and wrong, on the other the chain of causes and effects, are fastened to their throne. They govern us in all we do, in all we say, in all we think: every effort we can make to throw off our subjection, will serve but to demonstrate and confirm it. In words a man may pretend to abjure their empire: but in reality he will remain subject to it all the while. The *principle of utility* recognises this subjection, and assumes it for the foundation of that system, the object of which is to rear the fabric of felicity by the hands of reason and of law. Systems which attempt to question it, deal in sounds instead of sense, in caprice instead of reason, in darkness instead of light.

From *An Introduction to the Principles of Morals and Legislation* by Jeremy Bentham. Reprinted by permission of the Clarendon Press, Oxford.

But enough of metaphor and declamation: it is not by such means that moral science is to be improved.

II. The principle of utility is the foundation of the present work: it will be proper therefore at the outset to give an explicit and determinate account of what is meant by it. By the principle of utility is meant that principle which approves or disapproves of every action whatsoever, according to the tendency which it appears to have to augment or diminish the happiness of the party whose interest is in question: or, what is the same thing in other words, to promote or to oppose that happiness. I say of every action whatsoever; and therefore not only of every action of a private individual, but of every measure of government.

III. By utility is meant that property in any object, whereby it tends to produce benefit, advantage, pleasure, good, or happiness (all this in the present case comes to the same thing) or (what comes again to the same thing) to prevent the happening of mischief, pain, evil, or unhappiness to the party whose interest is considered: if that party be the community in general, then the happiness of the community: if a particular individual, then the happiness of that individual.

IV. The interest of the community is one of the most general expressions that can occur in the phraseology of morals: no wonder that the meaning of it is often lost. When it has a meaning, it is this. The community is a fictitious *body*, composed of the individual persons who are considered as constituting as it were its *members*. The interest of the community then is, what?—the sum of the interests of the several members who compose it.

V. It is in vain to talk of the interest of the community, without understanding what is the interest of the individual. A thing is said to promote the interest, or to be *for* the interest, of an individual, when it tends to add to the sum total of his pleasures: or, what comes to the same thing, to diminish the sum total of his pains.

VI. An action then may be said to be comformable to the principle of utility, or, for shortness sake, to utility (meaning with respect to the community at large), when the tendency it has to augment the happiness of the community is greater than any it has to diminish it.

VII. A measure of government (which is but a particular kind of action, performed by a particular person or persons) may be said to be conformable to or dictated by the principle of utility, when in like manner the tendency which it has to augment the happiness of the community is greater than any which it has to diminish it.

VIII. When an action, or in particular a measure of government, is supposed by a man to be conformable to the principle of utility, it may be convenient, for the purposes of discourse, to imagine a kind of law or dictate, called a law or dictate of utility: and to speak of the action in question, as being conformable to such law or dictate.

IX. A man may be said to be a partisan of the principle of utility, when the approbation or disapprobation he annexes to any action, or to any measure, is determined by and proportioned to the tendency which he conceives it to have to augment or to diminish the happiness of the community: or in other words, to its conformity or unconformity to the laws or dictates of utility.

X. Of an action that is conformable to the principle of utility one may always say either that it is one that ought to be done, or at least that it is not one that ought not to be done. One may say also, that it is right it should be done; at least that it is not wrong it should be done: that it is a right action; at least that it is not a wrong action. When thus interpreted, the words *ought,* and *right* and *wrong,* and others of that stamp, have a meaning: when otherwise, they have none.

XI. Has the rectitude of this principle been ever formally contested? It should seem that it had, by those who have not known what they have been meaning. Is it susceptible of any direct proof? it should seem not: for that which is used to prove everything else, cannot itself be proved: a chain of proofs must have their commencement somewhere. To give such proof is as impossible as it is needless.

XII. Not that there is or ever has been that human creature breathing, however stupid or perverse, who has not on many, perhaps on most occasions of his life, deferred to it. By the natural constitution of the human frame, on most occasions of their lives men in general embrace this principle, without thinking of it: if not for the ordering of their own actions, yet for the trying of their own actions, as well as of those of other men. There have been, at the same time, not many, perhaps, even of the most intelligent, who have been disposed to embrace it purely and without reserve. There are even few who have not taken some occasion or other to quarrel with it, either on account of their not understanding always how to apply it, or on account of some prejudice or other which they were afraid to examine into, or could not bear to part with. For such is the stuff that man is made of: in principle and in practice, in a right track and in a wrong one, the rarest of all human qualities is consistency.

XIII. When a man attempts to combat the principle of utility, it is with reasons drawn, without his being aware of it, from that very principle itself. His arguments, if they prove any thing, prove not that the principle is *wrong,* but that, according to the applications he supposes to be made of it, it is *misapplied.* Is it possible for a man to move the earth? Yes, but he must first find out another earth to stand upon.

Of Principles Adverse to That of Utility

I. If the principle of utility be a right principle to be governed by, and that in all cases, it follows from what has been just observed, that whatever principle differs from it in any case must necessarily be a wrong one. To prove any other principle, therefore, to be a wrong one, there needs no more than just to show it to be what it is, a principle of which the dictates are in some point or other different from those of the principle of utility: to state it is to confute it.

II. A principle may be different from that of utility in two ways: 1. By being constantly opposed to it: this is the case with a principle which may be termed the principle of *asceticism.* 2. By being sometimes opposed to it, and sometimes not, as it may happen: this is the case with another, which may be termed the principle of *sympathy* and *antipathy.*

III. By the principle of asceticism I mean that principle, which, like the principle of utility, approves or disapproves of any action, according to the tendency which it appears to have to augment or diminish the happiness of the party whose interest is in question; but in an inverse manner: approving of actions in as far as they tend to diminish his happiness; disapproving of them in as far as they tend to augment it.

IV. It is evident that any one who reprobates any the least particle of pleasure, as such, from whatever source derived, is *pro tanto* a partisan of the principle of asceticism. It is only upon that principle, and not from the principle of utility, that the most abominable pleasure which the vilest of malefactors ever reaped from his crime would be to be reprobated, if it stood alone. The case is, that it never does stand alone; but is necessarily followed by such a quality of pain (or, what comes to the same thing, such a chance for a certain quantity of pain) that the pleasure in comparison of it, is as nothing: and this is the true and sole, but perfectly sufficient, reason for making it a ground for punishment. . . .

X. The principle of utility is capable of being consistently pursued; and it is but tautology to say, that the more consistently it is pursued, the better it must ever be for humankind. The principle of asceticism never was, nor ever can be, consistently pursued by any living creature. Let but one tenth part of the inhabitants of this earth pursue it consistently, and in a day's time they will have turned it into a hell.

XI. Among principles adverse to that of utility, that which at this day seems to have most influence in matters of government, is what may be called the principle of sympathy and antipathy. By the principle of sympathy and antipathy, I mean that principle which approves or disapproves of certain actions, not on account of their tending to augment the happiness, nor yet on account of their tending to diminish the happiness of the party whose interest is in question, but merely because a man finds himself disposed to approve or disapprove of them: holding up that approbation or disapprobation as a sufficient reason for itself, and disclaiming the necessity of looking out for any extrinsic ground. Thus far in the general department of morals: and in the particular department of politics, measuring out the quantum (as well as determining the ground) of punishment, by the degree of the disapprobation.

XII. It is manifest, that this is rather a principle in name than in reality: it is not a positive principle of itself, so much as a term employed to signify the negation of all principle. What one expects to find in a principle is something that points out some external consideration, as a means of warranting and guiding the internal sentiments of approbation and disapprobation: this expectation is but ill fulfilled by a proposition, which does neither more nor less than hold up each of those sentiments as a ground and standard for itself.

XIII. In looking over the catalogue of human actions (says a partisan of this principle) in order to determine which of them are to be marked with the seal of disapprobation, you need but to take counsel of your own feelings: whatever you find in yourself a propensity to condemn, is wrong for that very reason. For the same reason it is also meet for punishment: in what proportion it is adverse to utility, or whether it be adverse to utility at all, is a matter that makes no difference. In that same *proportion* also is it meet for punishment: if you hate much, punish much: if you hate little, punish little: punish as you hate. If you hate not at all, punish not at all: the fine feelings of the soul are not to be overborne and tyrannized by the harsh and rugged dictates of political utility. . . .

XI. It is manifest, that the dictates of this principle will frequently coincide with those of utility, though perhaps without intending any such thing. Probably more frequently than not: and hence it is that the business of penal justice is carried on upon that tolerable sort of footing upon which we see it carried on in common at this day. For what more natural or more general ground of hatred to a practice can there be, than the mischievousness of such practice? What all men are exposed to suffer by, all men will be disposed to hate. It is far yet, however, from being a constant ground: for when a man suffers, it is not always that he knows what it is he suffers by. A man may suffer grievously, for instance, by a new tax, without being able to trace up the cause of his sufferings to the injustice of some neighbour, who has eluded the payment of an old one.

XVI. The principle of sympathy and antipathy is most apt to err on the side of severity. It is for applying punishment in many cases which deserve none: in many cases which deserve some, it is for applying more than they deserve. There is no incident imaginable, be it ever so trivial, and so remote from mischief, from which this principle may not extract a ground of punishment. Any difference in taste: any difference in opinion: upon one subject as well as upon another. No disagreement so trifling which perseverance and altercation will not render serious. Each becomes in the other's eyes an enemy, and, if laws permit, a criminal. This is one of the circumstances by which the human race is distinguished (not much indeed to its advantage) from the brute creation. . . .

XIX. There are two things which are very apt to be confounded, but which it imports us carefully to distinguish:—the motive or cause, which, by operating on the mind of an individual, is productive of any act: and the ground or reason which warrants a legislator, or other bystander, in regarding that act with an eye of approbation. When the act happens, in the particular instance in question, to be productive of effects which we approve of, much more if we happen to observe that the same motive may frequently be productive, in other instances, of the like effects, we are apt to transfer our approbation to the motive itself, and to assume, as the just ground for the approbation we bestow on the act, the circumstance of its originating from that motive. It is in this way that the sentiment of antipathy has often been considered as a just ground of action. Antipathy, for instance, in such or such a case, is the cause of an action which is attended with good effects: but this does not make it a right ground of action in that case, any more than in any other. Still farther. Not only the effects are good, but the agent sees beforehand that they will be so. This may make the action indeed a perfectly right action: but it does not make antipathy a right ground of action. For the same sentiment of antipathy, if implicitly deferred to, may be, and very frequently is, productive of the very worst effects. Antipathy, therefore, can never be a right ground of action. No more, therefore, can resentment, which, as will be seen more particularly hereafter, is but a modification of antipathy. The only right ground of action, that can possibly subsist, is, after all, the consideration of utility, which, if it is a right principle of action, and of approbation, in any one case, is so in every other. Other principles in abundance, that is, other motives, may be the reasons why such and such an act *has* been done: that is, the reasons or causes of its being done: but it is this alone that can be the reason why it might or ought to have been done. Antipathy or resentment requires always to be regulated, to prevent its doing mischief: to be regulated by what? always by the principle of utility. The principle of utility neither requires nor admits of any other regulator than itself.

Value of a Lot of Pleasure or Pain, How to Be Measured

I. Pleasures then, and the avoidance of pains, are the *ends* which the legislator has in view: it behooves him therefore to understand their *value*. Pleasures and pains are the *instruments* he has to work with: it behooves him therefore to understand their force, which is again, in other words, their value.

II. To a person considered *by himself*, the value of a pleasure or pain considered *by itself*, will be greater or less, according to the four following circumstances:

1. Its *intensity*.
2. Its *duration*.
3. Its *certainty* or *uncertainty*.
4. Its *propinquity* or *remoteness*.

III. These are the circumstances which are to be considered in estimating a pleasure or a pain considered each of them by itself. But when the value of any pleasure or pain is considered for the purpose of estimating the tendency of any *act* by which it is produced, there are two other circumstances to be taken into the account; these are,

5. Its *fecundity*, or the chance it has of being followed by sensations of the *same* kind: that is, pleasures, if it be a pleasure: pains, if it be a pain.
6. Its *purity*, or the chance it has of *not* being followed by sensations of the *opposite* kind: that is, pains, if it be a pleasure: pleasures, if it be a pain.

These two last, however, are in strictness scarcely to be deemed properties of the pleasure or the pain itself; they are not, therefore, in strictness to be taken into the account of the value of that pleasure or that pain. They are in strictness to be deemed properties only of the act, or other event, by which such pleasure or pain has been produced; and accordingly are only to be taken into the account of the tendency of such act or such event.

IV. To a *number* of persons, with reference to each of whom the value of a pleasure or a pain is considered, it will be greater or less, according to seven circumstances: to wit, the six preceding ones; *viz.*

1. Its *intensity*.
2. Its *duration*.
3. Its *certainty* or *uncertainty*.
4. Its *propinquity* or *remoteness*.

5. Its *fecundity.*
6. Its *purity.*

And one other; to wit:

7. Its *extent,* that is, the number of persons to whom it *extends;* or (in other words) who are affected by it.

V. To take an exact account then of the general tendency of any act, by which the interests of a community are affected, proceed as follows. Begin with any one person of those whose interests seem most immediately to be affected by it: and take an account.

1. Of the value of each distinguishable *pleasure* which appears to be produced by it in the *first* instance.

2. Of the value of each *pain* which appears to be produced by it in the *first* instance.

3. Of the value of each pleasure which appears to be produced by it *after* the first. This constitutes the *fecundity* of the first *pleasure* and the *impurity* of the first *pain.*

4. Of the value of each *pain* which appears to be produced by it after the first. This constitutes the *fecundity* of the first *pain,* and the *impurity* of the first pleasure.

5. Sum up all the values of all the *pleasures* on the one side, and those of all the pains on the other. The balance, if it be on the side of pleasure, will give the *good* tendency of the act upon the whole, with respect to the interests of that *individual* person: if on the side of pain, the *bad* tendency of it upon the whole.

6. Take an account of the *number* of persons whose interests appear to be concerned; and repeat the above process with respect to each. *Sum up* the numbers expressive of the degrees of *good* tendency, which the act has, with respect to each individual, in regard to whom the tendency of it is *good* upon the whole: do this again with respect to each individual, in regard to whom the tendency of it is *good* upon the whole: do this again with respect to each individual, in regard to whom the tendency of it is *bad* upon the whole. Take the *balance;* which, if on the side of *pleasure,* will give the general *good tendency* of the act, with respect to the total number or community of individuals concerned; if on the side of pain, the general *evil tendency,* with respect to the same community.

VI. It is not to be expected that this process should be strictly pursued previously to every moral judgment, or to every legislative or judicial operation. It may, however, be always kept in view: and as near as the process actually pursued on these occasions approaches to it, so near will such process approach to the character of an exact one.

VII. The same process is alike applicable to pleasure and pain, in whatever shape they appear: and by whatever denomination they are distinguished: to pleasure, whether it be called *good* (which is properly the cause or instrument of pleasure) or *profit* (which is distant pleasure, or the cause or instrument of distant pleasure), or *convenience,* or *advantage, benefit, emolument, happiness,* and so forth: to pain, whether it be called *evil* (which corresponds to *good*), or *mischief,* or *inconvenience,* or *disadvantage,* or *loss,* or *unhappiness,* and so forth.

VIII. Nor is this a novel and unwarranted, any more than it is a useless theory. In all this there is nothing but what the practice of mankind, wheresoever they have a clear view of their own interest, is perfectly conformable to. An article of property, an estate in land, for instance, is valuable, on what account? On account of the pleasures of all kinds which it enables a man to produce, and what comes to the same thing the pains of all kinds which it enables him to avert. But the value of such an article of property is universally understood to rise or fall according to the length or shortness of the time which a man has in it: the certainty or uncertainty of its coming into possession: and the nearness or remoteness of the time at which, if at all, it is to come into possession. As to the *intensity* of the pleasures which a man may derive from it, this is never thought of, because it depends upon the use which each particular person may come to make of it; which cannot be estimated till the particular pleasures he may come to derive from it, or the particular pains he may come to exclude by means of it, are brought to view. For the same reason, neither does he think of the *fecundity* or *purity* of those pleasures.

Thus much for pleasure and pain, happiness and unhappiness, in *general*.

23. The Deep Beauty of the Golden Rule   R. M. MacIver

Robert M. MacIver (1882–   ) is a prominent sociologist and political theorist who has a strong interest in a number of philosophical issues.

The subject that learned men call ethics is a wasteland on the philosophical map. Thousands of books have been written on this matter, learned books and popular books, books that argue and books that exhort. Most of them are empty and nearly all are vain. Some claim that pleasure is *the* good; some prefer the elusive and more enticing name of happiness; others reject such principles and speak of equally elusive goals such as self-fulfillment. Others claim that *the* good is to be found in looking away from the self, in devotion to the whole—which whole? in the service of God—whose God?—even in the service of the State—who prescribes the service? Here indeed, if anywhere, after listening to the many words of many apostles, one goes out by the same door as one went in.

The reason is simple. You say: "This is the way you should behave." But I say: "No, that is not the way." You say: "This is right." But I say: "No, that is wrong, and this is right." You appeal to experience. I appeal to experience against you. You appeal to authority: it is not mine. What is left? If you are strong, you can punish me for behaving my way. But does that prove anything except that you are stronger than I? Does it prove the absurd dogma that might makes right? Is the slavemaster right because he owns the whip, or Torquemada because he can send his heretics to the flames?

From this impasse no system of ethical rules has been able to deliver itself. How can ethics lay down final principles of behavior that are not your values against mine, your group's values against my group's?

Which, by the way, does not mean that your rules are any less valid for you because they are not valid for me. Only a person of shallow nature and autocratic leanings would draw that conclusion. For the sake of your integrity you must hold to your own values, no matter how much others reject them. Without *your* values you are nothing. True, you should search them and test them and learn by *your* experience and gain wisdom where you can. Your values are your guides through life but you need to use your own eyes. If I have different guides I shall go another way. So far as we diverge, values are relative as between you and me. But your values cannot be relative for you or mine for me.

That is not here the issue. It is that the relativity of values between you and me, between your group and my group, your sect and my sect, makes futile nearly all learned disquisitions about the first principles of ethics.

By ethics I mean the philosophy of how men should behave in their relations to one another. I am talking about philosophy, not about religion. When you have a creed, you can derive from it principles of ethics. Philosophy cannot begin with a creed, but only with reasoning about the nature of things. It cannot therefore presume that the values of other men are less to be regarded than the values of the proponent. If it does, it is not philosophy but dogma, dogma that is the enemy of philosophy, the kind of dogma that has been the source of endless tyranny and repression.

Can it be a philosophy worth the name that makes a universal of your values and thus rules mine out of existence, where they differ from yours?

How can reasoning decide between my values and yours? Values do not claim truth in any scientific sense; instead they claim validity, rightness. They do not declare what is so but what *should* be so. I cling to my values, you to yours. Your values, some of them, do not hold for me; some of them may be repulsive to me; some of them may threaten me. What then? To what court of reason shall we appeal? To what court that you and I both accept is there any appeal?

The lack of any court is the final *fact* about final values. It is a fundamental fact. It is a terrifying fact. It is also a strangely challenging fact. It gives man his lonely autonomy, his true responsibility. If he has anything that partakes of the quality of a God it comes from this fact. Man has more than the choice to obey or disobey. If he accepts authority he also chooses the authority he accepts. He is responsible not only to others but, more deeply, to himself.

Does all this mean that a universal ethical principle, applicable alike to me and you, even where our values diverge, is impossible? That there is no rule to go by, based on reason itself, in this world of irreconcilable valuations?

There is no rule that can prescribe both my values and yours or decide between them. There is one universal rule, and one only, that can be laid down, on ethical grounds—that is, apart from the creeds of particular religions and apart from the ways of the tribe that falsely and arrogantly universalize themselves.

Do to others as you would have others do to you. This is the only rule that stands by itself in the light of its own reason, the only rule that can stand by itself in the naked, warring universe, in the face of the contending values of men and groups.

What makes it so? Let us first observe that the universal herein laid down is one of procedure. It prescribes a mode of behaving, not a goal of action. On the level of goals, of *final* values, there is irreconcilable conflict. One rule prescribes humility, another pride; one prescribes abstinence, another commends the flesh-pots; and so forth through endless variations. All of us wish that *our* principle could be universal; most of us believe that it *should* be, that our *ought* ought to be all men's *ought*, but since we differ there can be, on this level, no possible agreement.

When we want to make our ethical principle prevail we try to persuade others, to "convert" them. Some may freely respond, if their deeper values are near enough to ours. Others will certainly resist and some will seek to persuade us in turn—why shouldn't they? They we can go no further except by resort to force and fraud. We can, if we are strong, dominate some and we can bribe others. We compromise our own values in doing so and we do not in the end succeed; even if we were masters of the whole world we could never succeed in making our principle universal. We could only make it falsely tyrannous.

So if we look for a principle in the name of which we can appeal to all men, one to which their reason can respond in spite of their differences, we must follow another road. When we try to make our values prevail over those cherished by others, we attack their values, their dynamic of behavior, their living will. If we go far enough we assault their very being. For the will is simply valuation in action. Now the deep beauty of the golden rule is that instead of attacking the will that is in other men, it offers their will a new dimension. "Do as you *would* have others . . ." As *you* would will others to do. It bids you expand your vision, see yourself in new relationships. It bids you transcend your insulation, see yourself in the place of others, see others in your place. It bids you test your values or at least your way of pursuing them. If you would disapprove that another should treat you as you treat him, the situations being reversed, is not that a sign that, by the standard of your own values, you are mistreating him?

This principle obviously makes for a vastly greater harmony in the social scheme. At the same time it is the only universal of ethics that does not take sides with or contend with contending values. It contains no dogma. It bids everyone follow his own rule, as it would apply *apart* from the accident of his particular fortunes. It bids him enlarge his own rule, as it would apply whether he is up or whether he is down. It is an accident that you are up and I am down. In another situation you would be down and I would be up. That accident has nothing to do with my *final* values or with yours. You have numbers and force on your side. In another situation I would have the numbers and the force. All situations of power are temporary and precarious. Imagine then the situations reversed and that you had a more wonderful power than is at the command of the most powerful, the power to make the more powerful act toward you as you would want him to act. If power is your dream, then dream of a yet greater power—and act out the spirit of your dream.

But the conclusive argument is not in the terms of power. It goes far deeper, down to the great truth that power so often ignores and that so often in the end destroys it, the truth that when you maltreat others you detach yourself from them, from the understanding of them, from the understanding of yourself. You insulate yourself, you narrow your own values, you cut yourself off from that which you and they have in common. And this commonness is more enduring and more satisfying than what you possess in insulation. You separate yourself, and for all your power you weaken yourself. Which is why power and fear are such close companions.

This is the reason why the evil you do to another, you do also, in the end, to yourself. While if you and he refrain from doing evil, one to another—not to speak of the yet happier consequences of doing positive good—this reciprocity of restraint from evil will redound to the good of both.

That makes a much longer story and we shall not here enter upon it. Our sole concern is to show that the golden rule is the *only* ethical principle, as already defined, that can have clear right of way everywhere in the kind of world we have inherited. It is the only principle that allows every man to follow his own intrinsic values while nevertheless it transforms the chaos of warring codes into a reasonably well-ordered universe.

Let us explain the last statement. What are a man's intrinsic values? Beyond his mere self-seeking every human being needs, and must find, some attachment to a larger purpose. These attachments, in themselves and apart from the way he pursues them, are his intrinsic values. For some men they are centered in the family, the clan, the "class," the community, the nation, the "race." It is the warfare of their group-attachments that creates the deadliest disturbances of modern society. For some men the focus of attachment is found in the greater "cause," the faith, the creed, the way of life. The conflict of these attachments also unlooses many evils on society and at some historical stages has brought about great devastation.

The greatest evils inflicted by man on man over the face of the earth are wrought not by the self-seekers, the pleasure lovers, or the merely amoral, but by the fervent devotees of ethical principles, those who are bound body and soul to some larger purpose, the nation, the "race," the "masses," the "brethren" whoever they may be. The faith they invoke, whatever it may be, is not large enough when it sets a frontier between the members and the non-members, the believers and the non-believers. In the heat of devotion to that larger but exclusive purpose there is bred the fanaticism that corrodes and finally destroys all that links man to the common humanity. In the name of the cause, they will torture and starve and trample under foot millions on millions of their fellowmen. In its name they will cultivate the blackest treachery. And if their methods fail, as fail in the end they must, they will be ready, as was Hitler, to destroy their own cause or their own people, the chosen ones, rather than accept the reality their blinded purpose denied.

How then can we say that the golden rule does not disqualify the intrinsic values of such people—even of people like Hitler or, say, Torquemada? In the name of his values Torquemada burned at the stake many persons who differed from their fellows mainly by being more courageous, honest, and faithful to their faith. What then were Torquemada's values? He was a servant of the Church and the Church was presumptively a servant of Jesus Christ. It was not the intrinsic values of his creed that moved him and his masters to reject the Christian golden rule. Let us concede they had some kind of devotion to religion. It was the distorted, fanatical way in which they pursued the dimmed values they cherished, it was not the values themselves, to which their inhumanity can be charged.

Let us take the case of Hitler. Apart from his passion for Germany, or the German "folk," he would have been of no account, for evil or for good. That passion of itself, that in his view intrinsic value, might have inspired great constructive service instead of destruction. It was the method he used, and not the values he sought to promote thereby, that led to ruin, his blind trust in the efficacy of ruthless might. Belonging to a "folk" that had been reduced in defeat from strength to humiliation, fed on false notions of history and responsive to grotesque fallacies about a "master race," he conceived the resurgence of Germany in the distorted light of his vindictive imagination. Had Hitler been a member of some small "folk," no more numerous, say, than the population of his native Austria, he might have cherished the same values with no less passion, but his aspirations would have taken a different form and would never have expressed themselves in horror and tragedy.

The golden rule says nothing against Hitler's mystic adoration of the German "race," against any man's intrinsic values. By "intrinsic values" we signify the goals, beyond mere self-seeking, that animate a human being. If your group, your nation, your "race," your church, is for you a primary attachment, continue to cherish it—give it all you have, if you are so minded. But do not use means that are repugnant to the standards according to which you would have others conduct themselves to you and your values. If your nation were a small one, would you not seethe with indignation if some large neighbor destroyed its independence? Where, then, is your personal integrity if, belonging instead to the large nation, you act to destroy the independence of a small one? You falsify your own values, in the longer run you do them injury, when you pursue them in ways that cannot abide the test of the golden rule.

It follows that while this first principle attacks no intrinsic values, no primary attachments of men to goods that reach beyond themselves, it nevertheless purifies every attachment, every creed, of its accidents, its irrelevancies, its excesses, its false reliance on power. It saves every human value from the corruption that comes from the arrogance of detachment and exclusiveness, from the shell of the kind of absolutism that imprisons its vitality.

At this point a word of caution is in order. The golden rule does not solve for us our ethical problems but offers only a way of approach. It does not prescribe our treatment of others but only the spirit in which we should treat them. It has no simple mechanical application and often enough is hard to apply—what general principle is not? It certainly does not bid us treat others as others *want* us to treat them—that would be an absurdity. The convicted criminal wants the judge to set him free. If the judge acts in the spirit of the golden rule, within the limits of the discretion permitted him as judge, he might instead reason somewhat as follows: "How would I feel the judge ought to treat *me* were I in this man's place? What could I—the man I am and yet somehow standing where this criminal stands—properly ask the judge to do for me, to me? In this spirit I shall assess his guilt and his punishment. In this spirit I shall give full consideration to the conditions under which he acted. I shall try to understand *him*, to do what I properly can for him, while at the same time I fulfill my judicial duty in protecting society against the dangers that arise if criminals such as he go free."

"Do to others as you would have others do to you." The disease to which all values are subject is the growth of a hard insulation. "I am right: I have the truth. If you differ from me, you are a heretic, you are in error. *Therefore* while you must allow me every liberty when you are in power I need not, in truth I ought not to, show any similar consideration for you." The barb of falsehood has already begun to vitiate the cherished value. While *you* are in power I advocate the equal rights of all creeds: when *I* am in power, I reject any such claim as ridiculous. This is the position taken by various brands of totalitarianism, and the communists in particular have made it a favorite technique in the process of gaining power, clamoring for rights they will use to destroy the rights of those who grant them. Religious groups have followed the same line. Roman Catholics, Calvinists, Lutherans, Presbyterians, and others have on occasion vociferously advocated religious liberty where they were in the minority, often to curb it where in turn they became dominant.

This gross inconsistency on the part of religious groups was flagrantly displayed in earlier centuries, but examples are still not infrequent. Here is one. *La Civilita Catholicâ,* a Jesuit organ published in Rome, has come out as follows:

"The Roman Catholic Church, convinced, through its divine prerogatives, of being the only true church, must demand the right to freedom for herself alone, because such a right can only be possessed by truth, never by error. As to other religions, the Church will certainly never draw the sword, but she will require that by legitimate means they shall not be allowed to propagate false doctrine. Consequently, in a state where the majority of the people are Catholic, the Church will require that legal existence be denied to error. . . . In some countries, Catholics will be obliged to ask full religious freedom for all, resigned at being forced to cohabilitate where they alone should rightly be allowed to live. . . . The Church cannot blush for her own want of tolerance, as she asserts it in principle and applies it in practice."[1]

Since this statement has the merit of honesty it well illustrates the fun-

---

[1]Quoted in the *Christian Century* (June 1948).

damental lack of rationality that lies behind all such violations of the golden rule. The argument runs: "Roman Catholics know they possess the truth; *therefore* they should not permit others to propagate error." By parity of reasoning why should not Protestants say—and indeed they have often said it—"We know we possess the truth; therefore we should not tolerate the errors of Roman Catholics." Why then should not atheists say: "We know we possess the truth; therefore we should not tolerate the errors of dogmatic religion."

No matter what we believe, we are equally convinced that *we* are right. We have to be. That is what belief means, and we must all believe something. The Roman Catholic Church is entitled to declare that all other religious groups are sunk in error. But what follows? That other groups have not the right to believe they are right? That you have the right to repress them while they have no right to repress you? That they should concede to you what you should not concede to them? Such reasoning is mere childishness. Beyond it lies the greater foolishness that truth is advanced by the forceful suppression of those who believe differently from you. Beyond that lies the pernicious distortion of meanings which claims that liberty is only "the liberty to do right"—the "liberty" for me to do what *you* think is right. This perversion of the meaning of liberty has been the delight of all totalitarians. And it might be well to reflect that it was the radical Rousseau who first introduced the doctrine that men could be "forced to be free."

How much do they have truth who think they must guard it within the fortress of their own might? How little that guarding has availed in the past! How often it has kept truth outside while superstition grew moldy within! How often has the false alliance of belief and force led to civil dissension and the futile ruin of war! But if history means nothing to those who call themselves "Christian" and still claim exclusive civil rights for their particular faith, at least they might blush before this word of one they call their Master: "All things therefore whatsoever ye would that men should do unto you, even so do ye also unto them; for this is the law and the prophets."

Contemporary Issues

Are We Obligated to Help Everyone?

24. Lifeboat Ethics: The Case Against Helping the Poor   Garrett Hardin

Garrett Hardin (1915–   ) is Professor of Human Ecology at the University of California, Santa Barbara. His books and articles on population control and other social issues have been widely read.

Environmentalists use the metaphor of the earth as a "spaceship" in trying to persuade countries, industries, and people to stop wasting and polluting our natural resources. Since we all share life on this planet, they argue, no single person or institution has the right to destroy, waste, or use more than a fair share of its resources.

But does everyone on earth have an equal right to an equal share of its resources? The spaceship metaphor can be dangerous when used by misguided idealists to justify suicidal policies for sharing our resources through uncontrolled immigration and foreign aid. In their enthusiastic but unrealistic generosity, they confuse the ethics of a spaceship with those of a lifeboat.

A true spaceship would have to be under the control of a captain, since no ship could possibly survive if its course were determined by committee. Spaceship Earth certainly has no captain; the United Nations is merely a toothless tiger, with little power to enforce any policy upon its bickering members.

If we divide the world crudely into rich nations and poor nations, two thirds of them are desperately poor, and only one third comparatively rich, with the United States the wealthiest of all. Metaphorically each rich nation can be seen as a lifeboat full of comparatively rich people. In the ocean outside each lifeboat swim the poor of the world, who would like to get in, or at least to share some of the wealth. What should the lifeboat passengers do?

First, we must recognize the limited capacity of any lifeboat. For example, a nation's land has a limited capacity to support a population, and, as the current energy crisis has shown us, in some ways we have already exceeded the carrying capacity of our land.

Adrift in a Moral Sea

So here we sit, say fifty people in our lifeboat. To be generous, let us assume it has room for ten more, making a total capacity of sixty. Suppose the fifty of us in the lifeboat see 100 others swimming in the water outside, begging for admission to our boat or for handouts. We have several options: we may be tempted to try to live by the Christian ideal of being "our brother's keeper," or by the Marxist ideal of "to each according to his needs." Since the needs of all in the water are the same, and since they can all be seen as "our brothers," we could take them all into our boat, making a total of 150 in a boat designed for sixty. The boat swamps, everyone drowns. Complete justice, complete catastrophe.

Since the boat has an unused excess capacity of ten more passengers, we could admit just ten more to it. But which ten do we let in? How do we choose? Do we pick the best ten, the neediest ten, "first come, first served"? And what do we say to the ninety we exclude? If we do let an extra ten into our lifeboat, we will have lost our "safety factor," an engineering principle of critical importance. For example, if we don't leave room for excess capacity as a safety factor in our country's agriculture, a new plant disease or a bad change in the weather could have disastrous consequences.

Suppose we decide to preserve our small safety factor and admit no more to the lifeboat. Our survival is then possible, although we shall have to be constantly on guard against boarding parties.

While this last solution clearly offers the only means of our survival, it is morally abhorrent to many people. Some say they feel guilty about their good luck. My reply is simple: "Get out and yield your place to others." This may solve the problem of the guilt-ridden person's conscience, but it does not change the ethics of the lifeboat. The needy person to whom the guilt-ridden person yields his place will not himself feel guilty about his good luck. If he did, he would not climb aboard. The net result of conscience-stricken people giving up their unjustly held seats is the elimination of that sort of conscience from the lifeboat.

This is the basic metaphor within which we must work out our solutions. Let us now enrich the image, step by step, with substantive additions from the real world, a world that must solve real and pressing problems of overpopulation and hunger.

This is the basic metaphor within which we must work out our solutions. Let us now enrich the image, step by step, with substantive additions from the real world, a world that must solve real and pressing problems of overpopulation and hunger.

The harsh ethics of the lifeboat become even harsher when we consider the reproductive differences between the rich nations and the poor nations. The people inside the lifeboats are doubling in numbers every eighty-seven years; those swimming around outside are doubling, on the average, every thirty-five years, more than twice as fast as the rich. And since the world's resources are dwindling, the difference in prosperity between the rich and the poor can only increase.

As of 1973, the U.S. had a population of 210 million people, who were increasing by 0.8 per cent per year. Outside our lifeboat, let us imagine another 210 million people (say the combined populations of Colombia, Ecuador, Venezuela, Morocco, Pakistan, Thailand, and the Philippines), who are increasing at a rate of 3.3 per cent per year. Put differently, the doubling time for this aggregate population is twenty-one years, compared to eighty-seven years for the U.S.

Multiplying the Rich and the Poor

Now suppose the U.S. agreed to pool its resources with those seven countries, with everyone receiving an equal share. Initially the ratio of Americans to non-Americans in this model would be one-to-one. But consider what the ratio would be after eighty-seven years, by which time the Americans would have doubled to a population of 420 million. By then, doubling every twenty-one years, the other group would have swollen to 354 billion. Each American would have to share the available resources with more than eight people.

But, one could argue, this discussion assumes that current population trends will continue, and they may not. Quite so. Most likely the rate of population increase will decline much faster in the U.S. than it will in the other countries, and there does not seem to be much we can do about it. In sharing with "each according to his needs," we must recognize that needs are determined by population size, which is determined by the rate of reproduction, which at present is regarded as a sovereign right of every nation, poor or not. This being so, the philanthropic load created by the sharing ethic of the spaceship can only increase.

The Tragedy of the Commons

The fundamental error of spaceship ethics, and the sharing it requires, is that it leads to what I call "the tragedy of the commons." Under a system of private property, the men who own property recognize their responsibility to care for it, for if they don't they will eventually suffer. A farmer, for instance, will allow no more cattle in a pasture than its carrying capacity justifies. If he overloads it, erosion sets in, weeds take over, and he loses the use of the pasture.

If a pasture becomes a commons open to all, the right of each to use it may not be matched by a corresponding responsibility to protect it. Asking everyone to use it with discretion will hardly do, for the considerate herdsman who refrains from overloading the commons suffers more than a selfish one who says his needs are greater. If everyone would restrain himself, all would be well; but it takes only one less than everyone to ruin a system of voluntary restraint. In a crowded world of less-than-perfect human beings, mutual ruin is inevitable if there are no controls. This is the tragedy of the commons.

One of the major tasks of education today should be the creation of such an acute awareness of the dangers of the commons that people will recognize its many varieties. For example, the air and water have become polluted because they are treated as commons. Further growth in the population, or per-capita conversion of natural resources into pollutants, will only make the problem worse. The same holds true for the fish of the oceans. Fishing fleets have nearly disappeared in many parts of the world;

technological improvements in the art of fishing are hastening the day of complete ruin. Only the replacement of the system of the commons with a responsible system of control will save the land, air, water, and oceanic fisheries.

The World Food Bank

In recent years there has been a push to create a new commons called a World Food Bank, an international depository of food reserves to which nations would contribute according to their abilities and from which they would draw according to their needs. This humanitarian proposal has received support from many liberal international groups, and from such prominent citizens as Margaret Mead, U.N. Secretary General Kurt Waldheim, and Senators Edward Kennedy and George McGovern.

A world food bank appeals powerfully to our humanitarian impulses. But before we rush ahead with such a plan, let us recognize where the greatest political push comes from, lest we be disillusioned later. Our experience with the Food for Peace program, or Public Law 480, gives us the answer. This program moved billions of dollars worth of U.S. surplus grain to food-short, population-long countries during the past two decades. But when P.L. 480 first became law, a headline in the business magazine *Forbes* revealed the real power behind it: "Feeding the World's Hungry Millions: How It Will Mean Billions for U.S. Business."

And indeed it did. In the years 1960 to 1970, U.S. taxpayers spent a total of $7.9 billion on the Food for Peace program. Between 1948 and 1970, they also paid an additional $50 billion for other economic-aid programs, some of which went for food and food-producing machinery and technology. Though all U.S. taxpayers were forced to contribute to the cost of P.L. 480, certain special-interest groups gained handsomely under the program. Farmers did not have to contribute the grain; the Government, or rather the taxpayers, bought it from them at full market prices. The increased demand raised prices of farm products generally. The manufacturers of farm machinery, fertilizers, and pesticides benefited by the farmers' extra efforts to grow more food. Grain elevators profited from storing the surplus until it could be shipped. Railroads made money hauling it to ports, and shipping lines profited from carrying it overseas. The implementation of P.L. 480 required the creation of a vast Government bureaucracy, which then acquired its own vested interest in continuing the program regardless of its merits.

Extracting Dollars

Those who proposed and defended the Food for Peace program in public rarely mentioned its importance to any of these special interests. The public emphasis was always on its humanitarian effects. The combination of silent selfish interests and highly vocal humanitarian apologists made a powerful and successful lobby for extracting money from taxpayers. We can expect the same lobby to push now for the creation of a World Food Bank.

However great the potential benefit to selfish interests, it should not be a decisive argument against a truly humanitarian program. We must ask if such a program would actually do more good than harm, not only momentarily but also in the long run. Those who propose the food bank usually refer to a current "emergency" or "crisis" in terms of world food supply. But what is an emergency? Although they may be infrequent and sudden, everyone knows that emergencies will occur from time to time. A well-run family, company, organization, or country prepares for the likelihood of accidents and emergencies. It expects them, it budgets for them, it saves for them.

Learning the Hard Way

What happens if some organizations or countries budget for accidents and others do not? If each country is solely responsible for its own well-being, poorly managed ones will suffer. But they can learn from experience. They may mend their ways, and learn to budget for infrequent but certain emergencies. For example, the weather varies from year to year, and periodic crop failures are certain. A wise and competent government saves out of the production of the good years in anticipation of bad years to come. Joseph taught this policy to Pharaoh in Egypt more than 2,000 years ago. Yet the great majority of the governments in the world today do not follow such a policy. They lack either the wisdom or the competence, or both. Should those nations that do manage to put something aside be forced to come to the rescue each time an emergency occurs among the poor nations?

"But it isn't their fault!" some kindhearted liberals argue. "How can we blame the poor people who are caught in an emergency? Why must they suffer for the sins of their governments?" The concept of blame is simply not relevant here. The real question is, what are the operational consequences of establishing a world food bank? If it is open to every country every time a need develops, slovenly rulers will not be motivated to take Joseph's advice. Someone will always come to their aid. Some countries will deposit food in the world food bank, and others will withdraw it. There will be almost no overlap. As a result of such solutions to food shortage emergencies, the poor countries will not learn to mend their ways, and will suffer progressively greater emergencies as their populations grow.

Population Control the Crude Way

On the average, poor countries undergo a 2.5 per cent increase in population each year; rich countries, about 0.8 per cent. Only rich countries have anything in the way of food reserves set aside, and even they do not have as much as they should. Poor countries have none. If poor countries received no food from the outside, the rate of their population growth would be periodically checked by crop failures and famines. But if they can always draw on a world food bank in time of need, their population can continue to grow unchecked, and so will their "need" for aid.

In the short run, a world food bank may diminish that need, but in the long run it actually increases the need without limit.

Without some system of worldwide food sharing, the proportion of people in the rich and poor nations might eventually stabilize. The overpopulated poor countries would decrease in numbers, while the rich countries that had room for more people would increase. But with a well-meaning system of sharing, such as a world food bank, the growth differential between the rich and the poor countries will not only persist, it will increase. Because of the higher rate of population growth in the poor countries of the world, 88 per cent of today's children are born poor, and only 12 per cent rich. Year by year the ratio becomes worse, as the fast-reproducing poor outnumber the slow-reproducing rich.

A world food bank is thus a commons in disguise. People will have more motivation to draw from it than to add to any common store. The less provident and less able will multiply at the expense of the abler and more provident, bringing eventual ruin upon all who share in the commons. Besides, any system of "sharing" that amounts to foreign aid from the rich nations to the poor nations will carry the taint of charity, which will contribute little to the world peace so devoutly desired by those who support the idea of a world food bank.

As past U.S. foreign-aid programs have amply and depressingly demonstrated, international charity frequently inspires mistrust and antagonism rather than gratitude on the part of the recipient nation.

Chinese Fish and Miracle Rice

The modern approach to foreign aid stresses the export of technology and advice, rather than money and food. As an ancient Chinese proverb goes: "Give a man a fish and he will eat for a day; teach him how to fish and he will eat for the rest of his days." Acting on this advice, the Rockefeller and Ford Foundations have financed a number of programs for improving agriculture in the hungry nations. Known as the "Green Revolution," these programs have led to the development of "miracle rice" and "miracle wheat," new strains that offer bigger harvests and greater resistance to crop damage. Norman Borlaug, the Nobel Prize-winning agonomist who, supported by the Rockefeller Foundation, developed "miracle wheat," is one of the most prominent advocates of a world food bank.

Whether or not the Green Revolution can increase food production as much as its champions claim is a debatable but possibly irrelevant point. Those who support this well-intended humanitarian effort should first consider some of the fundamentals of human ecology. Ironically, one man who did was the late Alan Gregg, a vice president of the Rockefeller Foundation. Two decades ago he expressed strong doubts about the wisdom of such attempts to increase food production. He likened the growth and spread of humanity over the surface of the earth to the spread of cancer in the human body, remarking that "cancerous growths demand food; but, as far as I know, they have never been cured by getting it."

Overloading the Environment

Every human born constitutes a draft on all aspects of the environment: food, air, water, forests, beaches, wildlife, scenery, and solitude. Food can, perhaps, be significantly increased to meet a growing demand. But what about clean beaches, unspoiled forests, and solitude? If we satisfy a growing population's need for food, we necessarily decrease its per capita supply of the other resources needed by men.

India, for example, now has a population of 600 million, which increases by 15 million each year. This population already puts a huge load on a relatively impoverished environment. The country's forests are now only a small fraction of what they were three centuries ago, and floods and erosion continually destroy the insufficient farmland that remains. Every one of the 15 million new lives added to India's population puts an additional burden on the environment, and increases the economic and social costs of crowding. However humanitarian our intent, every Indian life saved through medical or nutritional assistance from abroad diminishes the quality of life for those who remain, and for subsequent generations. If rich countries make it possible, through foreign aid, for 600 million Indians to swell to 1.2 billion in a mere twenty-eight years, as their current growth rate threatens, will future generations of Indians thank us for hastening the destruction of their environment? Will our good intentions be sufficient excuse for the consequences of our actions?

My final example of a commons in action is one for which the public has the least desire for rational discussion—immigration. Anyone who publicly questions the wisdom of current U.S. immigration policy is promptly charged with bigotry, prejudice, ethnocentrism, chauvinism, isolationism, or selfishness. Rather than encounter such accusations, one would rather talk about other matters, leaving immigration policy to wallow in the crosscurrents of special interests that take no account of the good of the whole, or the interests of posterity.

Perhaps we still feel guilty about things we said in the past. Two generations ago the popular press frequently referred to Dagos, Wops, Polacks, Chinks, and Krauts, in articles about how America was being "overrun" by foreigners of supposedly inferior genetic stock. But because the implied inferiority of foreigners was used then as justification for keeping them out, people now assume that restrictive policies could only be based on such misguided notions. There are other grounds.

A Nation of Immigrants

Just consider the numbers involved. Our Government acknowledges a net inflow of 400,000 immigrants a year. While we have no hard data on the extent of illegal entries, educated guesses put the figure at about 600,000 a year. Since the natural increase (excess of births over deaths) of the resident population now runs about 1.7 million per year, the yearly gain from immigration amounts to at least 19 per cent of the total annual increase, and may be as much as 37 per cent if we include the estimate for illegal immigrants. Considering the growing use of birth-control devices, the potential effect of educational campaigns by such organizations as Planned Parenthood Federation of America and Zero Population Growth, and the influence of inflation and the housing shortage, the fertility rate of American women may decline so much that immigration could account for all the yearly increase in population. Should we not at least ask if that is what we want?

For the sake of those who worry about whether the "quality" of the average immigrant compares favorably with the quality of the average resident, let us assume that immigrants and native-born citizens are of exactly equal quality, however one defines that term. We will focus here only on quantity; and since our conclusions will depend on nothing else, all charges of bigotry and chauvinism become irrelevant.

Immigration vs. Food Supply

World food banks *move food to the people,* hastening the exhaustion of the environment of the poor countries. Unrestricted immigration, on the other hand, *moves people to the food,* thus speeding up the destruction of the environment of the rich countries. We can easily understand why poor people should want to make this latter transfer, but why should rich hosts encourage it?

As in the case of foreign-aid programs, immigration receives support from selfish interests and humanitarian impulses. The primary selfish interest in unimpeded immigration is the desire of employers for cheap labor, particularly in industries and trades that offer degrading work. In the past, one wave of foreigners after another was brought into the U.S. to work at wretched jobs for wretched wages. In recent years the Cubans, Puerto Ricans, and Mexicans have had this dubious honor. The interests of the employers of cheap labor mesh well with the guilty silence of the country's liberal intelligentsia. White Anglo-Saxon Protestants are particularly reluctant to call for a closing of the doors to immigration, for fear of being called bigots.

But not all countries have such reluctant leadership. Most educated Hawaiians, for example, are keenly aware of the limits of their environment, particularly in terms of population growth. There is only so much room on the islands, and the islanders know it. To Hawaiians, immigrants from the other forty-nine states present as great a threat as those from other nations. At a recent meeting of Hawaiian government officials in Honolulu, I had the ironic delight of hearing a speaker, who like most of his audience was of Japanese ancestry, ask how the country might practically and constitutionally close its doors to further immigration. One member of the audience countered: "How can we shut the doors now? We have many friends and relatives in Japan that we'd like to bring here some day so that they can enjoy Hawaii too." The Japanese-American speaker smiled sympathetically and answered: "Yes, but we have children now, and someday we'll have grandchildren too. We can bring more people here from Japan only by giving away some of the land that we hope to pass on to our grandchildren some day. What right do we have to do that?"

At this point, I can hear U.S. liberals asking: "How can you justify slamming the door once you're inside? You say that immigrants should be kept out. But aren't we all immigrants, or the descendants of immigrants? If we insist on staying, must we not admit all others?" Our craving for intellectual order leads us to seek and prefer symmetrical rules and morals: a single rule for me and everybody else; the same rule yesterday, today, and tomorrow. Justice, we feel, should not change with time and place.

We Americans of non-Indian ancestry can look upon ourselves as the descendants of thieves who are guilty morally, if not legally, of stealing this land from its Indian owners. Should we then give back the land to the now living American descendants of those Indians? However morally or logically sound this proposal may be, I, for one, am unwilling to live by it and I know no one else who is. Besides, the logical consequence would be absurd. Suppose that, intoxicated with a sense of pure justice, we should decide to turn our land over to the Indians. Since all our wealth has also been derived from the land, wouldn't we be morally obliged to give that back to the Indians too?

Pure Justice vs. Reality

Clearly, the concept of pure justice produces an infinite regression to absurdity. Centuries ago, wise men invented statutes of limitations to justify the rejection of such pure justice, in the interest of preventing continual disorder. The law zealously defends property rights, but only relatively recent property rights. Drawing a line after an arbitrary time has elapsed may be unjust, but the alternatives are worse.

We are all the descendants of thieves, and the world's resources are inequitably distributed. But we must begin the journey to tomorrow from the point where we are today. We cannot remake the past. We cannot safely divide the wealth equitably among all peoples so long as people reproduce at different rates. To do so would guarantee that our grandchildren, and everyone else's grandchildren, would have only a ruined world to inhabit.

To be generous with one's own possessions is quite different from being generous with those of posterity. We should call this point to the attention of those who, from a commendable love of justice and equality, would institute a system of the commons, either in the form of a world food bank, or of unrestricted immigration. We must convince them, if we wish to save at least some parts of the world from environmental ruin.

Without a true world government to control reproduction and the use of available resources, the sharing ethic of the spaceship is impossible. For the foreseeable future, our survival demands that we govern our actions by the ethics of a lifeboat, harsh though they may be. Posterity will be satisfied with nothing less.

25. Famine, Affluence, and Morality   Peter Singer

Peter Singer, who teaches philosophy in Australia, has written books and articles on a variety of moral issues. His defense of the rights of animals has received much attention.

As I write this, in November 1971, people are dying in East Bengal from lack of food, shelter, and medical care. The suffering and death that are occurring there now are not inevitable, not unavoidable in any fatalistic sense of the term. Constant poverty, a cyclone, and a civil war have turned at least nine million people into destitute refugees; nevertheless, it is not beyond the capacity of the richer nations to give enough assistance to reduce any further suffering to very small proportions. The decisions and actions of human beings can prevent this kind of suffering. Unfortunately, human beings have not made the necessary decisions. At the individual level, people have, with very few exceptions, not responded to the situation in any significant way. Generally speaking, people have not given large sums to relief funds; they have not written to their parliamentary representatives demanding increased government assistance; they have not demonstrated in the streets, held symbolic fasts, or done anything else directed toward providing the refugees with the means to satisfy their essential needs. At the government level, no government has given the sort of massive aid that would enable the refugees to survive for more than a few days. Britain, for instance, has given rather more than most countries. It has, to date, given £14,750,000. For comparative purposes, Britain's share of the nonrecoverable development costs of the Anglo-French Concorde project is already in excess of £275,000,000, and on present estimates will reach £440,000,000. The implication is that the British government values a supersonic transport more than thirty times as highly as it values the lives of the nine million refugees. Australia is another country which, on a per capita basis, is well up in the "aid to Bengal" table. Australia's aid, however, amounts to less than one-twelfth of the cost of Sydney's new opera house. The total amount given, from all sources, now stands at about £65,000,000. The estimated cost of keeping the refugees alive for one year is £464,000,000. Most of the refugees have now been in the camps for more than six months. The World Bank has said that India needs a minimum of £300,000,000 in assistance from other countries before the end of the year. It seems obvious that assistance on this scale will not be forthcoming. India will be forced to choose between letting the refugees starve or diverting funds from her own development program, which will mean that more of her own people will starve in the future.[1]

Peter Singer, "Famine, Affluence, and Morality," *Philosophy & Public Affairs* 1, no. 3 (Spring, 1972). Copyright © 1972 by Princeton University Press. Reprinted by permission.

[1]There was also a third possibility: that India would go to war to enable the refugees to return to their lands. Since I wrote this paper, India has taken this way out. The situation is no longer that described above, but this does not affect my argument, as the next paragraph indicates.

These are the essential facts about the present situation in Bengal. So far as it concerns us here, there is nothing unique about this situation except its magnitude. The Bengal emergency is just the latest and most acute of a series of major emergencies in various parts of the world, arising both from natural and from man-made causes. There are also many parts of the world in which people die from malnutrition and lack of food independent of any special emergency. I take Bengal as my example only because it is the present concern, and because the size of the problem has ensured that it has been given adequate publicity. Neither individuals nor governments can claim to be unaware of what is happening there.

What are the moral implications of a situation like this? In what follows, I shall argue that the way people in relatively affluent countries react to a situation like that in Bengal cannot be justified; indeed, the whole way we look at moral issues—our moral conceptual scheme—needs to be altered, and with it, the way of life that has come to be taken for granted in our society.

In arguing for this conclusion I will not, of course, claim to be morally neutral. I shall, however, try to argue for the moral position that I take, so that anyone who accepts certain assumptions, to be made explicit, will, I hope, accept my conclusion.

I begin with the assumption that suffering and death from lack of food, shelter, and medical care are bad. I think most people will agree about this, although one may reach the same view by different routes. I shall not argue for this view. People can hold all sorts of eccentric positions, and perhaps from some of them it would not follow that death by starvation is in itself bad. It is difficult, perhaps impossible, to refute such positions, and so for brevity I will henceforth take this assumption as accepted. Those who disagree need read no further.

My next point is this: if it is in our power to prevent something bad from happening, without thereby sacrificing anything of comparable moral importance, we ought, morally, to do it. By "without sacrificing anything of comparable moral importance" I mean without causing anything else comparably bad to happen, or doing something that is wrong in itself, or failing to promote some moral good, comparable in significance to the bad thing that we can prevent. This principle seems almost as uncontroversial as the last one. It requires us only to prevent what is bad, and not to promote what is good, and it requires this of us only when we can do it without sacrificing anything that is, from the moral point of view, comparably important. I could even, as far as the application of my argument to the Bengal emergency is concerned, qualify the point so as to make it: if it is in our power to prevent something very bad from happening, without thereby sacrificing anything morally significant, we ought, morally, to do it. An application of this principle would be as follows: if I am walking past a shallow pond and see a child drowning in it, I ought to wade in and pull the child out. This will mean getting my clothes muddy, but this is insignificant, while the death of the child would presumably be a very bad thing.

The uncontroversial appearance of the principle just stated is deceptive. If it were acted upon, even in its qualified form, our lives, our society, and our world would be fundamentally changed. For the principle takes, firstly, no account of proximity or distance. It makes no moral difference whether the person I can help is a neighbor's child ten yards from me or a Bengali whose name I shall never know, ten thousand miles away. Secondly, the principle makes no distinction between cases in which I am the only person who could possibly do anything and cases in which I am just one among millions in the same position.

I do not think I need to say much in defense of the refusal to take proximity and distance into account. The fact that a person is physically near to us, so that we have personal contact with him, may make it more likely that we *shall* assist him, but this does not show that we *ought* to help him rather than another who happens to be further away. If we accept any principle of impartiality, universalizability, equality, or whatever, we cannot discriminate against someone merely because he is far away from us (or we are far away from him). Admittedly, it is possible that we are in a better position to judge what needs to be done to help a person near to us than one far away, and perhaps also to provide the assistance we judge to be necessary. If this were the case, it would be a reason for helping those near to us first. This may once have been a justification for being more concerned with the poor in one's town than with famine victims in India. Unfortunately for those who like to keep their moral responsibilities limited, instant communication and swift transportation have changed the situation. From the moral point of view, the development of the world into a "global village" has made an important, though still unrecognized, difference to our moral situation. Expert observers and supervisors, sent out by famine relief organizations or permanently stationed in famine-prone areas, can direct our aid to a refugee in Bengal almost as effectively as we could get it to someone in our own block. There would seem, therefore, to be no possible justification for discriminating on geographical grounds.

There may be a greater need to defend the second implication of my principle—that the fact that there are millions of other people in the same position, in respect to the Bengali refugees, as I am, does not make the situation significantly different from a situation in which I am the only person who can prevent something very bad from occurring. Again, of course, I admit that there is a psychological difference between the cases; one feels less guilty about doing nothing if one can point to others, similarly placed, who have also done nothing. Yet this can make no real difference to our moral obligations.[2] Should I consider that I am less obliged to pull the drowning child out of the pond if on looking around I see other people, no further away than I am, who have also noticed the child

---

[2]In view of the special sense philosophers often give to the term, I should say that I use "obligation" simply as the abstract noun derived from "ought," so that "I have an obligation to" means no more, and no less, than "I ought to." This usage is in accordance with the definition of "ought" given by the *Shorter Oxford English Dictionary:* "the general verb to express duty or obligation." I do not think any issue of substance hangs on the way the term is used; sentences in which I use "obligation" could all be rewritten, although somewhat clumsily, as sentences in which a clause containing "ought" replaces the term "obligation."

but are doing nothing? One has only to ask this question to see the absurdity of the view that numbers lessen obligation. It is a view that is an ideal excuse for inactivity; unfortunately most of the major evils—poverty, overpopulation, pollution—are problems in which everyone is almost equally involved.

The view that numbers do make a difference can be made plausible if stated in this way: if everyone in circumstances like mine gave £5 to the Bengal Relief Fund, there would be enough to provide food, shelter, and medical care for the refugees; there is no reason why I should give more than anyone else in the same circumstances as I am; therefore I have no obligation to give more than £5. Each premise in this argument is true, and the argument looks sound. It may convince us, unless we notice that it is based on a hypothetical premise, although the conclusion is not stated hypothetically. The argument would be sound if the conclusion were: if everyone in circumstances like mine were to give £5, I would have no obligation to give more than £5. If the conclusion were so stated, however, it would be obvious that the argument has no bearing on a situation in which it is not the case that everyone else gives £5. This, of course, is the actual situation. It is more or less certain that not everyone in circumstances like mine will give £5. So there will not be enough to provide the needed food, shelter, and medical care. Therefore by giving more than £5 I will prevent more suffering than I would if I gave just £5.

It might be thought that this argument has an absurd consequence. Since the situation appears to be that very few people are likely to give substantial amounts, it follows that I and everyone else in similar circumstances ought to give as much as possible, that is, at least up to the point at which by giving more one would begin to cause serious suffering for oneself and one's dependents—perhaps even beyond this point to the point of marginal utility, at which by giving more one would cause oneself and one's dependents as much suffering as one would prevent in Bengal. If everyone does this, however, there will be more than can be used for the benefit of the refugees, and some of the sacrifice will have been unnecessary. Thus, if everyone does what he ought to do, the result will not be as good as it would be if everyone did a little less than he ought to do, or if only some do all that they ought to do.

The paradox here arises only if we assume that the actions in question—sending money to the relief funds—are performed more or less simultaneously, and are also unexpected. For if it is to be expected that everyone is going to contribute something, then clearly each is not obliged to give as much as he would have been obliged to had others not been giving too. And if everyone is not acting more or less simultaneously, then those giving later will know how much more is needed, and will have no obligation to give more than is necessary to reach this amount. To say this is not to deny the principle that people in the same circumstances have the same obligations, but to point out that the fact that others have given, or may be expected to give, is a relevant circumstance: those giving after it has become known that many others are giving and those giving before are not in the same circumstances. So the seemingly absurd consequence of the principle I have put forward can occur only if people are in error about the actual circumstances—that is, if they think they are giving when others are not, but in fact they are giving when others are. The result of everyone doing what he really ought to do cannot be worse than the result of everyone doing less than he ought to do, although the result of everyone doing what he reasonably believes he ought to do could be.

If my argument so far has been sound, neither our distance from a preventable evil nor the number of other people who, in respect to that evil, are in the same situation as we are, lessens our obligation to mitigate or prevent that evil. I shall therefore take as established the principle I asserted earlier. As I have already said, I need to assert it only in its qualified form: if it is in our power to prevent something very bad from happening, without thereby sacrificing anything else morally significant, we ought, morally, to do it.

The outcome of this argument is that our traditional moral categories are upset. The traditional distinction between duty and charity cannot be drawn, or at least, not in the place we normally draw it. Giving money to the Bengal Relief Fund is regarded as an act of charity in our society. The bodies which collect money are known as "charities." These organizations see themselves in this way—if you send them a check, you will be thanked for your "generosity." Because giving money is regarded as an act of charity, it is not thought that there is anything wrong with not giving. The charitable man may be praised, but the man who is not charitable is not condemned. People do not feel in any way ashamed or guilty about spending money on new clothes or a new car instead of giving it to famine relief. (Indeed, the alternative does not occur to them.) This way of looking at the matter cannot be justified. When we buy new clothes not to keep ourselves warm but to look "well-dressed" we are not providing for any important need. We would not be sacrificing anything significant if we were to continue to wear our old clothes, and give the money to famine relief. By doing so, we would be preventing another person from starving. It follows from what I have said earlier that we ought to give money away, rather than spend it on clothes which we do not need to keep us warm. To do so is not charitable, or generous. Nor is it the kind of act which philosophers and theologians have called "supererogatory"—an act which it would be good to do, but not wrong not to do. On the contrary, we ought to give the money away, and it is wrong not to do so.

I am not maintaining that there are no acts which are charitable, or that there are no acts which it would be good to do but not wrong not to do. It may be possible to redraw the distinction between duty and charity in some other place. All I am arguing here is that the present way of drawing the distinction, which makes it an act of charity for a man, living at the level of affluence which most people in the "developed nations" enjoy, to give money to save someone else from starvation, cannot be supported. It is beyond the scope of my argument to consider whether the distinction should be redrawn or abolished altogether. There would be many other possible ways of drawing the distinction—for instance, one might decide that it is good to make other people as happy as possible, but not wrong not to do so.

Despite the limited nature of the revision in our moral conceptual scheme which I am proposing, the revision would, given the extent of both affluence and famine in the world today, have radical implications. These implications may lead to further objections, distinct from those I have already considered. I shall discuss two of these.

One objection to the position I have taken might be simply that it is too drastic a revision of our moral scheme. People do not ordinarily judge in the way I have suggested they should. Most people reserve their moral condemnation for those who violate some moral norm, such as the norm against taking another person's property. They do not condemn those who indulge in luxury instead of giving to famine relief. But given that I did not set out to present a morally neutral description of the way people make moral judgments, the way people do in fact judge has nothing to do with the validity of my conclusion. My conclusion follows from the principle which I advanced earlier, and unless that principle is rejected, or the arguments shown to be unsound, I think the conclusion must stand, however strange it appears.

It might, nevertheless, be interesting to consider why our society, and most other societies, do judge differently from the way I have suggested they should. In a well-known article, J. O. Urmson suggests that the imperatives of duty, which tell us what we must do, as distinct from what it would be good to do but not wrong not to do, function so as to prohibit behavior that is intolerable if men are to live together in society.[3] This may explain the origin and continued existence of the present division between acts of duty and acts of charity. Moral attitudes are shaped by the needs of society, and no doubt society needs people who will observe the rules that make social existence tolerable. From the point of view of a particular society, it is essential to prevent violations of norms against killing, stealing, and so on. It is quite inessential, however, to help people outside one's own society.

If this is an explanation of our common distinction between duty and supererogation, however, it is not a justification of it. The moral point of view requires us to look beyond the interests of our own society. Previously, as I have already mentioned, this may hardly have been feasible, but it is quite feasible now. From the moral point of view, the prevention of the starvation of millions of people outside our society must be considered at least as pressing as the upholding of property norms within our society.

It has been argued by some writers, among them Sidgwick and Urmson, that we need to have a basic moral code which is not too far beyond the capacities of the ordinary man, for otherwise there will be a general breakdown of compliance with the moral code. Crudely stated, this argument suggests that if we tell people that they ought to refrain from murder and give everything they do not really need to famine relief, they will do neither, whereas if we tell them that they ought to refrain from murder and that it is good to give to famine relief but not wrong not to do so,

[3] J. O. Urmson, "Saints and Heroes," in *Essays in Moral Philosophy*, ed. Abraham I. Melden (Seattle: University of Washington Press 1958), p. 214. For a related but significantly different view see also Henry Sidgwick, *The Methods of Ethics*, 7th edn. (London: Dover Press, 1907), pp. 220–21, 492–93.

they will at least refrain from murder. The issue here is: Where should we draw the line between conduct that is required and conduct that is good although not required, so as to get the best possible result? This would seem to be an empirical question, although a very difficult one. One objection to the Sidgwick-Urmson line of argument is that it takes insufficient account of the effect that moral standards can have on the decisions we make. Given a society in which a wealthy man who gives 5 per cent of his income to famine relief is regarded as most generous, it is not surprising that a proposal that we all ought to give away half our incomes will be thought to be absurdly unrealistic. In a society which held that no man should have more than enough while others have less than they need, such a proposal might seem narrow-minded. What it is possible for a man to do and what he is likely to do are both, I think, very greatly influenced by what people around him are doing and expecting him to do. In any case, the possibility that by spreading the idea that we ought to be doing very much more than we are to relieve famine we shall bring about a general breakdown of moral behavior seems remote. If the stakes are an end to widespread starvation, it is worth the risk. Finally, it should be emphasized that these considerations are relevant only to the issue of what we should require from others, and not to what we ourselves ought to do.

The second objection to my attack on the present distinction between duty and charity is one which has from time to time been made against utilitarianism. It follows from some forms of utilitarian theory that we all ought, morally, to be working full time to increase the balance of happiness over misery. The position I have taken here would not lead to this conclusion in all circumstances, for if there were no bad occurrences that we could prevent without sacrificing something of comparable moral importance, my argument would have no application. Given the present conditions in many parts of the world, however, it does follow from my argument that we ought, morally, to be working full time to relieve great suffering of the sort that occurs as a result of famine or other disasters. Of course, mitigating circumstances can be adduced—for instance, that if we wear ourselves out through overwork, we shall be less effective than we would otherwise have been. Nevertheless, when all considerations of this sort have been taken into account, the conclusion remains: we ought to be preventing as much suffering as we can without sacrificing something else of comparable moral importance. This conclusion is one which we may be reluctant to face. I cannot see, though, why it should be regarded as a criticism of the position for which I have argued, rather than a criticism of our ordinary standards of behavior. Since most people are self-interested to some degree, very few of us are likely to do everything that we ought to do. It would, however, hardly be honest to take this as evidence that it is not the case that we ought to do it.

It may still be thought that my conclusions are so wildly out of line with what everyone else thinks and has always thought that there must be something wrong with the argument somewhere. In order to show that my conclusions, while certainly contrary to contemporary Western moral standards, would not have seemed so extraordinary at other times and in other places, I would like to quote a passage from a writer not normally thought of as a way-out radical, Thomas Aquinas.

> Now, according to the natural order instituted by divine providence, material goods are provided for the satisfaction of human needs. Therefore the division and appropriation of property, which proceeds from human law, must not hinder the satisfaction of man's necessity from such goods. Equally, whatever a man has in superabundance is owed, of natural right, to the poor for their sustenance. So Ambrosius says, and it is also to be found in the *Decretum Gratiani:* "The bread which you withhold belongs to the hungry; the clothing you shut away, to the naked; and the money you bury in the earth is the redemption and freedom of the penniless."[4]

I now want to consider a number of points, more practical than philosophical, which are relevant to the application of the moral conclusion we have reached. These points challenge not the idea that we ought to be doing all we can to prevent starvation, but the idea that giving away a great deal of money is the best means to this end.

It is sometimes said that overseas aid should be a government responsibility, and that therefore one ought not to give to privately run charities. Giving privately, it is said, allows the government and the noncontributing members of society to escape their responsibilities.

This argument seems to assume that the more people there are who give to privately organized famine relief funds, the less likely it is that the government will take over full responsibility for such aid. This assumption is unsupported, and does not strike me as at all plausible. The opposite view—that if no one gives voluntarily, a government will assume that its citizens are uninterested in famine relief and would not wish to be forced into giving aid—seems more plausible. In any case, unless there were a definite probability that by refusing to give one would be helping to bring about massive government assistance, people who do refuse to make voluntary contributions are refusing to prevent a certain amount of suffering without being able to point to any tangible beneficial consequence of their refusal. So the onus of showing how their refusal will bring about government action is on those who refuse to give.

I do not, of course, want to dispute the contention that governments of affluent nations should be giving many times the amount of genuine, no-strings-attached aid that they are giving now. I agree, too, that giving privately is not enough, and that we ought to be campaigning actively for entirely new standards for both public and private contributions to famine relief. Indeed, I would sympathize with someone who thought that campaigning was more important than giving oneself, although I doubt whether preaching what one does not practice would be very effective. Unfortunately, for many people the idea that "it's the government's responsibility" is a reason for not giving which does not appear to entail any political action either.

Another, more serious, reason for not giving to famine relief funds is that until there is effective population control, relieving famine merely

[4]*Summa Theologica,* II-II, Question 66, Article 7, in *Aquinas, Selected Political Writings,* ed. A. P. d'Entreves, trans. J. G. Dawson (Oxford: Basil Blackwell, 1948), p. 171.

postpones starvation. If we save the Bengal refugees now, others, perhaps the children of these refugees, will face starvation in a few years' time. In support of this, one may cite the now well-known facts about the population explosion and the relatively limited scope for expanded production.

This point, like the previous one, is an argument against relieving suffering that is happening now, because of a belief about what might happen in the future; it is unlike the previous point in that very good evidence can be adduced in support of this belief about the future. I will not go into the evidence here. I accept that the earth cannot support indefinitely a population rising at the present rate. This certainly poses a problem for anyone who thinks it important to prevent famine. Again, however, one could accept the argument without drawing the conclusion that it absolves one from any obligation to do anything to prevent famine. The conclusion that should be drawn is that the best means of preventing famine, in the long run, is population control. It would then follow from the position reached earlier that one ought to be doing all one can to promote population control (unless one held that all forms of population control were wrong in themselves, or would have significantly bad consequences). Since there are organizations working specifically for population control, one would then support them rather than more orthodox methods of preventing famine.

A third point raised by the conclusion reached earlier relates to the question of just how much we all ought to be giving away. One possibility, which has already been mentioned, is that we ought to give until we reach the level of marginal utility—that is, the level at which, by giving more, I would cause as much suffering to myself or my dependents as I would relieve by my gift. This would mean, of course, that one would reduce oneself to very near the material circumstances of a Bengali refugee. It will be recalled that earlier I put forward both a strong and a moderate version of the principle of preventing bad occurrences. The strong version, which required us to prevent bad things from happening unless in doing so we would be sacrificing something of comparable moral significance, does seem to require reducing ourselves to the level of marginal utility. I should also say that the strong version seems to me to be the correct one. I proposed the more moderate version—that we should prevent bad occurrences unless, to do so, we had to sacrifice something morally significant—only in order to show that even on this surely undeniable principle a great change in our way of life is required. On the more moderate principle, it may not follow that we ought to reduce ourselves to the level of marginal utility, for one might hold that to reduce oneself and one's family to this level is to cause something significantly bad to happen. Whether this is so I shall not discuss, since, as I have said, I can see no good reason for holding the moderate version of the principle rather than the strong version. Even if we accepted the principle only in its moderate form, however, it should be clear that we would have to give away enough to ensure that the consumer society, dependent as it is on people spending on trivia rather than giving to famine relief, would slow down and perhaps disappear entirely. There are several reasons why this would be desirable in itself. The value and necessity of economic growth are now being questioned not only by conservationists, but by economists as well.[5] There is no doubt, too, that the consumer society has had a distorting effect on the goals and purposes of its members. Yet looking at the matter purely from the point of view of overseas aid, there must be a limit to the extent to which we should deliberately slow down our economy; for it might be the case that if we gave away, say, 40 per cent of our Gross National Product, we would slow down the economy so much that in absolute terms we would be giving less than if we gave 25 per cent of the much larger GNP that we would have if we limited our contribution to this smaller percentage.

I mention this only as an indication of the sort of factor that one would have to take into account in working out an ideal. Since Western societies generally consider one per cent of the GNP an acceptable level for overseas aid, the matter is entirely academic. Nor does it affect the question of how much an individual should give in a society in which very few are giving substantial amounts.

It is sometimes said, though less often now than it used to be, that philosophers have no special role to play in public affairs, since most public issues depend primarily on an assessment of facts. On questions of fact, it is said, philosophers as such have no special expertise, and so it has been possible to engage in philosophy without committing oneself to any position on major public issues. No doubt there are some issues of social policy and foreign policy about which it can truly be said that a really expert assessment of the facts is required before taking sides or acting, but the issue of famine is surely not one of these. The facts about the existence of suffering are beyond dispute. Nor, I think, is it disputed that we can do something about it, either through orthodox methods of famine relief or through population control or both. This is therefore an issue on which philosophers are competent to take a position. The issue is one which faces everyone who has more money than he needs to support himself and his dependents, or who is in a position to take some sort of political action. These categories must include practically every teacher and student of philosophy in the universities of the Western world. If philosophy is to deal with matters that are relevant to both teachers and students, this is an issue that philosophers should discuss.

Discussion, though, is not enough. What is the point of relating philosophy to public (and personal) affairs if we do not take our conclusions seriously? In this instance, taking our conclusion seriously means acting upon it. The philosopher will not find it any easier than anyone else to alter his attitudes and way of life to the extent that, if I am right, is involved in doing everything that we ought to be doing. At the very least, though, one can make a start. The philosopher who does so will have to sacrifice some of the benefits of the consumer society, but he can find compensation in the satisfaction of a way of life in which theory and practice, if not yet in harmony, are at least coming together.

[5]See, for instance, John Kenneth Galbraith, *The New Industrial State* (Boston: Houghton Mifflin, 1967); and E. J. Mishan, *The Costs of Economic Growth* (New York: Praeger, 1967).

The Enforcement of Morals

26. Morals and the Criminal Law   Sir Patrick Devlin

Sir Patrick Arthur Devlin (1905–   ), a former Lord Justice of Appeal and Lord of
Appeal in Ordinary and now High Steward of Cambridge University, England, has
produced writings in the philosophy of law and punishment that have stimulated
discussion on the part of philosophers.

. . . What is the connexion between crime and sin and to what extent,
if at all, should the criminal law of England concern itself with the
enforcement of morals and punish sin or immorality as such?

The statements of principle in the Wolfenden Report provide an
admirable and modern starting-point for such an inquiry. . . .

Early in the Report the Committee put forward:

Our own formulation of the function of the criminal law so far as it concerns the subjects of this enquiry. In this field, its function, as we see it, is
to preserve public order and decency, to protect the citizen from what is
offensive or injurious, and to provide sufficient safeguards against exploitation and corruption of others, particularly those who are specially vulnerable because they are young, weak in body or mind, inexperienced, or
in a state of special physical, official or economic dependence.

It is not, in our view, the function of the law to intervene in the private
lives of citizens, or to seek to enforce any particular pattern of behaviour,
further than is necessary to carry out the purposes we have outlined.

The Committee preface their most important recommendation

that homosexual behaviour between consenting adults in private should
no longer be a criminal offence, [by stating the argument] which we
believe to be decisive, namely, the importance which society and the law
ought to give to individual freedom of choice and action in matters of
private morality. Unless a deliberate attempt is to be made by society, acting through the agency of the law, to equate the sphere of crime with that
of sin, there must remain a realm of private morality and immorality which
is, in brief and crude terms, not the law's business. To say this is not to
condone or encourage private immorality.

Similar statements of principle are set out in the chapters of the Report
which deal with prostitution. No case can be sustained, the Report says,
for attempting to make prostitution itself illegal. The Committee refer to
the general reasons already given and add: 'We are agreed that private
immorality should not be the concern of the criminal law except in the
special circumstances therein mentioned.' They quote with approval the
report of the Street Offences Committee, which says: 'As a general prop-

osition it will be universally accepted that the law is not concerned with private morals or with ethical sanctions.' It will be observed that the emphasis is on *private* immorality. By this is meant immorality which is not offensive or injurious to the public in the ways defined or described in the first passage which I quoted. In other words, no act of immorality should be made a criminal offence unless it is accompanied by some other feature such as indecency, corruption, or exploitation. This is clearly brought out in relation to prostitution: 'It is not the duty of the law to concern itself with immorality as such . . . it should confine itself to those activities which offend against public order and decency or expose the ordinary citizen to what is offensive or injurious.' . . .

If this view is sound, it means that the criminal law cannot justify any of its provisions by reference to the moral law. It cannot say, for example, that murder and theft are prohibited because they are immoral or sinful. The State must justify in some other way the punishments which it imposes on wrongdoers and a function for the criminal law independent of morals must be found. This is not difficult to do. The smooth functioning of society and the preservation of order require that a number of activities should be regulated. The rules that are made for that purpose and are enforced by the criminal law are often designed simply to achieve uniformity and convenience and rarely involve any choice between good and evil. Rules that impose a speed limit or prevent obstruction on the highway have nothing to do with morals. Since so much of the criminal law is composed of rules of this sort, why bring morals into it at all? Why not define the function of the criminal law in simple terms as the preservation of order and decency and the protection of the lives and property of citizens, and elaborate those terms in relation to any particular subject in the way in which it is done in the Wolfenden Report? The criminal law in carrying out these objects will undoubtedly overlap the moral law. Crimes of violence are morally wrong and they are also offences against good order; therefore they offend against both laws. But this is simply because the two laws in pursuit of different objectives happen to cover the same area. Such is the argument. . . .

I think it is clear that the criminal law as we know it is based upon moral principle. In a number of crimes its function is simply to enforce a moral principle and nothing else. The law, both criminal and civil, claims to be able to speak about morality and immorality generally. Where does it get its authority to do this and how does it settle the moral principles which it enforces? Undoubtedly, as a matter of history, it derived both from Christian teaching. But I think that the strict logician is right when he says that the law can no longer rely on doctrines in which citizens are entitled to disbelieve. It is necessary therefore to look for some other source.

In jurisprudence, as I have said, everything is thrown open to discussion and, in the belief that they cover the whole field, I have framed three interrogatories addressed to myself to answer:

1. Has society the right to pass judgment at all on matters of mor-

als? Ought there, in other words, to be a public morality, or are morals always a matter for private judgment?
2. If society has the right to pass judgment, has it also the right to use the weapon of the law to enforce it?
3. If so, ought it to use that weapon in all cases or only in some; and if only in some, on what principles should it distinguish?

I shall begin with the first interrogatory and consider what is meant by the right of society to pass a moral judgment, that is, a judgment about what is good and what is evil. The fact that a majority of people may disapprove of a practice does not of itself make it a matter for society as a whole. Nine men out of ten may disapprove of what the tenth man is doing and still say that it is not their business. There is a case for a collective judgment (as distinct from a large number of individual opinions which sensible people may even refrain from pronouncing at all if it is upon somebody else's private affairs) only if society is affected. Without a collective judgment there can be no case at all for intervention. Let me take as an illustration the Englishman's attitude to religion as it is now and as it has been in the past. His attitude now is that a man's religion is his private affair; he may think of another man's religion that it is right or wrong, true or untrue, but not that it is good or bad. In earlier times that was not so; a man was denied the right to practice what was thought of as heresy, and heresy was thought of as destructive of society.

The language used in the passages I have quoted from the Wolfenden Report suggests the view that there ought not to be a collective judgment about immorality *per se*. Is this what is meant by 'private morality' and 'individual freedom of choice and action'? Some people sincerely believe that homosexuality is neither immoral nor unnatural. Is the 'freedom of choice and action' that is offered to the individual, freedom to decide for himself what is moral or immoral, society remaining neutral; or is it freedom to be immoral if he wants to be? The language of the Report may be open to question, but the conclusions at which the Committee arrive answer this question unambiguously. If society is not prepared to say that homosexuality is morally wrong, there would be no basis for a law protecting youth from 'corruption' or punishing a man for living on the 'immoral' earnings of a homosexual prostitute, as the Report recommends. This attitude the Committee makes even clearer when they come to deal with prostitution. In truth, the Report takes it for granted that there is in existence a public morality which condemns homosexuality and prostitution. What the Report seems to mean by private morality might perhaps be better described as private behaviour in matters of morals.

This view—that there is such a thing as public morality—can also be justified by *a priori* argument. What makes a society of any sort is community of ideas, not only political ideas but also ideas about the way its members should behave and govern their lives; these latter ideas are its morals. Every society has a moral structure as well as a political one: or rather, since that might suggest two independent systems, I should say that the structure of every society is made up both of politics and morals. Take, for example, the institution of marriage. Whether a man should be allowed to take more than one wife is something about which every society has to make up its mind one way or the other. In England we believe in the Christian idea of marriage and therefore adopt monogamy as a moral principle. Consequently the Christian institution of marriage has become the basis of family life and so part of the structure of our society. It is there not because it is Christian. It has got there because it is Christian, but it remains there because it is built into the house in which we live and could not be removed without bringing it down. The great majority of those who live in this country accept it because it is the Christian idea of marriage and for them the only true one. But a non-Christian is bound by it, not because it is part of Christianity but because, rightly or wrongly, it has been adopted by the society in which he lives. It would be useless for him to stage a debate designed to prove that polygamy was theologically more correct and socially preferable; if he wants to live in the house, he must accept it as built in the way in which it is.

We see this more clearly if we think of ideas or institutions that are purely political. Society cannot tolerate rebellion; it will not allow argument about the rightness of the cause. Historians a century later may say that the rebels were right and the Government was wrong and a percipient and conscientious subject of the State may think so at the time. But it is not a matter which can be left to individual judgment.

The institution of marriage is a good example for my purpose because it bridges the division, if there is one, between politics and morals. Marriage is part of the structure of our society and it is also the basis of a moral code which condemns fornication and adultery. The institution of marriage would be gravely threatened if individual judgments were permitted about the morality of adultery; on these points there must be a public morality. But public morality is not to be confined to those moral principles which support institutions such as marriage. People do not think of monogamy as something which has to be supported because our society has chosen to organize itself upon it; they think of it as something that is good in itself and offering a good way of life and that it is for that reason that our society has adopted it. I return to the statement that I have already made, that society means a community of ideas; without shared ideas on politics, morals, and ethics no society can exist. Each one of us has ideas about what is good and what is evil; they cannot be kept private from the society in which we live. If men and women try to create a society in which there is no fundamental agreement about good and evil they will fail; if, having based it on common agreement, the agreement goes, the society will disintegrate. For society is not something that is kept together physically; it is held by the invisible bonds of common thought. If the bonds were too far relaxed the members would drift apart. A common morality is part of the bondage. The bondage is part of the price of society; and mankind, which needs society, must pay its price. . . .

You may think that I have taken far too long in contending that there is such a thing as public morality, a proposition which most people would readily accept, and may have left myself too little time to discuss the next question which to many minds may cause greater difficulty: to what extent should society use the law to enforce its moral judgments? But I believe that the answer to the first question determines the way in which the second should be approached and may indeed very nearly dictate the answer to the second question. If society has no right to make judgments on morals, the law must find some special justification for entering the field of morality: if homosexuality and prostitution are not in themselves wrong, then the onus is very clearly on the law-giver who wants to frame a law against certain aspects of them to justify the exceptional treatment. But if society has the right to make a judgment and has it on the basis that a recognized morality is as necessary to society as, say, a recognized government, then society may use the law to preserve morality in the same way as it uses it to safeguard anything else that is essential to its existence. If therefore the first proposition is securely established with all its implications, society has a prima facie right to legislate against immorality as such.

The Wolfenden Report, notwithstanding that it seems to admit the right of society to condemn homosexuality and prostitution as immoral, requires special circumstances to be shown to justify the intervention of the law. I think that this is wrong in principle and that any attempt to approach my second interrogatory on these lines is bound to break down. I think that the attempt by the Committee does break down and that this is shown by the fact that it has to define or describe its special circumstances so widely that they can be supported only if it is accepted that the law *is* concerned with immorality as such.

The widest of the special circumstances are described as the provision of 'sufficient safeguards against exploitation and corruption of others, particularly those who are specially vulnerable because they are young, weak in body or mind, inexperienced, or in a state of special physical, official or economic dependence.' The corruption of youth is a well-recognized ground for intervention by the State and for the purpose of any legislation the young can easily be defined. But if similar protection were to be extended to every other citizen, there would be no limit to the reach of the law. The 'corruption and exploitation of others' is so wide that it could be used to cover any sort of immorality which involves, as most do, the co-operation of another person. Even if the phrase is taken as limited to the categories that are particularized as 'specially vulnerable,' it is so elastic as to be practically no restriction. This is not merely a matter of words. For if the words used are stretched almost beyond breaking-point, they still are not wide enough to cover the recommendations which the Committee makes about prostitution.

Prostitution is not in itself illegal and the Committee does not think that it ought to be made so. If prostitution is private immorality and not the law's business, what concern has the law with the ponce or the brothel-keeper or the householder who permits habitual prostitution? The Report recommends that the laws which make these activities criminal offences should be maintained or strengthened and brings them (so far as it goes into principle; with regard to brothels it says simply that the law rightly frowns on them) under the head of exploitation. There may be cases of exploitation in this trade, as there are or used to be in many others, but in general a ponce exploits a prostitute no more than an impressario exploits an actress. The Report finds that 'the great majority of prostitutes are women whose psychological makeup is such that they choose this life because they find in it a style of living which is to them easier, freer and more profitable than would be provided by any other occupation. . . . In the main the association between prostitute and ponce is voluntary and operates to mutual advantage.' The Committee would agree that this could not be called exploitation in the ordinary sense. They say: 'It is in our view an over-simplification to think that those who live on the earnings of prostitution are exploiting the prostitute as such. What they are really exploiting is the whole complex of the relationship between prostitute and customer; they are, in effect, exploiting the human weaknesses which cause the customer to seek the prostitute and the prostitute to meet the demand.'

All sexual immorality involves the exploitation of human weaknesses. The prostitute exploits the lust of her customers and the customer the moral weakness of the prostitute. If the exploitation of human weaknesses is considered to create a special circumstance, there is virtually no field of morality which can be defined in such a way as to exclude the law.

I think, therefore, that it is not possible to set theoretical limits to the power of the State to legislate against immorality. It is not possible to settle in advance exceptions to the general rule or to define inflexibly areas of morality into which the law is in no circumstances to be allowed to enter. Society is entitled by means of its laws to protect itself from dangers, whether from within or without. Here again I think that the political parallel is legitimate. The law of treason is directed against aiding the king's enemies and against sedition from within. The justification for this is that established government is necessary for the existence of society and therefore its safety against violent overthrow must be secured. But an established morality is as necessary as good government to the welfare of society. Societies disintegrate from within more frequently than they are broken up by external pressures. There is disintegration when no common morality is observed and history shows that the loosening of moral bonds is often the first stage of disintegration, so that society is justified in taking the same steps to preserve its moral code as it does to preserve its government and other essential institutions. The suppression of vice is as much the law's business as the suppression of subversive activities; it is no more possible to define a sphere of private morality than it is to define one of private subversive activity. It is wrong to talk of private morality or of the law not being concerned with immorality as such or to try to set rigid bounds to the part which the law may play in the suppression of vice. There are no theoretical limits to the power of the State to legislate against treason and sedition, and likewise I think there can be no theoretical limits to legislation against immorality. You may argue that if a man's sins affect only himself it cannot be the concern of society. If he chooses to get drunk every night in the privacy of his own home, is any one except himself the worse for it? But suppose a quarter or a half of the population got drunk every night, what sort of society would it be? You cannot set a theoretical limit to the number of people who can get drunk before society is entitled to legislate against drunkenness. The same may be said of gambling. The Royal Commission on Betting, Lotteries, and Gaming took as their test

the character of the citizen as a member of society. They said: 'Our concern with the ethical significance of gambling is confined to the effect
which it may have on the character of the gambler as a member of society.
If we were convinced that whatever the degree of gambling this effect
must be harmful we should be inclined to think that it was the duty of the
state to restrict gambling to the greatest extent practicable.'

In what circumstances the State should exercise its power is the third
of the interrogatories I have framed. But before I get to it I must raise a
point which might have been brought up in any one of the three. How
are the moral judgments of society to be ascertained? By leaving it until
now, I can ask it in the more limited form that is now sufficient for my
purpose. How is the law-maker to ascertain the moral judgments of society? It is surely not enough that they should be reached by the opinion of
the majority; it would be too much to require the individual assent of
every citizen. English law has evolved and regularly uses a standard which
does not depend on the counting of heads. It is that of the reasonable
man. He is not to be confused with the rational man. He is not expected
to reason about anything and his judgment may be largely a matter of
feeling. It is the viewpoint of the man in the street—or to use an archaism
familiar to all lawyers—the man in the Clapham omnibus. He might also
be called the right-minded man. For my purpose I should like to call him
the man in the jury box, for the moral judgment of society must be something about which any twelve men or women drawn at random might
after discussion be expected to be unanimous. This was the standard the
judges applied in the days before Parliament was as active as it is now and
when they laid down rules of public policy. They did not think of themselves as making law but simply as stating principles which every right-
minded person would accept as valid. It is what Pollock called 'practical
morality,' which is based not on theological or philosophical foundations
but 'in the mass of continuous experience half-consciously or unconsciously accumulated and embodied in the morality of common sense.' He
called it also 'a certain way of thinking on questions of morality which we
expect to find in a reasonable civilized man or a reasonable Englishman,
taken at random.'

Immorality then, for the purpose of the law, is what every right-
minded person is presumed to consider to be immoral. Any immorality is
capable of affecting society injuriously and in effect to a greater or lesser
extent it usually does; this is what gives the law its *locus standi*. It cannot be
shut out. But—and this brings me to the third question—the individual
has a *locus standi* too; he cannot be expected to surrender to the judgment
of society the whole conduct of his life. It is the old and familiar question
of striking a balance between the rights and interests of society and those
of the individual. This is something which the law is constantly doing in
matters large and small. To take a very down-to-earth example, let me
consider the right of the individual whose house adjoins the highway to
have access to it; that means in these days the right to have vehicles sta-
tionary in the highway, sometimes for a considerable time if there is a lot
of loading or unloading. There are many cases in which the courts have
had to balance the private right of access against the public right to use

the highway without obstruction. It cannot be done by carving up the highway into public and private areas. It is done by recognizing that each have rights over the whole; that if each were to exercise their rights to the full, they would come into conflict; and therefore that the rights of each must be curtailed so as to ensure as far as possible that the essential needs of each are safeguarded.

I do not think that one can talk sensibly of a public and private morality any more than one can of a public or private highway. Morality is a sphere in which there is a public interest and a private interest, often in conflict, and the problem is to reconcile the two. This does not mean that it is impossible to put forward any general statements about how in our society the balance ought to be struck. Such statements cannot of their nature be rigid or precise; they would not be designed to circumscribe the operation of the law-making power but to guide those who have to apply it. While every decision which a court of law makes when it balances the public against the private interest is an *ad hoc* decision, the cases contain statements of principle to which the court should have regard when it reaches its decision. In the same way it is possible to make general statements of principle which it may be thought the legislature should bear in mind when it is considering the enactment of laws enforcing morals.

I believe that most people would agree upon the chief of these elastic principles. There must be toleration of the maximum individual freedom that is consistent with the integrity of society. It cannot be said that this is a principle that runs all through the criminal law. Much of the criminal law that is regulatory in character—the part of it that deals with *malum prohibitum* rather than *malum in se*—is based upon the opposite principle, that is, that the choice of the individual must give way to the convenience of the many. But in all matters of conscience the principle I have stated is generally held to prevail. It is not confined to thought and speech; it extends to action, as is shown by the recognition of the right to conscientious objection in war-time; this example shows also that conscience will be respected even in times of national danger. The principle appears to me to be peculiarly appropriate to all questions of morals. Nothing should be punished by the law that does not lie beyond the limits of tolerance. It is not nearly enough to say that a majority dislike a practice; there must be a real feeling of reprobation. Those who are dissatisfied with the present law on homosexuality often say that the opponents of reform are swayed simply by disgust. If that were so it would be wrong, but I do not think one can ignore disgust if it is deeply felt and not manufactured. Its presence is a good indication that the bounds of toleration are being reached. Not everything is to be tolerated. No society can do without intolerance, indignation, and disgust; they are the forces behind the moral law, and indeed it can be argued that if they or something like them are not present, the feelings of society cannot be weighty enough to deprive the individual of freedom of choice. I suppose that there is hardly anyone nowadays who would not be disgusted by the thought of deliberate cruelty to animals. No one proposes to relegate that or any other form of sadism to the realm of private morality or to allow it to be practised in public or in private. It would be possible no doubt to point out that until a comparatively short while ago nobody thought very much of cruelty to animals and also that pity and kindliness and the unwillingness to inflict pain are virtues more generally esteemed now than they have ever been in the past. But matters of this sort are not determined by rational argument. Every moral judgment, unless it claims a divine source, is simply a feeling that no right-minded man could behave in any other way without admitting that he was doing wrong. It is the power of a common sense and not the power of reason that is behind the judgments of society. But before a society can put a practice beyond the limits of tolerance there must be a deliberate judgment that the practice is injurious to society. There is, for example, a general abhorrence of homosexuality. We should ask ourselves in the first instance whether, looking at it calmly and dispassionately, we regard it as a vice so abominable that its mere presence is an offence. If that is the genuine feeling of the society in which we live, I do not see how society can be denied the right to eradicate it. Our feeling may not be so intense as that. We may feel about it that, if confined, it is tolerable, but that if it spread it might be gravely injurious; it is in this way that most societies look upon fornication, seeing it as a natural weakness which must be kept within bounds but which cannot be rooted out. It becomes then a question of balance, the danger to society in one scale and the extent of the restriction in the other. On this sort of point the value of an investigation by such a body as the Wolfenden Committee and of its conclusions is manifest.

The limits of tolerance shift. This is supplementary to what I have been saying but of sufficient importance in itself to deserve statement as a separate principle which law-makers have to bear in mind. I suppose that moral standards do not shift; so far as they come from divine revelation they do not, and I am willing to assume that the moral judgments made by a society always remain good for that society. But the extent to which society will tolerate—I mean tolerate, not approve—departures from moral standards varies from generation to generation. It may be that over-all tolerance is always increasing. The pressure of the human mind, always seeking greater freedom of thought, is outwards against the bonds of society forcing their gradual relaxation. It may be that history is a tale of contraction and expansion and that all developed societies are on their way to dissolution. I must not speak of things I do not know; and anyway as a practical matter no society is willing to make provision for its own decay. I return therefore to the simple and observable fact that in matters of morals the limits of tolerance shift. Laws, especially those which are based on morals, are less easily moved. It follows as another good working principle that in any new matter of morals the law should be slow to act. By the next generation the swell of indignation may have abated and the law be left without the strong backing which it needs. But it is then difficult to alter the law without giving the impression that moral judgment is being weakened. This is now one of the factors that is strongly militating against any alteration to the law on homosexuality.

A third elastic principle must be advanced more tentatively. It is that as far as possible privacy should be respected. This is not an idea that has ever been made explicit in the criminal law. Acts or words done or said in public or private are all brought within its scope without distinction in principle. But there goes with this a strong reluctance on the part of judges and legislators to sanction invasions of privacy in the detection of crime. The police have no more right to trespass than the ordinary citizen has; there is no general right of search; to this extent an Englishman's home is still his castle. The Government is extremely careful in the exercise even of those powers which it claims to be undisputed. Telephone tapping and interference with the mails afford a good illustration of this. A Committee of three Privy Councillors who recently inquired into these activities found that the Home Secretary and his predecessors had already formulated strict rules governing the exercise of these powers and the Committee were able to recommend that they should be continued to be exercised substantially on the same terms. But they reported that the power was 'regarded with general disfavour.'

This indicates a general sentiment that the right to privacy is something to be put in the balance against the enforcement of the law. Ought the same sort of consideration to play any part in the formation of the law? Clearly only in a very limited number of cases. When the help of the law is invoked by an injured citizen, privacy must be irrelevant; the individual cannot ask that his right to privacy should be measured against injury criminally done to another. But when all who are involved in the deed are consenting parties and the injury is done to morals, the public interest in the moral order can be balanced against the claims of privacy. The restriction on police powers of investigation goes further than the affording of a parallel; it means that the detection of crime committed in private and when there is no complaint is bound to be rather haphazard and this is an additional reason for moderation. These considerations do not justify the exclusion of all private immorality from the scope of the law. I think that, as I have already suggested, the test of 'private behaviour' should be substituted for 'private morality' and the influence of the factor should be reduced from that of a definite limitation to that of a matter to be taken into account. Since the gravity of the crime is also a proper consideration, a distinction might well be made in the case of homosexuality between the lesser acts of indecency and the full offence, which on the principles of the Wolfenden Report it would be illogical to do.

The last and the biggest thing to be remembered is that the law is concerned with the minimum and not with the maximum; there is much in the Sermon on the Mount that would be out of place in the Ten Commandments. We all recognize the gap between the moral law and the law of the land. No man is worth much who regulates his conduct with the sole object of escaping punishment, and every worthy society sets for its members standards which are above those of the law. We recognize the existence of such higher standards when we use expressions such as 'moral obligation' and 'morally bound.' The distinction was well put in the judgment of African elders in a family dispute: 'We have power to make you divide the crops, for this is our law, and we will see this is done. But we have not power to make you behave like an upright man.'

It can only be because this point is so obvious that it is so frequently ignored. Discussion among law-makers, both professional and amateur, is too often limited to what is right or wrong and good or bad for society. There is a failure to keep separate the two questions I have earlier posed—the question of society's right to pass a moral judgment and the question of whether the arm of the law should be used to enforce the judgment. The criminal law is not a statement of how people ought to behave; it is a statement of what will happen to them if they do not behave; good citizens are not expected to come within reach of it or to set their sights by it, and every enactment should be framed accordingly.

The arm of the law is an instrument to be used by society, and the decision about what particular cases it should be used in is essentially a practical one. Since it is an instrument, it is wise before deciding to use it to have regard to the tools with which it can be fitted and to the machinery which operates it. Its tools are fines, imprisonment, or lesser forms of supervision (such as Borstal and probation) and—not to be ignored—the degradation that often follows upon the publication of the crime. Are any of these suited to the job of dealing with sexual immorality? The fact that there is so much immorality which has never been brought within the law shows that there can be no general rule. It is a matter for decision in each case; but in the case of homosexuality the Wolfenden Report rightly has regard to the views of those who are experienced in dealing with this sort of crime and to those of the clergy who are the natural guardians of public morals.

The machinery which sets the criminal law in motion ends with the verdict and the sentence; and a verdict is given either by magistrates or by a jury. As a general rule, whenever a crime is sufficiently serious to justify a maximum punishment of more than three months, the accused has the right to the verdict of a jury. The result is that magistrates administer mostly what I have called the regulatory part of the law. They deal extensively with drunkenness, gambling, and prostitution, which are matters of morals or close to them, but not with any of the graver moral offences. They are more responsive than juries to the ideas of the legislature; it may not be accidental that the Wolfenden Report, in recommending increased penalties for solicitation, did not go above the limit of three months. Juries tend to dilute the decrees of Parliament with their own ideas of what should be punishable. Their province of course is fact and not law, and I do not mean that they often deliberately disregard the law. But if they think it is too stringent, they sometimes take a very merciful view of the facts. Let me take one example out of many that could be given. It is an offence to have carnal knowledge of a girl under the age of sixteen years. Consent on her part is no defence; if she did not consent, it would of course amount to rape. The law makes special provision for the situation when a boy and girl are near in age. If a man under twenty-four can prove that he had reasonable cause to believe that the girl was over the age of sixteen years, he has a good defence. The law regards the offence as sufficiently serious to make it one that is triable only by a judge at assizes. 'Reasonable cause' means not merely that the boy honestly believed that the girl was over sixteen but also that he must have had reasonable grounds for his belief. In theory it ought not to be an easy defence to make out but in fact it is extremely rare for anyone who advances it to be convicted. The fact is that the girl is often as much to blame as the boy. The object of the law, as judges repeatedly tell juries, is to protect young girls against themselves; but juries are not impressed.

The part that the jury plays in the enforcement of the criminal law, the fact that no grave offence against morals is punishable without their verdict, these are of great importance in relation to the statements of principle that I have been making. They turn what might otherwise be pure exhortation to the legislature into something like rules that the law-makers cannot safely ignore. The man in the jury box is not just an expression; he is an active reality. It will not in the long run work to make laws about morality that are not acceptable to him.

This then is how I believe my third interrogatory should be answered—not by the formulation of hard and fast rules, but by a judgment in each case taking into account the sort of factors I have been mentioning. The line that divides the criminal law from the moral is not determinable by the application of any clear-cut principle. It is like a line that divides land and sea, a coastline of irregularities and indentations. There are gaps and promontories, such as adultery and fornication, which the law has for centuries left substantially untouched. Adultery of the sort that breaks up marriage seems to me to be just as harmful to the social fabric as homosexuality or bigamy. The only ground for putting it outside the criminal law is that a law which made it a crime would be too difficult to enforce; it is too generally regarded as a human weakness not suitably punished by imprisonment. All that the law can do with fornication is to act against its worst manifestations; there is a general abhorrence of the commercialization of vice, and that sentiment gives strength to the law against brothels and immoral earnings. There is no logic to be found in this. The boundary between the criminal law and the moral law is fixed by balancing in the case of each particular crime the pros and cons of legal enforcement in accordance with the sort of considerations I have been outlining. The fact that adultery, fornication, and lesbianism are untouched by the criminal law does not prove that homosexuality ought not to be touched. The error of jurisprudence in the Wolfenden Report is caused by the search for some single principle to explain the division between crime and sin. The Report finds it in the principle that the criminal law exists for the protection of individuals; on this principle fornication in private between consenting adults is outside the law and thus it becomes logically indefensible to bring homosexuality between consenting adults in private within it. But the true principle is that the law exists for the protection of society. It does not discharge its function by protecting the individual from injury, annoyance, corruption, and exploitation; the law must protect also the institutions and the community of ideas, political and moral, without which people cannot live together. Society cannot ignore the morality of the individual any more than it can his loyalty; it flourishes on both and without either it dies. . . .

Society cannot live without morals. Its morals are those standards of conduct which the reasonable man approves. A rational man, who is also a good man, may have other standards. If he has no standards at all he is not a good man and need not be further considered. If he has standards, they may be very different; he may, for example, not disapprove of homosexuality or abortion. In that case he will not share in the common morality; but that should not make him deny that it is a social necessity. A rebel may be rational in thinking that he is right but he is irrational if he thinks that society can leave him free to rebel. . . .

27. Immorality and Treason   H. L. A. Hart

Herbert Lionel Adolphus Hart (1907–   ) spent some time as a lawyer in London and then returned to Oxford University where, in 1952, he became professor of jurisprudence. The impact of Hart's writings has been felt widely in contemporary philosophy of law.

The Wolfenden Committee on Homosexual Offences and Prostitution recommended by a majority of 12 to 1 that homosexual behaviour between consenting adults in private should no longer be a criminal offence. One of the Committee's principal grounds for this recommendation was expressed in its report in this way: 'There must remain a realm of private morality and immorality which in brief and crude terms is not the law's business.' I shall call this the liberal point of view: for it is a special application of those wider principles of liberal thought which John Stuart Mill formulated in his essay on Liberty. Mill's most famous words, less cautious perhaps than the Wolfenden Committee's, were:

> The only purpose for which power can be rightfully exercised over any member of a civilized community against his will is to prevent harm to others. His own good, either physical or moral, is not a sufficient warrant. He cannot rightfully be compelled to do or forbear . . . because in the opinion of others to do so would be wise or even right.

Repudiation of the Liberal Point of View

The liberal point of view has often been attacked, both before and after Mill. I shall discuss here the repudiation of it made by Sir Patrick Devlin, in his recent lecture, which has now been published. This contains an original and interesting argument designed to show that '*prima facie* society has the right to legislate against immorality as such' and that the Wolfenden Committee were mistaken in thinking that there is an area of private immorality which is not the law's business. Sir Patrick's case is a general one, not confined to sexual immorality, and he does not say whether or not he is opposed to the Wolfenden Committee's recommendation on homosexual behaviour. Instead he gives us a hypothetical principle by which to judge this issue. He says: 'If it is the genuine feeling of

Reprinted from *The Listener*, July 30, 1959 by permission of the author.

our society and homosexuality is a vice so abominable that its mere presence is an offence,' society has the right to eradicate it by the use of the
criminal law.

The publication by Sir Patrick of this lecture is in itself an interesting
event. It is many years since a distinguished English lawyer delivered himself of general reasoned views about the relationship of morality to the
criminal law. The last to do so with comparable skill and clarity was, I
think, the great Victorian judge James Fitzjames Stephen. It is worth
observing that Stephen, like Sir Patrick, repudiated the liberal point of
view. Indeed his gloomy but impressive book *Liberty, Equality, Fraternity*
was a direct reply to Mill's essay *On Liberty*. The most remarkable feature
of Sir Patrick's lecture is his view of the nature of morality—the morality
which the criminal law may enforce. Most previous thinkers who have
repudiated the liberal point of view have done so because they thought
that morality consisted either of divine commands or of rational principles
of human conduct discoverable by human reason. Since morality for them
had this elevated divine or rational status as the law of God or reason, it
seemed obvious that the state should enforce it, and that the function of
human law should not be merely to provide men with the opportunity for
leading a good life, but actually to see that they led it. Sir Patrick does not
rest his repudiation of the liberal point of view on these religious or rationalist conceptions. Indeed much that he writes reads like an abjuration of
the notion that reasoning or thinking has much to do with morality.
English popular morality has no doubt its historical connection with the
Christian religion: 'That,' says Sir Patrick, 'is how it got there.' But it does
not owe its present status or social significance to religion any more than
to reason.

What, then, is it? According to Sir Patrick it is primarily a matter of
feeling. 'Every moral judgment,' he says, 'is a feeling that no right-minded
man could act in any other way without admitting that he was doing
wrong.' Who then must feel this way if we are to have what Sir Patrick
calls a public morality? He tells us that it is 'the man in the street,' 'the man
in the jury box,' or (to use the phrase so familiar to English lawyers) 'the
man on the Clapham omnibus.' For the moral judgments of society so far
as the law is concerned are to be ascertained by the standards of the reasonable man, and he is not to be confused with the rational man. Indeed,
Sir Patrick says 'he is not expected to reason about anything and his judgment may be largely a matter of feeling.'

Intolerance, Indignation, and Disgust

But what precisely are the relevant feelings, the feelings which may
justify use of the criminal law? Here the argument becomes a little complex. Widespread dislike of a practice is not enough. There must, says Sir
Patrick, be 'a real feeling of reprobation.' Disgust is not enough either.
What is crucial is a combination of intolerance, indignation, and disgust.
These three are the forces behind the moral law, without which it is not
'weighty enough to deprive the individual of freedom of choice.' Hence

there is, in Sir Patrick's outlook, a crucial difference between the mere adverse moral judgment of society and one which is inspired by feeling raised to the concert pitch of intolerance, indignation, and disgust.

This distinction is novel and also very important. For on it depends the weight to be given to the fact that when morality is enforced individual liberty is necessarily cut down. Though Sir Patrick's abstract formulation of his views on this point is hard to follow, his examples make his position fairly clear. We can see it best in the contrasting things he says about fornication and homosexuality. In regard to fornication, public feeling in most societies is not now of the concert-pitch intensity. We may feel that it is tolerable if confined: only its spread might be gravely injurious. In such cases the question whether individual liberty should be restricted is for Sir Patrick a question of balance between the danger to society in the one scale, and the restriction of the individual in the other. But if, as may be the case with homosexuality, public feeling is up to concert pitch, if it expresses a 'deliberate judgment' that a practice as such is injurious to society, if there is 'a genuine feeling that it is a vice so abominable that its mere presence is an offence,' then it is beyond the limits of tolerance, and society may eradicate it. In this case, it seems, no further balancing of the claims of individual liberty is to be done, though as a matter of prudence the legislator should remember that the popular limits of tolerance may shift: the concert-pitch feeling may subside. This may produce a dilemma for the law; for the law may then be left without the full moral backing that it needs, yet it cannot be altered without giving the impression that the moral judgment is being weakened.

A Shared Morality

If this is what morality is—a compound of indignation, intolerance, and disgust—we may well ask what justification there is for taking it, and turning it as such, into criminal law with all the misery which criminal punishment entails. Here Sir Patrick's answer is very clear and simple. A collection of individuals is not a society; what makes them into a society is among other things a shared or public morality. This is as necessary to its existence as an organized government. So society may use the law to preserve its morality like anything else essential to it. 'The suppression of vice is as much the law's business as the suppression of subversive activities.' The liberal point of view which denies this is guilty of 'an error in jurisprudence': for it is no more possible to define an area of private morality than an area of private subversive activity. There can be no 'theoretical limits' to legislation against immorality just as there are no such limits to the power of the state to legislate against treason and sedition.

Surely all this, ingenious as it is, is misleading. Mill's formulation of the liberal point of view may well be too simple. The grounds for interfering with human liberty are more various than the single criterion of 'harm to others' suggests: cruelty to animals or organizing prostitution for gain do not, as Mill himself saw, fall easily under the description of harm to others. Conversely, even where there is harm to others in the most literal sense, there may well be other principles limiting the extent to which he often stresses between theoretical and practical limits. But with criteria, not a single criterion, determining when human liberty may be restricted. Perhaps this is what Sir Patrick means by a curious distinction which he often stresses between theoretical and practical limits. But with all its simplicities the liberal point of view is a better guide than Sir Patrick to clear thought on the proper relation of morality to the criminal law: for it stresses what he obscures—namely, the points at which thought is needed before we turn popular morality into criminal law.

Society and Moral Opinion

No doubt we would all agree that a consensus of moral opinion on certain matters is essential if society is to be worth living in. Laws against murder, theft, and much else would be of little use if they were not supported by a widely diffused conviction that what these laws forbid is also immoral. So much is obvious. But it does not follow that everything to which the moral vetoes of accepted morality attach is of equal importance to society; nor is there the slightest reason for thinking of morality as a seamless web: one which will fall to pieces carrying society with it, unless all its emphatic vetoes are enforced by law. Surely even in the face of the moral feeling that is up to concert pitch—the trio of intolerance, indignation, and disgust—we must pause to think. We must ask a question at two different levels which Sir Patrick never clearly enough identifies or separates. First, we must ask whether a practice which offends moral feeling is harmful, independently of its repercussion on the general moral code. Secondly, what about repercussion on the moral code? Is it really true that failure to translate this item of general morality into criminal law will jeopardize the whole fabric of morality and so of society?

We cannot escape thinking about these two different questions merely by repeating to ourselves the vague nostrum: 'This is part of public morality and public morality must be preserved if society is to exist.' Sometimes Sir Patrick seems to admit this, for he says in words which both Mill and the Wolfenden Report might have used, that there must be the maximum respect for individual liberty consistent with the integrity of society. Yet this, as his contrasting examples of fornication and homosexuality show, turns out to mean only that the immorality which the law may punish must be generally felt to be intolerable. This plainly is no adequate substitute for a reasoned estimate of the damage to the fabric of society likely to ensue if it is not suppressed.

Nothing perhaps shows more clearly the inadequacy of Sir Patrick's approach to this problem than his comparison between the suppression of sexual immorality and the suppression of treason or subversive activity. Private subversive activity is, of course, a contradiction in terms because 'subversion' means over-throwing government, which is a public thing. But it is grotesque, even where moral feeling against homosexuality is up to concert pitch, to think of the homosexual behaviour of two adults in private as in any way like treason or sedition either in intention or effect. We can make it *seem* like treason only if we assume that deviation from a general moral code is bound to affect that code, and to lead not merely to its modification but to its destruction. The analogy could begin to be plausible only if it was clear that offending against this item of morality was likely to jeopardize the whole structure. But we have ample evidence for believing that people will not abandon morality, will not think any better of murder, cruelty and dishonesty, merely because some private sexual practice which they abominate is not punished by the law.

Because this is so the analogy with treason is absurd. Of course 'No man is an island': what one man does in private, if it is known, may affect others in many different ways. Indeed it may be that deviation from general sexual morality by those whose lives, like the lives of many homosexuals, are noble ones and in all other ways exemplary will lead to what Sir Patrick calls the shifting of the limits of tolerance. But if this has any analogy in the sphere of government it is not the overthrow of ordered government, but a peaceful change in its form. So we may listen to the promptings of common sense and of logic, and say that though there could not logically be a sphere of private treason there is a sphere of private morality and immorality.

Sir Patrick's doctrine is also open to a wider, perhaps a deeper, criticism. In his reaction against a rationalist morality and his stress on feeling, he has I think thrown out the baby and kept the bath water; and the bath water may turn out to be very dirty indeed. When Sir Patrick's lecture was first delivered *The Times* greeted it with these words: 'There is a moving and welcome humility in the conception that society should not be asked to give its reason for refusing to tolerate what in its heart it feels intolerable.' This drew from a correspondent in Cambridge the retort: 'I am afraid that we are less humble than we used to be. We once burnt old women because, without giving our reasons, we felt in our hearts that witchcraft was intolerable.'

This retort is a bitter one, yet its bitterness is salutary. We are not, I suppose, likely, in England, to take again to the burning of old women for witchcraft or to punishing people for associating with those of a different race or colour, or to punishing people again for adultery. Yet if these things were viewed with intolerance, indignation, and disgust, as the second of them still is in some countries, it seems that on Sir Patrick's principles no rational criticism could be opposed to the claim that they should be punished by law. We could only pray, in his words, that the limits of tolerance might shift.

Curious Logic

It is impossible to see what curious logic has led Sir Patrick to this result. For him a practice is immoral if the thought of it makes the man on the Clapham omnibus sick. So be it. Still, why should we not summon all the resources of our reason, sympathetic understanding, as well as critical intelligence, and insist that before general moral feeling is turned into criminal law it is submitted to scrutiny of a different kind from Sir Patrick's? Surely, the legislator should ask whether the general morality is based on ignorance, superstition, or misunderstanding; whether there is a false conception that those who practise what it condemns are in other ways dangerous or hostile to society; and whether the misery to many parties, the blackmail and the other evil consequences of criminal punishment, especially for sexual offences, are well understood. It is surely extraordinary that among the things which Sir Patrick says are to be considered before we legislate against immorality these appear nowhere; not even as 'practical considerations,' let alone 'theoretical limits.' To any theory which, like this one, asserts that the criminal law may be used on the vague ground that the preservation of morality is essential to society and yet omits to stress the need for critical scrutiny, our reply should be: 'Morality, what crimes may be committed in thy name!'

As Mill saw, and de Tocqueville showed in detail long ago in his critical by sympathetic study of democracy, it is fatally easy to confuse the democratic principle that power should be in the hands of the majority with the utterly different claim that the majority, with power in their hands, need respect no limits. Certainly there is a special risk in a democracy that the majority may dictate how all should live. This is the risk we run, and should gladly run; for it is the price of all that is so good in democratic rule. But loyalty to democratic principles does not require us to maximize this risk: yet this is what we shall do if we mount the man in the street on the top of the Clapham omnibus and tell him that if only he feels sick enough about what other people do in private to demand its suppression by law no theoretical criticism can be made of his demand.

Suggestions for Further Reading

Anthologies

Rachels, James (ed.). *Moral Problems.* 2nd ed. New York: Harper, 1975. Recent essays on such currently discussed moral issues as sex, abortion, punishment, and death.

Singer, Marcus (ed.). *Morals and Values.* New York: Scribner, 1977. A good collection of readings on the main problems of ethical theory.

Taylor, Paul (ed.). *Problems of Moral Philosophy.* Belmont, Calif.: Wadsworth, 1978. A good anthology of important writings on a wide range of ethical problems.

Wasserstrom, Richard (ed.). *Today's Moral Problems.* New York: Macmillan, 1979. Recent essays on a variety of moral issues.

Individual Works

Barnes, Hazel E. *An Existentialist Ethics.* New York: Knopf, 1967. A clear presentation of an existentialist approach to ethics, as well as a consideration and rejection of a number of other contemporary ethical views.

Binkley, Luther. *Contemporary Ethical Theories.* New York: Citadel, 1961. A clear discussion of the twentieth-century analytic philosophers' approach to ethics.

Brandt, William. *Ethical Theory.* Englewood Cliffs, N.J.: Prentice-Hall, 1959. This is an excellent but somewhat difficult introduction to ethical theory. There are excellent bibliographies on almost all major topics in ethical theory.

Fletcher, Joseph. *Situation Ethics: The New Morality.* Philadelphia: Westminster, 1966. A contemporary Christian view of ethics, which stresses love as the basis for decision-making in ethics.

Frankena, William. *Ethics.* Englewood Cliffs, N.J.: Prentice-Hall, 1963. Provides a clear, concise statement of the major ethical problems and positions.

Hospers, John. *Human Conduct.* New York: Harcourt, 1961. An excellent, clearly written textbook, which is highly recommended for the beginning student.

Mill, John Stuart. *Utilitarianism.* Indianapolis: Bobbs, 1957. A classic statement of the utilitarian position, which differs from Bentham's version in several important ways.

Olson, Robert G. *The Morality of Self-interest.* New York: Harcourt, 1965. An interesting defense of a version of egoism.

Rand, Ayn. *The Virtue of Selfishness.* New York: Signet, 1964. An interesting, but at times confusing, defense of egoism by a popular novelist and an intellectual leader of the libertarian movement.

Russell, Bertrand. *Human Society in Ethics and Politics.* New York: Simon & Schuster, 1952. A clearly written analysis of a variety of ethical issues by a great modern philosopher.

Smart, J. J. C. and Bernard Williams. *Utilitarianism: for and Against.* London: Cambridge U.P., 1973. Smart gives a detailed description and defense of utilitarianism and Williams offers a variety of criticisms.

Dictionary of the History of Ideas: Studies of Selected Pivotal Ideas. Philip P. Weiner, editor-in-chief. New York: Scribners, 1973. Substantial and clearly written essays emphasizing the historical development of topics discussed in this part. Designed to inform the nonspecialist, each essay concludes with a select bibliography.

Encyclopedia of Philosophy. Paul Edwards, editor-in-chief. New York: Macmillan, 1967. The student will find many worthwhile articles on the subject treated in this part, and excellent bibliographies.

Four: Democracy and Society

Introduction

Consider these two situations. It is April 14 late in the evening. Completing your federal income tax form, you discover to your dismay that you owe an additional tax of two hundred dollars to the U.S. government. After triple-checking your return, you sigh and write out a personal check in the amount required. For it is either pay or be fined or perhaps be clapped into jail. Nothing voluntary here. You are being coerced by other human beings; if you do not comply, you will suffer. Muttering, you trudge to the mailbox located on the next block. Returning to your home, a man you've never seen before points a revolver at you and demands that you give him all of your money. Nothing voluntary here, either. Choking down your anger, you give the robber the fifty dollars in your wallet. The story ends somewhat happily. You reach home safe but poorer.

Do these two situations differ in any significant way? Or are they the same except for incidental details? Both involve financial loss and coercion that you would prefer to avoid. Is the government nothing more than a robber on a more ambitious scale? Is the robber really an individual entrepreneur heroically defying a company monopoly? Of course, many would hold that the two situations are not comparable at all. The federal income tax is legitimate, legal, justifiable; whereas robbery is criminal, illegal, unjustifiable. The income tax constitutes a self-assessment; through your elected representatives you've consented to it. You have not consented to be robbed. As a result of the sixteenth amendment, the federal income tax is constitutional. Armed robbery is unconstitutional. Certainly armed robbery is undemocratic. The federal income tax possesses a political philosophy to give it rational support; armed robbery remains innocent of any political philosophy justifying it.

The field of political philosophy offers a rich and varied landscape of problems, methods of analysis, and solutions. This section focuses on one problem: Can the democratic state be justified rationally? Can its superiority to other forms of government be shown on rational grounds? All governments, whether allegedly democratic or not, claim to be legitimate. That is to say, they assert that they not only have the allegiance of those subject to their authority but that they also deserve loyalty. Democratic governments are no exception to this generalization. The government of the United States claims not only that its citizens must support it by paying taxes and, if necessary, must protect and defend it by fighting and dying in war; it

239

further holds that American citizens ought to be ready and willing to make these sacrifices. If any individual American citizen or group of American citizens refuse to obey the government, then those in authority not only can use the police power to compel obedience but are justified in doing so. A legitimate government maintains that its physical authority ultimately rests on moral authority. Governments justify their existence and policies by appealing to a political philosophy. Democratic governments claim to be promoting the political philosophy of democracy. Defending the cause of the Union at Gettysburg, Lincoln did not rest that defense on the threat of force; he declared that the nation was "conceived in liberty and dedicated to the proposition that all men are created equal." A political philosophy, whatever else it may comprise, consists of propositions claiming to be true and consistent with one another. And governments, particularly when their authority is seriously and sharply questioned, picture themselves implementing some political philosophy. Therefore, the political philosophy of democracy is not to be identified with familiar democratic practices such as universal suffrage, the two-party system, political conventions, a president and a congress, specific legislation, and so on; these actual governmental forms and exercises presumably are the most effective means so far devised for translating the abstract propositions of democratic political philosophy into concrete reality. A democratic government is supposed to be democratic political philosophy in action.

Of course, the political philosophy of democracy includes many more propositions than merely one or two basic ones such as that all men are created equal. Any serious political philosophy turns out to be more complex than that in the sense of being composed of a large number of propositions. Incidentally, this fact accounts for the inconsistency among some of the propositions that often exists unnoticed in the crowd. However, let us concentrate on the proposition that all men are created equal for the moment in order to facilitate the task of briefly sketching what a philosopher in his professional capacity does when he scrutinizes a political philosophy. Democratic politicians seek to implement the political philosophy of democracy, espouse principles, and renew people's dedication to those tenets. The philosopher works along different lines. He seeks to articulate each and every proposition constituting the political philosophy of democracy and to state them as free from ambiguity, vagueness, and emotional connotations as possible. What does the proposition "All men are created equal" mean? Is this the best statement of the proposition? Each word in the statement of the proposition can be found in the dictionary and the words are combined in a grammatically correct way. Does "created" imply some conception of a divine creation of man so that democratic political philosophy would have to include certain theological statements about God and the origin of man? Certainly some proponents of democracy have argued that democracy rests on supernatural and revealed religion, that it really is

God's will. Some critics of democracy also have agreed with the religious defenders of democracy that it has a divine basis, that democracy is Christian ethics translated into a secular vocabulary. However, these critics have gone on to argue that the soundness and even the sense of Christian ethics is inextricably bound up with acceptance of the whole Christian faith. But in terms of the scientific outlook of the present the Christian faith changes from truth to myth and so democracy along with it becomes no more than a dream, no matter how appealing. In reply, religious exponents of democracy have contended that the warranted conclusion to draw is that if democracy is to survive and prosper, everyone should "get religion." Our religiously pluralistic society has encouraged defenders of this religious basis of democracy to enlarge that basis beyond Christianity to embrace other religions and even further to just embrace religion in general. Further, how is the proposition that each individual is of unique worth to be rendered consistent with the principle that all men are created equal? What is meant by "equality?" Equal talents? Equal incomes? Equality before the law? Equality of opportunity? Every adult citizen who is not obviously insane or retarded can fulfill competently the duties of any elective office? Does "equality" mean all of these, some of these, or none of these? Finally, granted clarity and agreement on the meaning of the proposition "All men are created equal," is the proposition true or false? At least what evidence, were it to be found, would be accepted as falsifying the proposition? Is "All men are created equal" an empirical generalization such as water freezes at 32 degrees F.? If it is, then producing one human being created unequal would prove the generalization false. Or is the proposition "All men are created equal" prescriptive, rather than descriptive? Instead of asserting some state of affairs, is the proposition simply the expression of a desire: I or we wish, that all men were created equal? But, then, if it were prescriptive, the proposition "All men are created equal" would be neither true nor false. A wish is neither true nor false.

The aim in this introduction is not to answer these questions but to suggest the distinctive character of the philosophic approach to political thought, an enterprise consisting in the combination of clarification of concepts, determination of logical consistency, formulation and assessment of criteria of truth and falsity, and the ultimate weighing of the truth claims of the principles appealed to to justify political action. Political philosophy is distinct from day-to-day political debate and descriptive accounts of actual political behavior, although the latter may influence political philosophy and vice versa. Some political philosophies are so comprehensive they range from offering shrewd practical advice on how to be a successful tyrant or win a revolution to envisioning a total form or way of life covering all aspects of individual and collective human life; from how to win elections or seize control of the state to doctrines about the nature of human nature, the direction of history, and the nature of reality, from maneuvers to metaphysics. Certainly, in terms of speculative boldness and development, political philosophy extends beyond what social scientists would consider genuinely scientific theorizing. This bulging over the boundaries of the strictly scientific often has enhanced the power of political philosophies to elicit an active devotion from millions, which at times is religious in both intensity and endurance. From Plato to Karl Popper, influencing the actions of men has been one of the main goals of political philosophers.

For a moment let us return to the cases of paying one's taxes and being robbed. The federal income tax is constitutional and the law of the land and so presumably it represents the will of a majority of American citizens. Yet there are Americans who do not want, do not consent, to pay income taxes any more than they do to being robbed. What rationally persuasive grounds can be found in democratic political philosophy why a dissenting minority should abide by the will of a majority and not seek to do everything possible to successfully evade it? Does a majority vote really reflect the will of a majority of the citizens? Convincing answers to these questions are not as easy to find as one might first suppose. Laws are devised and passed by elected representatives and not by a direct vote of the people. Representatives in government are cultivated constantly by skillful lobbyists representing not the people in general but powerful, wealthy special interest groups. Before laws can be voted on by a legislature as a whole, they must be reported out of a legislative committee composed only of a small number of legislators. As a result of the seniority system in the U.S. Congress, the powerful chairmanships of these committees often are held by representatives who are re-elected many times by a small minority of the American people in districts and states where the candidate faces no significant political opposition. The cost of campaigning for high national office has grown to the point where only wealthy individuals or those who have put themselves heavily in debt to wealthy individuals, corporations, unions, and other groups can afford it. The president of the United States, ostensibly representing all of the American people, is not elected directly by the people. Provided he has the necessary number of electoral votes, a candidate can become president of the United States even though he does not gain a majority of the popular vote. Furthermore, a majority of the eligible voters often do not even vote. Finally, few candidates for public office are elected unanimously; voters cast ballots against them by voting for opponents or by abstaining from voting entirely. That is to say, at any given time a considerable number of Americans are opposed to those governing them and do not consider their elected rulers to be representing their will at all.

However, let us suppose that the machinery of democratic government functioned perfectly and infallibly registered the will of the people. Is what the majority believes to be true or good always so? At one time a majority of Europeans believed the earth to be flat. A few generations ago a majority of

Americans believed that slavery was right and just. Of course, by sheer overwhelming weight of numbers a majority could force a dissenting minority to go along with its wishes, however much the minority might disagree silently. But all this would prove is the superior might of the majority, not its superior knowledge or virtue. If a dissenting minority should submit to a majority merely because decision, however arrived at, is better than indecisive drifting, a dictator securely in power could supply the decisiveness in a less inconstant manner than could a vague, shifting majority confused by conflicting propaganda. The quality of a majority decision is the resultant of the quality of the individuals who compose the majority; for example, a majority composed of stupid people would be more likely to reach foolish decisions than wise ones. Such a majority of poor quality might accidentally produce some wise decisions; nevertheless, fortuitous wisdom hardly seems a very persuasive reason for always accepting the will of the majority. Should not the vote of an intelligent, informed, responsible, civic-minded person count two, three, or more times the vote of some lout who must be dragged out of a saloon on Election Day and lured to the polls to vote with the promise of a free drink afterwards? Perhaps individuals should earn the privilege of the vote by first making some worthwhile contribution to society or only on the condition that they be self-supporting or have I.Q.s over 80. It has been argued that those who possess more property and more capital hold a greater stake in the fate of the country because they have more to lose than those who possess less and, therefore, should determine government policy. Those with little or nothing to lose are likely to act selfishly, rashly, and irresponsibly. Wealthy officeholders would be immune to bribes since they don't need more money, already having more than enough.

A rational justification of democracy would be impossible without weighing the merits of alternative forms of government. Everyone is familiar with the *mot* to the effect that democracy is the worst form of government except for all the other forms of government that have been tried. Yet the claimed superior worth of democracy hardly goes uncontested. The political philosophy of communism, now subscribed to by millions of people, views American democracy as a sham doomed to disappear in the future. The political philosophy of anarchism opposes American democracy because it sees all government as inherently evil.

These foregoing remarks are not intended to settle the issue of the merits of democracy; they are intended to point up the fact that it is a real, vital issue.

John Dewey long has been recognized as one of the foremost philosophical defenders of democracy. Throughout an unusually long productive life, Dewey sought to reinterpret nineteenth-century American democracy in a way that would be consonant with the scientific-industrial society of the twentieth century. He envisions democracy as a total way of life and not merely as a form of government. For Dewey, democracy is the complete realization of what it means to be a community. The political practices associated with democracy are the "best means" so far invented for achieving the "participation of every mature human being in the formation of the values that regulate the living of men together." Dewey sees this "formation" of values as a never finished, ongoing process, rather than as the discovery of some eternal, absolute system of values. The spirit of democracy is a liberal one, a spirit that ceaselessly criticizes its first principles. Such criticism does not weaken society, as both reactionary and radical dogmatists contend; it strengthens democracy. Hence, the basic freedom in a democracy must be freedom of mind, an essential condition for the flourishing of the liberal spirit.

Dewey appeals to the nature of human nature to justify democracy. No one is wise or good enough to rule others without their consent. The Plato of the *Republic* is wrong; no one can be *made* wise or good enough. There is no expertise of ruling and consequently no experts at the task to whom we should submit ourselves totally. The main reason for this irremediable lack of experts at ruling is that no ruler or set of rulers can ever know enough to justify their absolute authority. As Dewey puts it, only the person who wears the shoe best knows where it pinches. And he must be able to make the rulers pay attention to his pain. A democratic form of government, however imperfect it may be, has been more effective in accomplishing this securing of the attention of rulers and getting them to act to remove the pain than has any king or dictatorship, whether exercised by the proletariat or by some other group or individual. Unless rulers can be checked and brought to heel by the ruled, the former, no matter how well intentioned, invariably will oppress the latter. And all oppression is evil. This restraint of the few by the many is the *leitmotiv* of any democratic society. The less gifted, the layman, always must be able to control the more gifted, the expert, or else sooner or later the latter will ride roughshod over the former. This is a hard saying for many academics and other intellectuals, all too many of whom have willingly served "benevolent" despots while dreaming in their sleep of being such despots.

Dewey finds this democratic subordination of the rulers to the ruled, whether in government or any other social institution, very imperfectly realized in any existing society. For him democracy is a faith, an ideal. A faith, an ideal can only be assessed by discovering what consequences flow from acting on it. And we cannot discover those consequences except by acting. To use an illustration Dewey does not employ, the merits of Woodrow Wilson's ideal of a League of Nations could not be rationally justified by abstract speculation alone but only by trying to put it into practice. Did the failure of the actual League of Nations prove Wilson's ideal a fatuous one? No, the Wilsonian faith was reincarnated in the United Nations whose ultimate fate has not yet been decided. And the nature of the decision depends on what we do now and in the future. Similarly, the merit of any individual cannot be assessed by any principle such as family, race, religion, or other criterion antecedent to what he does and its consequences. Democratic equality must not be confused with equality of abilities; it is equality of opportunity, opportunity for each individual to show what he *can* do. Ideals, individuals, institutions, and philosophies must be tested by their results, not by their origins or some fixed nature ascribed to them. Therefore, the only adequate test of democracy would be the fuller practice of democracy. The cure for the ills of democracy is more democracy. Many of our social institutions developed before the advent of modern democracy and so reflect the undemocratic habits of an authoritarian past. Education is the key to the success of democracy; modern education must be so designed as to nurture democratic habits in the young. For the anarchists are wrong in contending all government to be evil; group life, particularly in our complex society, necessitates planning, organization— that is, government of some form. The issue is not whether there shall be government or no government but rather what kind of government will elicit from each member of the community whatever of value he has to contribute through his voluntary participation.

The American critic of ideas H. L. Mencken has been particularly critical of the democratic idea. Mencken also was a journalist who reported on nearly every national political convention of the first half of the twentieth century and possessed an intimate knowledge of American politics and politicians. Mencken believed that most defenders of democracy viewed the workings of democratic government through an idealistic haze and so did not see them as they actually were but as they wanted them to be. Mencken sees democratic politics as a "mere battle of rival rogues" to get into office and then to stay in office. Without exception, all politicians are frauds, the worst being the reformers who try to disguise their fraudulence with moral pretense. No politician could ever fully tell what he honestly believes and hope to get elected. Democracy demands its leaders be dishonest. Democracy does not promote human dignity; it destroys it as surely as any authoritarian regime, indeed more surely by steady moral erosion than by violent suppression.

To Mencken, the political philosophy of democracy rests on false premises. The common man is not the repository of some special wisdom; on the contrary, he is incurably stupid and incompetent, dominated by the emotion of fear, above all, the fear of ideas. He does not yearn for liberty; he dreads it. What he wants is security, a cowlike contentment. A small minority composed of unusual people like Dewey desire intellectual freedom; Dewey, in Mencken's view, succumbs to the common error of supposing that most men want that he wants. No wonder liberals again and again are surprised and outraged when they fall victim to periodic witch hunts. If the liberals were realistic, they would expect this in a democracy. They then would see that more democracy would not cure the ills of democracy but would instead utterly destroy the liberty they cherish so highly. The common man does not want equality of opportunity, which would give the superior man the opportunity to develop his superiority and thereby triumph over his inferiors. The common man does not want to be "underprivileged"; he longs for the advantage over his betters, not equality with them. The unmistakable sign of the inferiority of the common man is his preoccupation with morality. Hence, in a democracy where the common man rules, every issue becomes a moral issue. For morality is the chief weapon in the arsenal of the weak, inferior man in his struggle with his natural superiors whom he seeks to enfeeble by poisoning them with bad conscience. Those who feel threatened or incapable of mastering their environment gabble most about "justice" and their "sacred rights." John D. Rockefeller, Sr., amassing a gigantic fortune by ruthlessly destroying his business competitors while teaching Sunday school every week, symbolizes the dream of the common man come true. America has generated an aristocracy; but, alas, it has turned out to be merely common after all—a fearful, selfish, hypocritical plutocracy.

According to Mencken's criticism, not only is the political philosophy of democracy dependent on false propositions but it also promotes meretricious values. It exalts dunderheads, cowards, cads; it persecutes intelligent, honest, courageous men who will not lie and who cannot be bought. The communists are correct in seeing human history as a protracted struggle but interpret it too narrowly as a war of economic classes. In reality, this long civil war within humanity is broader and more fundamental than economics; it is the conflict between a superior minority struggling to grow and progress against the repeated efforts of an inferior and envious majority to hold it back. The political philosophy of democracy amounts to nothing more than the war propaganda of that reactionary majority. And the war? It is the forays of those denied admittance to gain entrance to an exclusive club. When at last they succeed, they fail. For when all can belong, the club has lost its exclusivity and membership loses all value. Meanwhile, the original members have formed another exclusive club now ripe for attack. And so the self-defeating war goes on, thrilling, sometimes hilarious, always cruel.

Lenin champions a portion of the inferior and reactionary majority Mencken condemns: the proletariat. For Lenin, capitalists constitute a fearful, selfish, reactionary minority oppressing a noble and progressive majority, whereas members of Mencken's superior minority and inferior majority are to be found in all social and economic classes. True democracy, Lenin contends, will be realized only in the classless society that will follow the seizure of the state by the workers and their elimination of the capitalists. The so-called democracy of capitalism—"democracy for the rich," as Lenin calls it—is a sham because its narrow restrictions "exclude and squeeze out the poor from politics and from an active share in democracy." Lenin agrees that the cure for the ills of democracy is more democracy: proletarian democracy. This greater democracy will never come by liberal reform as Dewey and other bourgeois democrats suppose but only by violent revolution. The limits of capitalist democracy are revealed by the refusal of the capitalist class to consent to its elimination by its own wage slaves. The true democracy of the classless society with its full participation of to each according to his need and from each according to his ability will mean more freedom for the proletarian because the dictatorship of the proletariat will deprive the capitalist of his freedom to exploit the workers and shove him along the way to extinction. And as the capitalist exploiter disappears, the state will "wither away" because there will be no need for the machinery of organized suppression, which is the essence of the state. Debate concerning whether or not the revolution, the dictatorship of the proletariat, the withering away of the state, and the advent of the classless society *ought* to happen or not would be useless; they must occur; they are inevitable according to absolute dialectical laws of historical development discovered by Karl Marx. The only question is whether or not one recognizes and accepts the truth of Marxism. Those who do not face certain defeat and oblivion.

Kropotkin argues that anarchism is the only way out of the political and social dilemma in which we find ourselves as the result of nineteenth-century social and political developments. The dilemma is that political freedom and economic freedom appear to be mutually exclusive; and men ardently desire both freedoms. If government is not to be too strong to be oppressive, then the capitalist will be left free to oppress the worker; if the government is to be strong enough to prevent the capitalist from enslaving the workers, then the government will enslave all citizens. Either we have wage-slavery or we have state-slavery. Capitalist democracy and the communist dictatorship of the proletariat are equally evil. Confronted with a dilemma, men first try to convince themselves that one alternative is a lesser evil than the other. However, twentieth-century experience with capitalist democracy and its economic booms and busts and imperialist wars and with communist dictatorships of the proletariat actually established clearly proves that both alternatives are equally repugnant. Kropotkin argues that anarchism can provide both economic and political freedom by abolishing both private property and the state. Anarchism means the elimination of coercion whether employed by capitalists or commissars. Anarchism will replace coercion, not with disorder as critics charge but with voluntary consent and cooperation. Such free consent and cooperation is not artificial but "a pronounced tendency of human society." Human history shows mankind moving toward greater and greater individual freedom and the elimination of the tyranny of man over man. Voluntary cooperation has been encouraged by biological evolution because it promotes the preservation of the species. Indeed, Kropotkin maintains, free consent and cooperation have been more important during the course of biological evolution for the "survival of the fittest" than have struggle and conflict. In Kropotkin's reading, history and evolution point to anarchism as the next stage of the human career. Not surprisingly, Kropotkin repudiates the deliberate violence of bomb throwing and assassination of public officials that are sometimes associated with anarchism, often by critics seeking to discredit anarchism. Other political philosophies admit the desirability of anarchism as an ideal but either reject it as forever impractical or place its realization somewhere in the remote future or in an equally remote past. Kropotkin's analysis contends that anarchism is realizable now; we are prompted to it by our current political dilemma, by history and by evolution.

Although the readings by Dewey, Mencken, Lenin, and Kropotkin make incompatible claims, there are significant areas of agreement within them. The harmony is worth pointing out in view of the intense partisan emotion that is often aroused by political controversy. The student should seek to formulate both the propositions on which these philosophers agree and those on which they disagree. Are these propositions really propositions, factual claims? What conceivable evidence would prove them true or false? What value judgments, avowed and hidden, do these philosophers make and how do they defend them? Are these political philosophies internally consistent?

Today the appropriateness of programs of preferential treatment of certain groups in a democracy officially dedicated to equality arouses continuing and bitter controversy. Carl Cohen argues that what is at issue is the desirability of preference by race, not the appropriateness of affirmative action. Racial injustice should not be tolerated but eliminated promptly and energetically. Is preference by race a just means to use for the purpose of removing racial injustice? This issue has been raised by racially preferential admissions to law schools and medical schools but certainly is not confined to such a context. In Cohen's view neither the requirements of justice nor American society's interest in integration validly support a policy of preferential treatment by race. What we should strive for is equal treatment rather than preferential treatment. The results of preferential treatment by race injure more than benefit, no matter what the race.

Richard Wasserstrom does not claim to have proven the rightness and desirability of programs of preferential treatment. What he does argue is that such programs are not racist and sexist nor unjust or unprincipled. There is no inconsistency in arguing for preferential programs and against racism and sexism. Contemporary social reality in the United States is such that programs of preferential treatment could be an effective means for achieving equality and integration. Without vigorous implementation of policies such as preferential treatment, our many racist and sexist institutions are unlikely to reform.

28. A Defense of Democracy   John Dewey

John Dewey (1859–1952) wrote systematic treatises on subjects in all major fields of philosophy and earned a worldwide reputation as one of America's greatest philosophers.

. . . Democracy is much broader than a special political form, a method of conducting government, of making laws and carrying on governmental administration by means of popular suffrage and elected officers. It is that, of course. But it is something broader and deeper than that. The political and governmental phase of democracy is a means, the best means so far found, for realizing ends that lie in the wide domain of human relationships and the development of human personality. It is, as we often say, though perhaps without appreciating all that is involved in the saying, a way of life, social and individual. The key-note of democracy as a way of life may be expressed, it seems to me, as the necessity for the participation of every mature human being in formation of the values that regulate the living of men together: which is necessary from the standpoint of both the general social welfare and the full development of human beings as individuals.

Universal suffrage, recurring elections, responsibility of those who are in political power to the voters, and the other factors of democratic government are means that have been found expedient for realizing democracy as the truly human way of living. They are not a final end and a final value. They are to be judged on the basis of their contribution to the end. It is a form of idolatry to erect means into the end which they serve. Democratic political forms are simply the best means that human wit has devised up to a special time in history. But they rest back upon the idea that no man or limited set of men is wise enough or good enough to rule others without their consent; the positive meaning of this statement is that all those who are affected by social institutions must have a share in producing and managing them. The two facts that each one is influenced in what he does and enjoys and in what he becomes by the institutions under which he lives, and that therefore he shall have, in a democracy, a voice in shaping them, are the passive and active sides of the same fact.

The development of political democracy came about through substitution of the method of mutual consultation and voluntary agreement for the method of subordination of the many to the few enforced from above. Social arrangements which involve fixed subordination are maintained by coercion. The coercion need not be physical. There have existed, for short periods, benevolent despotisms. But coercion of some sort there has been; perhaps economic, certainly psychological and moral. The very fact of exclusion from participation is a subtle form of suppression. It gives indi-

From "Democracy and Educational Administration," *School and Society,* Vol. 45, No. 1162, April 3, 1937. Reprinted by permission of USA TODAY, successor to SCHOOL AND SOCIETY.

viduals no opportunity to reflect and decide upon what is good for them. Others who are supposed to be wiser and who in any case have more power decide the question for them and also decide the methods and means by which subjects may arrive at the enjoyment of what is good for them. This form of coercion and suppression is more subtle and more effective than is overt intimidation and restraint. When it is habitual and embodied in social institutions, it seems the normal and natural state of affairs. The mass usually become unaware that they have a claim to a development of their own powers. Their experience is so restricted that they are not conscious of restriction. It is part of the democratic conception that they as individuals are not the only sufferers, but that the whole social body is deprived of the potential resources that should be at its service. The individuals of the submerged mass may not be very wise. But there is one thing they are wiser about than anybody else can be, and that is where the shoe pinches, the troubles they suffer from.

The foundation of democracy is faith in the capacities of human nature; faith in human intelligence and in the power of pooled and cooperative experience. It is not belief that these things are complete but that if given a show they will grow and be able to generate progressively the knowledge and wisdom needed to guide collective action. Every autocratic and authoritarian scheme of social action rests on a belief that the needed intelligence is confined to a superior few, who because of inherent natural gifts are endowed with the ability and the right to control the conduct of others; laying down principles and rules and directing the ways in which they are carried out. It would be foolish to deny that much can be said for this point of view. It is that which controlled human relations in social groups for much the greater part of human history. The democratic faith has emerged very, very recently in the history of mankind. Even where democracies now exist, men's minds and feelings are still permeated with ideas about leadership imposed from above, ideas that developed in the long early history of mankind. After democratic political institutions were nominally established, beliefs and ways of looking at life and of acting that originated when men and women were externally controlled and subjected to arbitrary power, persisted in the family, the church, business and the school, and experience shows that as long as they persist there, political democracy is not secure.

Belief in equality is an element of the democratic credo. It is not, however, belief in equality of natural endowments. Those who proclaimed the idea of equality did not suppose they were enunciating a psychological doctrine, but a legal and political one. All individuals are entitled to equality of treatment by law and in its administration. Each one is affected equally in quality if not in quantity by the institutions under which he lives and has an equal right to express his judgment, although the weight of his judgment may not be equal in amount when it enters into the pooled result to that of others. In short, each one is equally an individual and entitled to equal opportunity of development of his own capacities, be they large or small in range. Moreover, each has needs of his own, as significant to him as those of others are to them. The very fact of natural and psychological inequality is all the more reason for establishment by law of equality of opportunity, since otherwise the former becomes a means of oppression of the less gifted.

While what we call intelligence be distributed in unequal amounts, it is the democratic faith that it is sufficiently general so that each individual has something to contribute, whose value can be assessed only as enters into the final pooled intelligence constituted by the contributions of all. Every authoritarian scheme, on the contrary, assumes that its value may be assessed by some *prior* principle, if not of family and birth or race and color or possession of material wealth, then by the position and rank a person occupies in the existing social scheme. The democratic faith in equality is the faith that each individual shall have the chance and opportunity to contribute whatever he is capable of contributing and that the value of his contribution be decided by its place and function in the organized total of similar contributions, not on the basis of prior status of any kind whatever.

I have emphasized in what precedes the importance of the effective release of intelligence in connection with personal experience in the democratic way of living. I have done so purposely because democracy is so often and so naturally associated in our minds with freedom of *action*, forgetting the importance of freed intelligence which is necessary to direct and to warrant freedom of action. Unless freedom of individual action has intelligence and informed conviction back of it, its manifestation is almost sure to result in confusion and disorder. The democratic idea of freedom is not the right of each individual to *do* as he pleases, even if it be qualified by adding "provided he does not interfere with the same freedom on the part of others." While the idea is not always, not often enough, expressed in words, the basic freedom is that of freedom of *mind* and of whatever degree of freedom of action and experience is necessary to produce freedom of intelligence. The modes of freedom guaranteed in the Bill of Rights are all of this nature: Freedom of belief and conscience, of expression of opinion, of assembly for discussion and conference, of the press as an organ of communication. They are guaranteed because without them individuals are not free to develop and society is deprived of what they might contribute.

... There is some kind of government, of control, wherever affairs that concern a number of persons who act together are engaged in. It is a superficial view that holds government is located in Washington and Albany. There is government in the family, in business, in the church, in every social group. There are regulations, due to custom if not to enactment, that settle how individuals in a group act in connection with one another.

It is a disputed question of theory and practice just how far a democratic political government should go in control of the conditions of action within special groups. At the present time, for example, there are those who think the federal and state governments leave too much freedom of independent action to industrial and financial groups, and there are others who think the government is going altogether too far at the present time. I do not need to discuss this phase of the problem, much less to try to settle it. But it must be pointed out that if the methods of regulation and administration in vogue in the conduct of secondary social groups are non-democratic, whether directly or indirectly or both, there is bound to be an unfavorable reaction back into the habits of feeling, thought and action of citizenship in the broadest sense of that word. The way in which any organized social interest is controlled necessarily plays an important part in forming the dispositions and tastes, the attitudes, interests, purposes and desires, of those engaged in carrying on the activities of the group. For illustration, I do not need to do more than point to the moral, emotional and intellectual effect upon both employers and laborers of the existing industrial system. Just what the effects specifically are is a matter about which we know very little. But I suppose that every one who reflects upon the subject admits that it is impossible that the ways in which activities are carried on for the greater part of the waking hours of the day; and the way in which the share of individuals are involved in the management of affairs in such a matter as gaining a livelihood and attaining material and social security, can not but be a highly important factor in shaping personal dispositions; in short, forming character and intelligence.

In the broad and final sense all institutions are educational in the sense that they operate to form the attitudes, dispositions, abilities and disabilities that constitute a concrete personality. The principle applies with special force to the school. For it is the main business of the family and the school to influence directly the formation and growth of attitudes and dispositions, emotional, intellectual and moral. Whether this educative process is carried on in a predominantly democratic or non-democratic way becomes, therefore, a question of transcendent importance not only for education itself but for its final effect upon all the interests and activities of a society that is committed to the democratic way of life. . . .

There are certain corollaries which clarify the meaning of the issue. Absence of participation tends to produce lack of interest and concern on the part of those shut out. The result is a corresponding lack of effective responsibility. Automatically and unconsciously, if not consciously, the feeling develops, "This is none of our affair; it is the business of those at the top; let that particular set of Georges do what needs to be done." The countries in which autocratic government prevails are just those in which there is least public spirit and the greatest indifference to matters of general as distinct from personal concern. . . . Where there is little power, there is correspondingly little sense of positive responsibility. It is enough to do what one is told to do sufficiently well to escape flagrant unfavorable notice. About larger matters, a spirit of passivity is engendered. . . .

It still is also true that incapacity to assume the responsibilities involved in having a voice in shaping policies is bred and increased by conditions in which that responsibility is denied. I suppose there has never been an autocrat, big or little, who did not justify his conduct on the ground of the unfitness of his subjects to take part in government. . . . But, as was said earlier, habitual exclusion has the effect of reducing a sense of responsibility for what is done and its consequences. What the argument for democracy implies is that the best way to produce initiative and constructive power is to exercise it. Power, as well as interest, comes by use and practice. . . .

The fundamental beliefs and practices of democracy are now challenged as they never have been before. In some nations they are more than challenged. They are ruthlessly and systematically destroyed. Everywhere there are waves of criticism and doubt as to whether democracy can meet pressing problems of order and security. The causes for the destruction of political democracy in countries where it was nominally established are complex. But of one thing I think we may be sure. Wherever it has fallen it was too exclusively political in nature. It had not become part of the bone and blood of the people in daily conduct of its life. Democratic forms were limited to Parliament, elections and combats between parties. What is happening proves conclusively, I think, that unless democratic habits of thought and action are part of the fiber of a people, political democracy is insecure. It can not stand in isolation. It must be buttressed by the presence of democratic methods in all social relationships. The relations that exist in educational institutions are second only in importance in this respect to those which exist in industry and business, perhaps not even to them.

I recur then to the idea that the particular question discussed is one phase of a wide and deep problem. I can think of nothing so important in this country at present as a rethinking of the whole problem of democracy and its implications. Neither the rethinking nor the action it should produce can be brought into being in a day or year. The democratic idea itself demands that the thinking and activity proceed cooperatively. . . .

29. The Disease of Democracy   H. L. Mencken

Henry Louis Mencken (1880–1956), journalist, literary critic, essayist, philologist, and editor, primarily thought of himself as a critic of ideas, particularly those ideas his fellow Americans considered so obviously true they needed no critical examination. His *The Philosophy of Friedrich Nietzsche,* published in 1908, was one of the first intelligent and sympathetic books on the thought of the German philosopher to appear in the United States.

. . . Whether it be called a constitutional monarchy, as in England, or a representative republic, as in France, or a pure democracy, as in some of the cantons of Switzerland, it is always essentially the same. There is, first, the mob, theoretically and in fact the ultimate judge of all ideas and the source of all power. There is, second, the camorra of self-seeking minorities, each seeking to inflame, delude and victimize it. The political process thus becomes a mere battle of rival rogues. But the mob remains quite free to decide between them. It may even, under the hand of God, decide for a minority that happens, by some miracle, to be relatively honest and enlightened. If, in common practice, it sticks to the thieves, it is only because their words are words it understands and their ideas are ideas it cherishes. It has the power to throw them off at will, and even at whim, and it also has the means.

A great deal of paper and ink has been wasted discussing the difference between representative government and direct democracy. The theme is a favourite one with university pundits, and also engages and enchants the stall-fed Rousseaus who arise intermittently in the cow States, and occasionally penetrate to Governors' mansions and the United States Senate. It is generally held that representative government, as practically encountered in the world, is full of defects, some of them amounting to organic disease. Not only does it take the initiative in lawmaking out of the hands of the plain people, and leave them only the function of referees; it also raises certain obvious obstacles to their free exercise of that function. Scattered as they are, and unorganized save in huge, unworkable groups, they are unable, it is argued, to formulate their virtuous desires quickly and clearly, or to bring to the resolution of vexed questions the full potency of their native sagacity. Worse, they find it difficult to enforce their decisions, even when they have decided. Every Liberal knows this sad story and has shed tears telling it. The remedy he offers almost always consists of a resort to what he calls a pure democracy. That is to say he proposes to set up the recall, the initiative and referendum, or something else of the sort, and so convert the representative into a mere clerk or messenger. The final determination of all important public questions, he argues, ought to be in the hands of the voters themselves. They alone can muster enough wisdom for the business, and they alone are without guile. The cure for the evils of democracy is more democracy.

All this, of course, is simply rhetoric. Every time anything of the kind is tried it fails ingloriously. Nor is there any evidence that it has ever succeeded elsewhere, to-day or in the past. . . .

The truth is that the difference between representative democracy and direct democracy is a great deal less marked than political sentimentalists assume. Under both forms the sovereign mob must employ agents to execute its will, and in either case the agents may have ideas of their own, based upon interests of their own, and the means at hand to do and get what they will. Moreover, their very position gives them a power of influencing the electors that is far above that of any ordinary citizen: they become politicians *ex officio,* and usually end by selling such influence as remains after they have used all they need for their own ends. Worse, both forms of democracy encounter the difficulty that the generality of citizens, no matter how assiduously they may be instructed, remain congenitally unable to comprehend many of the problems before them, or to consider all of those they do comprehend in an unbiased and intelligent manner. Thus it is often impossible to ascertain their views in advance of action, or even, in many cases, to determine their conclusions *post hoc.* The voters gathered in a typical New England town-meeting were all ardent amateurs of theology, and hence quite competent, in theory, to decide the theological questions that principally engaged them: nevertheless, history shows that they were led facilely by professional theologians, most of them quacks with something to sell. In the same way, the great masses of Americans of to-day, though they are theoretically competent to decide all the larger matters of national policy, and have certain immutable principles, of almost religious authority, to guide them, actually look for leading to professional politicians, who are influenced in turn by small but competent and determined minorities, with special knowledge and special interests. It was thus that the plain people were shoved into the late war, and it is thus that they will be shoved into the next one. They were, in overwhelming majority, against going in, and if they had had any sense and resolution they would have stayed out. But these things they lacked. . . .

There is the art of the demagogue, and there is the art of what may be called, by a shot-gun marriage of Latin and Greek, the demaslave. They are complementary, and both of them are degrading to their practitioners. The demagogue is one who preaches doctrines he knows to be untrue to men he knows to be idiots. The demaslave is one who listens to what these idiots have to say and then pretends that he believes it himself. Every man who seeks elective office under democracy has to be either the one thing or the other and most men have to be both. The whole process is one of false pretences and ignoble concealments. No educated man stating plainly the elementary notions that every educated man holds about the matters that principally concern government, could be elected to office in a democratic state, save perhaps by a miracle. His frankness would arouse fears, and those fears would run against him; it is his business to arouse fears that will run in favour of him. Worse, he must not only consider the weaknesses of the mob, but also the prejudices of the minorities that prey upon it. Some of these minorities have developed a highly efficient technique of intimidation. They not only know how to arouse the fears of the mob; they also know how to awaken its envy, its dislike of privilege, its hatred of its betters. How formidable they may become is shown by the example of the Anti-Saloon League in the United States—a minority body in the strictest sense, however skillful its mustering of popular support, for it nowhere includes a majority of the voters among its subscribing members, and its leaders are nowhere chosen by democratic methods. And how such minorities may intimidate the whole class of place-seeking politicians has been demonstrated brilliantly and obscenely by the same corrupt and unconscionable organization. It has filled all the law-making bodies of the nation with men who have got into office by submitting cravenly to its dictation, and it has filled thousands of administrative posts, and not a few judicial posts, with vermin of the same sort.

Such men, indeed, enjoy vast advantages under democracy. The mob, insensitive to their dishonour, is edified and exhilarated by their success. The competition they offer to men of a decenter habit is too powerful to be met, so they tend, gradually, to monopolize all the public offices. Out of the muck of their swinishness the typical American law-maker emerges. He is a man who has lied and dissembled, and a man who has crawled. He knows the taste of boot-polish. He has suffered kicks in the tonneau of his pantaloons. He has taken orders from his superiors in knavery and he has wooed and flattered his inferiors in sense. His public life is an endless series of evasions and false pretenses. He is willing to embrace any issue, however idiotic, that will get him votes, and he is willing to sacrifice any principle, however sound, that will lose them for him. I do not describe the democratic politician at his inordinate worst; I describe him as he is encountered in the full sunshine of normalcy. He may be, on the one hand, a cross-roads idler striving to get into the State Legislature by grace of the local mortgage-sharks and evangelical clergy, or he may be, on the other, the President of the United States. It is almost an axiom that no man may make a career in politics in the Republic without stooping to such ignobility: it is as necessary as a loud voice. Now and then, to be sure, a man of sounder self-respect may make a beginning, but he seldom gets very far. Those who survive are nearly all tarred, soon or late, with the same stick. They are men who, at some time or other, have compromised with their honour, either by swallowing their convictions or by whooping for what they believe to be untrue. They are in the position of the chorus girl who, in order to get her humble job, has had to admit the manager to her person. And the old birds among them, like chorus girls of long experience come to regard the business resignedly and even complacently. It is the price that a man who loves the clapper-clawing of the vulgar must pay for it under the democratic system. He becomes a coward and a trimmer *ex-officio*. Where his dignity was in the days of his innocence there is now only a vacuum in the wastes of his subconscious. Vanity remains to him, but not pride. . . .

To sum up: the essential objection to feudalism (the perfect antithesis to democracy) was that it imposed degrading acts and attitudes upon the vassal; the essential objection to democracy is that, with few exceptions, it imposes degrading acts and attitudes upon the men responsible for the welfare and dignity of the state. The former was compelled to do homage to his suzerain, who was very apt to be a brute and an ignoramus. The latter are compelled to do homage to their constituents, who in overwhelming majority are certain to be both.

Democracy and Liberty

THE WILL TO PEACE.   Whenever the liberties of *Homo vulgaris* are invaded and made a mock of in a gross and contemptuous manner, as happened, for example, in the United States during the reign of Wilson, Palmer, Burleson and company, there are always observers who marvel that he bears the outrage with so little murmuring. Such observers only display their unfamiliarity with the elements of democratic science. The truth is that the common man's love of liberty, like his love of sense, justice and truth, is almost wholly imaginary. As I have argued, he is not actually happy when free; he is uncomfortable, a bit alarmed, and intolerably lonely. He longs for the warm, reassuring smell of the herd, and is willing to take the herdsman with it. Liberty is not a thing for such as he. He cannot enjoy it rationally himself, and he can think of it in others only as something to be taken away from them. It is, when it becomes a reality, the exclusive possession of a small and disreputable minority of men, like knowledge, courage and honour. A special sort of man is needed to understand it, nay, to stand it—and he is inevitably an outlaw in demo-cratic societies. The average man doesn't want to be free. He simply wants to be safe.

Nietzsche, with his usual clarity of vision, saw the point clearly. Liberty, he used to say, was something that, to the general, was too cold to be borne. Nevertheless, he apparently believed that there was an unnatural, drug-store sort of yearning for it in *all* men, and so he changed Schopen-hauer's will-to-live into a will-to-power, *i.e.,* a will-to-free-function. Here he went too far, and in the wrong direction: he should have made it, on the lower levels, a will-to-peace. What the common man longs for in this world, before and above all his other longings, is the simplest and most ignominious sort of peace—the peace of a trusty in a well-managed peni-tentiary. He is willing to sacrifice everything else to it. He puts it above his dignity and he puts it above his pride. Above all, he puts it above his liberty. The fact, perhaps, explains his veneration for policemen, in all the forms they take—his belief that there is a mysterious sanctity in law, how-ever absurd it may be in fact. A policeman is a charlatan who offers, in return for obedience, to protect him (*a*) from his superiors, (*b*) from his equals, and (*c*) from himself. This last service, under democracy, is com-monly the most esteemed of them all. In the United States, at least theo-retically, it is the only thing that keeps ice-wagon drivers, Y.M.C.A. secre-taries, insurance collectors and other such human camels from smoking opium, ruining themselves in the night clubs, and going to Palm Beach with Follies girls. It is a democratic invention.

Here, though the common man is deceived, he starts from a sound premise: to wit, that liberty is something too hot for his hands—or, as Nietzsche puts it, too cold for his spine. Worse, he sees in it something that is a weapon against him in the hands of his enemy, the man of supe-rior kidney. Be true to your nature, and follow its teachings: this Emer-sonian counsel, it must be manifest, offers an embarrassing support to every variety of the *droit de seigneur.* The history of democracy is a history of efforts to force successive minorities to be *un*true to their nature. Democracy, in fact, stands in greater peril of the free spirit than any sort of despotism ever heard of. The despot, at least, is always safe in one respect: his own belief in himself cannot be shaken. But democracies may be demoralized and run amok, and so they are in vast dread of heresy, as a Sunday-school superintendent is in dread of scarlet women, light wines and beer, and the unreadable works of Charles Darwin. It would be uni-maginable for a democracy to submit serenely to such gross dissents as Frederick the Great not only permitted, but even encouraged. Once the mob is on the loose, there is no holding it. So the subversive minority must be reduced to impotence; the heretic must be put down.

If, as they say, one of the main purposes of all civilized government is to preserve and augment the liberty of the individual, then surely democ-racy accomplishes it less efficiently than any other form. Is the individual worth thinking of at all? Then the superior individual is worth more thought than his inferiors. But it is precisely the superior individual who is the chief victim of the democratic process. It not only tries to regulate his acts; it also tries to delimit his thoughts; it is constantly inventing new forms of the old crime of imagining the King's death. The Roman *lex de majestate* was put upon the books, not by an emperor, nor even by a consul, but by Saturninus, a tribune of the people. Its aim was to protect the state against aristocrats, *i.e.,* against free spirits, each holding himself answerable only to his own notions. The aim of democracy is to break all such free spirits to the common harness. It tries to iron them out, to pump them dry of self-respect, to make docile John Does of them. The measure of its success is the extent to which such men are brought down, and made common. The measure of civilization is the extent to which they resist and survive. Thus the only sort of liberty that is real under democracy is the liberty of the have-nots to destroy the liberty of the haves. . . .

For all I know, democracy may be a self-limiting disease, as civilization itself seems to be. There are obvious paradoxes in its philosophy, and some of them have a suicidal smack. It offers John Doe a means to rise above his place beside Richard Roe, and then, by making Roe his equal, it takes away the chief usufructs of the rising. I here attempt no pretty logical gymnastics: the history of democratic states is a history of disingenuous efforts to get rid of the second half of that dilemma. There is not only the natural yearning of Doe to use and enjoy the superiority that he has won; there is also the natural tendency of Roe, as an inferior man, to acknowledge it. Democracy, in fact, is always inventing class distinctions, despite its theoretical abhorrence of them. The baron has departed, but in his place stand the grand goblin, the supreme worthy archon, the sovereign grand commander. Democratic man, as I have remarked, is quite unable to think of himself as a free individual; he must belong to a group, or shake with fear and loneliness—and the group, of course, must have its leaders. It would be hard to find a country in which such brummagem serene highnesses are revered with more passionate devotion than they get in the United States. The distinction that goes with mere office runs far ahead of the distinction that goes with actual achievement. A Harding is regarded as genuinely superior to a Halsted, no doubt because his doings are better understood. But there is a form of human striving that is understood by democratic man even better than Harding's, and that is the striving for money. Thus the plutocracy, in a democratic state, tends to take the place of the missing aristocracy, and even to be mistaken for it. It is, of course, something quite different. It lacks all the essential characters of a true aristocracy: a clean tradition, culture, public spirit, honesty, honour, courage—above all, courage. It stands under no bond of obligation to the state; it has no public duty; it is transient and lacks a goal. Its most puissant dignitaries of to-day came out of the mob only yesterday— and from the mob they bring all its peculiar ignobilities. As practically encountered, the plutocracy stands quite as far from the *honnête homme* as it stands from the Holy Saints. Its main character is its incurable timorousness; it is for ever grasping at the straws held out by demagogues. Half a dozen gabby Jewish youths, meeting in a back room to plan a revolution—in other words, half a dozen kittens preparing to upset the Matterhorn—are enough to scare it half to death. Its dreams are of banshees, hobgoblins, bugaboos. The honest, untroubled snores of a Percy or a Hohenstaufen are quite beyond it.

The plutocracy, as I say, is comprehensible to the mob because its aspirations are essentially those of inferior men: it is not by accident that Christianity, a mob religion, paves heaven with gold and precious stones, *i.e.,* with money. There are, of course, reactions against this ignoble ideal among men of more civilized tastes, even in democratic states, and sometimes they arouse the mob to a transient distrust of certain of the plutocratic pretensions. But that distrust seldom arises above mere envy, and the polemic which engenders it is seldom sound in logic or impeccable in motive. What it lacks is aristocratic disinterestedness, born of aristocratic security. There is no body of opinion behind it that is, in the strictest sense, a free opinion. Its chief exponents, by some divine irony, are pedagogues of one sort or another—which is to say, men chiefly marked by their haunting fear of losing their jobs. Living under such terrors, with the plutocracy policing them harshly on one side and the mob congenitally suspicious of them on the other, it is no wonder that their revolt usually peters out in metaphysics, and that they tend to abandon it as their families grow up, and the costs of heresy become prohibitive. The pedagogue, in the long run, shows the virtues of the Congressman, the newspaper editorial writer or the butler, not those of the aristocrat. When, by any chance, he persists in contumacy beyond thirty, it is only too commonly a sign, not that he is heroic, but simply that he is pathological. So with most of his brethren of the Utopian Fife and Drum Corps, whether they issue out of his own seminary or out of the wilderness. They are fanatics; not statesmen. Thus politics, under democracy, resolves itself into impossible alternatives. Whatever the label on the parties, or the war cries issuing from the demagogues who lead them, the practical choice is between the plutocracy on the one side and a rabble of preposterous impossibilists on the other. One must either follow the New York *Times,* or one must be prepared to swallow Bryan and the Bolsheviki. It is a pity that this is so. For what democracy needs most of all is a party that will separate the good that is in it theoretically from the evils that beset it practically, and then try to erect that good into a workable system. What it needs beyond everything is a party of liberty. It produces, true enough, occasional libertarians, just as despotism produces occasionally regicides, but it treats them in the same drum-head way. It will never have a party of them until it invents and installs a genuine aristocracy, to breed them and secure them.

LAST WORDS.   I have alluded somewhat vaguely to the merits of democracy. One of them is quite obvious: it is, perhaps, the most charming form of government ever devised by man. The reason is not far to seek. It is based upon propositions that are palpably not true—and what is not true, as everyone knows, is always immensely more fascinating and satisfying to the vast majority of men than what is true. Truth has a harshness that alarms them, and an air of finality that collides with their incurable romanticism. They turn, in all the great emergencies of life, to the ancient promises, transparently false but immensely comforting, and of all those ancient promises there is none more comforting than the one to the effect that the lowly shall inherit the earth. It is at the bottom of the dominant religious system of the modern world, and it is at the bottom of the dominant political system. The latter, which is democracy, gives it an even higher credit and authority than the former, which is Christianity. More, democracy gives it a certain appearance of objective and demonstrable truth. The mob man, functioning as citizen, gets a feeling that he is really important to the world—that he is genuinely running things. Out of his maudlin herding after rogues and mountebanks there comes to him a sense of vast and mysterious power—which is what makes archbishops, police sergeants, the grand goblins of the Ku Klux and other such magnificoes happy. And out of it there comes, too, a conviction that he is somehow wise, that his views are taken seriously by his betters—which is what makes United States Senators, fortune-tellers and Young Intellectuals happy. Finally, there comes out of it a glowing consciousness of a high duty triumphantly done—which is what makes hangmen and husbands happy.

All these forms of happiness, of course, are illusory. They don't last. The democrat, leaping into the air to flap his wings and praise God, is for ever coming down with a thump. The seeds of his disaster, as I have shown, lie in his own stupidity: he can never get rid of the naive delusion—so beautifully Christian!—that happiness is something to be got by taking it away from the other fellow. But there are seeds, too, in the very nature of things: a promise, after all, is only a promise, even when it is supported by divine revelation, and the chances against its fulfillment may be put into a depressing mathematical formula. Here the irony that lies under all human aspiration shows itself: the quest for happiness, as always, brings only *un*happiness in the end. But saying that is merely saying that the true charm of democracy is not for the democrat but for the spectator. That spectator, it seems to me, is favoured with a show of the first cut and calibre. Try to imagine anything more heroically absurd! What grotesque false pretences! What a parade of obvious imbecilities! What a welter of fraud! But is fraud unamusing? Then I retire forthwith as a psychologist. The fraud of democracy, I contend, is more amusing than any other—more amusing even, and by miles, than the fraud of religion. Go into your praying-chamber and give sober thought to any of the more characteristic democratic inventions: say, Law Enforcement. Or to any of the typical democratic prophets: say, the late Archangel Bryan. If you don't come out paled and palsied by mirth then you will not laugh on the Last Day itself, when Presbyterians step out of the grave like chicks from the egg, and wings blossom from their scapulae, and they leap into interstellar space with roars of joy.

I have spoken hitherto of the possibility that democracy may be a self-limiting disease, like measles. It is, perhaps, something more: it is self-devouring. One cannot observe it objectively without being impressed by its curious distrust of itself—its apparently ineradicable tendency to abandon its whole philosophy at the first sign of strain. I need not point to what happens invariably in democratic states when the national safety is menaced. All the great tribunes of democracy, on such occasions, convert themselves, by a process as simple as taking a deep breath, into despots of an almost fabulous ferocity. Lincoln, Roosevelt and Wilson come instantly to mind: Jackson and Cleveland are in the background, waiting to be recalled. Nor is this process confined to times of alarm and terror: it is going on day in and day out. Democracy always seems bent upon killing the thing it theoretically loves. I have rehearsed some of its operations against liberty, the very cornerstone of its political metaphysic. It not only wars upon the thing itself; it even wars upon mere academic advocacy of it. I offer the spectacle of Americans jailed for reading the Bill of Rights as perhaps the most gaudily humorous ever witnessed in the modern world. Try to imagine monarchy jailing subjects for maintaing the divine right of Kings! Or Christianity damning a believer for arguing that Jesus Christ was the Son of God! This last, perhaps, has been done: anything is possible in that direction. But under democracy the remotest and most fantastic possibility is a commonplace of every day. All the axioms resolve themselves into thundering paradoxes, many amounting to downright contradictions in terms. The mob is competent to rule the rest of us—but it must be rigorously policed itself. There is a government, not of men, but of laws—but men are set upon benches to decide finally what the law is and may be. The highest function of the citizen is to serve the state— but the first assumption that meets him, when he essays to discharge it, is an assumption of his disingenuousness and dishonour. Is that assumption commonly sound? Then the farce only grows the more glorious.

I confess, for my part, that it greatly delights me. I enjoy democracy immensely. It is incomparably idiotic, and hence incomparably amusing. Does it exalt dunderheads, cowards, trimmers, frauds, cads? Then the pain of seeing them go up is balanced and obliterated by the joy of seeing them come down. Is it inordinately wasteful, extravagant, dishonest? Then so is every other form of government: all alike are enemies to laborious and virtuous men. Is rascality at the very heart of it? Well, we have borne that rascality since 1776, and continue to survive. In the long run, it may turn out that rascality is necessary to human government, and even to civilization itself—that civilization, at bottom, is nothing but a colossal swindle. I do not know: I report only that when the suckers are running well the spectacle is infinitely exhilarating. But I am, it may be, a somewhat malicious man: my sympathies, when it comes to suckers, tend to be coy. What I can't make out is how any man can believe in democracy who feels for and with them, and is pained when they are debauched and made a show of. How can any man be a democrat who is sincerely a democrat?

30. A Communist Critique of Democracy   V. I. Lenin

Vladimir Ilyich Lenin (1870–1924), Communist theoretician and Russian revolutionary leader, was Soviet premier from 1918 until his death.

In the current arguments about the state, the mistake is constantly made against which Engels cautions . . . it is constantly forgotten that the

From *State and Revolution*, The Little Lenin Library, vol. 14 (New York: International Publishers, 1932). Reprinted by permission of the publisher. The title of this selection was chosen by the editors.

destruction of the state means also the destruction of democracy; that the withering away of the state also means the withering away of democracy.

At first sight such a statement seems exceedingly strange and incomprehensible; indeed, some one may even begin to fear lest we be expecting the advent of such an order of society in which the principle of the subordination of the minority to the majority will not be respected—for is not a democracy just the recognition of this principle?

No, democracy is *not* identical with the subordination of the minority to the majority. Democracy is a *state* recognizing the subordination of the minority to the majority, *i.e.*, an organization for the systematic use of *violence* by one class against the other, by one part of the population against another.

We set ourselves the ultimate aim of destroying the state, *i.e.*, every organized and systematic violence, every use of violence against man in general. We do not expect the advent of an order of society in which the principle of subordination of minority to majority will not be observed. But, striving for Socialism, we are convinced that it will develop into Communism; that, side by side with this, there will vanish all need for force, for the *subjection* of one man to another, and of one part of the population to another, since people will *grow accustomed* to observing the elementary conditions of social existence *without force and without subjection.*

In order to emphasize this element of habit, Engels speaks of a *new generation,* "reared under new and free social conditions," which "will be able to throw on the scrap heap all this state rubbish"—every kind of state, including even the democratic-republican state.

For the elucidation of this, the question of the economic basis of the withering away of the state must be. . . .

It is clear that there can be no question of defining the exact moment of the *future* withering away—the more so as it must obviously be a rather lengthy process. . . .

The whole theory of Marx is an application of the theory of evolution—in its most consistent, complete, well considered and fruitful form—to modern capitalism. It was natural for Marx to raise the question of applying this theory both to the *coming* collapse of capitalism and to the *future* evolution of *future* Communism.

On the basis of what *data* can the future evolution of future Communism be considered?

On the basis of the fact that *it has its origin* in capitalism, that it develops historically from capitalism, that it is the result of the action of a social force to which capitalism *has given birth.* There is no shadow of an attempt on Marx's part to conjure up a Utopia, to make idle guesses about that which cannot be known. Marx treats the question of Communism in the same way as a naturalist would treat the question of the evolution of, say, a new biological species, if he knew that such and such was its origin, and such and such the direction in which it changed.

Marx, first of all, brushes aside the confusion the Gotha Programme brings into the question of the interrelation between state and society.

"Contemporary society" is the capitalist society—he writes—which exists in all civilised countries, more or less free of mediaeval admixture, more or less modified by each country's particular historical development, more or less developed. In contrast with this, the "contemporary state" varies with every state boundary. It is different in the Prusso-German Empire from what it is in Switzerland, and different in England from what it is in the United States. The "contemporary state" is therefore a fiction.

Nevertheless, in spite of the motley variety of their forms, the different states of the various civilised countries all have this in common: they are all based on modern bourgeois society, only a little more or less capitalistically developed. Consequently, they also have certain essential characteristics in common. In this sense, it is possible to speak of the "contemporary state" in contrast to the future, when its present root, bourgeois society, will have perished.

Then the question arises: what transformation will the state undergo in a Communist society? In other words, what social functions analogous to the present functions of the state will then still survive? This question can only be answered scientifically, and however many thousand times the word people is combined with the word state, we get not a flea-jump closer to the problem. . . . *

Having thus ridiculed all talk about a "people's state," Marx formulates the question and warns us, as it were, that to arrive at a scientific answer one must rely only on firmly established scientific data.

The first fact that has been established with complete exactness by the whole theory of evolution, by science as a whole—a fact which the Utopians forgot, and which is forgotten by the present-day opportunists who are afraid of the Socialist revolution—is that, historically, there must undoubtedly be a special stage or epoch of *transition* from capitalism to Communism.

Between capitalist and Communist society—Marx continues—lies the period of the revolutionary transformation of the former into the latter. To this also corresponds a political transition period, in which the state can be no other than *the revolutionary dictatorship of the proletariat.**

This conclusion Marx bases on an analysis of the role played by the proletariat in modern capitalist society, on the data concerning the evolution of this society, and on the irreconcilability of the opposing interests of the proletariat and the bourgeoisie.

Earlier the question was put thus: to attain its emancipation, the proletariat must overthrow the bourgeoisie, conquer political power and establish its own revolutionary dictatorship.

Now the question is put somewhat differently: the transition from capitalist society, developing towards Communism, towards a Communist society, is impossible without a "political transition period," and the state in this period can only be the revolutionary dictatorship of the proletariat.

What, then, is the relation of this dictatorship to democracy?

We have seen that the *Communist Manifesto* simply places side by side the two ideas: the "transformation of the proletariat into the ruling class" and the "establishment of democracy." On the basis of all that has been

*[*Critique of the Social-Democratic Programmes.*—Ed.]
*[Ibid.—Ed.]

said above, one can define more exactly how democracy changes in the transition from capitalism to Communism.

In capitalist society, under the conditions most favourable to its development, we have more or less complete democracy in the democratic republic. But this democracy is always bound by the narrow framework of capitalist exploitation, and consequently always remains, in reality, a democracy for the minority, only for the possessing classes, only for the rich. Freedom in capitalist society always remains just about the same as it was in the ancient Greek republics: freedom for the slave-owners. The modern wage-slaves, owing to the conditions of capitalist exploitation, are so much crushed by want and poverty that "democracy is nothing to them," "politics is nothing to them"; that, in the ordinary peaceful course of events, the majority of the population is debarred from participating in social and political life. . . .

Democracy for an insignificant minority, democracy for the rich—that is the democracy of capitalist society. If we look more closely into the mechanism of capitalist democracy, everywhere, both in the "petty"—so-called petty—details of the suffrage (residential qualification, exclusion of women, etc.), and in the technique of the representative institutions, in the actual obstacles to the right of assembly (public buildings are not for "beggars"!), in the purely capitalist organization of the daily press, etc., etc.—on all sides we see restriction after restriction upon democracy. These restrictions, exceptions, exclusions, obstacles for the poor, seem slight, especially in the eyes of one who has himself never known want and has never been in close contact with the oppressed classes in their mass life (and nine-tenths, if not ninety-nine hundredths, of the bourgeois publicists and politicians are of this class), but in their sum total these restrictions exclude and squeeze out the poor from politics and from an active share in democracy.

Marx splendidly grasped this *essence* of capitalist democracy, when, in analyzing the experience of the Commune, he said that the oppressed were allowed, once every few years, to decide which particular representatives of the oppressing class should be in parliament to represent and repress them!

But from this capitalist democracy—inevitably narrow, subtly rejecting the poor, and therefore hypocritical and false to the core—progress does not march onward, simply, smoothly and directly, to "greater and greater democracy," as the liberal professors and petty-bourgeois opportunists would have us believe. No, progress marches onward, *i.e.,* towards Communism, through the dictatorship of the proletariat; it cannot do otherwise, for there is no one else and no other way to *break the resistance* of the capitalist exploiters.

But the dictatorship of the proletariat—*i.e.,* the organisation of the vanguard of the oppressed as the ruling class for the purpose of crushing the oppressors—cannot produce merely an expansion of democracy. *Together* with an immense expansion of democracy which *for the first time* becomes democracy for the poor, democracy for the people, and not democracy for the rich folk, the dictatorship of the proletariat produces a series of restrictions of liberty in the case of the oppressors, the exploiters, the capitalists. We must crush them in order to free humanity from wage-slavery; their resistance must be broken by force; it is clear that where there is suppression there is also violence, there is no liberty, no democracy.

Engels expressed this splendidly in his letter to Bebel when he said, as the reader will remember, that "as long as the proletariat still *needs* the state, it needs it not in the interests of freedom, but for the purpose of crushing its antagonists; and as soon as it becomes possible to speak of freedom, then the state, as such, ceases to exist."

Democracy for the vast majority of the people, and suppression by force, *i.e.,* exclusion from democracy, of the exploiters and oppressors of the people—this is the modification of democracy during the *transition* from capitalism to Communism.

Only in Communist society, when the resistance of the capitalists has been completely broken, when the capitalists have disappeared, when there are no classes (i.e., there is no difference between the members of society in their relation to the social means of production), *only then* "the state ceases to exist," and *"it becomes possible to speak of freedom."* Only then a really full democracy, a democracy without any exceptions, will be possible and will be realised. And only then will democracy itself begin to *wither away* due to the simple fact that, freed from capitalist slavery, from the untold horrors, savagery, absurdities and infamies of capitalist exploitation, people will gradually *become accustomed* to the observance of the elementary rules of social life that have been known for centuries and repeated for thousands of years in all school books; they will become accustomed to observing them without force, without compulsion, without subordination, without the *special apparatus* for compulsion which is called the state.

The expression "the state *withers away*," is very well chosen, for it indicates both the gradual and the elemental nature of the process. Only habit can, and undoubtedly will, have such an effect; for we see around us millions of times how readily people get accustomed to observe the necessary rules of life in common, if there is no exploitation, if there is nothing that causes indignation, that calls forth protest and revolt and has to be *suppressed*.

Thus, in capitalist society, we have a democracy that is curtailed, poor, false; a democracy only for the rich, for the minority. The dictatorship of the proletariat, the period of transition to Communism, will, for the first time, produce democracy for the people, for the majority, side by side with the necessary suppression of the minority—the exploiters. Communism alone is capable of giving a really complete democracy, and the more complete it is the more quickly will it become unnecessary and wither away of itself.

In other words: under capitalism we have a state in the proper sense of the word, that is, special machinery for the suppression of one class by another, and of the majority by the minority at that. Naturally, for the successful discharge of such a task as the systematic suppression by the exploiting minority of the exploited majority, the greatest ferocity and savagery of suppression are required, seas of blood are required, through which mankind is marching in slavery, serfdom, and wage-labour.

Again, during the *transition* from capitalism to Communism, suppression is *still* necessary; but it is the suppression of the minority of exploiters by the majority of exploited. A special apparatus, special machinery for suppression, the "state," is *still* necessary, but this is now a transitional state, no longer a state in the usual sense, for the suppression of the minority of exploiters, by the majority of the wage slaves *of yesterday,* is a matter comparatively so easy, simple and natural that it will cost far less bloodshed than the suppression of the risings of slaves, serfs or wage labourers, and will cost mankind far less. This is compatible with the diffusion of democracy among such an overwhelming majority of the population, that the need for *special machinery* of suppression will begin to disappear. The exploiters are, naturally, unable to suppress the people without a most complex machinery for performing this task; but *the people* can suppress the exploiters even with very simple "machinery," almost without any "machinery," without any special apparatus, by the simple *organisation of the armed masses* (such as the Soviets of Workers' and Soldiers' Deputies, we may remark, anticipating a little).

Finally, only Communism renders the state absolutely unnecessary, for there is *no one* to be suppressed—"no one" in the sense of a *class,* in the sense of a systematic struggle with a definite section of the population. We are not Utopians, and we do not in the least deny the possibility and inevitability of excesses on the part of *individual persons,* nor the need to suppress *such* excesses. But, in the first place, no special machinery, no special apparatus of repression is needed for this; this will be done by the armed people itself, as simply and as readily as any crowd of civilised people, even in modern society, parts a pair of combatants or does not allow a woman to be outraged. And, secondly, we know that the fundamental social cause of excesses which consist in violating the rules of social life is the exploitation of the masses, their want and their poverty. With the removal of this chief cause, excesses will inevitably begin to *"wither away."* We do not know how quickly and in what succession, but we know that they will wither away. With their withering away, the state will also *wither away.* . . .

31. Anarchism: The Rejection of Democracy and Capitalism   Peter Kropotkin

Prince Peter Kropotkin (1842–1921), member of the Czarist nobility, geographer, and author, was one of the ablest, and most influential anarchist theoreticians of his time. He lived in exile for forty-two years until he was permitted to return to Russia in 1917.

Anarchism, the no-government system of socialism, has a double origin. It is an outgrowth of the two great movements of thought in the economic and the political fields which characterize the nineteenth cen-

From "Anarchist Communism: Its Basis and Principles," reprinted in Roger N. Baldwin (ed.). *Kropotkin's Revolutionary Pamphlets,* New York: Dover Publications, Inc., 1970.

tury, and especially its second part. In common with all socialists, the anarchists hold that the private ownership of land, capital, and machinery has had its time; that it is condemned to disappear; and that all requisites for production must, and will, become the common property of society, and be managed in common by the producers of wealth. And in common with the most advanced representatives of political radicalism, they maintain that the ideal of the political organization of society is a condition of things where the functions of government are reduced to a minimum, and the individual recovers his full liberty of initiative and action for satisfying, by means of free groups and federations—freely constituted—all the infinitely varied needs of the human being.

As regards socialism, most of the anarchists arrive at its ultimate conclusion, that is, at a complete negation of the wage-system and at communism. And with reference to political organization, by giving a further development to the above-mentioned part of the radical program, they arrive at the conclusion that the ultimate aim of society is the reduction of the functions of government to *nil*—that is, to a society without government, so an-archy. The anarchists maintain, moreover, that such being the ideal of social and political organization, they must not remit it to future centuries, but that only those changes in our social organization which are in accordance with the above double ideal, and constitute an approach to it, will have a chance of life and be beneficial for the commonwealth.

As to the method followed by the anarchist thinker, it entirely differs from that followed by the utopists. The anarchist thinker does not resort to metaphysical conceptions (like "natural rights," the "duties of the State," and so on) to establish what are, in his opinion, the best conditions for realizing the greatest happiness of humanity. He follows, on the contrary, the course traced by the modern philosophy of evolution. He studies human society as it is now and was in the past; and without either endowing humanity as a whole, or separate individuals, with superior qualities which they do not possess, he merely considers society as an aggregation of organisms trying to find out the best ways of combining the wants of the individual with those of cooperation for the welfare of the species. He studies society and tries to discover its *tendencies,* past and present, its growing needs, intellectual and economic, and in his ideal he merely points out in which direction evolution goes. He distinguishes between the real wants and tendencies of human aggregations and the accidents (want of knowledge, migrations, wars, conquests) which have prevented these tendencies from being satisfied. And he concludes that the two most prominent although often unconscious, tendencies throughout our history have been: first, a tendency towards integrating labor for the production of all riches in common, so as finally to render it impossible to discriminate the part of the common production due to the separate individual; and second, a tendency towards the fullest freedom of the individual in the prosecution of all aims, beneficial both for himself and for society at large. The ideal of the anarchist is thus a mere summing-up of what he considers to be the next phase of evolution. It is no longer a matter of faith; it is a matter for scientific discussion.

In fact, one of the leading features of this century is the growth of socialism and the rapid spreading of socialist views among the working-classes. How could it be otherwise? We have witnessed an unparalleled sudden increase of our powers of production, resulting in an accumulation of wealth which has outstripped the most sanguine expectations. But owing to our wage system, this increase of wealth—due to the combined efforts of men of science, of managers, and workmen as well—has resulted only in an unprecedented accumulation of wealth in the hands of the owners of capital; while an increase of misery for great numbers, and an insecurity of life for all, have been the lot of the workmen. The unskilled laborers, in continuous search for labor, are falling into an unheard-of-destitution. And even the best paid artisans and skilled workmen labor under the permanent menace of being thrown, in their turn, into the same conditions as the unskilled paupers, in consequence of some of the continuous and unavoidable fluctuations of industry and caprices of capital.

The chasm between the modern millionaire who squanders the produce of human labor in a gorgeous and vain luxury, and the pauper reduced to a miserable and insecure existence, is thus growing wider and wider, so as to break the very unity of society—the harmony of its life—and to endanger the progress of its further development.

At the same time, workingmen are less and less inclined to patiently endure this division of society into two classes, as they themselves become more and more conscious of the wealth-producing power of modern industry, of the part played by labor in the production of wealth, and of their own capacities of organization. In proportion as all classes of the community take a more lively part in public affairs, and knowledge spreads among the masses, their longing for equality becomes stronger, and their demands for social reorganization become louder and louder. They can be ignored no more. The worker claims his share in the riches he produces; he claims his share in the management of production; and he claims not only some additional well-being, but also his full rights in the higher enjoyments of science and art. These claims, which formerly were uttered only by the social reformer, begin now to be made by a daily growing minority of those who work in the factory or till the acre. And they so conform to our feelings of justice that they find support in a daily growing minority among the privileged classes themselves. Socialism becomes thus *the* idea of the nineteenth century; and neither coercion nor pseudo-reforms can stop its further growth.

Much hope of improvement was placed, of course, in the extension of political rights to the working classes. But these concessions, unsupported as they were by corresponding changes in economic relations, proved delusions. They did not materially improve the conditions of the great bulk of the workmen. Therefore, the watchword of socialism is: "Economic freedom as the only secure basis for political freedom." And as long as the present wage system, with all its bad consequences, remains unaltered, the socialist watchword will continue to inspire the workmen. Socialism will continue to grow until it has realized its program.

Side by side with this great movement of thought in economic matters, a like movement has been going on with regard to political rights, political organization, and the functions of government. Government has been submitted to the same criticism as capital. While most of the radicals saw in universal suffrage and republican institutions the last word of political wisdom, a further step was made by the few. The very functions of government and the State, as also their relations to the individual, were submitted to a sharper and deeper criticism. Representative government having been tried by experiment on a wide field, its defects became more and more prominent. It became obvious that these defects are not merely accidental but inherent in the system itself. Parliament and its executive proved to be unable to attend to all the numberless affairs of the community and to conciliate the varied and often opposite interests of the separate parts of a State. Election proved unable to find out the men who might represent a nation, and manage, otherwise than in a party spirit, the affairs they are compelled to legislate upon. These defects become so striking that the very principles of the representative system were criticized and their justness doubted.

Again, the dangers of a centralized government became still more conspicuous when the socialists came to the front and asked for a further increase of the powers of government by entrusting it with the management of the immense field covered now by the economic relations between individuals. The question was asked whether a government entrusted with the management of industry and trade would not become a permanent danger for liberty and peace, and whether it even would be able to be a good manager?

The socialists of the earlier part of this century did not fully realize the immense difficulties of the problem. Convinced as they were of the necessity of economic reforms, most of them took no notice of the need of freedom for the individual. And we have had social reformers ready to submit society to any kind of theocracy, or dictatorship in order to obtain reforms in a socialist sense. Therefore we have seen in England and also on the Continent the division of men of advanced opinions into political radicals and socialists—the former looking with distrust on the latter, as they saw in them a danger for the political liberties which have been won by the civilzed nations after a long series of struggles. And even now, when the socialists all over Europe have become political parties, and profess the democratic faith, there remains among most impartial men a well-founded fear of the *Volksstaat* or "popular State" being as great a danger to liberty as any form of autocracy if its government be entrusted with the management of all the social organization including the production and distribution of wealth.

Recent evolution, however, has prepared the way for showing the necessity and possibility of a higher form of social organization which may guarantee economic freedom without reducing the individual to the role of a slave to the State. The origins of government have been carefully studied, and all metaphysical conceptions as to its divine or "social contract" derivation having been laid aside, it appears that it is among us of a relatively modern origin, and that its powers have grown precisely in proportion as the division of society into the privileged and unprivileged classes was growing in the course of ages. Representative government has also been reduced to its real value—that of an instrument which has rendered services in the struggle against autocracy, but not an ideal of free political organization. As to the system of philosophy which saw in the State a leader of progress, it was more and more shaken as it became evident that progress is the most effective when it is not checked by State interference. It has thus become obvious that a further advance in social life does not lie in the direction of a further concentration of power and regulative functions in the hands of a governing body, but in the direction of decentralization, both territorial and functional—in a subdivision of public functions with respect both to their sphere of action and to the character of the functions; it is in the abandonment to the initiative of freely constituted groups of all those functions which are now considered as the functions of government. . . .

Anarchists recognize the justice of both the just-mentioned tendencies towards economic and political freedom, and see in them two different manifestations of the very same need of equality which constitutes the very essence of all struggles mentioned by history. Therefore, in common with all socialists, the anarchist says to the political reformer: "No substantial reform in the sense of political equality and no limitation of the powers of government can be made as long as society is divided into two hostile camps, and the laborer remains, economically speaking, a slave to his employer." But to the state socialist we say also: "You cannot modify the existing conditions of property without deeply modifying at the same time the political organization. You must limit the powers of government and renounce parliamentary rule. To each new economic phase of life corresponds a new political phase. Absolute monarchy corresponded to the system of serfdom. Representative government corresponds to capital-rule. Both, however, are class-rule. But in a society where the distinction between capitalist and laborer has disappeared, there is no need of such a government; it would be an anachronism, a nuisance. Free workers would require a free organization, and this cannot have any other basis than free agreement and free cooperation, without sacrificing the autonomy of the individual to the all-pervading interference of the State. The no-capitalist system implies the no-government system."

Meaning thus the emancipation of man from the oppressive powers of capitalism and government as well, the system of anarchism becomes a synthesis of the two powerful currents of thought which characterize our century.

In arriving at these conclusions anarchism proves to be in accordance with the conclusions arrived at by the philosophy of evolution. By bringing to light the plasticity of organization, the philosophy of evolution has shown the admirable adaptability of organisms to their conditions of life, and the ensuing development of such faculties as render more complete both the adaptations of the aggregates to their surroundings and those of each of the constituent parts of the aggregate to the needs of free cooperation. It has familiarized us with the circumstance that throughout organic nature the capacities for life in common grow in proportion as the integration of organisms into compound aggregates becomes more and more complete; and it has enforced thus the opinion already expressed by social moralists as to the perfectibility of human nature. It has shown us that, in the long run of the struggle for existence, "the fittest" will prove to be those who combine intellectual knowledge with the knowledge necessary for the production of wealth, and not those who are now the richest because they, or their ancestors, have been momentarily the strongest.

By showing that the "struggle for existence" must be conceived not merely in its restricted sense of a struggle between individuals for the means of subsistence but in its wider sense of adaptation of all individuals of the species to the best conditions for the survival of the species, as well as for the greatest possible sum of life and happiness for each and all, it has permitted us to deduce the laws of moral science from the social needs and habits of mankind. It has shown us the infinitesimal part played by positive law in moral evolution, and the immense part played by the natural growth of altruistic feelings, which develop as soon as the conditions of life favor their growth. It has thus enforced the opinion of social reformers as to the necessity of modifying the conditions of life for improving man, instead of trying to improve human nature by moral teachings while life works in an opposite direction. Finally, by studying human society from the biological point of view, it has come to the conclusions arrived at by anarchists from the study of history and present tendencies as to further progress being in the line of socialization of wealth and integrated labor combined with the fullest possible freedom of the individual. . . .

Taking all this into account, and still more the practical aspects of the question as to how private property *might* become common property, most of the anarchists maintain that the very next step to be made by society, as soon as the present regime of property undergoes a modification, will be in a communist sense. We are communists. But our communism is not that of the authoritarian school: it is anarchist communism, communism without government, free communism. It is a synthesis of the two chief aims pursued by humanity since the dawn of its history—economic freedom and political freedom.

I have already said that anarchism means no-government. We know well that the word "anarchy" is also used in current phraseology as synonymous with disorder. But that meaning of "anarchy," being a derived one, implies at least two suppositions. It implies, first, that wherever there is no government there is disorder; and it implies, moreover, that order, due to a strong government and a strong police, is always beneficial. Both implications, however, are anything but proved. There is plenty of order—we should say, of harmony—in many branches of human activity where the government, happily, does not interfere. As to the beneficial effects of order, the kind of order that reigned at Naples under the Bourbons surely was not preferable to some disorder started by Garibaldi; while the Protestants of this country will probably say that the good deal of disorder made by Luther was preferable, at any rate, to the order which reigned under the Pope. While all agree that harmony is always desirable, there is no such unanimity about order, and still less about the "order" which is supposed to reign in our modern societies. So that we have no objection whatever to the use of the word "anarchy" as a negation of what has been often described as order.

By taking for our watchword anarchy in its sense of no-government, we intend to express a pronounced tendency of human society. In history we see that precisely those epochs when small parts of humanity broke down the power of their rulers and reassumed their freedom were epochs of the greatest progress, economic and intellectual. Be it the growth of the free cities, whose unrivalled monuments—free work of free associations of workers—still testify to the revival of mind and of the well-being of the citizen; be it the great movement which gave birth to the Reformation— those epochs when the individual recovered some part of his freedom witnessed the greatest progress. And if we carefully watch the present development of civilized nations, we cannot fail to discover in it a marked and ever-growing movement towards limiting more and more the sphere of action of government, so as to leave more and more liberty to the initiative of the individual. After having tried all kinds of government, and endeavored to solve the insoluble problem of having a government "which might compel the individual to obedience, without escaping itself from obedience to collectivity," humanity is trying now to free itself from the bonds of any government whatever, and to respond to its needs of organization by the free understanding between individuals pursuing the same common aims.

Home Rule, even for the smallest territorial unit or group, becomes a growing need. Free agreement is becoming a substitute for law. And free cooperation a substitute for governmental guardianship. One after the other those activities which were considered as the functions of government during the last two centuries are disputed; society moves better the less it is governed. And the more we study the advance made in this direction, as well as the inadequacy of governments to fulfill the expectations placed in them, the more we are bound to conclude that humanity, by steadily limiting the functions of government, is marching towards reducing them finally to *nil*. We already foresee a state of society where the liberty of the individual will be limited by no laws, no bonds—by nothing else but his own social habits and the necessity, which everyone feels, of finding cooperation, support, and sympathy among his neighbors. . . .

The objections to the above may be easily foreseen. It will be said of course: "But what is to be done with those who do not keep their agreements? What with those who are not inclined to work? What with those who would prefer breaking the written laws of society, or—on the anarchist hypothesis—its unwritten customs? Anarchism may be good for a higher humanity,—not for the men of our own times."

First of all, there are two kinds of agreements: there is the free one which is entered upon by free consent, as a free choice between different courses equally open to each of the agreeing parties. And there is the enforced agreement, imposed by one party upon the other, and accepted by the latter from sheer necessity; in fact, it is no agreement at all; it is a mere submission to necessity. Unhappily, the great bulk of what are now described as agreements belong to the latter category. When a workman sells his labor to an employer and knows perfectly well that some part of the value of his produce will be unjustly taken by the employer; when he sells it without even the slightest guarantee of being employed so much as six consecutive months, it is a sad mockery to call that a free contract. Modern economists may call it free, but the father of political economy— Adam Smith—was never guilty of such a misrepresentation. As long as three-quarters of humanity are compelled to enter into agreements of that description, force is of course necessary, both to enforce the supposed agreements and to maintain such a state of things. Force—and a great deal of force—is necessary to prevent the laborers from taking possession of what they consider unjustly appropriated by the few; and force is necessary to continually bring new "uncivilized nations" under the same conditions.

But we do not see the necessity of force for enforcing agreements freely entered upon. We never heard of a penalty imposed on a man who belonged to the crew of a lifeboat and at a given moment preferred to abandon the association. All that his comrades would do with him, if he were guilty of a gross neglect, would probably be to refuse to have anything further to do with him. Nor did we hear of fines imposed on a contributor to the dictionary for a delay in his work, or of *gendarmes* driving the volunteers of Garibaldi to the battlefield. Free agreements need not be enforced.

As to the so-often repeated objection that no one would labor if he were not compelled to do so by sheer necessity, we heard enough of it before the emancipation of slaves in America, as well as before the emancipation of serfs in Russia. And we have had the opportunity of appreciating it at its just value. So we shall not try to convince those who can be convinced only by accomplished facts. As to those who reason, they ought to know that, if it really was so with some parts of humanity at its lowest stages, or if it is so with some small communities, or separate individuals, brought to sheer despair by ill success in their struggle against unfavorable conditions, it is not so with the bulk of the civilized nations. With us, work is a habit, and idleness an artificial growth. Of course, when to be a manual worker means to be compelled to work all one's life long for ten hours a day, and often more, at producing some part of something—a pin's head, for instance; when it means to be paid wages on which a family can live only on the condition of the strictest limitation of all its needs; when it means to be always under the menace of being thrown tomorrow out of employment—and we know how frequent are the industrial crises, and what misery they imply; when it means, in a very great number of cases, premature death in a paupers' infirmary, if not in the workhouse; when to be a manual worker signifies to wear a life-long stamp of inferiority in the eyes of those very people who live on the work of these "hands;" when it always means the renunciation of all those higher enjoyments that science and art give to man—oh, then there is no wonder that everybody—the manual workers as well—has but one dream: that of rising to a condition where others would work for him.

Overwork is repulsive to human nature—not work. Overwork for supplying the few with luxury—not work for the well-being of all. Work is a physiological necessity, a necessity of spending accumulated bodily energy, a necessity which is health and life itself. If so many branches of useful work are so reluctantly done now, it is merely because they mean overwork, or they are improperly organized. But we know—old Franklin knew it—that four hours of useful work every day would be more than sufficient for supplying everybody with the comfort of a moderately well-to-do middle-class house, if we all gave ourselves to productive work, and if we did not waste our productive powers as we do waste them now.

As to the childish question, repeated for fifty years: "Who would do disagreeable work?" frankly I regret that none of our *savants* has ever been brought to do it, be it for only one day in his life. If there is still work which is really disagreeable in itself, it is only because our scientific men have never cared to consider the means of rendering it less so. They have always known that there were plenty of starving men who would do it for a few cents a day.

As to the third—the chief—objection, which maintains the necessity of a government for punishing those who break the law of society, there is so much to say about it that it hardly can be touched incidentally. The more we study the question, the more we are brought to the conclusion that society itself is responsible for the anti-social deeds perpetrated in its midst, and that no punishment, no prisons, and no hang-men can diminish the numbers of such deeds; nothing short of a reorganization of society itself.

Three quarters of all the acts which are brought before our courts every year have their origin, either directly or indirectly, in the present disorganized state of society with regard to the production and distribution of wealth—not in perversity of human nature. As to the relatively few antisocial deeds which result from anti-social inclinations of separate individuals, it is not by prisons, nor even by resorting to the hangmen, that we can diminish their numbers. By our prisons, we merely multiply them and render them worse. By our detectives, our "price of blood," our executions, and our jails, we spread in society such a terrible flow of basest passions and habits, that he who should realize the effects of these institutions to their full extent would be frightened by what society is doing under the pretext of maintaining morality. We *must* search for other remedies, and the remedies have been indicated long since.

Of course now, when a mother in search of food and shelter for her children must pass by shops filled with the most refined delicacies of refined gluttony; when gorgeous and insolent luxury is displayed side by side with the most execrable misery; when the dog and the horse of a rich man are far better cared for than millions of children whose mothers earn a pitiful salary in the pit or the manufactory; when each "modest" evening dress of a lady represents eight months, or one year, of human labor; when enrichment at somebody else's expense is the avowed aim of the "upper classes," and no distinct boundary can be traced between honest and dishonest means of making money—then force is the only means for maintaining such a state of things. Then an army of policemen, judges, and hangmen becomes a necessary institution.

But if all our children—all children are *our* children—received a sound instruction and education—and we have the means of giving it; if every family lived in a decent home—and they *could* at the present high pitch of our production; if every boy and girl were taught a handicraft at the same time as he or she receives scientific instruction, and *not* to be a manual producer of wealth were considered as a token of inferiority; if men lived in closer contact with one another, and had continually to come into contact on those public affairs which now are vested in the few; and if, in consequence of a closer contact, we were brought to take as lively an interest in our neighbors' difficulties and pains as we formerly took in those of our kinsfolk—then we should not resort to policemen and judges, to prisons and executions. Anti-social deeds would be nipped in the bud, not punished. The few contests which would arise would be easily settled by arbitrators; and no more force would be necessary to impose their decisions than is required now for enforcing the decisions of the family tribunals of China.

And here we are brought to consider a great question: what would become of morality in a society which recognized no laws and proclaimed the full freedom of the individual[?] Our answer is plain. Public morality is independent from, and anterior to, law and religion. Until now, the teachings of morality have been associated with religious teachings. But the influence which religious teachings formerly exercised on the mind has faded of late, and the sanction which morality derived from religion has no longer the power it formerly had. Millions and millions grow in our cities who have lost the old faith. Is it a reason for throwing morality overboard, and for treating it with the same sarcasm as primitive cosmogony?

Obviously not. No society is possible without certain principles of morality generally recognized. If everyone grew accustomed to deceiving his fellow-men; if we never could rely on each other's promise and words; if everyone treated his fellow as an enemy, against whom every means of warfare is justifiable—no society could exist. And we see, in fact, that notwithstanding the decay of religious beliefs, the principles of morality remain unshaken. We even see irreligious people trying to raise the current standard of morality. The fact is that moral principles are independent of religious beliefs: they are anterior to them. The primitive Tchuktchis have no religion: they have only superstitions and fear of the hostile forces of nature; and nevertheless we find with them the very same principles of morality which are taught by Christians and Buddhists, Mussulmans and Hebrews. Nay, some of their practices imply a much higher standard of tribal morality than that which appears in our civilized society.

In fact, each new religion takes its moral principles from the only real stock of morality—the moral habits which grow with men as soon as they unite to live together in tribes, cities, or nations. No animal society is possible without resulting in a growth of certain moral habits of mutual support and even self-sacrifice for the common well-being. These habits are a necessary condition for the welfare of the species in its struggle for life—cooperation of individuals being a much more important factor in the struggle for the preservation of the species than the so-much-spoken-of physical struggle between individuals for the means of existence. The "fittest" in the organic world are those who grow accustomed to life in society;

and life in society necessarily implies moral habits. As to mankind, it has during its long existence developed in its midst a nucleus of social habits, of moral habits, which cannot disappear as long as human societies exist. And therefore, notwithstanding the influences to the contrary which are now at work in consequence of our present economic relations, the nucleus of our moral habits continues to exist. Law and religion only formulate them and endeavor to enforce them by their sanction.

Whatever the variety of theories of morality, all can be brought under three chief categories: the morality of religion; the utilitarian morality; and the theory of moral habits resulting from the very needs of life in society. Each religious morality sanctifies its prescriptions by making them originate from revelation; and it tries to impress its teachings on the mind by a promise of reward, or punishment, either in this or in a future life. The utilitarian morality maintains the idea of reward, but it finds it in man himself. It invites men to analyze their pleasures, to classify them, and to give preference to those which are most intense and most durable. We must recognize, however, that, although it has exercised some influence, this system has been judged too artificial by the great mass of human beings. And finally—whatever its varieties—there is the third system of morality which sees in moral actions—in those actions which are most powerful in rendering men best fitted for life in society—a mere necessity of the individual to enjoy the joys of his brethren, to suffer when some of his brethren are suffering; a habit and a second nature, slowly elaborated and perfected by life in society. That is the morality of mankind; and that is also the morality of anarchism.

Such are, in a very brief summary, the leading principles of anarchism. Each of them hurts many a prejudice, and yet each of them results from an analysis of the very tendencies displayed by human society. Each of them is rich in consequences and implies a thorough revision of many a current opinion. And anarchism is not a mere insight into a remote future. Already now, whatever the sphere of action of the individual, he can act, either in accordance with anarchist principles or on an opposite line. And all that may be done in that direction will be done in the direction to which further development goes. All that may be done in the opposite way will be an attempt to force humanity to go where it will *not* go.

Contemporary Issues

Equality and Preferential Treatment

32. Who Are Equals?   Carl Cohen

Carl Cohen (1931–   ), professor of philosophy at the University of Michigan, has established his professional reputation in the areas of political and social philosophy and philosophy of law. His publications include *Communism, Fascism and Democracy; Democracy;* and *Democracy and Civil Disobedience.*

> *"Equals ought to have equality. But there still remains a question: equality or inequality of what?"*
>
> Aristotle, *Politics,* Bk. III, Chap. 12

The Fourteenth Amendment to the U.S. Constitution reads in part: "No State shall . . . deny to any person within its jurisdiction the equal protection of the laws." What is the point of this passage? What would a law be like that did not apply equally to those to whom it applied at all? Imagine the law: "All citizens eighteen years of age and over shall have the right to vote." Under it, the seventeen-year-old and the nineteen-year-old are treated very differently; but all nineteen-year-old citizens are treated in one way (if the law is obeyed) and all seventeen-year-old citizens in another—neither group is denied the equal protection of the law. Suppose, when I went to register to vote, the county clerk responded to my request with an embarrassed smile, saying: "Ah yes, Mr. Cohen, but, you see, you're Jewish, so—I'm afraid—we can't register you." Well—we'd make short work of him.

Now suppose the law were different. Suppose it read: "All citizens eighteen years of age and over—except Jews—shall have the right to vote." The clerk will not smile when he is handed my application in this case. "I'm sorry, Mr. Cohen," one can hear the mechanical voice of that bureaucrat, "but the law prescribes that Jews may not vote." I am stunned as I read the printed act of Congress he puts before me; but there it is: non-Jews (over eighteen) vote, Jews don't. Suppose the clerk is efficient and incorruptible—all Jews are treated alike with utmost scrupulosity. Then it would appear that all were treated justly under that law, receiving its equal protection.

Surely we never supposed that the equal protection of the law entails identical treatment for everyone. We know that would be absurd. Employers have legal obligations that employees have not. Students have legal rights (and duties) that teachers have not. Rich people must pay taxes that poor people need not. Our legal codes are replete with distinctions—hundreds and thousands of distinctions determining the applicability of

From the *Phi Kappa Phi Journal,* Vol. LVIII, No. 1 (Winter, 1978). The name of this journal published by the Honor Society of Phi Kappa Phi recently was changed to *National Forum.* Reprinted with permission of the author and *National Forum.*

the laws. I may be angered by a distinction drawn—yet I will reluctantly agree that if that is the law, and since I am in a specific category, it is fair for me to be obliged under that law, as others are who are in the same class.

We argue about these distinctions—but in three very different ways. We may argue (lawyers are constantly arguing) about who are and who are not in the same class. When you defend a contested deduction on your income tax against the IRS, or I insist that as a college professor I am not a "public official" in the sense that would require public disclosure of my finances, we are disputing over the application of the legal categories drawn, not over the categories themselves.

We may argue—as students of political science, or as legislators—that it is wise (or unwise) to introduce certain categorial distinctions. For example, should the law distinguish between large and small entrepreneurs in the application of industrial safety regulations? Should the law distinguish between different categories of employment in establishing minimum wage requirements? (And so on.)

We may argue about whether categories of a particular kind should be permitted in the law at all. Some legislation duly enacted, or administrative regulations duly authorized, may distinguish categories of persons we think ought not be distinguished. Some discriminations are worse than unwise; they are unjust.

Return now to the Fourteenth Amendment and its "equal protection clause." The prohibition in that clause bears chiefly on arguments of the third sort. It does not bar legislatures from categorizing, but is interpreted so as to require categories used in laws to have a rational foundation. Some categorial distinctions will by that clause be prohibited altogether. Under Hitler's Nuremberg Laws all Jews were treated alike, but justice in America does not permit that sort of equal protection. The central thrust of the Fourteenth Amendment was, and is, to forbid the use—in law, or by administrators under color of law—of categories intrinsically unfair.

But which categories are unfair? The Amendment itself was clearly designed to insure that blacks, former slaves, were to be as free as whites. The laws were to protect all races equally. Now, more than a century later, seeking to give redress for long-standing racial injustice, we encounter the problem of fairness from the other side. May we, in the honest effort to achieve real equality among the races, distinguish between black and white (and yellow and brown, etc.) giving preference to some over others? Does our commitment to the equal protection of the laws permit it?

When the courts, and especially the United States Supreme Court, speak to such questions, they decide not simply what the U.S. Constitution requires, but what (in their view) justice requires. High courts must frame principles to guide the resolution of disputes between real parties, in the case before them and in future cases. Judicial reasoning is often profoundly moral reasoning. Actual cases, faced and decided, are the grist which the mill of American justice grinds. We do well to philosophize with the courts, and as they do, in living contexts.

The context now forcing a deeper understanding of "the equal protection of the laws" is that of racially preferential admissions to law schools and medical schools. Some call the problem that of "reverse discrimination," others "benign quotas." Let the name not prejudice the issue. What is *not* before us, or the courts, is the appropriateness of affirmative action. None of the participants in this dispute question the pressing need to take vigorous action, affirmative action, to correct long-standing racial injustice. What is at issue is *what* we may justly do to advance this objective— what categories we may (or must not) use, how we may (or must not) apply them.

The case of *The Regents of the University of California v. Allan Bakke* . . . puts this problem in sharp focus. Allan Bakke was twice rejected (in 1973 and 1974) by the medical school of the University of California at Davis. His undergraduate performance was fine, his test scores excellent, his character and interview performance admirable; he ranked very high among the more than 3,000 applicants for 100 seats. But 16 of those seats were reserved for minority-group applicants, who faced admission standards deliberately and markedly lower than did majority-group students like Bakke. The University of California (like many of its sister universities) was determined to enroll a representative proportion of blacks and members of other minority groups in its medical school—however distasteful the double standard believed necessary to accomplish that end.

The Davis medical school established a special committee to fill the reserved slots, and the committee evaluated the minority-group candidates, who competed only against one another. Officially, any disadvantaged person could seek admission under the special program; in fact, all persons admitted under that program, from its inception in 1969, were minority-group members. Officially, that committee reported to the admissions committee; in fact, the applicants chosen by the special committee were invariably admitted. In each of the years Bakke was rejected, some minority-group admittees had grade-point averages so low (2.11 in 1973, 2.21 in 1974) that, if they had been white, they would have been summarily rejected.

The University of California does not deny that the overall ranking of many of the minority-group applicants who were accepted—after interviews, and with character, interests, test scores, and averages all considered—was substantially below that of many majority applicants who were rejected. Bakke contends that had his skin been of a darker color he would certainly have been admitted. He argues that, refused admission solely because of his race, he was denied "the equal protection of the laws" guaranteed him by the Fourteenth Amendment to the U.S. Constitution.

All sides in this litigation agree that professional schools may properly use, in screening for admission, a host of factors other than test-scores and grade-point averages: dedication or dexterity, compassion or professional aims. All sides agree that persons unfairly injured are entitled to full, appropriate, and timely redress. What remains at issue in this case is one thing only: *preference by race.*

The advocates of racially preferential systems reason as follows: Equal protection of the laws requires different treatment for people in different circumstances. Minority-group members are in very special circumstances. Preference by race is here a reasonable instrument to achieve, for members of minority groups, objectives both just and compelling.

Such preference (not denied by the medical school) is thus defended by two central arguments. The first is grounded in alleged demands of justice: Only by deliberately preferring minority applicants can we give adequate compensation for generations of oppressive maltreatment. The second is grounded in the alleged needs of society: If we do not continue to give deliberate racial preference, our medical and law schools will again become what they long were—white enclaves. *Compensation* is the heart of the first argument, *integration* of the second. Both arguments are profoundly mistaken.

Redress is rightly given for injury—not for being black or brown. Members of minority groups have been cruelly damaged, but whatever damage is rightly compensated for (cultural or economic deprivation, inferior schooling, or other), *any* applicant so unfairly damaged is fully entitled to the same special consideration, regardless of his race or ethnic group. The prohibition of special favor by race—any race—is the central thrust of a constitutional guarantee that all will receive the protection of the laws equally. Classification by race for the distribution of goods or opportunities is intrinsically odious, always invidious, and morally impermissible, no matter how laudable the goals in view.

What of the school-desegregation cases in which the U.S. Supreme Court has approved the use of racial categories to insure racial integration? Don't these show that racial preference is permissible if the aim is good? Certainly not. In these cases attention to race was allowed in order to ascertain whether school boards that had been discriminating wrongfully by race had really ceased to do so. Racial identification was there permitted—but only to insure that all students, of whatever race, received absolutely equal treatment. The distinction between that use of racial counting, and the use of racial categories to reintroduce special preference, is sharp and profound.

Can the University of California be defended on the ground that its system of racial preference is not injurious but benign? No. Results, not intentions, determine benignity. All racial quotas have injurious results and therefore cannot be benign. When the goods being distributed are in short supply, and some get more of those goods because of their race, then others get less because of their race. There is no escaping that cold logic. Bakke and others like him are seriously penalized for no other reason than their race. Such a system, as even the Washington State Supreme Court in the *DeFunis* case agreed, "is certainly not benign with respect to non-minority students who are displaced by it."

All this says not an iota against compensation. If redress is due, let us give it, and give it fully. If compensation is to be offered through special favor in professional-school admissions—a questionable mode of payment but a possible one—then let us be certain we look in every case to the injury for which we give redress, and not to the race of the applicant.

If the requirements of justice cannot support racial preference, perhaps the society's interest in integration can. The Supreme Court of California, while upholding Bakke's claim, allowed, *arguendo,* that integration is a compelling interest. "Integration" has different meanings, of course. That ambiguity invites the university's most appealing complaint. "You have told us to integrate," the university has said, in effect, "and when we devise admissions systems designed to do just that, you tell us we may not use racial preference. But the problem is a racial one. We cannot achieve racial balance unless we give special preference to racial minorities. Do not ask the impossible of us. And do not ask us to do in indirect ways what you will not permit us to do directly."

That argument by the University of California is not sound. A considered reply to it (here much compressed) is fourfold.

First, some of the ends in view are important, some are questionable. That the entire package is "compelling" is very doubtful.

(a) Better medical and legal services for minorities is a pressing need, but it is far from obvious that minority professionals reared in city slums will return to practice there. And it is patently unfair to burden them with this restrictive expectation. If the intention to give service to particular segments of the community is to be a consideration in admission to professional school, let that be known, and let all persons, of whatever race, make their case for establishing such intentions, if they claim them.

(b) Some defend preferential admission on the ground that many persons seeking professional help will be "more comfortable" with a lawyer or a doctor of their own race or religion. Possibly true. But the argument based upon this interest, now to serve as a justification of institutionalized racial preference, has long been used to exclude blacks from white hospitals and Jews from gentile law firms. It is an argument in which bigots of every color will take satisfaction.

(c) Diversity of cultural background in the professional schools, and in the professions themselves, will increase the richness of education and of service, and will provide role-models for youngsters from cultural groups long oppressed. These are genuine and worthy interests, but are they compelling in the requisite sense? What *is* compelling is integration in the classical sense: the removal of every obstruction to genuinely equal opportunity, the elimination of every racial qualification. Integration in the now fashionable sense—entailing some *de facto* mix of races approaching proportionality—may be desirable in some contexts and undesirable in others, but is in any case certainly not compelling.

Second, the Supreme Court of California emphasized that no party has shown preference by race in admissions (which all agree is objectionable) to be necessary to achieve appropriate social goals. Even if arbitrary numerical ratios are established as the only acceptable standard of success, that cannot be shown. But from whence comes that standard? The entire history of our nation has been one of ethnic layering, in which different interests and activities tend to be pursued by different cultural and ethnic groups. That is not unwholesome. The effort to homogenize society in spite of this natural tendency is already proving to be divisive, frustrating, and unworkable. Substantial increases of diversity in some professions are reasonably sought. With nonpreferential forms of affirmative action pursued vigorously, and admissions criteria enlarged and enriched and applied evenhandedly to all applicants, diversity and *de facto* integration may be much advanced. Still more might be accomplished if various compensatory schemes were introduced, but they must be applied in a racially neutral way. Some majority applicants who deserve compensatory preference will also benefit under such programs, but this is entirely fitting.

There is nothing crafty about this reply. The claim that these are but devious ways to reach the same ends is simply false, and betrays an inclination to introduce racial preference somehow, "through the back door," if necessary. That would be ugly. There is no reason to fear or to be ashamed of an honest admissions program, or of an honest compensatory program, honestly applied. The racial count that results may not be the same as that when racial preference is used, but perhaps it ought not be. Even if the count were the same, the individuals (admitted using principles, not race) would be different, and that makes all the difference. It is certain that substantial progress in diversifying and integrating professional school classes can be achieved without racial preference.

Third, we must see that granting favor on the basis of race alone is a nasty business, however honorable the goal. The moral issue comes in classic form: Terribly pressing objectives (integrated professions, adequate legal and medical service for members of minority groups) appear to require impermissible means. Might we not wink at the Constitution, this once, in view of the importance and decency of our objectives?

Such winking is precisely the hope of every party having aims that are, to that party's profound conviction, of absolutely overriding importance. Constitutional short-cuts have been and will be urged for the sake of national security (e.g., the internment of Japanese-Americans during World War II), for the enforcement of criminal laws (e.g., admission of illegally seized evidence), and in other spheres. But wink we must not! Each party in its turn must abide the restrictions of constitutional process. The single most important feature of a constitution, if it is more than paper, is its preclusion of unjust means. Hence the preciousness and power of the guarantee of equality before the law. When good process and laudable objectives conflict, long experience teaches the priority of process. Means that are corrupt will infect the result and (with societies as with individuals) will corrupt the user in the end. So it is with wire-tapping, with censorship, and with every short-cut taken knowingly at the expense of the rights of individuals. So it is also with racial preference, even when well-intended.

The fourth response to the integration argument is as compelling as the first three, but adds bitter irony. Hating the taste of racial preference in admissions, the advocates of these programs swallow them only because of a conviction that they are so good for us. Bitter but (they think) medicinal. In this, too, they are mistaken. Racial preference is good for nobody, black or white, majority or minority. It will not integrate the races but will *dis*integrate them, forcing attention to race, creating anxiety and agitation about race in all the wrong contexts, exciting envy, ill-will, and widespread resentment of unfair penalties and undeserved rewards.

It will not serve the minority well if it becomes clear that minority-group students admitted preferentially are less qualified to pursue their studies and to practice their professions. A black psychiatrist at Case Western Reserve University Hospital, Dr. Charles DeLeon, told the *New York Times* in 1974: "I wouldn't hit a dog with some of the minority students I've seen, and I have an idea that you honkies are taking in these dummies so that eight years from now you'll be able to turn around and say, 'Look how bad they all turned out.'"

Above all, racial preference clouds the accomplishments and undermines the reputations of those superbly qualified minority-group professionals who neither need nor get special favor. When, in the minds of everyone, black and white, a physician's dark skin is automatically linked to charity and payoff, who among members of minority groups is served? It is a cruel result.

Racial preference is dynamite. Many who play with such preference are now blinded by honest zeal and hide from themselves the explosions in the sequel. Justice John Marshall Harlan, dissenting in 1896 from the Supreme Court ruling that established the "separate but equal" doctrine, insisted that the U.S. Constitution was and must be color-blind. Some would have the law be color-conscious now so that it can indeed become color-blind in the future. That cannot be. One is reminded of political leaders who "suspend" constitutions to "build a firmer base for democracy." Once established as constitutionally acceptable grounds for discriminatory distribution, racial categories will wax, not wane, in importance. No prescription for racial disharmony can be surer of success.

Official favoritism by race or national origin is poison in society. In American society, built of manifold racial and ethnic layers, it is deadly poison. How gravely mistaken it will be to take new doses of the same stuff, while still suffering the pains of recovery from the old.

33. A Defense of Programs of Preferential Treatment   Richard A. Wasserstrom

Richard A. Wasserstrom (1936–   ), is professor of law and philosophy at the University of California, Los Angeles. In 1963–64 he was an attorney in the civil rights division of the U.S. Department of Justice. He is the author of *The Judicial Decision* and has edited *War and Morality, Morality and the Law,* and *Today's Moral Problems,* Second Edition.

Many justifications of programs of preferential treatment depend upon the claim that in one respect or another such programs have good consequences or that they are effective means by which to bring about some desirable end, e.g., an integrated, equalitarian society. I mean by "programs of preferential treatment" to refer to programs such as those at issue in the *Bakke* case—programs which set aside a certain number of places (for example, in a law school) as to which members of minority groups (for example, persons who are non-white or female) who possess certain minimum qualifications (in terms of grades and test scores) may be preferred for admission to those places over some members of the majority group who possess higher qualifications (in terms of grades and test scores).

Many criticisms of programs of preferential treatment claim that such

From the *Phi Kappa Phi Journal*, Vol. LVIII, No. 1 (Winter, 1978). The name of this journal published by the Honor Society of Phi Kappa Phi recently was changed to *National Forum*. Reprinted with permission of the author and *National Forum*.

programs, even if effective, are unjustifiable because they are in some important sense unfair or unjust. In this paper I present a limited defense of such programs by showing that two of the chief arguments offered for the unfairness or injustice of these programs do not work in the way or to the degree supposed by critics of these programs.

The first argument is this. Opponents of preferential treatment programs sometimes assert that proponents of these programs are guilty of intellectual inconsistency, if not racism or sexism. For, as is now readily acknowledged, at times past employers, universities, and many other social institutions did have racial or sexual quotas (when they did not practice overt racial or sexual exclusion), and many of those who were most concerned to bring about the eradication of those racial quotas are now untroubled by the new programs which reinstitute them. And this, it is claimed, is inconsistent. If it was wrong to take race or sex into account when blacks and women were the objects of racial and sexual policies and practices of exclusion, then it is wrong to take race or sex into account when the objects of the policies have their race or sex reversed. Simple considerations of intellectual consistency—of what it means to give racism or sexism as a reason for condemning these social policies and practices— require that what was a good reason then is still a good reason now.

The problem with this argument is that despite appearances, there is no inconsistency involved in holding both views. Even if contemporary preferential-treatment programs which contain quotas are wrong, they are not wrong for the reasons that made quotas against blacks and women pernicious. The reason why is that the social realities do make an enormous difference. The fundamental evil of programs that discriminated against blacks or women was that these programs were a part of a larger social universe which systematically maintained a network of institutions which unjustifiably concentrated power, authority, and goods in the hands of white male individuals, and which systematically consigned blacks and women to subordinate positions in the society.

Whatever may be wrong with today's affirmative-action programs and quota systems, it should be clear that the evil, if any, is just not the same. Racial and sexual minorities do not constitute the dominant social group. Nor is the conception of who is a fully developed member of the moral and social community one of an individual who is either female or black. Quotas which prefer women or blacks do not add to an already relatively overabundant supply of resources and opportunities at the disposal of members of these groups in the way in which the quotas of the past did maintain and augment the overabundant supply of resources and opportunities already available to white males.

The same point can be made in a somewhat different way. Sometimes people say that what was wrong, for example, with the system of racial discrimination in the South was that it took an irrelevant characteristic, namely race, and used it systematically to allocate social benefits and burdens of various sorts. The defect was the irrelevance of the characteristic used—race—for that meant that individuals ended up being treated in a manner that was arbitrary and capricious.

I do not think that was the central flaw at all. Take, for instance, the most hideous of the practices, human slavery. The primary thing that was wrong with the institution was not that the particular individuals who were assigned the place of slaves were assigned there arbitrarily because the assignment was made in virtue of an irrelevant characteristic, their race. Rather, it seems to me that the primary thing that was and is wrong with slavery is the practice itself—the fact of some individuals being able to own other individuals and all that goes with that practice. It would not matter by what criterion individuals were assigned; human slavery would still be wrong. And the same can be said for most if not all of the other discrete practices and institutions which comprised the system of racial discrimination even after human slavery was abolished. The practices were unjustifiable—they were oppressive—and they would have been so no matter how the assignment of victims had been made. What made it worse, still, was that the institutions and the supporting ideology all inter-locked to create a system of human oppression whose effects on those living under it were as devastating as they were unjustifiable.

Again, if there is anything wrong with the programs of preferential treatment that have begun to flourish within the past ten years, it should be evident that the social realities in respect to the distribution of resources and opportunities make the difference. Apart from everything else, there is simply no way in which all of these programs taken together could plausibly be viewed as capable of relegating white males to the kind of genuinely oppressive status characteristically bestowed upon women and blacks by the dominant social institutions and ideology.

The second objection is that preferential-treatment programs are wrong because they take race or sex into account rather than the only thing that does matter—that is, an individual's qualifications. What all such programs have in common and what makes them all objectionable, so this argument goes, is that they ignore the persons who are more qual-ified by bestowing a preference on those who are less qualified in virtue of their being either black or female.

There are, I think, a number of things wrong with this objection based on qualifications, and not the least of them is that we do not live in a society in which there is even the serious pretense of a qualification requirement for many jobs of substantial power and authority. Would anyone claim, for example, that the persons who comprise the judiciary are there because they are the most qualified lawyers or the most qualified persons to be judges? Would anyone claim that Henry Ford II is the head of the Ford Motor Company because he is the most qualified person for the job? Part of what is wrong with even talking about qualifications and merit is that the argument derives some of its force from the erroneous notion that we would have a meritocracy were it not for programs of pref-erential treatment. In fact, the higher one goes in terms of prestige, power and the like, the less qualifications seem ever to be decisive. It is only for certain jobs and certain places that qualifications are used to do more than establish the possession of certain minimum competencies.

But difficulties such as these to one side, there are theoretical difficul-ties as well which cut much more deeply into the argument about qualifi-cations. To begin with, it is important to see that there is a serious inconsistency present if the person who favors "pure qualifications" does so on the ground that the most qualified ought to be selected because this promotes maximum efficiency. Let us suppose that the argument is that, if we have the most qualified performing the relevant tasks, we will get those tasks done in the most economical and efficient manner. There is nothing wrong, in principle, with arguments based upon the good consequences that will flow from maintaining a social practice in a certain way. But it is inconsistent for the opponent of preferential treatment to attach much weight to qualifications on this ground, because it was an analogous appeal to the good consequences that the opponent of preferential treatment thought was wrong in the first place. That is to say, if the chief thing to be said in favor of strict qualifications and preferring the most qualified is that it is the most efficient way of getting things done, then we are right back to an assessment of the different consequences that will flow from different programs, and we are far removed from the considerations of justice or fairness that were thought to weigh so heavily against these programs.

It is important to note, too, that qualifications—at least in the educational context—are often not connected at all closely with any plausible conception of social effectiveness. To admit the most qualified students to law school, for example—given the way qualifications are now determined—is primarily to admit those who have the greatest chance of scoring the highest grades at law school. This says little about efficiency except perhaps that these students are the easiest for the faculty to teach. However, since we know so little about what constitutes being a good, or even successful lawyer, and even less about the correlation between being a very good law student and being a very good lawyer, we can hardly claim very confidently that the legal system will operate most effectively if we admit only the most qualified students to law school.

To be at all decisive, the argument for qualifications must be that those who are the most qualified deserve to receive the benefits (the job, the place in law school, etc.) because they are the most qualified. The introduction of the concept of desert now makes it an objection as to justice or fairness of the sort promised by the original criticism of the programs. But now the problem is that there is no reason to think that there is any strong sense of "desert" in which it is correct that the most qualified deserve anything.

Let us consider more closely one case, that of preferential treatment in respect to admission to college or graduate school. There is a logical gap in the inference from the claim that a person is most qualified to perform a task, e.g., to be a good student, to the conclusion that he or she deserves to be admitted as a student. Of course, those who deserve to be admitted should be admitted. But why do the most qualified deserve anything? There is simply no necessary connection between academic merit (in the sense of being the most qualified) and deserving to be a member of a student body. Suppose, for instance, that there is only one tennis court in the community. Is it clear that the two best tennis players ought to be the ones permitted to use it? Why not those who were there first? Or those who will enjoy playing the most? Or those who are the worst and, therefore, need the greatest opportunity to practice? Or those who have the chance to play least frequently?

We might, of course, have a rule that says that the best tennis players get to use the court before the others. Under such a rule the best players would deserve the court more than the poorer ones. But that is just to push the inquiry back one stage. Is there any reason to think that we ought to have a rule giving good tennis players such a preference? Indeed, the arguments that might be given for or against such a rule are many and varied. And few if any of the arguments that might support the rule would depend upon a connection between ability and desert.

Someone might reply, however, that the most able students deserve to be admitted to the university because all of their earlier schooling was a kind of competition, with university admission being the prize awarded to the winners. They deserve to be admitted because that is what the rule of the competition provides. In addition, it might be argued, it would be unfair now to exclude them in favor of others, given the reasonable expectations they developed about the way in which their industry and performance would be rewarded. Minority-admission programs, which inevitably prefer some who are less qualified over some who are more qualified, all possess this flaw.

There are several problems with this argument. The most substantial of them is that it is an empirically implausible picture of our social world. Most of what are regarded as the decisive characteristics for higher education have a great deal to do with things over which the individual has neither control nor responsibility: such things as home environment, socioeconomic class of parents, and, of course, the quality of the primary and secondary schools attended. Since individuals do not deserve having had any of these things vis-à-vis other individuals, they do not, for the most part, deserve their qualifications. And since they do not deserve their abilities they do not in any strong sense deserve to be admitted because of their abilities.

To be sure, if there has been a rule which connects, say, performance at high school with admission to college, then there is a weak sense in which those who do well at high school deserve, for that reason alone, to be admitted to college. In addition, if persons have built up or relied upon their reasonable expectations concerning performance and admission, they have a claim to be admitted on this ground as well. But it is certainly not obvious that these claims of desert are any stronger or more compelling than the competing claims based upon the needs of or advantages to women or blacks from programs of preferential treatment. And as I have indicated, all rule-based claims of desert are very weak unless and until the rule which creates the claim is itself shown to be a justified one. Unless one has a strong preference for the status quo, and unless one can defend that preference, the practice within a system of allocating places in a certain way does not go very far at all in showing that that is the right or the just way to allocate those places in the future.

A proponent of programs of preferential treatment is not at all committed to the view that qualifications ought to be wholly irrelevant. He or she can agree that, given the existing structure of any institution, there is probably some minimal set of qualifications without which one cannot participate meaningfully within the institution. In addition, it can be granted that the qualifications of those involved will affect the way the institution works and the way it affects others in the society. And the consequences will vary depending upon the particular institution. But all of this only establishes that qualifications, in this sense, are relevant, not that they are decisive. This is wholly consistent with the claim that race or sex should today also be relevant when it comes to matters such as admission to college or law school. And that is all that any preferential-treatment program—even one with the kind of quota used in the *Bakke* case—has ever tried to do.

I have not attempted to establish that programs of preferential treatment are right and desirable. There are empirical issues concerning the consequences of these programs that I have not discussed, and certainly not settled. Nor, for that matter, have I considered the argument that justice may permit, if not require, these programs as a way to provide compensation or reparation for injuries suffered in the recent as well as distant past, or as a way to remove benefits that are undeservedly enjoyed by those of the dominant group. What I have tried to do is show that it is wrong to think that programs of preferential treatment are objectionable in the centrally important sense in which many past and present discriminatory features of our society have been and are racist and sexist. The social realities as to power and opportunity do make a fundamental difference. It is also wrong to think that programs of preferential treatment are in any strong sense either unjust or unprincipled. The case for programs of preferential treatment could, therefore, plausibly rest both on the view that such programs are not unfair to white males (except in the weak, rule-dependent sense described in the foregoing) and on the view that it is unfair to continue the present set of unjust—often racist and sexist—institutions that comprise the social reality. And the case for these programs could rest as well on the proposition that, given the distribution of power and influence in the United States today, such programs may reasonably be viewed as potentially valuable, effective means by which to achieve admirable and significant social ideals of equality and integration.

Suggestions for Further Reading

Anthologies

Beck, Robert N. *Perspectives in Social Philosophy: Readings in Philosophic Sources of Social Thought.* New York: Holt, 1967. This book contains generous selections from the writings of classical and contemporary political philosophers. There are sections devoted to existentialism and analytic philosophy.

Cohen, Marshall et al. (eds.). *Equality and Preferential Treatment.* Princeton, New Jersey: Princeton U.P., 1978. An interesting recent collection of essays on this controversial subject.

Cranston, Maurice (ed.). *Western Political Philosophers: A Background Book.* New York: Capricorn, 1967. A series of concise and lucid essays by contemporary philosophers and political scientists on Plato, Aristotle, Aquinas, Machiavelli, Hobbes, Locke, Rousseau, Burke, Hegel, Marx, and Mill. The beginning student, particularly, will find this book helpful.

Pennock, J. Roland and Chapman, John W. (eds.). *Equality.* Nomos IX. Yearbook of the American Society for Political and Legal Philosophy. New York: Atherton, 1967. A collection of essays by philosophers, political scientists, and lawyers on various aspects of egalitarianism. Other volumes in this series are devoted to *Authority, Community, Liberty, Justice, Revolution,* and other topics of political philosophy.

Somerville, John and Santoni, Ronald E. (eds.). *Social and Political Philosophy: Readings from Plato to Gandhi.* New York: Doubleday, Anchor, 1963. Extensive selections (in some instances the unabridged work) from some of the most famous and influential writings in social and political thought by philosophers and political leaders.

Individual Works

Beck, Robert N. *Handbook in Social Philosophy.* New York: Macmillan, 1979. An examination of such topics as state power and authority, political obligation, and the ideal of justice in terms of various contemporary philosophical perspectives.

Deininger, Whitaker T. *Problems in Social and Political Thought: A Philosophical Introduction.* New York: Macmillan, 1965. An expository text focusing on the contributions of both classical and contemporary philosophers. Designed for the beginning student.

De Tocqueville, Alexis. *Democracy in America.* Edited and abridged by Richard D. Heffner. New York: New American Library, a Mentor Book, 1956. Although written over a hundred years ago, this work remains one of the most perceptive studies of American democracy. With the passage of time, it seems to grow more, not less, pertinent.

Dewey, John. *Freedom and Culture.* New York: Capricorn, 1963.

———. *Individualism: Old and New.* New York: Capricorn, 1962.

———. *Liberalism and Social Action.* New York: Capricorn, 1963.

———. *The Public and Its Problems.* Chicago: Alan Swallow, 1957. The major works on social and political philosophy by the great American philosopher of liberal democracy.

Frankel, Charles. *The Democratic Prospect.* New York: Harper, Harper Colophon Book, 1964. A contemporary defense of democracy by an American philosopher.

Goldman, Emma. *Red Emma Speaks: Selected Writings and Speeches by Emma Goldman.* Compiled and edited by Alix Kates Shulman, New York: Random, Vintage Books, 1972. A comprehensive collection of essays by a famous American anarchist.

Hook, Sidney. *Reason, Social Myths and Democracy.* New Preface by the author. New York: Harper, Harper Torchbooks, 1966. A vigorous, clear, and critical examination of various political philosophies with particular emphasis on Marxism and democracy by a former student of John Dewey and an able defender of his philosophy.

Macpherson, Crawford B. *The Life and Times of Liberal Democracy.* New York: Oxford U.P., 1977. A brief, clear attempt to set forth the essence of liberal democracy as now conceived.

Mencken, H. L. *Minority Report: H. L. Mencken's Notebooks.* New York: Knopf, 1956. This book consists of memoranda Mencken jotted down over many years. Yet these seemingly disconnected notes, often witty and biting, express a coherent and fundamental criticism of the American democratic scheme of things.

Quinton, Anthony. (ed.). *Political Philosophy.* New York: Oxford U.P., 1967. A judicious collection of recent influential writings on various issues in the area of political philosophy.

Raphael, D. D. *Problems of Political Philosophy.* London: Pall Mall, 1970. A recent, clearly written introduction for the beginning student.

Rawls, John. *A Theory of Justice.* Cambridge: Belknap Press of Harvard U.P., 1971. An outstanding systematic work in social and political philosophy by an American philosopher. It already has provoked a great deal of discussion. Recommended for the more advanced student.

Reitman, Jeffrey H. *In Defense of Political Philosophy.* New York: Harper, Harper Torchbooks, 1972. The book vigorously argues against R. P. Wolff's *In Defense of Anarchism* (See Wolff, *In Defense of Anarchism*) and for majoritarian democracy.

Russell, Bertrand. *Power: A New Social Analysis.* New York: Barnes & Noble, Unwin Books, 1962.

————. *Roads to Freedom: Socialism, Anarchism and Syndicalism.* New York: Barnes & Noble, Unwin Books, 1965. The first book, *Power,* is Russell's attempt at a comprehensive statement of his social and political philosophy. In the second book, Russell fully describes and discusses political doctrines, particularly the Guild Socialism Russell himself still favored in 1948 and now stimulating renewed interest because of current dissatisfaction with both capitalist democracy and Marxian communism.

Spencer, Herbert. *The Man Versus the State.* Edited by Donald Macrae, Baltimore: Penguin, 1969. As the result of the growing conviction that governments have become too strong for the preservation of men's liberties, the writings of the great nineteenth-century champion of *laissez faire* individualism against an inherently oppressive state have sparked renewed interest.

Taylor, Richard. *Freedom, Anarchy, and the Law: An Introduction to Political Philosophy.* Englewood Cliffs, N.J.: Prentice-Hall, 1973. Beginning and advanced students will find this lucid work stimulating and a pleasure to read.

Wolff, Robert Paul. *In Defense of Anarchism.* New York: Harper, Harper Torchbooks, 1970. This iconoclastic work by an American philosopher has provoked much discussion. (See Reitman, *In Defense of Political Philosophy.*)

Young, Michael. *The Rise of Meritocracy, 1870–2033.* Baltimore, Penguin, 1968. The famous, stimulating, imaginative vision of a kind of "meritocracy" where I.Q. plus effort equal merit that our present society could easily become.

Dictionary of the History of Ideas: Studies of Selected Pivotal Ideas. Philip P. Wiener, editor-in-chief. New York: Scribners, 1973. Substantial and clearly written essays emphasizing the historical development of topics discussed in this part. Designed to inform the nonspecialist, each essay concludes with a select bibliography.

Encyclopedia of Philosophy. Paul Edwards, editor-in-chief. New York: Macmillan, 1967. The beginning student will find many worthwhile articles on the subjects treated in this part, and excellent bibliographies.

Philosophy and Public Affairs. Princeton, N.J.: Princeton U.P. A quarterly journal. Philosophers and philosophically inclined writers from various disciplines bring their methods to bear on problems that concern everyone interested in social and political issues.

Five: Mind and Body

Introduction

In Karel Čapek's well-known play *R.U.R.* (Rossum's Universal Robots), scientists have learned to manufacture robots capable of doing all the manual and intellectual activities humans perform. Humans consider the robots to be lacking a soul since they are nothing more than a machine produced by a complex physical process, and use the robots in any way that serves man's needs. The robots, whose manufacture resulted from a new method of organizing matter, look and act very much like humans except that they lack emotions and feelings, which were purposely omitted to increase productivity. Since the robot's insensitivity to pain often leads to accidents, a scientist at Rossum's robot factory experiments with changes in their formula to give them human emotions. His experiments succeed; but the new sensitive robots consider themselves man's equal and, frustrated by their inferior status, rebel and destroy man.

This play raises the question of whether the robots, though only complex machines, differ significantly from the men who created them. The answers to this question can have important effects on man's view of himself and his place in the world. One traditional religious view of man, which gives him special importance, is that he alone, because he possesses an immaterial soul, was made in the image of God. But if man can be shown to be nothing more than a complex machine, this view of his special status must be given up. The doctrine that man is spiritual as well as physical has been thought to be of crucial importance for other reasons. The claim that man is immortal is based on his supposed possession of a soul that can continue in existence after the body's destruction. Some philosophers have argued that since a physical world would be controlled by invariable laws, the doctrine of free will can be maintained only if man has a spiritual aspect, and only if man possesses free will can he be morally responsible. In light of such implications, the philosopher is concerned to determine if man really is more than a complex physical object.

The problem of the nature of man, whether he is wholly physical or not, is called the mind-body problem. One prominent view of reality—*materialism*—holds that man, as is every other object in the universe, is totally a physical being. The universe is considered to consist of the motion of particles of matter in a void or space. Any claim that man has a soul or mind is regarded as a myth. The fact that man can do such things as talk and reason is attributed to his highly developed nervous system and brain. Death occurs when the body ceases to function. Any continuation of life after death is not the disembodied personal immortality defended by various religions, but the continued existence of the molecules that make up the body. This metaphysical materialism should not be confused with a popular use of the term *materialism* to refer to those who have no high ethical aims and who are primarily concerned with acquiring worldly goods and pleasures.

Opposed to the materialist view are those who believe that man is more than a material body; he also has a nonmaterial mind or soul. The idea of a person's being more than his body arose for a number of reasons. One possible reason is that primitive man could not comprehend why some bodies were alive and others dead when they apparently had the same physical parts. They endowed the living body with an invisible spirit or soul which the dead body lacked. The idea of a soul that apparently left the body at the time of death became the foundation for the belief in immortality, i.e., the continued existence of the soul after death.

In speculation about the soul, present-day philosophers generally equate it with the mind, which they claim is that part of us that thinks and has images and sensations. These philosophers posit a nonmaterial mind because, for one reason, the various images and thoughts we have do not have any size, weight, or location and so cannot be material. Further, it is often claimed that a mind is necessary to explain purposive behavior. Purposive behavior is behavior that is determined by one's apprehension and desire for some future goal, in contrast to behavior determined by prior physical causes. Philosophers who hold that man has both a physical body and a nonphysical mind are *dualists.*

The most generally held form of dualism and the form that is perhaps closest to our ordinary conception of man is *interactionism.* The interactionists maintain that both mind and body can causally affect each other. Thus, events in the mind can produce bodily behavior, and bodily events can produce mental occurrences. An example of events in the mind causing bodily events would be a thought of a girl friend causing one to pick up the phone and call her. An example of a physical event causing a mental event would be a case where stubbing one's toe produces a sensation of pain.

Many philosophers have thought the interactionist view unsatisfactory. The major difficulty is that there seems to be no good explanation of how a mental event, such as a thought, can cause physical behavior. We ordinarily think of causation in terms of one physical event producing another. A simple example would be a moving billiard ball's hitting a second ball and moving it. But how can a thought produce movement in a person's body? And where does the mind act on the body to cause it to move? One might be inclined to say that the mind affects some portion of the brain, but physiologists have found no place where the brain seems to be stimulated by any invisible cause. Similarly, how can the body produce sensations or images in the mind, which is nonphysical?

Confronted with such difficulties, some philosophers who believe that mental phenomena cannot be reduced to physical ones have given up interactionism in favor of *epiphenomenalism.* This view holds that physical events can cause mental events, but that occurrences in the mind are not able to cause any physical events. Rather than interaction, we have a one-way causal relation: from the body to the mind. This view, too, has had its share of critics. This view, like interactionism, needs to explain how a physical event in the body can cause an event to take place in the mind. Another problem is that paradoxical results follow from this theory. One such result is that all thoughts and reasoning are totally without significance in the determination of our behavior. It is certainly hard to believe that the world would be exactly as it is today even though none of men's thoughts about democracy, religion, and morality had ever occurred.

An ingenious theory that asserts the existence of minds but avoids the problems of the various dualist theories is *idealism.* Idealists affirm the existence of minds along with perceptions and feelings but deny the existence of any material objects existing apart from minds. Those objects that we ordinarily consider to exist in an external world are, in fact, nothing but appearances in minds. Although the idealist view of the world as consisting solely of disembodied minds and their contents seems very odd, it should not be dismissed without a careful assessment. Perhaps the most serious difficulty confronting the idealist is that of providing an explanation of the cause of our perceptions. If there is nothing independent of our minds causing our perceptions of such objects as tables and chairs, why do we perceive them at all?

In the first group of readings that follow, several of these positions are defended. In "How to Bury the Mind-Body Problem," Richard Taylor defends materialism. He contends that the main reason for the belief in the existence of minds is the false assumption that matter cannot think: that thinking, choosing, and reasoning cannot be done by "mere bodies." He bolsters his case for materialism by exhibiting the weaknesses in the major arguments used to support the existence of minds. In defending the interactionist position, C. E. M. Joad argues that the materialist cannot adequately explain purposive behavior or the way in which meaning is apprehended. He conceives of the mind as an active, creative force, which carries on activities that could not be conceived as resulting from the function of the brain. In opposition to the materialist view, Joad maintains that a perfect knowledge of a person's brain would fail to tell us what he was thinking since different thoughts could result in the same brain state. In "Sense Without Matter," A.

A. Luce rejects materialism by denying that we have any knowledge of matter or any need to postulate its existence. The sensations we have cannot, however, exist alone; and, so, we must postulate the existence of minds.

Although the development of robots has long been a subject for science-fiction stories and plays, such as *R.U.R.,* it is becoming a subject of increasing interest to philosophers and scientists as a result of the recent development of computers. Some theorists maintain that computers will eventually be developed to the point where they can perform all of the rational processes of human beings. And with the development of computerized robots, we would have a machine that could do everything a human being can do. In fact, it is argued, such a machine would be a human being, and a human being would have been shown to be nothing more than a machine. But is it possible to develop a machine that can perform all of the "mental" feats of a human being? And if such a machine could be developed, would it still lack something that humans possess? If we produce a machine that can do everything a human being can do, then have we shown that humans are really nothing more than physical objects?

In "In Praise of Robots," Carl Sagan contends not only that machines are capable of intelligence; but also that, in the future, machines will take over many onerous and dangerous jobs now performed by humans. Sagan believes that we must accept intelligent machines and learn to cooperate with them if we are to produce a better, more productive society in the future. In considering whether machines are intelligent, John H. Troll argues that machines can never be developed that can perform all of the mental processes of human beings. He contends that the kind of thinking that humans do in seeing relations between events and making generalizations is not something that can be programmed into a computer. If this kind of thinking cannot be done by computers, then, Troll contends, they will never be able to engage in creative thought or decide which of the various concepts they manipulate are meaningful.

A major issue that arises from a discussion of the mind-body problem is that of immortality. Continued existence after physical death would require that man have a nonphysical part that can survive without the body. The acceptance of dualism is not, however, by itself sufficient to show that there actually is immortality. It is certainly possible that the mind ceases to function when the body does. So, to have rational grounds for the belief in immortality, one would not only have to show that one has a mind or soul but also that there is evidence that such continued existence occurs.

In "Immortality: An Absurd Supposition," Baron d'Holbach argues that even if the doubtful claim that men have souls were admitted, there would be no reason to believe that the soul is immortal. One objection to the belief in an immortal soul is that men need senses and a brain to have thoughts and feelings; but death, which destroys our body, would eliminate the necessary physical basis of mental life. Further, Holbach believes that men should not attempt to conceal their mortality from themselves by preposterous stories of souls in another realm. C. J. Ducasse maintains that the arguments used to show that life after death is impossible are faulty. Against the claim that all the evidence we have shows that the mind ceases to function at the time of death, Ducasse cites possible evidence to the contrary from investigations in psychical phenomena. He is careful to point out, however, that even if such evidence is authentic, it still may not indicate continued existence. Ducasse maintains that the desire to show immortality to be impossible stems from the assumption that materialism is true. Rejection of that assumption as least opens the way for belief in immortality.

Materialism

34. How to Bury the Mind-Body Problem   Richard Taylor

Richard Taylor (1919–   ), professor of philosophy at the University of Rochester, has written highly acclaimed books and articles on a variety of philosophical problems.

The mind-body problem, in all its variants, is a philosophical fabrication resting on no genuine data at all. It has arisen from certain presuppositions about matter and human nature familiar to philosophy from the time of the Pythagoreans, presuppositions which have persisted just to the extent that they have been left unexamined. And they have not been questioned very much simply because they are so familiar.

There are vexing, unsolved problems of psychology and problems of mental health, but there are no mind-body problems. And there are problems of "philosophical psychology," as they are sometimes called today— problems of perception, sensation, the analysis of deliberation, of purposeful behavior, and so on—but there are no mind-body problems.

The reason why there are no mind-body problems is the most straightforward imaginable: It is because there are no such things as *minds* in the first place. There being no minds, there are in strictness no mental states or events; there are only certain familiar states, capacities, and abilities which are conventionally but misleadingly called "mental." They are so-called, partly in deference to certain philosophical presuppositions, and partly as a reflection of our lack of understanding of them, that is of our ignorance.

From the American Philosophical Quarterly, Vol. 6, No. 2 (April, 1969). Reprinted with permission of the author and *The American Philosophical Quarterly*.

Men and women are not minds, nor do they "have" minds. It is not merely that they do not "have" minds the way they have arms and legs; they do not have minds in any proper sense at all. And just as no man or woman has or ever has had any mind, so also are cats, dogs, frogs, vegetables, and the rest of living creation without minds—though philosophers of the highest rank, such as Aristotle, have felt driven to say that all living things, vegetables included, must have souls (else how could they be *living* things?) just as others of similar eminence, like Descartes, have thought that men must have minds, else how could they be *thinking* things? Today, when philosophers talk about mind-body problems, and advance various claims concerning the possible relationships between "mental" and "physical" states and events, they are, of course, talking about men. But they might as well be talking about frogs, because the presuppositions that give rise to these theories apply to other animals as well as to men.

I. Philosophical Arguments for the Existence or Nonexistence of Things

There cannot be any philosophical argument proving that something does or does not exist, so long as the description or definition of it is self-consistent. Thus there cannot be a philosophical argument proving that men do or do not, as some medieval thinkers believed, have an indestructible bone in their bodies. One can only say that such a bone has never been found (which is not a philosophical argument) and then exhibit the groundlessness or falsity of the presuppositions that gave rise to the belief in the first place. (In this case it was certain presuppositions concerning the requirements of the resurrection of the body.) Similarly, there can be no philosophical argument proving that men do or do not have souls, spirits, or minds, or that there are not *sui generis* mental states or events, assuming that these can be described in a self-consistent way. One can only note that such things have never been found in any man, living or dead, and then exhibit the arbitrariness and apparent falsity of the presuppositions that give rise to these opinions in the first place. Now of course, as far as *finding* them goes, many philosophers claim to find them all the time, *within themselves*. They are alleged to be *private* things, deeply hidden, discernible only by their possessors. All they really "find," however, are the most commonplace facts about themselves that are perfectly well known to anyone who knows anything at all—but of this, more later.

II. The Grand Presupposition of the Mind-Body Problem

What I must do now, then, is consider the presupposition that has given birth to the so-called "mind-body" problem, and show that there is nothing in it at all that anyone needs to believe; that, on the contrary, we have good evidence that it is false.

The presupposition can be tersely expressed by saying: *Matter cannot think.* That is the way a Cartesian would put it, but philosophers now spell it out a little better. Thus, we are apt to be told that thinking, choosing, deliberating, reasoning, perceiving, and even feeling, are not concepts of physics and chemistry, so that these terms have no application to bodies. Since, however, men do think, choose, deliberate, reason, perceive and feel, it follows that men are not "mere bodies." They are instead minds or souls or, as it is more common to say today "selves" or "persons," and such terms as "is thinking," "is choosing," "is perceiving," etc., are not physical or bodily but *personal* predications. A man may be in one clear sense a physical object, having arms and legs and so on, but a person is not just that visible and palpable object; there is more to a self or person than this. For it is the self or person that thinks, chooses, deliberates, feels, and so on, and not his body or some part of it.

Again—and this is really only another way of expressing the same presupposition—we are apt to be told that thoughts, choices, reasons, feelings, etc., are not physical things. It makes no sense to ask how large a thought is, whether it is soluble in alcohol, and so on. Yet these things do exist—any man can be aware of them, "within himself." Hence, that "self" within which such things occur must be something more than or other than the body. It might be just the totality of all those nonphysical ("mental") things, but in any case it is mental in nature, so a self or person is not the same thing as his body.

Or again, in case one boggles at calling thoughts, feelings, and the like, "things," at least (it is said) no one can deny that they are events or states. But they are not events or states that occur or obtain in the laboratories of physicists and chemists—except in the sense that they sometimes occur in physicists and chemists themselves, who sometimes happen to be in laboratories. No one could ever truly represent whatever might be happening in a test tube or vacuum tube as the transpiring of a thought or feeling. These things just do not—indeed, obviously could not—happen in test tubes or vacuum tubes, because they are not the *kind* of event involving changes of matter. They are a kind of "mental" event. And since these things do, obviously, happen in men, then things happen in men which are nonphysical, "mental," in nature. And so on.

III. "Selves" or "Persons" as Minds and Bodies

The word "self" and the plural "selves" are fairly common items of contemporary philosophical vocabulary. These words never occur outside of philosophy, except as suffixes to personal pronouns, but in philosophical contexts they are sometimes taken to denote rather extraordinary things. Selves are, indeed, about the strangest inhabitants of nature that one can imagine—except that, as sometimes described in philosophy, they are not even imaginable in the first place, being quite nonphysical. You cannot poke a self with a stick; the nearest you can come to that is to poke his body. The self that has that body is not supposed to be quite the same thing as his body—that is a (mere) physical object, a possible subject matter for physics and chemistry. *That* is not what thinks, reasons, deliberates, and so on; it is the self that does things like this.

At the same time, selves are never doubted to be the same things as *persons,* and persons are thought to be the same things as people, as men.

And there is no doubt at all that men are visible, palpable objects, having arms and legs and so on: That they are in short, physical objects. So the thing becomes highly ambiguous. We do not, in contexts in which it would seem silly or embarrassing to do so, have to say that selves (men) are spirit beings (minds) which in some sense or other happen to "have" bodies. Clearly men are visible and palpable things, that is, are bodies. We can say that all right. But at the same time we need not say—indeed, *must* not say—that men are just (mere) bodies. There is, after all, a difference between a man's body, and that which thinks, perceives, feels, deliberates, and so on; and those are things that men (selves) do, not things that bodies do. Or again, there is, after all, a difference between bodily predicates (weighs 160 pounds, falls, is warm) and personal predicates (chooses, believes, loves his country, etc.). The former can be predicated of a man's body, just like any other body, but it would "make no sense" to predicate the latter of any (mere) body, and hence of any man's body. They are only predicated of persons. So even though selves are persons and persons are men and men are visible, palpable beings, we must not think that they are just nothing but physical beings. They are physical bodies with minds, or, as some would prefer, minds with physical bodies or, as most writers on this subject want to say, they are somehow *both*.

So the "mental" is discriminated from the (merely) "physical," and the mind-body problem emerges at once: What is the *connection* between them? What is the relationship between men's minds and their bodies? or between mental and physical events? Or between personal and physical predicates? Anyone who raises this question—for these all amount to one and the same question—can see at once that it is going to be extremely difficult to answer. And this means that it is capable of nourishing a vast amount of philosophy. It has, in fact, kept philosophers on scattered continents busy for hundreds of years, and even today claims much of the time of philosophical faculties and their proteges. It seems a conceit to undertake to put an end to all this, but that is what I propose now to do.

IV. Mentalism and Materialism

Consider the following two theses:

> (I) A person is not something that has, possesses, utilizes, or contains a mind. That is, a person is not one thing and his mind another thing. A person or self and his mind are one and the same thing.
> (II) A person is not something that has, possesses, utilizes, or occupies a body. That is, a person is not one thing and his body another thing. A person or self and his body are one and the same thing.

We can call these two theses "mentalism" and "materialism" respectively, since the first asserts that men are minds and not bodies, and the second that they are bodies and not minds.

Now the first thing to note about these two rather crudely stated theses is that both of them cannot be true, since each asserts what the other denies. They could, of course, both be false, since a person might be identical neither with his body nor with his mind (though it is hard to think of any other candidate for the title of "person"), or a person might somehow be identical with the two of them at once. These two simple theses are, nevertheless, a good starting point for discussion, and I am going to maintain that (II), the materialist thesis, is absolutely true.

Philosophers have tended to regard (I), or some more sophisticated version of it, as correct, and to dismiss (II) as unworthy of consideration. In fact, however—and it is hard to see how this could have been so generally overlooked—*any* philosophical argument in favor of (I) against (II) is just as good an argument for (II) against (I). This I shall illustrate shortly.

In the meantime, let us give what is due to the humble fact that there are considerations drawn from common sense, indeed from the common knowledge of mankind, which favor, without proving (II). It is common knowledge that there are such things as human bodies, that there are men and women in the world. There is also one such body which everyone customarily, and without the least suggestion of absurdity, refers to as himself; he sees himself in the mirror, dresses himself, scratches himself, and so on. This is known, absolutely as well as anything can be known, and if any man were to profess doubt about it—if he doubted, for example, that there are such physical objects in the world as men and women, and therefore doubted the reality of his own body—then that man would have to be considered *totally* ignorant. For there is nothing more obvious than this. A man would be ignorant indeed if he did not know that there are such things as the sun, moon, earth, rivers, and lakes. I have never met anyone so ignorant as that. But a man who did not even know that there are men and women in the world, and that he—his body—was one of them, would be totally ignorant.

Now there is no such common knowledge of the existence of minds or souls. No one has ever found such a thing anywhere. Belief in such things rests either on religious persuasion or on philosophical arguments, sometimes on nothing but the connotations of familiar words. Such beliefs are opinions, easily doubted, and nothing that anyone knows. If a man denies that such things exist, as many have, then he exhibits no ignorance; he expresses only scepticism or doubt concerning certain religious or philosophical presuppositions or arguments.

If, accordingly, we are seeking some sort of thing with which to identify persons, then this is a *prima facie* consideration in favor of identifying them with their bodies, with things we know to be real, rather than with things postulated to suit the requirements of philosophical arguments or religious faith. This does not prove that men are nothing but bodies, of course, but it is enough to show that, since we know there are such things as persons, and we know there are such things as men (living human bodies), we had better regard these as the very same things *unless* there are some facts which would prohibit our doing so. And I shall maintain that there are no such facts. There are only philosophical arguments, not one of which proves anything.

The Arguments for Mentalism. I shall now consider the arguments I know, already adumbrated, in favor of what I have called mentalism. Of course not all philosophers who take seriously the mind-body problem subscribe to this simple thesis as I have formulated it, but the more sophisticated versions can be considered as we go along, and it will be seen that the arguments for these are equally inconclusive.

The First Argument. There are certain predicates that undoubtedly apply to persons, but not to their bodies. Persons and their bodies cannot, therefore, be the same. One can sometimes truly say of a person, for example, that he is intelligent, sentimental, that he loves his country, believes in God, holds strange theories on the doctrine of universals, and so on. But it would sound very odd—indeed, not even make sense—to assert any such things of any physical object whatever and hence of any man's body. It would at best be a confusion of categories to say that a certain man's *body* loves its country, for example.

Reply. If the foregoing is considered a good argument for the nonidentity of persons and bodies, then the following is obviously just as good an argument for not identifying them with their minds: There are certain predicates that undoubtedly apply to persons, but not to their minds. A person and his mind cannot, therefore, be the same. One can sometimes truly say of a person, for example, that he is walking, ran into a post, is feverish, or that he fell down. But it would sound very odd—indeed not even make sense—to assert such things of any mind whatever. It would at best be a confusion of categories to say, for instance, that a certain man's *mind* ran into a post.

Considerations such as these have led many philosophers to affirm that a person or the "true self" is neither a mind, nor a body. Hence, a person must be (a) something else altogether or, as some would prefer to say, the term "person" must express a "primitive" concept or (b) both mind and body; i.e., a person must be something having both mental and physical properties.

The former of these alternatives is simply evasive. Persons are real beings, so there must be existing things which are persons. If when we bump into a man we are not bumping into a person, and if at the same time we are not referring to a person when we say of someone that he is thinking, then it is quite impossible to see what is left to fill the role of a person. The word "person" may indeed be a primitive one, but this, I think, only means that such arguments as the two just cited are equally good and equally bad.

The second alternative that persons are beings having both mental and physical properties, is obviously only as good as the claim that there are such things as "mental properties" to begin with. Indeed, it is not even that good, for just as a physical property can be nothing but a property of a physical thing, i.e., a body, so also a mental property can be nothing but the property of a mental thing, i.e., a mind. For something to count as a physical property of something it is sufficient, and necessary, that the thing in question is a physical object. By the same token, for something to count as a mental property it is sufficient, and necessary, that it be the property that some mind possesses. Any property whatsoever that can be truly claimed to be the property of some body, animate or inanimate, is a physical property; the assertion that some body possesses a nonphysical property is simply a contradiction. This second alternative, that persons are beings possessing both physical and mental properties, therefore amount to saying that a person is at one and the same time *two* utterly different things—a body with its physical properties and a mind with its mental properties. These are not supposed to be two things in the same sense that a family, for instance, is a plurality of beings consisting of husband, wife, and perhaps one or more children, but two wholly disparate kinds of beings having, as Descartes put it, nothing in common. Now this is no resolution of the antithesis between what I have called mentalism and materialism. It is only a reformulation of that issue. For now we can surely ask: Which of these two is the person, the true self? The body which has a mind, or the mind which has a body? And we are then back where we started.

The Second Argument. This argument consists of pointing out the rather remarkable things that a person can do but which, it is alleged, no physical object, of whatever complexity, can do, from which it of course follows that a person is not a physical object and hence not identical with his own body. A person, for example, can reason, deliberate about ends and means, plan for the future, draw inferences from evidence, speculate, and so on. No physical objects do such things, and even complicated machines can at best only simulate these activities. Indeed, it would not even make sense to say that a man's body was, for example, speculating on the outcome of an election, though this would not be an absurd description of some person. A person, therefore, is not the same thing as his body, and can only be described in terms of certain concepts of mind.

Reply. This argument is not very different from the first; it only substitutes activities for properties which are baptized "mental." And one reply to it is the same as to the first argument; namely, that since persons often do things that no mind could do—for instance, they run races, go fishing, raise families, and so on—then it follows that persons are not minds.

A far better reply, however, and one that is not so question-begging as it looks, is to note that since men do reason, deliberate, plan, speculate, draw inferences, run races, go fishing, raise families, and so on, and since the men that do all such things are the visible, palpable beings that we see around us all the time, then it follows that *some* physical objects—namely, men—do all these things. All are, accordingly, the activities of physical objects; they are not activities divided between a physical object, the visible man, on the one hand, and some invisible thing, his mind, on the other.

Consider the statement: "I saw George yesterday; he was trying to figure out the best way to get from Albany to Montpelier." Now this statement obviously refers, in a normal context, to a person, and it is perfectly clear that the name "George" and the pronoun "he" refer to *one and the same* being, that person. And what they both refer to is something that was seen, a certain man's body; they do not refer to some unseen thing, of which that body is some sort of visible manifestation. If that were so, then the statement would not really be true. And in any case, it would be embarrassingly silly to suppose that a more accurate rendition of the thought expressed in this statement might be: "I saw George's body yesterday. His mind was trying to figure out how to get (how to get what?) from Albany to Montpelier." It is, accordingly, one and the same thing which (a) is seen, and (b) figures and plans, and that thing is undoubtedly the physical object George. Now if conventions incline us to describe figuring out something as a "mental" activity, then we shall have to say that some purely physical objects—namely, living men—engage in mental activities. But this is simply misleading, if not contradictory, for it suggests that we are ascribing to a physical object an activity of something that is not physical, but mental. It would, therefore, be far better to say that some physical objects, namely, men or persons, sometimes perform physical activities such as figuring and planning which are quite unlike those we are accustomed to finding in certain other physical objects such as machines and the like.

The Third Argument. This argument, the commonest of all, is to the effect that while there may or may not be such things as "minds" (whatever that might mean), there are indisputably certain nonphysical things which are quite properly called "mental," as anyone can verify within himself. Indeed, it is sometimes claimed that nothing, not even the reality of our own bodies, is as certain as the existence of these mental things, which are perceived "directly."

Reply. What are here referred to as mental entities are, of course, such things as thoughts, mental images, after-images, sensations, feelings, and so on. Pains are frequently mentioned in this context, being, presumably, things whose existence no one would question. Having got to this point then the next step, of course, is to speculate on the connection between these mental things and certain "physical" states of the body. They evidently are not the same, and yet it is hard to see what the connection could be. Speculation also extends to such questions as whether two or more men might have "the same" pain, or why it is impossible that they should in view of the fact that they can hold common possession of ordinary "physical" things like clocks and books. Again, curiosity is aroused by the fact that a mental image, for instance, seems to have color, and yet it somehow can be perceived only by one person, its owner. Again, images sometimes seem to have shape—enough so that a perceiver can distinguish one from another, for instance—and yet no assignable size. Here, really, is a gold mine for philosophical speculation, and such speculations have filled, as they still fill, volumes.

Now surely there is a *better* way to express all that is known to be true in all this, and it is a way that does not even permit these odd theories to get started. What we know is true, and all we know is true, is that men think, sense, imagine, feel, etc. It is sheer redundancy to say that men think things called "thoughts," sense things called "sensations," imagine "images," and feel "feelings." There are no such things. And to say there are no such things is *not* to deny that men think, sense, imagine, and feel.

What, for instance, does it mean to say a man feels a pain in his foot? Absolutely nothing, except that his foot hurts. But this hurting, what sort of thing is it? It is not a thing at all; not a thing felt, and certainly not a mental thing that is felt *in his foot*. It is a state, and in no sense a state of his mind, but a straightforward state of his foot. But can that be a *physical* state? Well, it is assuredly a state of his foot, and that is a physical object; there is nothing else—no spirit foot, no spirit being, no spirit mind—that it can be a state of. Why, then, cannot other people have that same state? Why cannot other people feel the same pain I feel in my foot? And if it is a physical state, why cannot we open the foot and *see* it there? Or make some straightforward test of its presence in another man's foot?

To ask questions like these is just not to understand what is meant by describing an object as being in a certain state. Consider a piece of molten lead. Now this molten state, what sort of thing is it? The answer is that it is not a thing at all; it is a state or condition of a thing. Is it a physical state? Well, it is a state of the lead, and that is a physical object; there is nothing else for it to be a state of. Why, then, cannot another piece of lead have that same state? Why cannot something else have the molten state of this piece of lead? Of course something else can, in the only meaningful sense that can be attached to such a question; that is, another piece of lead, or some things which are not lead can melt the same way this piece of lead melted. To ask why another piece of lead cannot have the molten state of this piece of lead is, of course, unintelligible, unless it is interpreted the way just suggested, in which case the answer is that it can. But similarly, to ask why another man cannot have the pain that this man is feeling is also unintelligible, unless construed as the question why other men cannot suffer pain, in which case its presupposition is wrong—they can. And if the piece of lead's being melted is a "physical" state, why can we not separate the lead into drops and see that state? Simply because it is a state of the lead, and not some other thing contained in the lead. Indeed, to separate it into drops *is* to see, not its meltedness (there is no such thing), but that it is melted—that is just the test. We do not have to *ask* the lead whether it is melted, and rely upon its testimony; we can tell by its behavior. And in the same way we can sometimes—admittedly not always—see that a man is suffering, without having to ask him. That we sometimes go wrong here does not result from the fact that his suffering is something quite hidden within him, which he alone can find and then report; there is nothing hidden, and nothing for him to find. Still, there is a straightforward way of testing whether a piece of lead is melted, and there is no similarly straightforward way of testing whether a man's foot hurts—he may only be pretending it does. Does this indicate that there might be a pain, which he has found in his foot but might conceal, as he might conceal the contents of his wallet? Surely not; it shows only that men, unlike pieces of lead, are capable of dissimulating. No philosophy was needed to unearth that commonplace fact. It is easier to test for the presence of some states of properties than others, and this is true not only of the states of men's bodies, but of everything under the sun. But things that are hard to establish do not, just by virtue of that, warrant the title of "mental."

Similar remarks can be made about images, which are frequent candidates for the role of mental entities. When queried about their mental imagery, people often will describe it in colorful detail and even with pride, not unlike the regard one might have for a precious gem accessible only to himself. It turns out, though, that all one thereby describes is his power of imagination, which is, of course, sometimes quite great. To say that one has a lively imagination, even great powers of imagination, does not mean that he can create with his mind, *ex nihilo,* things called "images" and composed of some mental, nonphysical, spiritual material. There is no material that is nonmaterial, and there are no images composed of this or anything else—except, of course, those physical objects (pictures, etc.) visible to anyone who can see, which are rightly called images of things. When someone *sees* something, there is (i) the man who sees, and (ii) the thing seen; for instance, some building or scene. There is not, between these, a third thing called the appearance of what is seen; philosophers are pretty much agreed on this. But similarly, when someone *imagines* something or, as it is misleadingly put, "forms an image" of it, there is (i) the man who imagines, and (ii) sometimes, but not always, something that he imagines; for instance, some building or scene, which might or might not be real. There is not, between these, a third thing called the image of what is imagined. There is just the imagining of the thing in question. And to say that a man is imagining something is to say what he is doing, or perhaps to refer to some state he is in; it is not to refer to some inner thing that he creates and, while it lasts, exclusively possesses.

It is enough, it seems to me, to point this out; that is, to point out that we can say all we want to say about men's powers of imagination without ever introducing the substantive "an image." Philosophy is robbed of nothing by the disposal of these, and there is absolutely no fact about human nature which requires us to affirm their existence. But if one does insist upon the reality of mental images, and professes, for instance, to find them right in his own mind by introspecting—and it is astonishing how eager students of philosophy seem to be to make this claim—then we can ask some very embarrassing questions. Suppose, for instance, one professes to be able to form a very clear image of, say, the campus library—he can bring it before his mind, hold it there, perhaps even turn it bottom side up, and banish it at will. We ask him, then to hold it before his mind and count the number of steps in the image, the number of windows, the number and disposition of pigeons on the roof, and so on. He could do these things if he had a photograph of the thing before him. But he cannot do them with the image, in spite of the fact that it is supposed to be right there "before his mind," easily and "directly" inspectable. He can tell how many steps there are only if he has sometime counted the steps on the building itself (or in a photograph of it) and now *remembers*— but that is not counting the steps in the image. Or he can *imagine* that it has, say, 30 steps, and then *say* "30"—but that is not counting anything either; it is only a performance. The image he professes to "have" there, so clearly and with such detail, does not even exist. He claims to have produced in his mind an image of the library; but all he has actually done is imagine the library.

What, then, is imagining something? Is it an activity, a state, or what? It does not really matter here how we answer that; it is only *not* the producing of an entity called a "mental image." Let us suppose for this context, then, that to be imagining something is to be in a certain *state*. Is it, then, a *physical* state? Well, it is a state of a man, just as drunkenness, sleep, perspiration, obesity, etc., are sometimes states of this man or that. What is meant by asking whether these are "physical" states, other than asking whether they are states of a physical object? What shall we say of being in a state of sleep, for instance? It is the state of a man, and a man is a physical—that is, a visible and palpable—being. You cannot poke a man's state of imagining something with a stick; all you can do is poke him. That is true. But you cannot poke his somnolence with a stick either. There is nothing to poke; there is only the man sleeping, or the man imagining, or the man becoming drunk, or whatever.

How then can a man, if he is nothing but a (mere) physical object, be in such a state as this, that is, of imagining something? If he is only a body and can do this, why cannot sticks and stones be in such a state, for are they not bodies too? The answer is: For just the same reason that sticks and stones cannot be drunken, asleep, perspiring, obese, or hungry; namely, that they are sticks and stones and not men. The reason is not that they lack minds. Even if they had them, they still could not be drunken, asleep, perspiring, obese or hungry, for they would still be sticks and stones and not men.

The Fourth (and Last) Argument. It is fairly common for people, including philosophers, to say that they can perfectly well imagine surviving the death of their bodies, which would be quite impossible for anyone who supposed that he and his body were one and the same thing. Admittedly no one knows whether there is any survival of death, but it is at least not necessarily false. The doctrine of metempsychosis, for example, though there may be no reason for believing it, cannot be shown to be impossible just on philosophical grounds. It would be impossible, however, if a person and his body were identical, and so would any other form of survival. We know the fate of the body: dust. If I am the same as my body, then it is logically impossible that I should not share that fate.

Reply. All this argument shows is that not everyone, perhaps even no one, *knows* that he and his body are one and the same thing. It does not in the least show that, in fact, they are not. Some things, like the Evening Star and the Morning Star, which some are accustomed to thinking of and describing as different things, nevertheless do turn out to be the same.

Suppose a god were to promise me a life after death—promising, perhaps, to have me (the very person that I am) reborn elsewhere with a different body. Now such a promise might quicken a real hope in me, provided I am capable (as everyone is) of thinking of myself as being something different from my body. But the fact that I can think such a distinction does not show that there is one, and in case there is not—in case I happen to be identical with my body—then of course no god could fulfill such a promise. Consider this analogy: If an enemy of our country did not know that Albany is (the same thing as) the capital of New York, then he might be very interested in a proposal to bomb the one but to spare the other. It would nevertheless be a proposal that no one could carry out. The fact that someone who is ignorant of this identity can entertain the possibility of its being carried out does not show that it is possible; it shows only that he does not know that it is not.

V. The Soul as Life and the Soul as Thought

It is useful in concluding, I think, to compare the philosophical conception of the mind with what was once the philosophical conception of life. It was once pretty much taken for granted that men and other animals *possess* something which inanimate things lack, namely, life, and that it is *because* they possess this that they can do all sorts of things that inanimate things cannot do, such as move themselves, assimilate nourishment, reproduce their kind, and so on. Aristotle classified the souls of living things according to the abilities they imparted to their owners, and thought that even vegetables had souls. Indeed, an animal's *life* and *soul* were generally thought to be one and the same thing. The very word "animal" has its origin in this belief. Socrates, according to Plato, was even able to convince himself of his own immortality on the basis of this notion for, he thought, if it is only because he has a life or soul to begin with that he is a living man, then it is idle to fear the death of that very soul. Life seemed to him identical with his soul, but accidental to his body, indeed even foreign to such a thing of clay. A similar model was at work in Descartes' philosophy when he declared that the soul could never stop thinking. Thought seemed to him identical with his soul, but positively foreign to his body.

Now of course we still talk of life that way, but we no longer take such common modes of speech as descriptive of any reality. We speak of a man "losing" his life, of a man "taking" another's life, of the "gift" of life, and even of the "breath" of life which God is supposed to infuse into an otherwise *lifeless* body. But these are plainly metaphors. No one supposes that a man or animal moves, assimilates nourishment, reproduces, and so on *because* it is possessed of life. We no longer think of life as something added to an animal body, some separable thing that quickens matter. To distinguish something as a living animal is only to call attention to the very complicated way the matter of its body is organized and to a large class of capacities which result from such organization. A living body is simply one in which certain processes, some of them frightfully complex and ill understood, take place. A living body, in short, differs from a nonliving one, not in what it possesses, but in what it does, and these are facts about it that can be verified in a straightforward way.

I have been urging a similar way of speaking of the mind; not as something mysteriously *embodied* here and there, and something that is supposed to *account* for the more or less intelligent behavior of certain beings. A being capable of more or less intelligent thought and action differs from one lacking such capacities, not in something it possesses, but precisely in what it does. And this, incidentally, explains why a man tends to regard it as a deep insult to be told that he has no mind. It is not because he is thus divested in our eyes of some possession dearly prized, but rather, because such a remark is quite rightly taken to mean that he lacks certain important and distinctively human abilities and capacities. If a man is assured that his possession of certain more or less intellectual abilities is in no way in question, he feels divested of nothing upon learning that among his parts or possessions there is none that is properly denoted "a mind."

VI. Does Matter Think?

Probably every philosopher has felt more or less acutely at one time or another a profound puzzlement in the idea of (mere) matter doing those various things rightly ascribable only to persons. How, it is wondered, can a body think, deliberate, imagine things, figure and plan, and so on?

This is really no proper source of bafflement, however. No one can say, *a priori,* what the highly organized material systems of one's body are or are not capable of. It was once thought incredible that matter, unquickened by any soul, could be alive, for matter seemed to inquirers to be inert or lifeless by its very nature. Yet we see around us all the time specimens of living matter—in the merest insects, for instance—so philosophical prejudice has had to yield to the fact. Similarly, I submit, we see around us all the time specimens of thinking matter; that is, material beings which deliberate, imagine, plan, and so on. For men do in fact do these things, and when we see a man, we are seeing a material being—a dreadfully complex and highly organized one, to be sure, but no less a visible and palpable object for that. In any case, the seeming mystery or incredibility that may attach to the idea of matter exercising intellectual capacities is hardly dissolved by postulating something *else* to exercise those capacities. If there is a difficulty in comprehending how a body can do such things, there is surely no less difficulty in seeing how something which is not a body can do them any better.

Interactionism

35. The Mind as Distinct from the Body   C. E. M. Joad

Cyril Edwin Mitchinson Joad (1891–1953) was a prolific English author, whose books and articles and speeches on philosophy exerted broad public appeal in his lifetime.

The issue between those who endeavour to interpret mind action in terms of body action, and those who contend for the unique, distinct, and in some sense independent status of mind, is not capable of definite settle-

From *How Our Minds Work* by C. E. M. Joad. Published by Philosophical Library. Reprinted by permission of the publishers.

ment. . . . The most that can be done is to suggest certain objections that can be and have been brought against the materialist position, . . . and at the same time to indicate a number of independent considerations which seem to demand a different kind of approach to psychology, and a different interpretation of its problems. This interpretation, to put it briefly, insists that a living organism is something over and above the matter of which its body is composed; that it is, in short, an expression of a principle of life, and that life is a force, stream, entity, spirit, call it what you will, that cannot be described or accounted for in material terms; that in human beings this principle of life expresses itself at the level of what is called mind, that this mind is distinct from both body and brain, and, so far from being a mere register of bodily occurrences, is able, acting on its own volition, to produce such occurrences, and that no account of mind action which is given in terms of brain action, gland activity or bodily responses to external stimuli can, therefore, be completely satisfactory. This is the view which in some form or other is held by those who find a materialist explanation of psychology unsatisfactory, and in this chapter we shall be concerned with the reasons for it.

Biological Considerations

Purposiveness.   Some of these reasons, and perhaps the most important, are derived in part from regions which lie outside the scope of psychology proper; they belong to biology, and are based on a consideration of the characteristics which all living beings are found to possess in common. With regard to one of these "alleged" characteristics of living organisms it is necessary to say a few words, since it constitutes a starting point for the method of interpretation with which we shall be concerned in this chapter. The characteristic in question is that to which we give the name of purposiveness, and because of this characteristic it is said that any attempt to interpret the behaviour of living creatures in terms of material response to stimuli must inevitably break down. Purposiveness implies the capacity to be influenced by and to work for a purpose; this in its turn involves the apprehension, whether conscious or unconscious, of some object which lies in the future and which the purpose seeks to achieve; it therefore necessitates the existence of a mind. If, therefore, purposiveness is a true characteristic of living creatures, then we have established a good starting point for our "mental" approach to psychology.

What, therefore, is meant by saying that living creatures are purposive? Primarily, that in addition to those of their movements which may be interpreted as responses to existing situations, they also act in a way which seems to point to the existence of a spontaneous impulse or need to bring about some other situation which does not yet exist. This impulse or need is sometimes known as a conation; a good instance of the sort of thing that is meant is the impulse we feel to maintain the species by obtaining food or seeking a mate. The impulse is chiefly manifested in the efforts a living organism will make to overcome any obstacle which impedes the fulfilment of its instinctive need. It will try first one way of dealing with it and then another, as if it were impelled by some overmastering force which drove it forward to the accomplishment of a particular purpose. Thus the salmon, proceeding up stream, leaping over rocks and breasting the current in order to deposit her spawn in a particular place, is acting in a way which it is difficult to explain in terms of a response to external stimuli. An organism again will seek to preserve the trend of natural growth and development by which alone the purpose of existence will be fulfilled; in its endeavour to reach and to maintain what we may call its natural state or condition, it is capable, if need arises, of changing or modifying its bodily structure. If you take the hydroid plant Antennularia and remove it from the flat surface to which it is accustomed to adhere, it will begin to proliferate long wavy roots or fibers in the effort to find something solid to grip, while everybody has heard of the crab's habit of growing a new leg in place of one that has been knocked off.

Activity of this kind seems difficult to explain on materialist lines as the response to a stimulus; it appears rather to be due to the presence of a living, creative impulse to develop in the face of any obstacle in a certain way. That a living organism works as a machine works, by reacting in the appropriate way to the appropriate stimulus, is admitted; all that is contended is that it acts in other ways as well, that these other activities depend not only upon the quality of stimulus received, but upon the intensity of the creature's conative impulse, and that the existence of the impulse is only explicable on the assumption that the creature is animated by the need to fulfil a purpose.

Foresight and Expectation. When we apply this conclusion to human psychology, we are immediately struck by the fact that the individual not only exhibits in common with other organisms this characteristic of purposive behaviour, but is in many cases conscious of the nature of the purpose which inspires his behaviour. The man who studies in order to pass an examination is not only impelled by a push from behind; he is drawn forward by a pull from in front. This pull from in front can only become operative if he can be credited with the capacity to conceive the desirability of a certain state of affairs—namely, the passing of the examination, which does not yet exist; he shows, in other words, foresight and expectation. It is activites of this kind which seem most insistently to involve the assumption of a mind to do the foreseeing and expecting. In other words, the capacity to be influenced by events which lie in the future seems inexplicable on the stimulus-response basis; the *thought* of what does not exist may be allowed to influence the mind, but it is difficult to see how the non-existent can stimulate the body. . . .

The Apprehension of Meaning

An important fact about our mental life is that we are capable of appreciating meaning. A statement of fact written on a piece of paper is, so far as its material content is concerned, merely a number of black marks inscribed on a white backgound. Considered, then, as a collection of visual, physical stimuli, it is comparatively unimportant; what is important is the meaning which is attached to these marks. If they inform us, for example, that we have received a legacy of ten thousand pounds it is not the black marks on the white background but the meaning they convey that effects a disturbance in our emotional life, sufficiently profound to keep us awake all night. Now the meaning of the marks is obviously not a physical stimulus; it is something immaterial. How, then, is its effect to be explained in terms of bodily responses to physical stimuli, which the mind merely registers? Let us take one or two further examples in order to present the difficulty in a concrete form.

Let us suppose that I am a geometrician and am thinking about the properties of a triangle. As I do not wish at this point to enter into the vexed question of whether *some* physical stimulus is or is not necessary to initiate every chain of reasoning, we will assume that in this case there was a physical stimulus—it may have been a chance remark about Euclid, or the appearance of a red triangular road signpost while I am driving a car—a stimulus which we will call X, which prompted me to embark upon the train of speculations about the triangle. My reasoning proceeds until I arrive at a conclusion, which takes the form of a geometrical proposition expressed in a formula. I carry this formula in my head for a number of days and presently write it down. In due course I write a book, setting forth my formula and giving an account of the reasoning which led me to it. The book is read and understood by A. Presently it is translated into French, and is read and understood by B. Later still I deliver a lecture on the subject which is heard and understood by C. As A, B, and C have each of them understood my formula and the reasoning upon which it is based, we may say that the reasoning process has had for them the same meaning throughout. If it had not, they would not all have reached the same conclusion and understood the same thing by it. Yet in each of the four cases the sensory stimulus was different; for myself it was X, for A it was a number of black marks on a white background, for B a number of different black marks on a white background, and for C a number of vibrations in the atmosphere impinging upon his eardrums. It seems incredible that all these different stimuli should have been able to produce a consciousness of the same meaning, if our respective reactions to them were confined to physical responses (which must in each case have been different) which were subsequently reflected in our minds by a process of mental registration of the different responses. The stimuli being different, the intervention of something possessed of the capacity to grasp the *common* element among these physically different entities alone seems able to account for the facts, but the common element is the meaning, which is immaterial and can be grasped, therefore, only by a mind.

Let us take another example instanced by Professor McDougall:

A man receives a telegram which says "Your son is dead." The visual physical stimulus here is, as before, a collection of black marks on an orange field. The reaction experienced in terms of his bodily behaviour may take the form of a complete cessation of all those symptoms usually associated with life—that is to say, he may faint. When he recovers consciousness his thoughts and actions throughout the whole of the remainder of his life may be completely changed. Now that all these complicated reactions are not constituted by and do not even spring from a response to the *physical* stimulus, may be seen by comparing the reactions of an acquaintance who reads the telegram, and so subjects himself to the same stimulus. Moreover, the omission of a single letter, converting the telegram into "Our son is dead," would cause none of the reactions just described, but might result at most in the writing of a polite letter of condolence.

The independence of the bodily reactions of the physical stimuli actually presented is in these cases very marked, and, unless we are to introduce conceptions such as the intellectual apprehension of the *meaning* of the marks, it seems impossible to explain their effect. Yet such a conception again involves the active intervention of mind.

Synthesizing Power of Mind. This conclusion is reinforced by what we may call the synthesizing power of mind. Synthesizing means putting together, and one of the most remarkable powers that we possess is that of taking a number of isolated sensations and forming them into a whole. We shall have occasion to return to this point at greater length in connection with our account of sensation in the next chapter. For the present we will content ourselves with giving one or two examples of mental synthesis.

Let us consider for a moment the case of aesthetic appreciation. The notes of a symphony considered separately consist merely of vibrations in the atmosphere. Each note may, when sounded in isolation produce a pleasant sensation, and as one note is struck after another we get a sequence of pleasant sensations. But although this is a sufficient description of the symphony considered as a collection of material events, and of our reactions to these events considered merely in terms of sensations, it is quite clear that we normally think of a symphony as being something more than this. We think of it in fact as a whole, and it is as a whole that it gives what is called aesthetic pleasure. Now in thinking of the symphony in this way our mind is going beyond the mere sequence of pleasant sensations which its individual notes produce, and putting them together into some sort of pattern. If the notes were arranged in a different order, although the actual vibrations which impinged upon our senses would be the same, the pleasurable aesthetic effect would be destroyed.

It seems to follow that our pleasure in a symphony cannot be wholly accounted for, although it may depend upon our physical responses to the stimuli of the individual notes; in order to obtain aesthetic pleasure we must somehow be able to perceive it as more than the sum total of the individual notes—that is, as a whole pattern or arrangement. The pleasure ceases when the *wholeness* of the object perceived is destroyed, as it is, for example, by the transposition of certain notes. We may compare the difference between the physical sensations which are our responses to the visual stimuli of the colours and canvas of which a picture is composed, with our synthesized perception of a picture as a work of art.

We must conclude, then, that we possess the power of realizing external objects not merely as collections of physical stimuli, which of course they are, but as wholes in which the actual sensory elements are combined to form a single object of a higher order. This faculty of combining or putting together seems to involve the existence not only of a mind, but of a mind of an active, creative type which is able to go out beyond the raw material afforded by our bodily sensations, and to apprehend ideal objects as wholes which are more than the collection of physical events which compose their constituent parts.

Summary of Argument

The conclusion to which the arguments of this chapter appear to point is that, in addition to the body and brain, the composition of the living organism includes an immaterial element which we call mind; that this element, although it is in very close association with the brain, is more than a mere glow or halo surrounding the cerebral structure, the function of which is confined to reflecting the events occurring in that structure; that, on the contrary, it is in some sense independent of the brain, and in virtue of its independence is able in part to direct and control the material constituents of the body, using them to carry out its purposes in relation to the external world of objects, much as a driver will make use of the mechanism of his motorcar. Mind so conceived is an active, dynamic, synthesizing force; it goes out beyond the sensations provided by external stimuli and arranges them into patterns, and it seems to be capable on occasion of acting without the provocation of bodily stimuli to set it in motion. It is, in other words, creative, that is, it carries on activities which even the greatest conceivable extension of our physiological knowledge would not enable us to infer from observing the brain. How, then, are we to conceive of the relationship of the mind to the brain?

An actor in a play of Shakespeare not only speaks words, but makes gestures, so that if you were completely deaf you would still be able to infer something of what the play was about from seeing the gestures. It is obvious, however, that there is much more in the play than the pantomime of the players. There are, for example, the words, the characters, the plot, and the poetry. Now to use a simile of the philosopher Bergson, the brain is the organ of pantomime. If you were to observe a man's brain you would know just as much of his thoughts as found vent in gestures. You would know, in other words, all that his thoughts imply in the way of actions or the beginnings of actions,[1] but the thoughts themselves would escape you just as the words and meaning of the play would escape the deaf spectator. This is what is meant by saying that the mind overflows the brain. If our knowledge of both psychology and physiology were perfect, we should be able to describe the movements of the brain without observing it, provided we had complete understanding of a man's state of mind; but we should not from the most minute and thorough inspection of the brain be able to tell what the man was thinking, since just as one gesture of the actor may stand for many different thoughts, so one state of the brain may represent any one of a host of states of mind.

---

[1] Among the beginnings of actions may be mentioned those movements of the larynx which are involved in talking.

Idealism

36. Sense Without Matter   A. A. Luce

Arthur Aston Luce (1882–   ), professor of Metaphysics at Trinity College, Dublin, is the author of many books and articles on immaterialism and the philosophy of George Berkeley.

According to the ancient theory of sense-perception, founded on Aristotle's teaching, there are two factors to be distinguished in every case of sense-perception: (1) the sensible qualities or appearances, i.e. the sense-data actually perceived by sense; and (2) the material substance, itself unperceived and unperceivable, that supports the qualities or appearances. In this account of things matter is essential to sense-perception, but is just what we do not perceive; that is why I call it a *residuum.* In so far as there is a theory of matter, this is it. Matter, when taken precisely and positively and apart from its appearances, is to be regarded as spread like a carpet, an unqualitied carpet, under all the outward and obvious aspects of the things of sense. More technically, matter is the substrate, *per se* unperceived and unperceivable, that "supports" sensible qualities, like red and rough and loud, qualities *per se* unsubstantial; matter substantiates them, and let them "materialise." Both factors are, they say, necessary to real existence and sense-perception. Sensible qualities are, they say, flimsy, transient and variable; matter gives them solidity and permanence and invariability. Matter, they say, is all in the dark night, and but for the sensible qualities that reveal it we should know nothing at all about it. Our external world, luminous and solid, is thus the product of these two factors, sensible quality and matter. Every external thing, or body, is the product of the same two factors. The shoe, the ship, the piece of sealing-wax, each is twofold, like a nut. Each has shell and kernel. The shell is the red, the brown, the hard, the soft, the sound, the smell, the taste and whatever else in it is actually sensed or to be sensed; the rest of it is kernel, substance, substrate, matter, which, as matter, is utterly unperceivable.

There it is in its naked simplicity, in its shameless obscurity—this old Greek guess, the theory of matter or material substance. Hammered for centuries into the heads of uncomprehending youth, conned and repeated by rote by learned and unlearned alike, it has entered into the public mind, as did the flatness of the earth; and both superstitions die hard. The theory is venerated, not understood; it is indeed unintelligible,

Reprinted with permission of Thomas Nelson & Sons Limited from *Sense Without Matter* (1954) by A. A. Luce. The book has been reprinted in the United States by Greenwood Press.

and it is venerated all the more on that account. It is venerated for its comparative antiquity; it is valued more as a blanket than as a carpet; it solves no problems; it gives no support, but it removes certain difficulties out of sight. It holds up an ideal of permanence in the flux of things in a changing world; it contains the welcome suggestion of a hidden hand and of an absolute standard behind the scenes, and it offers these things without making any demand on man's moral and spiritual nature. But is it true? No, it is not true. Does it shed light? No, it sheds no light. It is redolent of the *a priori* and the abstract. I doubt if it ever aimed at truth, as the realist understands that term. I doubt if it was ever intended to provide a true-to-fact account of what actually happens when a man sees and touches. It tries to ease certain difficulties in the theories of perception and of change; but it obscures other problems, and removes them out of sight; it makes darkness visible; it sheds no light. . . .

I am indeed asking, "Does matter exist?" And I answer, "No"; but I am also asking a deeper, constructive question, viz.: "What precisely do I see and touch?" If we know precisely what we see and touch and otherwise sense, the question about matter settles itself automatically. We are studying sense-perception in order to find out precisely what man perceives by sense. Matter has always been the intellectual refuge of scepticism and half-knowledge. The materialist distrusts his senses, depreciates their position and rejects their evidence. He holds that sense without matter does not make sense. That contention goes far and cuts deep, and warps a man's attitude, not only to things of spirit, but to reality all along the line. The materialist holds that without matter the sensible could not exist as a *thing*, could not cause, and would be indistinguishable from dream. . . .

I open my eyes and see. What precisely do I see? I stretch out my hand and touch. What precisely do I touch? What precisely do we see and touch, when we see and touch? That is our question. We have many names in ordinary life for the myriad things we see and touch—shoes, ships, sealing-wax, apples, pears and plums; those names are precise enough for action, but they are not precise enough for thought; thought is concerned with common features and resemblances, more than with differences and distinctions. Now, when I see ships and shoes and apples and so forth, what precisely do I see that is common to all those sights? I see colours and shades of colour, light and its modes, illuminated points and lines and surfaces. Those are the things I actually see, and I call them inclusively visual data; they are the elemental objects of the sense of sight. And when I touch shoes and ships and apples and so forth, what precisely do I touch that is common to all those touches? I touch hard, soft, solid, fluid, resistant, yielding, and (in the wider sense of "touch") hot, cold, warm and tepid. Those are the things I actually touch, and I call them inclusively tactual data; they are the elemental objects of the sense of touch. . . .

The theory of matter, as we have seen, requires us to hold that in every instance of sense-perception there are two factors to be recognised and distinguished, viz. the actual object of sense, the sense-data actually perceived by eye or ear or hand or other sense organ, and the material substance, itself unperceived and unperceivable, that supports the sense-data. The case against the theory is, in outline, that the theory postulates an intolerable division, based on an improbable guess. It is not a theory reasonably distinguishing homogeneous parts in a thing, like shell and kernel, pea and pod. It is a theory requiring us to break up the one homogeneous thing into two heterogeneous and inconsistent parts, and, incidentally, to pin our faith to the existence of material substance, for which there is not the slightest evidence from fact.

Let us take an instance, and see how the theory of matter works out. See yonder mahogany table. Its colour is brown, in the main, though it is veined and grained in lighter colours. Its touch is hard and smooth. It has a smell and a taste and a sound; but I hardly ever need to bother about them; for I know the table ordinarily by its colours and by the cut and shape of its lines of light and its shading, and if I am in doubt I can handle it, and feel it and lift it up. It is a sensible table. It is a sensible table through and through. I can bore holes in it, can plane away its surfaces, can burn it with fire and reduce it to ashes; and I shall never come on anything in it that is not an actual or possible object of sense; it is composed entirely of sense-data and *sensibilia*. Now the theory of matter brings in totally different considerations; it asks me to believe that all these sense-data and *sensibilia* do not constitute the real table. I am asked to believe that beneath the table I see and touch stands another table, a supporting table, a table of a totally different nature that cannot be seen or touched or sensed in any other way, a table to be taken on trust, and yet a highly important table, because it is the real, invariable, material table, while the table I see and touch is only apparent, variable, inconstant and volatile. The visible-tangible, sensible table has colour and hardness and the other qualities by which things of sense are known and distinguished. The real table has none of these.

What an impossible duality! Yonder mahogany table proves to be two tables. It is a sensible table, and it is a material table. If I take the theory seriously, and go through with it, I am bound to believe the same of everything else around me; wherever I look, I am condemned to see double, and to grope my way through life with divided aim and reduced efficiency.

No rational account of the coexistence of the two tables has ever been given, nor could be given. Some say that the "real table" is the *cause* of the apparent table, but how the cause works is a mystery. Some say that the "real table" is the original, and the apparent table a copy; but what would be the use of a copy that is totally unlike its original? And who, or what, does the copying, and how? The two tables are left there, juxtaposed, unrelated and unexplained. They are not two aspects of the one thing; they are not two parts of the one thing; they have nothing in common; they are not comparable; they could not stem from the one stock; they are heterogeneous; they are at opposite poles of thought; they differ as light from darkness; if the one is, the other is not. No mixing of the two is possible; they cannot be constituents of the one thing; for they are contradictories; if the table is really coloured, then it is not matter; if the table is really matter, then it is not coloured. The supposition of two heteroge-

neous bodies in the one thing of sense is self-contradictory, destroying the
unity of the thing. . . .

Then consider the question of evidence. What evidence is there for
the existence of matter? What evidence is there for non-sensible matter?
Why should I believe in the matter of materialism? Set aside the misunderstanding that confuses matter with the sensible; set aside the prejudice
that would identity with matter the chemical atom, or the subatomic
objects of nuclear physics; set aside the legend of the constant sum-total
of energy from which all springs and to which all returns; set aside mere
tradition and voice of uninformed authority. And what philosophical
evidence is there for the matter of materialism? There is no evidence at
all. Writers on matter appeal to prejudice and ignorance in favour of matter; they assume and take it for granted that everyone accepts the existence of matter; they never attempt to prove its existence directly. There
is no direct evidence to be had. They try to establish it indirectly. There
could not be an external *thing*, they say, unless there were matter; unless
there were matter, they say, there would be no cause of change in the
external world, nor any test for true and false. . . .

I have examined the typical case of seeing and touching, and have
shown that there is no place for matter there. I have examined the normal
perceptual situation, and have shown that it contains no evidence for matter, and that the forcible intrusion of matter destroys the unity of the
thing perceived and of the world of sense. The onus of proof is on the
materialist, and the immaterialist can fairly challenge him to produce his
evidence. If there is matter, produce it. If there is evidence for matter,
produce it. Neither matter, nor valid evidence for matter, has ever yet
been produced.

The nearest approach to evidence for matter proves on careful study
to be bad evidence. It is not evidence for matter; it is evidence for spirit
spoilt. I refer to the notion of *support.* The strength of materialism (and its
ultimate weakness) is its exploitation of the sub-rational feeling that somehow the pillars of the house rest on matter. People turn to matter for
support; they are dimly aware of the need for support; but if they analysed that need, they would look for the support elsewhere.

Sense-data need support, and from the time of Aristotle to the present
day men have claimed that matter supplies the desired support. But could
matter, if it existed, supply the kind of support that sense-data need? Literal support is not in question. Sense-data do not need literal support,
and if they did need it, matter *ex hypothesi* could not supply it. In the literal
sense sense-data are *given* supported; they are supported by other sense-
data. The table supports the books; the books rest on it; without it they
would fall. I can see and feel the books and the table in effective contact.
That support is visible and tangible. Literal support means sensible support, which is just what matter *e vi termini* could not give; for matter cannot be seen or touched or otherwise sensed. The legs of the table support
the table; the floor supports both; the earth supports the floor; in all such
cases support and things supported are homogeneous; both are *sensibilia*.
Matter is not a *sensibile*. Matter and sense are heterogeneous *ex hypothesi*,

and therefore matter, if there were such a thing, could not literally support sense-data.

Sense-data cannot stand alone. Like letters of the alphabet or figures or any other symbols they need the support of mind or spirit. By their very mould and nature they are not absolute, but are relative to mind or spirit. An alphabet *in vacuo* would be nonsense. The footprint in the sand implies one to leave the imprint, and the same *understood* implies one to understand it. To "understand" is to stand under and support, as the taking mind stands under and supports the work of the making mind. The materialist's quest of matter as an absolute object of perception, distinct from sense-data, is wrong-headed in principle; he leaves out of the account his own mind. His mind supports his object, as the reader's understanding mind supports the meaning of the printed page, and takes out of it what the writer's mind put into it. Sense-data are not mind or modes of mind; they do not think or will or plan or purpose; but they are from mind and for the mind, and they imply mind and cannot be understood apart from mind. That is why they cannot stand alone; that is why they require support; that is why they require *that sort* of support that only mind or spirit can give. To look to matter for such support would be absurd; for matter is defined as that which is not mind or spirit. Matter cannot support the objects of our senses in theory or practice, literally or metaphorically, and to look to matter for support is to lean on a broken reed.

Let me clinch the argument with an appeal to observable fact in a concrete case. If matter is, I ask, *where* is it? If matter is, it is in things, and in all external things, and the type of external thing selected is neither here nor there. I will choose a homely, explorable thing that we can know through and through, a mutton chop. If matter is, it is in this mutton chop. I ask, where? Where is it in this mutton chop? Where could it be? Take away from this given chop all its sense-data, including its obtainable sense-data. Take away those of the outside and those of the inside, those of the meat and the bone, those of the fat and the lean, be it cooked or uncooked. take away all that we do sense and all that we might sense, and what is left? There are its visual data, its browns and reds and blacks and whites, and all the other colours and hues of its surface and potential surfaces and centre. There are its tactual data, its rough and smooth, hard and soft, resistant and yielding, solid and fluid, and those varied palpables that admit my knife or hinder its easy passage. It has auditory data; its fat and lean and bone make different sounds when struck by knives and forks. Many smells and savours go to its composing, raw or cooked. Air and moisture link it to its sensible context, and show as steam and vapour under heat. The chop has sensible shapes that may concern artists and even geometricians; it has sensible contents and sensible forms that are specially the concern of chemist and physicist; they are no less sensible and no less real than those contents and forms that are of importance to the butcher and the housewife and the cook. Take them all away in thought. Take away all the *sensa* and the *sensibilia* of this mutton chop, and what is left? Nothing! Nothing is left. In taking away its *sensa* and *sensibilia* you have taken away all the mutton chop, and nothing is left, and its matter is nowhere. Its matter, other than its sense-data, is nothing at all, nothing but a little heap of powdered sentiment, nothing but the ghost of the conventional thing, nothing but the sceptic's question-mark. . . .

Is matter wanted as a cause? Are sense-data or sensible qualities (call them what you wish) effects of matter? Are the immediate objects of our senses caused by matter? Are sense-data so lacking in causal power that material substance must be postulated and assumed? Is material substance the power behind the scenes, the secret spring of causal action? . . .

Is matter wanted as a cause? Several questions are here combined. What is meant by "cause"? Can sense-data cause? Can they make changes begin to be? If they can, is there any need for matter? If they cannot, how could matter help? If sense-data are passive, how could material substance activate them, and confer on them the power of the cause?

These questions answer themselves in the light of the foregoing analysis of "cause." The term "cause" is ambiguous. In one sense, sense-data can cause, in the other sense, not. Sense-data are not spirits; they cannot make changes begin to be; they cannot directly alter the course of events; for they are passive; but indirectly they give rise to effects; they are signs of what is coming; men read those signs and act on them and make changes begin to be. The sign works through the mind that reads it and understands it and acts on it, just as the works of Shakespeare work through minds that read them and understand them and act on them. The passive sign gives rise indirectly to changes it does not produce. In that respect, and in that respect only, the passive objects of sense around us are causes. In strict speech they are not causes, but are like causes, and not unnaturally, but wrongly, they become credited with the power of making changes begin to be. For practical purposes it is enough for us to know that smoke and fire are almost invariably found together. When we see the smoke we expect the fire, and we are on our guard and take precautions. That is the full extent of the causal connection. The smoke is a passive sign of what is coming; it involves you and me in action, but does not act itself. The black smoke is there, and it will soon burst into a red flame unless I extinguish it. That is the only sense in which the black smoke is the cause of the red flame. The smoke does not make the fire begin to be. The smoke is not the true cause of the fire. The smoke is but the customary antecedent; when we see or smell it, we expect its consequent. The two are indissolubly connected in our minds because they are very frequently associated in nature. The association is there in nature, as in the mind; sometimes we see the smoke before the fire, sometimes the fire before the smoke. Hence it matters little which we call *cause,* and which we call *effect;* they are two parts of the one process; all we need to know is that the two events are causally connected in the sense that the one makes us expect the other. It is no truer that the fire is the cause of the smoke than that the smoke is the cause of the fire. Both propositions are on the one level as regards truth and falsity. In respect of significance or cue-causation, both events are indifferently causes and effects. In respect of efficient or true causation, neither is cause, neither is effect of the other.

Then comes the question about matter. Sense-data *per se* are passive; they may be viewed as acting indirectly through their significance for minds. Does matter enter into the cause? Is material substance the hidden hand behind the scenes? No; matter has nothing to say to causation in either sense of the term. *Ex hypothesi* matter has no significance for mind, and has not the power of the cause. Matter could not cause, nor enable sense-data to do so. There is no room for matter in the causal relation. All that matter does is to mystify, and people are too ready to be mystified. They see that the objects of sense cannot truly cause, and yet that some cause of change is required; and instead of thinking the problem out along the lines sketched above, they jump at the hypothesis of material substance. It shelves the problem and puts it out of sight; it is a facile solution that saves men the trouble of thinking. They say to themselves, "Matter is something we know not what; it acts we know not how". And so all issues in mystery.

Putting aside mystery and mystification, we see that what calls for explanation is some sensible event, some event in the world of sense. We *see* the water rise, and the litmus-paper change colour; we feel the wax soft and then still softer. A sensible change has occurred, and as rational sentients we are bound to ask, "What did it? What caused this change in the world of sense?" To reply, "The material substance of moon or wax or acid did it", or, "Material substance in general did it", may give some mystic satisfaction to mystic minds; but such replies have no explanatory value; they shed no light on the problem. Man wants to know causes, and needs to know causes, in order to have some control over events. If he cannot shape the course of events, he must shape his behaviour to suit the events. He needs to be able to move muscle and limb at the right time and to push and pull the things of sense in immediate contact with his body. To do so to the best advantage man needs a certain attitude to things; he needs confidence in the universe; he needs to be able to trust the course and composition of the universe, its order and regularity, its wisdom and its goodness. Man is spirit and sense. To form and guide his experience man needs a knowledge of spiritual causes and sensible effects. Matter comes under neither category; *ex hypothesi* matter is neither spiritual nor sensible; therefore it can contribute nothing to a knowledge of causes; it cannot be seen or touched, and therefore it cannot tell me when or how to push and pull the things I see and touch around me. Even if matter existed and possessed some occult power of altering sensible things and effecting visible and tangible changes, we never could *know* that this matter effected that change; we never could connect cause and its effect; we should be none the wiser for the existence of matter; we should have nothing to build on, no foundation for experience or for future action. We never could *know* that this invisible was the cause of that visible change, or that that intangible was the cause of this tangible change. In a word, if matter were a cause, we should never have the evidence of sense as to the cause of a sensible effect. Matter would be of no practical use

with regard to knowledge of causes, and it would make no practical difference in life and experience. The invention of matter and its intrusion
into the causal relation is purely psychological. It gives some sort of relief
to the feelings; it cannot be too easily disproved, and it asks nothing of
our moral and spiritual nature.

We men originate changes, and we know that we do so. We push; we
pull; we strive, purpose and endeavour; we produce effects, often at sec-
ond-hand, and working with the effects of another's will, but we produce
effects, and we recognise the effects as effects of our causal power. We
are true causes; we are true causes that endure; therefore we are substantial causes; we are substances that cause. We understand spiritual causation from within, to some extent at least, and it is the only true causation
that we understand at all; and we know it by the effort involved. In prospect or retrospect I know what it is to climb a ladder. I connect causally
myself at the foot of it and myself at the top; climbing a ladder is quite
different from falling off a ladder; causal effort is required. I can look at
fire and wax without any similar sense of effort; I can keep on looking. I
can watch the wax soften and melt on the hearth-stone. I have no sense of
effort; it is a smooth, expected transition; it is a relation between two
events or states; it is the relation of simple series in time, the relation of
before and after, completely devoid of any suggestion of true causality.
To mount a five-foot ladder and climb down again involves an effort of
mind and body. If I am hoisted up five feet and let down again, no effort
by me is involved. In the former case I cause the rise and the fall; in the
latter case, not. Effort marks the difference; that feeling of effort, be it
muscular, mental or mixed, is the index of finite, causal power. Causal
power belongs to the *anima,* to the finite *anima* or spirit, and it does not
belong to the inanimate.

How then to account for the opposite view? Why do people make the
mistake, I will not say of imagining causation where there is none, but of
crediting the inanimate thing or event with the power of the cause? Why
do they attribute causal power to the sun and moon instead of to the
Power that moves them? Several answers might be given; one deserves
special mention here, and that is sympathy or empathy. It may be a relic
of the old notions, classed as animist or hylozoist, or it may be a very
natural result of our real oneness with the things around us. We do feel
with them and for them and in them. We do project ourselves into them,
as little Alice projects herself into her doll. When Homer makes the river
fight, or Wordsworth sets his daffodils a-dancing, they are projecting their
own efforts into the external world, and thereby enlivening their themes
and winning their readers' sympathies. There lies one great source of the
supposed inanimate second cause. There is no such cause, but we invent
it. We invent it empathetically. As do the poets and the other masters of
language, we project into a passive object splinters and sparks of our own
activity. We throw forward into the inanimate thing the effort we should
make and the action we should take, if we were it. Smoke follows fire,
often, always. It is cause and effect, we say. We see the fire, and we expect
the smoke, or we smell the smoke and we go looking for the fire. These
inanimate, passive things, easily moved, are cues for the action; they are

like causes; they make us think causally. But that is not enough for all of us; for we are sympathetic, imaginative creatures. We are not content with cue causes; we are not content with sequences; we are not content with the observed fact that where there is smoke there is fire. We proceed to embellish and embroider the fact by reading ourselves into the situation; we mentally puff a lighted cigar, and there is the smoke; empathetically we say that the fire produces the smoke, and we vaguely view the tongues of flame puffing forth the smoke. The embroidery and embellishment are not true to fact; but they are part of the art of using rich, imaginative language. If taken literally, they misrepresent the primary facts of our sentient existence.

Causal matter is a parallel development. The causal sensible has been developed empathetically from the passive, inanimate thing of sense; and the supposed causal powers of matter have by a similar process of self-projection been embroidered upon the original hypothesis of the passive substrate. Aristotle distinguished the material cause from the efficient cause. His efficient cause was what I have termed the true cause; his material cause was like my cue cause. His efficient cause got things done, and made changes begin to be; his material cause was the inactive *sine qua non* of the doing. The function of Aristotelian matter was to support, and not to act. Aristotelian matter was passive; it was a limiting concept, almost a negation; it was not a thing, nor a quality, nor a quantity; for it had to consist with sensible things and sensible qualities and sensible quantities; it was potentiality and possibility, just a short of nothing. Later philosophers referred to matter as "a dead, inactive lump". An object so slight and negative and ineffective might well have been lost to sight altogether, and very naturally there has long been an oscillation between the two poles of thought about matter. Some understand it as active, some as passive. Some adhere to the original notion of it as passive substrate, visualising it as a carpet spread under the things of sense, or as a prop supporting them. Others have gone over to the active theory, making matter the secret source of change in the world of sense, the "hidden hand" behind sensible phenomena.

The modern trends of chemistry and physics have furthered the tendency to regard matter as an active cause. Many people today, I fancy, identify matter vaguely with atomic energy or with the rapid movement of the tiny parts and particles of elements. In olden days Jove's thunderbolt was the secret weapon of the gods; today atomic energy has taken its place as the power behind the scenes. The bomb that controls the policies of nations controls the trend of thought, and in popular imagination appears as proof positive of active matter. Gunpowder and high explosives, when they were first invented, affected popular thought in a similar way. No new factors bearing on the issue for intellect have come to light in our day. No new proof of a non-sensible substrate of the world of sense has been discovered. The bomb is nothing new by way of proof of matter; only the horror, the suddenness and the vast scale of the consequent destruction have reinforced whatever argument is there. The fact is that electrons, neutrons and the other scientific objects and working concepts of today are no nearer possessing the power of the true cause than were acids, alkalis, phlogiston and gravity; but they are more remote from the macroscopic, and in consequence they strike the imagination more forcibly than did the objects and concepts of the older sciences. The bomb may be designed, constructed and described by various concepts and symbols, but such concepts and symbols do not alter the fact that the bomb itself is sensible through and through. In whole and part and particle it can be seen and touched and heard; it contains and releases and conveys motions that can be seen and touched and heard. Atomic energy, however subtle its constitution, however penetrating its results, belongs entirely to the province of sense; its only causality is that of significance, the causality of the sign or cue cause. The bomb, live, exploding, or exploded, is a multiple sign of sights and sounds and feelings that go with and after it; pity and fear and panic movements of escape are aroused in us by the sight or thought of it, and naturally we project into it those incipient movements that we begin, not it. Our sympathies are strongly aroused. "I have a pain in your chest," wrote Madame de Sevigné to her daughter. We feel in the bomb what we might feel in ourselves, and thus we credit it with those efforts and activites that are really our own. Empathy accounts for our *mis*-takes, but does not alter the facts of existence. Empathy cannot transmute passive into active, or make a cue cause into a true cause. The bomb is no true cause; for it is entirely an effect; finite spirits have made it, using and misusing the effects of Will Infinite.

The causal argument for the existence of matter has thus been examined and refuted. I will recapitulate before I leave it. The causal argument owes its cogency to the assumption that colours and touches and all the other objects we actually perceive by sense cannot cause the changes we observe in the world of sense. That assumption is true in one sense of the term "cause", and false in another. It is true that colours and other such objects are passive things, unable to initiate motion or make the smallest change begin to be. But that rule would apply equally to matter, if matter existed; for it is only another way of saying that spirits alone are truly active, and matter, being by definition non-spiritual, would necessarily be ruled out as cause. If, on the other hand, is meant by "cause" merely the inoperative, antecedent sign, created and conserved by cosmic power, in that sense colours and similar objects are causes; for sentients can read their meaning, can grasp their significance, and can act accordingly. To postulate matter as causal sign would be doubly absurd. If you have a perfectly good and adequate sensible sign, there is no need for the material sign, or room for it. And secondly, matter *ex hypothesi* cannot be seen or touched or otherwise perceived by sense, and therefore it could not act as a sign for sentient beings. In sum, no argument for the existence of matter can validly be drawn from the concept of cause or the facts of causation.

Contemporary Issues

Are Men Machines?

37. In Praise of Robots   Carl Sagan

Carl Sagan (1934–   ) is David Duncan professor of Astronomy and Space Sciences and Director of the Laboratory for Planetary Studies at Cornell University.

The word "robot," first introduced in the 1920's by the Czech writer Karel Čapek, is derived from the Slavic root for "worker." But it signifies a machine rather than a human worker. Robots, especially robots in space, have lately been getting a bad press. We have read that a human being was necessary to make the terminal landing adjustments on Apollo 11, without which the first manned lunar landing would have ended in disaster; that a mobile robot on the lunar surface could never have been so clever as the astronauts in selecting samples to be returned to earth-bound geologists; and that machines could never have repaired, as men did, the sunshade that was so vital for the continuance of the Skylab missions.

All these comments turn out, naturally enough, to have been written by humans. I wonder if a small self-congratulatory element, a whiff of human chauvinism, has not crept into these judgments. Just as whites can sometimes detect racism and men can occasionally discern sexism, I wonder whether we cannot here glimpse some comparable affliction of the human spirit—a disease that as yet has no name. The word "humanism" has been preempted by other and more benign activities of mankind. From the analogy with sexism and racism I suppose the name for this malady could be "speciesism"—the prejudice that there are no beings so fine, so capable, and so reliable as human beings.

This is a prejudice because it is, at the very least, a prejudgment—a conclusion drawn before all the facts are in. Such comparisons of men and machines in space are comparisons of smart men with dumb machines. We have not asked what sorts of machines could have been built for the thirty or so billion dollars that the Apollo and Skylab missions together cost.

Each human being is a superbly constructed, astonishingly compact, self-ambulatory computer—capable on occasion of independent decision making and real control of his or her environment. But there are serious limitations to employing human beings in certain environments. For example, without a great deal of protection, human beings would be inconvenienced on the ocean floor, the surface of Venus, the deep interior of Jupiter, or even on long space missions. Perhaps the only interesting information from Skylab that could not have been obtained by machines is that when human beings remain in space for a period of months, they undergo a spectacular loss of bone calcium and phosphorus. This seems to imply that human beings will be incapacitated under zero gravity on missions of six to nine months or more. The minimum interplanetary voyages have characteristic lengths of a year or two. Spinning the spacecraft can produce a kind of artificial gravity, but it is inconvenient and costly.

Because we value human beings highly, we are reluctant to send them on extremely risky missions. If we do send human beings to exotic environments, we must also send along their food, their air, their water, amenities for entertainment and waste recycling, and companions. Machines, however, need no elaborate life-support systems, no entertainment, no companionship, and we do not yet feel strong ethical prohibitions against sending them on one-way or suicide missions.

Certainly for simple missions, machines have proved themselves many times over. Unmanned vehicles performed the first photography of the whole earth and the far side of the moon, the first landings on the moon and Venus, and in the Mariner 9 mission to Mars, the first thorough reconnaissance of another planet. Here on earth it is increasingly common for high-technology manufacturing—in chemical and pharmaceutical plants, for example—to be performed largely or entirely under computer control. In all these activities machines are able, to some extent, to sense errors, correct mistakes, and alert distant human controllers about perceived problems. The powerful arithmetical abilities of computing machines—now hundreds of millions of times faster than unaided human beings—is legendary. But what about really complex discussions? Can machines, in any sense, think through a new problem? Can they make discussions of the branched-contingency-tree variety, which we think of as characteristically human? (That is, I ask question 1; if the answer is A, I ask question 2; if the answer is B, I ask question 3; and so on.)

Some decades ago the English mathematician Alan Mathison Turing described what would be necessary for him to believe in machine intelligence. The condition was simply that he could be in teletype or typewriter communication with a machine and be unable to tell that it was not a human being. Turing imagined the following conversation between a man and a machine:

> *Q.* In the first line of your sonnet, which reads "Shall I compare thee to a summer's day," would not "a spring day" do as well or better?
> *A.* It wouldn't scan.
> *Q.* How about "a winter's day?" That would scan all right.
> *A.* Yes, but nobody wants to be compared to a winter's day.
> *Q.* Would you say Mr. Pickwick reminded you of Christmas?
> *A.* In a way.
> *Q.* Yet Christmas is a winter's day, and I do not think Mr. Pickwick would mind the comparison.
> *A.* I don't think you're serious. By a winter's day one means a typical winter's day, rather than a special one like Christmas.

No machine of this sophistication has yet been built, but so far only a limited amount of effort and money has been put into artificial intelligence, and there are only a half-dozen centers of such activity in the world. One of the more striking results, obtained in a very limited universe of discourse—that of children's blocks—comes from work done at the Artificial Intelligence Laboratory of the Massachusetts Institute of Technology. Here is a dialogue between a man and a machine:

Man. What does the box contain?
Machine. The blue pyramid and the blue box.
Man. How many blocks are not in the box?
Machine. Four of them.
Man. Is at least one of them narrower than the one that I told
you to pick up?
Machine. Yes, the red cube.
Man. Is there a steeple?
Machine. Sorry, I don't know the word "steeple."
Man. A steeple is a stack that contains two green cubes and a pyramid, for example.
Machine. I understand.
Man. Are there any steeples now?
Machine. No.
Man. Build one.

The machine does. It reaches out its mechanical hand, moves the cubes, builds the structure that has just been described.

Man. When did you pick up the pyramid?
Machine. While I was stacking up the red cube, the large red block, and the large green cube.
Man. Why?
Machine. To get rid of it.
Man. Why did you clear off that cube?
Machine. To put it on the large green cube.

As another example, a computer program that imitates a psychiatrist was also once developed at MIT. This is a much simpler program than the blocks program because it does not attempt to "understand" much of what is said to it, but only manipulates the phrases in sentences it has heard in accordance with a contingency tree sensitive to certain words that are considered especially important by humans. This program involves nondirective psychotherapy, which generally speaking, requires extremely simple computer programs. Here is a remarkable dialogue between a human being and a computer psychotherapist. (It is one of the most interesting of such conversations. Many other such machine/human psychiatric dialogues are not nearly so striking. But I suppose most human/human psychiatric dialogues are not very striking either.) In order to keep the respective roles of therapist and patient clear in this interaction, the computer therapist types upper case and the patient types lower case:

> men are all alike.
> IN WHAT WAY?
> they're always bugging us about something or other.
> CAN YOU THINK OF A SPECIFIC EXAMPLE?
> well, my boyfriend made me come here.
> YOUR BOYFRIEND MADE YOU COME HERE?
> he noticed that i'm depressed much of the time.
> I AM SORRY TO HEAR YOU ARE DEPRESSED.
> he's right. i am unhappy.
> DO YOU THINK COMING HERE WILL HELP YOU NOT TO BE UNHAPPY?
> i need some help, that much is clear.
> WHAT WOULD IT MEAN TO YOU IF YOU GOT SOME HELP?
> perhaps i could learn to get along with my mother.
> TELL ME MORE ABOUT YOUR FAMILY.
> my mother takes care of me.
> WHO ELSE IN YOUR FAMILY TAKES CARE OF YOU?
> my father.
> YOUR FATHER?
> you are like my father in some ways.
> WHAT RESEMBLANCE DO YOU SEE?
> you are not very aggressive, but i don't think you want me to notice
>   that.
> WHAT MAKES YOU THINK I AM NOT VERY AGGRESSIVE?
> you don't argue with me.
> WHY DO YOU THINK I DON'T ARGUE WITH YOU?
> you are afraid of me.
> DOES IT PLEASE YOU TO BELIEVE I AM AFRAID OF YOU?
> it pleases my father to think i am afraid of him.
> WHAT ELSE COMES TO MIND WHEN YOU THINK OF YOUR FATHER?
> bullies.
> DOES THAT HAVE ANYTHING TO DO WITH THE FACT THAT YOUR
>   BOYFRIEND MADE YOU COME HERE?

This astonishing—one is very tempted to say perceptive—response from the computer is, of course, preprogrammed. But then, so are the responses of human psychotherapists. No such computer program is adequate for psychiatric use today, but the same can be remarked about some human psychotherapists. In a period when more and more people in our society seem to be in need of psychiatric counseling, and when time-sharing of computers is widespread, I can imagine the development of a network of computer psychotherapeutic terminals, something like arrays of large telephone booths, in which, for a few dollars a session, we would be able to talk with an attentive, tested, and largely nondirective psychotherapist. Insuring the confidentiality of the psychiatric dialogue is probably the most important step to be worked out.

Another sign of the intellectual accomplishments of machines is found in games. Even exceptionally simple computers—those that can be wired by a bright ten-year-old—can be programmed to play perfect tic-tac-toe. One computer has played master-class checkers—it has beaten the Connecticut state champion. Chess is a much more difficult game than tic-tac-toe or checkers. Here, programming a machine to win is not easy, and novel strategies have been used, including several successful attempts to have a computer learn from its own experience in playing previous chess games. For example, computers can learn empirically that it is better in the beginning game to control the center of the chess board than the periphery.

So far no computer has become a chess master; the ten best chess players in the world have nothing to fear from any present machine. But several computers have played well enough to be ranked somewhere in the middle range of serious, tournament-playing chess players. I have heard machines demeaned (often with a just audible sigh of relief) because chess is an area in which human beings are still superior. This reminds me of the old joke in which a stranger remarks with wonder on the accomplishments of a checker-playing dog, whose owner replies. "Oh it's not all that remarkable. He loses two games out of three." A machine that plays chess in the middle range of human expertise is a very capable machine; even if there are thousands of better human chess players, there are millions of worse ones. To play chess requires a great deal of strategy and foresight, analytical powers, the ability to cross-corelate large numbers of variables and to learn from experience. These are excellent qualities not only for individuals whose job it is to discover and explore but also for those who watch the baby and walk the dog.

Chess-playing computers, because they have very complex programs, and because, to some extent, they learn from experience, are sometimes unpredictable. Occasionally they perform in a way that their programmers would never have anticipated. Some philosophers have argued for free will in human beings on the basis of our sometimes unpredictable behavior. But the case of the chess-playing computer clearly tells us that, when viewed from the outside, behavior may be unpredictable only because it is the result of a complex although entirely determined set of steps on the inside. Among its many other uses, machine intelligence can help illuminate the ancient philosophical debate on free will and determinism.

With this more or less representative set of examples of the state of development of machine intelligence, I think it is clear that a major effort over the next decade, involving substantial investments of money, could produce much more sophisticated programs. I hope that the inventors of such machines and programs will become generally recognized as the consummate artists they are. . . .

To construct something with the intelligence of an insect may not seem a very impressive feat. But it is a feat that took nature four billion years to accomplish. We have been exploring space for less than a hundred-millionth of that time. A machine of this intelligence is a great human achievement.

As the field of machine intelligence advances and as more and more distant objects in the solar system become accessible to exploration, we will see the development of increasingly sophisticated onboard computers—instruments that slowly climb the phylogenetic tree from insect intelligence to crocodile intelligence to squirrel intelligence and, in the not very remote future, I think, to dog intelligence. Any flight to very great distances must have a computer capable of determining whether it is working properly. There will be no possibility of sending to earth for a repairman. The machine must be able to sense it is sick and skillfully doctor its own illnesses. A computer is needed that is able either to fix or replace its own failed parts or sensors or structural components. Such a computer, which has been called STAR—for Self-Testing And Repairing computer—is on the threshold of development. It employs redundant components, as biology does—we have two lungs and two kidneys partly because each is protection against failure of the other. But a computer can be much more redundant than a human being—we have, after all, only one head and one heart.

In view of the weight premium on deep-space exploratory ventures, there will be strong pressures for continued miniaturization of intelligent machines. Remarkable miniaturization has already occurred; vacuum tubes have been replaced by transistors and wired circuits by printed circuit boards. A few years ago a circuit that occupied much of a 1930's radio set was regularly being printed on the equivalent of the head of a pin. Today the same circuit can be printed on the point of a pin, and the head can accommodate a fair fraction of a small computer.

If intelligent machines for terrestrial mining and space exploratory applications are pursued, the time is not far off when household and other domestic robots will become commercially feasible. Unlike the classical anthropoid robots of science fiction, there is no reason for such machines to look any more human than a vacuum cleaner does. They will be specialized for their functions. There are many common tasks, ranging from bar tending to floor washing, that involve a limited array of intellectual capabilities, although they require substantial stamina and patience. All-purpose ambulatory household robots, capable of performing the domestic functions of a proper nineteenth-century British butler, are probably many decades off. But more specialized machines, adapted to specific household functions, are already on the horizon.

Conceivably, many other civic tasks and essential functions of everyday life could also be carried out by intelligent machines. A recent newspaper report states that garbage collectors in Anchorage, Alaska, have won a wage settlement guaranteeing them a yearly salary of $18,000. Economic pressures alone may make a persuasive case for the development of automated garbage-collecting machines. For the development of domestic and civic robots to be a general social good, the effective reemployment of those displaced by robots must, of course, be arranged; but over a human generation that should not be too difficult—particularly if enlightened educational reforms are initiated.

We appear to be on the verge of developing a wide variety of intelligent machines capable of performing tasks too dangerous, too expensive, too onerous, or too boring for human beings. The development of these machines is, in my mind, one of the few legitimate spin-offs of the space program. The main obstacle to their development seems to be a human problem: the quiet feeling that comes stealthily and unbidden to claim that there is something unpleasant or "inhuman" about machines performing certain tasks as well as, or better than, humans; the feeling that generates a sense of loathing for creatures made of silicon and germanium rather than proteins and nucleic acids.

Our survival as a species depends on our transcending these primitive chauvinisms. Adjustment to intelligent machines is, in part, a matter of acclimatization. There are cardiac pacemakers in existence that sense the beat of the human heart. Only at the slightest hint of fibrillation does the pacemaker stimulate the heart. This is a mild but useful sort of machine intelligence. I cannot imagine the wearer of this device resenting its intelligence. I think that there will shortly be a similar sort of acceptance for much more intelligent and sophisticated machines. We have a generation of youngsters who are growing up with pocket computers, machine languages, computer graphics, electronic music, automated instruction, and computer games. They are unlikely to find anything alien about machine intelligence. There is nothing inhuman about an intelligent machine; it is, indeed, the expression of those superb intellectual capabilities that only human beings, of all the creatures on our planet, now possess.

A legitimate concern in the development of machine intelligence is its potential for misuse by unscrupulous governmental, military, and police agencies. Here, as in many other areas of modern technology, the same devices can be used either for enormous good or enormous evil. A world with central data banks containing dossiers on all its citizens, with robot policemen and robot judges, and with automated battlefields is not a world in which I personally would care to live and bring up children. It would be a nightmare world. But a world with adequate food, mineral, and energy resources; a world that provides its human inhabitants with ample leisure and an intellectually and spiritually rich environment with which to make that leisure meaningful; a world engaged in the exploration of other distant and exotic worlds—that is a world I would find extremely attractive. Both of these future worlds are accessible through machine intelligence. To avoid the nightmare and realize the dream requires a wholesale restructuring of the planet's political institutions—a restructuring that is clearly required quite apart from the implications of intelligent machines. If we survive, I think our future will depend to a significant degree on a partnership between human and machine intelligence.

38. The Thinking of Men and Machines   John H. Troll

John Hans Troll (1919–   ), a physicist by training and designer of the Sidewinder Guidance Missile System. For many years he has worked on thinking machines of various kinds and has acted as consultant for companies manufacturing electronic computers.

From *The Atlantic Monthly*, July, 1954. Copyright © 1954 by The Atlantic Monthly Company, Boston, Mass. Reprinted by permission of the author.

The uneasy, half-embarrassed rivalry between man and machine has reached a peak with the thinking machine. We have become used to machines that are more powerful, more durable, more accurate, and faster than we are, but machines that challenge our intelligence are hard to take. At this point the competition becomes uncomfortable.

Machines and tools have always been created in the image of man. The hammer grew from the balled fist, the rake from the hand with fingers outstretched for scratching, the shovel from the hand hollowed to scoop. As machines became more than simple tools, outstripping their creators in performance, demanding and obtaining increasing amounts of power, and acquiring superhuman speeds and accuracies, their outward resemblance to the natural model disappeared; only the names of the machine's parts show vestiges of their human origin. The highly complex machinery of the modern industrial age has arms that swing, fingers that fold, legs that support, teeth that grind, and male and female parts that mate. Machines feed on material, run when things go well, and spit and cough when they don't.

But the newest machines possess human traits that had always been considered far beyond mechanization. Here we find not only electric eyes that see and sensing devices that feel, but also memories that recall and logic sections that classify, arrange, and select. These machines can make choices, comparisons, and decisions, learn from past experience, and reach logical conclusions on the basis of premises. It may no longer be denied: these machines can really think.

This realization has renewed the furtive rivalry between man and machine. The battle is being fought underground because even to concede the existence of such a constest would be undignified. Like a small child jealous of the attention paid a puppy, men do not often admit openly that this inhuman contrivance of nuts and bolts and evilly gleaming electron tubes is a threat. But as the child will get even with the puppy by tweaking its tail when no one is looking, so man, consciously or unconsciously, likes to throw monkey wrenches into machines and see them get their comeuppance.

Newspaper editors a few years back felt that there would be interest in a story about a Japanese arithmetician who, with an abacus—a simple device made of a few counting beads—won a race against a mechanical calculating machine. The story was prominently featured in the world press. If the mechanical calculator had won, there would have been no story.

No one likes to depend on a rival. Consequently there is a general desire to distrust and by-pass machines. Pilots during the Second World War preferred to fly by the seat of their pants—a device so notoriously insensitive that it won't tell the pilot when he flies upside down—rather than by their highly precise and reliable instruments. Many posters and disciplinary actions were necessary to make pilots use their instruments.

When Univac, one of the computers used on election night, made an amazingly accurate prediction of the outcome on the basis of very early returns, it was disbelieved by the experts who designed and constructed it. Even when by all rational standards it becomes evident that the machine knows better, man is reluctant to let it have the last word.

An even more telling sign of this half-secret battle of man and the technical monster of his creation is the character of the Utopias of our time. Where Thomas More of the sixteenth century and Edward Bellamy of the nineteenth found ideal, beautifully harmonious societies in their imaginary travels, with satisfactory solutions to the pressing problems of their days, George Orwell and Aldous Huxley in our age see only a night-marishly heightened outgrowth of the modern world. In their Utopias, standardization, an integral part of the machine culture, extends to the hygienically controlled production of humans; machines take all the major roles in human enjoyment, dominating even sex and simple sports; machines write all novels and plays and newspapers and create all art and entertainment; machines watch and spy day and night, destroying all vestiges of human individuality. Is the arrival of the thinking machine the first sign that these nightmares are about to become a reality? Is man hopelessly outmatched in this bout with the machine?

Take for instance the calculation involved in the design of photographic lenses. Before the arrival of computers, one could design lenses by painstaking pencil and paper work. By this method an experienced lens designer took about six years to design one of the complicated lenses. The desk calculator cut this time to about fifteen weeks, and now a giant computer like the Bureau of Standards SEEAC does the job in a single hour.

Let us look at this lens-design problem a little closer to learn something about the way such a machine operates. A good optical lens like those used in the best cameras differs from simple lenses or from eyeglasses mainly in that it consists of many glasses of various shapes all cemented together. The designers must prescribe the exact shape of each of these glasses making up a lens so that all rays originating from a point, say from a star we want to photograph, will meet in another point behind the lens, forming an image of the star. Actually, these rays cannot be made to meet in a point, which would be ideal, but will all fall within a circle. The smaller the circle, the better defined the image and the better the lens.

The design procedure is part calculation, part trial and error. There are, of course, an infinite number of angles at which the rays may enter the lens. A good many of these must be traced through the lens. That is, we must find the change in angle for each ray as it enters and leaves each glass. As a result, we know the angle of the ray when it leaves the last glass surface and therefore where it will meet the other rays. Though the arithmetical procedure to find these changes of angles for each ray is not complicated, it requires accuracies to about seven decimals, and many rays have to be considered. After all the required rays are traced we find the diameter of the circle within which they meet. If we find it small enough to suit our requirements, the job is done. But if it appears too large, we must change by a slight amount one of the shapes of the glass surfaces. Now we trace all the rays for the new condition and see whether we have improved the design or made it worse. It used to take a man six years to complete such a job.

How much of this work can the computer take over for us? Almost all of it. It requires only an adequate set of instructions. These must contain a formula which shows what the angle of a ray is when leaving a surface if we know the angle of entrance, some properties of the glass, the shape of the surface, and the color of the ray. In addition, the instructions tell the computer how good a lens it must design and what initial shapes to start with.

Next, we tell the machine how to proceed. Our program may read: "Start with a ray 45 degrees off to the center axis. Figure its entrance and exit angles through each of the eleven surfaces. Note the angle of exit from the last surface; do the same with the ray at 44 degrees, then 43 degrees, and so forth, in intervals of one degree until the ray at 0 degrees has been traced. Compare the resulting circle where the rays meet with the desired one; if it is the same size or smaller, print out the answer; if it is larger, change the shape of the first surface and repeat the ray tracing. If the new answer is better than the old one but still not right, change the surface again in the same direction. If the new answer is worse, change in the opposite direction. When the best answer is still not right, change the second surface the same way, and so through all other surfaces until the answer is right."

The actual instructions to the computer appear not in words but in a mathematical shorthand written on magnetic tape or in the form of punched holes in a paper tape very much like the good old player piano roll—quite a remarkable device in days when no one thought of computers. It could memorize long piano pieces, know which notes to play, when and how loud, and yet no one worried about its being a thinking machine.

Now that the machine has received its instructions, it can go to work. Strangely enough, it performs in an eerie silence. There are no motors whirring, no bells clanging, not even a hum as it races through millions of trial-and-error calculations with a speed that is literally close to that of lightning. Only the even red glow of the tubes shows that anything is going on. When the computer is finished, there is the clacking of an electric typewriter printing out the solution.

If anything goes wrong, the machine stops and types out what is the matter. Often it can tell which of its many tubes has failed, or what additional information it requires to complete the problem. Most computers are designed so that they never give wrong answers; if something fails, the machine gives no answer. Once an answer is printed, you can depend upon it. Moreover, computers constantly check their work and will repeat any calculation that appears incorrect.

Can we call such a process thinking? We have seen that it involves remembering, sorting, classifying, and choosing alternatives on the basis of logic. When men do this sort of work, it has always been considered thinking. And so in fairness to the machine we must concede that within the usual meaning of the word it can and does think. And since in the course of its work the machine discards solutions in favor of better ones, acting on past experience, it cannot be denied that it also learns. Since it thinks fast, it learns fast—much faster than man. Moreover, it makes no mistakes and while working on a problem never forgets. Does this mean that the machine is more intelligent than man?

To state it generally, today's thinking machines are in their element and truly superior to men when they draw conclusions about particular cases to which a general rule applies. There are computers in development that can make quick and accurate strategic decisions in air battles, taking into consideration the positions of the friendly and enemy aircraft—provided they are given a basic tactical rule they can follow. And by the same token, there is no reason why tomorrow's computer could not predict the sales volume for an article, corrected for season, weather, the general state of prosperity, Mr. Dior's dictates, and the prevailing feminine mood, as long as it has past sales trends that it can use as a rule.

But the unquestioned obedience to the initial rules which makes for the machine's superhuman precision also sets a limit to its general intelligence. For the results of its thinking can only be as good as the rules that it has been taught to follow. If the rules showed themselves to be totally wrong for the situation, the machine would cling to them stubbornly, threatening, like the broom of the sorcerer's apprentice, destruction for its master and itself.

There is another kind of thinking—the thinking that sees relations between individual events and forms rules on this basis, and, having formed them, discards or modifies what no longer fits. Men do this kind of thinking so effortlessly that we often do not even consider it thought. If we see a circle, for instance, we immediately recognize it as such regardless of its material or its size. We need not examine each point on the circle separately and compare it with a formula. Moreover, we can tell things that are approximately circular without much strain. Machines cannot sense shapes that are not given point by point or as a mathematical formula.

It is this form of thinking that we use when we recognize someone on the street. We do not, computer fashion, check a lot of details: "5 feet 7 inches tall, size 32 blouse, brown eyes, blond hair, arm length 33 inches, finger lengths 3 inches, 4 inches," and so forth; we can say immediately, "Hello, Mary." It matters little whether Mary has lost or gained weight, has grown taller or dyed her hair. In fact, we need no precise quantitative information about her at all. On a purely statistical basis, the amount of information required to distinguish her definitely among the 75 million females living in this country would be formidable. Yet we need to know astonishingly little to be quite certain that this is Mary. We may recognize her on a cold winter day though she is covered with bulky clothes from head to foot and nothing shows but the tip of a red nose—or we might recognize her from the rear without even this meager clue. People can recognize one another at unexpected meetings after twenty years, when they have last seen one another in grammar school and when they have grown, acquired beards or figures, changed their voices and their clothing—when, in fact, not a particle of their bodies is the same.

Despite the nearly miraculous feat involved in recognition, it requires no outstanding mental ability. Children and even pets are quite good at it. Yet such an activity exceeds the capabilities of the most complex thinking machines. It depends entirely on forming a general picture, an idea—something more than a simple checking off, or adding, or averaging of all the individual parts.

How we form such ideas or generalizations has always been considered one of the most puzzling aspects of the human mind. The ancient Greeks, and particularly Plato, saw it closely related to the recognition process. He believed that true reality in the form of ideas was stored in a place visited by man's soul before birth, and that the earthly realization of particular objects was a recall of memories acquired during this prenatal experience. Ideas can not only serve in helping us to recognize what we have seen but can be applied to predict the unknown on the basis of similarity. A cab driver in New York told me that he was able to cut his working day to a respectable eight hours while most of his colleagues had to work ten or twelve. Yet he made just as much money and had as many fares as they did. His secret: he learned to recognize the peculiar characteristics of people making up their minds to take a cab. He could spot such people in a crowd or walking out of a building. Before he let me off, he pointed to a man who was just walking along and said, "He wants a cab." He pulled up next to him and the man got in as I got out.

Most good salesmen know who can be called by his first name and slapped on the back after a few minutes' acquaintance and who must always be addressed as "Mr." and treated with formality. Confidence men are very adept at determining what kind of man makes a good "mark," and they don't have at their disposal a set of standardized psychological tests. Their occupation is safe from the intrusion of the thinking machine.

All of us form definite first impressions and adjust our behavior accordingly. We feel whether the new aquaintance is friendly, whether he is a threat or harmless, whether he is bright or dull, and how we may best be able to get along with him. We recognize and adjust to behavior just as we recognize a person, not by the busy examination of many detailed facts but by organizing these facts into a new entity.

A similar process is involved when a doctor makes a diagnosis. There are really an infinite number of possible diseases that a doctor may be faced with, and if he had to proceed entirely on serial examination of all the symptoms, most of his patients would die—most likely of old age— before he was able to make a single diagnosis; yet the good diagnostician often identifies a disease immediately, and at other times requires only relatively few specific tests to come to a conclusion. His mental picture of the disease is a whole, not a collection of many details, and he can therefore recognize it when he sees something that matches this mental picture.

A singular human attribute is not only the formation of ideas but the ability to connect such ideas in a useful fashion. The human memory is a filing system that has a far greater capacity than that of the largest thinking machine built. A mechanical brain that had as many tubes or relays as the human brain has nerve cells (some ten billion) would not fit into the Empire State Building, and would require the entire output of Niagara Falls to supply the power and the Niagara River to cool it. Moreover, such a computer could operate but a fraction of a second at a time before several thousand of its tubes would fail and have to be replaced.

One of the largest of today's computers, the Eniac, has about 10,000 tubes and has therefore about as many brain cells as a flatworm.

The human brain, with one million times as many cells, is unique not only for its ability to store vast amounts of information in a small storage space and for requiring vanishing amounts of operating power, but also for the speed and ease with which any remembered item can be produced. The human filing system is so flexible that it can be reshuffled instantly from an infinity of new viewpoints. The most elaborate filing systems or library catalogues are arranged by author, subject, and sometimes date of publication, with cross-references between these files. The human file of ideas, however, classifies each idea in an infinite variety of ways; the word "red" can be connected with "green" or "hot" or "blush" or "Skelton" or "Communist" or "blood" or "herring," to mention only a few. Computers can refer to their memories only in a systematic fashion, well planned and explained beforehand, but cannot create new cross-indexing for themselves.

Yet connection of ideas forms an important aspect of thinking. Without it, Newton could not have associated the apocryphal apple with the motion of the planets because the cross-index, "apple falling—*see* rate—*see* square law—*see* planets' motion," had not existed. Nor could Norbert Wiener and Shannon have seen that there is a similarity between the way a message loses intelligibility in transmission and an object loses heat to the surrounding area. Nor could physicists have seen that there are similarities in the ways sound, light, and heat behave, so that picturing them as waves would work for all. Nor could Freud have recognized a connection between accidental slips of the tongue and jokes, dreams, and neuroses.

The sort of thinking that can be called truly creative is such forming and organizing of ideas and the connecting of these ideas into new larger entities. And this is precisely what falls beyond the computer's scope. With its electronics, memories, logic systems, lightning speeds, accuracy, and infallibility, a computer cannot create an idea or ask a question that could form a basis for a new outlook.

Nor does it seem likely that tomorrow's computers will do this. The machines of the future may overcome some of the other handicaps, such as their enormous size and power requirements. There are signs that they may even beget their own kind—but never ideas.

True, a computer could be designed which would randomly and madly connect all sorts of facts and then test them for internal consistencies. It would certainly come up with a million theories. But it would have no criterion for selecting the ones that are meaningful.

For what is meaningful is a function of man's need to survive and to create a world for himself that he can manage physically and mentally.

Thinking machines, more than any other invention in the history of mankind, can aid this creation of a workable and understandable environment by checking man's ideas for validity and internal consistency, by saving him millions of trials and errors, and by speeding up immeasurably the acquisition of new facts and knowledge. But it always takes a human to come up with the approach, the generalization, the idea which furnishes the basis for the machine's lightning checking, applying, and finding of new facts. How such basic ideas are conceived we do not know. Yet only they can be called truly creative thought—a process which must forever remain in the province of the human spirit. The bad dreams of our Utopians will not come true; even the most complex, advanced thinking machines will not replace or dominate this spirit.

Do We Survive Death?

39. Immortality: An Absurd Supposition   Baron d'Holbach

WHAT IS THE SOUL? WE KNOW NOTHING ABOUT IT. IF THIS PRETENDED SOUL WAS OF ANOTHER ESSENCE FROM THAT OF THE BODY, THEIR UNION WOULD BE IMPOSSIBLE.

The superiority which men arrogate to themselves over other animals is principally founded upon the opinion of possessing exclusively an immortal soul. But as soon as we ask what this soul is, they begin to stammer. It is an unknown substance; it is a secret force distinguished from their bodies; it is a spirit of which they can form no idea. Ask them how this spirit, which they suppose like their God, totally deprived of a physical substance, could combine itself with their material bodies? They will tell you that they know nothing about it; that it is a mystery to them; that this combination is the effect of the Almighty power. These are the clear ideas which men form of the hidden, or, rather, imaginary substance which they consider the motor of all their actions! If the soul is a substance essentially different from the body, and which can have no affinity with it, their union would be, not a mystery, but a thing impossible. Besides, this soul, being of an essence different from that of the body, ought to act necessarily in a different way from it. However, we see that the movements of the body are felt by this pretended soul, and that these two substances, so different in essence, always act in harmony. You will tell us that this harmony is a mystery; and I will tell you that I do not see my soul, that I know and feel but my body; that it is my body which feels, which reflects, which judges, which suffers, and which enjoys, and that all of its faculties are the necessary results of its own mechanism or of its organization.

THE EXISTENCE OF A SOUL IS AN ABSURD SUPPOSITION, AND THE EXISTENCE OF AN IMMORTAL SOUL IS A STILL MORE ABSURD SUPPOSITION.

Although it is impossible for men to have the least idea of the soul, or of this pretended spirit which animates them, they persuade themselves, however, that this unknown soul is exempt from death; everything proves to them that they feel, think, acquire ideas, enjoy or suffer, but by the means of the senses or of the material organs of the body. Even admitting the existence of this soul, one can not refuse to recognize that it depends wholly on the body, and suffers conjointly with it all the vicissitudes which

From *Superstition in All Ages* by Jean Meslier. Published by Peter Eckler in 1890.

it experiences itself; and however it is imagined that it has by its nature nothing analogous with it; it is pretended that it can act and feel without the assistance of this body; that deprived of this body and robbed of its senses, this soul will be able to live, to enjoy, to suffer, be sensitive of enjoyment or of rigorous torments. Upon such a tissue of conjectural absurdities the wonderful opinion of the immortality of the soul is built.

If I ask what ground we have for supposing that the soul is immortal: they reply, it is because man by his nature desires to be immortal, or to live forever. But I rejoin, if you desire anything very much, is it sufficient to conclude that this desire will be fulfilled? By what strange logic do they decide that a thing can not fail to happen because they ardently desire it to happen? Man's childish desires of the imagination, are they the measure of reality? Impious people, you say, deprived of the flattering hopes of another life, desire to be annihilated. Well, have they not just as much right to conclude by this desire that they will be annihilated, as you to conclude that you will exist forever because you desire it?

IT IS EVIDENT THAT THE WHOLE OF MAN DIES.

Man dies entirely. Nothing is more evident to him who is not delirious. The human body, after death, is but a mass, incapable of producing any movements the union of which constitutes life. We no longer see circulation, respiration, digestion, speech, or reflection. It is claimed then that the soul has separated itself from the body. But to say that this soul, which is unknown, is the principle of life, is saying nothing, unless that an unknown force is the invisible principle of imperceptible movements. Nothing is more natural and more simple than to believe that the dead man lives no more, nothing more absurd than to believe that the dead man is still living.

We ridicule the simplicity of some nations whose fashion is to bury provisions with the dead—under the idea that this food might be useful and necessary to them in another life. Is it more ridiculous or more absurd to believe that men will eat after death than to imagine that they will think; that they will have agreeable or disagreeable ideas; that they will enjoy; that they will suffer; that they will be conscious of sorrow or joy when the organs which produce sensations or ideas are dissolved and reduced to dust? To claim that the souls of men will be happy or unhappy after the death of the body is to pretend that man will be able to see without eyes, to hear without ears, to taste without a palate, to smell without a nose, and to feel without hands and without skin. Nations who believe themselves very rational, adopt, nevertheless, such ideas.

INCONTESTABLE PROOFS AGAINST THE SPIRITUALITY OF THE SOUL.

The dogma of the immortality of the soul assumes that the soul is a simple substance, a spirit; but I will always ask, what is a spirit? It is, you say, a substance deprived of expansion, incorruptible, and which has nothing in common with matter. But if this is true, how came your soul into existence? how did it grow? how did it strengthen? how weaken itself, get out of order, and grow old with your body? In reply to all these questions, you say that they are mysteries; but if they are mysteries, you understand nothing about them. If you do not understand anything about them, how can you positively affirm anything about them? In order to believe or to affirm anything, it is necessary at least to know what that consists of which we believe and which we affirm. To believe in the existence of your immaterial soul is to say that you are persuaded of the existence of a thing of which it is impossible for you to form any true idea; it is to believe in words without attaching any sense to them; to affirm that the thing is as you claim, is the highest folly or assumption. . . .

IT IS FALSE THAT MATERIALISM CAN BE DEBASING TO THE HUMAN RACE.

Materialism, it is objected, makes of man a mere machine, which is considered very debasing to the human race. But will the human race be more honored when it can be said that man acts by the secret impulsions of a spirit, or a certain something which animates him without his knowing how? It is easy to perceive that the superiority which is given to mind over matter, or to the soul over the body, is based upon the ignorance of the nature of this soul; while we are more familiarized with matter or the body, which we imagine we know, and of which we believe we have understood the springs; but the most simple movements of our bodies are, for every thinking man, enigmas as difficult to divine as thought.

The esteem which so many people have for the spiritual substance appears to result from the impossibility they find in defining it in an intelligible way. The contempt which our metaphysicians show for matter comes from the fact that "familiarity breeds contempt." When they tell us that the soul is more excellent and noble than the body, they tell us nothing, except that what they know nothing about must be more beautiful than that of which they have some faint ideas.

THE DOGMA OF ANOTHER LIFE IS USEFUL BUT FOR THOSE WHO PROFIT BY IT AT THE EXPENSE OF THE CREDULOUS PUBLIC.

We are constantly told of the usefulness of the dogma of life hereafter. It is pretended that even if it should be a fiction, it is advantageous, because it imposes upon men and leads them to virtue. But is it true that this dogma renders men wiser and more virtuous? The nations where this fiction is established, are they remarkable for the morality of their conduct? Is not the visible world always preferred to the invisible world? If those who are charged to instruct and to govern men had themselves enlightenment and virtue, they would govern them far better by realities than by vain chimeras; but deceitful, ambitious, and corrupt, the legislators found it everywhere easier to put the nations to sleep by fables than to teach them truths; than to develop their reason; than to excite them to virtue by sensible and real motives; than to govern them in a reasonable way.

Theologians, no doubt, have had reasons for making the soul immaterial. They needed souls and chimeras to populate the imaginary regions which they have discovered in the other life. Material souls would have been subjected, like all bodies, to dissolution. Moreover, if men believe that everything is to perish with the body, the geographers of the other world would evidently lose the chance of guiding their souls to this unknown abode. They would draw no profits from the hopes with which they feast them, and from the terrors with which they take care to overwhelm them. If the future is of no real utility to the human race, it is at least of the greatest advantage to those who take upon themselves the responsibility of conducting mankind thither.

IT IS FALSE THAT THE DOGMA OF ANOTHER LIFE CAN BE CONSOLING; AND IF IT WERE, IT WOULD BE NO PROOF THAT THIS ASSERTION IS TRUE.

But, it will be said, is not the dogma of the immortality of the soul consoling for beings who often find themselves very unhappy here below? If this should be an illusion, is it not a sweet and agreeable one? Is it not a benefit for man to believe that he can live again and enjoy, sometime, the happiness which is refused to him on earth? Thus, poor mortals! you make your wishes the measure of the truth! Because you desire to live forever, and to be happier, you conclude from thence that you will live forever, and that you will be more fortunate in an unknown world than in the known world, in which you so often suffer! Consent, then, to leave without regret this world, which causes more trouble than pleasure to the majority of you. Resign yourselves to the order of destiny, which decrees that you, like all other beings, should not endure forever. But what will become of me? you ask! What you were several millions of years ago. You were then, I do not know what; resign yourselves, then, to become again in an instant, I do not know what; what you were then; return peaceably to the universal home from which you came without your knowledge into your material form, and pass by without murmuring, like all the beings which surround you!

40. Is Life After Death Possible?   C. J. Ducasse

The question whether human personality survives death is sometimes asserted to be one upon which reflection is futile. Only empirical evidence, it is said, can be relevant, since the question is purely one of fact.

But no question is purely one of fact until it is clearly understood; and this one is, on the contrary, ambiguous and replete with tacit assumptions. Until the ambiguities have been removed and the assumptions critically examined, we do not really know just what it is we want to know when we ask whether a life after death is possible. Nor, therefore, can we tell until then what bearing on this question various facts empirically known to us may have.

To clarify its meaning is chiefly what I now propose to attempt. I shall ask first why a future life is so generally desired and believed in. Then I shall state, as convincingly as I can in the time availiable, the arguments commonly advanced to prove that such a life is impossible. After that, I shall consider the logic of these arguments, and show that they quite fail to establish the impossibility. Next, the tacit but arbitrary assumption, which makes them nevertheless appear convincing, will be pointed out. And finally, I shall consider briefly a number of specific forms which a life after death might take, if there is one.

Let us turn to the first of these tasks.

Why Man Desires Life After Death

To begin with, let us note that each of us here has been alive and conscious at all times in the past which he can remember. It is true that sometimes our bodies are in deep sleep, or made inert by anesthetics or injuries. But even at such times we do not experience unconsciousness in ourselves, for to experience it would mean being conscious of being unconscious, and this is a contradiction. The only experience of unconsciousness in ourselves we ever have is, not experience of total unconsciousness, but of unconsciousness *of this or that;* as when we report: "I am not conscious of any pain," or "of any bell-sound," or "of any difference between those two colors," etc. Nor do we ever experience unconsciousness in another person, but only the fact that, sometimes, some or all of the ordinary activities of his body cease to occur. That consciousness itself is extinguished at such times is thus only a hypothesis which we construct to account for certain changes in the behavior of another person's body or to explain in him or in ourselves the eventual lack of memories relating to the given period.

Being alive and conscious is thus, with all men, a lifelong experience and habit; and conscious life is therefore something they naturally—even if tacitly—expect to continue. As J. B. Pratt has pointed out, the child takes the continuity of life for granted. It is the fact of death that has to be taught him. But when he has learned it, and the idea of a future life is then put explicitly before his mind, it seems to him the most natural thing in the world.[1]

The witnessing of death, however, is a rare experience for most of us, and, because it breaks so sharply into our habits, it forces on us the question whether the mind, which until then was manifested by the body now dead, continues shomehow to live on, or, on the contrary, has become totally extinct. This question is commonly phrased as concerning "the immortality of the soul." and immortality, strictly speaking, means survival forever. But assurance of survival for some considerable period— say a thousand, or even a hundred, years—would probably have almost as much present psychological value as would assurance of survival strictly forever. Most men would be troubled very little by the idea of extinction at so distant a time—even less troubled than is now a healthy and happy youth by the idea that he will die in fifty or sixty years. Therefore, it is

[1]J. B. Pratt, *The Religious Consciousness,* p. 225.

survival for some time, rather than survival specifically forever, that I shall alone consider.

The craving for continued existence is very widespread. Even persons who believe that death means complete extinction of the individual's consciousness often find comfort in various substitute conceptions of survival. They may, for instance, dwell on the continuity of the individual's germ plasm in his descendants. Or they find solace in the thought that, the past being indestructible, their individual life remains eternally an intrinsic part of the history of the world. Also—and more satisfying to one's craving for personal importance—there is the fact that since the acts of one's life have effects, and these in turn further effects, and so on, therefore what one has done goes on forever influencing remotely, and sometimes greatly, the course of future events.

Gratifying to one's vanity, too, is the prospect that, if the achievements of one's life have been great or even only conspicuous, or one's benefactions or evil deeds have been notable, one's name may not only be remembered by acquaintances and relatives for a little while, but may live on in recorded history. But evidently survival in any of these senses is but a consolation prize—but a thin substitute for the continuation of conscious individual life, which may not be a fact, but which most men crave nonetheless.

The roots of this craving are certain desires which death appears to frustrate. For some, the chief of these is for reunion with persons dearly loved. For others, whose lives have been wretched, it is the desire for another chance at the happiness they have missed. For others yet, it is desire for further opportunity to grow in ability, knowledge or character. Often, there is also the desire, already mentioned, to go on counting for something in the affairs of men. And again, a future life for oneself and others is often desired in order that the redressing of the many injustices of this life shall be possible. But it goes without saying that, although desires such as these are often sufficient to cause belief in a future life, they constitute no evidence at all that it is a fact.

In this connection, it may be well to point out that, although both the belief in survival and the belief in the existence of a god or gods are found in most religions, nevertheless there is no necessary connection between the two beliefs. No contradiction would be involved in supposing either that there is a God but no life after death or that there is a life after death but no God. The belief that there is a life after death may be tied to a religion, but it is no more intrinsically religious than would be a belief that there is life on the planet Mars. The after-death world, if it exists, is just another region or dimension of the universe.

But although belief in survival of death is natural and easy and has always been held in one form or another by a large majority of mankind, critical reflection quickly brings forth a number of apparently strong reasons to regard that belief as quite illusory. Let us now review them.

The Arguments Against Survival

There are, first of all, a number of facts which definitely suggest that both the existence and the nature of consciousness wholly depend on the presence of a functioning nervous system. It is pointed out, for example, that wherever consciousness is observed, it is found associated with a living and functioning body. Further, when the body dies, or the head is struck a heavy blow, or some anesthetic is administered, the familiar outward evidences of consciousness terminate, permanently or temporarily. Again, we know well that drugs of various kinds—alcohol, caffein, opium, heroin, and many others— cause specific changes at the time in the nature of a person's mental states. Also, by stimulating in appropriate ways the body's sense organs, corresponding states of consciousness—namely, the various kinds of sensations—can be caused at will. On the other hand, cutting a sensory nerve immediately eliminates a whole range of sensations.

Again, the contents of consciousness, the mental powers, or even the personality, are modified in characteristic ways when certain regions of the brain are destroyed by disease or injury or are disconnected from the rest by such an operation as prefrontal lobotomy. And that the nervous system is the indispensable basis of mind is further suggested by the fact that, in the evolutionary scale, the degree of intelligence of various species of animals keeps pace closely with the degree of development of their brain.

That continued existence of mind after death is impossible has been argued also on the basis of theoretical considerations. It has been argued also on the basis of theoretical considerations. It has been contended, for instance, that what we call states of consciousness—or more particularly, ideas, sensations, volitions, feelings, and the like—are really nothing but the minute physical or chemical events which take place in the tissues of the brain. For, it is urged, it would be absurd to suppose that an idea or a volition, if it is not itself a material thing or process, could cause material effects such as contractions of muscles.

Moreover, it is maintained that the possibility of causation of a material event by an immaterial, mental cause is ruled out *a priori* by the principle of the conservation of energy; for such causation would mean that an additional quantity of energy suddenly pops into the nervous system out of nowhere.

Another conception of consciousness, which is more often met with today than the one just mentioned, but which also implies that consciousness cannot survive death, is that "consciousness" is only the name we give to certain types of behavior, which differentiate the higher animals from all other things in nature. According to this view, to say, for example, that an animal is conscious of a difference between two stimuli means nothing more than that it responds to each by different behavior. That is, the difference of *behavior* is what consciousness of difference between the stimuli *consists in;* and is not, as is commonly assumed, only the behavioral *sign* of something mental and not public, called "consciousness that the stimuli are different."

Or again, consciousness, of the typically human sort called thought, is identified with the typically human sort of behavior called speech; and this, again not in the sense that speech *expresses* or *manifests* something different from itself, called "thought," but in the sense that speech—

whether uttered or only whispered—*is* thought itself. And obviously, if thought, or any mental activity, is thus but some mode of behavior of the living body, the mind cannot possibly survive death.

Still another difficulty confronting the hypothesis of survival becomes evident when one imagines in some detail what survival would have to include in order to satisfy the desires which cause man to crave it. It would, of course, have to include persistence not alone of consciousness, but also of personality; that is, of the individual's character, acquired knowledge, cultural skills and interests, memories, and awareness of personal identity. But even this would not be enough, for what man desires is not bare survival, but to go on living in some objective way. And this means to go on meeting new situations and, by exerting himself to deal with them, to broaden and deepen his experience and develop his latent capacities.

But it is hard to imagine this possible without a body and an environment for it, upon which to act and from which to receive impressions. And, if a body and an environment were supposed, but not material and corruptible ones, then it is paradoxical to think that, under such radically different conditions, a given personality could persist.[2]

To take a crude but telling analogy, it is past belief that, if the body of any one of us were suddenly changed into that of a shark or an octopus, and placed in the ocean, his personality could, for more than a very short time, if at all, survive intact so radical a change of environment and of bodily form.

The Arguments Examined

Such, in brief, are the chief reasons commonly advanced for holding that survival is impossible. Scrutiny of them, however, will, I think, reveal that they are not as strong as they first seem and far from strong enough to show that there can be no life after death.

Let us consider first the assertion that "thought," or "consciousness," is but another name for subvocal speech, or for some other form of behavior, or for molecular processes in the tissues of the brain. As Paulsen and others have pointed out,[3] no evidence ever is or can be offered to support that assertion, because it is in fact but a disguised proposal to make the words "thought," "feeling," "sensation," "desire," and so on, denote facts quite different from those which these words are commonly employed to denote. To say that those words are but other names for certain chemical or behavioral events is as grossly arbitrary as it would be to say that "wood" is but another name for glass, or "potato" but another name for cabbage. What thought, desire, sensation, and other mental states are like, each of us can observe directly by introspection; and what introspection reveals is that they do not in the least resemble muscular contraction, or glandular secretion, or any other known bodily events. No tampering with language

---

[2]Cf. Gardner Murphy, "Difficulties Confronting the Survival Hypothesis," *Journal of the American Society for Psychical Research* for April, 1945, p. 72; Corliss Lamont, "The Illusion of Immortality" (New York, 1935), pp. 26 ff.

[3]F. Paulsen, "Introduction to Philosophy" (trans. by F. Thilly, 2d ed.), pp. 82–83.

can alter the observable fact that thinking is one thing and muttering quite another; that the feeling called anger has no resemblace to the bodily behavior which usually goes with it; or that an act of will is not in the least like anything we find when we open the skull and examine the brain. Certain mental events are doubtless connected in some way with certain bodily events, but they are not those bodily events themselves. The connection is not identity.

This being clear, let us next consider the arguments offered to show that mental processes, although not identical with bodily processes, nevertheless depend on them. We are told, for instance, that some head injuries, or anesthetics, totally extinguish consciousness for the time being. As already pointed out, however, the strict fact is only that the usual bodily signs of consciousness are then absent. But they are also absent when a person is asleep; and, yet, at the same time, dreams, which are states of consciousness, may be occurring.

It is true that when the person concerned awakens, he often remembers his dreams, whereas the person that has been anesthetized or injured has usually no memories relating to the period of apparent blankness. But this could mean that his consciousness was, for the first time, dissociated from its ordinary channels of manifestation, as was reported of the co-conscious personalities of some of the patients of Dr. Morton Prince.[4] Moreover, it sometimes occurs that a person who has been in an accident reports lack of memories not only for the period during which his body was unresponsive but also for a period of several hours *before* the accident, during which he had given to his associates all the ordinary external signs of being conscious as usual.

But, more generally, if absence of memories relating to a given period proved unconsciousness for that period, this would force us to conclude that we were unconscious during the first few years of our lives, and indeed have been so most of the time since; for the fact is that we have no memories whatever of most of our days. That we were alive and conscious on any long past specific date is, with only a few exceptions, not something we actually remember, but only something which we infer must be true.

Evidence from Psychical Research

Another argument advanced against survival was, it will be remembered, that death must extinguish the mind, since all manifestations of it then cease. But to assert that they invariably then cease is to ignore altogether the considerable amount of evidence to the contrary, gathered over many years and carefully checked by the Society for Psychical Research. *This evidence, which is of a variety of kinds, has been reviewed by Professor Gardner Murphy in an article published in the Journal of the Society.[5] He mentions first the numerous well-authenticated cases of

[4]"My Life as a Dissociated Personality" (edited by Morton Prince; Boston: Badger).

[5]"An Outline of Survival Evidence," *Journal of the American Society for Psychical Research,* January, 1945.

*[The contention that cases of apparitions have been well authenticated is disputed by a number of scholars. See C. E. M. Hansel, *ESP: A Scientific Evaluation* (New York: Scribners, 1966) and Milbourne Christopher, *ESP, Seers & Psychics* (New York: Crowell, 1970).—Ed.]

apparition of a dead person to others as yet unaware that he had died or even been ill or in danger. The more strongly evidential cases of apparition are those in which the apparition conveys to the person who sees it specific facts until then secret. An example would be that of the apparition of a girl to her brother nine years after her death, with a conspicuous scratch on her cheek. Their mother then revealed to him that she herself had made that scratch accidentally while preparing her daughter's body for burial, but that she had then at once covered it with powder and never mentioned it to anyone.

Another famous case is that of a father whose apparition some time after death revealed to one of his sons the existence and location of an unsuspected second will, benefiting him, which was then found as indicated. Still another case would be the report by General Barter, then a subaltern in the British Army in India, of the apparition to him of a lieutenant he had not seen for two or three years. The lieutenant's apparition was riding a brown pony with black mane and tail. He was much stouter than at their last meeting, and, whereas formerly clean-shaven, he now wore a peculiar beard in the form of a fringe encircling his face. On inquiry the next day from a person who had known the lieutenant at the time he died, it turned out that he had indeed become very bloated before his death; that he had grown just such a beard while on the sick list; and that he had some time before bought and eventually ridden to death a pony of that very description.

Other striking instances are those of an apparition seen simultaneously by several persons. It is on record that an apparition of a child was perceived first by a dog, that the animal's rushing at it, loudly barking, interrupted the conversation of the several persons present in the room, thus drawing their attention to the apparition, and that the latter then moved through the room for some fifteen seconds, followed by the barking dog.[6]

Another type of empirical evidence of survival consists of communications, purporting to come from the dead, made through the persons commonly called sensitives, mediums, or automatists. Some of the most remarkable of these communications were given by the celebrated American medium, Mrs. Piper, who for many years was studied by the Society for Psychical Research, London, with the most elaborate precautions against all possibility of fraud. Twice, particularly, the evidences of identity supplied by the dead persons who purportedly were thus communicating with the living were the very kinds, and of the same precision and detail, which would ordinarily satisfy a living person of the identity of another living person with whom he was not able to communicate directly, but only through an intermediary, or by letter or telephone.[7]

[6]The documents obtained by the Society for Psychical Research concerning this case, that of the lieutenant's apparition, and that of the girl with the scratch, are reproduced in Sir Ernest Bennett's "Apparitions and Haunted Houses" (London: Faber and Faber, 1945), pp. 334–337, 28–35, and 145–150 respectively.

[7]A summary of some of the most evidential facts may be found in the book by M. Sage, entitled "Mrs. Piper and the Society for Psychical Research" (New York: Scott-Thaw Co., 1904); others of them are related in some detail in Sir Oliver Lodge's "The Survival of Man," Sec. IV (New York: Moffat, Yard and Co., 1909) and in A. M. Robbins' "Both Sides of the Veil," Part II (Boston: Sherman, French, and Co., 1909). The fullest account is in the *Proceedings of the Society for Psychical Research*.

Again, sometimes the same mark of identity of a dead person, or the same message from him, or complementary parts of one message, are obtained independently from two mediums in different parts of the world.

Of course, when facts of these kinds are recounted, as I have just done, only in abstract summary, they make little if any impression upon us. And the very word "medium" at once brings to our minds the innumerable instances of demonstrated fraud perpetrated by charlatans to extract money from the credulous bereaved. But the modes of trickery and sources of error, which immediately suggest themselves to us as easy, natural explanations of the seemingly extraordinary facts, suggest themselves just as quickly to the members of the research committees of the Society for Psychical Research. Usually, these men have had a good deal more experience than the rest of us with the tricks of conjurers and fraudulent mediums, and take against them precautions far more strict and ingenious than would occur to the average sceptic.[8]

But when, instead of stopping at summaries, one takes the trouble to study the detailed, original reports, it then becomes evident that they cannot all be just laughed off; for to accept the hypothesis of fraud or malobservation would often require more credulity than to accept the facts reported.

To *explain* those facts, however, is quite another thing. Only two hypotheses at all adequate to do so have yet been advanced. One is that the communications really come, as they purport to do, from persons who have died and have survived death. The other is the hypothesis of telepathy—that is, the supposition, itself startling enough, that the medium is able to gather information directly from the minds of others, and that this is the true source of the information communicated. To account for all the facts, however, this hypothesis has to be stretched very far, for some of them require us to suppose that the medium can tap the minds even of persons far away and quite unknown to him, and can tap even the subconscious parts of their minds.

Diverse highly ingenious attempts have been made to devise conditions that would rule out telepathy as a possible explanation of the communications received; but some of the most critical and best-documented investigators still hold that it has not yet been absolutely excluded. Hence, although some of the facts recorded by psychical research constitute, prima facie, strong empirical evidence of survival, they cannot be said to establish it beyond question. But they do show that we need to revise rather radically in some respects our ordinary ideas of what is and is not possible in nature.

Can Mental States Cause Bodily Events?

Let us now turn to another of the arguments against survival. That states of consciousness entirely depend on bodily processes, and therefore

[8]Cf. H. Carrington, "The Physcial Phenomena of Spiritualism, Fraudulent and Genuine" (Boston: Small, Maynard & Co., 1908).

cannot continue when the latter have ceased, is proved, it is argued, by the fact that various states of consciousness—in particular, the several kinds of sensations—can be caused at will by appropriately stimulating the body.

Now, it is very true that sensations and some other mental states can be so caused; but we have just as good and abundant evidence that mental states can cause various bodily events. John Laird mentions, among others, the fact that merely willing to raise one's arm normally suffices to cause it to rise; that a hungry person's mouth is caused to water by the idea of food; that feelings of rage, fear or excitement cause digestion to stop; that anxiety causes changes in the quantity and quality of the milk of a nursing mother; that certain thoughts cause tears, pallor, blushing or fainting; and so on.[9] The evidence we have that the relation is one of cause and effect is exactly the same here as where bodily processes cause mental states.

It is said, of course, that to suppose something non-physical, such as thought, to be capable of causing motion of a physical object, such as the body, is absurd. But I submit that if the heterogeneity of mind and matter makes this absurd, then it makes equally absurd the causation of mental states by stimulation of the body. Yet no absurdity is commonly found in the assertion that cutting the skin causes a feeling of pain, or that alcohol, caffein, bromides, and other drugs, cause characteristic states of consciousness. As David Hume made clear long ago, no kind of causal connection is intrinsically absurd. Anything might cause anything; and only observation can tell us what in fact can cause what.

Somewhat similar remarks would apply to the allegation that the principle of the conservation of energy precludes the possibility of causation of a physical event by a mental event. For if it does, then it equally precludes causation in the converse direction, and this, of course, would leave us totally at a loss to explain the occurrence of sensations. But, as Keeton and others have pointed out,[10] that energy is conserved is not something observation has revealed or could reveal, but only a postulate—a defining postulate for the notion of an "isolated physical system."

That is, conservation of energy is something one has to have if, but only if, one insists on conceiving the physical world as wholly self-contained, independent, isolated. And just because the metaphysics which the natural sciences tacitly assume does insist on so conceiving the physical world, this metaphysics compels them to save conservation by postulations *ad hoc* whenever dissipation of energy is what observation reveals. It postulates, for instance, that something else, which appears at such times but was not until then regarded as energy, is energy too, but it is then said, "in a different form."

Furthermore, as Broad has emphasized, all that the principle of conservation requires is that when a quantity Q of energy disappears at one place in the physical world an equal quanity of it should appear at some

[9]John Laird, "Our Minds and Their Bodies" (London, 1925), pp. 16–19.
[10]M. T. Keeton, "Some Ambiguities in the Theory of the Conservation of Energy, *Philosophy of Science*, Vol. 8, No. 3, July 1941.

other place there. And the supposition that, in some cases, what causes it to disappear here and appear there is some mental event, such perhaps as a volition, does not violate at all the supposition that energy is conserved.[11]

A word, next, on the parallelism between the degree of development of the nervous systems of various animals and the degree of their intelligence. This is alleged to prove that the latter is the product of the former. But the facts lend themselves equally well to the supposition that, on the contrary, an obscurely felt need for greater intelligence in the circumstances the animal faced was what brought about the variations which eventually resulted in a more adequate nervous organization.

In the development of the individual, at all events, it seems clear that the specific, highly complex nerve connections which become established in the brain and cerebellum of, for instance, a skilled pianist are the results of his will over many years to acquire the skill.

We must not forget in this context that there is a converse, equally consistent with the facts, for the theory, called epiphenomenalism, that mental states are related to the brain much as the halo is to the saint, that is, as effects but never themselves as causes. The converse theory, which might be called hypophenomenalism, and which is pretty well that of Schopenhauer, is that the instruments which the various mechanisms of the body constitute are the objective products of obscure cravings for the corresponding powers; and, in particular, that the organization of the nervous system is the effect and material isomorph of the variety of mental functions exercised at a given level of animal or human existence. . . .

[11]C. D. Broad, "The Mind and Its Place in Nature," pp. 103 ff.

Suggestions for Further Reading

Anthologies

Anderson, Alan Ross (ed.). *Minds and Machines.* Englewood Cliffs, N.J.: Prentice-Hall, 1964. A collection of interesting contemporary articles on the question of whether men are machines. The articles are difficult but worthwhile reading.

Flew, Anthony (ed.). *Body, Mind, and Death.* New York: Macmillan, 1966. Some important articles on the mind-body problem from Plato to the present day. The introduction and annotated bibliography are excellent.

Laslett, Peter (ed.). *The Physical Basis of the Mind.* Oxford: Basil Blackwell, 1951. A series of eight radio broadcasts given by British scientists and philosophers. The talks are very clear and interesting.

Individual Works

Adler, Mortimer, *The Difference of Man and the Difference It Makes.* Cleveland: World, 1967. The relation of the problem of the existence of mind to the issue of how men differ from animals. There is also a good discussion of whether men differ essentially from computing machines.

Beloff, John. *The Existence of Mind.* New York: Citadel, 1964. An examination of the arguments for and against dualism.

Ducasse, C. J. *Nature, Mind, and Death.* LaSalle, Ill.: Open Court, 1951. A good discussion of the mind-body problem and its relation to the question of immortality.

Hospers, John. *An Introduction to Philosophical Analysis,* 2nd ed. Englewood Cliffs, N.J.; Prentice-Hall, 1967. Chapter 20 contains a very lucid statement of the main arguments and positions.

Lamont, Corliss. *The Illusion of Immortality,* 2nd ed. London: C. A. Watts, 1952. An attack on the belief in immortality. The book is clearly written but the arguments are not very rigorous.

Taylor, Richard. *Metaphysics,* 2nd ed. Englewood-Cliffs, N.J.: Prentice-Hall, 1974. Chapters 2–4 provide a clear discussion of the mind-body controversy and a defense of materialism.

Shaffer, Jerome. *Reality, Knowledge, and Value.* New York: Random, 1971. Chapters 8–14 provide a very readable account of the main issues in the mind-body controversy.

Dictionary of the History of Ideas: Studies of Selected Pivotal Ideas. Philip P. Weiner, editor-in-chief. New York: Scribners, 1973. Substantial and clearly written essays emphasizing the historical development of topics discussed in this part. Designed to inform the nonspecialist, each essay concludes with a select bibliography.

Encyclopedia of Philosophy. Paul Edwards, editor-in-chief. New York: Macmillan, 1967. The student will find many worthwhile articles on the subject treated in this part, and excellent bibliographies.

Six:
Knowledge
and Science

Introduction

All men want knowledge, admire it, even revere it. Platitudinous as this state-ment may appear, it is certainly ambiguous. No doubt this accounts for the fact that so many people think the statement true. For knowledge as some-thing sought, as a value, suggests two quite different things: (1) knowledge as a good or end-in-itself independent of any use to which it may be put; (2) knowledge as a means necessary for the securing of some other value. We call men who dedicate themselves to the disinterested pursuit of knowledge, to the free play of ideas, "intellectuals," and "theoreticians." In this sense, philosophers traditionally have seen themselves and have been seen by oth-ers as superintellectuals, as the theoretician's theoretician. Historical legend has it that the first philosopher known to us, Thales of Miletus in Asia Minor (circa 585 B.C.), afflicted with the reproaches of his fellow citizens that he was a man of knowledge but also a poor man (and so what worth did knowledge have?), used his knowledge of nature to predict that the next crop of olives would be a bumper one. Keeping the practical results of his knowledge to himself, as would become a hardheaded businessman, Thales then bought up all of the olive presses in the region, thereby securing a monopoly for him-self. When the unusually abundant harvest of olives duly took place, Thales rented out his olive presses at a high price and so made a large amount of money by cornering the market. Philosophers could make money if they wanted to do so, he reportedly declared, but willingly were poor because they valued knowledge above everything else, even wealth. No doubt Thales would never enroll in a business school; however, if he did, he would earn all A's.

Socrates refused to accept money for his teaching, not wishing to be financially dependent on anyone. (No wonder he scorned politicians.) Socrates distrusted wealth; for of what use is wealth but to stimulate and delight the senses, so sapping one's rational energies and distracting one's reason from the pursuit of truth. Refusing to stop asking questions as the price of life and freedom, condemned to death, drinking the hemlock, dying, Socrates has become a symbol of the fearless and unrelenting search for knowledge in spite of the opposition of the ignorant majority. The god Apollo announced that Socrates was the wisest man in Greece. Aristotle, the most influential philosopher in the Western world and the first great biologist, conceived man's highest destiny, because man is the only animal possessing reason, to be the full and unimpeded functioning of that reason, sheer knowing for its own sake. In knowing, man comes closest to being a god. If there are gods, knowing would be the only activity compatible with their exalted status. Practical activities, such as healing broken legs or multiplying loaves and fishes, would be beneath divine dignity. In the seventeenth century, the philosopher Spinoza equated God and Nature. In the glow of his own "intellectual love of God," Spinoza revealed how knowing the unchanging truth for its own sake can elicit all of the traditional religious emotions of devotion to what is greater and worthier than one's self and how knowing for its own sake can satisfy the old religious yearning for triumph over devouring time and for unshakable peace. The pursuit of knowledge as the ultimate Good thus emits cosmic, religious echoes. The devotees of knowing for its own sake have moved with a priestly mien whether they wore the toga or the white laboratory coat of the modern scientist. In our day, Albert Einstein is the symbol of the philosopher-scientist, the pure Knower, the inspired theoretician—Einstein, with the massive brow, the lined face, the flowing white hair suggesting a symphony conductor or other artist, and the luminous eyes through which the universe gazes into you.

Nevertheless, the pursuit of knowledge for its own sake evokes the supreme allegiance of only a small minority of Americans and people in other countries. The great majority values knowledge as technique, as know-how, as a necessary means to other more important values, such as excitement and amusement. A little over a century ago, a Jewish prophet, who had read Greek and German philosophy, wrote that until his day philosophers had been content to understand the world but that the real task of philosophy was to change the world. Most Americans and all thoroughly modern people of other countries agree in this with Marx. The great majority of contemporary men and women prize knowledge as power, science as technology, as a kind of magic that works, a cornucopia pouring forth an unending and swelling stream of wealth with its attendant power and luxury. A small minority of intellectuals excepted, most contemporaries know very well what they want— wealth, power, luxury. For them, the problem concerns means: how to produce wealth, power, luxury, and all things dependent on them ever more abundantly. If the cost of that production means a polluted environment, chemically fouled lakes and streams, dying wildlife, and degraded human life, so far we have been willing to pay that cost. And should that cost become exorbitant, even deadly, we are sustained by the faith that the cure for the ills of technology is a bigger and better technology.

Only because science has shown itself so fecund in producing these goods and in progressively eliminating undesirable side effects has it been allowed to develop to its present level. For science, particularly on its theoretical side as a pursuit of knowledge for its own sake, was and is one of the most subversive agents ever invented by man. It is no coincidence that controversy whirls around the figures of Copernicus, Galileo, Darwin, Einstein, and Freud like black clouds rumbling with thunder and flashing with lightning. They symbolize the disturbing fact that science constantly shows us that the world and man really are quite different from what most people thought they were. Hence, for most people the value of knowing for its own sake must be subordinated to other values. Millions of Americans drive automobiles and at the same time reject the proposition that man is a mammal. The pursuit of knowledge is splendid but such an enterprise must be compatible with national security. Of course we must hold all of our theories tentatively, but we know that any average American is superior in every way to any foreigner.

No, the great majority of men and women tolerate science, admire it, or revere it only to the degree and extent that science is a necessary means to various desired nonscientific ends. When science fails to provide the necessary means, people turn to kinds of "knowledge" other than the scientific. Does scientific psychology look dubiously upon extrasensory perception, does it cast doubt on the claim that those messages really came from beloved Uncle Max dead these many years? Then, scientific psychology is dogmatic, materialistic, too narrow, at best merely partial knowledge. If astronomy won't tell us if we will be lucky or unlucky today, then astrology will. Does science seem to make it difficult to believe God exists? Then our hearts inform us that he does exist. Does science fail to prove convincingly that we should all love one another and stop hating? Then mystical insight will.

This ambiguity of knowledge as an end for its own sake and as a means to realizing other values provides the humus out of which philosophical reflection on knowledge and science grows. Hence, philospphers study and discuss what they technically call *epistemology:* the investigation of the origin, nature, methods, and limits of knowledge. Philosophers wonder about and often answer such questions as: What is the nature of knowledge? What criteria distinguish genuine knowledge from the spurious article? Does all knowledge come from sense experience, or can our reason know that certain propositions must be true independently of sense experience? What is science? What is the scientific method? Is there a scientific method? Is all knowledge worthy of the name produced by science and science alone? Is there anything that science cannot find out? More radically, can we know anything at all or is it all merely a matter of shifting opinions, what we call "knowledge" being merely those illusions, or perhaps even delusions, agreed upon?

Obviously, there is no point in trying to find out something unless we doubt we know everything. Socrates claimed to know only that he did not know. Such doubting of the truth of what is claimed to be known, called *skepticism* in philosophy, can be made systematic and pushed further than Socrates did. Some philosophers have universalized skepticism to include everything, maintaining that nothing exists; or that, if anything did exist, it cannot be known; or that, if anything can be known, it cannot be communicated. In order to be called a philosophy, skepticism must be defended with arguments. For example, consider the claim that we can never learn anything new. This conclusion follows from the proposition that we cannot find something unless we first know what we are looking for. Unless we know what we are seeking, we won't know when we have found it. Therefore, we only can find out what we already know, or we can never learn what we don't know. It is not recommended that students use this argument in answering examination questions. Add to the argument the observation that all men are born ignorant, and you generate the conclusion that no one can ever learn anything. You say you have learned many things? Then refute the argument of the skeptic, or admit that you have been deceived in thinking you've learned many things. The thoroughgoing skeptic argues that we never can be sure that any proposition is true because first we must have reliable criteria to distinguish truth from falsity. But how do we know that we can rely on the criteria? First, the criteria must be justified. But how do we know that we can rely on the justification of the criteria? First, the justification must be justified. And, before that, we must justify the justification of the justification. An infinite regress is generated—that is, no criteria separating truth from falsehood can ever be justified. There are many variations of this kind of argument. Our senses deceive us. Therefore, we appeal to our reason to tell us when our senses are or are not deceiving us. But first we must know whether or not our reason is deceiving us; and so the infinite regress opens before us. Again, some maintain we should only accept as true those propositions confirmed by observation. But why should we accept the principle that we should only accept as true those propositions confirmed by observation? And then why accept the additional principles used to justify that principle? And so on and on and on.

At first one might suppose naïvely that he could find refuge from the skeptic in Divine revelation, mystical insight, or visions induced by LSD and other drugs. However, many of the revelations, insights, and visions contradict one another, to say nothing of common sense and science; and so the question of truth and falsity cannot be evaded permanently. Therefore, the skeptic patiently waits for our inevitable return.

And yet does there not remain one great practical and theoretical refutation of a universal skepticism? That is, does not the great body of modern science and its successful application nearly everywhere in contemporary life clearly prove that we can distinguish truth from falsehood, can know, and can learn?

In the steady light of science, the arguments of the skeptic seem to fade into mere verbal ingenuity, into sleight of hand with language. Indeed, the skeptical arguments, compared with the achievements of science, do not seem worth the trouble needed to expose clearly their logical fallacies. On the contrary, they can simply be dismissed as philosophical curiosities. Or can they?

In the first reading in this part, Bertrand Russell seeks to prove that skepticism finds renewed vigor and sustenance in the very citadel of science, its supposed conqueror. One of the greatest of recent philosophers, Russell throughout a long life sought knowledge for its own sake; he yearned for the Truth, Certainty. But Russell finds that science fails to supply the indubitable truth he seeks. All science ultimately rests on sense perception, on what we see, hear, smell, taste. All sense perception is a matter of cause and effect. All causes differ from their effects because otherwise all causes would be identical with their effects. Whatever we perceive (colors, sounds, smells, and so on) is an effect. Therefore, we never perceive causes. All causes are postulates, entities inferred by inductive reasoning. But in inductive reasoning (that is, any attempt to infer a conclusion on the basis of what we perceive), the evidence is never sufficient to prove the conclusion true beyond any doubt. The conclusion of an inductive argument always *may* be false. We can never be sure which scientific theories, if any, are true. Consequently, science does not vanquish skepticism, after all. The common, everyday world we perceive—the world of blue sky, green grass and trees, houses, substantial people, beautiful sunsets—turns out to be an illusion whose cause we never can be sure we know. Modern science agrees with Shakespeare's mellow skeptic, Prospero, in *The Tempest:* "We are such stuff as dreams are made on. . . ."

René Descartes, like Bertrand Russell, sought intellectual certainty. To know something is to be unable to doubt its truth. Hence, Descartes searches for a proposition he cannot doubt. If he can discover such a proposition, he can then examine it to learn what characteristics it possesses that make it impervious to any doubt. These characteristics will provide the criteria of certainty. Once we know these criteria of certainty, we can sort out all propositions that satisfy these criteria of certainty from those that do not. Descartes discovers he cannot, in the very act of doubting, doubt the proposition that he is doubting. Since doubting is a kind of thinking, Descartes declares: I think, therefore I am *(Cogito ergo sum.)*. Why can't he doubt this? Because it is so clear and distinct to his reason. Clearness and distinctness to one's reason are the criteria of certainty. Descartes soon finds other propositions perfectly clear and distinct, such as: every event has a cause; no cause can be less perfect than its effect; and others. Mathematics, above all, is clear and distinct to our reason. Therefore, mathematical physics must be true. Whatever cannot be treated by mathematical physics must be relegated to the province of faith and subjective opinion. Notice that Descartes' criteria of certainty are clearness and distinctness to reason, not to sense perception. Descartes illustrates a form of philosophical *rationalism* that holds that there are some propositions our reason can know to be true independently of sense experience. Given our supply of propositions known to be true, we can then logically deduce still other propositions that must be true until all of human knowledge stands complete in one vast deductive system. Only in this way can the threat of universal skepticism be overcome successfully, the rationalist claims.

The issue is now focused sharply. Are there any propositions about the world which can be proved from self-evident premises by self-evident steps? The philosophical *rationalist* maintains that there are. The philosophical *empiricist* denies that there are any such propositions. W. V. Quine and J. S. Ullian defend the central tenet of empiricism, that the ultimate evidence for. our whole system of beliefs consists of our own direct observations. They deny that empiricism will necessarily result in subjectivism, as the skeptic and rationalist claim. Publicly agreed-upon observations can be obtained if we do not identify observations with events of sensation but instead ask what counts as an *observation sentence.* What makes a sentence an observation sentence is that a second witness would be bound to agree to it on the spot, provided he understands the language of the sentence. Although an observation may be made by an individual, the truth of an observation sentence is a public or intersubjective affair. Observation sentences are nearly infallible.

"The Detective as Scientist" by Irving M. Copi, an outstanding contemporary logician, provides a clear and authoritative account of the fundamental structure or logic of that process of inquiry or problem-solving we have come to call "science" or the "scientific method" and which has proven so increasingly successful since the seventeenth century. However, science is not only a problem-solving enterprise; it does more than discover heretofore unsuspected facts, test new theories, and inspire ingenious technologies. Modern science is a cultural phenomenon of enormous and growing importance. The science of any period is affected by the culture of that period and, in turn, influences the culture in which it is carried on. More and more pervasively, science influences our culture more than the latter affects it. A sign of this shift in authority is the increasing controversy over the value of science. Henry Margenau, a scientist and a philosopher, sees science as generating a new philosophy, as transforming our intellectual outlook, progressively altering all of our beliefs, including our conception of what knowledge is and how it is obtained and, above all, man's conception of his own nature.

Socrates adopted counsel far more ancient than he knew when he urged his fellow Athenians: Know thyself. Socrates argued that self-knowledge, as well as knowledge of the lack of such knowledge, was the most important kind of knowledge, more important than understanding the nature of the heavens or the causes of thunderstorms and earthquakes. For Socrates was convinced that the nature of man had significant implications for how he should live, for the nature of the good life for man. This conviction did not perish with Socrates' body; it is held by many men today. It almost seems to be one of those "Eternal Ideas" postulated by Plato, Socrates' greatest student, as does the idea of Socrates as a martyr to the truth. What is the nature of human nature? Does man possess a fixed, definite nature or not? What does modern science have to say, if anything, in answer to these old questions? And so we come to the first ancient contemporary issue: Nature versus nurture.

According to Edward O. Wilson, the new, developing science of sociobiology is the study " . . . of all aspects of social behavior up to and including the evolution of social behavior in man." In his view, human evolution by natural selection means that chance and environmental necessity produced man. We possess the brains we have because they promote the survival and multiplication of the genes that direct their assembly. He sees the human mind as a device for survival and reproduction. The mind is the effect of the brain. Biological determinism forms Wilson's main theme. Sociobiology, as Wilson envisages it, does not simply assert that there are genetically determined limits to the range of potential human behaviors, but speculates on the existence of genes for specific and variable traits in human nature, such as spite, aggression, homosexuality, altruism, and characteristic behavioral differences between men and women in Western society. He does not deny the occurrence of nongenetic learning but warns against its exaggeration. Wilson rejects all traditional religious and ideological explanations of human behavior. However, the human mind is genetically determined to create moralities, religions, and mythologies. Wilson has his own superior mythology to propose: scientific materialism with its evolutionary epic. Although scientific materialism cannot be proven true beyond question, it can be brought " . . . as close to truth as the human mind is constructed to judge the truth."

Stuart Hampshire criticizes what he holds to be a philosophic theory implicit in Wilson's sociobiology, i.e., a form of mind-body dualism which philosophers call "epiphenomenalism." This kind of dualism asserts that mind differs from body but that mental events are always and only effects of bodily events and never causes of the latter. This dualism can be broadened into one of culture (the subject of the social sciences, particularly anthropology) and physical nature or physical theory (the province of the physical sciences). The concept of sociobiology is that of a single science which would account for the workings of both sides of this dualism in the context of a more comprehensive "synthesis" of the physical and the social, the object and the agent. Hampshire contends, on the contrary, that this dualism represents two irreplaceable forms or types of inquiry about human beings which we must pursue because of our own nature as "embodied and self-conscious thinkers." One type of inquiry, characteristic of man as a disinterested observer, strives for a purely theoretical understanding of human beings as objects subject to universal laws of nature; the other type, characteristic of man as a social agent, is an attempt on the part of human beings to understand their own thinking. The pecularity of our species is to alternate between these two types of inquiry. A complete and undistorted understanding of man requires both forms of inquiry. Sociobiology, as a synthesis or "super-inquiry" embracing both of these types of inquiry, poses an impossible ideal. It ignores the diversity of cultures, of languages, of particular social contexts, of human thought which cannot be explained by universal laws, which are "universal" in that they ignore such dispersion. Phenomena can be explained only by like phenomena, by phenomena of the same logical type. Thoughts can only be understood by continuities of thought, not by the laws of motion. A contemporary, sophisticated scientific materialist, Hampshire argues, will not conceive of the relation between mind and body as a causal one, as does the epiphenomenalist, but as a parallel relation between two contexts equally real and equally necessary for an adequate understanding of ourselves.

Our second contemporary issue stars those two combatants: mysticism versus reason. Should man unreservedly submit himself to the authority of science and technology and reject all conflicting authorities? Or should man look to mysticism as a cognitive authority of weight equal or even superior to that of science? Or should mysticism be spurned as a bogus cognitive authority since contemplation, or the mystical experience, is a noncognitive experience, however valuable it may be psychologically? If many of our problems stem from science, particularly the uses to which scientific knowledge has been put by nonscientists such as politicians and generals, is not more science the cure for the ills of a partially scientific society? Or is our society suffering from an excess of science? Theodore Roszak argues that we suffer from too much science; John Passmore contends that we suffer from too little science.

In the selection entitled "Mysticism and Ecology: The Rhapsodic Intellect" the American historian Theodore Roszak, one of the leading exponents of a "counter culture" to our scientific-technological one, sees these issues brought insistently to the fore in what he terms "the subversive science" of ecology. Ecology deserves the adjective "subversive" because, in Roszak's interpretation, it radically differs from traditional science. Unlike traditional science, ecology eschews "mathematical generalization" or "materialist reductionism"; rather, this new science of the relations of organisms and their environments aims at an intuitive grasp of wholes rather than an analysis of wholes into constituent parts. It seeks to contemplate the world rather than to manipulate it. This emphasis on intuition and contemplation brings ecology closer to art, religion, and, in general, mysticism and away from rationalistic science. The lover of art, the religious devotee, and the mystical seer do not seek power over the work of art, God, and Reality so that these objects can be changed; they seek joyous union with them. Roszak holds that aesthetic, religious, or mystical contemplation provides a more satisfactory model for man to follow in adjusting to his total environment than does the imperialistic attitude of domination inherent in traditional science. The conflict between mysticism and reason resolves into a conflict of values. A power philosophy ultimately results in destruction for both the subjects and the wielders of power. The corruption and degradation of both primitive peoples and their conquerors and exploiters provides a specific symbolic instance of the havoc that is inevitably caused by any attitude placing the highest value on power and control. Roszak's main objection to traditional science appears to be that it is animated by and encourages a philosophy championing man's power and total control over his environment; that is, traditional science simply substitutes all of nature for those primitive, "natural" peoples whom nineteenth-century imperialists sought to "civilize," that is, outfit them with plug hats and brassieres and infect them with diseases.

Roszak wants to purge science or reason of its nationalist imperialist coloring, to liberate it from servitude to a philosophy of power that is prosaically utilitarian and numb to the rich diversity of human values. Traditional science must be cut down to size so that men no longer idolize it but view it more realistically and justly as merely one human value and skill among others. This healthy humbling of Big Science will be achieved by integrating it into "rhapsodic intellect." To accomplish this integration of scientific intellect into a broader, multifunctional intellect, we must rise to the insight that there are different kinds of knowledge and various ways of being rational. Traditional science gives "literal" knowledge; myth and mysticism and their expression in art and religion supply "resonant" knowledge. Literal knowledge is true belief and can be verbalized in propositional form and its fruit is power over nature and man. Resonant knowledge is direct, living personal experience, and its fruit comprehensive vision or total orientation. This comprehensive vision or total orientation is a whole or integration of diverse values. Roszak does not deny the value of literal knowledge; he does, however, deny that it is the sole value or even the supreme value. Equally, perhaps more important, are the values offered by art, religion, mysticism. What ultimately determines that literal knowledge ought *not* to be the sole or supreme value? Not appeal to literal fact, but the direct, personal experience of the rich and diverse range of human values, that is, "resonant" knowledge. This resonant knowledge is the experience of values, not a set of true beliefs that are articulable as propositions. Resonant knowledge is knowledge by acquaintance; literal knowledge is knowledge by description. In still another sense, Roszak finds science, art, religion, mysticism to be all equally forms of knowledge, to be rational; they are all means, "know-hows," skills for achieving various values, whether those of power over the environment or those of a contemplative union with the environment. The synthesis of literal and resonant knowledge constitutes the "rhapsodic intellect" whose expression is the "subversive science" of ecology.

The philosopher John Passmore considers the "resonant" knowledge that Roszak so highly prizes to be rubbish in need of quick removal. To Passmore mysticism is the great menace to the future well-being of human civilization, not reason or science and technology. The main conclusion that Passmore defends is that ecological problems, if they can be solved at all, can be solved only by "thoughtful action" and not by transforming nature into a mystery. A "science" that does not solve problems is not really a science. Passmore argues that much of the plausibility of the mystic's case depends upon a mistaken interpretation of science as intrinsically "atomistic," as incapable of grasping certain important truths pertaining to phenomena as a "whole" or system instead of the "parts" of phenomena isolated by scientific analysis. There are no significant truths that, in principle, can be discerned only by mystical insight and not by science. Science not only analyzes into parts but also studies natural systems or "wholes" and their interrelations. The conception of nature as sacred, as not to be tampered with or changed but only contemplated, sounds self-defeating coming from professed ecologists because if our ecological problems are to be solved we will have to tamper with or manipulate and control nature. We need more power over nature, not less. Ecology is a science and, therefore, its aim is to remove mysteries, not to contemplate or create them. The view of man as master of nature, so often associated with science and technology, is open to various interpretations, not all of them derogatory, by any means. There is, for example, the interpretation that man is "capable of transforming the world into a civilized state," a capacity worthy of praise rather than condemnation. That the world as it is today is too civilized hardly seems obviously true. Passmore frankly claims that certain forms of society can be defended rationally as being higher or better than other forms. Not even ecological mystics really want to return to a neolithic stage of culture—at least, not if they enjoy "literal" knowledge of the nature of neolithic culture. Industrial growth constitutes a complex problem for rational ecologists. However, it is clear that undiscriminating and wholesale condemnation and opposition to industrial growth is an inadequate response more likely to worsen our situation rather than improve it. Industrial growth has had beneficial consequences and the slowing down or halting of such growth could produce very damaging results. In this area the "question of questions" for Passmore is whether or not we can change our economic practices enough to meet the ecological challenge without increasing the power of the government to totalitarian dimensions. In any event, mystical contemplation will not eliminate pollution. Reason may not solve the problem either; but it affords the only possibility of doing so.

The Nature of Knowledge

Skepticism

41. Philosophic Doubts   Bertrand Russell

. . .Philosophy arises from an unusually obstinate attempt to arrive at real knowledge. What passes for knowledge in ordinary life suffers from three defects: it is cocksure, vague, and self-contradictory. The first step towards philosophy consists in becoming aware of these defects, not in order to rest content with a lazy scepticism, but in order to substitute an amended kind of knowledge which shall be tentative, precise, and self-consistent. There is of course another quality which we wish our knowledge to possess, namely, comprehensiveness: we wish the area of our knowledge to be as wide as possible. But this is the business of science rather than philosophy. A man does not necessarily become a better philosopher through knowing more scientific facts; it is principles and methods and general conceptions that he should learn from science if philosophy is what interests him. . . .

I mentioned a moment ago three defects in common beliefs, namely, that they are cocksure, vague, and self-contradictory. It is the business of philosophy to correct these defects so far as it can, without throwing over knowledge altogether. To be a good philosopher, a man must have a strong desire to know, combined with great caution in believing that he knows; he must also have logical acumen and the habit of exact thinking. All these, of course, are a matter of degree. Vagueness, in particular, belongs, in some degree, to all human thinking; we can diminish it indefinitely, but we can never abolish it wholly. Philosophy, accordingly, is a continuing activity, not something in which we can achieve final perfection once for all. In this respect, philosophy has suffered from its association with theology. Theological dogmas are fixed, and are regarded by the orthodox as incapable of improvement. Philosophers have too often tried to produce similarly final systems: they have not been content with the gradual approximations that satisfied men of science. In this they seem to me to have been mistaken. Philosophy should be piecemeal and provisional like science; final truth belongs to heaven, not to this world.

The three defects which I have mentioned are interconnected, and by becoming aware of any one we may be led to recognise the other two. I will illustrate all three by a few examples.

Let us take first the belief in common objects, such as tables and chairs and trees. We all feel quite sure about these in ordinary life, and yet our reasons for confidence are really very inadequate. Naïve common sense supposes that they are what they appear to be, but that is impossible, since they do not appear exactly alike to any two simultaneous observers; at least, it is impossible if the object is a single thing, the same for all observ-

From *An Outline of Philosophy* by Bertrand Russell. Reprinted by permission of George Allen & Unwin Ltd., London, 1927.

ers. If we are going to admit that the object is not what we see, we can no longer feel the same assurance that there is an object; this is the first intrusion of doubt. However, we shall speedily recover from this setback, and say that of course the object is "really" what physics says it is. Now physics says that a table or a chair is "really" an incredibly vast system of electrons and protons in rapid motion, with empty space in between. This is all very well. But the physicist, like the ordinary man, is dependent upon his senses for the existence of the physical world. If you go up to him solemnly and say, "Would you be so kind as to tell me, as a physicist, what a chair really is?" you will get a learned answer. But if you say, without preamble, "Is there a chair there?" he will say, "Of course there is; can't you see it?" To this you ought to reply in the negative. You ought to say, "No, I see certain patches of colour, but I don't see any electrons or protons, and you tell me that they are what a chair consists of." He may reply: "Yes, but a large number of electrons and protons close together look like a patch of colour." "What do you mean by 'look like'?" you will then ask. He is ready with an answer. He means that light-waves start from the electrons and protons (or, more probably, are reflected by them from a source of light), reach the eye, have a series of effects upon the rods and cones, the optic nerve, and the brain, and finally produce a sensation. But he has never seen an eye or an optic nerve or a brain, any more than he has seen a chair: he has only seen patches of colour which, he says, are what eyes "look like." That is to say, he thinks that the sensation you have when (as you think) you see a chair, has a series of causes, physical and psychological, but all of them, on his own showing, lie essentially and forever outside experience. Nevertheless, he pretends to base his science upon observation. Obviously there is here a problem for the logician, a problem belonging not to physics, but to quite another kind of study. This is a first example of the way in which the pursuit of precision destroys certainty.

The physicist believes that he infers his electrons and protons from what he perceives. But the inference is never clearly set forth in a logical chain, and, if it were, it might not look sufficiently plausible to warrant much confidence. In actual fact, the whole development from common-sense objects to electrons and protons has been governed by certain beliefs, seldom conscious, but existing in every natural man. These beliefs are not unalterable, but they grow and develop like a tree. We start by thinking that a chair is as it appears to be, and is still there when we are not looking. But we find, by a little reflection, that these two beliefs are incompatible. If the chair is to persist independently of being seen by us, it must be something other than the patch of colour we see, because this is found to depend upon conditions extraneous to the chair, such as how the light falls, whether we are wearing blue spectacles, and so on. This forces the man of science to regard the "real" chair as the cause (or an indispensable part of the cause) of our sensations when we see the chair. Thus we are committed to causation as an *a priori* belief without which we should have no reason for supposing that there is a "real" chair at all. Also, for the sake of permanence we bring in the notion of substance: the "real" chair is a substance, or collection of substances, possessed of permanence and the power to cause sensations. This metaphysical belief has operated, more or less unconsciously, in the inference from sensations to electrons and protons. The philosopher must drag such beliefs into the light of day, and see whether they still survive. Often it will be found that they die on exposure.

Let us now take up another point. The evidence for a physical law, or for any scientific law, always involves both memory and testimony. We have to rely both upon what we remember to have observed on former occasions, and on what others say they have observed. In the very beginnings of science, it may have been possible sometimes to dispense with testimony; but very soon every scientific investigation began to be built upon previously ascertained results, and thus to depend upon what others had recorded. In fact, without the corroboration of testimony we should hardly have had much confidence in the existence of physical objects. Sometimes people suffer from hallucinations, that is to say, they think they perceive physical objects, but are not confirmed in this belief by the testimony of others. In such cases, we decide that they are mistaken. It is the similarity between the perceptions of different people in similar situations that makes us feel confident of the external causation of our perceptions; but for this, whatever naïve beliefs we might have had in physical objects would have been dissipated long ago. Thus memory and testimony are essential to science. Nevertheless, each of these is open to criticism by the sceptic. Even if we succeed, more or less, in meeting his criticism, we shall, if we are rational, be left with a less complete confidence in our original beliefs than we had before. Once more, we shall become less cocksure as we become more accurate.

Both memory and testimony lead us into the sphere of psychology. I shall not at this stage discuss either beyond the point at which it is clear that there are genuine philosophical problems to be solved. I shall begin with memory.

Memory is a word which has a variety of meanings. The kind that I am concerned with at the moment is the recollection of past occurrences. This is so notoriously fallible that every experimenter makes a record of the result of his experiment at the earliest possible moment: he considers the inference from written words to past events less likely to be mistaken than the direct beliefs which constitute memory. But some time, though perhaps only a few seconds, must elapse between the observation and the making of the record, unless the record is so fragmentary that memory is needed to interpret it. Thus we do not escape from the need of trusting memory to some degree. Moreover, without memory we should not think of interpreting records as applying to the past, because we should not know that there was any past. Now, apart from arguments as to the proved fallibility of memory, there is one awkward consideration which the sceptic may urge. Remembering, which occurs now, cannot possibly— he may say—prove that what is remembered occurred at some other time, because the world might have sprung into being five minutes ago, exactly as it then was, full of acts of remembering which were entirely misleading. Opponents of Darwin, such as Edmund Gosse's father, urged a very similar argument against evolution. The world, they said, was created in 4004 B.C., complete with fossils, which were inserted to try our faith. The world was created suddenly, but was made such as it would have been if it had evolved. There is no logical impossibility about this view. And similarly there is no logical impossibility in the view that the world was created five minutes ago, complete with memories and records. This may seem an improbable hypothesis, but it is not logically refutable.

Apart from this argument, which may be thought fantastic, there are reasons of detail for being more or less distrustful of memory. It is obvious that no *direct* confirmation of a belief about a past occurrence is possible, because we cannot make the past recur. We can find confirmation of an indirect kind in the revelations of others and in contemporary records. The latter, as we have seen, involve some degree of memory, but they may involve very little, for instance when a shorthand report of a conversation or speech has been made at the time. But even then, we do not escape wholly from the need of memory extending over a longer stretch of time. Suppose a wholly imaginary conversation were produced for some criminal purpose, we should depend upon the memories of witnesses to establish its fictitious character in a law-court. And all memory which extends over a long period of time is very apt to be mistaken; this is shown by the errors invariably found in autobiographies. Any man who comes across letters which he wrote many years ago can verify the manner in which his memory has falsified past events. For these reasons, the fact that we cannot free ourselves from dependence upon memory in building up knowledge is, *prima facie*, a reason for regarding what passes for knowledge as not quite certain. . . .

Testimony raises even more awkward problems. What makes them so awkward is the fact that testimony is involved in building up our knowledge of physics, and that, conversely, physics is required in establishing the trustworthiness of testimony. Moreover, testimony raises all the problems connected with the relation of mind and matter. Some eminent philsosphers, *e.g.* Leibniz, have constructed systems according to which there would be no such thing as testimony, and yet have accepted as true many things which cannot be known without it. I do not think philosophy has quite done justice to this problem, but a few words will, I think, show its gravity.

For our purposes, we may define testimony as noises heard, or shapes seen, analogous to those which we should make if we wished to convey an assertion, and believed by the hearer or seer to be due to someone else's desire to convey an assertion. Let us take a concrete instance: I ask a policeman the way, and he says, "Fourth to the right, third to the left." That is to say, I hear these sounds, and perhaps I see what I interpret as his lips moving. I assume that he has a mind more or less like my own, and has uttered these sounds with the same intention as I should have had if I had uttered them, namely to convey information. In ordinary life, all this is not, in any proper sense, an inference; it is a belief which arises in us on the appropriate occasion. But if we are challenged, we have to substitute inference for spontaneous belief, and the more the inference is examined the more shaky it looks.

The inference that has to be made has two steps, one physical and one psychological. The physical inference is of the sort we considered a moment ago, in which we pass from a sensation to a physical occurrence.

We hear noises, and think they proceed from the ploiceman's body. We see moving shapes, and interpret them as physical motions of his lips. This inference, as we saw earlier, is in part justified by testimony; yet now we find that it has to be made before we can have reason to believe that there is any such thing as testimony. And this inference is certainly sometimes mistaken. Lunatics hear voices which other people do not hear; instead of crediting them with abnormally acute hearing, we lock them up. But if we sometimes hear sentences which have not proceeded from a body, why should this not always be the case? Perhaps our imagination has conjured up all the things that we think others have said to us. But this is part of the general problem of inferring physical objects from sensations, which, difficult as it is, is not the most difficult part of the logical puzzles concerning testimony. The most difficult part is the inference from the policeman's body to his mind. I do not mean any special insult policemen; I would say the same of politicians and even of philosophers.

The inference to the policeman's mind certainly *may* be wrong. It is clear that a maker of waxworks could make a life-like policeman and put a gramophone inside him, which would cause him periodically to tell visitors the way to the most interesting part of the exhibition at the entrance to which he would stand. They would have just the sort of evidence of his being alive that is found convincing in the case of other policemen. Descartes believed that animals have no minds, but are merely complicated automata. Eighteenth-century materialists extended this doctrine to men. But I am not now concerned with materialism; my problem is a different one. Even a materialist must admit that, when he talks, he means to convey something, that is to say, he uses words as signs, not as mere noises. It may be difficult to decide exactly what is meant by this statement, but it is clear that it means something, and that it is true of one's own remarks. The question is: Are we sure that it is true of the remarks we hear, as well as of those we make? Or are the remarks we hear perhaps just like other noises, merely meaningless disturbances of the air? The chief argument against this is analogy: the remarks we hear are so like those we make that we think they must have similar causes. But although we cannot dispense with analogy as a form of inference, it is by no means demonstrative, and not infrequently leads us astray. We are therefore left, once more, with a *prima facie* reason for uncertainty and doubt.

This question of what we mean ourselves when we speak brings me to another problem, that of introspection. Many philosophers have held that introspection gave the most indubitable of all knowledge; others have held that there is no such thing as introspection. Descartes, after trying to doubt everything, arrived at "I think, therefore I am," as a basis for the rest of knowledge. Dr. John B. Watson the behaviourist holds, on the contrary, that we do not think, but only talk. Dr. Watson, in real life, gives as much evidence of thinking as anyone does, so, if *he* is not convinced that he thinks, we are all in a bad way. At any rate, the mere existence of such an opinion as his, on the part of a competent philosopher, must suffice to show that introspection is not so certain as some people have thought. But let us examine this question a little more closely.

The difference between introspection and what we call perception of external objects seems to me to be connected, not with what is primary in our knowledge, but with what is inferred. We think, at one time, that we are seeing a chair; at another, that we are thinking about philosophy. The first we call perception of an external object; the second we call introspection. Now we have already found reason to doubt external perception, in the full-blooded sense in which common sense accepts it. . . . [W]hat is indubitable in "seeing a chair" is the occurrence of a certain pattern of colours. But this occurrence, we shall find, is connected with me just as much as with the chair; no one except myself can see exactly the pattern that I see. There is thus something subjective and private about what we take to be external perception, but this is concealed by precarious extensions into the physical world. I think introspection, on the contrary, involves precarious extensions into the mental world; shorn of these, it is not very different from external perception shorn of its extensions. To make this clear, I shall try to show what we know to be occurring when, as we say, we think about philosophy.

Suppose, as the result of introspection, you arrive at a belief which you express in the words: "I am now believing that mind is different from matter." What do you know, apart from inferences, in such a case? First of all, you must cut out the word "I": the person who believes is an inference, not part of what you know immediately. In the second place, you must be careful about the word "believing". I am not now concerned with what this word should mean in logic or theory of knowledge; I am concerned with what it can mean when used to describe a direct experience. In such a case, it would seem that it can only describe a certain kind of feeling. And as for the proposition you think you are believing, namely, "mind is different from matter", it is very difficult to say what is really occurring when you think you believe it. It may be mere words, pronounced, visualised, or in auditory or motor images. It may be images of what the words "mean," but in that case it will not be at all an accurate representation of the logical content of the proposition. You may have an image of a statue of Newton "voyaging through strange seas of thought alone," and another image of a stone rolling downhill, combined with the words "how different!" Or you may think of the difference between composing a lecture and eating your dinner. It is only when you come to expressing your thought in words that you approach logical precision.

Both in introspection and in external perception, we try to express what we know in WORDS.

We come here, as in the question of testimony, upon the social aspect of knowledge. The purpose of words is to give the same kind of publicity to thought as is claimed for physical objects. A number of people can hear a spoken word or see a written word, because each is a physical occurrence. If I say to you, "mind is different from matter," there may be only a very slight resemblance between the thought that I am trying to express and the thought which is aroused in you, but these two thoughts have just this in common, that they can be expressed by the same words. Similarly, there may be great differences between what you and I see when, as we say, we look at the same chair; nevertheless we can both express our perceptions by the same words.

A thought and a perception are thus not so very different in their own nature. If physics is true, they are different in their correlations: when I see a chair, others have more or less similar perceptions, and it is thought that these are all connected with light-waves coming from the chair, whereas, when I think a thought, others may not be thinking anything similar. But this applies also to feeling a toothache, which would not usually be regarded as a case of introspection. On the whole, therefore, there seems no reason to regard introspection as a different *kind* of knowledge from external perception. . . .

As for the *trustworthiness* of introspection, there is again a complete parallelism with the case of external perception. The actual datum, in each case, is unimpeachable, but the extensions which we make instinctively are questionable. Instead of saying, "I am believing that mind is different from matter," you ought to say, "certain images are occurring in a certain relation to each other, accompanied by a certain feeling." No words exist for describing the actual occurrence in all its particularity; all words, even proper names, are general, with the possible exception of "this," which is ambiguous. When you translate the occurrence into words, you are making generalisations and inferences, just as you are when you say "there is a chair." There is really no vital difference between the two cases. In each case, what is really a datum is unutterable, and what can be put into words involves inferences which may be mistaken.

When I say that "inferences" are involved, I am saying something not quite accurate unless carefully interpreted. In "seeing a chair," for instance, we do not first apprehend a coloured pattern, and then proceed to infer a chair: belief in the chair arises spontaneously when we see the coloured pattern. But this belief has causes not only in the present physical stimulus, but also partly in past experience, partly in reflexes. In animals, reflexes play a very large part; in human beings, experience is more important. The infant learns slowly to correlate touch and sight, and to expect others to see what he sees. The habits which are thus formed are essential to our adult notion of an object such as a chair. The perception a chair by means of sight has a physical stimulus which affects only sight directly, but stimulates ideas of solidity and so on through early experience. The inference might be called "physiological." As inference of this sort is evidence of past correlations, for instance between touch and sight, but may be mistaken in the present instance; you may, for example, mistake a reflection in a large mirror for another room. Similarly in dreams we make mistaken physiological inferences. We cannot therefore feel certainty in regard to things which are in this sense inferred, because, when we try to accept as many of them as possible, we are nevertheless compelled to reject some for the sake of self-consistency.

We arrived a moment ago at what we called "physiological inference" as an essential ingredient in the common-sense notion of a physical object. Physiological inference, in its simplest form, means this: given a stimulus S, to which, by a reflex, we react by a bodily movement R, and a stimulus S′ with a reaction R′, if the two stimuli are frequently experienced together, S will in time produce R′.[1] That is to say, the body will act as if

---

[1] *E.g.* if you hear a sharp noise and see a bright light simultaneously, often, in time, the noise without the light will cause your pupils to contract.

S' were present. Physiological inference is important in theory of knowledge, ... I have mentioned it partly to prevent it from being confused with logical inference, and partly in order to introduce the problem of *induction*, ...

Induction raises perhaps the most difficult problem in the whole theory of knowledge. Every scientific law is established by its means, and yet it is difficult to see why we should believe it to be a valid logical process. Induction, in its bare essence, consists of the argument that, because A and B have been often found together and never found apart, therefore, when A is found again, B will probably also be found. This exists first as a "physiological inference," and as such is practised by animals. When we first begin to reflect, we find ourselves making inductions in the physiological sense, for instance, expecting the food we see to have a certain kind of taste. Often we only become aware of this expectation through having it disappointed, for instance if we take salt thinking it is sugar. When mankind took to science, they tried to formulate logical principles justifying this kind of inference.... [T]hey seem to me very unsuccessful. I am convinced that induction must have validity of some kind in some degree, but the problem of showing how or why it can be valid remains unsolved. Until it is solved, the rational man will doubt whether his food will nourish him, and whether the sun will rise tomorrow. I am not a rational man in this sense, but for the moment I shall pretend to be. And even if we cannot be completely rational, we should probably all be the better for becoming somewhat more rational than we are. At the lowest estimate, it will be an interesting adventure to see whither reason will lead us.

The problems we have been raising are none of them new, but they suffice to show that our everyday views of the world and of our relations to it are unsatisfactory....

Rationalism

42. Meditations I and II   René Descartes

René Descartes (1596–1650), inventor of analytic geometry and one of the greatest of French philosophers, has affected profoundly the problems, methods, and solutions of modern philosophy.

Meditation I

Of the Things of Which We May Doubt.   Several years have now elapsed since I first became aware that I had accepted, even from my youth, many false opinions for true, and that consequently what I afterwards based on

From *The Meditations and Selections from the Principles of René Descartes,* translated by John Veitch, The Open Court Publishing Co., La Salle, Illinois, 1905.

such principles was highly doubtful; and from that time I was convinced of the necessity of undertaking once in my life to rid myself of all the opinions I had adopted, and of commencing anew the work of building from the foundation, if I desired to establish a firm and abiding super-structure in the sciences. But as this enterprise appeared to me to be one of great magnitude, I waited until I had attained an age so mature as to leave me no hope that at any stage of life more advanced I should be better able to execute my design. On this account, I have delayed so long that I should henceforth consider I was doing wrong were I still to con-sume in deliberation any of the time that now remains for action. Today, then, since I have opportunely freed my mind from all cares, and am happily disturbed by no passions, and since I am in the secure possession of leisure in a peaceable retirement, I will at length apply myself earnestly and freely to the general overthrow of all my former opinions. But, to this end, it will not be necessary for me to show that the whole of these are false—a point, perhaps, which I shall never reach; but as even now my reason convinces me that I ought not the less carefully to withhold belief from what is not entirely certain and indubitable, than from what is man-ifestly false, it will be sufficient to justify the rejection of the whole if I shall find in each some ground for doubt. Nor for this purpose will it be necessary even to deal with each belief individually, which would be truly an endless labour; but, as the removal from below of the foundation nec-essarily involves the downfall of the whole edifice, I will at once approach the criticism of the principles on which all my former beliefs rested.

All that I have, up to this moment, accepted as possessed of the highest truth and certainty, I received either from or through the senses. I observed however, that these sometimes misled us; and it is the part of prudence not to place absolute confidence in that by which we have even once been deceived.

But it may be said, perhaps that, although the senses occasionally mis-lead us respecting minute objects, and such as are so far removed from us as to be beyond the reach of close observation, there are yet many other of their informations (presentations), of the truth of which it is manifestly impossible to doubt; as for example, that I am in this place, seated by the fire, clothed in a winter dressing-gown, that I hold in my hands this piece of paper, with other intimations of the same nature. But how could I deny that I possess these hands and this body, and withal escape being classed with persons in a state of insanity, whose brains are so disordered and clouded by dark bilious vapours as to cause them pertinaciously to assert that they are monarchs when they are in the greatest poverty; or clothed in gold and purple when destitute of any covering; or that their head is made of clay, their body of glass, or that they are gourds? I should cer-tainly be not less insane than they, were I to regulate my procedure according to examples so extravagant.

Though this be true, I must nevertheless here consider that I am a man, and that, consequently, I am in the habit of sleeping, and represent-ing to myself in dreams those same things, or even sometimes others less probable, which the insane think are presented to them in their waking moments. How often have I dreamt that I was in these familiar circumstances,—that I was dressed, and occupied this place by the fire, when I was lying undressed in bed? At the present moment, however, I certainly look upon this paper with eyes wide awake; the head which I now move is not asleep; I extend this hand consciously and with express purpose, and I perceive it; the occurrences in sleep are not so distinct as all this. But I cannot forget that, at other times, I have been deceived in sleep by similar illusions; and, attentively considering those cases, I perceive so clearly that there exist no certain marks by which the state of waking can ever be distinquished from sleep, that I feel greatly astonished; and in amazement I almost persuade myself that I am now dreaming.

Let us suppose, then, that we are dreaming, and that all these particulars—namely, the opening of the eyes, the motion of the head, the forth-putting of the hands—are merely illusions; and even that we really possess neither an entire body nor hands such as we see. Nevertheless, it must be admitted at least that the objects which appear to us in sleep are, as it were, painted representations which could not have been formed unless in the likeness of realities; and, therefore, that those general objects, at all events,—namely, eyes, a head, hands, and an entire body—are not simply imaginary, but really existent. For, in truth, painters themselves, even when they study to represent sirens and satyrs by forms the most fantastic and extraordinary, cannot bestow upon them natures absolutely new, but can only make a certain medley of the members of different animals; or if they chance to imagine something so novel that nothing at all similar has ever been before, and such as is, therefore, purely fictitious and abso-lutely false, it is at least certain that the colours of which this is composed are real.

And on the same principle, although these general objects, viz. a body, eyes, a head, hands, and the like, be imaginary, we are nevertheless abso-lutely necessitated to admit the reality at least of some other objects still more simple and universal than these, of which, just as of certain real colours, all those images of things, whether true and real, or false and fantastic, that are found in our consciousness, are formed.

To this class of objects seem to belong corporeal nature in general and its extension; the figure of extended things, their quantity or magnitude, and their number, as also the place in, and the item during, which they exist, and other things of the same sort. We will not, therefore, perhaps reason illegitimately if we conclude from this that Physics, Astronomy, Medicine, and all the other sciences that have for their end the consider-ation of composite objects, are indeed of a doubtful character; but that Arithmetic, Geometry, and the other sciences of the same class, which regard merely the simplest and most general objects, and scarcely inquire whether or not these are really existent, contain somewhat that is certain and indubitable; for whether I am awake or dreaming, it remains true that two and three makes five, and that a square has but four sides; nor does it seem possible that truths so apparent can ever fall under a suspi-cion of falsity or incertitude.

Nevertheless, the belief that there is a God who is all-powerful, and who created me, such as I am, has, for a long time, obtained steady pos-session of my mind. How, then, do I know that he has not arranged that there should be neither earth, nor sky, nor any extended thing, nor figure, nor magnitude, nor place, providing at the same time, however, for the rise in me of the perceptions of all these objects, and the persuasion that these do not exist otherwise than as I perceive them? And further, as I sometimes think that others are in error respecting matters of which they believe themselves to possess a perfect knowledge, how do I know that I am not also deceived each time I add together two and three, or number the sides of a square, or form some judgement still more simple, if more simple indeed can be imagined? But perhaps Deity has not been willing that I should be thus deceived, for He is said to be supremely good. If, however, it were repugnant to the goodness of Deity to have created me subject to constant deception, it would seem likewise to be contrary to this goodness to allow me to be occasionally deceived; and yet it is clear that this is permitted. Some, indeed, might perhaps be found who would be disposed rather to deny the existence of a Being so powerful than to believe that there is nothing certain. But let us for the present refrain from opposing this opinion, and grant that all which is here said of a Deity is fabulous; nevertheless in whatever way it be supposed that I reached the state in which I exist, whether by fate, or chance, or by an endless series of antecedents and consequents, or by any other means, it is clear (since to be deceived and to err is a certain defect) that the probability of my being so imperfect as to be the constant victim of deception, will be increased exactly in proportion as the power possessed by the cause, to which they assign my origin, is lessened. To these reasonings I have assuredly nothing to reply, but am constrained at last to avow that there is nothing of all that I formerly believed to be true of which it is impossible to doubt, and that not through thoughtlessness or levity, but from cogent and maturely considered reasons; so that henceforward, if I desire to discover anything certain, I ought not the less carefully to refrain from assenting to those same opinions than to what might be shown to be manifestly false.

But it is not sufficient to have made these observations; care must be taken likewise to keep them in remembrance. For those old and customary opinions perpetually recur—long and familiar usage giving them the right to occupying my mind, even almost against my will, and subduing my belief; nor will I lose the habit of deferring to them and confiding in them so long as I shall consider them to be what in truth they are, viz., opinions to some extent doubtful, as I have already shown, but still highly probable, and such as it is much more reasonable to believe than deny. It is for this reason I am persuaded that I shall not be doing wrong, if, taking an opposite judgment of deliberate design, I become my own deceiver, by supposing, for a time, that all those opinions are entirely false and imaginary, until at length, having thus balanced my old by my new prejudices, my judgment shall no longer be turned aside by perverted usage from the path that may conduct to the perception of truth. For I am assured that, meanwhile, there will arise neither peril nor error from this course, and that I cannot for the present yield too much distrust, since the end I now seek is not action but knowledge.

I will suppose, then, not that Deity, who is sovereignly good and the fountain of truth, but that some malignant demon, who is at once exceedingly potent and deceitful, has employed all his artifice to deceive me; I will suppose that the sky, the air, the earth, colours, figures, sounds, and all external things, are nothing better than the illusions of dreams, by means of which this being has laid snares for my credulity; I will consider myself as without hands, eyes, flesh, blood, or any of the senses, and as falsely believing that I am possessed of these; I will continue resolutely fixed in this belief, and if indeed by this means it be not in my power to arrive at the knowledge of truth, I shall at least do what is in my power, viz., suspend my judgment, and guard with settled purpose against giving my assent to what is false, and being imposed upon by this deceiver, whatever be his power and artifice.

But this undertaking is arduous, and a certain indolence insensibly leads me back to my ordinary course of life; and just as the captive, who, perchance, was enjoying in his dreams an imaginary liberty; when he begins to suspect that it is but a vision, dreads awakening, and conspires with the agreeable illusions that the deception may be prolonged; so I, of my own accord, fall back into the train of my former beliefs, and fear to arouse myself from my slumber, lest the time of laborious wakefulness that would succeed this quiet rest, in place of bringing any light of day, should prove inadequate to dispel the darkness that will arise from the difficulties that have now been raised.

Meditation II

Of the Nature of the Human Mind; and That It Is More Easily Known Than the Body.   The Meditation of yesterday has filled my mind with so many doubts, that it is no longer in my power to forget them. Nor do I see, meanwhile, any principle on which they can be resolved; and, just as if I had fallen all of a sudden into very deep water, I am so greatly disconcerted as to be unable either to plant my feet firmly on the bottom or sustain myself by swimming on the surface, I will, nevertheless, make an effort, and try anew the same path on which I had entered yesterday, that is, proceed by casting aside all that admits of the slightest doubt, not less than if I had discovered it to be absolutely false; and I will continue always in this track until I shall find something that is certain, or at least, if I can do nothing more, until I shall know with certainty that there is nothing certain. Archimedes, that he might transport the entire globe from the place it occupied to another, demanded only a point that was firm and immovable; so also, I shall be entitled to entertain the highest expectations, if I am fortunate enough to discover only one thing that is certain and indubitable.

I suppose, accordingly, that all the things which I see are false (fictitious); I believe that none of those objects which my fallacious memory represents ever existed; I suppose that I possess no senses; I believe that body, figure, extension, motion, and place are merely fictions of my mind. What is there, then, that can be esteemed true? Perhaps this only, that there is absolutely nothing certain.

But how do I know that there is not something different altogether from the objects I have now enumerated, of which it is impossible to entertain the slightest doubt? Is there not a God, or some being, by whatever name I may designate him, who causes these thoughts to arise in my mind? But why suppose such a being, for it may be I myself am capable of producing them? Am I, then, at least not something? But I before denied that I possessed senses or a body; I hesitate, however, for what follows from that? Am I so dependent on the body and the senses that without these I cannot exist? But I had the persuasion that there was absolutely nothing in the world, that there was no sky and no earth, neither minds nor bodies; was I not, therefore, at the same time, persuaded that I did not exist? Far from it; I assuredly existed, since I was persuaded. But there is I know not what being, who is possessed at once of the highest power and the deepest cunning, who is constantly employing all his ingenuity in deceiving me. Doubtless, then, I exist, since I am deceived; and, let him deceive me as he may, he can never bring it about that I am nothing, so long as I shall be conscious that I am something. So that it must, in fine, be maintained, all things being maturely and carefully considered, that this proposition, I am, I exist, is necessarily true each time it is expressed by me, or conceived in my mind.

But I do not yet know with sufficient clearness what I am, though assured that I am; and hence, in the next place, I must take care, lest perchance I inconsiderately substitute some other object in room of what is properly myself, and thus wander from truth, even in that knowledge which I hold to be of all others the most certain and evident. For this reason, I will now consider anew what I formerly believed myself to be, before I entered on the present train of thought; and of my previous opinion I will retrench all that can in the least be invalidated by the grounds of doubt I have adduced, in order that there may at length remain nothing but what is certain and indubitable. What then did I formerly think I was? Undoubtedly I judged that I was a man. But what is a man? Shall I say a rational animal? Assuredly not; for it would be necessary forthwith to inquire into what is meant by animal, and what by rational, and thus, from a single question, I should insensibly glide into others, and these more difficult than the first; nor do I now possess enough of leisure to warrant me in wasting my time amid subtleties of this sort. I prefer here to attend to the thoughts that sprung up of themselves in my mind, and were inspired by my own nature alone, when I applied myself to the consideration of what I was. In the first place, then, I thought that I possessed a countenance, hands, arms, and all the fabric of members that appears in a corpse, and which I called by the name of body. It further occurred to me that I was nourished, that I walked, perceived, and thought, and all those actions I referred to the soul; but what the soul itself was I either did not stay to consider, or, if I did, I imagined that it was something extremely rare and subtile, like wind, or flame, or ether, spread through my grosser parts. As regarded the body, I did not even doubt of its nature, but thought I distinctly knew it, and if I had wished to describe it according to the notions I then entertained, I should have explained myself in this manner: By body I understand all that can be terminated by a certain figure; that can be comprised in a certain place, and so fill a certain space as therefrom to exclude every other body; that can be perceived either by touch, sight, hearing, taste, or smell; that can be moved in different ways, not indeed of itself, but by something foreign to it by which it is touched and from which it receives the impression; for the power of self-motion, as likewise that of perceiving and thinking, I held as by no means pertaining to the nature of body; on the contrary, I was somewhat astonished to find such faculties existing in some bodies.

But as to myself, what can I now say that I am, since I suppose there exists an extremely powerful, and, if I may so speak, malignant being, whose whole endeavours are directed towards deceiving me? Can I affirm that I possess any one of all those attributes of which I have lately spoken as belonging to the nature of body? After attentively considering them in my own mind, I find none of them that can properly be said to belong to myself. To recount them were idle and tedious. Let us pass, then, to the attributes of the soul. The first mentioned were the powers of nutrition and walking; but, if it be true that I have no body, it is true likewise that I am capable neither of walking nor of being nourished. Perception is another attribute of the soul; but perception too is impossible without the body: besides, I have frequently during sleep, believed that I perceived objects which I afterwards observed I did not in reality perceive. Thinking is another attribute of the soul; and here I discover what properly belongs to myself. This alone is inseparable from me. I am—I exist: this is certain; but how often? As often as I think; for perhaps it would even happen, if I should wholly cease to think, that I should at the same time altogether cease to be. I now admit nothing that is not necessarily true: I am there-fore, precisely speaking, only a thinking thing, that is, a mind, under-standing, or reason,—terms whose signification was before unknown to me. I am, however, a real thing, and really existent; but what thing? The answer was, a thinking thing. The question now arises, am I aught besides? I will stimulate my imagination with a view to discover whether I am not still something more than a thinking being. Now it is plain I am not the assemblage of members called the human body; I am not a thin and penetrating air diffused through all these members, or wind, or flame, or vapour, or breath, or any of all the things I can imagine; for I supposed that all these were not, and, without changing the supposition, I find that I still feel assured of my existence.

But it is true, perhaps, that those very things which I suppose to be nonexistent, because they are unknown to me, are not in truth different from myself whom I know. This is a point I cannot determine, and do not now enter into any dispute regarding it. I can only judge of things that are known to me: I am conscious that I exist, and I who know that I exist inquire into what I am. It is, however, perfectly certain that the knowledge of my existence, thus precisely taken, is not dependent on things, the existence of which is as yet unknown to me: and consequently it is not dependent on any of the things I can feign in imagination. Moreover, the phrase itself, I frame an image, reminds me of my error; for I should in truth frame one if I were to imagine myself to be anything, since to imag-ine is nothing more than to contemplate the figure or image of a corporeal thing; but I already know that I exist, and that it is possible at the same time that all those images, and in general all that relates to the nature of body, are merely dreams or chimeras. From this I discover that it is not more reasonable to say, I will excite my imagination that I may know more distinctly what I am, than to express myself as follows: I am now awake, and perceive something real; but because my perception is not sufficiently clear, I will of express purpose go to sleep that my dreams may represent to me the object of my perception with more truth and clearness. And, therefore, I know that nothing of all that I can embrace in imagination belongs to the knowledge which I have of myself, and that there is need to recall with the utmost care the mind from this mode of thinking, that it may be able to know its own nature with perfect distinctness.

But what, then, am I? A thinking thing, it has been said. But what is a thinking thing? It is a thing that doubts, understands, conceives, affirms, denies, wills, refuses, that imagines also, and perceives. Assuredly it is not little, if all these properties belong to my nature. But why should they not belong to it? Am I not that very being who now doubts of almost everything; who, for all that, understands and conceives certain things; who affirms one alone as true, and denies the others; who desires to know more of them, and does not wish to be deceived; who imagines many things, sometimes even despite his will; and is likewise percipient of many, as if through the medium of the senses. Is there nothing of all this as true as that I am, even although I should be always dreaming, and although he who gave me being employed all his ingenuity to deceive me? Is there also any one of these attributes that can be properly distinguished from my thought, or that can be said to be separate from myself? For it is of itself so evident that it is I who doubt, I who understand, and I who desire, that it is here unnecessary to add anything by way of rendering it more clear. And I am as certainly the same being who imagines; for, although it may be (as I before supposed) that nothing I imagine is true, still the power of imagination does not cease really to exist in me and to form part of my thought. In fine, I am the same being who perceives, that is, who apprehends certain objects as by the organs of sense, since, in truth, I see light, hear a noise, and feel heat. But it will be said that these presentations are false, and that I am dreaming. Let it be so. At all events it is certain that I seem to see light, hear a noise, and feel heat; this cannot be false, and this is what in me is properly called perceiving, which is nothing else than thinking. From this I begin to know what I am with somewhat greater clearness and distinctness than heretofore.

But, nevertheless, it still seems to me, and I cannot help believing, that corporeal things, whose images are formed by thought, which fall under the senses, and are examined by the same, are known with much greater distinctness than that I know not what part of myself which is not imaginable; although, in truth, it may seem strange to say that I know and comprehend with greater distinctness things whose existence appears to me doubtful, that are unknown, and do not belong to me, than others of whose reality I am persuaded, that are known to me, and appertain to my proper nature; in a word, than myself. But I see clearly what is the state of the case. My mind is apt to wander, and will not yet submit to be restrained within the limits of truth. Let us therefore leave the mind to itself once more, and, according to it every kind of liberty, permit it to consider the objects that appear to it from without, in order that, having afterwards withdrawn it from these gently and opportunely, and fixed it on the consideration of its being and the properties it finds in itself, it may then be the more easily controlled.

Let us now accordingly consider the objects that are commonly thought to be the most easily, and likewise the most distinctly known, viz., the bodies we touch and see; not, indeed, bodies in general, for these general notions are usually somewhat more confused, but one body in particular. Take, for example, this piece of wax; it is quite fresh, having been but recently taken from the bee-hive; it has not yet lost the sweetness of the honey it contained; it still retains somewhat of the odour of the flowers from which it was gathered; its colour, figure, size, are apparent to the sight, it is hard, cold, easily handled; and sounds when struck upon with the finger. In fine, all that contributes to make a body as distinctly known as possible, is found in the one before us. But, while I am speaking, let it be placed near the fire—what remained of the taste exhales, the smell evaporates, the colour changes, its figure is destroyed, its size increases, it becomes liquid, it grows hot, it can hardly be handled, and, although struck upon, it emits no sound. Does the same wax still remain after this change? It must be admitted that it does remain; no one doubts it, or judges otherwise. What, then, was it I knew with so much distinctness in the piece of wax? Assuredly, it could be nothing of all that I observed by means of the senses, since all the things that fell under taste, smell, sight, touch, and hearing are changed, and yet the same wax remains. It was perhaps what I now think, viz., that this wax was neither the sweetness of honey, the pleasant odour of flowers, the whiteness, the figure, nor the sound, but only a body that a little before appeared to me conspicuous under these forms, and which is now perceived under others. But, to speak precisely, what is it that I imagine when I think of it in this way? Let it be attentively considered, and, retrenching all that does not belong to the wax, let us see what remains. There certainly remains nothing, except something extended, flexible, and movable. But what is meant by flexible and movable? Is it not that I imagine that the piece of wax, being round, is capable of becoming square, or of passing from a square into a triangular figure? Assuredly such is not the case, because I conceive that it admits of an infinity of similar changes; and I am, moreover, unable to compass this infinity by imagination, and consequently this conception which I have of the wax is not the product of the faculty of imagination. But what now is this extension? Is it not also unknown? For it becomes greater when the wax is melted, greater when it is boiled, and greater still when the heat increases; and I should not conceive clearly and according to truth, the wax as it is, if I did not suppose that the piece we are considering admitted even of a wider variety of extension that I ever imagined. I must, therefore, admit that I cannot even comprehend by imagination what the piece of wax is, and that it is the mind alone which perceives it. I speak of one piece in particular; for, as to wax in general, this is still more evident. But what is the piece of wax that can be perceived only by the understanding or mind? It is certainly the same which I see, touch, imagine; and, in fine, it is the same which, from the beginning, I believed it to be. But (and this it is of moment to observe) the perception of it is neither an act of sight, of touch, nor of imagination, and never was either of these, though it might formerly seem so, but is simply an intuition of the mind, which may be imperfect and confused, as it formerly was, or very clear and distinct, as it is at present, according as the attention is more or less directed to the elements which it contains, and of which it is composed.

But, meanwhile, I feel greatly astonished when I observe the weakness of my mind, and its proneness to error. For although, without at all giving expression to what I think, I consider all this in my own mind, words yet occasionally impede my progress, and I am almost led into error by the terms of ordinary language. We say, for example, that we see the same wax when it is before us, and not that we judge it to be the same from its retaining the same colour and figure: whence I should forthwith be disposed to conclude that the wax is known by the act of sight, and not by the intuition of the mind alone, were it not for the analogous instance of human beings passing on in the street below, as observed from a window. In this case I do not fail to say that I see the men themselves, just as I say that I see the wax; and yet what do I see from the window beyond hats and cloaks that might cover artificial machines, whose motions might be determined by springs? But I judge that there are human beings from these appearances, and thus I comprehend, by the faculty of judgment alone which is in the mind, what I believed I saw with my eyes.

The man who makes it his aim to rise to knowledge superior to the common, ought to be ashamed to seek occasions of doubting from the vulgar forms of speech: instead, therefore, of doing this, I shall proceed with the matter in hand, and inquire whether I had a clearer and more perfect perception of the piece of wax when I first saw it, and when I thought I knew it by means of the external sense itself, or, at all events, by the common sense, as it is called, that is, by the imaginative faculty; or whether I rather apprehend it more clearly at present, after having examined with greater care, both what it is, and in what way it can be known. It would certainly be ridiculous to entertain any doubt on this point. For what, in that first perception, was there distinct? What did I perceive which any animal might not have perceived? But when I distinguish the wax from its exterior forms, and when, as if I had stripped it of its vestments, I consider it quite naked, it is certain, although some error may still be found in my judgment, that I cannot, nevertheless, thus apprehend it without possessing a human mind.

But, finally, what shall I say of the mind itself, that is, of myself? For as yet I do not admit that I am anything but mind. What, then! I who seem to possess so distinct an apprehension of the piece of wax,—do I not know myself, both with greater truth and certitude, and also much more distinctly and clearly? For if I judge that the wax exists because I see it, it assuredly follows, much more evidently, that I myself am or exist, for the same reason: for it is possible that what I see may not in truth be wax, and that I do not even possess eyes with which to see anything; but it cannot be that when I see, or, which comes to the same thing, when I think I see, I myself who think am nothing. So likewise, if I judge that the wax exists because I touch it, it will still also follow that I am; and if I determine that my imagination, or any other cause, whatever it be, persuades me of the existence of the wax, I will still draw the same conclusion. And what is here remarked of the piece of wax, is applicable to all the other things that are external to me. And further, if the notion or perception of wax appeared to me more precise and distinct, after that not only sight and touch, but many other causes besides, rendered it manifest to my apprehension, with how much greater distinctness must I not know myself, since all the reasons that contribute to the knowledge of the nature of wax, or of any body whatever, manifest still better the nature of my mind? And there are besides so many other things in the mind itself that contribute to the illustration of its nature, that those dependent on the body, to which I have here referred, scarcely merit to be taken into account.

But, in conclusion, I find I have insensibly reverted to the point I desired; for, since it is now manifest to me that bodies themselves are not properly perceived by the senses nor by the faculty of imagination, but by the intellect alone; and since they are not perceived because they are seen and touched, but only because they are understood or rightly comprehended by thought, I readily discover that there is nothing more easily or clearly apprehended than my own mind. But because it is difficult to rid one's self so promptly of an opinion to which one has been long accustomed, it will be desirable to tarry for some time at this stage, that, by long continued meditation, I may more deeply impress upon my memory this new knowledge.

Empiricism

43. Observation   Willard Van Orman Quine and Joseph Silbert Ullian

Willard Van Orman Quine (1908–   ) is Edgar Pierce Professor of Philosophy at Harvard University. His fourteen books include *Word and Object, Methods of Logic,* and *The Roots of Reference.* Joseph Silbert Ullian (1930–   ) is professor of Philosophy at Washington University, where he has taught since 1965. He has written extensively on topics in philosophy, logic, and computer science.

Some of us are more easily satisfied than others. Each of us is more easily satisfied on some issues than on others: more easily satisfied on the issues that matter less. But there is a limit: when we get down to our own direct observation, there is nowhere deeper to look. Someone else's report, even of direct observation, has not quite this finality for us. We may have good reason to trust such a report, but in trusting it we are making an inference from other evidence, other observations of our own. What we are directly observing is rather the report itself, the spoken or written words. We have then to draw on past linguistic experience of the veracity of this or other speakers. A memory or even a written record of our own direct observation is still at some remove from the original observation itself, though we can seldom ask better. What we are directly observing in the case of our own written record is, like our friend's report, only inferentially related to our original observation; though in our own case we have the best of reasons to abide by the inference.

Thus the ultimate evidence that our whole system of beliefs has to answer up to consists strictly of our own direct observations—including our observations of our notes and of other people's reports. Naturally we leave many points unchecked. Lore is handed down from our forebears. Such actual evidence as any one of us does have, however, is in the end the direct evidence of the senses. Likewise such evidence as there is and ever was, collectively, for the whole overwhelming edifice of science, has consisted only in the direct evidence of many peoples' senses.

The world with its quarks and chromosomes, its distant lands and spiral nebulae, is like a vast computer in a black box, forever sealed except for its input and output registers. These we directly observe, and in the light of them we speculate on the structure of the machine, the universe. Thus it is that we think up the quarks and chromosomes, the distant lands and the nebulae; they would account for the observable data. When an observation turns out expectedly, we may try modifying our theory of that structure at one or another point.

When an observation shows that a system of beliefs must be overhauled, it leaves us to choose which of those interlocking beliefs to revise; this important fact has come up repeatedly. The beliefs face the tribunal of observation not singly but in a body. But note now that the observation sentence itself, the sentence that reports or predicts a present or imminent observation, is peculiar on this score. It does face the tribunal singly, in the usual case, and simply stands or falls with the observation that it reports or predicts. And, standing or falling, it sustains or lets down the system of beliefs that implied it.

What are observations? Some philosophers have taken them to be sensory events: the occurrence of smells, feels, noises, color patches. This way lies frustration. What we ordinarily notice and testify to are rather the objects and events out in the world. It is to these that our very language is geared, because language is a social institution, learned from other people who share the scene to which the words refer. Observation sentences, like theoretical sentences, are for the most part sentences about external objects. This is why they can enter into logical relations with scientific theory, confirming or refuting it.

In an early page we asked what sorts of things were the objects of belief. Then we gratefully dropped that question, noticing that we could instead talk of sentences and of believing them true. Now a similar maneuver conduces to clarity in dealing with the notion of observation: let us ask no longer what counts as an observation, but turn rather to language and ask what counts as an observation sentence.

What makes a sentence an observation sentence is not what sort of event or situation it describes, but how it describes it. Thus, I may see the dean of the law school mail a birthday check to his daughter in Belgium. Saying so in these terms does not qualify as an observation sentence. If on the other hand I describe that same event by saying that I saw a stout man with a broad face, a gray moustache, rimless spectacles, a Homburg hat, and a walking stick, putting a small white flat flimsy object into the slot of a mailbox, this is an observation sentence. What makes it an observation sentence is that any second witness would be bound to agree with me on all points then and there, granted merely an understanding of my language. The witness would not be bound to agree that it was the dean, whom he or she might not know, nor expected to know anything about the check or a daughter in Belgium.

In short, an observation sentence is something that we can depend on other witnesses to agree to at the time of the event or situation described. A witness might of course forget and give divergent testimony later, or might fail to notice a feature at the time until it was pointed out. But the witness can check and assent if asked at the time. The reason for such agreement is that the terms used in an observation sentence are terms that we can all apply to their objects on sight: terms like "mailbox," "stout man," "gray moustache," "rimless spectacles," "Homburg hat," "walking stick." They are terms unlike "dean of the law school," "birthday," "daughter in Belgium"; for in applying these terms to the present situation we depend on past experiences that few have been privileged to share.

"The cat is on the mat" qualifies as an observation sentence. "My cat is on the mat" does not, on our definition, since another witness might not know whose cat it was. Even our observation sentence may sometimes be truthfully uttered without reporting a present observation; thus "The cat is on the mat" may sometimes express a belief based on earlier observation or mere hearsay. In calling it an *observation sentence* we mean that it is a form of words that *can* be used to report a present event or situation, and that other witnesses can then be counted on to concur if queried at the time.

It is easy to see why some of our sentences are bound to be of this kind, if we reflect on how we learn language. Some terms, and short sentences containing them, are learned in the sensible presence of something that the term describes, or in the circumstances that the sentence reports. This way of learning expressions is what philosophers call *ostensive*. It is a simple matter of learning to associate the heard words with things simultaneously observed—a matter, as modern psychologists put it, of conditioning. Thus, we may venture to volunteer or assent to the word "yellow" in the presence of something yellow, on hearing others do so. This way of responding will be reinforced, as psychologists say, by social approval or successful communication, and so become habitual. The part of language that we learn first must be learned ostensively, thus not depending on other language-learning.

Further vocabulary is acquired afterward by processes that depend on prior acquisitions. Learning by ostension depends on no prior acquisitions. By ostension we learn to use and react to observation sentences.

Typical observation sentences are about bodies: "This is a table," "This table is square," "The cat is on the mat." Always the situation that makes an observation sentence true will be a situation that is intersubjectively observable; that is, it will be the sort of situation to which multiple witnesses could, if present, attest. Further, it will be a situation that the witnesses can witness one another's witnessing of. These crucial traits are assured by the distinctive nature of ostension. The learner of the language has to be able to observe the relevant situation simultaneously with hearing the veteran speaker affirm the sentence, and must also be able to observe that the speaker's affirming of the sentence is accompanied by observations of that same situation. Correspondingly, the veteran speaker who ventures to judge the learner's performance has to be able to observe that the learner, when affirming the sentence, is observing the appropriate situation.

There are two traits of observation sentences which, when considered side by side, invite a philosophical question. The distinguishing feature of observation sentences is that they can be checked on the spot. Yet these sentences are commonly about enduring bodies—cats, mats, tables. How is this possible? That there are enduring bodies at all, behind the passing show of sensory appearance, is a point of physical theory—a rudimentary point, but still something beyond the observable present occasion. How then can a sentence about bodies be at the same time an observation sentence, for which the whole occasion for affirmation is the observable present?

This puzzle comes of viewing the matter from the wrong end. The special virtue of observation sentences is that we can, in principle, learn them by ostension as wholes, keyed as wholes to the appropriate observable occasions, before ever learning to link the component words to enduring bodies. "The cat is on the mat" can be learned ostensively as a unitary string of syllables in association with a certain range of possible scenes. All of us necessarily learned some observation sentences thus. Then, as we gradually caught on to the theory of enduring bodies, we came to treat some of the component words as referring to bodies. Learning by ostension, as a trained animal might, to associate whole observation sentences with appropriate patterns of stimulation, is a first indispensable step toward learning physical theory. We get on into the theory afterward, bit by bit, as we learn to dismember the observation sentences and make further use of their component words. It is to this primary, ostensive learning of observation sentences as wholes that physical theory itself owes its vital continuing connection with sensory evidence.

Probably none of us in fact learned "The cat is on the mat" outright by ostension, but we could have. A likelier example is "(This is a) ball," or "Yellow." An important trait of language is that people learn it by different routes, and no record of the route is preserved in the words learned. What makes a sentence an observation sentence is not that it *was* learned ostensively but that it is of a sort that *could* have been. And what sort is that? We already said: it is a sentence whose whole occasion of affirmation, nearly enough, is the intersubjectively observable present occasion. This is a straightforward trait attaching to some sentences and not others. And it is a trait that is socially traceable, for what it comes to is just that all speakers of the language, nearly enough, will assent to the sentence under the same concurrent stimulations. "The table is square" and "The cat is on the mat" will pass this test and so qualify as observation sentences. "This is a bachelor" will not qualify as an observation sentence, since one of two tested speakers may happen to know that the man pointed to is a bachelor while the other does not.

Ostension accounts for our acquisition of only a modest part of our language. A major source is an elaborate and largely unconscious process of abstraction and generalization, working partly from what we have previously learned by ostension and depending heavily on imitation of observed use. We guess the force of one sentence by noting its use in relation to other sentences; we grasp the use of a word by abstraction from sentences in which it turns up; and we learn how to build new sentences by copying the structure observed in old ones. There is much that could be said, and much more still to be learned, about these methods.

A less mysterious form that such derivative acquisition can take, though not the most frequent, is definition. The simplest form of definition, in turn, is that in which the new expression is equated outright to some expression that is presumed to have been already intelligible. Thus, if we suppose the words "parent," "brother," "married," and "man" already to have been somehow acquired, we might explain "uncle" and "bachelor" by equating them to "parent's brother" and "unmarried man." Other definitions are contextual; in these the new expression is not equated to anything outright, but systematic instructions are given for translating all desired sentences containing the expression. For instance, we might define "brother," not by formulating any direct substitute for the word by itself, but by systematically explaining all sentences in which the word occurs followed by "of." This we could do by translating "brother of x" as "male other than x whose parents are the parents of x." Or again, we might define the connective "if and only if," not outright, but by systematically explaining all the compound sentences that are obtained by putting "if and only if" between sentences. We simply explain "p if and only if q" as "if p then q and if q then p."

Observation sentences are the bottom edge of language, where it touches experience: where speech is conditioned to stimulation. It is ultimately through them that language in general gains its meaning, its bearing on reality. This is why it is they that convey the basic evidence for all belief, all scientific theory. They play this fundamental role not only when someone is checking over his or her beliefs after a prediction has gone wrong, but equally when someone is marshaling evidence for a belief that has been challenged by a colleague. And it is here that the social trait just now attributed to observation sentences is crucial—that all speakers assent to such a sentence under the same stimulations. As dissident theorists converge toward observation sentences, they converge to agreement.

An observation may be made by an individual; but, as we have emphasized, the truth of the observation sentence is an intersubjective matter. Here a favorite old irrationalist doctrine finds both its seductiveness and its rebuttal. The hoary view contends that truth is relative to believer; there's truth for me and truth for you, and their reconciliation is generally neither possible nor desirable. Now the variable ownership of acts of observation might be cited in support of this doctrine. For haven't we said that observations are the ultimate basis for belief systems? And can't we be expected, you and I, to make different observations? Maybe so; but which observation sentences are *true* will not thus depend on either of us, nor on any other observer. The firmness of our respective grounds for accepting a given observation sentence may vary, and so may our appraisal of that sentence; but its truth cannot. Happily, we need not acquiesce in the ultimacy of disagreement in order to appreciate its sources. Intersubjective conflict, to be sure, is unlike intrasubjective conflict in one important way: the former, but not the latter, may be recognized as such without thereby gaining impetus for giving way. But where your beliefs and mine are mutually inconsistent we cannot both be right, any more than I alone can be right in each of several incompatible beliefs.

So we all contribute, with our respective observations, to the knowledge that we all share. We find here an element that at once makes science hard and makes it possible. It is hard because it must build a coherent system from the diverse evidence gleaned and reported by people of different times, places, cultures, and interests; it is possible because there is thus so much to draw on.

Are observation sentences infallible? Nearly, if we set aside those offered disingenuously and those uttered by speakers who have not quite learned the language. It would strain the very meaning of the words, in such sentences, to suppose any appreciable fallibility; for the words are themselves acquired through the association of observation sentences with the observable circumstances of their utterance.

A trace of fallibility, indeed, there is. Normally, observation is the tug that tows the ship of theory; but in an extreme case the theory pulls so hard that observation yields. It can happen that a theory has long gone unchallenged, neatly conforming to countless relevant observations on every hand, and that now one observation conflicts with it. Chances are that we will waive the one wayward observation. This still does not mean going back on our definition of an observation sentence. We defined it as a sentence to which all witnesses are bound to accede at the time of the observed event; we left them free to change their minds afterward. In the cases where we waive an observation—and they had better be pretty special—we are changing our minds after the occasion, or, more usually, doubting someone else's report.

It is never a matter of rejecting an observation sentence on the occasion of the observation. And an observation sentence ceases to be an observation sentence, after all, when we change the tense of its verb. Reports of past observations involve inference, as lately remarked. It is only these, and not strictly observation sentences, that we are second-guessing when we waive the wayward observation.

Despite any such legalisms, however, our memories are not to be lightly dismissed, much less our records. Nor are the reports of observation by trusted colleagues, though the trust in this quarter admits of degrees. It is only a strong and long unchallenged theory that will occasionally resist the adverse testimony of a remembered or recorded or reported observation. In such an extremity we may attribute the wayward evidence to unexplained interference, even to hallucination. If such alleged cases of hallucination tend to cluster in a few persons, who may then be seen as prone to hallucination, so much the better for our scientific conscience. There is then hope of accommodating the very waywardness of those wayward observations in a theory too, a theory of psychopathology. Law may thus be sought in the apparent breaches of law.

Even when observations persist in conflicting with a theory, the theory will not necessarily be abandoned forthwith. It will linger until a plausible substitute is found; the conflicting observations will stand unexplained, and the sense of crisis will mount.

> Galileo's contributions to the study of motion depended closely upon difficulties discovered in Aristotle's theory by scholastic critics. Newton's new theory of light and color originated in the discovery that none of the existing . . . theories would account for the length of the spectrum, and the wave theory that replaced Newton's was announced in the midst of growing concern about anomalies in the relation of diffraction and polarization effects to Newton's theory. Thermodynamics was born from the collision of two existing nineteenth-century physical theories, and quantum mechanics from a variety of difficulties surrounding black-body radiation, specific heats, and the photoelectric effect. Furthermore, in all these cases except that of Newton the awareness of anomaly had lasted so long and penetrated so deep that one can appropriately describe the fields affected by it as in a state of growing crisis. Because it demands . . . major shifts in the problems and techniques of normal science, the emergence of new theories is generally preceded by a period of pronounced professional insecurity. As one might expect, that insecurity is generated by the persistent failure of the puzzles of normal science to come out as they should. Failure of existing rules is the prelude to a search for new ones.[1]

There are some points at which, without deliberate consideration of theories, all of us find it second nature to edit observation. We learn to take it that sticks appearing bent while partially immersed in water should in fact be judged straight. We learn not to suppose that the moon is larger when near the horizon than when higher in the sky. When the colors before us begin to vibrate, we do not imagine that the properties of light have changed. But in all these examples, again, we are at pains in the end to accommodate the waywardness of the observations in a theory too. The illusion of the immersed sticks is covered by a physical theory of refraction; the illusion of the low moon is coped with by some psychological hypotheses; and a general visual disruption is apt to set us speculating about something we ate or drank. Observations thus stubbornly retain their primacy. They remain the boundary conditions of our body of beliefs.

It must be confessed however that not all observations, or reports of observations, are so conscientiously accommodated. Some of them, uncongenial to existing theory, get passed over with even less acknowledgment than it would take to rate them as hallucinations. Persistent reports of occult experiences receive this short treatment, as also, of late, many of

[1]T. S. Kuhn, *The Structure of Scientific Revolutions* (Chicago and London: The University of Chicago, 1962), pp. 67f.

the reports of unindentified flying objects. Note, however, that a good scientist does not treat an uncongenial observation in this high-handed way when the observation is induced by an experiment of his own. For his experiment will have been designed for the very purpose of deciding between two alternative moves in the development of his theory, two pre-conceived alternative beliefs. But he will perhaps dismiss a puzzling observation, reported to him with palpable sincerity or even made by himself, if he has in mind no specific change of theory that might accommodate the observation and still jibe with previous data. Up to a point this high-handedness is justifiable. If a scientist were to interrupt existing projects in order to find a plausible hypothesis for every puzzling experience outside the laboratory, and if he were to lend a patient and judicious ear to every crank and gossip, he would learn less.

Scientists are so good nowadays at discovering truth that it is trivial to condone their methods and absurd to criticize them. At the same time it is evident that waiving observations is always a delicate business. A theory that is sustained only at the cost of systematic waiving is an undependable instrument of prediction and not a good example of scientific method.

Just because it is not feasible to accommodate all observations all the time, some philosophers have wanted to scout the whole idea of observation. Their doubts have been aggravated by a further consideration: the air of subjectivity that seems to them to render the very idea of observation hopelessly vague. Where the untrained eye observes a wired metal box, the trained eye observes a condenser. Where the untrained eye observes nothing, the trained eye observes the recent trace of a deer. But again these discrepancies are no ground for misgivings when properly viewed; they are only a play on the careless use of a word.

For philosophical purposes the notion of observation, and of observation sentence, needs to be taken with an unimaginative literalness. A straightforward criterion to the purpose is already before us: that all reasonably competent speakers of the language be disposed, if asked, to assent to the sentence under the same stimulations of their sensory surfaces. On this criterion "That's a condenser" simply does not count as an observation sentence, trained eye notwithstanding. Naturally the experts, being reasonable, will stop pressing for further evidence anyway as soon as they can agree. They can agree that it is a condenser, so they stop there, rather than press on compulsively to genuine observation sentences, in our sense of the term; but they always could press on. If they care to use the term *observation* for their intermediate stopping point, let us not dispute about the term. They might be said to be simply narrowing the category of "competent speakers of the language" to their specialized group.

We remarked that some philosophers have identified observations with events of sensation. It is thus not to be wondered at that, in some philosophical writings, the title of *observation sentence* is reserved for sentences very different from observation sentences as we have defined them. It is reserved for introspective reports such as "I am in pain" and "I seem to see blue now." Such reports also have been rated as infallible. It must be conceded that they tend to be incontestable, because of the speaker's privileged access to his or her private experience. But on this very point they differ diametrically from observation sentences in our sense. The situations that make them true are not ones to which multiple witnesses could attest. What is open to public observation in such a case is rather the introspective report itself. What is comparable to the cat's being on the mat is not the person's feeling pain or seeing blue, but the reporting pain or blue—the verbal behavior. This verbal behavior is indeed available as a datum for further theorizing; it is a datum to which multiple witnesses might attest.

The Nature of Science

44. The Detective as Scientist   Irving M. Copi

Irving Marmer Copi (1917–   ), an American professor of philosophy, has written extensively and lucidly on logic, scientific method, and the philosophy of language.

. . . A perennial favorite in this connection is the detective, whose problem is not quite the same as that of the pure scientist, but whose approach and technique illustrate the method of science very clearly. The classical example of the astute detective who can solve even the most baffling mystery is A. Conan Doyle's immortal creation, Sherlock Holmes. Holmes, his stature undiminished by the passage of time, will be our hero in the following account:

1. The Problem. Some of our most vivid pictures of Holmes are those in which he is busy with magnifying glass and tape measure, searching out and finding essential clues which had escaped the attention of those stupid bunglers, the "experts" of Scotland Yard. Or those of us who are by temperament less vigorous may think back more fondly on Holmes the thinker, " . . . who, when he had an unsolved problem upon his mind, would go for days, and even for a week, without rest, turning it over, rearranging his facts, looking at it from every point of view until he had either fathomed it or convinced himself that his data were insufficient."[1] At one such time, according to Dr. Watson:

> He took off his coat and waistcoat, put on a large blue dressing-gown, and then wandered about the room collecting pillows from his bed and cushions from the sofa and armchairs. With these he constructed a sort of Eastern divan, upon which he perched himself cross-legged, with an ounce of shag tobacco and a box of matches laid out in front of him. In the dim light of the lamp I saw him sitting there, an old briar pipe between his lips, his eyes fixed vacantly upon the corner of the ceiling, the blue smoke curling up from him, silent, motionless, with the light shining upon his strong-set aquiline features. So he sat as I dropped off to sleep, and so he sat when a sudden ejaculation caused me to wake up, and I found the summer sun shining into the apartment. The pipe was still between his lips, the smoke still curled upward, and the room was full of a dense tobacco haze,

[1]"The Man with the Twisted Lip."

but nothing remained of the heap of shag which I had seen upon the previous night.[2]

But such memories are incomplete. Holmes was not always searching for clues or pondering over solutions. We all remember those dark periods—especially in the earlier stories—when, much to the good Watson's annoyance, Holmes would drug himself with morphine or cocaine. That would happen, of course, between cases. For when there is no mystery to be unraveled, no man in his right mind would go out to look for clues. Clues, after all, must be clues for something. Nor could Holmes, or anyone else, for that matter, engage in profound thought unless he had something to think about. Sherlock Holmes was a genius at solving problems, but even a genius must have a problem before he can solve it. All reflective thinking, and this term includes criminal investigation as well as scientific research, is a problem-solving activity, as John Dewey and other pragmatists have rightly insisted. There must be a problem felt before either the detective or the scientist can go to work.

Of course the active mind sees problems where the dullard sees only familiar objects. One Christmas season Dr. Watson visited Holmes to find that the latter had been using a lens and forceps to examine " . . . a very seedy and disreputable hard-felt hat, much the worse for wear, and cracked in several places."[3] After they had greeted each other, Holmes said of it to Watson, "I beg that you will look upon it not as a battered billycock but as an intellectual problem."[4] It so happened that the hat led them into one of their most interesting adventures, but it could not have done so had Holmes not seen a problem in it from the start. A problem may be characterized as a fact or group of facts for which we have no acceptable explanation, which seem unusual, or which fail to fit in with our expectations or preconceptions. It should be obvious that *some* prior beliefs are required if anything is to appear problematic. If there are no expectations, there can be no surprises.

Sometimes, of course, problems came to Holmes already labeled. The very first adventure recounted by Dr. Watson began with the following message from Gregson of Scotland Yard:

> My Dear Mr. Sherlock Holmes:
>   There has been a bad business during the night at 3, Lauriston Gardens, off the Brixton Road. Our man on the beat saw a light there about two in the morning, and as the house was an empty one, suspected that something was amiss. He found the door open, and in the front room, which is bare of furniture, discovered the body of a gentleman, well dressed, and having cards in his pocket bearing the name of 'Enoch J. Drebber, Cleveland, Ohio, U.S.A.' There had been no robbery, nor is there any evidence as to how the man met his death. There are marks of blood in the room, but there is no wound upon his person. We are at a loss as to how he came into the empty house; indeed, the whole affair is a puzzler. If you can come round to the house any time before twelve, you

[2]Ibid.
[3]"The Adventure of the Blue Carbuncle."
[4]Ibid.

will find me there. I have left everything in statu quo until I hear from you. If you are unable to come, I shall give you fuller details, and would esteem it a great kindness if you would favour me with your opinion.

Yours faithfully,

TOBIAS GREGSON[5]

Here was a problem indeed. A few minutes after receiving the message, Sherlock Holmes and Dr. Watson "were both in a hansom, driving furiously for the Brixton Road."

2. Preliminary Hypotheses.   On their ride out Brixton way, Holmes "prattled away about Cremona fiddles and the difference between a Stradivarius and an Amati." Dr. Watson chided Holmes for not giving much thought to the matter at hand, and Holmes replied: "No data yet . . . It is a capital mistake to theorize before you have all the evidence. It biases the judgment."[6] This point of view was expressed by Holmes again and again. On one occasion he admonished a younger detective that "The temptation to form premature theories upon insufficient data is the bane of our profession."[7] Yet for all of his confidence about the matter, on this one issue Holmes was completely mistaken. Of course one should not reach a *final judgment* until a great deal of evidence has been considered, but this procedure is quite different from *not theorizing.* As a matter of fact, it is strictly impossible to make any serious attempt to collect evidence unless one *has* theorized beforehand. As Charles Darwin, the great biologist and author of the modern theory of evolution, observed: " . . . all observation must be for or against some view, if it is to be of any service." The point is that there are too many particular facts, too many data in the world, for anyone to try to become acquainted with them all. Everyone, even the most patient and thorough investigator, must pick and choose, deciding which facts to study and which to pass over. He must have some working hypothesis for or against which to collect relevant data. It need not be a *complete* theory, but at least the rough outline must be there. Otherwise how could one decide what facts to select for consideration out of the totality of all facts, which is too vast even to begin to sift?

Holmes' actions were wiser than his words in this connection. After all, the words were spoken in a hansom speeding towards the scene of the crime. If Holmes really had no theory about the matter, why go to Brixton Road? If facts and data were all that he wanted, any old facts and any old data, with no hypotheses to guide him in their selection, why should he have left Baker Street at all? There were plenty of facts in the rooms at 221-B, Baker Street. Holmes might just as well have spent his time counting all the words on all the pages of all the books there, or perhaps making very accurate measurements of the distances between each separate pair of articles of furniture in the house. He could have gathered data to his heart's content and saved himself cab fare into the bargain!

It may be objected that the facts to be gathered at Baker Street have

[5]*A Study in Scarlet.*
[6]Ibid.
[7]*The Valley of Fear.*

nothing to do with the case, whereas those which awaited Holmes at the scene of the crime were valauble clues for solving the problem. It was, of course, just this consideration which led Holmes to ignore the "data" at Baker Street and hurry away to collect those off Brixton Road. It must be insisted, however, that the greater relevance of the latter could not be *known* beforehand but only conjectured on the basis of previous experience with crimes and clues. It was in fact a *hypothesis* which led Holmes to look in one place rather than another for his facts, the hypothesis that there was a murder, that the crime was committed at the place where the body was found, and that the murderer had left some trace or clue which could lead to his discovery. Some such hypothesis is always required to guide the investigator in his search for relevant data, for in the absence of any preliminary hypothesis, there are simply too many facts in this world to examine. The preliminary hypothesis ought to be highly tentative, and it must be based on previous knowledge. But a preliminary hypothesis is as necessary as the existence of a problem for any serious inquiry to begin.

It must be emphasized that a preliminary hypothesis, as here conceived, need not be a complete solution to the problem. The hypothesis that the man was murdered by someone who had left some clues to his identity on or near the body of his victim was what led Holmes to Brixton Road. This hypothesis is clearly incomplete: it does not say who committed the crime, or how it was done, or why. Such a preliminary hypothesis may be very different from the final solution to the problem. It will never be complete: it may be a tentative explanation of only part of the problem. But however partial and however tentative, a preliminary hypothesis is required for any investigation to proceed.

3. Collecting Additional Facts. Every serious investigation begins with some fact or group of facts which strike the investigator as problematic and which initiate the whole process of inquiry. The initial facts which constitute the problem are usually too meagre to suggest a wholly satisfactory explanation for themselves, but they will suggest—to the competent investigator—some preliminary hypotheses which lead him to search out additional facts. These additional facts, it is hoped, will serve as clues to the final solution. The inexperienced or bungling investigator will overlook or ignore all but the most obvious of them; but the careful worker will aim at completeness in his examination of the additional facts to which his preliminary hypotheses lead him. Holmes, of course, was the most careful and painstaking of investigators.

Holmes insisted on dismounting from the hansom a hundred yards or so from their destination and approached the house on foot, looking carefully at its surroundings and especially at the pathway leading up to it. When Holmes and Watson entered the house, they were shown the body by the two Scotland Yard operatives, Gregson and Lestrade. ("There is no clue," said Gregson. "None at all," chimed in Lestrade.) But Holmes had already started his own search for additional facts, looking first at the body:

... his nimble fingers were flying here, there, and everywhere, feeling, pressing, unbuttoning, examining. . . . So swiftly was examination made, that one would hardly have guessed the minuteness with which it was conducted. Finally, he sniffed the dead man's lips, and then glanced at the soles of his patent leather boots.[8]

Then turning his attention to the room itself.

> . . . he whipped a tape measure and a large round magnifying glass from his pocket. With these two implements he trotted noiselessly about the room, sometimes stopping, occasionally kneeling, and once lying flat upon his face. So engrossed was he with his occupation that he appeared to have forgotten our presence, for he chattered away to himself under his breath the whole time, keeping up a running fire of exclamations, groans, whistles, and little cries suggestive of encouragement and of hope. As I watched him I was irresistibly reminded of a pure-blooded, well-trained foxhound as it dashes backward and forward through the covert, whining in its eagerness, until it comes across the lost scent. For twenty minutes or more he continued his researches, measuring with the most exact care the distance between marks which were entirely invisible to me, and occasionally applying his tape to the walls in an equally incomprehensible manner. In one place he gathered up very carefully a little pile of gray dust from the floor and packed it away in an envelope. Finally he examined with his glass the word upon the wall, going over every letter of it with the most minute exactness. This done, he appeared to be satisfied, for he replaced his tape and his glass in his pocket.
>
> "They say that genius is an infinite capacity for taking pains," he remarked with a smile. "It's a very bad definition, but it does apply to detective work."[9]

One matter deserves to be emphasized very strongly. Steps 2 and 3 are not completely separable but are usually very intimately connected and interdependent. True enough, we require a preliminary hypothesis to begin any intelligent examination of facts, but the additional facts may themselves suggest new hypotheses, which may lead to new facts, which suggest still other hypotheses, which lead to still other additional facts, and so on. Thus having made his careful examination of the facts available in the house off Brixton Road, Holmes was led to formulate a further hypothesis which required the taking of testimony from the constable who found the body. The man was off duty at the moment, and Lestrade gave Holmes the constable's name and address.

> Holmes took a note of the address.
>
> "Come along, Doctor," he said: "we shall go and look him up. I'll tell you one thing which may help you in the case," he continued, turning to the two detectives. "There has been murder done, and the murderer was a man. He was more than six feet high, was in the prime of life, had small feet for his height, wore coarse, square-toed boots and smoked a Trichinopoly cigar. He came here with his victim in a four-wheeled cab, which was drawn by a horse with three old shoes and one new one on his off fore-leg. In all probability the murderer had a florid face, and the fingernails of his right hand were remarkably long. These are only a few indications, but they may assist you."

[8]*A Study in Scarlet.*
[9]Ibid.

Lestrade and Gregson glanced at each other with an incredulous smile.
"If this man was murdered, how was it done?" asked the former.
"Poison," said Sherlock Holmes curtly, and strode off.[10]

4. Formulating the Hypothesis. At some stage or other of his investigation, any man—whether detective, scientist, or ordinary mortal—will get the feeling that he has all the facts needed for his solution. He has his "2 and 2," so to speak, but the task still remains of "putting them together." At such a time Sherlock Holmes might sit up all night, consuming pipe after pipe of tobacco, trying to think things through. The result or end product of such thinking, if it is successful, is a hypothesis which accounts for all the data, both the original set of facts which constituted the problem, and the additional facts to which the preliminary hypotheses pointed. The actual discovery of such an explanatory hupothesis is a process of creation, in which imagination as well as knowledge is involved. Holmes, who was a genius at inventing hypotheses, described the process as reasoning "backward." As he put it,

> Most people if you describe a train of events to them, will tell you what the result would be. They can put those events together in their minds, and argue from them that something will come to pass. There are few people, however, who, if you told them a result, would be able to evolve from their own inner consciousness what the steps were which led up to that result.[11]

Here is Holmes' description of the process of formulating an explanatory hypothesis. However that may be, when a hypothesis has been proposed, its evaluation must be along the lines that were sketched in Section III [Omitted Here]. Granted its relevance and testability, and its compatibility with other well-attested beliefs, the ultimate criterion for evaluating a hypothesis is its predictive power.

5. Deducing Further Consequences. A really fruitful hypothesis will not only explain the facts which originally inspired it, but will explain many others in addition. A good hypothesis will point beyond the initial facts in the direction of new ones whose existence might otherwise not have been suspected. And of course the verification of those further consequences will tend to confirm the hypothesis which led to them. Holmes' hypothesis that the murdered man had been poisoned was soon put to such a test. A few days later the murdered man's secretary and traveling companion was also found murdered. Holmes asked Lestrade, who had discovered the second body, whether he had found anything in the room which could furnish a clue to the murderer. Lestrade answered, "Nothing," and went on to mention a few quite ordinary effects. Holmes was not satisfied and pressed him, asking, "And was there nothing else?" Lestrade answered, "Nothing of any importance," and named a few more details, the last of which was "a small chip ointment box containing a couple of pills." At this information,

[10] Ibid.
[11] Ibid.

> Sherlock Holmes sprang from his chair with an exclamation of delight. "The last links," he cried, exultantly. "My case is complete."
>
> The two detectives stared at him in amazement.
>
> "I have now in my hands," my companion said, confidently, "all the threads which have formed such a tangle. . . . I will give you a proof of my knowledge. Could you lay your hands upon those pills?"
>
> "I have them," said Lestrade, producing a small white box . . . [12]

On the basis of his hypothesis about the original crime, Holmes was able to predict that the pills found at the scene of the second crime must contain poison. Here deduction has an essential role in the process of any scientific or inductive inquiry. The ultimate value of any hypothesis lies in its predictive or explanatory power, which means that additional facts must be deducible from an adequate hypothesis. From his theory that the first man was poisoned and that the second victim met his death at the hands of the same murderer, Holmes inferred that the pills found by Lestrade must be poison. His theory, however sure he may have felt about it, was only a theory and needed further confirmation. He obtained that confirmation by testing the consequences deduced from the hypothesis and finding them to be true. Having used deduction to make a prediction, his next step was to test it.

6. Testing the Consequences. The consequences of a hypothesis, that is, the predictions made on the basis of that hypothesis, may require various means for their testing. Some require only observation. In some cases, Holmes needed only to watch and wait—for the bank robbers to break into the vault, in the "Adventure of the Red-headed League," or for Dr. Roylott to slip a venomous snake through a dummy ventilator, in the "Adventure of the Speckled Band." In the present case, however, an experiment had to be performed.

Holmes asked Dr. Watson to fetch the landlady's old and ailing terrier, which she had asked to have put out of its misery the day before. Holmes then cut one of the pills in two, dissolved it in a wineglass of water, added some milk, and

> . . . turned the contents of the wineglass into a saucer and placed it in front of the terrier, who speedily licked it dry. Sherlock Holmes's earnest demeanour had so far convinced us that we all sat in silence, watching the animal intently, and expecting some startling effect. None such appeared, however. The dog continued to lie stretched upon the cushion, breathing in a laboured way, but apparently neither the better nor the worse for its draught.
>
> Holmes had taken out his watch, and as minute followed minute without result, an expression of the utmost chagrin and disappointment appeared upon his features. He gnawed his lip, drummed his fingers upon the table, and showed every other symptom of acute impatience. So great was his emotion that I felt sincerely sorry for him, while the two detectives smiled derisively, by no means displeased at this check which he had met.
>
> "It can't be a coincidence," he cried, at last springing from his chair and pacing wildly up and down the room: "it is impossible that it should

[12]Ibid.

be a mere coincidence. The very pills which I suspected in the case of Drebber are actually found after the death of Stangerson. And yet they are inert. What can it mean? Surely my whole chain of reasoning cannot have been false. It is impossible! And yet this wretched dog is none the worse. Ah, I have it! I have it!" With a perfect shriek of delight he rushed to the box, cut the other pill in two, dissolved it, added milk, and presented it to the terrier. The unfortunate creature's tongue seemed hardly to have been moistened in it before it gave a convulsive shiver in every limb, and lay as rigid and lifeless as if it had been struck by lightning.

Sherlock Holmes drew a long breath, and wiped the perspiration from his forehead.[13]

By the favorable outcome of his experiment, Holmes' hypothesis had received dramatic and convincing confirmation.

7. *Application.* The detective's concern, after all, is a practical one. Given a crime to solve, he has not merely to explain the facts but to apprehend and arrest the criminal. The latter involves making application of his theory, using it to predict where the criminal can be found and how he may be caught. He must deduce still further consequences from the hypothesis, not for the sake of additional confirmation but for practical use. From his general hypothesis Holmes was able to infer that the murderer was acting the role of a cabman. We have already seen that Holmes had formed a pretty clear description of the man's appearance. He sent out his army of "Baker Street Irregulars," street urchins of the neighborhood, to search out and summon the cab driven by just that man. The successful "application" of this hypothesis can be described again in Dr. Watson's words. A few minutes after the terrier's death.

... there was a tap at the door, and the spokesman of the street Arabs, young Wiggins, introduced his insignificant and unsavoury person.

"Please, sir," he said touching his forelock, "I have the cab downstairs."

"Good boy," said Holmes, blandly. "Why don't you introduce this pattern at Scotland Yard?" he continued, taking a pair of steel handcuffs from a drawer. "See how beautifully the spring works. They fasten in an instant."

"The old pattern is good enough," remarked Lestrade, "if we can only find the man to put them on."

"Very good, very good," said Holmes, smiling. "The cabman may as well help me with my boxes. Just ask him to step in, Wiggins."

I was surprised to find my companion speaking as though he were about to set out on a journey, since he had not said anything to me about it. There was a small portmanteau in the room, and this he pulled out and began to strap. He was busily engaged at it when the cabman entered the room.

"Just give me a help with this buckle, cabman," he said, kneeling over his task, and never turning his head.

The fellow came forward with a somewhat sullen, defiant air, and put down his hands to assist. At that instant there was a sharp click, the jangling of metal, and Sherlock Holmes sprang to his feet again.

"Gentlemen," he cried, with flashing eyes, "let me introduce you to Mr.

[13]Ibid.

Jefferson Hope, the murderer of Enoch Drebber and of Joseph Stangerson."[14]

Here we have a picture of the detective as scientist, reasoning from observed facts to a testable hypothesis which not only explains the facts but permits of practical application.

45. The Coming Philosophy of Science   Henry Margenau

Henry Margenau (1901–   ), a well-known physicist and philosopher, is the author of specialized books in physics and of such recent works as *Ethics and Science, The Scientist,* and *Integrative Principles of Modern Thought.*

In Western culture science is a pragmatic pursuit; it is the discovery of useful facts, whatever they may be. Its virtue lies in the honesty and accuracy with which these facts are gathered and in the completeness of the pattern that, as part of formulated knowledge, they finally compose. This factualness of science makes it blind to the differences between the trivial and the significant, the odious and the exquisite, the good and the bad; indeed the identification of science with the realm of discoverable fact has largely removed it from most basic human concerns and made it into a gigantic robot driving toward material progress.

It is this *obvious* movement from discovery to the generation of a better material milieu that has captured our attention, engaged our fancy, and warped our appreciation of the true and abiding function of science in human culture. For it leaves out of consideration an obscurer movement, which accompanies the other with fateful inevitability, and which goes from discovery to understanding, wisdom, philosophy, straight into the affairs of the human spirit.

Let me characterize this other movement, first in general terms. An important scientific discovery is never a mere addition to knowledge; it is usually a challenge to established beliefs, a deflection from current trends of thought, and often an apostasy to common sense. But this is hard to see, partly because the neon lights of publicity, which shine on the open pageantry of the obvious manifestations of scientific progress, have dulled our vision; partly because one has to apprehend more than facts to discern the deeper effects of science. So this movement—from discovery through new theory, modification of what is called common sense, toward subtler changes in our cosmological beliefs, in the theory of knowledge, in the nature of the universe, and indeed of man—goes on in obscurity, without recognition and applause. It goes with a fateful tread, slowly and

From *The Key Reporter,* Vol. XXV, No. 1 (Autumn, 1959). Reprinted with permission of *The Key Reporter* and Phi Beta Kappa.

[14]Ibid.

sometimes erratically, like an object lumbering downhill without intelligent guidance, meeting many obstacles in its path; but it moves to its end, and its end decides the intellectual and cultural climate in which men live. And ultimately sociology, ethics, politics, and even religion are infected by the germ that is born when a truly great discovery in pure science is made.

One example of the obscure movement will illustrate my point. I shall leave aside those, like the rise of materialism in the wake of certain discoveries in science, that are already recognized by historians.

The laws of mechanics were formulated at the beginning of the seventeenth century by a group of men among whom Galileo and Newton were pre-eminent. The crucial features of these laws are their invariability, their claim of universal validity, and the peculiar manner in which they make space and time, previously regarded by many as physical agents, into formal concepts that in their relation to phenomena are neutral, impotent, and absolute. In the decades following Galileo and Newton many attempts were made to translate these novel aspects of nature's law into the language of philosophy. The culminating success in these endeavors was achieved by Kant, whose theory of categories took care of the apodictic nature of the laws of mechanics, and whose theory of space and time as pure forms of intuition accounted beautifully for their importance as physical agents and their absoluteness in man's understanding of the world. The tremendous historical success of so peculiar a philosophical doctrine as Kant's can never be understood, unless it is projected against the scientific background it was able to rationalize and comprehend. And it is also clear how Kant's conception of natural law transformed itself in his own teaching into the categorical imperative and the abstract notion of duty that governed the ethical behavior of the continent of Europe for a century or more. Thus the cultural lag between scientific discovery and its philosophic understanding—or, if you prefer, acclimatization—was of the order of a hundred years.

It is important to record that in the distant past even the obvious movement required hundreds of years to reach its culmination. The discovery of gunpowder is known to have occurred in the twelfth century in central Europe, but powder was not used in warfare until the fourteenth century. This slow pace has changed today: fission was discovered in 1939; the first atomic bomb exploded in 1944. Five years saw the conversion of a modern discovery into the most destructive of weapons.

Has the obscure trend launched by science been similarly accelerated? The quantum theory was developed around 1910, and it presented one of the most incisive challenges man's thinking has ever received. Today physicists apply the fundamental equations of quantum mechanics whenever a problem calls for them; they have perfected techniques for solving them through admirable researches; but the fundamental meaning of these equations is by no means clear. The very men who created the quantum theory—Bohr, Schrödinger, Heisenberg, Born, De Broglie, and many others—have shifted a large part of their attention in recent years to the business of clarifying what their earlier discoveries mean. The sad thing is that they do not agree, and that the present generation of physicists pays little attention to them. The century of gestation for the obscure development is not yet up.

It stands to reason that man's thinking will be troubled by paradoxes and trapped in pseudoproblems if it embraces only *part* of the truth, and the texture of truth cannot be whole if the technological consequences of science are clear but its philosophic import is beclouded with contradictions. This is the state in which we live, a state of crises, incoherences, and contrasts. Let our society become aware of this and give heed and encouragement to the most urgent task: to humanize science, to search for its meaning to man, to harmonize its *ideal* structure, not only its technological effects, with our way of life.

I shall not survey what needs to be done today to bring about such harmony. Instead, I shall undertake the perhaps impossible task of guessing the features of the coming philosophy, which will be a true transcription of the ideal resources, attitudes, and commitments of present science. Four new facets of the growing crystal of science impress me as most significant and pregnant with suggestions for philosophy.

First is a courageous, healthful skepticism regarding the finality of all basic truths called axioms or postulates. Euclid's geometry was based on axioms and postulates the truth of which was for nearly two millenia regarded as indubitable. Their validity was not open to proof, but to inspection: any curious person, through his light of inner reason, could discern the eternal verity of Euclud's axioms. That conviction was rudely shattered when non-Euclidean geometries were discovered, when mathematicians saw for the first time, about a hundred years ago, that truth in geometry was internal consistency, that there were many rival systems of posulates, all of which led to formally coherent theoretical structures but only one of which did justice to the facts of the world as known. Postulates, it was thus recognized, did not carry within themselves the affidavits of their validity. They were not produced and justified by an infallible *lumen naturale*. Their logical status was one of tentative acceptance, subject to change when the observable facts called for it.

Science had thus renounced absolute truth. But it made this sacrifice gladly, for it gained thereby an affinity and a measure of deepened understanding for other areas of human concern. By recognizing its own need for commitment to postulates and axioms of which it cannot be sure in *a priori* or in final fashion, it made common cause with those disciplines in which commitment to norms, ideals, and values is essential to progress. Science saw the similarity between its own need to avow axioms and man's wider need to accept faith.

Suspension of Common Sense

Science also relies increasingly on reason, often very abstract reason, and tends to be critical of "common sense." It intends no disparagement of the kind of human wisdom that often goes by that name, especially in areas where science itself is incompetent. But when a clear claim of reason contradicts cherished beliefs it *does* ask their surrender, and it sometimes haughtily affirms that science itself gave rise to common sense, regarding the latter merely as the residue of scientific knowledge left in the wake of advancing science and absorbed by the scientifically illiterate. "*Allez en avant, la foi vous viendra,*" was d'Alembert's admonition, and it intended to say that the scientist should not worry too much about apparent absurdities in his manifestoes. The clearest example of the awkward truth of d'Alembert's announcement is seen in the theory of relativity, where strange propositions, first courageously embraced by men like Einstein in full cognizance of their contradiction to common sense, were later proved true in observations, and have now gained universal acceptance, except by a few cranks who militantly refuse to understand them.

Another tendency prominently displayed by modern physics is the repudiation of mechanical models. "Classical" (i.e., superannuated) science had cast its thought overwhelmingly into visual molds, employing in its explanation infinitesimal replicas of the mechanisms encountered in the macroscopic world. The microcosm of science was replete with minute wheels and gears, rods and strings, dumbbells and miniature solar systems, and these devices were taken at face value even though no feasible process could expose them to view. They were known to be too small to be seen, not merely because microscopes of sufficient power had not been constructed, but in consequence of the fundamental fact that they are *in principle* below the limit of detection by optical light, being smaller than one of its wavelengths. It seems odd in retrospect that the view sometimes voiced by positivists of the classical era was not more seriously considered—the view contending that entities too small to be perceived may have properties that likewise defy perception and require for their apprehension more subtle attributes than the objects of our daily experience.

This recognition, the awareness that objects composing the physical microcosm cannot be understood in terms of the facile concepts of the visual world, has come to the fore in quantum mechanics. An electron, according to this new branch of science, has, under certain conditions, no determinate position, energy, or speed at all; it may be in a state that can be pictured only as a cloud or wave of probability from which it emerges as a real (in the older sense) physical entity only when a measurement is made. Very abstract, non-intuitable concepts like probabilities and probability amplitudes replace the older mechanical models; pictures give way to pure forms, solid stuff to abstract fields, particles to mathematical singularities, and reason takes the place of cruder kinds of intuition. Refinement, sublimation of the method of science, are the names some have applied to this change; others voice their disapproval by calling it a recession from reality. Whether we like it or not, the change has taken place and has left an indelible imprint on modern science.

Finally, there is an element of daring which the surveyor of the scientific scene can clearly see. The word "evolution," with all the literal and figurative allusions it suggests, describes rather well the attitude of nineteenth-century science. But today, it seems, one ought to replace the past-centered *ex* by the forward-looking *ad,* the twisting *volvere* by the coming *venire,* the past participle by the future one, and thus convert "evolution" into "adventure." This word portrays the mood of present science and does justice to its soaring spirit, its flight into pure reason, its courage to release tremendous energies, its drive to conquer space, and its denial of common sense.

I now turn to the difficult portion of my chosen task: to the questionable—and indeed fallible—sketch of the nascent philosophy that is to provide an organic unity for the components of scientific method so briefly summarized. The details of this philosophy elude me. I do not know whether it will be a systematic, closely reasoned structure or a melee of rhapsodic insights, because the traditional century of maturation has only half elapsed. But if I am not entirely deceived, its method will reflect the ongoing concerns, the dynamism of science itself. Like science, this philosophy will conceive its goal to be an ideal one, attainable only as a limiting answer to finite and often repeated human questions. Knowing the tentative nature of postulates, it will harbor no static certainties; while it will recognize meaningful eternal questions, it will brook no eternal answers, nor will it entertain timeless truths. Facilities for improvement, for progressive correction in the face of the never ending surge of fresh and unexpected facts, will be implanted in its very method of inquiry as a safeguard against stagnation and the encroachment of dogmatism.

A History but Not a Fate

Such will be its method, if my instinct is correct. And among its problems will be human freedom. Old-style physical science kept the riddle of freedom from being seriously debated by locking it in the dusty storeroom of mechanical models, where it subsided like a conundrum among weighty problems. Mechanisms obeying Newton's laws permit no freedom; if they are taken to describe exhaustively man's make-up, then his life and his actions are as narrowly determined as the path of a missile; he has a fate but not a history.

Quantum theory rescues man's destiny from the fateful web of physical determination. It injects uncertainties into the concatenation of events, and these uncertainties *may* harbor freedom. No physicist has shown how freedom results from the laws of quantum mechanics, but there is clearly room for it. Some writers, eager to make a case for freedom, have mistaken it for absence of determination, thus committing the error of supposing that to be free is to be unpredictable. For if only the probabilities of quantum mechanics determined our behavior, we should be forced to act erratically, the quality of our actions would be determined in the mean, and a case for moral responsibility could hardly be made.

To state the issue correctly, one should say that freedom is no longer a pseudoproblem or a subjective affair of introspection that has no correlate in the external world: it has been taken out of the wastebasket of paradoxes and placed on the shelf of challenging problems to be solved. To obtain the solution, the scientist can go—and has gone—a certain distance; the philosopher versed in science must do the rest.

A Key to Encrusted Mysteries

Lastly, there is hope that the coming philosophy will achieve a major synthesis of hereditary contrasts. History has saddled our thinking with antinomies, with conceptual poles before which inquiry is arrested. We are awed by the mind-body problem, the conflicts between subject and object, the world and its knower, the cosmic spectacle and the spectator. At the risk of sacrilege to these encrusted mysteries, I suggest that science now holds a key to their solution, and to a solution other than the easy one that claims that these antinomies are without empirical content. This key is in the discovery of what engineers called "feedback," economists "transactions," physicists "the irreducible interference between measurement and the measured variable." Stripped to its fundamentals—and the terms *feedback* and *transactions* are here meant to describe basic processes of knowledge—this discovery denies the existence of a barrier separating the knower from the known; it removes the curtain between the spectacle and the spectator and makes him part of the cosmic show. On the plane of elemental essences, as in atomic physics, every observation modifies what is being observed, the knower enters into nature in every measurement, and every sequence of events hinges on incidents of human intervention.

The new philosophy will, I am sure, render a more coherent account of this situation than my crude allusions can suggest. It will doubtless demonstrate, in accordance with the implications of science, that there remains no ivory tower for detached speculation that makes no difference to the world. Facts have turned into acts, freedom is no longer an illusion, stagnant truth has become an eternal challenge. When these insights are finally organized into an embracive philosophy, the picture of man will likewise be altered: he will appear as an agent of greater power, creativity, and responsibility than before, but he will be humble before truth.

Contemporary Issues

Science and Human Nature: Nature Versus Nurture

46. Sociobiology   Edward Osborne Wilson

Edward Osborne Wilson (1929–   ) is Baird Professor of Science and curator of entomology at Harvard University. His recent books arguing for the development of a new science of sociobiology are: *Sociobiology: The New Synthesis* and *On Human Nature.*

The first dilemma has been created by the seemingly fatal deterioration of the myths of traditional religion and its secular equivalents, principal among which are ideologies based on a Marxian interpretation of history. The price of these failures has been a loss of moral consensus, a greater sense of helplessness about the human condition and a shrinking of concern back toward the self and the immediate future. The intellectual solution of the first dilemma can be achieved by a deeper and more courageous examination of human nature that combines the findings of biology with those of the social sciences. The mind will be more precisely explained as an epiphenomenon of the neuronal machinery of the brain. That machinery is in turn the product of genetic evolution by natural selection acting on human populations for hundreds of thousands of years in their ancient environments. By a judicious extension of the methods and ideas of neurobiology, ethology, and sociobiology a proper foundation can be laid for the social sciences, and the discontinuity still separating the natural sciences on the one side and the social sciences and humanities on the other might be erased.

If this solution to the first dilemma proves even partially correct, it will lead directly to the second dilemma: the conscious choices that must be made among our innate mental propensities. The elements of human nature are the learning rules, emotional reinforcers, and hormonal feedback loops that guide the development of social behavior into certain channels as opposed to others. Human nature is not just the array of outcomes attained in existing societies. It is also the potential array that might be achieved through conscious design by future societies. By looking over the realized social systems of hundreds of animal species and deriving the principles by which these systems have evolved, we can be certain that all human choices represent only a tiny subset of those theoretically possible. Human nature is, moreover, a hodgepodge of special genetic adaptations to an environment largely vanished, the world of the Ice-Age hunter-gatherer. Modern life, as rich and rapidly changing as it appears to those caught in it, is nevertheless only a mosaic of cultural hypertrophies of the archaic behavioral adaptations. And at the center of the second dilemma is found a circularity: we are forced to choose among the elements of human nature by reference to value systems which these same elements created in an evolutionary age now long vanished.

Fortunately, this circularity of the human predicament is not so tight that it cannot be broken through an exercise of will. The principal task of human biology is to identify and to measure the constraints that influence the decisions of ethical philosophers and everyone else, and to infer their significance through neurophysiological and phylogenetic reconstructions of the mind. This enterprise is a necessary complement to the continued study of cultural evolution. It will alter the foundation of the social sciences but in no way diminish their richness and importance. In the process it will fashion a biology of ethics, which will make possible the selection of a more deeply understood and enduring code of moral values. . . .

The search for values will then go beyond the utilitarian calculus of genetic fitness. Although natural selection has been the prime mover, it works through a cascade of decisions based on secondary values that have historically served as the enabling mechanisms for survival and reproductive success. These values are defined to a large extent by our most intense emotions: enthusiasm and a sharpening of the senses from exploration; exaltation from discovery; triumph in battle and competitive sports; the restful satisfaction from an altruistic act well and truly placed; the stirring of ethnic and national pride; the strength from family ties; and the secure biophilic pleasure from the nearness of animals and growing plants.

There is a neurophysiology of such responses to be deciphered, and their evolutionary history awaits reconstruction. A kind of principle of the conservation of energy operates among them, such that the emphasis of any one over others still retains the potential summed power of all. Poets have noted it well, as in the calm phrasing of Mary Barnard's Sappho:

> Some say a cavalry corps,
> some infantry, some, again,
> will maintain that the swift oars
>
> of our fleet are the finest
> sight on dark earth; but I say
> that whatever one loves, is.

Although the means to measure these energies are lacking, I suspect psychologists would agree that they can be rechanneled substantially without losing strength, that the mind fights to retain a certain level of order and emotional reward. Recent evidence suggests that dreams are produced when giant fibers in the brainstem fire upward through the brain during sleep, stirring the cerebral cortex to activity. In the absence of ordinary sensory information from the outside, the cortex responds by calling up images from the memory banks and fabricating plausible stories. In an analogous manner the mind will always create morality, religion, and mythology and empower them with emotional force. When blind ideologies and religious beliefs are stripped away, others are quickly manufactured as replacements. If the cerebral cortex is rigidly trained in the techniques of critical analysis and packed with tested information, it will reorder all that into some form of morality, religion, and mythology. If the mind is instructed that its pararational activity cannot be combined with the rational, it will divide itself into two compartments so that both activities can continue to flourish side by side.

This mythopoeic drive can be harnessed to learning and the rational search for human progress if we finally concede that scientific materialism is itself a mythology defined in the noble sense. So let me give again the reasons why I consider the scientific ethos superior to religion: its repeated triumphs in explaining and controlling the physical world; its self-correcting nature open to all competent to devise and conduct the tests; its readiness to examine all subjects sacred and profane; and now the possibility of explaining traditional religion by the mechanistic models of evolutionary biology. The last achievement will be crucial. If religion, including the dogmatic secular ideologies, can be systematically analyzed and explained as a product of the brain's evolution, its power as an external source of morality will be gone forever and the solution of the second dilemma will have become a practical necessity.

The core of scientific materialism is the evolutionary epic. Let me repeat its minimum claims: that the laws of the physical sciences are consistent with those of the biological and social sciences and can be linked in chains of causal explanation; that life and mind have a physical basis; that the world as we know it has evolved from earlier worlds obedient to the same laws; and that the visible universe today is everywhere subject to these materialist explanations. The epic can be indefinitely strengthened up and down the line, but its most sweeping assertions cannot be proved with finality.

What I am suggesting, in the end, is that the evolutionary epic is probably the best myth we will ever have. It can be adjusted until it comes as close to truth as the human mind is constructed to judge the truth. And if that is the case, the mythopoeic requirements of the mind must somehow be met by scientific materialism so as to reinvest our superb energies. There are ways of managing such a shift honestly and without dogma. One is to cultivate more intensely the relationship between the sciences and humanities. The great British biologist J. B. S. Haldane said of science and literature, "I am absolutely convinced that science is vastly more stimulating to the imagination than are the classics, but the products of the stimulus do not normally see the light because scientific men as a class are devoid of any perception of literary form." Indeed, the origin of the universe in the big bang of fifteen billion years ago, as deduced by astronomers and physicists, is far more awesome than the first chapter of Genesis or the Ninevite epic of Gilgamesh. When the scientists project physical processes backward to that moment with the aid of mathematical models they are talking about everything—literally everything—and when they move forward in time to pulsars, supernovas, and the collision of black holes they probe distances and mysteries beyond the imaginings of earlier generations. Recall how God lashed Job with concepts meant to overwhelm the human mind:

> Who is this whose ignorant words
> cloud my design in darkness?

> Brace yourself and stand up like a man;
> I will ask questions, and you shall answer . . .
> Have you descended to the springs of the sea
> or walked in the unfathomable deep?
> Have the gates of death been revealed to you?
> Have you ever seen the door-keepers of the place of darkness?
> Have you comprehended the vast expanse of the world?
> Come, tell me all this, if you know.

And yes, we *do* know and we have told. Jehovah's challenges have been met and scientists have pressed on to uncover and to solve even greater puzzles. The physical basis of life is known; we understand approximately how and when it started on earth. New species have been created in the laboratory and evolution has been traced at the molecular level. Genes can be spliced from one kind of organism into another. Molecular biologists have most of the knowledge needed to create elementary forms of life. Our machines, settled on Mars, have transmitted panoramic views and the results of chemical soil analysis. Could the Old Testament writers have conceived of such activity? And still the process of great scientific discovery gathers momentum.

Yet, astonishingly, the high culture of Western civilization exists largely apart from the natural sciences. In the United States, intellectuals are virtually defined as those who work in the prevailing mode of the social sciences and humanities. Their reflections are devoid of the idioms of chemistry and biology, as though humankind were still in some sense a numinous spectator of physical reality. In the pages of *The New York Review of Books, Commentary, The New Republic, Daedalus, National Review, Saturday Review,* and other literary journals articles dominate that read as if most of basic science had halted during the nineteenth century. Their content consists largely of historical anecdotes, diachronic collating of outdated, verbalized theories of human behavior, and judgments of current events according to personal ideology—all enlivened by the pleasant but frustrating techniques of effervescence. Modern science is still regarded as a problem-solving activity and a set of technical marvels, the importance of which is to be valuated in an ethos extraneous to science. It is true that many "humanistic" scientists step outside scientific materialism to participate in the culture, sometimes as expert witnesses and sometimes as aspiring authors, but they almost never close the gap between the two worlds of discourse. With rare exceptions they are the tame scientists, the token emissaries of what must be viewed by their hosts as a barbaric culture still ungraced by a written language. They are degraded by the label they accept too readily: popularizers. Very few of the great writers, the ones who can trouble and move the deeper reaches of the mind, ever address real science on its own terms. Do they know the nature of the challenge?

The desired shift in attention could come more easily now that the human mind is subject to the network of causal explanation. Every epic needs a hero: the mind will do. Even astronomers, accustomed to thinking about ten billion galaxies and distances just short of infinity, must agree that the human brain is the most complex device that we know and the crossroads of investigation by every major natural science. The social scientists and humanistic scholars, not omitting theologians, will eventually have to concede that scientific naturalism is destined to alter the foundations of their systematic inquiry by redefining the mental process itself.

I began this book with an exposition of the often dialectic nature of scientific advance. The discipline abuts the antidiscipline; the antidiscipline succeeds in reordering the phenomena of the discipline by reduction to its more fundamental laws; but the new synthesis created in the discipline profoundly alters the antidiscipline as the interaction widens. I suggested that biology, and especially neurobiology and sociobiology, will serve as the antidiscipline of the social sciences. I will now go further and suggest that the scientific materialism embodied in biology will, through a reexamination of the mind and the foundations of social behavior, serve as a kind of antidiscipline to the humanities. No Comtian revolution will take place, no sudden creation of a primitively scientific culture. The translation will be gradual. In order to address the central issues of the humanities, including ideology and religious belief, science itself must become more sophisticated and in part specially crafted to deal with the peculiar features of human biology.

I hope that as this syncretism proceeds, a true sense of wonder will reinvade the broader culture. We need to speak more explicitly of the things we do not know. The epic of which natural scientists write in technical fragments still has immense gaps and absorbing mysteries, not the least of which is the physical basis of the mind. Like blank spaces on the map of a partly explored world, their near borders can be fixed but their inner magnitude only roughly guessed. Scientists and humanistic scholars can do far better than they have at articulating the great goals toward which literate people move as on a voyage of discovery. Unknown and surprising things await. They are as accessible as in those days of primitive wonder when the early European explorers went forth and came upon new worlds, and the first microscopists watched bacteria swim across drops of water. As knowledge grows, science must increasingly become the stimulus to imagination.

Such a view will undoubtedly be opposed as elitist by some who regard economic and social problems as everywhere overriding. There is an element of truth in that objection. Can anything really matter while people starve in the Sahel and India and rot in the prisons of Argentina and the Soviet Union? In response it can be asked, do we want to know, in depth and for all time, why we care? And when these problems are solved, what then? The stated purpose of governments everywhere is human fulfillment in some sense higher than animal survival. In almost all socialist revolutions the goals of highest priority, next to consecration of the revolution, are education, science, and technology—the combination that leads inexorably back to the first and second dilemmas.

This view will be rejected even more firmly by those whose emotional needs are satisfied by traditional organized religion. God and the church, they will claim, cannot be extinguished *ex parte* by a rival mythology based on science. They will be right. God remains a viable hypothesis as the prime mover, however undefinable and untestable that conception may be. The rituals of religion, especially the rites of passage and the sanctification of nationhood, are deeply entrenched and incorporate some of the most magnificent elements of existing cultures. They will certainly continue to be practiced long after their etiology has been disclosed. The anguish of death alone will be enough to keep them alive. It would be arrogant to suggest that a belief in a personal, moral God will disappear, just as it would be reckless to predict the forms that ritual will take as scientific materialism appropriates the mythopoeic energies to its own ends.

I also do not envision scientific generalization as a substitute for art or as anything more than a nourishing symbiont of art. The artist, including the creative writer, communicates his most personal experience and vision in a direct manner chosen to commit his audience emotionally to that perception. Science can hope to explain artists, and artistic genius, and even art, and it will increasingly use art to investigate human behavior, but it is not designed to transmit experience on a personal level or to reconstitute the full richness of the experience from the laws and principles which are its first concern by definition.

Above all, I am not suggesting that scientific naturalism be used as an alternative form of organized formal religion. My own reasoning follows in a direct line from the humanism of the Huxleys, Waddington, Monod, Pauli, Dobzhansky, Cattell, and others who have risked looking this Gorgon in the face. Each has achieved less than his purpose, I believe, for one or the other of two reasons. He has either rejected religious belief as animism or else recommended that it be sequestered in some gentle preserve of the mind where it can live out its culture-spawned existence apart from the mainstream of intellectual endeavor. Humanists show a touching faith in the power of knowledge and the idea of evolutionary progress over the minds of men. I am suggesting a modification of scientific humanism through the recognition that the mental processes of religious belief—consecration of personal and group identity, attention to charismatic leaders, mythopoeism, and others—represent programmed predispositions whose self-sufficient components were incorporated into the neural apparatus of the brain by thousands of generations of genetic evolution. As such they are powerful, ineradicable, and at the center of human social existence. They are also structured to a degree not previously appreciated by most philosophers. I suggest further that scientific materialism must accommodate them on two levels: as a scientific puzzle of great complexity and interest, and as a source of energies that can be shifted in new directions when scientific materialism itself is accepted as the more powerful mythology.

That transition will proceed at an accelerating rate. Man's destiny is to know, if only because societies with knowledge culturally dominate societies that lack it. Luddites and anti-intellectuals do not master the differential equations of thermodynamics or the biochemical cures of illness. They stay in thatched huts and die young. Cultures with unifying goals will learn more rapidly than those that lack them, and an autocatalytic growth of learning will follow because scientific materialism is the only mythology that can manufacture great goals from the sustained pursuit of pure knowledge.

I believe that a remarkable effect will be the increasingly precise specification of history. One of the great dreams of social theorists—Vico, Marx, Spencer, Spengler, Teggart, and Toynbee, among the most innovative—has been to devise laws of history that can foretell something of the future of mankind. Their schemes came to little because their understanding of human nature had no scientific basis; it was, to use a favored expression of scientific reporting, orders of magnitude too imprecise. The invisible hand remained invisible; the summed actions of thousands or millions of poorly understood individual human beings was not to be computed. Now there is reason to entertain the view that the culture of each society travels along one or the other of a set of evolutionary trajectories whose full array is constrained by the genetic rules of human nature. While broadly scattered from an anthropocentric point of view, this array still represents only a tiny subset of all the trajectories that would be possible in the absence of the genetic constraints.

As our knowledge of human nature grows, and we start to elect a system of values on a more objective basis, and our minds at last align with our hearts, the set of trajectories will narrow still more. We already know, to take two extreme and opposite examples, that the worlds of William Graham Sumner, the absolute Social Darwinist, and Mikhail Bakunin, the anarchist, are biologically impossible. As the social sciences mature into predictive disciplines, the permissible trajectories will not only diminish in number but our descendants will be able to sight farther along them.

Then mankind will face the third and perhaps final spiritual dilemma. Human genetics is now growing quickly along with all other branches of science. In time, much knowledge concerning the genetic foundation of social behavior will accumulate, and techniques may become available for altering gene complexes by molecular engineering and rapid selection through cloning. At the very least, slow evolutionary change will be feasible through conventional eugenics. The human species can change its own nature. What will it choose? Will it remain the same, teetering on a jerrybuilt foundation of partly obsolete Ice-Age adaptations? Or will it press on toward still higher intelligence and creativity, accompanied by a greater—or lesser—capacity for emotional response? New patterns of sociality could be installed in bits and pieces. It might be possible to imitate genetically the more nearly perfect nuclear family of the white-handed gibbon or the harmonious sisterhoods of the honeybees. But we are talking here about the very essence of humanity. Perhaps there is something already present in our nature that will prevent us from ever making such changes. In any case, and fortunately, this third dilemma belongs to later generations.

In the spirit of the enrichment of the evolutionary epic, modern writers often summon the classical mythic heroes to illustrate their view of the predicament of humankind: the existential Sisyphus, turning fate into the only means of expression open to him; hesitant Arjuna at war with his conscience on the Field of Righteousness; disastrous Pandora bestowing the ills of mortal existence on human beings; and uncomplaining Atlas, steward of the finite Earth. Prometheus has gone somewhat out of fashion in recent years as a concession to resource limitation and managerial prudence. But we should not lose faith in him. Come back with me for a moment to the original, Aeschylean Prometheus:

Chorus   Did you perhaps go further than you have told us?
Prometheus   I caused mortals to cease foreseeing doom.
Chorus   What cure did you provide them with against that sickness?
Prometheus   I placed in them blind hopes.

The true Promethean spirit of science means to liberate man by giving him knowledge and some measure of dominion over the physical environment. But at another level, and in a new age, it also constructs the mythology of scientific materialism, guided by the corrective devices of the scientific method, addressed with precise and deliberately affective appeal to the deepest needs of human nature, and kept strong by the blind hopes that the journey on which we are now embarked will be farther and better than the one just completed.

47. The Illusion of Sociobiology   Stuart Newton Hampshire

Stuart Newton Hampshire (1914–   ) is Warden of Wadham College, Oxford University, England. He was Professor of Philosophy at Princeton University from 1963 to 1970. His writings include: *Thought and Action, Freedom of Mind and Other Essays, Modern Writers and Other Essays,* and *Two Theories of Morality.*

The tradition of mixing the concepts of biology with philosophy and *Weltanschauung* stretches back into the last century and has Comte and Spencer as its unfortunate leaders: unfortunate, because their works are by now largely unreadable. Professor Wilson is sharply aware that his writing belongs to this tradition and he is aware of the dangers and deceptions within the tradition; particularly the danger that yesterday's scientific speculations soon acquire a fusty look. Having been born in the excitement of today's discoveries, they are then extrapolated into a golden scientific future, which turns out to be quite different.

Jacques Monod's *Chance and Necessity* was an immediate predecessor of this book in usefully creating a stir, and Professor Wilson also mentions the Huxleys and C. H. Waddington. They all called upon moral and political philosophers to take due account of the theory of evolution and of natural selection, and specifically to adapt their moral values to correspond to the scientifically ascertainable needs of the human race. They all accused philosophers, and humanists of all kinds, of being unnecessarily ignorant of the exactly known formative influences on human nature and of a willful innocence which left them pontificating in a void. Like the priests whom they supposed they had outgrown and displaced, philosophers were accused of turning their backs on ascertained facts in order to be consoled by their own moral inventions.

Professor Wilson says all these things in his new book,* but with much more care and with more qualifications. He has not neglected philosophy in the academic sense, and he knows what limits philosophers are likely to place on inferences from scientific theories to moral requirements. He is much less dogmatic and confident of his conclusions than Monod was.

Briefly summarized, his argument runs like this: we have need now of a new discipline, called sociobiology, which will exhibit the junction of biology, in all its recently developing branches, with the social sciences. This new combined discipline will investigate the constraints that limit the options open to us when we wish to improve ways of life and social organization. There are fixities in human nature, as there are also points of plasticity and variability about which we may be uninformed. There are many sources within biology which can yield evidence about these constraints: studies of primate behavior, of brain physiology, studies of identical twins, learning theory, and, above all, studies within genetics of inherited traits and capacities, and of the physical basis of the transmission of them.

Professor Wilson alludes to some recent and current work in these fields, and much of his argument consists of predictions of future developments in these flourishing sciences. They should, he thinks, provide in future the explanatory background to accumulating knowledge in the social sciences; and by social science he seems to mean principally anthropology and sociology. He quotes liberally from social anthropologists to illustrate presumed constancies in sexual roles and in habits of religious observance. He infers that these have a hereditary basis and that they can be seen to confer a natural advantage on human populations organized in social groups. He means a natural advantage in the biologists' sense of contributing to the adaptation of a population and hence to its survival, though not necessarily to the survival of the individuals who carry the advantage. Sexuality itself can be seen as a naturally selected device to ensure pair-bonding, and it is simply bad biology to think of sexual intercourse as primarily designed for reproduction, as the natural-law doctrine of the Catholic Church requires. Biology, in this view, corrects moral and social theory.

Professor Wilson characteristically avoids the better known errors of inferring from the behavior of primates to the behavior of man, and he avoids the use of concepts like aggression and territoriality in making such inferences. He remarks that "there is no evidence that a widespread unitary aggressive instinct exists." He dismisses the claims, familiar in bestsellers on popular biology, that men are uniquely destructive within their own species, or that the persistence of warfare and factional infighting is to be interpreted as a variant of defense of territory, as known in some other species. He does not fall back into any of these variants of simplified social Darwinism.

*[*On Human Nature*. Cambridge: Harvard U.P., 1978—ed.]

The theory holding his argument together is that genes establish limits within which culture can develop both as unexamined social convention and as conscious belief. Sometimes a cultural trait is a hypertrophy, or enlargement, of a physically founded disposition, and sometimes culture develops by playing variations on a basic, physically determined theme. For example, a tendency to polygyny—the mating of the male with more than one female—probably has an inherited physical basis and confers a natural advantage on the species; but the forms that it takes—polygamy, monogamy, mistresses, multiple marriages and divorces—may be very various.

Professor Wilson even surmises that there is an inherited need, represented in gene pools, for some kind of reverence for the sacred, and that this need, passed from generation to generation by physical, not cultural, transmission, sets a limit upon the possibilities of a bare, scientific enlightenment as a basis for social cohesion. Just as the inherited need for pair-bonding and some family ties probably makes ideal communal living impracticable, so, according to Wilson, there is an inherited need for some "sacralization," with its accompanying myth, a need built into the human constitution. This is due to the long-tested and selected advantage to a population of preserving social cohesion over many generations; and "sacralization" is a means to social cohesion.

The disputable hypothesis here concerns the method of transmission of these supposed human constancies rather than the constancies themselves. Professor Wilson is distinguishing between, on the one hand, human traits which have been naturally selected as conferring an advantage on descendants and which have therefore been physically transmitted through a population, and on the other, human traits which are transmitted through specific social customs, and he argues that there is a physically inherited tendency of men to conform to social customs, whatever the customs may be.

The substance of his thesis is the guess that many more of the recognized human constancies than is generally thought are physically, rather than socially, determined, Standing behind this thesis is a philosophical claim that is not fully worked out but that is clearly implied and once or twice stated: that thought and belief and sentiment, and all that composes culture, are epiphenomena in human nature. That is, human nature is in the first place constituted by a transmission of genetic material which incorporates a program for human behavior—a program, however, that has a certain range of indeterminacy and that leaves options open.

The preprogramming, Wilson acknowledges, is unspecific when compared with the preprogramming of other species, and the cortex, and the human brain as a whole, is (as far as we know) a uniquely elaborate piece of machinery, designed through natural selection to record and respond to an immense variety of stimuli, with an immense variety of patterns of behavior. More particularly, the human brain is now adapted not only to learning languages but also to pursuing knowledge indefinitely, and these inbuilt dispositions lead to complexities and elaborations in behavior which cannot be computed, even in outline. The question of whether there is a sense in which the multiply varied human responses must be assumed to be determined, even though they are probably incalculably complex, Wilson leaves to one side, wisely.

Professor Wilson naturally concludes that we can now apply the knowledge of biological possibilities and limits that we have just acquired in more intelligent social planning. His last chapter has the title "Hope," and this application of biology to social science and planning is the hope. Men have, he says, inherited mythopoeic tendencies which served them well in primitive conditions, and he believes that scientific materialism by itself will not be rich enough as a replacement for religion and as solid social cement. What he calls "the evolutionary epic" is "probably the best myth we will ever have. It can be adjusted until it comes as close to truth as the human mind is constructed to judge the truth." If the rather obscure end of this last sentence is overlooked, one can hear once again the steady hum of scientific optimism which was first given classical form in Condorcet's great "*Esquisse d'un tableau historique des progrès de l'esprit humain.*"*

This very bare summary of the argument is unfair if it has not given an impression of the good sense with which Wilson's claims for scientific enlightenment are advanced, and of the caution with which the underlying issues of choice and determinism are reasonably left on one side. But still the argument of the book, and the philosophical assumptions behind it, seem to be misconceived and wrong.

One root of my disagreement is that Professor Wilson's scientific materialism stops short of being materialistic enough. For instance, in the chapter on religion he asks: "Is the readiness to be indoctrinated a neurologically based learning rule that evolved through the selection of clans competing against each other?" The concept of indoctrination, I think, has no place in a physical science, and vast obscurities are concealed in that phrase "neurologically based." One man's indoctrination is another man's learning, according to their evaluations of the propositions learned: do they have a different physical basis? Or again: "The mind is predisposed—one can speculate that learning rules are physiologically programmed—to participate in a few processes of sacralization. . . ." But sacralization is not a concept that can be fitted into physical theory, if only because no criterion or sufficient test of whether a process is a process of sacralization is to be found in observable behavior. The thought of the subject is essential, as it is also essential to distinguishing indoctrination from other learning processes.

Another example of an inherited trait cited by Wilson will serve as a contrast: the dispositions that are involved in competitions among males for dominance in a group, and in recognizing and deferring to the dominant male. Being value-free and having behavioral criteria, these can be sufficiently revealed to observation, or can be tested by experiment; skilled observation may be sufficient to show, without indeterminacy, whether or not the dispositions are present. Therefore male dominance

*[*Outline of a Historical View of the Progress of the Human Mind*—ed.]

is a concept that can be introduced into a scientific theory without obscurity or indeterminacy.

Where the line is properly to be drawn between that which is observable and that which is not observable or testable is within limits open to discussion and argument; and more or less austere and restrictive definitions can be accepted for different purposes and in different sciences. Similarly, what counts as thought is also variable, although only within limits. The objection that I am bringing against Professor Wilson's kind of scientific materialism, so called, is not just a methodological one, nor is it a technical point in the philosophy of science. Nor is it an objection which empiricist philosophers of the present day would particularly stress rather more than rationalists. It is a more general issue which has been at the center of philosophy since the seventeenth century, and the objections to sociobiology as a possible science cannot be understood until this issue has been clarified.

Like most men who in the last resort follow established common-sense habits of thought, and who temper common sense with love of the natural sciences, Professor Wilson is an "interactionist," believing that there will turn out to be natural laws, scientifically established, exhibiting a two-way causation between mental and bodily states. But he is an interactionist who thinks he is a materialist, because he also believes that the dominance of physical causes in interactions between mind and body have not been understood up until now.

This is why he speaks of thought and of culture as epiphenomena in relation to the physical causes operative in heredity. This view of causal dependencies between body and mind is the natural response of common-sense thinking to the accelerating success of the physical sciences; and yet it is, I believe, an incoherent view when its full implications are traced; it is a halfway house, a working compromise. The implicit incoherences of the compromise lead to no trouble, and are scarcely even noticed, until a theoretician, scientist, or philosopher comes forward with a speculative project such as sociobiology.

The incoherences come to the surface as soon as we enter the sphere of systematic theory. We can happily talk about psychogenic lesions and psychosomatic illnesses as a way of recording regular correlations between the physical and mental that we have noticed in ordinary experience—so long as we do not ask for systematic explanations of them. As unquestioning and practical interactionists, we have an embarrassing thought and we find that we immediately blush; the correlation between our thought and its physical effect seems clear; we take a tranquilizer and immediately have more serene thoughts. This level of knowledge of causal connections between mind and matter is exactly like the empirical knowledge of causes which enables most of us to manipulate physical things without knowing the laws of mechanics which would explain their reactions. But if we have serious plans to future research, we had better find an engineer who knows some mechanics and physical theory; and sociobiology is intended to be a science and not merely an unexplained list of useful causal correlations.

The incoherence of Professor Wilson's project for sociobiology is prob-ably best explained by the example of Descartes; he was certainly not an epiphenomenalist in Professor Wilson's sense, but he did foresee the essential problem which a systematic physics would present to common-sense thinking. Every physical motion, whether on an astronomical scale or a subatomic scale, has to be explicable by universal laws of motion, quantitatively expressed, and these laws are themselves intelligibly related parts of a single systematic theory. This requirement applies to the motions of a man's body, and of his limbs, no less than to any other observable object. So when I go for a walk and wave to a friend, these observable movements must have a complete explanation, with any degree of precision required, within the laws of physics and by reference to initial conditions stated in physical terms.

When adequate explanation, in the sense of lawlike and systematic explanation, is in question, physical changes can only be explained by physical changes, and no spiritual forces can burst in from outside, as it were, as if by miracle. So much for what Descartes required of the physical sciences. Equally, and on the other side, thought has its own connected-ness and continuity, a connectedness that is quite different from that of things extended in space; and a thought can only be adequately explained through its connection with another thought in accordance with universal laws of thought. There are evidently looser causal connections, well known at the empirical level, between states of body and states of mind which include thoughts; and we rely on this empirical knowledge from day to day. But it is not knowledge which has the structure and organiza-tion of a science.

Descartes was a dualist in the sense that he represented the created world as divided into two self-contained domains of objects in space and of thoughts, and the two domains have a meeting point in human person-ality. Professor Wilson, in his plans for sociobiology, represents thought, as it enters into culture and social customs, as in part to be explained scientifically by physical determinants, without claiming that there can be an adequate explanation of physical states outside physics. Biology there-fore advances into the territory of the social sciences, but no reverse pro-cess of social scientists explaining physical phenomena to biologists is called for.

Professor Wilson has the Cartesian spirit in that he predicts more secure foundations for knowledge in the human sciences on the basis of the sensational discoveries in molecular biology in the last thirty years, as did Descartes on the basis of Galileo's physics. But he seems not to have heeded the case repeatedly made against Descartes. When I go for a walk and wave to a friend, the scientific descriptions of motion and change in the language of physics and biology make no reference to the gesture of waving, or to friends, or even to going for a walk. These are concepts from the mixed descriptions of common sense, and common sense is not principally concerned with the purely physical mechanisms that will explain the observed physical events scientifically. This mixed vocabulary was not designed for the purposes of scientific theory or for adequate explanation. Rather it has developed to meet the needs of communication between persons, and, most important, to meet the needs of decision-making and of discussing intentions and sentiments with others.

The beliefs, desires, sentiments, and intentions that initiate and guide my actions have been formed in my head, or heart, for some good or bad reasons, and often for reasons which I then explain to others. At the same time I see the behavior of others as indications of their beliefs, desires, and sentiments and as realizing their intentions. Our verbs of action and names and descriptions of persons and things—e.g., "waving," "friendly,"—depend for their meaning largely on the social institutions, customs, and rituals to which they refer, or which provide a necessary context for them.

A keen-eyed observer from outer space, where they have quite different ways of life, would not see the point of much of our behavior, and would not be able to infer the beliefs, desires, and sentiments which inspire it. He would not recognize the furniture, or classify patterns of behavior as we do. The options open to him in his planning would be correspondingly different. Similarly, an old man arriving in contemporary California from some backward area might not be able to identify what middle-aged professors are doing running through the streets in shorts: they are running, plainly, but with what intention or meaning? "Jogging" is the name of a new institution, with a particular context of belief and desire, and to identify someone's running as jogging implicitly invokes this background and setting.

It is a general characteristic of common-sense and prescientific descriptions of conduct that the imputation of intentions and sentiments to the subject always invokes a context wider than any one particular occasion. What a man can be truly described as intentionally doing depends on the range of his beliefs and interests, and these in turn depend in part upon his culture, in the sense of the social customs and the language which he has learned; and what the action is depends also on the social circumstances surrounding it. Tarzan might go through the same motions on a sunny afternoon in the jungle as the California professor; but certainly he is not jogging.

These features of common-sense discourse about persons are not accidental or alterable. They arise from the fact that we must use the same vocabulary in thinking about our own present decisions as in thinking about our past behavior and about the behavior of others; while we have to invent a special vocabulary, with its own distinct type of concepts, for purely theoretical and scientific purposes. To take one example of the necessarily mixed categories of common sense: when I ask myself why I am doing something, I ask myself for the reasons that explain my action; when from curiosity I ask myself for an explanation of this same conduct in retrospect, this reason becomes also a cause, or causal factor. But it is not the kind of cause that has its place in explaining the operations of a physical mechanism, whether at the biological or chemical or fundamental physical level. Its operation is not experimentally established, and it does not have the degree of independence of its effect, and also of its unobserved setting, which experimental confirmation requires.

If I want an explanation that will be not only exact and testable but also that will fit into a general and systematic theory, then I must change the terms under which my conduct is considered. In satisfying these demands for comprehensive and exact explanation, I shall find that I am investigating the mechanisms of the performance rather than the performance identified and described as a social and cultural phenomenon, and as an expression of thought. The descriptions of behavior which can be fitted into a scheme of scientific explanation must be appropriately determinate and exact; they must not depend for their interpretation on the context of use and they must be equally testable by all observers. Psychological terms, drawn from the common vocabulary, do not satisfy these two central conditions.

The central incoherence in the idea of sociobiology arises at the junction of two forms of explanation which, serving different purposes, cannot be welded into a continuous whole: physical theory lies on one side of the coin, and what Professor Wilson calls culture, the domain of the social sciences, and particularly of anthropology, lies on the other side. It is important that one should not see this irreparable break as a division in reality, but rather as a division between two divergent sets of human interests, both irreplaceable interests. The division between the extended, or spatial, world and the world of thought has generally been represented by philosophers as a metaphysical division and as such left altogether unexplained. Professor Wilson similarly conveys a picture of the superstructure of culture imposed on the main structure of man's physical nature, with the consequent idea of a single science which would represent the workings of both.

But this picture can be, and should be, reversed, by taking as the starting point not the ultimate nature of reality, but the needs of human beings, one species among other products of evolution, who happen to have developed a physical mechanism, the human brain and central nervous system. This mechanism confers some peculiar powers: principally the power to develop forms of speech, and therefore forms of reflection and of self-consciousness, which permit forward planning of future action and also the search for laws of nature, and these in turn open up new technologies at an accelerating pace.

These technologies will increasingly be used not only to develop greater powers of perception, but to improve the performance of the brain and of adjuncts of the brain. The structure and development of scientific knowledge can be studied as a form of human behavior, but this second-order study subdivides into two quite different enterprises. The first is the study of the physical mechanisms of human intelligence, principally (at the present state of knowledge) the physiology of the brain and machine simulation of mechanisms of thought. The second includes a historical study of the habits of thought and of the social settings which are likely to be favorable to the development of knowledge. It includes as well a study of the strategies which, at different stages of knowledge, are likely to be most successful. And these second kinds of studies require philosophical, as well as historical, reflection.

I am not arguing that there are only two types and forms of inquiry:

inquiry into thought and culture, and inquiry into physical mechanisms. My argument does not support a dualism in this sense. Rather my claim is that human beings, while studying themselves and their own kind, must pursue at least two irreplaceable types of inquiry because of their own nature as embodied and self-conscious thinkers. One is an inquiry aiming at a purely theoretical understanding of their own physical functioning, in which human beings are seen as objects that conform to universal laws of nature; the other is an inquiry aiming at an understanding of their own thinking, and the thinking of others, in various normal social settings and in different languages.

The alternation between two viewpoints, one from that of disinterested observer and the other from that of social agent, constitutes the peculiarity of our species. Professor Wilson's materialism stops short of recognizing that physical theory, as it has developed, is not concerned with matter, as this word was originally understood; rather physical theory retains its identity as an inquiry in virtue of its purpose and of its structure, as being always experimental and comprehensive and exact. The force of gravity was sometimes thought, in the eighteenth century, to be too immaterial to be acceptable in physics, and the forces and particles that constitute the elements of the physical world, as revealed in modern physics, are more and more remote from the medium-sized material things such as a man's palpable body. No one can predict what will be the elements picked out as fundamental in physical theory fifty years from now, if the human race suffers no catastrophe. But we can be fairly sure that the mechanisms of genetic endowment, and of the operations of the brain, will be increasingly understood as deterministic, or semi-deterministic, systems, some of which can be to some unknown degree controlled by physical inputs through new technologies.

This understanding of bodily processes does not entail a loss of the autonomy of thought which follows its own laws in deciding which manipulations of physical reality, including the human body, should be undertaken and with what purposes in view. The notion that men think with their brains before making decisions, and that their brains function in conformity with physical laws, should be no more disturbing than the recognition that men see with their eyes, which equally conform to the laws of physics. The thought that enters into their decisions and actions, like the thought that enters into their recognition of objects seen, is governed to some degree by logic and to some degree by the syntax and vocabulary of a particular language, and to some degree also by the association of ideas in an individual's imagination. Very different thoughts, conforming to the laws of thought, will accompany the same physical transaction in different men or in the same man at different times.

In his trenchant polemic against sociobiology and Professor Wilson,* Professor Marshall Sahlins remarks, for example, that the same genealogical and physical family relationships bear utterly different labels in the context of different social customs in different societies. As an anthropologist he denies that there can be a valid argument from general geneal-

*The Use and Abuse of Biology, by Marshall Sahlins (University of Michigan Press, 1976).

ogical facts to the natural-selection advantage conferred by particular sexual customs and particular family relationships. For these customs and relations are not characteristic of the entire species, and they serve the function of providing social cohesion under different social conditions, and not the function of ensuring the better survival of a gene pool under comparable physical conditions.

Professor Wilson in effect ignores the distinguishing feature of human beings: *false speciation,* as it is sometimes called—namely, the attachment of normal men through thought and language to the habits, and way of life, of a particular subgroup, accompanied by some measure of hostility or indifference to the habits and ways of life of other subgroups of the same species. That human beings are innately disposed to learn some language, but are not innately disposed to learn one particular language, is a fact about human beings which provokes a question in natural history: what advantage was conferred on the species by the disposition to learn diverse languages and to fall into tightly coherent social groups which are often hostile to one another?

This question may be unanswerable, or unanswerable within the limits of present knowledge. But it is at least evident that this linguistic dispersion of the species is only one part of a deep-seated characteristic of dispersion, and that therefore the truly scientific study of human nature, necessarily concerned with universal laws, will leave the explanation of human thought, conscious and unconscious, untouched, except for the abstractions of logic, which are detached from the grammar of any particular language and also from any particular social context.

It is not difficult to understand, from direct experience, that our thought interprets bodily movements and physical change, whether they are our own movements or not, in accordance with regular sequences or chains of thought. These sequences have to be understood in their own terms as thoughts, governed by the continuities of thought and not by laws of motion. I have to know something about the concepts that are liable to be present to a man's mind and the alternative actions that he is likely to consider, if I am to explain his thought and intentions. To explain his thought at any particular time, as also to explain my own, entails filling in the context of surrounding thought. To explain the intentions and purposes that animate my behavior at any time entails specifying my desires and my beliefs about my situation; and it also entails filling in the context of thought surrounding these particular desires and beliefs.

Asking why I have particular thoughts immediately raises the need for a justification and endorsement of them; most of the thoughts that are dragged into my conscious scrutiny have probably been formed in preconscious thought, far away from critical scrutiny. Fitting my thoughts into a coherent pattern of thought is both correction and explanation, and is not the discovery or the invention of a mechanism.

Social anthropology, often cited by Professor Wilson, is a disciplined inquiry into human nature and culture which is a "social science" for the purposes of university administration. But neither in method nor in purpose does the inquiry have much in common with the physical sciences. It is not an experimental science, and it does not attain, or generally aim at, comprehensive, exact, and systematic theories. Rather it tries to interpret the distinguishing habits of thought and the intentions incorporated in the social customs of the indefinitely varied social groups which are open to study. Its method is interpretation and translation, and the provision of a context of thought for beliefs and desires which otherwise, and considered in isolation, are unintelligible. Anthropologists try to exhibit as coherent, in all their variety, customs and conventions and religious and sexual practices and family arrangements and arts and games. These are all expressions of thought, not objects of exact and systematic scientific theory.

In arguing against Professor Wilson's sociobiology and scientific materialism, I have continually mentioned thought, and the explanation of thought; and Professor Sahlins, like many other anthropologists, writes about "symbolic" systems as his objects of study, using Ernst Cassirer's terminology. To the degree this usage omits considerations of the full range of thought, with all its complexities of practical reasoning and reflection, it seems too restrictive.

Also, there is a philosophical point to be made by the use of the word *thought* when materialism is in question. The distinction between understanding and explaining thought by reference to causes, and understanding and explaining physical change by reference to causes, is a distinction made unavoidable by the most elementary facts about us: particularly, the fact that we are born with the physical equipment that makes it possible for us to think and to talk to others about our activities and movements tomorrow. The most tough-minded scientific materialist, who is *ex hypothesis* an active thinker, has to think of his future in the light of his accumulating knowledge of the natural course of events. He knows that accretions to his knowledge of independent causes will present him with new possibilities of action, to which he may wish to respond differently.

All this he knows most vividly and directly through the control of his own body, which places him in the observed physical world and ties him to it and makes him conform to its physical laws. He is not only, or principally, the observer of his body; he is also the thoughtful interpreter of its movements; his thought lends them sense and direction, in so far as he interprets them as conforming to his desires and beliefs. He will think of his body's movements as his "actions" when they conform to his leading desire and when he knows or believes that the immediate cause of the movement is in him, and in the physical embodiment of his desire in the structures of his brain.

If he is a thoroughgoing scientific materialist, unlike Professor Wilson, he will not think of the relation between his desire and its physical embodiment in the brain as a causal relation; he will point to a parallel between this relation and the relation of the physical processes of color vision to the recognition of colors. Just as the same genealogical relations—e.g., that between maternal grandmother and son, or between aunt and nephew—may be interpreted by different concepts in different kinship systems and different languages, so there will be many different intentions embodied in movements which, from the standpoint of a scientific observer, are the same movement. One does not therefore need to go to the exalted level of the academic disciplines to find that the scientific materialist is one who believes that the world as we observe it proceeds in accordance with the laws of physics, and that our desires, beliefs, and other thoughts, including the belief in materialism, have a perceptible, and therefore physical, embodiment in the brain, as our perceptions have a physical embodiment in the eyes. But the scientific materialist should also recognize that the nature of these thoughts, including the belief in materialism itself, can only be adequately explained by their contexts and by the connections peculiar to thought.

The sense in which Professor Wilson is not sufficiently a materialist is that he expects too much from immaterial causes in science, and from a technology based on them; and this is the vice of all those who still expect too much from the social sciences, and particularly from sociology. It is by operation on the physical mechanisms of heredity and intelligence that we can expect planned changes, for better or worse, of a kind that could not be achieved by persuasion and argument—that is, by thought.

Sociobiology as a project has the ring of Condorcet's optimism, of the hopes of the Enlightenment and of Comtean positivism; it suggests a picture of the history of different societies and cultures as best understood as a history of humanity's successive adaptations to a natural environment. Apart from being philosophically incoherent, this seems to me a dangerous illusion about history. Catastrophe is also a feature both of natural history in biological time and of the comparatively short history of human cultures. Improbably favorable mutations that lead to better adaptations to particular environments in the short run can also lead to maladaptation and extinction in the longer run. Do we know that the developments of the brain associated with intelligent speech and self-consciousness and social diversity may not in the longer run prove disastrous? If forced to speculate in the longer run, I think that it is a reasonable belief, on present evidence, that the species will not for very long survive and will prove to have been in this sense an evolutionary failure. Dispersion through language and custom may be a net disadvantage in the long run.

Obviously this is as much mere speculation as a contrary belief would be. But the better contribution of a biologist might be to indicate the chanciness of human survival and the very narrow limits of human knowledge. Seen from the standpoint of contemporary physics and contemporary biology alone, and without the consolations of revealed religion, human knowledge of the universe must always be a very small thing and the future development of science entirely unpredictable. Our categories and concepts are limited by our powers of observation and of thought, and we do not know how far we may extend these powers by manipulation of their physical embodiments. But we have no assurance of a unique destiny for the human race, unless from supernatural evidences.

Recognition of the contingency of evolution and of natural selection should reasonably be combined with recognition of present uncertainty. Neither with respect to survival nor with respect to the perspective from which we learn about the universe are we uniquely privileged, as far as we know; and the record does not suggest that we have a very distinguished and happy future. The monuments of human thought, and not least the physical sciences, are evidently impressive. But our knowledge and understanding will always be narrowly limited by our inherited physical constitutions, and there is no reason to believe that we have some central or essential part in nature's whole design. The universe would proceed regularly on its way without human beings. If it does, perhaps the dolphins, and also the whales, will move untroubled through the silent seas, evolving still along their own appropriate path.

Science and Ecology: Mysticism Versus Reason

48. Mysticism and Ecology: The Rhapsodic Intellect   Theodore Roszak

Theodore Roszak (1933–   ) is Professor of History and Chairman of General Studies at California State University, Hayward. He is the author of *The Making of a Counter Culture, Where the Wasteland Ends,* and *Person/Planet: The Creative Disintegration of Industrial Society.* He has become well known as an advocate of a "counter culture" to our contemporary scientific-technological one.

To Know and to Know

There is a moment in Tolstoy's *The Death of Ivan Ilyich* when the dying Ivan wanders back in memory to an episode in his early education. He recalls a lesson in logic . . . the familiar textbook syllogism that begins "All men are mortal."

"*All men are mortal*" . . . he knew it then, as a boy: an indisputable fact. And here on his deathbed, he confronts the fact again. "All men are mortal." But now there is a special light that plays over the words, gravely changing their character. It is as if Ivan has for the first time come to know his mortality. And yet he has always known it, as a matter of simple deduction from the premise. He has always known it . . . but never known it, not as he knows it here and now. There is nothing he can add to the fact; he cannot increase its "information content." Nothing about the first has changed . . . and yet everything about it has changed. Ivan has at last learned what these four words really *mean.* He cannot say anything more or different than when he was a schoolboy in his logic class; yet what he knows now carries the weight of increased *meaning.* Ivan does not know more; he knows deeper.

But where is this increased meaning to be found? No longer in the words, but in the whole man who hears and speaks them. It is in *the feel of the words* as they pass through his mind and in the power they have acquired to change his life. The words are the same, but now when Ivan ponders them, there is a *resonance* that was not there before. The meaning is in the resonance. And the resonance swells within him until it rocks the foundations of his life.

There are ways of knowing and ways of knowing. Tolstoy's Ivan Ilyich is a study in existential knowledge, knowledge that possesses the resonance of personal crisis. The knowledge of transcendent symbols has much the same character. It too must have its resonance: the resonance of root meaning. In both cases, we are carried beyond verbal surfaces. In both cases, knowledge is deepened and personalized by the impact of urgent experience, but without increase of information. Se we are left knowing more than we can say—unless perhaps we have the gift of rhapsodic declaration. We are in the position of the Zen master who began as a novice knowing that mountains are only mountains, rivers only rivers, and finished as a sage knowing that mountains are only mountains, rivers only rivers . . . ah, but finished knowing it *wisely*. How to talk about such things?

I have argued that the alternative to the idolatrous reality we inherit from "single vision and Newton's sleep" is the reclamation of transcendent symbols. This is to appeal for a richer kind of knowledge, yet nothing that distinguishes itself by yielding additional data about the world. That is the dilemma of the symbols. They fill our lives, our art, our language; but those who do not attend to the resonance of symbols will invariably move along the surface of experience, mistaking the densified derivative for its transcendent original. Failing to see the vital difference, they will insist that one tell them what *more* there is to know than they already know. Single vision, we must remember, deals in the same repertory of symbols as do religion, ritual, art. It covers much the same *quantity* of cultural space, but without qualitative depth. Its habit is always to interpret the symbol down and away from its transcendent source, to densify it into articulate fact, empirical object, and then to say, "See! *Here* we have the real meaning of the thing."

The Old Gnosis has, over the past century or more, been run through any number of ingeniously reductive "interpretations." Its economic, psychological, sociological meanings have all been filtered out for study. And of course these secular accretions are also there to be examined. They are part of the human story. But not all. There is that which remains behind when the accretions have been peeled away from the symbols. *Root* meaning. The gold amid the dross. God's portion.

Resonance and Literalism

The peculiar degeneration of consciousness from which we suffer— the diminishing awareness of symbolic resonance—is especially a crisis of language. In our culture, almost uniquely, we have inverted the hierarchical relationship between rhapsodic declaration and literal prose, between matters of myth and matters of fact. Rhapsody and myth—the prime linguistic carriers of symbolic resonance—have long since ceased to be regarded as sources of knowledge. Whatever else Christianity borrowed from Judaism, it left behind the lyric spirit of prophecy, preferring desiccated theological discourse. It worked that weakness for literalism well into the grain of western consciousness until, in the modern period, most of our keenest minds had come passionately to believe, like Dickens' Mr. Gradgrind, that "in this life, we want nothing but Facts, sir; nothing but Facts." What else could follow from this but a culture whose realities are restricted to flat, functional prose, unambiguous quantities, and Baconian inductions. As a result, the one-dimensional language of the logician, scholar, and critic—and eventually of the technician and scientist—has been promoted to a position of omnipotence among us. Has there ever been such a culture of explainers and clarifiers, expounders and logic choppers?

Think how fanatically verbal our education is, our *good* education that strives for "excellence" by force-feeding children with reading-writing-and-arithmetic from the earliest possible age, and never ceases exercising that narrow range of skills from nursery school to graduate school. Lecture, textbook, recitation, examination, note taking, research, criticism, debate, discussion ... from Dick and Jane to the seminar table and learned journal. If there is more to the human anatomy than the reading eye, the logical ear, and the articulating voice box, our schools know nothing of it. God help the painters and dancers, the musicians and contemplatives among our students! When we educate, it is invariably on the assumption that the meanings of things can be exhausted by making good, clear, logical talk about them. Where there should be the resonance of experience, we demand more language. Or better still: numbers. For modern mathematics has achieved the special status of a language devoid even of those last quavers of resonance that cling stubbornly to words: ambiguity, emotional shading, etymological echoes. To suggest in any of our academies that there are things words and numbers cannot and ought not try to cope with is to commit an anti-intellectual outrage. Like Ivan Ilyich, we are the prisoners of literal surfaces. For Ivan, it came as an astonishment and terror to realize that the logical premise "all men are mortal" had an experience attached to it. Besides the word "death," there was also ... *death*. So too the symbols demand experience of us. They must be received with the openness of our total being. And when they take hold, they strike us dumb.

To live fully is to live resonantly. Language isolated from its nonverbal resonances can adequately express only the monotones of life: simple information, unambiguous operations. Yet the major effort of analytical and positivist philosophy over the past several generations has not been to amplify resonance, but to imperiously drive all meaning into just such monotonous linguistic formulations ... and then to shoot on sight whatever refuses to be herded into this intellectual concentration camp. As if language had become the private property of logicians, technicians, and scientists, and henceforth all communication must be modeled on the hard-edged exactitudes of laboratory research—without even allowance for the contribution that intuition, hunches, wordplay, metaphor, and rule-of-thumb make to all worthwhile research.

Here we have another ironic example of how Christian religious psychology has paved the way for the skeptical positivism that was to be religion's deadliest opposition. The literalist mentality has never been more at home than in Christianity, where it has systematically reduced religion to abstract discussions of Belief and Doctrine. "A God to whom human words cannot point," Harvey Cox has said, "is not the God of the Bible." Sad to say. For where religion invests so exclusively in discursive theology, insisting that the word divorced from vision and conduct can embody the spirit, the effect is to scotch the resonant meaning of language. So we have those grotesque idiocies of Christian history that have made religion stink in the nostrils of so many decent people: the official catechism learned by rote, wars fought over articles of faith, the judgment of people by the creeds they mouth, the persecution of heretical professions.

All this comes of unloading upon ordinary language a burden it cannot bear. The proper question to ask of any people's religion is, "What have they experienced and how may we share in this experience?" Christianity has single-mindedly pressed another question: "What do they say they believe and how does it square with our creed?"

I vividly recall my own mind-murdering struggles with the Catholic catechism in childhood. Question and answer, question and answer . . . a jackbooted parade of lifeless verbal formulas, every one of them to be recited letter perfect, every one of them to be literally believed under threat of corporal punishment. Dogma and doctrine were marched through my brain like storm troops flattening every natural barrier childish inquisitiveness might raise. It was open warfare on young imagination. Can there be any question what damage has been done to the visionary powers in our culture by generation after generation of such ruthless creed-mongering? For the good of my soul, I was being programmed like a human computer with data points of the true faith. Among all my socalled religious instructors, there was not one, I think, who knew that even Saint Thomas laid aside his theology once the supreme vision had settled upon him, saying, "All that I have written seems to me like straw compared with what has now been revealed to me."

Understandable enough that the rebellious positivist should despise the authoritarian folly of dogmatic theology to the point of dismissing all religious discourse as "meaningless." It was my own reaction to the inanity of Christian literalism. But this only repeats the dogmatist's error. It overlooks that the meaning of visionary and metaphysical parlance is in the resonance of its symbolism. That is where its power lies to shape conscience and consciousness without resort to inculcation. In his conviction that language without resonance is the full measure of reality, the positivist is really the secret blood brother of the dogmatic theologian. The one nails his literalism to creed and scripture, the other to empirical verification. The one dismisses whatever lacks doctrinal authority, the other whatever lacks empirical fact. Between them, as between two millstones, the symbols have been ground to dust. And from those little literal bits we have pieced together the language of operational efficiency and single vision. . . .

Ecology and the Uses of Mysticism

The psychic distance that separates the scientist's objectified uniformity of nature from the Oneness of the Old Gnosis is immense. It is the distance separating St. Francis from Albert Camus' Stranger. Existentially speaking, it is all the difference between the life of one who is at home in the universe and the life of one who feels himself to be a cosmic freak.

Universal law, the mathematical continuum, the physical continuity of life . . . none of these do justice to the symbolic resonance of the chemical marriage. But there is a better place to listen for the resonance in the contemporary world. The science we call ecology is the nearest approach that objective consciousness makes to the sacramental vision of nature which underlies the symbol of Oneness. In fact, the ecologists at times fall so much under the spell of the Old Gnosis that they very nearly wander over that frontier of the mind which divides respectable science from nature mysticism.

Ecology has been called "the subversive science"—and with good reason. Its sensibility—wholistic, receptive, trustful, largely non-tampering, deeply grounded in aesthetic intuition—is a radical deviation from traditional science. Ecology does not systematize by mathematical generalization or materialist reductionism, but by the almost sensuous intuiting of natural harmonies on the largest scale. Its patterns are not those of numbers, but of unity in process; its psychology borrows from Gestalt and is an awakening awareness of wholes greater than the sum of their parts. In spirit, the discipline is contemplative and therapeutic, a concernful listening with the third ear. Lynn White, Jr., has appropriately nominated St. Francis as the patron saint of ecology; I would be inclined to name the Hermetic philosophers and Romantic poets as its founding fathers. And from somewhere further back still, the vision of the Tao feeds into the study.

Moreover, like all the healing arts, ecology is through and through judgmental in character. It cannot be value-neuter. Perhaps this is its most marked contrast with the other sciences. The patterns ecologists study include man in body, mind, and deed, and therefore they prescribe a standard of health. What violates the natural harmony must be condemned; what enhances it, be endorsed. For the ecologist, being right means living right; the virtues of prudence, gentleness, mutual aid flow gracefully from his study. Ecology is the closest our science has yet come to an integrative wisdom. It, and not physics, deserves to become the *basic* science of the future.

It is all to the good—gloriously so—that our science should be enriched by this new sensibility. But this *is* a departure from scientific tradition, and it comes late in the day. How great a departure may be gauged by Otis D. Duncan's undisguised ambivalence in his article on human ecology in the latest edition of the *Encyclopaedia Britannica* (1971).

The holistic emphasis implied by the very idea of human ecology has been a continual threat to the unity of the discipline. Comprehensive treaties on the subject typically have represented expressions of social philosophy rather than empirically grounded statements of scientific theory. Indeed, numerous commentators have put forth the view that human ecology must remain primarily a philosophic viewpoint rather than aspire to the status of a systematic discipline.

In other words, the more life-saving wisdom ecology offer us, the less right it has to "aspire" to the lofty "status" of a true science. The scientific community properly makes haste to embrace the ecologists as their spokesmen in the environmental crisis. But, in truth, this is rather like the Catholic Church, at a late stage, canonizing a Joan of Arc, whom its previous custodians had burned at the stake for witchcraft.

Still, better late than never.

Yet there is a deeper issue here—one which even our keenest ecologists have yet to confront. And when they do, will they be able to keep their discipline on the safe side of scientific respectability? Potentially, there is heresy hidden within this new ecological sensibility that now spreads through the industrial world, though perhaps only those who come to ecology already dubious about the sufficiency of the scientific vision of nature can as yet recognize that fact.

Let me illustrate what I mean. The point I am after emerges clearly in the following highly imaginative reading of primitive ritual. The passage comes from the landscape architect and city planner Ian McHarg and nicely reveals the ecological insight he brings to all his work.

> Among the Iroquois the bear was highly esteemed. . . . When the hunted bear was confronted, the kill was preceded by a long monologue in which the needs of the hunter were fully explained and assurances were given that the killing was motivated by need, and not the wish to dishonor. Now if you would wish to develop an attitude to prey that would ensure stability in a hunting society, then such views are the guarantee. . . . The hunter who believes that all matter and actions are sacramental and consequential will bring deference and understanding to his relations with the environment. He will achieve a steady state with his environment—he will live in harmony with nature and survive because of it.

McHarg's sensitive interpretation is welcome relief from the ethnocentrism that would have us think our prescientific ancestors were not quite wholly and competently human. Here we have the sort of sympathetic insight that is now making anthropological activists of so many young people, influencing them toward a "neolithic conservatism" (Paul Goodman's phrase) that seeks to revive the primitive folkways.

But read the passage again, and notice: McHarg's appreciation of what he calls "the pantheist view" (the transcendent experience of Oneness) is entirely functional. His conclusion is that the sensibility he describes just happened, by a stroke of luck, to be serviceable; it worked to produce a ritually regulated ecosystem. Now, he argues, industrial society must invent a similarly successful expedient for dealing with its environment. But when McHarg takes up discussion of that prospect, he begins by asking "where else can we turn for an accurate model of the world and ourselves but to science?"

And here is the crux of the matter. *Is this purely functionalist analysis of the perennial nature mysticism sufficient?* Or do we not see here once again a transcendent symbol in the process of densification? Ecology stands at a critical crossroads. Is it, too, to become another anthropocentric technique of efficient manipulation, a matter of enlightened self-interest and expert, long-range resource budgeting? Or will it meet the nature mystics on their own terms and so recognize that we are to embrace nature as if indeed it were a beloved person in whom, as in ourselves, something sacred dwells?

The counsel of ecology is caution. But *why* should we be cautious? Only because our own poor hides are at stake? That is one answer. And by the terms of that answer, nature remains objectivized, if more expediently exploited. But there is another possibility. We must deal cautiously with nature because caution is an expression of love, and our love is invited—in no merely metaphorical sense.

Sooner or later (in fact, the time is now) ecology will have to come to grips with the sensibility of that Iroquois hunter—with the vision of all the nature mystics—by way of something more than a reductionist functionalism. It will have to confront in all honesty the paramount fact that modern science in its profoundist ecological insight is indebted to religious traditions reaching back to shamanic origins. For the experience of nature's Oneness burned bright in human awareness long before Newton found the numbers with which to caricature that great truth.

Ecology already hovers on the threshold of heresy. Will it be brave enough to step across and, in so doing, revolutionize the sciences as a whole? If that step is to be taken, it will not be a matter of further research, but of transformed consciousness. Kathleen Raine, in a single line of poetry, gives us the razor's edge of the issue neatly honed: "It is not birds that speak, but men learn silence."

For many of our cultural drop-outs who have already learned that silence—which is the symbolic resonance—ecology represents a last tenuous connection with the scientific mainstream. It is the one science that seems capable of assimilating moral principle and visionary experience, and so of becoming a science of the whole person. But there is no guarantee ecology will reach out to embrace these other dimensions of the mind. It could finish—at least in its professionally respectable version—as no more than a sophisticated systems approach to the conservation of natural resources. The question remains open: which will ecology be, the last of the old sciences or the first of the new?

A Science of Rhapsodic Intellect

. . . Because science dominates the reality game of high industrial society, I am convinced that a hard critique of its psychology now has everything to do with restoring our cultural health. If we fail to alter that game radically, neither sanity nor democracy has much chance of holding out against the technocratic imperatives of the artificial environment. For that matter, science itself is not likely to survive as more than a caricature of its finest aspirations unless it joins in the adventure of expanding consciousness—though this is sure to cost it most of the privileges it now enjoys as the brain trust of the technocracy.

There have been many wise prescriptions offered for the ills of our single-visioned science. Abraham Maslow has called for an "hierarchical integration" of many modes of knowing, including those we are learning from the Zen and Taoist traditions. Lewis Mumford has long been advocating a science based on "an organic world-picture," rather than mechanistic models. Lancelot Law Whyte has sought to unite art, ethics, and natural philosophy within a "science of form" whose genealogy traces back to Goethe. Thomas Blackburn has employed the concept of complementarity as a model for integrating sensuous experience, intuition, and objectivity. Arthur Koestler has become a major public voice for those biologists and psychologists who dissent from reductionist and behavioral methods, demanding a new emphasis on wholes and systems. My views share a large common ground with all these thinkers. The essence of their critique and mine is that science is far too narrowly grounded in the personality. It closes out too much experience and in this way drastically distorts what it studies. As a result, it has become a highly productive research machinery; but what it pours forth does not add up to a life-enhancing natural philosophy.

But I believe science has more to do than live down its reductionist and mechanist vices; it must also purge itself of the idolatrous sensibility it inherits from its Judeo-Christian background. No change of scientific mind will go far enough that does not return us to the sacramental vision of nature. On this point, my own thinking echoes that of Seyyed Hossein Nasr. Like him, I believe our science must once more learn to contemplate nature "not as an independent domain of reality but as a mirror reflecting a higher reality, a vast panorama of symbols which speak to man and have meaning for him." In brief, the task is to create a science of rhapsodic intellect.

Perhaps this is too much to ask of a tightly organized profession seemingly in the flood tide of success and bedazzled by its capacity to proliferate "hard results." Single vision is so far removed from the participative and multidimensional consciousness which rhapsodic intellect requires. And yet, in another sense, rhapsodic intellect beings as close to home as the symbols that guide the scientific mind in its downward course through time and matter. If only the scientists might recapture for us and for themselves the root meaning of those symbols and realize the debt they owe to the visionary powers from which the symbols stem. Even in the barest mathematical formulations of science the symbols linger on, waiting to be warmed into life. The numbers have not always been so bereft of resonance as modern philosophy has labored to make them. They too were once objects of contemplation. Within the Pythagorean tradition— which is doubtless a comparatively late version of the old number magic— every act of calculation served as an expression of partial harmonies within the One.

A reductionist mathematics, eager to get on with its manipulative measurements, sees more utility in atomizing the One and then counting up its parts into discrete and meaningless agglomerations: heaps of things here and there in the void. "The atoms of Democritus and Newton's particles of light . . ." But that is not the only way to experience number. There is also an *internal* counting which preserves the sense that all things are parts of the whole, that the many is a playful flux within the One. For such a sense of number, every equation is a balancing out of polarities, a making of one out of two. As for the geometric forms: they have never lost their charm for the artist, and probably not for the mathematician either. It is unlikely that any amount of utilitarian objectivizing will ever wholly dispel the symbolic resonance that arises from that strange tension between shaping line and unshaped space, between bounded and boundless. The forms and numbers need lose none of their usefulness for remaining in touch with their old mysteries. Though of course meditation takes time from calibration; it slows down the research and is nothing that can be run off by a computer.

But all this is only to observe once again the paradox that makes transcendent and densified symbols both identical and yet antithetical—like the positive and negative versions of the same photograph. Which should warn us that a science of rhapsodic intellect can never be achieved on the cheap by simply tacking an afterthought on the business as usual of nonstop research. Nor can it be done by processing young scientists through an additional course of study in Taoist nature mysticism. It is a matter of changing the fundamental sensibility of scientific thought—and doing so even if we must drastically revise the professional character of science and its place in our culture. There is no doubt in my mind that such a revision would follow. Rhapsodic intellect would slacken the pace and scale of research to a degree that would be intolerable by current professional standards. It would subordinate much research to those contemplative encounters with nature that deepen, but do not increase knowledge. And it would surely end some lines of research entirely out of repugnance for their reductionism, insensitivity, and social risk.

What place would science then occupy in our culture? Stephen Toulmin has compared scientific thought to the activity of map making, suggesting that the relationship of theory to nature is much like that of a map to a landscape. I find this a fruitful analogy to ponder—though like all analogies it has its limits. Like a map, a sound body of scientific knowledge helps us to plot short-run successful journeys through those parts of the world that have been charted. It is an ingenious utilitarian device which allows us somewhat greater certainty in our prediction and adaptation. Without question, this is a precious human skill, and a fascination in its own right. But just as no map can ever be more than a selective approximation of its terrain, so no theory can be more than a schematic representation of nature. That does not make it a "mere" model, for there is always some point of real contact between the theory and the portion of nature it relates to. But that point of contact is no more than a point, and it can be devilishly difficult to say precisely what its character is, beyond saying that it orders the world for more successful manipulation.

Scientific knowledge, like a map, ignores a great deal for the very sake of such utility. That is the basis of its selectivity. We forfeit the whole value of a map if we forget that it is *not* the landscape itself or anything remotely like an exhaustive depiction of it. If we do forget, we grow rigid as a robot obeying a computer program; we lose the intelligent plasticity and intuitive judgment that every wayfarer must preserve. We may then know the map in fine detail, but our knowledge will be purely academic, inexperienced, shallow. To that extent, it may finally become disastrously impractical, thus defeating the original purpose of the map. As every wise explorer in history has known, not even the best map can replace the advice of a native guide, who may not even know what a map is. But the guide knows the pitfalls, shortcuts, and hidden resources of the country. He knows where the dangerous beasts are and the fever spots. He knows how to listen for the secret messages of the land and how best to live there.

When we insist on making scientific expertise the arbiter of all knowledge, it is exactly like believing that cartographers know more about the terrain than the natives who live there, or the artists who have come to paint its beauties, or the priests who tend its holy places. And that is (to borrow a phrase from Bentham) folly on stilts. It leads to the absurd arrogance of the book-learned sociologist who insists that, on the basis of his behavioral models, he knows more about slums and ghettos than the people who live in them. Or the sort of systems analysis that includes every kind of expertise, but never the experience of the people on the receiving end of the planning. Or the sort of psychotherapy that assumes the doctors know more about alcoholism or drug addiction or psychosis than those who have lived through the terrors. Or the sort of astrophysics that finds it sufficient to know everything about the stars except why they were once regarded as divine.

When scientists think about nature or society or people, they are really thinking about a vast collection of contrived schemes and models which are indispensable to the research their profession respects as worthwhile. The artificiality of these schemes is extreme and the gaps between them will always be large enough to let whole worlds of experience fall through. To believe that all the schemes will one day be pieced together into a perfect replica of reality is like attempting to construct a "perfect" map that leaves nothing out. If that could be done, it would provide a map as big and miscellaneous as its terrain—and therefore wholly impractical. But the very justification for the scientist's highly abstracted way of viewing the world is its selective, well-defined utility. Even the intellectual fascination of working out the puzzles of theory is related to utility as its validating touchstone. What comes of the enterprise is, after some fashion, supposed to "work"—if only to help sharpen the pure researcher's ability to anticipate the outcome of his next experiment.

Our culture has become extremely good at this style of thinking over the past three centuries. We have polished it into a superb skill—in the natural sciences at least. (The behavioral sciences are a dubious project rather like making maps of imaginary landscapes that change by the hour and are recreated afresh by their inhabitants in the light of what every new map reveals.) The pride we take in this skill is legitimate. But it is a restrictively specialized vision of reality. Discussion among scientists is like discussion of the advanced problems of map making in a cartography seminar. The cartographers are talking about their maps and not landscapes. That is why what they say frequently becomes so paradoxical when translated into ordinary language. When they forget the difference between map and landscape—and when they permit or persuade us to forget that difference—all sorts of liabilities ensue. The risk then is that we may drift hopelessly out of touch with the landscape itself, so much so that whatever progress we continue making in the techniques of cartography is only an expedition deeper into learned stupidity. At which point, it would be better to close down the science for the sake of regaining the sense we were born with.

Worse still, we are in danger of letting ourselves be mystified by experts whose rarefied knowledge now seems vastly beyond our reach. And that is the beginning of technocratic politics. In effect, the artificial environment gives us a map to live in, instead of a landscape—and so a world peculiarly beholden to the skills of mapmakers.

But worst of all, to mistake maps for landscapes is to degrade every other way of knowing the world's terrain into some sort of illusion, and in this way to close off the richest sources of joy and enlightenment in the personality. Then we forget that to map a forest means less than to write poems about it; to map a village means less than to visit among its people; to map a sacred grove means less than to worship there. Making maps may be absorbing and useful; it may take enormous intellectual talent and great training; but it is the most marginal way of knowing the landscape.

Does it lower the status of science to view it in this way? Obviously it does. But then science has been lionized out of all proportion by the necessities of urban-industrial life and by the political opportunism of the technocracy. Science never deserved to stand on the cultural pinnacle it now so gracelessly occupies; it will find itself a more becoming human activity once it steps down from that summit. As a human skill it is as worth pursuing as any; but its product, unless integrated into an ideal of rhapsodic intellect, has nothing to do with what gives life meaning.

What chance is there that such a transformation of sensibilities will take place within the scientific community? I think not much. Rhapsodic intellect would mean a revolution of consciousness, and true revolutions never happen from within the palace—especially when the living inside is so easy. If the sacramental vision of nature is ever restored to science as a discipline of the sacred, the job will be done from outside the profession— by mavericks and dissenters who have sacrificed the mandarin privileges of their profession for the sake of staying close to the Old Gnosis. In the technocratic society, a natural philosopher pays a heavy price for believing that wisdom counts for more than expertise. Big Science passes over such poor investments in favor of high-yield research specialists. But already there is a sizable contingent of adventurous science drop-outs young and old willing to keep company and mingle sensibilities with artists, nature mystics, far-out philosophers, and assorted cultural subversives. It is an alliance that will surely bear fruit in time.

Our science (like our technics) is maniacal because it bears the cultural burden of finding meaning for its society where meaning cannot possibly be found: in a reality of densified symbols. The task is an exercise in futility. For a densified symbol is precisely one that has been alienated from its root meaning. It is only good for power-knowledge. Nevertheless, science continues to thrust its way fanatically into ever denser regions of being, hoping to strike through to some ultimate truth that will vindicate its quest . . . the secret of life concocted in a test tube . . . the origin of the universe . . . the mechanisms of intelligence. . . . But all it finds are reductionist caricatures, nihilist know-how.

If the Reality Principle of the modern world is ever transformed, the change will happen, perversely and heretically, at the fringes of our culture and work its way in toward the center. The scientists, the guardians of single vision in urban-industrial society and the intellectual linchpin of the technocracy, may be among the last to hear the news.

49. Removing the Rubbish   John Passmore

John Arthur Passmore (1914–   ) is a well-known historian of philosophy and philosopher. He holds a post at the Institute of Advanced Studies, the Australian National University, Canberra. He is very interested in science, as well as in the theater, literature, music, and the fine arts.

For me to claim that I have solved any of the world's ecological problems would be inconsistent with one of my central theses. For ecological problems, or so I have argued, can be solved only by the joint efforts of scientists, technologists, economists, statesmen, administrators. And a philosopher is none of these, let alone all of them conjointly. Then what have I done? To compare small things with great, I have sought, like John Locke, 'to be employed as an under-labourer in clearing ground a little and removing some of the rubbish that lies in the way of knowledge'— and, by way of knowledge, to effective action. Let me now look more consecutively at what I have tried to clear away.

First, mystical 'rubbish,' the view that mysticism can save us, where technology cannot. Science and technology, democracy and free enterprise have always had their enemies; mysticism, primitivism, authoritarianism have always had their adherents. The ecologically-based protest— not only against shortsightedness and greed but, more fundamentally, against those attitudes to nature and society which are used to justify shortsightedness and greed—is, I have freely admitted, fully justified in itself. But it is being deployed as a new and powerful weapon in the old battle between rationality and mysticism, as when Fraser Darling tries to persuade us that the West can solve its ecological problems only by adopting 'the philosophy of wholeness', or 'the truth of Zoroastrianism . . . that we are all of one stuff, difference is only in degree, and God can be conceived as being in all and of all, the sublime and divine immanence.' (In the currently fashionable manner Darling turns to Zoroaster for what he could easily have found further West.) A moment later we find him urging us to 'exercise the ideal of our aristocratic nature, to be the servant of the planet to which we were born and to which we are still bound.'[1] His simultaneous appeal to immanence and aristocracy—his simultaneous assertion and denial, that is, of fundamental differences—is only too typical, in its intellectual incoherence, of the Western mystical tradition. And the ideal of the aristocrat who is also a servant—whether of God, of the people, or of the planet—is just as characteristic of authoritarianism. The 'philosophy of wholeness,' as in classical German Idealism, serves to link the two: the 'total whole' is at once a social and a metaphysical absolute, in which the individual is totally submerged. Fraser Darling is not introducing a new element into Western civilisation; rather, he is trying to make dominant one of the most dangerous illusions to which it has been subject, the mystical, totalistic illusion. Against this attempt, I have particularly protested.

There are, of course, special reasons why ecology should so often have been thought of as being in essence mystical, as anti-scientific or as entailing 'a philosophy of wholeness.' The general tendency of Western science has been analytic, atomistic; it has explained large-scale behaviour in terms of the behaviour of particles. So classical soil-science analyses a clod of earth into a collection of molecules held together by physical forces. This way of looking at such a clod is of great importance in explaining, let us say, the behaviour of an area of land under the impact of heavy rain or of deep ploughing. The ecologist thinks of the land not as a set of clods but rather as an ingredient in an energy system, a larger whole. 'Land,' writes Aldo Leopold, 'is not merely soil; it is a fountain of energy flowing through a circuit of soils, plants, and animals. Food chains are the living channels which conduct energy upward; death and decay return it to the soil.'[2] Changes in the soil's fertility he explains by pointing to break-downs in such chains, such cycles. Similarly, whereas the atomistic biologist studies an organism as a system of cells—and, beyond that, of molecules—the ecologist looks at its place in a broader system, its habitat, and at the relationship between that organism-in-its-habitat and still wider systems.

That does not mean, however, that the ecologist can eschew laboratory studies. If he hopes to understand, let us say, the way in which mercuric salts are built up in the human organism, he needs to investigate *both* the nature of the food chain which enables mercuric salts deposited in an estuary to find their way into the brains of human beings *and* what happens in the tissues of each of the members of that food chain. Nor does the mere fact that the ecologist makes use of such concepts as energy cycles or food chains in any way suggest that ecology is supra-scientific.

This is a crucial point. Science is not *intrinsically* atomistic. It explains the behaviour of the tides, for example, by referring them to forces oper-

---

[1] F. Fraser Darling: 'Man's responsibility for the environment', in F. J. Ebling (ed.). *Biology and Ethics,* Symposium of the Institute of Biology, no. 18 (London, 1969), p. 119. On this general theme see also George Seddon: 'The rhetoric and ethics of the environmental protest movement', *Meanjin,* 31:4 (December 1972), pp. 427–37.

[2] Aldo Leopold: *A Sand County Almanac,* p. 253.

ating in the solar system, Sometimes, in order to explain a thing's behaviour, one needs only to look at the forms of activity which go on within it—or, as it would more commonly be put, at the particles which make it up; sometimes one needs to look, rather, at the wider forms of activity within which its own forms of activity go on. But, more often than not, one needs to look at both—explaining a person's behaviour, for example, partly in terms of his 'genetic constitution,' the forms of activity he has inherited, partly in terms of the culture within which he was educated. He stammers, let us say, because he was born left-handed into a culture which demands right-handedness from its members.

No doubt, the ecologist's talk of chains and cycles may ring ancient bells by associative resonance; we think, perhaps, of the classical 'great chain of being' or of those cycles beloved by mystics—'a perpetual circle for the Good, from the Good, in the Good, and to the Good.'[3] But such associations are not justified by the actual procedures of ecologists. The 'wholes' in which ecology is interested are not mystical unities—my back garden could constitute an ecosystem—nor are they, although Fraser Darling suggests otherwise, the kind of metaphysical whole within which all differences are converted into differences in degree. Indeed, although ecology can be studied at a high level of abstractions in terms of energy transfers, one of its main contributions to human understanding lies in its emphasis on the importance of individual differences, the far-reaching consequences which can result from what at first sight appears to be a very slight change in the membership of a system. Only in so far as it has wrongly been supposed that science must be atomistic does the Western scientific tradition have any quarrel with the rise in ecology. This is not the sort of quarrel which can be resolved only by abandoning science in favour of mysticism.

Nor, to solve our ecological problems, are we forced once more to think of nature as sacred. That doctrine, too, 'lies in the way to knowledge.' So to revert, I have suggested, would be to go back on the whole tradition of Western science, perhaps the greatest of man's achievements. For to regard nature as sacred is to think of it in the manner the Jews and the Greeks deliberately rejected, as having a 'mysterious life' which it is improper, sacrilegious, to try to understand or control, a life we should submit to and worship.[4] Science, in contrast, converts mysteries into problems, to which it can hope to find solutions.

Such a reversion, furthermore, is neither necessary nor sufficient to save the biosphere. It is certainly not sufficient; societies for whom nature is sacred have nonetheless destroyed their natural habitation. A passage from Plato's *Critias* will illustrate this point. He is describing Attica: 'There are remaining only the bones of the wasted body, as they may be called . . . all the richer and softer parts of the soil having fallen away, and the

---

[3]C. E. Rolt (ed.): *Dionysius the Areopagite on the Divine Names and the Mystical Theology* (London, 1920), p. 107. Compare the diagram from the fourteenth-century mystic Henry Suso in A. Nygren: *Agape and Eros*, trans. P. S. Watson (London, 1953), facing p. 616, with the diagram in 'Ecology: the new great chain of being', *Natural History*, 77: 10 (December 1968), p. 9.

[4]On this theme, see Henry Frankfort: *Kingship and the Gods*.

mere skeleton of the land being left. But in the primitive state of the country, its mountains were high hills covered with soil, and the plains . . . were full of rich earth, and there was abundance of wood in the mountains.'[5] This decline, Plato tells us, is testified to by the fact that 'sacred memorials' remain at points, by his time dry, where once flowed rivers and streams. Man does not necessarily preserve, that is, the stream he has dedicated to a god; simple ignorance or greed can be as damaging as technological know-how. Nowhere, as we have said, is ecological destruction more apparent than in today's Japan, for all its tradition of nature-worship.

Indeed, to carry this argument further, the belief that nature is sacred can tell against attempts to preserve it. Just in virtue of its divinity, it may be argued, nature can be trusted to look after itself. Consider the case of Emerson. 'In the woods,' he tells us, 'we return to reason and faith.' 'There,' he continues, 'I feel that nothing can befall me in life,—no disgrace, no calamity . . . which nature cannot repair; . . . the currents of the Universal Being circulate through me; I am part or parcel of God.'[6] Yet Emerson was indulgent towards the plunderers of the American countryside then making their way to the American West. 'The recuperative powers of Nature' were, in his eyes, a sufficient guarantee that the self-reliance he admired would not issue in final devastation.[7] A nature which can heal men can surely heal itself, a nature that is divine men cannot destroy. To take our ecological crises seriously, so I have constantly argued, is to recognise, first, man's utter dependence on nature, but secondly, nature's vulnerability to human depredations—the *fragility*, that is, of both man and nature, for all their notable powers of recuperation. And this means that neither man nor nature is sacred or quasi-divine.*

There is more than a little paradox in the view, when it comes from ecologically-minded preservationists, that we need to revert to older, mystical attitudes to nature. For ecology, however much some of those who praise ecology would like to persuade us otherwise, is a serious scientific attempt, dependent on the aid of such technological innovations as the computer, to understand what scientists still find mysterious—the ways in which populations respond to environmental fluctuations. This manner of looking at ecology is unpopular with those, like Theodore Roszak, who hoped that ecology would replace scientific analysis by 'a new science in which the object of knowledge will be rather like the poet's beloved: something to be contemplated but not analysed, something that

[5] Plato: *Critias*, trans. B. Jowett (Oxford, 1892), III*b, c.*
[6] R. W. Emerson: *Nature: Addresses and Lectures* (Boston, 1876), p. 10.
[7] Compare S. L. Udall: *The Quiet Crisis* (New York, 1963), pp. 48–55.
*It may be true that in hunting societies—the example most often cited—the belief that nature is sacred and animals are capable of understanding served in some measure as a protection against the destruction of species. (Although man the hunter, it would now seem, was largely responsible for the disappearance of a great many of the large mammals—the giant kangaroo in Australia, the moa in New Zealand, the woolly mammoth in North America.) But as matters stand, such beliefs are not merely so out of harmony with our traditions that to attempt to revive them would be to attempt the impossible; they simply would not serve.

is permitted to retain its mysteries.'[8] But if Roszak and his counter-cultural followers are disappointed to discover that ecology is after all another branch of science, that it *dispels* mysteries, many of us see in that fact, rather, a demonstration that Western science is still fecund, still capable of contributing to the solution of the problems which beset human beings, even when they are problems of the scientist's own making.

That science is still so fecund is just as well, seeing that, as I have often had occasion to remark, ignorance is one of the most potent obstacles to our solving our ecological problems, an ignorance which only science can dispel. No doubt, the modern West has more knowledge at its disposal than has had any previous society. But it has neither the kind nor the degree of knowledge which it now needs. Our knowledge of the ways in which societies work is not at all comparable in extent with our knowledge of the workings, let us say, of the planetary system; we know little about the atmosphere, the seas, the life cycles of the scarcely numerable varieties of plant and animal life. While absolutely speaking we know a great deal, we are proportionally ignorant, proportionally in relation to what we need to know. The farmer tilling his fields by conventional methods and living in a traditional society did not need to know a great deal. But the task we have now to undertake, in attempting to estimate the long-term effects of our actions both on the biosphere and on human societies, is so immense that in relation to it our ignorance is almost total.

To correct this situation may well require, I am fully prepared to admit, a minor revolution within science. The scientist will be forced, in the unenthusiastic words of one of my scientific colleagues, 'to slosh about in that primordial ooze known as interdisciplinary studies.' He will need to pay more respect to such scientists as work outside laboratories. There is a pecking-order in science; almost everybody pecks the 'natural historian.' The field naturalist is unlikely to find himself awarded a Nobel Prize or even a Fellowship of the Royal Society. But there are already signs that such a revolution is under way, if still very tentatively.* Field studies are beginning to regain something of their previous status—Darwin did not, after all, work in a laboratory—and more and more distinguished scientists are at least dipping their fingers into the 'primordial ooze.' To say that science has need of new directions, however, is one thing, to say that the West ought to abandon its hard-won tradition of critical investigation is quite another; that tradition it needs more than ever before.

What about the view, so often associated with science and technology, that man is master of the world? Must not that at least, if not science itself,

---

[8]Theodore Roszak: 'Ecology and mysticism', *Humanist* 86:5 (May 1971), p. 136. See also Norman Brown: *Life Against Death* (London, 1959), pt. 5, ch. 15, p. 236, and my summary in *The Perfectibility of Man,* pp. 306. See also Passmore: 'The revolt against science', *Search 3,* 11–12 (November–December 1972). pp. 415–22.

*One of the most significant examples that has come my way is A. B. Pippard's Inaugural Lecture as Cavendish Professor of Physics in the University of Cambridge. It is time, he there suggests, for scientists to turn their attention 'towards the difficult and less elegant phenomena of the real physical world' in contrast with their past concentration on simpler and more elegant natural laws. Coming from a Cavendish Professor, that is really something. See A. B. Pippard: *Reconciling Physics with Reality* (Cambridge, 1972).

be abandoned? Man's dominion can be understood, I have suggested, in a number of different ways, varying in their degree of 'arrogance.' On the minimal interpretation, it 'licenses' men to sustain themselves by making use, in the manner of any other animal, of what they find around them. Or, to drop the confusing quasi-legal talk of 'licences', 'dominion', 'rights', talk of which we have had more than enough, it says that there is nothing morally wrong in men's behaving in this way. Even thus interpreted it is rejected by the sterner ascetics, by, for example, the third-century neo-Platonist Porphyry, who would restrict the diet of such men as hope to perfect themselves to those fruits which plants do not need for reproduction.[9] (This is at least an improvement on the sole bill of fare permitted, on similar grounds, by Samuel Butler's *Erewhon* prophets—rotting fruit and decaying cabbage leaves.) But wherever the boundaries are drawn, I have argued, we can certainly say this much: man can live at all only as a predator, whether on plants or animals. And in order to establish a civilisation he has to go beyond this point; he has to domesticate herds or plant crops and must so far act as lord and master over at least a segment of nature. In so far as he necessarily acts in this way, it is pointless to suggest that man should do *nothing* to disturb existing ecological systems, should *in no sense* attempt to master them.

At the opposite extreme, 'lordship over nature' is interpreted as entailing that nature is wax in man's hands. Interpreted thus, I have agreed, it must certainly be rejected. Indeed, it was never plausible. Cicero's Balbus, boasting that as a result of their navigational inventions men had now mastered the wind and the waves, had never experienced, so much is clear, the force of a tropical cyclone. Even now, in claiming mastery over nature, men are whistling to keep their courage up. If their science, once converted into technology, enables them to control their immediate natural environment more effectively than can any other animal, it also constantly reminds them, as Karl Popper has particularly emphasised, of what they cannot do. As ecology has now sufficiently demonstrated, the doctrine that nature is infinitely malleable is not merely an illusion—comforting, perhaps, to human beings in their helplessness and encouraging to them in their aspirations—but a dangerous delusion.

An intermediate interpretation, however, can be framed thus: men, uniquely, are capable of transforming the world into a civilised state; that is their major responsibility to their fellow-men. The virtues of civilisation, no doubt, are now sometimes questioned. Once more the 'noble savage' hunts his ecological way through intellectual drawing-rooms. . . .

If we ask, indeed, what human beings add to the world by their presence in it, there is, I should say, only one possible reply: civilisation. Were it not for his ability to civilise, man would be no more than a predator amongst the rest, more powerful, more aggressive, more violent, more skillful in capturing his prey but in no other respects superior, and in many respects inferior, to the prey he hunts. And man's great memorials—his science, his philosophy, his technology, his architecture, his countryside—are all of them founded upon his attempt to understand and

---

[9]Porphyry: *De Abstinentia* IV, 20.

subdue nature. Through their struggles with nature men have discovered their potentialities and developed those forms of enterprise which constitute their civilisation. I have included the countryside in the list of man's memorials, because even the landscapes we now so greatly admire—the landscapes of Tuscany or of England or of Kyushu—are largely the creation of human enterprise, of human struggles. When Cowper wrote 'God made the country; man made the town,' he was simply mistaken. The eighteenth-century English countryside Cowper knew and loved was largely of human creation. (What god, for the matter of that, would not be proud of having created eighteenth-century Bath?) That is what, however obscurely, Hegel and his followers saw, and passed on to the Marxists. It is not merely out of arrogance that men think of themselves as having a 'duty to subdue nature'; it is only they who can create. So far, and only so far, they can rightfully claim 'dominion over nature.'

Nor, however implausible the doctrine that nature exists only to serve man, is there any objection to the weaker view, to which Descartes subscribes, that whatever exists in nature is of some use to us. This is not, as it might at first seem to be, an empirical hypothesis, for there is no way of falsifying it. It always remains possible that something will turn out to be useful which we have cast aside as useless. But it can act as a guiding principle, encouraging men to look for uses in unexpected places, discouraging the destruction of what might eventually turn out to be of vital importance to them. In that form, it should certainly not be cast aside as 'rubbish.'

The danger in destroying is, of course, a point on which the ecological critics have particularly insisted. And quite clearly one has to concede, as Ehrlich puts it, that 'any tinkering with an ecosystem may result in unforeseen and deleterious consequences.'[10] But, as we have repeatedly had occasion to note, man has had no option but to live dangerously. If he had let himself be too alarmed by the fact that, in a certain sense, he does not know what he is doing, he would never have ventured beyond his immediate environment. Nor would he, certainly, ever have embarked on the domestication of animals, let alone agriculture or industry. Indeed, if we follow to its logical conclusion Ehrlich's description of man as a dangerous tinkerer, we can scarcely stop short of that picture of man's relationships with nature composed at the very end of the nineteenth century by W. S. Blunt, the ecologist's poet-laureate.*

Here is 'unspoiled Nature' as Blunt sees it:

> Thou dost remember, Lord, the glorious World it was,
> The beauty, the abundance, the unbroken face
> Of undulent forest spread without or rent or seam
> Thy lakes, Thy floods, Thy marshes, tameless, unbetrayed,
> All virgin of the spoiler, all inviolate,
> In beauty undeflowered, where fear was not nor hate.

---

[10]P. R. and A. H. Ehrlich: *Population Resources Environment,* p. 182.

*This poem, Blunt tells us, was 'written to some extent in collaboration with the late Herbert Spencer'. It sounds like it.

And here is man, that 'lewd bare-buttocked ape':

> Man the senseless knave
> Who struck fire from his flint to burn Thy gorses brave,
> Thy heaths for his lean kine, who, being the one unclean,
> Defiled Thy flower-sweet Earth with ordure heaps obscene,
> To plant his rice, his rye.[11]

But the virtues of civilisation, many of us would wish to argue, are not to be so lightly set aside. It is one thing to recognise that human action has unintended consequences; quite another to suggest that man is nothing but the defiler of nature. Lewd he often is, no doubt, but the bareness of his buttocks is not the only thing which distinguishes him from the ape; if the 'glorious world' of Blunt's imagination was a world without hate—although scarcely, as he suggests, without fear—it was also a world without love, without art, without science, without philosophy, with no Venice, no Nara, no Salzburg.* These are as much consequences of man's 'tinkering' as are 'ordure heaps obscene.' That we ought to attempt to try to preserve the spirit that creates them, I shall not even bother to argue.

It is a much more particular assumption, however, that the democratic institutions, the spirit of enterprise, the liberal attitude, characteristic of the modern West are worth preserving and maintaining. That requires separate argument. No one with any knowledge of history could have any illusions about Western civilisation, modern or ancient, with its record of violence, cruelty, fanaticism, puritanism and avarice. What is particularly tragic is the way in which the best and the worst have so often gone together, as the history of Florence from the thirteenth to the fifteenth century vividly exemplifies. Everything was there, genius in literature, painting, sculpture, science; cruelty and violence of the lowest, least forgivable, kind; even the egalitarian terrorism of Giano della Bella. But it remains true, I believe, that nowhere outside Western civilisation have men so often risen to such great heights. This by no means implies that cultures which are not Western in type are valueless. No one who has even the slightest acquaintance whether with their cultural achievements or their social structures could possibly take that view. In its dealings with other cultures, I should freely grant, the West has often shown itself at its arrogant, bigoted, greedy worst. But neither the simple sensualities of Tahiti nor the complex ritual of ancient Japan enabled the human spirit

---

[11]Wilfrid Scawen Blunt: 'Satan absolved: a Victorian mystery' (1899), in *The Poetical Works of W. S. Blunt* (London, 1914), vol. 2, pp. 266, 275.

*Ian McHarg, in a much-reprinted paper rhetorically entitled 'Is man a planetary disease?', is prepared to lay it down that 'Algae know about creativity but man does not'. There is no depth of masochistic nonsense to which in their moods of self-denigration men will not descend. In Roeg's 1970 film *Walkabout* not man in general but only civilised man is diagnosed as a disease. The gentle self-reliant aborigine is contrasted with civilised men and women who are cruel, cold, mean-spirited, sexually repressed, devoted only to their possessions, utterly ruthless. Western art is depicted as childish play, its science as trivialities in a desert, its literature as a rambling story at once pointless and cruel, its education system as a training in futile snobberies, its industry as rusted *debris,* its technology as an instrument of slaughter, its mathematics as empty formulae. If this indictment—or the picture of civilisation in Godard's *Weekend*—is at all points justified then, certainly, I should have no policy to advocate except mass suicide. The alternative—the hunting savage—arouses in my heart no enthusiasm whatsoever.

to expand to its fullest extent. A craftsman, a certain type of artist, might have found in such a society all that he needed, but a philosopher, a scientist, a dramatist, would not. The West has not conquered the world solely by the force of its arms or the flashier attractions of its consumer goods. The richness and diversity of Western culture even a country like Japan has found profoundly stimulating, for all the importance of its own achievements.

One of the more fashionable forms of contemporary cant condemns as 'racialist'—now an all-encompossing form of abuse—the description of any form of society as 'higher' or 'more advanced' or 'better' than any other. No doubt, as I have granted, a less 'advanced' society can possess virtues which a more 'advanced' society lacks. The fact remains that there are familiar and quite proper ways of grading societies: in terms of the diversity of their culture, their humanitarianism, the degree of liberty they offer their citizens. By any of these criteria the liberal democratic West stands high. (Nor will it do to reply that this is not surprising, since the West invented these criteria. What other criteria are we offered?) Its range of cultural achievements in science, in philosophy, in art, is unequalled; few of its citizens starve in the streets or live by exhibiting their deformities; never before has personal liberty been so widely diffused. If we judge modern Western democracies imperfect this is only by applying to them those absolute standards which the West has taught us. We take it for granted that they contain no Untouchables, no Etas; we condemn them, quite rightly, because they still discriminate against certain of their members, still confine personal liberty by absurd and pointless laws, still do not adequately educate their citizens, still do not do all that they might to help those—inside or outside their territories—whose life is nasty, brutish and short. If the liberal democracies collapse, this will be because they have aroused in their citizens aspirations which no society will ever completely satisfy, not because those aspirations are worthless.* To *seek* their destruction, with whatever noble aims in mind, is to attempt to destroy the only sort of society which has ever come near to fulfilling those aspirations.

The view that ecological problems are more likely to be solved in an authoritarian than in any such a liberal democratic society rests on the implausible assumption that the authoritarian state would be ruled by ecologist-kings. In practice, there is more hope of action in democratic societies. In the United States, particularly, the habit of local action, the capacity of individuals to initiate legal proceedings, the tradition of public disclosure, are powerful weapons in the fight against ecological destruction. The democratic states should rather be condemned. I have sug-

*It is very misleading, of course, to speak of the 'West' in a monolithic way. I have often been told, if I wrote in modified praise of Western civilisation, that I have forgotten Newark and New York. The tragedy of New York no one could forget; that city and its inhabitants should be preserved for eternity in plasticised aspic as a memorial to the grandeur and the misery of the human condition. Newark, I confess, but seldom crosses my mind, less often than, let us say, Aarhus. Why should it? But Newark is no more typical of the West than is Calcutta of India or Osaka of Japan. I see no reason for believing, either, that it shows the West, as in a science-fiction mirror, what it is certain to become. Indeed, it is reminiscent of the eighteenth century rather than prophetic of the twenty-first. In many fundamental respects, America is a very old-fashioned country.

gested, when they are tempted into exactly the same vices as the totalitarian states: spying, soothing utterances from central authorities, facesaving, bureaucratic inertia, censorship, concealment.*

What about the metaphysical outlook characteristic of the West? That, I have tried to show, is exceptionally complex and diversified, by no means to be summed up as the view that nature is wax in man's hands. Nor is the West, I should add, irrevocably committed to that Aristotelian-type metaphysics for which nature consists of substances with distinct properties, each of which can be separately modified without altering anything else. One of the most important alternative suggestions, dating back in essence to Heraclitus, is that the world consists of complex systems of interacting processes varying in their stability. Each such system—of which a human being is one—can survive, like a flame, only so long as it can interact with surrounding systems in certain particular ways, drawing upon and giving out to the systems around it. It can die by choking on its own wastes or because it has exhausted its resources. That way of looking at the world, which ecological investigations help to substantiate, makes it perfectly plain why 'You can't do one thing at a time'; it destroys, too, the belief that human beings are somehow different, outside the eco-system, whether as villainous intruders or heroic manipulators. But it does so in a manner not in the least mystical, not in the least anti-scientific in spirit, not in the least implying that there is something intrinsically wrong with any attempt to make the world a better place.

On such a view man's uniqueness is not metaphysical; it lies, like the peculiarities of a flame, in the special character of his relations with other systems, his ability deliberately to transform them. Christians have thought otherwise. Ecological critics of the West are justified in arguing that Christianity has encouraged man to think of himself as metaphysically unique, as supernaturally above, rather than naturally immersed in, the ebb and flow of processes. What is ecologically dangerous in Christianity, indeed, is not that it denies the sacredness of nature but that it encourages men to believe that they are 'sons of God' and therefore secure, their continued existence on earth guaranteed by God. So far it encourages *hubris;* it makes of nature something which can be ravaged with impurity. Man, it must certainly be recognised, has no tenure in the biosphere.

Christian theology, however, has in the past proved itself to be remarkably flexible. Theologians are now busily attempting to work out new attitudes to nature, still consonant in a general way with traditional Christianity but reverting in important respects to a prelapsarian conception of man and man's role and denying that men have a 'sacredness' which animals do not possess.[12] For my part I more than doubt whether Christian

---

*In so far as the ecological movement necessarily involves a critique of the creeping bureaucratisation so characteristic of our society, it has a social and political importance extending well beyond its immediate ecological ends; in so far as its practical policies would tend to encourage that bureaucratisation, it represents a social danger. For not only are man and nature fragile, so too is liberal civilisation, as the tragic history of inter-war Germany so vividly reminds us.

[12]See, for example, J. B. Coff: *Is it too Late: A Theology of Ecology* (Beverly Hills, 1972), and what was said above about Barth and Schweitzer.

theology can thus reshape itself without ceasing to be distinctively Christian, whether it can bring itself to deny, in the light of its central theology, either that man is *metaphysically* unique—as a soul to be saved—or that in the end his survival is *metaphysically* guaranteed.* Only if men see themselves, I should rather argue, for what they are, quite alone, with no one to help them except their fellow-men, products of natural processes which are wholly indifferent to their survival, will they face their ecological problems in their full implications. Not by the extension, but by the total rejection, of the concept of the sacred will they move towards that sombre realisation.

The rejection of Christianity by no means immediately entails, however, the acceptance of a doctrine more conscious of human limitations, as is sufficiently obvious both in the Soviet Union and contemporary China. Nothing could be more ecologically damaging than the Hegelian-Marxist doctrine that nature, before man operates upon it, is mere potentiality. Two traditional attitudes are, I suggested, more promising—the first, that man should think of himself as a steward; the second, that in his attempts to transform nature he should cooperate with it. The 'stewardship' attitude is often said to be peculiarly Christian; this I have denied. It is linked rather with the idea that man forms part of a chain of improvement, that he has responsibilities to those who come after him, responsibilities arising out of his attempt to preserve and develop what he loves. In its fullest implications this is a peculiarly Western and modern concept, dating back to Kant. Its ecological importance is manifest.

As for the view that man should co-operate with nature, this cannot, of course, be taken literally. Nature is not a semi-divine entity with aims which human beings can share. Against any such an interpretation, Robert Boyle rightly protested. Interpreted less literally, however, it suggests, as we have already seen, a policy of ecological wisdom: to try to control pests by diversifying crops rather than by insecticides, to construct tourist hotels so that they make use of, rather than cut across, existing drainage contours, to grow what can be grown with least damage to the countryside. And so on, modestly but effectively. Read thus, it is by no means rubbish.

To accept it does not commit us, however, to Barry Commoner's 'third law of ecology'—'nature knows best.'[13] It is true enough—as, like Ehrlich, Commoner argues—that every human intervention in an ecosystem is likely to disturb the workings of that system in a way that is detrimental to some member of it. So much is true of every change, man-induced or nature-induced. But it by no means follows, as his 'law' might seem to suggest, that every such change, or even most such changes, will be detri-

---

*Much stress is now laid, however, on Paul's 'the whole creation groaneth and travaileth in pain together until now' (Rom. VII:22). This is taken to imply that not only man but the whole creation anticipates salvation. There have for long been those, indeed, who expect immortality for animals, although no one in the West, perhaps, has gone so far as those Eastern teachers for whom even a blade of grass can aspire to Buddhahood. Christianity would be wholly transformed, however, were it to be supposed that cats and dogs were as much 'sons of God' as are human beings and are called upon in the same way to seek after salvation.

[13]*The Closing Circle*, p. 41.

mental to *human beings*. Unlike the watches to which he compares them, ecological systems were not designed for man's use. When men picked seeds off plants and sowed them on cleared ground, they acted in a way that was detrimental to the organic life which was accustomed to feed on the fallen seeds. But only the most unreconstructed primitivist would suggest that the actions of our agricultural forefathers were destructive of human interests. A nature left entirely alone as 'knowing best' would support only the dreariest and most monotonous of lives. Even the primitive hunter found it necessary to burn; the fires he lit have transformed the face of the earth.[14]

It is, indeed, absurd to suggest that man can find in nature, at hand for his taking, all that he needs to live a good life. So much, in principle, the authors of Genesis saw: nature has its 'thorns and thistles' which man has no option but to root out. In his essay on 'Nature', J. S. Mill mounts a general attack on the injunction that men ought to 'cooperate with nature.' 'Her powers,' as Mill put it, 'are often towards man in the position of enemies, from whom he must wrest, by force and ingenuity, what little he can for his own use.'[15] One may well warm to the enthusiasm with which Mill attacks the more sentimental nature-lovers. Anyone who lives on the inhospitable shores of Australia will certainly appreciate his feelings. To think of nature as an 'enemy', however, is not the alternative to thinking of it as a 'friend'. Natural processes, as I have constantly emphasised, go on in their own way, indifferent to human interests. But we shall do best to learn how they operate, not supposing that they will immediately respond to our whims or miraculously suspend their modes of operation so as to permit us harmlessly to convert rainforests into agricultural lands or rivers into sewers.

What of the view that the West now needs not only a new concept of nature but a new set of moral principles to act as a guide in its relationships with nature? That, I have argued, is not entirely wrong-headed. During most of the West's history, as we have observed, its moral philosophers, Stoic or Christian, denied that man's relationship with nature is governed by any moral considerations whatsoever. From Montaigne onwards, however, to say nothing of his neo-Platonic predecessors, sceptics and humanists took a different view. And by the end of the eighteenth century, as I have pointed out, even Christians began to argue, although often against fierce opposition from their co-religionists, that callousness towards animal suffering was morally wrong. Nor is cruelty to animals a unique instance of such a change of heart. Well over a hundred years ago an editorial writer in the Melbourne *Age*—and newspaper editorials are not given to moral innovations—could assert that 'he who cuts down a tree unnecessarily is a criminal.' One has only to look at some regions of England, or France, or Italy, to see that, as much as in Japan, the land, for all the hardship involved in working it, has been loved. As Leopold recognized, there are 'seeds' in the West of the morality he advocates in

---

[14]O. C. Stewart: 'Fire as the first great force employed by man', in W. L. Thomas, Jr. (ed.): *Man's Role in Changing the Face of the Earth* (Chicago, 1956), pp. 115–33.

[15]J. S. Mill: *Three Essays on Religion*. p. 15.

which the active cherishing of nature is accounted good and its wanton destruction evil, even if it would be unsafe to assume, with Victor Hugo, that such a new morality will *inevitably* come to dominate the West.

The traditional moral teaching of the West, Christian or utilitarian. has always taught men, however, that they ought not so to act as to injure their neighbours. And we have now discovered that the disposal of wastes into sea or air, the destruction of ecosystems, the procreation of large families, the depletion of resources, constitute injury to our fellow-men, present and future. To that extent, conventional morality, without any supplementation whatsoever, suffices to justify our ecological concern, our demand for action against the polluter, the depleter of natural resources, the destroyer of species and wildernesses.

One of my colleagues, an ardent preservationist, condemns me as a 'human chauvinist.' What he means is that in my ethical arguments, I treat human interests as paramount. I do not apologise for that fact; an 'ethic dealing with man's relation to land and to the plants and animals growing on it' would not only be about the behaviour of human beings, as is sufficiently obvious, but would have to be justified by reference to human interests. The land which a bad farmer allows to slip into a river did not have a 'right' to stay where it was. The supposition that anything but a human being has 'rights' is, or so I have suggested, quite untenable.

This insistence on the primacy of human interest does not imply, however, that the only question at issue is whether someone's *income* will decline as a result of the silting of the river. The silting of a sparkling river, the replacement of a forested slope by an eroded hillside, is a loss to mankind even if it does not lessen anyone's income. To cause it to happend constitutes an act of vandalism, the destruction of something worth enjoying for its own sake. Only in so far as Western moralists have suggested otherwise, have suggested that no form of human activity has any value unless it involves a direct relationship with God or, for moralists of a more secular cast of mind, a relationship to a narrowly conceived economic prosperity, can the West plausibly be said to need a 'new ethic.' What it needs, for the most part, is not so much a 'new ethic' as a more general adherence to a perfectly familiar ethic.

For the major sources of our ecological disasters—apart from ignorance—are greed and short-sightedness, which amount to much the same thing. (The greedy man pursues the object of his greed in a manner which is indifferent to the means employed and to the wider consequences of his pursuit. The short-sighted man, more commonly described as 'practical,' displays that special form of indifference to consequences which refuses to look beyond the present or the immediate future.) There is no novelty in the view that greed is evil; no need of a new ethic to tell us as much.

Our society, however, has officially denounced greed while in practice subscribing to Horace's maxim: 'By right means if you can, but by any means make money.' (Just as it officially denounces violence while in fact admiring it, glorying in it—as its favourite forms of literature make perfectly clear—except when it is employed by those it condemns on other grounds.) To tell men that they must now moderate their zeal for posses-

sions, must give up what have been highly profitable pursuits, must surrender established economic rights, is to risk condemnation as a fanatic.
No doubt it is formally recognised that there are ways of making money
that are not entirely virtuous. But even the successful thief often excites
admiration rather than contumely; the most devastating of land-devel-
opers may hope to be rewarded, in British countries, with such signs of
public esteem as a knighthood. As the young Marx once worte, 'money is
the jealous God of Israel before whom no other god may exist'—and the
worship of it, as he also argued, has given birth to an 'actual contempt for
and practical degradation of nature.'[16] It is not 'rubbish' to suggest that
our society actually, although not in its explicitly-enunciated moral principles, does honour to violence, short-sightedness and greed. What this
brings out, once more, is that new modes of behaviour are much more
important than new moral principles.

I am not, when I condemn greed, condemning the making of
money—that would be like a eunuch condemning sexual intercourse. All
I am condemning is the view that every pursuit is valuable just in so far as
it is a way of making money or that money-making is the ratinal norm in
comparison with which all other pursuits are irrational and abnormal.
Every free society has been a commercial society, and the connection is
not a merely accidental one. But certainly there is little hope for us unless
we can moderate our desire to possess.* We shall do so, however, only if
we can learn to be more sensuous in our attitude to the world, more ready
to enjoy the present moment for itself, as an object of immediate pleasure,
instead of frenetically seeking the power and security that possessions
offer.

It is at this point that the moral outlook of the West is not merely
inadequate but dangerous—in virtue of the puritanism it inherited from
Augustine and, beyond Augustine, from Plato. We have already seen
how, for example, this puritanism adversely affects the prospects for population control, by restricting the publicising of birth control methods and
by condemning all sexual relationships which do not have procreation as
their aim. But the more general puritan attack on sensuousness, its denial
that the enjoyment of sensual pleasures for their own sake can ever be
right and proper, has also had, as we have also suggested, more widespread, less obvious, ecological consequences. Admittedly, one has only to
look back on the art, the architecture, the literature, the man-made landscapes, the townscapes, of our Western past to observe that the puritanic
tradition has never wholly destroyed, even in the West, man's sensuous
delight in the surfaces of things, in sights and smells, in sounds and tastes
and touches. But it is as if the smoke of the industrial revolution had
destroyed men's eyes, ears, noses and sense of touch, or as if only by seiz-
ing upon and making their own the familiar tenets of what had been a
minority puritanism could men justify the ugliness which they were cre-

---

[16]Karl Marx: 'On the Jewish question', in L. D. Easton and K. H. Guddat: *Writings of the
Young Marx on Philosophy and Society* (New York, 1967), pp. 245–6.

*The 'we' in this sentence is not that patronising 'we' which means 'everybody except me
and the enlightened few I am addressing'. It means all of us: 'You! hypocrite lecteur!—mon
semblable,—mon fragere.'

ating around them. A more sensuous society could never have endured the desolate towns, the dreary and dirty houses, the uniquely ugly chapels, the slag heaps, the filthy rivers, the junk yards which constitute the 'scenery' of the post-industrial West and which it has exported to the East. Only if men can first learn to look sensuously at the world will they learn to care for it. Not only to look at it, but to touch it, smell it, taste it. As we said, Plato—like every other authoritarian, like Stalin and Skinner in our own century, like the Protestant Church (legate in its own eyes of an authoritarian deity)—severely condemns the sensuous man, the lover of sights and sounds. And one must grant to him that a purely sensuous life, in which sensuousness is never kindled into love, love with the responsibility and care it brings in its train, is impoverished, sub-human and incapable by itself of solving ecological, or any other, problems. But, on the other side, the attempt to be 'super-human' by rising totally above sensuousness issues, as I have elsewhere argued in more detail, is a way of life no less impoverished, no less sub-human, and is utterly destructive, into the bargain, of man-nature relationships.*

The traditions I have so far explored, whether with sympathy or antipathy, have a long history. I have said almost nothing as yet about a factor which many would regard as far more ecologically significant than metaphysical principles and moral ideas—industrial growth. I cannot conclude without considering, however inadequately, the problems it raises. Industrial growth is a new phenomenon and the attitudes of mind it has generated, however powerfully, are still so new that it is somewhat odd to call them traditions. It is only very recently that nations have boasted of their Gross National Product, that a society has condemned itself, or been condemned, because its per capita growth rate is low, that consumers have come to expect an endless flow of new types of product, that industry has been geared to meet the needs of an affluent society. Here, many would say, lies the real crux of our problem. The changes of heart to which I have drawn attention—the intimations of a new, more considerate attitude to nature—are, on this view, of no fundamental importance. It is the crudest sort of sentimentalism—rubbish, my critics would say—to see in the spectacle of Boy Scouts collecting bottles or 'conservation' groups preventing the construction of this or that freeway anything more than a middle-class game. At best the participants in such enterprises are like children constructing a sand barrier to protect their castle from the tide-turned sea. At worst they distract attention from the fundamental issues. For what is at fault, so it is said, is the total system, the scientific-technological-industrial complex on which the midle-class reformers depend for their livelihood and their social position.

*Only a Canute who took his courtiers seriously and pretended to sweep back the tide by sweeping with the ebb would think it necessary to defend sensuality, I shall no doubt be told, in so 'permissive' an age. But permissiveness is not necessarily sensuous. More often than not, it takes the form of obscenity—a sub-variety of violence (who has ever seen a sensuous American film?)—or of grossness as in the Berlin of the 'Thirties, with those female mud-wrestlers and transvestite sexual grostesqueries so vividly depicted in Fosse's film version of *Cabaret*. In spirit, both obscenity and grossness are Augustinian. Remember, too, that 'sensuous' does not mean 'sexual.' For more on the importance and the limits of sensuality see *The Perfectibility of Man*.

This is one of the points where I find myself least certain of my ground. The issues involved are so large, so complex, so difficult that I can do little more than raise them. To what degree is the further emancipation of the human spirit, in the East as well as in the West, inevitably tied up with the advance of industry? Can resources safely be diverted from industrial development to less-despoiling tertiary activities? Can industries be cabined and confined without undermining the spirit of enterprise which has brought them to birth? On the face of it, one can no doubt reply that the historical connections between industry and freedom are not inevitable. There can be heavy industry, as in Russia, where there is little or no freedom; neither Greek democracy nor the Enlightenment came into being within a highly industrialised society. There are good reasons for believing, furthermore, that the emergence of large industrial complexes represents a threat to, rather than a necessary condition of, the further emancipation of mankind. Yet one is still left uneasy about our capacity, without destroying liberty, effectively to redeploy our forces.

Not uncommonly, we are told that what has to be abandoned is the ideal, much loved by politicians, of economic growth. This concept, however, is far from being a perspicuous one, and its ambiguities are of first importance. If economic growth is defined as the more effective utilisation of scarce resources, better economising, then what is commonly described as economic growth may in fact be economic recession. Let us take a simple case. A park is built over to provide new office areas. The park had made available such scarce commodities in an urban context as space, light, quiet, air, the sight and smell of flowers and trees and shrubs. Should not the construction of such buildings count as economic recession and the reverse process, the destruction of buildings to construct parks, as economic growth?

Not, no doubt, if growth is measured in terms of the Gross National Product, as this is conventionally defined. And this means that the supposition that the Gross National Product is a satisfactory measure of the quality of a society's life must certainly be abandoned; there is something wrong with any measure which suggests that it constitutes 'economic growth' when parks, shops, hotels, theatres, neighbourhoods, are destroyed in order to substitute banks and insurance offices. But throughout the developed world, in Japan as well as the United States, attempts are being made to find a better index of economic growth than the Gross National Product—'an amenities index,' or a 'stock index,' which would take into account the destruction of amenities and natural resources as well as the flow-through of goods. The problems of constructing such an index are manifold; we have already touched on some of them. It is so much easier to quantify and compare the value of marketable goods than it is to compare the loss in amenity arising out of the destruction of a park with the economic gains from the offices which have taken its place.

Even presuming, however, that a solution can be found to this technical problem, we have still to ask whether our society can *afford* to substitute parks for office buildings, or more generally to reduce its Gross National Product (It must be remembered that population is bound for some time to increase.) This is a point in respect to which some conservationists are remarkably insouciant. 'By the use of such specious arguments as the loss of jobs, the lowering of living standards, and the raising of prices,' one of them has written of the anti-ecologists, 'they are endeavouring to turn the citizen away from those who are striving to save a viable environment for future generations.'[17] But the spectacle of an unemployed man or an old-age pensioner faced by rising prices is at least as pitiable as the spectacle of an oil-soaked mutton bird. Arguments which direct attention to economic costs are not necessarily 'specious.'

On the other side, the question now is whether the liberal-democratic West can afford *not* to cut down its industrial activity or, at the very least, to alter its direction. We can perhaps speak of an 'ecological transition,' a point at which a country's industrial activity reduces rather than enhances the quality of life of its citizens, at which increased industrial activity, at least in its conventional forms, is profitable only when its costs are estimated by grossly inadequate methods of accounting, accounting which entirely ignores the public squalor it creates. Its citizens have a per capita income more than enough to permit them to live enjoyable lives, so far as that capacity depends on income; they have a national product sufficient to support adequate social services. Sweden, Japan, the United States, to take only three examples, have all passed that point; they can afford to devote part of their income to the solution of their ecological problems and to compensate, by way of better social services, for the resulting increases in prices. Whether they will do so is, of course, quite a different matter. But in fact their rate of population growth is already moving towards zero; to varying degrees, Japan more slowly, they are introducing sharp-toothed legislation against pollution; they are at least more aware than they were of the need to preserve wildernesses and wild species. Their middle-class ecological reformers reflect rather than disguise deep social forces. It is not absurd to hope that they may be able to find the resources to solve their major ecological problems.

One difficulty is to avoid the costs of industrial slow-downs, or redeployment, from falling very unevenly. It is not the reformers who would lose their jobs if, to take a very minor proposal, regulations were introduced which made it illegal for automobile companies to change their models except in so far as by so doing they saved resources or diminished pollution. No doubt, every citizen might have to meet increased taxation. But that is nothing compared with seeing one's entire mode of life vanish overnight. It is cruel foolishness to suggest that people would be perfectly content to turn their lathes into pitchforks.

So far we have looked at changes in the rate of industrial growth only from the point of view of developed countries. But it could also greatly affect the developing countries, whose conviction that they would bear the brunt of any attempt on the part of Western nations to solve the world's ecological problems is clearly reflected in a number of the consensus resolutions put forward by the 1972 Stockholm Conference. Consider, for example, the eleventh 'principle': 'The environmental policies of all States

---

[17]Denis Puleston: 'Protecting the environment', *New Scientist* (28 September 1972), p. 558.

should enhance and not adversely affect the present or future development potential of developing countries.' Or even more strikingly, the twenty-third principle, not in the original proposals but introduced in the course of discussion: 'Without prejudice to such criteria as may be agreed upon by the international community . . . it will be essential in all cases to consider the system of values prevailing in each country, and the extent of the applicability of standards which are valid for the most advanced countries but which may be *inappropriate and of unwarranted social cost for the developing countries.'* In other words, do not expect the developing countries to proceed as if they had reached the point of 'ecological transition!'

It is sometimes suggested that the West cannot afford to lower its rate of industrial development precisely because it has the responsibility on its shoulders for the developing countries. This, as it stands, is hypocrisy. Aid to developing countries represents a miniscule fraction of the national income of most of the developed countries; the proportion is unlikely to increase. Much of the aid, furthermore, is useless, its nature determined by the interests of the donor rather than by the needs of the recipient. If—with the caveats we have already entered—the West were to give up its pollution-creating synthetic products and lower its tariffs, it might substantially improve the position of the developing countries while at the same time alleviating its own ecological problems. But that would involve real sacrifices.

One must not, however, exaggerate. Some forms of aid have been genuinely helpful. And the effectiveness of other forms of aid has been nullified by greed and corruption at the point of reception rather than at the point of donation. The developing countries are not unnaturally fearful lest, should the developed countries begin to concentrate on their ecological problems, even this degree of aid will cease. They fear, too, that if they attempt to limit industrial growth, the industrial countries will reduce their imports from the developing countries. If, in the course of writing this book, I have ever felt cheerfulness breaking in, a moment's reflection on the plight of the developing countries has been sufficient to dispel it.

So long as one keeps one's eyes solely on the liberal democratic West, the prospect is a little more encouraging, if only because the solutions for a number of problems converge. It is not only in order to solve their ecological problems that the Western countries need to transfer resources from industry to tertiary services; new transport systems, decentralisation, population control, are as essential for urban as for ecological renewal. In order to solve that set of problems which Galbraith has collectively designated as 'public squalor,' the West, to a striking degree, would have to embark on precisely the courses of action which are essential for the solution of its ecological problems. (The opposite situation holds in the developing countries; there lies the tragedy.)

What troubles me, however, is that it is hard to see any way in which the West can change its economic habits which does not entail the shifting of decisions about choices from the market to governments. This has already happened, of course, to a large degree; those income-earners—most of us—who have not learned the art of tax-evasion will have a large part, perhaps the greater part, of their income spent for them by the government. Whether this process can be carried further in a manner which does not entail the gradual emergence of a bureaucratic police state and the stifling of enterprise is, for me, the question of questions. Is Sweden, as has recently been argued, the prime example of creeping totalitarianism?

To sum up, I find it impossible to sum up, to arrive at any neat, tidy, quotable conclusions. As I have written, I have become more and more conscious of the complexity of every problem I have touched upon. I have tried to clear some intellectual ground, so that the alternatives before us are a little less obscured by undergrowth, but the problems remain. Yet nothing could be worse than to allow ourselves to slip into the doomsday mood of paranoic melancholia. The elderly, especially, are only too liable to this mood, whether taking pleasure in the reflection that by dying they will miss nothing but calamities or seeking an illusory grandeur as prophets of death and destruction. But in the young, too, apocalyptic prophecy can serve as a substitute for the overwhelming responsibility of action.

There is certainly a risk that we shall be utterly discouraged by the implications of Barry Commoner's 'first ecological law'—'everything is connected to everything else'—for this makes it appear that to act at all is the height of imprudence. But fortunately I do not, before I swat a mosquito, have to calculate the consequences of my act on the sun's output of cosmic rays or the eutrophication of Lake Erie. It is just not true that everything I do has effects on *everything* else. What we do need always to remember, however—and this is sufficiently alarming—is that the unintended consequences of our actions are often surprisingly remote in time and place from those actions. (Skin cancer forty years after exposure to the sun; the excess fertiliser from my garden feeding algae in a remote stream.) Commoner's 'law' somewhat resembles the old Heraclitean dictum 'expect the unexpected.' Valuable as a warning, it is useless as a guide to action.

What in general I have emphasised is that, if the world's ecological problems are to be solved at all, it can only be by that old-fashioned procedure, thoughtful action. We may, of course, think to no purpose; by acting thoughtfully we may make matters worse. As we know quite well in our personal lives, we are sometimes saved by rashness, destroyed by prudence. Looking before we leap may make cowards of us. But there is no alternative policy. Mystical contemplation will not clean our streams or feed our peoples; no invisible guiding hand, whether Providence or History, guarantees our salvation. In the biosphere, as I said, man has no tenure; his own folly may, at any time, lose him his precarious occupancy.

How and what we think, however, is determined not only by our brain structure but by the nature of the possibilities our society leaves open to us, the forms of thinking its traditions permit and encourage. The modern West, I have argued, leaves more options open than most other societies; its traditions, intellectual, political, moral, are complex, diversified and fruitfully discordant. That gives it the capacity to grow, to change: it nurtures within itself the seeds of innumerable revolutions. It is inventive—not only technologically, but politically, administratively, intellectually. Its flexibility gives it a better, not a lesser, chance of solving its problems. Admittedly, its central Stoic-Christian traditions are not favourable to the solution of its ecological problems—those traditions which deny that man's relationships with nature are governed by any moral principles and assign to nature the very minimum of independent life. But they, I have sought to show, are not the only Western traditions and their influence is steadily declining.

If, a century hence, men live worse lives than they do today, that will not be because the traditions of the West have bemused them; greed, ignorance, shortsightedness, fanaticism, are not Western inventions. How in fact they will live I have not dared to guess. My sole concern is that we should do nothing which will reduce their freedom of thought and action, whether by destroying the natural world which makes that freedom possible or the social traditions which permit and encourage it.

Suggestions for Further Reading

Anthologies

Ammerman, Robert R. and Singer, Marcus G. (eds.). *Belief, Knowledge and Truth.* New York: Scribners, 1970. A rich selection, ranging from elementary to difficult, from philosophical writings on skepticism, empiricism, rationalism, and other issues in the theory of knowledge from ancient Greece to the present. An extensive bibliography of books and articles.

Braybrooke, David (ed.). *Philosophical Problems of the Social Sciences.* New York: Macmillan, Sources in Philosophy Series, 1965. Contains a substantial introductory essay by the editor and a selection of recent philosophical writings treating problems suggested by psychology, history, economics, and the other social sciences. This book of readings is designed for the beginning student.

Caplan, Arthur L. (ed.). *The Sociobiology Debate. Readings on Ethical and Scientific Issues.* New York: Harper & Row, 1978. A collection of classic scientific articles, important writings in the recent sociobiology controversy and new writings by philosophers, biologists, anthropologists, and political theorists.

Gardner, Martin (ed.). *Great Essays in Science.* New York: Pocket Books, 1957. A highly readable collection of writings on the nature of science and its social implications by scientists and philosophers. This book is more entertaining than many novels.

Mitcham, Carl and Mackey, Robert (eds.). *Philosophy and Technology: Readings in the Philosophical Problems of Technology.* New York: Free Press, 1972. A well-balanced selection of writings by American, British, and European thinkers on the nature of technology; ethical, political, and religious critiques of technology; and metaphysical analyses of technology. A good selection and annotated bibliography of works in English, French, and German enhances the value of this book.

Natanson, Maurice (ed.). *Philosophy of the Social Sciences.* New York: Random, 1963. This anthology provides examples of the application of the phenomenological method to the study of human society. Extensive bibliography. For the more advanced student.

Shapere, Dudley (ed.). *Philosophical Problems of Natural Science.* New York: Macmillan, Sources in Philosophy Series, 1965. Contains a substantial introductory essay by the editor and a selection of recent philosophical writings dealing with the structural and historical analyses of science. This book of readings is designed for the beginning student.

Suppe, Frederick (ed.). *The Structure of Scientific Theories,* 2nd ed. Urbana, Illinois: Univ. of Ill. Press, 1978. A good anthology of recent writings in the philosophy of science. For the advanced student.

Individual Works

Ayer, A. J. *The Problem of Knowledge.* Baltimore: Penguin, 1956. A more advanced yet clearly written philosophical investigation of the nature, scope, and limits of human knowledge. This book was designed not only for the professional philosopher but for the general reader as well. Particular attention is called to Chapter 2, "Skepticism and Certainty."

Cohen, Morris R. *Reason and Nature,* 2nd ed. New York: Free Press, 1964, A classic work by an American philosopher who was a champion of the supremacy of critical reason in human life. Cohen devotes considerable attention to the ethical, legal, religious, and historic implications of scientific knowledge and method. A scholarly work, yet written so lucidly that the beginning student can read it with pleasure.

Gardner, Martin. *Fads and Fallacies in the Name of Science,* 2nd ed. New York: Dover, 1957. A fascinating examination of extrasensory perception, the hollow earth hypothesis, dianetics, orgone boxes, and other theories and devices that the author criticizes as being pseudoscience.

Hospers, John. *An Introduction to Philosophical Analysis,* 2nd ed. Englewood Cliffs, N.J.: Prentice-Hall, 1967. This expository text contains a clear, contemporary, and elementary discussion of rationalism and empiricism for the beginning student.

Huxley, Thomas Henry. *Selections from the Essays of T. H. Huxley,* edited by Alburey Castell, New York: Appleton, 1948. A collection of some of the most famous essays treating such topics as science and education, science and religion, and science and ethics.

Nagel, Ernest. *The Structure of Science.* New York: Harcourt, 1961. A recent comprehensive treatment of the nature of explanation in the natural and social sciences by an outstanding American philosopher of science. A book for the more advanced student.

Otto, Max C. *Science and the Moral Life.* New York: New American Library, Mentor Book, 1949. An unusually felicitous defense of a scientific humanism in the tradition of William James and John Dewey. With a sophistication developed to the point of simplicity, this book is designed for the layman in philosophy.

Popper, Karl. *Objective Knowledge: An Evolutionary Approach.* New York: Oxford University Press, 1972. A recent work by an internationally outstanding contemporary philosopher of science.

Putman, Hilary. *Meaning and the Moral Sciences.* Boston: Routledge and Kegan Paul, 1978. A recent, provocative work illustrating new trends of thought by a prominent American philosopher of science.

Ravetz, Jerome R. *Scientific Knowledge and Its Social Problems.* New York: Oxford U.P.: 1973. A recent and influential discussion of the nature of science and its impact on society and nature.

Russell, Bertrand. *The Scientific Outlook.* New York: Norton, 1962. The first two parts of this book deal with the natures of scientific knowledge and scientific technique. In the third part entitled "The Scientific Society," Russell rewrites and updates Plato's *Republic.* In the course of his philosophical critique of the scientific society, Russell discusses all of the objections to such a society to be found in George Orwell's *1984,* Aldous Huxley's *Brave New World,* and other similar fictional and nonfictional critiques.

Stapledon, Olaf. *Last and First Men and Star Maker.* New York: Dover, 1968. Two science fiction novels by a philosopher that convey the haunting beauty and disturbing strangeness of the world revealed by science better than most abstract treatises. These powerfully imaginative works reveal why many men find the scientific understanding and manipulation of the world and man so fascinating and hopeful and many others find it so appalling and depressing.

Dictionary of the History of Ideas: Studies of Selected Pivotal Ideas. Philip P. Wiener, editor-in-chief. New York: Scribners, 1973. Substantial and clearly written essays emphasizing the historical development of topics discussed in this part. Designed to inform the nonspecialist, each essay concludes with a select bibliography.

Encyclopedia of Philosophy. Paul Edwards, editor-in-chief. New York: Macmillan, 1967. The beginning student will find many worthwhile articles on the subjects treated in this part, and excellent bibliographies.

Introduction

An ancient legend tells of a fabulously wealthy king who, being bored with life, sent heralds into all parts of his kingdom offering the rewards of fame and fortune to any subject who could invent a new pleasure. A quaint, charming, and innocuous fable, you say. However, let us, as artists often do, update this legend by dressing it in contemporary costume. Suppose, then, that the President of the United States were to announce on television his intention of presenting a freedom medal at a gala White House ceremony to any American citizen who could invent a new pleasure. What would be the reactions of the President's fellow countrymen and of the other nations of the world? Does anyone really expect that such a promulgation would be discussed seriously, calmly, objectively, logically? No one really does. Everyone knows that in the United States the reaction would be amused puzzlement followed by furious denunciations on the floor of Congress of this moral affront to every decent man and woman in the country, indignant editorials in the mass media bristling with alarm at this additional sign of corruption in high places, thinly veiled hints from the opposition political party of insanity in the national leadership, and a hail of angry resolutions from patriotic and professional organizations vowing to fight the policy to the bitter end. From London, we would hear: "In his television broadcast yesterday, the President of the United States gave what is perhaps the most convincing proof of the crass materialism rampant in our former colony. Being a young country, America has not learned as yet that the old, traditional pleasures are best." From Paris, we would hear: "And you Americans have always called France an immoral country." Moscow and Peking would agree: "The request of the President of the United States for the invention of a new pleasure shows the desperation of the bourgeoisie to escape the reality of inevitable revolution."

The call for an inventor of a new pleasure symbolizes mankind's call for the artist to create new works of art. We desire the pleasure that works of art can give and sometimes reward the artist handsomely. And yet, paradoxically, we fear that pleasure we want so much and distrust the man who provides it. From time to time we see darker tints in the golden wine of art, and suspect that it may contain some deadly poison. To some the musical *Hair* represents one of the outstanding artistic works of the last decade. To others it is a blatant encouragement of sexual promiscuity, marijuana smoking, and social anarchy, and to some, the tremendous success of this musical all over the world only supplies further indication of the danger of art. Joseph Stalin

463

allegedly once remarked that Dostoevski was a great artist but also a terrible reactionary whose writings should be banned. Many people consider Ezra Pound one of the great poets of our century and yet the United States Government charged him with treason. To many people, twentieth-century art in general represents a magnificent period of experimentation, originality, and enduring achievement. To others it reeks of degeneration. This paradoxical relationship of man to art is not unique to our day; we can trace it back to ancient Greece. Plato felt it keenly. It is the kind of problem demanding the philosopher's skill at analysis, criticism, and clarification in order to elucidate the real issues, if any, involved and the direction in which a genuine resolution of them may be found. And so, Socrates-like, the philosopher asks questions. Does art exercise any effect at all on human conduct? If art does influence human conduct, is that influence trivial or significant and how would this be determined rationally? Granted an important impact of art on morality, is it preponderantly for good or for evil? If for evil, is censorship the best way to eliminate or minimize that evil? Or would the disadvantages of censorship outweigh any benefits that might flow from it? We are familiar with the claim of some moral system or ideology to enjoy the unqualified right of judging art. Perhaps a more cogent case can be made for reversing that relationship, setting up art as the arbiter of morality and maintaining that the categories of good and evil are fundamentally aesthetic ones. Should the creation and enjoyment of art be accorded the supreme position in human life and all other human values be subordinated to aesthetic values? Is the attitude of aesthetic detachment an adequate basis for a philosophy of life?

In the dialogue entitled *The Republic,* Plato takes up many of these questions. The stated general purpose of *The Republic* is to define *justice* by describing a rational Utopia where the wisest men (that is, philosophers) rule. Employing the character of Socrates as his mouthpiece, Plato sets forth what he feels to be the proper role of art in a society that is thoroughly and relentlessly devoted to the promotion of human welfare. Since man is a rational animal, his welfare will be achieved by subordinating all other human values to the complete realization of his intellectual capacity. Of course, the only problem in a perfect society lies in perpetuating it. Plato resolves this problem into one of ensuring that the rulers will always be intellectuals by organizing the entire society into a comprehensive educational system, placing each individual in the position for which he is best suited according to his abilities. Education as a placement agency should be familiar to contemporary students. Therefore, for Plato the role of art in society becomes its role in education.

Here it should be pointed out that the meaning of art in Plato is not confined to what today we would call the "fine arts" but includes all human skills from training dogs and building ships to painting pictures and sculpting statues.

The highest art, as Plato sees it, is living the good or rational life. Plato evaluates what we refer to as the "fine arts" in terms of the ways in which they help and hinder the making of the good life. Plato is convinced that art in our sense of the "fine arts," appealing primarily to the senses and the desire for pleasure rather than to reason and the desire for knowledge, possesses a tremendous capacity for affecting the molding of human character for good and for evil. Therefore, in *The Republic* Socrates presents the case for an official policy of censorship designed, not to eliminate all of the fine arts, but to deliberately and systematically promote their good effects and prevent them from exercising their harmful powers and thereby advance the highest art of living the rational life.

In the next selection drawn from his *Politics,* Aristotle, Plato's star pupil, presents the case against establishing a censorship of the arts on the grounds that it would be socially unhygienic. Art produces a catharsis, a kind of purging of our emotions, reducing their strength to the point where they can be controlled by reason and thereby preventing them from being socially and individually destructive. Art "imitates" life, not in the sense that it literally copies life, but in the sense that it produces in us emotions evoked by situations encountered in actual life. Since music is most effective in arousing such emotions, it is the most imitative of the arts. However, art differs from life in that works of art do not incite to action but effect the opposite. Therefore, art is a form of therapy, a sort of safety valve. However, difficult as it may be to settle the issue, both Plato and Aristotle cannot be correct: Art cannot both cause and not cause crime and general moral degeneration.

When philosophers find themselves faced with conflicting theories, neither of which can be easily determined to be true, a common strategy consists in seeking an alternative theory. The theories of both Plato and Aristotle agree on the assumption that art causally affects human conduct; they differ on the general character of that influence, Plato arguing that it is often detrimental to morality and Aristotle that it is on the whole benign. Jean-Paul Sartre, a leading contemporary Existentialist philosopher, rejects this common assumption of Plato and Aristotle, contending that art and morality, Beauty and the Good, are completely independent of each other. The work of art is an autonomous product and should be judged only in terms of aesthetic standards and not in terms of moral, political, theological, or other nonaesthetic ones. Sartre argues that human conduct obviously is an "existential" matter, for human conduct is the making of choices. To choose is to "exist," in the sense in which Sartre employs the concept *existence.* To "exist" is to be real. However, contemplation of a work of art necessitates suspending the making of choices; it means ceasing to act, ignoring past and future, and becoming absorbed in the present. Hence, the work of art does not "exist"; it is a timeless essence, a nonmaterial image—in short, it is purely imaginary. Art belongs to imagination, morality belongs to existence.

Art and morality, Beauty and Goodness, occupy distinct and separate planes, and so the problem of whether the influence of art is predominantly for good or for evil is a pseudoproblem. Art is neither moral nor immoral but nonmoral.

Much of the debate concerning art and morality reveals a strong and persistent bias on the part of most participants in favor of the moral man rather than of the aesthetically sensitive man in the general sense of assigning greater dignity, scope, and intrinsic importance to morality in contrast with art. D. W. Prall, the American aesthetician, seeks to reverse this emphasis, subordinating morality to art. Prall maintains that all moral values derive from aesthetic values. The discrimination of good and evil is ultimately accomplished by the eye of the artist. Aesthetic employment is the only real end-in-itself, all other worthwhile nonaesthetic values being but various means to its attainment.

John Dewey sees the relationship of art and morality in a still different form, not as a relationship of dependence of one on the other or as a relationship of independence of one from the other, but as reciprocal connection. More precisely, the relationship between art and morality *ought* to be one of mutual interdependence if art were not narrowly conceived as the pleasure of an idle moment, as entertainment, and morality crudely seen as the mechanical awarding of praise and blame according to some rigid and oversimplified code. If we construed art and morality more intelligently, neither would be confined artificially to separate compartments, but would be seen to be elements of all human culture: art imaginatively discerning the ideal and morality being a collective name for all shared human values. Traditional, "academic" art may merely decorate and enhance conventional values. However, new art is new because it makes us sensitive to new values, to novel ideals, and thereby encourages moral innovation. Art as the imaginative discernment of possibilities redeems human life from the damnation of routine and boredom.

F. E. Sparshott, a Canadian philosopher, carefully articulates and distinguishes the issues and the accompanying opposing arguments in the snarled controversy about censorship and the arts. Sparshott's acute and comprehensive analysis should stimulate and clarify the reader's philosophical reflections on the contemporary issue of art and pornography. The author's elucidation shows that the issue of whether or not art should be censored is not a simple matter of white *versus* black but instead a complex, subtle, and profound controversy.

The vexed issue of whether or not the arts should be censored is as old as Plato and as fresh as today's news. Walter Berns presents a recent, sophisticated version of the case of censorship of the arts. Berns does not deny that many people like pornography, and even delight in the obscene.

However, the fact that somebody wants something is not proof that that something is good for him or for anybody else. The desired is not necessarily the desirable. Many people desperately want heroin but this does not make heroin good for them. Society should uphold moral standards because their destruction means the ultimate destruction of society itself. The maintenance of moral standards requires good character, which, in turn, necessitates self-restraint. Self-restraint is impossible without a sense of shame. A sense of shame is incompatible with an attitude that everything is permitted, with everybody doing his or her "thing." The legalization of pornography, of obscene art, encourages an attitude that everything is permitted and thus undermines morality. Berns adds the corollary that democracy—self-governance—rests on the capacity for self-restraint. The uncensored circulation of pornography thus threatens the existence of democracy. Furthermore, the upholding of moral standards strengthens all standards of what is worthwhile and thereby supports the aesthetic distinction between art and trash. In short, censorship is a form of self-restraint or self-discipline; self-restraint is essential to the maintenance of all standards, be they moral ones, aesthetic ones, political ones, or others.

In Berns's interpretation, obscenity has a justifiable place in art when it is used as a means to increase our understanding of what is right by law and what is right by nature rather than as a means for destroying standards. Of course, censors will be fallible human beings; however, if they err, it is better that they do so on the side of standards of decency rather than on the side of obscenity. Too much is at stake: the future of morality, democracy—yes, art itself.

In opposing censorship of the arts, Marshall Cohen argues that the harm caused by censorship outweighs any harm produced by obscenity and pornography. Indeed, most of the baneful effects that Berns ascribes to obscenity are imaginary. Cohen admits the plausibility of the claim that "society has a right to protect its moral environment." Yet there is no evading the fact that censorship means a curtailment of freedom of thought and speech. What is the aim of censorship: to preserve moral standards or to prevent criticism of them? Perhaps some of our moral standards are in reality so pernicious in their effects that they should not be merely criticized but eliminated? If our moral and other standards cannot withstand attack, they are not worth preserving. Censorship easily, perhaps inevitably, considering the vagueness of the meaning of "obscene" and "pornographic" to say nothing of "smut" and "dirt," becomes a means for stopping moral change and with it moral improvement. In seeking to make something better, we always run the risk of making it worse.

Cohen recognizes that many people find pornography repugnant. But to oppose censorship is not to force pornography on those who do not want it.

It is possible for pornography to be freely available and also to avoid invasion of privacy. Cohen does not object to prevention of public nuisances. Should the law prohibit commercial exploitation of a morbid interest in sex? Cohen argues against such a prohibition on the ground of difficulty of distinguishing between "morbid" and "healthy" interest and between "commercial exploitation" and accepted "capitalist sales techniques." What would happen if censorship of the arts ended up with censorship of capitalism? The dangers of censorship are far greater than its benefits.

50. Moral and Immoral Art   Plato

Plato (427–347 B.C.), an Athenian aristocrat, was converted by Socrates from poetry to philosophy. With the exception of Aristotle, no philosopher has exerted a greater formative influence on Western culture. In many of the Platonic dialogues, Socrates is made to express ideas doubtless those of Plato. In the following selection, Socrates discusses moral and immoral art with Adeimantus and Glaucon, both young men and brothers of Plato.

Socrates (narrator): Come then, and let us pass a leisure hour in story-telling, and our story shall be the education of our heroes.

Adeimantus: By all means.

And what shall be their education? Can we find a better than the traditional sort?—and this has two divisions, gymnastic for the body, and music for the soul.

True.

Shall we begin education with music, and go on to gymnastic afterwards?

By all means.

And when you speak of music, do you include literature or not?

I do.

And literature may be either true or false?

Yes.

And the young should be trained in both kinds, and we begin with the false?

I do not understand your meaning, he said.

You know, I said, that we begin by telling children stories which, though not wholly destitute of truth, are in the main fictitious; and these stories are told them when they are not of an age to learn gymnastics.

Very true.

That was my meaning when I said that we must teach music before gymnastics.

From "The Republic," by Plato from The Dialogues of Plato, translated by Benjamin Jowett, 3rd ed., 1892 (as reprinted in the Random House volume, by Raphael Demos, 1937). Reprinted by permission of the Clarendon Press, Oxford.

Quite right, he said.

You know also that the beginning is the most important part of any work, especially in the case of a young and tender thing; for that is the time at which the character is being formed and the desired impression is more readily taken.

Quite true.

And shall we just carelessly allow children to hear any casual tales which may be devised by casual persons, and to receive into their minds ideas for the most part the very opposite of those which we should wish them to have when they are grown up?

We cannot.

Then the first thing will be to establish a censorship of the writers of fiction, and let the censors receive any tale of fiction which is good, and reject the bad; and we will desire mothers and nurses to tell their children the authorised ones only. Let them fashion the mind with such tales, even more fondly than they mould the body with their hands; but most of those which are now in use must be discarded.

Of what tales are you speaking? he said.

You may find a model of the lesser in the greater, I said; for they are necessarily of the same type, and there is the same spirit in both of them.

Very likely, he replied; but I do not as yet know what you would term the greater.

Those, I said, which are narrated by Homer and Hesiod, and the rest of the poets, who have ever been the great story-tellers of mankind.

But which stories do you mean, he said; and what fault do you find with them?

A fault which is most serious, I said; the fault of telling a lie, and, what is more, a bad lie.

But when is this fault committed?

Whenever an erroneous representation is made of the nature of gods and heroes,—as when a painter paints a portrait not having the shadow of a likeness to the original.

Yes, he said, that sort of thing is certainly very blameable; but what are the stories which you mean?

First of all, I said, there was the greatest of all lies, in high places, which the poet told about Uranus, and which was a bad lie too,—I mean what Hesiod says that Uranus did, and how Cronus retaliated on him.[1] The doings of Cronus, and the sufferings which in turn his son inflicted upon him, even if they were true, ought certainly not to be lightly told to young and thoughtless persons; if possible, they had better be buried in silence. But if there is an absolute necessity for their mention, a chosen few might hear them in a mystery, and they should sacrifice not a common [Eleusinian] pig, but some huge and unprocurable victim; and then the number of hearers will be very few indeed.

Why, yes, said he, those stories are extremely objectionable.

[1]Hesiod, Theogony, 154, 459.

Yes, Adeimantus, they are stories not to be repeated in our State; the young man should not be told that in committing the worst of crimes he is far from doing anything outrageous; and that even if he chastises his father when he does wrong, in whatever manner, he will only be following the example of the first and greatest among the gods.

I entirely agree with you, he said; in my opinion these stories are quite unfit to be repeated.

Neither, if we mean our future guardians to regard the habit of quarreling among themselves as of all things the basest, should any word be said to them of the wars in heaven, and of the plots and fightings of the gods against one another, for they are not true. No, we shall never mention the battles of the giants, or let them be embroidered on garments; and we shall be silent about the innumerable other quarrels of gods and heroes with their friends and relatives. If they would only believe us we would tell them that quarreling is unholy, and that never up to this time has there been any quarrel between citizens; this is what old men and old women should begin by telling children; and when they grow up, the poets also should be told to compose for them in a similar spirit. But the narrative of Hephaestus binding Here his mother, or how on another occasion Zeus sent him flying for taking her part when she was being beaten, and all the battles of the gods in Homer—these tales must not be admitted into our State, whether they are supposed to have an allegorical meaning or not. For a young person cannot judge what is allegorical and what is literal; anything that he receives into his mind at that age is likely to become indelible and unalterable; and therefore it is most important that the tales which the young first hear should be models of virtuous thoughts. . . .

And if any one asserts that the violation of oaths and treaties, which was really the work of Pandarus,[2] was wrought about by Athene and Zeus, or that the strife and contention of the gods was instigated by Themis and Zeus,[3] he shall not have our approval; neither will we allow our young men to hear the words of Aeschylus, that

> God plants guilt among men when he desires utterly to destroy a house.

And if a poet writes of the sufferings of Niobe—the subject of the tragedy in which these iambic verses occur—or of the house of Pelops, or of the Trojan way or on any similar theme, either we must not permit him to say that these are the works of God, or if they are of God, he must devise some explanation of them such as we are seeking; he must say that God did what was just and right, and they were the better for being punished; but that those who are punished are miserable, and that God is the author of their misery—the poet is not to be permitted to say; though he may say that the wicked are miserable because they require to be punished, and are benefited by receiving punishment from God; but that God being good is the author of evil to any one is to be strenuously denied, and not

[2]Iliad ii. 69.
[3]Ib. xx.

to be said or sung or heard in verse or prose by any one whether old or young in any well-ordered commonwealth. Such a fiction is suicidal, ruinous, impious.

I agree with you, he replied, and am ready to give my assent to the law.

Let this then be one of our rules and principles concerning the gods, to which our poets and reciters will be expected to conform—that God is not the author of all things, but the good only.

That will do, he said.

And what do you think of a second principle? Shall I ask you whether God is a magician, and of a nature to appear insidiously now in one shape, and now in another—sometimes himself changing and passing into many forms, sometimes deceiving us with the semblance of such transformations; or is he one and the same immutably fixed in his own proper image?

I cannot answer you, he said, without more thought.

Well, I said; but if we suppose a change in anything, that change must be effected either by the thing itself, or by some other thing?

Most certainly.

And things which are at their best are also least liable to be altered or discomposed; for example, when healthiest and strongest, the human frame is least liable to be affected by meats and drinks, and the plant which is in the fullest vigour also suffers least from winds or the heat of the sun or any similar causes.

Of course.

And will not the bravest and wisest soul be least confused or deranged by any external influence?

True.

And the same principle, as I should suppose, applies to all composite things—furniture, houses, garments: when good and well made, they are least altered by time and circumstances.

Very true.

Then everything which is good, whether made by art or nature, or both, is least liable to suffer change from without?

True.

But surely God and the things of God are in every way perfect?

Of course they are.

Then he can hardly be compelled by external influence to take many shapes?

He cannot.

But may he not change and transform himself?

Clearly, he said, that must be the case if he is changed at all.

And will he then change himself for the better and fairer, or for the worse and more unsightly?

If he change at all he can only change for the worse, for we cannot suppose him to be deficient either in virtue or beauty.

Very true, Adeimantus; but then, would any one, whether God or man, desire to make himself worse?

Impossible.

Then it is impossible that God should ever be willing to change; being, as is supposed, the fairest and best that is conceivable, every God remains absolutely and for ever in his own form.

That necessarily follows, he said, in my judgment.

Then, I said, my dear friend, let none of the poets tell us that

> The gods, taking the disguise of strangers from other lands, walk up and down cities in all sorts of forms,[4]

and let no one slander Proteus and Thetis, neither let any one, either in tragedy or in any other kind of poetry, introduce Here disguised in the likeness of a priestess asking an alms

> For the life-giving daughters of Inachus the river of Argos;

—let us have no more lies of that sort. Neither must we have mothers under the influence of the poets scaring their children with a bad version of these myths—telling how certain gods, as they say, 'Go about by night in the likeness of so many strangers and in divers forms;' but let them take heed lest they make cowards of their children, and at the same time speak blasphemy against the gods.

Heaven forbid, he said.

But although the gods are themselves unchangeable, still by witchcraft and deception they may make us think that they appear in various forms?

Perhaps, he replied.

Well, but can you imagine that God be willing to lie, whether in word or deed, or to put forth a phantom of himself?

I cannot say, he replied.

Do you not know, I said, that the true lie, if such an expression may be allowed, is hated of gods and men?

What do you mean? he said.

I mean that no one is willingly deceived in that which is the truest and highest part of himself, or about the truest and highest matters; there, above all, he is most afraid of a lie having possession of him.

Still, he said, I do not comprehend you.

The reason is, I replied, that you attribute some profound meaning to my words; but I am only saying that deception, or being deceived or uninformed about the highest realities in the highest part of themselves, which is the soul, and in that part of them to have and to hold the lie, is what mankind least like;—that, I say, is what they utterly detest.

There is nothing more hateful to them.

And, as I was just now remarking, this ignorance in the soul of him who is deceived may be called the true lie; for the lie in words is only a kind of imitation and shadowy image of a previous affection of the soul, not pure unadulterated falsehood. Am I not right?

Perfectly right.

The true lie is hated not only by the gods, but also by men?

Yes.

Whereas the lie in words is in certain causes useful and not hateful; in dealing with enemies—that would be an instance; or again, when those whom we call our friends in a fit of madness or illusion are going to do

[4]Hom. Od. xvii. 485.

some harm, then it is useful and is a sort of medicine or preventive; also in the tales of mythology, of which we were just now speaking—because we do not know the truth about ancient times, we make falsehood as much like truth as we can, and so turn it to account.

Very true, he said.

But can any of these reasons apply to God? Can we suppose that he is ignorant of antiquity, and therefore has recourse to invention?

That would be ridiculous, he said.

Then the lying poet has no place in our idea of God?

I should say not.

Or perhaps he may tell a lie because he is afraid of enemies?

That is inconceivable.

But he may have friends who are senseless or mad?

But no mad or senseless person can be a friend of God.

Then no motive can be imagined why God should lie?

None whatever.

Then the superhuman and divine is absolutely incapable of falsehood?

Yes.

Then is God perfectly simple and true both in word and deed; he changes not; he deceives not, either by sign or word, by dream or waking vision. . . .

And can he be fearless of death, or will he choose death in battle rather than defeat and slavery, who believes the world below to be real and terrible?

Impossible.

Then we must assume a control over the narrators of this class of tales as well as over the others, and beg them not simply to revile, but rather to commend the world below, intimating to them that their descriptions are untrue, and will do harm to our future warriors.

That will be our duty, he said.

Then, I said, we shall have to obliterate many obnoxious passages, beginning with the verses,

> I would rather be a serf on the land of a poor and portionless man than rule over all the dead who have come to nought.[5]

We must also expunge the verse, which tells us how Pluto feared,

> Lest the mansions grim and squalid which the gods abhor should be seen both of mortals and immortals.[6]

And again:—

> O heavens! verily in the house of Hades there is soul and ghostly form but no mind at all![7]

Again of Tiresias:—

> [To him even after death did Persephone grant mind,] that he alone should be wise; but the other souls are flitting shades.[8]

[5]Od. ix. 489.
[6]Il. xx. 64.
[7]Il. xxiii. 103.
[8]Od. x. 495.

Again:—

> The soul flying from the limbs had gone to Hades, lamenting her fate, leaving manhood and youth.[9]

Again:—

> And the soul, with shrilling cry, passed like smoke beneath the earth.[10]

And,—

> As bats in hollow of mystic cavern, whenever any of them has dropped out of the string and falls from the rock, fly shrilling and cling to one another, so did they with shrilling cry hold together as they moved.[11]

And we must beg Homer and the other poets not to be angry if we strike out these and similar passages, not because they are unpoetical, or unattractive to the popular ear, but because the greater the poetical charm of them, the less they are meet for the ears of boys and men who are meant to be free, and who should fear slavery more than death.

Undoubtedly.

Also we shall have to reject all the terrible and appalling names which describe the world below—Cocytus and Styx, ghosts under the earth, and sapless shades, and any similar words of which the very mention causes a shudder to pass through the inmost soul of him who hears them. I do not say that these horrible stories may not have a use of some kind; but there is a danger that the nerves of our guardians may be rendered too excitable and effeminate by them. . . .

Again, truth should be highly valued; if, as we were saying, a lie is useless to the gods, and useful only as a medicine to men, then the use of such medicines should be restricted to physicians; private individuals have no business with them.

Clearly not, he said.

Then if any one at all is to have the privilege of lying, the rulers of the State should be the persons; and they, in their dealings either with enemies or with their own citizens, may be allowed to lie for the public good. But nobody else should meddle with anything of the kind; and although the rulers have this privilege, for a private man to lie to them in return is to be deemed a more heinous fault than for the patient or the pupil of a gymnasium not to speak the truth about his own bodily illnesses to the physician or to the trainer, or for a sailor not to tell the captain what is happening about the ship and the rest of the crew, and how things are going with himself or his fellow sailors.

Most true, he said.

If, then, the ruler catches anybody beside himself lying in the State,

> Any of the craftsmen, whether he be priest or physician or carpenter.[12]

he will punish him for introducing a practice which is equally subversive and destructive of ship or State.

[9]Il. xvi. 856.
[10]Ib. xxiii. 100.
[11]Od. xxiv. 6.
[12]Od. xvii. 383 sq.

Most certainly, he said, if our idea of the State is ever carried out.[13]
In the next place our youth must be temperate?
Certainly.
Are not the chief elements of temperance, speaking generally, obedience to commanders and self-control in sensual pleasures?
True.
Then we shall approve such language as that of Diomede in Homer,

> Friend, sit still and obey my word,[14]

and the verses which follow,

> The Greeks marched breathing prowess,[15]
> . . . . in silent awe of their leaders,[16]

and other sentiments of the same kind.
We shall.
What of this line,

> O heavy with wine, who hast the eyes of a dog and the heart of a stag,[17]

and of the words which follow? Would you say that these, or any similar impertinences which private individuals are supposed to address to their rulers, whether in verse or prose, are well or ill spoken?
They are ill spoken.
They may very possibly afford some amusement, but they do not conduce to temperance. And therefore they are likely to do harm to our young men—you would agree with me there?
Yes.
And then, again, to make the wisest of men say that nothing in his opinion is more glorious than

> When the tables are full of bread and meat, and the cup-bearer carries round wine which he draws from the bowl and pours into the cups,[18]

is it fit or conducive to temperance for a young man to hear such words? Or the verse

> The saddest of fates is to die and meet destiny from hunger?[19]

What would you say again to the tale of Zeus, who, like other gods and men were asleep and he the only person awake, lay devising plans, but forgot them all in a moment through his lust, and was so completely overcome at the sight of Here that he would not even go into the hut, but wanted to lie with her on the ground, declaring that he had never been in such a state of rapture before, even when they first met one another

> Without the knowledge of their parents;[20]

[13]Or, 'if his words are accompanied by actions.'
[14]Il. iv. 412.
[15]Od. iii. 8.
[16]Ib. iv. 431.
[17]Ib. i. 225.
[18]Ib. ix. 8.
[19]Ib. xii. 342.
[20]Il. xiv. 281.

or that other tale of how Hephaestus, because of similar goings on, cast a chain around Ares and Aphrodite?[21]

Indeed, he said, I am strongly of opinion that they ought not to hear that sort of thing.

But any deeds of endurance which are done or told by famous men, these they ought to see and hear; as, for example, what is said in the verses,

> He smote his breast, and thus reproached his heart,
> Endure, my heart; far worse hast thou endured![22]

Certainly, he said.

In the next place, we must not let them be receivers of gifts or lovers of money.

Certainly not.

Neither must we sing to them of

> Gifts persuading gods, and persuading reverend kings.[23]

Neither is Phoenix, the tutor of Achilles, to be approved or deemed to have given his pupil good counsel when he told him that he should take the gifts of the Greeks and assist them;[24] but that without a gift he should not lay aside his anger. Neither will we believe or acknowledge Achilles himself to have been such a lover of money that he took Agamemnon's gifts, or that when he had received payment he restored the dead body of Hector, but that without payment he was unwilling to do so.[25]

Undoubtedly, he said, these are not sentiments which can be approved.

. . . [W]e must come to an understanding about the mimetic art,—whether the poets, in narrating their stories, are to be allowed by us to imitate, and if so, whether in whole or in part, and if the latter, in what parts; or should all imitation be prohibited?

You mean, I suspect, to ask whether tragedy and comedy shall be admitted into our State?

Yes, I said; but there may be more than this in question: I really do not know as yet, but whither the argument may blow, thither we go.

And go we will, he said.

Then, Adeimantus, let me ask you whether our guardians ought to be imitators; or rather, has not this question been decided by the rule already laid down that one man can only do one thing well, and not many; and that if he attempt many, he will altogether fail of gaining much reputation in any?

Certainly.

And this is equally true of imitation; no one man can imitate many things as well as he would imitate a single one?

He cannot.

---

[21]Od. viii. 266.
[22]Ib. xx. 17.
[23]Quoted by Suidas as attributed to Hesiod.
[24]Il. ix. 515.
[25]Ib. xxiv. 175.

Then the same person will hardly be able to play a serious part in life, and at the same time to be an imitator and imitate many other parts as well; for even when two species of imitation are nearly allied, the same persons cannot succeed in both, as, for example, the writers of tragedy and comedy—did you not just now call them imitations?

Yes, I did; and you are right in thinking that the same persons cannot succeed in both.

Any more than they can be rhapsodists and actors at once?

True.

Neither are comic and tragic actors the same; yet all these things are but imitations.

They are so.

And human nature, Adeimantus, appears to have been coined into yet smaller pieces, and to be as incapable of imitating many things well, as of performing well the actions of which the imitations are copies.

Quite true, he replied.

If then we adhere to our original notion and bear in mind that our guardians, setting aside every other business, are to dedicate themselves wholly to the maintenance of freedom in the State, making this their craft, and engaging in no work which does not bear on this end, they ought not to practise or imitate anything else; if they imitate at all, they should imitate from youth upward only those characters which are suitable to their profession—the courageous, temperate, holy, free, and the like; but they should not depict or be skilful at imitating any kind of illiberality or baseness, lest from imitation they should come to be what they imitate. Did you never observe how imitations, beginning in early youth and continuing far into life, at length grow into habits and become a second nature, affecting body, voice, and mind?

Yes, certainly, he said.

Then, I said, we will not allow those for whom we profess a care and of whom we say that they ought to be good men, to imitate a woman, whether young or old, quarrelling with her husband, or striving and vaunting against the gods in conceit of her happiness, or when she is in affliction, or sorrow, or weeping; and certainly not one who is in sickness, love or labour.

Very right, he said.

Neither must they represent slaves, male or female, performing the offices of slaves?

They must not.

And surely not bad men, whether cowards or any others, who do the reverse of what we have just been prescribing, who scold or mock or revile one another in drink or out of drink, or who in any other manner sin against themselves and their neighbours in word or deed, as the manner of such is. Neither should they be trained to imitate the action or speech of men or women who are mad or bad; for madness, like vice, is to be known but not to be practised or imitated.

Very true, he replied.

Neither may they imitate smiths or other artificers or oarsmen, or boatswains, or the like?

How can they, he said, when they are not allowed to apply their minds to the callings of any of these?

Nor may they imitate the neighing of horses, the bellowing of bulls, the murmur of rivers and roll of the thunder, and all that sort of thing?

Nay, he said, if madness be forbidden, neither may they copy the behaviour of madmen.

You mean, I said, if I understand you aright, that there is one sort of narrative style which may be employed by a truly good man when he has anything to say, and that another sort will be used by a man of an opposite character and education.

And which are these two sorts? he asked.

Suppose, I answered, that a just and good man in the course of a narration comes on some saying or action of another good man,—I should imagine that he will like to personate him, and will not be ashamed of this sort of imitation: he will be most ready to play the part of the good man when he is acting firmly and wisely; in a less degree when he is overtaken by illness or love or drink; or has met with any other disaster. But when he comes to a character which is unworthy of him, he will not make a study of that; he will disdain such a person, and will assume his likeness, if at all, for a moment only when he is performing some good action; at other times he will be ashamed to play a part which he has never practised, nor will he like to fashion and frame himself after the baser models; he feels the employment of such an art, unless in jest, to be beneath him, and his mind revolts at it. . . .

But shall our superintendence go no further, and are the poets only to be required by us to express the image of the good in their works, on pain, if they do anything else, of expulsion from our State? Or is the same control to be extended to other artists, and are they also to be prohibited from exhibiting the opposite forms of vice and intemperance and meanness and indecency in sculpture and building and the other creative arts; and is he who cannot conform to this rule of ours to be prevented from practising his art in our State, lest the taste of our citizens be corrupted by him? We would not have our guardians grow up amid images of moral deformity, as in some noxious pasture, and there browse and feed upon many a baneful herb and flower day by day, little by little, until they silently gather a festering mass of corruption in their own soul. Let our artists rather be those who are gifted to discern the true nature of the beautiful and graceful; then will our youth dwell in a land of health, amid fair sights and sounds, and receive the good in everything; and beauty, the effluence of fair works, shall flow into the eye and ear, like a health-giving breeze from a purer region, and insensibly draw the soul from earliest years into likeness and sympathy with the beauty of reason.

Glaucon   There can be no nobler training than that, he replied.

And therefore, I said, Glaucon, musical training is a more potent instrument than any other, because rhythm and harmony find their way into the inward places of the soul, on which they mightily fasten, imparting grace, and making the soul of him who is rightly educated graceful, or of him who is ill-educated ungraceful; and also because he who has received this true education of the inner being will most shrewdly perceive omissions or faults in art and nature, and with a true taste, while he praises and rejoices over and receives into his soul the good, and becomes noble and good, he will justly blame and hate the bad, now in the days of his youth, even before he is able to know the reason why; and when reason comes he will recognise and salute the friend with whom his education has made him long familiar.

Yes, he said, I quite agree with you in thinking that our youth should be trained in music and on the grounds which you mention.

Just as in learning to read, I said, we were satisfied when we knew the letters of the alphabet, which are very few, in all their recurring sizes and combinations; not slighting them as unimportant whether they occupy a space large or small, but everywhere eager to make them out; and not thinking ourselves perfect in the art of reading until we recognise them wherever they are found.

True—

Or, as we recognise the reflection of letters in the water, or in a mirror, only when we know the letters themselves; the same art and study giving us the knowledge of both:

Exactly—

Even so, as I maintain, neither we nor our guardians, whom we have to educate, can ever become musical until we and they know the essential forms, in all their combinations, and can recognise them and their images wherever they are found, not slighting them either in small things or great, but believing them all to be within the sphere of one art and study.

Most assuredly.

And when a beautiful soul harmonizes with a beautiful form, and the two are cast in one mould, that will be the fairest of sights to him who has an eye to see it?

The fairest indeed.

And the fairest is also the loveliest?

That may be assumed.

And the man who has the spirit of harmony will be most in love with the loveliest; but he will not love him who is of an inharmonious soul?

That is true, he replied, if the deficency be in his soul; but if there be any merely bodily defect in another he will be patient of it, and will love all the same. . . .

51. Art as Social Therapy Aristotle

Aristotle (384–322 B.C.), son of a Macedonian physician, most famous student of Plato, and tutor of the Young Alexander the Great, was called simply "The Philosopher" in medieval universities, so great was his stature. His writings seem to be notes made for or taken from his lectures. His early writings, now lost, are said

to have shown great literary skill. Minus the influence of Aristotle's philosophy,
Western civilization would not be what it was and is.

No one will doubt that the legislator should direct his attention above
all to the education of youth; for the neglect of education does harm to
the constitution. The citizen should be molded to suit the form of government under which he lives. For each government has a peculiar character
which continues to preserve it. The character of democracy creates
democracy, and the character of oligarchy creates oligarchy; and always
the better the character, the better the government.

Again, for the exercise of any faculty or art a previous training and
habituation are required; clearly therefore for the practice of virtue. And
since the whole city has one end, it is manifest that education should be
public, and not private,—not as at present, when every one looks after his
own children separately, and gives them separate instruction of the sort
which he thinks best; the training in things which are of common interest
should be the same for all. Neither must we suppose that any one of the
citizens belongs to himself, for they all belong to the state, and are each of
them a part of the state and the care of each part is inseparable from the
care of the whole. In this particular as in some others the Lacedaemonians
are to be praised, for they take the greatest pains about their children,
and make education the business of the state.

That education should be regulated by law and should be an affair of
state is not to be denied, but what should be the character of this public
education, and how young persons should be educated, are questions
which remain to be considered. As things are, there is disagreement about
the subjects. For mankind are by no means agreed about the things to be
taught, whether we look to virtue or the best life. Neither is it clear
whether education is more concerned with intellectual or with moral virtue. The existing practice is perplexing; no one knows on what principle
we should proceed—should the useful in life, or should virtue, or should
the higher knowledge, be the aim of our training; all three opinions have
been entertained. Again, about the means there is no agreement; for different persons, starting with different ideas about the nature of virtue,
naturally disagree about the practice of it. There can be no doubt that
children should be taught those useful things which are really necessary,
but not all useful things; for occupations are divided into liberal and illiberal; and to young children should be imparted only such kinds of knowledge as will be useful to them without vulgarizing them. And any occupation, art, or science, which makes the body or soul or mind of the
freeman less fit for the practice or exercise of virtue, is vulgar; wherefore
we call those arts vulgar which tend to deform the body, and likewise all
paid employments, for they absorb and degrade the mind. There are also
some liberal arts quite proper for a freeman to acquire, but only in a

From 'Politics,' by Aristotle, translated by Benjamin Jowett from *The Oxford Translation of Aristotle,*
edited by W. D. Ross, Vol. X, 1921. Reprinted by permission of the Clarendon Press, Oxford. Footnotes
have been omitted.

certain degree, and if he attend them too closely, in order to attain perfection in them, the same evil effects will follow. The object also which a man sets before him makes a great difference; if he does or learns anything for his own sake or for the sake of his friends, or with a view to excellence, the action will not appear illiberal; but if done for the sake of others, the very same action will be thought menial and servile. The received subjects of instruction, as I have already remarked, are partly of a liberal and partly of an illiberal character.

The customary branches of education are in number four; they are— (1) reading and writing, (2) gymnastic exercises, (3) music, to which is sometimes added (4) drawing. Of these, reading and writing and drawing are regarded as useful for the purposes of life in a variety of ways, and gymnastic exercises are thought to infuse courage. Concerning music a doubt may be raised—in our own day most men cultivate it for the sake of pleasure, but originally it was included in education, because nature herself, as has been often said, requires that we should be able, not only to work well, but to use leisure well; for, as I must repeat once again, the first principle of all action is leisure. Both are required, but leisure is better than occupation and is its end; and therefore the question must be asked, what ought we to do when at leisure? Clearly we ought not to be amusing ourselves, for then amusement would be the end of life. But if this is inconceivable, and amusement is needed more amid serious occupations than at other times (for he who is hard at work has need of relaxation, and amusement gives relaxation, whereas occupation is always accompanied with exertion and effort), we should introduce amusements only at suitable times, and they should be our medicines, for the emotion which they create in the soul is a relaxation, and from the pleasure we obtain rest. But leisure of itself gives pleasure and happiness and enjoyment of life, which are experienced, not by the busy man, but by those who have leisure. For he who is occupied has in view some end which he has not attained; but happiness is an end, since all men deem it to be accompanied with pleasure and not with pain. This pleasure, however, is regarded differently by different persons, and varies according to the habit of individuals; the pleasure of the best man is the best, and springs from the noblest sources. It is clear then that there are branches of learning and education which we must study merely with a view to leisure spent in intellectual activity, and these are to be valued for their own sake; whereas those kinds of knowledge which are useful in business are to be deemed necessary, and exist for the sake of other things. And therefore our fathers admitted music into education, not on the ground either of its necessity, or utility, for it is not necessary, nor indeed useful in the same manner as reading and writing, which are useful in money-making, in the management of a household, in the acquisition of knowledge and in political life, nor like drawing, useful for a more correct judgment of the works of artists, nor again like gymnastic, which gives health and strength; for neither of these is to be gained from music. There remains, then, the use of music for intellectual enjoyment in leisure; which is in fact evidently the reason of its introduction, this being one of the ways in which it is thought that a freeman should pass his leisure; as Homer says—

> But he who alone should be called to the pleasant feast,

and afterwards he speaks of others whom he describes as inviting

> The bard who would delight them all.

And in another place Odysseus says there is no better way of passing life than when men's hearts are merry and

> The banqueters in the hall, sitting in order, hear the voice of the minstrel.

It is evident, then, that there is a sort of education in which parents should train their sons, not as being useful or necessary, but because it is liberal or noble. Whether this is of one kind only, or of more than one, and if so, what they are, and how they are to be imparted, must hereafter be determined. Thus much we are now in a position to say, that the ancients witness to us; for their opinion may be gathered from the fact that music is one of the received and traditional branches of education. Further, it is clear that children should be instructed in some useful things,—for example, in reading and writing,—not only for their usefulness, but also because many other sorts of knowledge are acquired through them. With a like view they may be taught drawing, not to prevent their making mistakes in their own purchases, or in order that they may not be imposed upon in the buying or selling of articles, but perhaps rather because it makes them judges of the beauty of the human form. To be always seeking after the useful does not become free and exalted souls. Now it is clear that in education practice must be used before theory, and the body be trained before the mind; and therefore boys should be handed over to the trainer, who creates in them the proper habit of body, and to the wrestling-master, who teaches them their exercises. . . .

Concerning music there are some questions which we have already raised; these we may now resume and carry further; and our remarks will serve as a prelude to this or any other discussion of the subject. It is not easy to determine the nature of music, or why any one should have a knowledge of it. Shall we say, for the sake of amusement and relaxation, like sleep or drinking, which are not good in themselves, but are pleasant, and at the same time 'make care to cease', as Euripides says? And for this end men also appoint music, and make use of all three alike,—sleep, drinking, music,—to which some add dancing. Or shall we argue that music conduces to virtue, on the ground that it can form our minds and habituate us to true pleasures as our bodies are made by gymnastic to be of a certain character? Or shall we say that it contributes to the enjoyment of leisure and mental cultivation, which is a third alternative? Now obviously youths are not to be instructed with a view to their amusement, for learning is no amusement, but is accompanied with pain. Neither is intellectual enjoyment suitable to boys of that age, for it is the end, and that which is imperfect cannot attain the perfect or end. But perhaps it may be said that boys learn music for the sake of the amusement which they will have when they are grown up. If so, why should they learn themselves, and not, like the Persian and Median kings, enjoy the pleasure and instruction which is derived from hearing others? (for surely persons who have made music the business and profession of their lives will be better performers than those who practise only long enough to learn). If they must learn music, on the same principle they should learn cookery, which is absurd. And even granting that music may form the character, the objection still holds: why should we learn ourselves? Why cannot we attain true pleasure and form a correct judgment from hearing others, like the Lacedaemonians?—for they, without learning music, nevertheless can correctly judge, as they say, of good and bad melodies. Or again, if music should be used to promote cheerfulness and refined intellectual enjoyment, the objection still remains—why should we learn ourselves instead of enjoying the performances of others? We may illustrate what we are saying by our conception of the Gods; for in the poets Zeus does not himself sing or play on the lyre. Nay, we call professional performers vulgar; no freeman would play or sing unless he were intoxicated or in jest. But these matters may be left for the present.

The first question is whether music is or is not to be a part of education. Of the three things mentioned in our discussion, which does it produce?—education or amusement or intellectual enjoyment, for it may be reckoned under all three, and seems to share in the nature of all of them. Amusement is for the sake of relaxation, and relaxation is of necessity sweet, for it is the remedy of pain caused by toil; and intellectual enjoyment is universally acknowledged to contain an element not only of the noble but of the pleasant, for happiness is made up of both. All men agree that music is one of the pleasantest things, whether with or without song; as Musaeus says,

> Song is to mortals of all things the sweetest.

Hence and with good reason it is introduced into social gatherings and entertainments, because it makes the hearts of men glad: so that on this ground alone we may assume that the young ought to be trained in it. For innocent pleasures are not only in harmony with the perfect end of life, but they also provide relaxation. And whereas men rarely attain the end, but often rest by the way and amuse themselves, not only with a view to a further end, but also for the pleasure's sake, it may be well at times to let them find a refreshment in music. It sometimes happens that men make amusement the end, for the end probably contains some element of pleasure, though not any ordinary or lower pleasure; but they mistake the lower for the higher, and in seeking for the one find the other, since every pleasure has a likeness to the end of action. For the end is not eligible for the sake of any future good, nor do the pleasures which we have described exist for the sake of any future good but of the past, that is to say, they are the alleviation of past toils and pains. And we may infer this to be the reason why men seek happiness from these pleasures. But music is pursued, not only as an alleviation of past toil, but also as providing recreation. And who can say whether, having this use, it may not also have a nobler one? In addition to this common pleasure, felt and shared in by all (for the pleasure given by music is natural, and therefore adapted to all ages and characters), may it not have also some influence over the character and the soul? It must have such an influence if characters are affected by it. And that they are so affected is proved in many ways, and not least by the power which the songs of Olympus exercise; for beyond question they inspire enthusiasm, and enthusiasm is an emotion of the ethical part of the soul. Besides, when men hear imitations, even apart from the rhythms and tunes themselves, their feelings move in sympathy. Since then music is a pleasure, and virtue consists in rejoicing and loving and hating aright, there is clearly nothing which we are so much concerned to acquire and to cultivate as the power of forming right judgments, and of taking delight in good dispositions and noble actions. Rhythm and melody supply imitations of anger and gentleness, and also of courage and temperance, and of all the qualities contrary to these, and of the other qualities of character, which hardly fall short of the actual affections, as we know from our own experience, for in listening to such strains our souls undergo a change. The habit of feeling pleasure or pain at mere representations is not far removed from the same feeling about realities; for example, if any one delights in the sight of a statue for its beauty alone, it necessarily follows that the sight of the original will be pleasant to him. The objects of no other sense, such as taste or touch, have any resemblance to moral qualities; in visible objects there is only a little, for there are figures which are of a moral character, but only to a slight extent, and all do not participate in the feeling about them. Again, figures and colours are not imitations, but signs, of moral habits, indications which the body gives of states of feeling. The connexion of them with morals is slight, but in so far as there is any, young men should be taught to look, not at the works of Pauson, but at those of Polygnotus, or any other painter or sculptor who expresses moral ideas. On the other hand, even in mere melodies there is an imitation of character, for the musical modes differ essentially from one another, and those who hear them are differently affected by each. Some of them make men sad and grave, like the so-called Mixolydian, others enfeeble the mind, like the relaxed modes, another, again, produces a moderate and settled temper, which appears to be the peculiar effect of the Dorian; the Phrygian inspires enthusiasm. The whole subject has been well treated by philosophical writers on this branch of education, and they confirm their arguments by facts. The same principles apply to rhythms; some have a character of rest, others of motion, and of these latter again, some have a more vulgar, others a nobler movement. Enough has been said to show that music has a power of forming the character, and should therefore be introduced into the education of the young. The study is suited to the stage of youth, for young persons will not, if they can help, endure anything which is not sweetened by pleasure, and music has a natural sweetness. There seems to be in us a sort of affinity to musical modes and rhythms, which makes some philosophers say that the soul is a tuning, others, that it possesses tuning.

And now we have to determine the question which has been already raised, whether children should be themselves taught to sing and play or not. Clearly there is a considerable difference made in the character by the actual practice of the art. It is difficult, if not impossible, for those who do not perform to be good judges of the performance of others. Besides, children should have something to do, and the rattle of Archytas, which people give to their children in order to amuse them and prevent them from breaking anything in the house, was a capital invention, for a young thing cannot be quiet. The rattle is a toy suited to the infant mind, and education is a rattle or toy for children of a larger growth. We conclude then that they should be taught music in such a way as to become not only critics but performers.

The question what is or is not suitable for different ages may be easily answered; nor is there any difficulty in meeting the objection of those who say that the study of music is vulgar. We reply (1) in the first place, that they who are to be judges must also be performers, and that they should begin to practise early, although when they are older they may be spared the execution; they must have learned to appreciate what is good and to delight in it, thanks to the knowledge which they acquired in their youth. As to (2) the vulgarizing effect which music is supposed to exercise, this is a question which we shall have no difficulty in determining, when we have considered to what extent freemen who are being trained to political virtue should pursue the art, what melodies and what rhythms they should be allowed to use, and what instruments should be employed in teaching them to play; for even the instrument makes a difference. The answer to the objection turns upon these distinctions; for it is quite possible that certain methods of teaching and learning music do really have a degrading effect. It is evident then that the learning of music ought not to impede the business of riper years, or to degrade the body or render it unfit for civil or military training, whether for bodily exercises at the time or for later studies.

The right measure will be attained if students of music stop short of the arts which are practised in professional contests, and do not seek to acquire those fantastic marvels of execution which are now the fashion in such contests, and from these have passed into education. Let the young practise even such music as we have prescribed, only until they are able to feel delight in noble melodies and rhythms, and not merely in that common part of music in which every slave or child and even some animals find pleasure.

From these principles we may also infer what instruments should be used. The flute, or any other instrument which requires great skill, as for example the harp, ought not to be admitted into education, but only such as will make intelligent students of music or of the other parts of education. Besides, the flute is not an instrument which is expressive of moral character; it is too exciting. The proper time for using it is when the performance aims not at instruction, but at the relief of the passions. And there is a further objection; the impediment which the flute presents to the use of the voice detracts from its educational value. The ancients therefore were right in forbidding the flute to youths and freemen, although they had once allowed it. For when their wealth gave them a greater inclination to leisure, and they had loftier notions of excellence, being also elated with their success, both before and after the Persian War, with more zeal than discernment they pursued every kind of knowledge, and so they introduced the flute into education. At Lacedaemon there was a choragus who led the chorus with a flute, and at Athens the instrument became so popular that most freemen could play upon it. The popularity is shown by the tablet which Thrasippus dedicated when he furnished the chorus to Ecphantides. Later experience enabled men to judge what was or was not really conducive to virtue, and they rejected both the flute and several other old-fashioned instruments, such as the Lydian harp, the many-stringed lyre, the 'heptagon', 'triangle', 'sambuca', and the like— which are intended only to give pleasure to the hearer, and require extraordinary skill of hand. There is a meaning also in the myth of the ancients, which tells how Athene invented the flute and then threw it away. It was not a bad idea of theirs, that the Goddess disliked the instrument because it made the face ugly; but with still more reason may we say that she rejected it because the acquirement of flute-playing contributes nothing to the mind, since to Athene we ascribe both knowledge and art.

Thus then we reject the professional instruments and also the professional mode of education in music (and by professional we mean that which is adopted in contests), for in this the performer practises the art, not for the sake of his own improvement, but in order to give pleasure, and that of a vulgar sort, to his hearers. For this reason the execution of such music is not the part of a freeman but of a paid performer, and the result is that the performers are vulgarized, for the end at which they aim is bad. The vulgarity of the spectator tends to lower the character of the music and therefore of the performers; they look to him—he makes them what they are, and fashions even their bodies by the movements which he expects them to exhibit.

We have also to consider rhythms and modes, and their use in education. Shall we use them all or make a distinction? and shall the same distinction be made for those who practise music with a view to education, or shall it be some other? Now we see that music is produced by melody and rhythm, and we ought to know what influence these have respectively on education, and whether we should prefer excellence in melody or excellence in rhythm. But as the subject has been very well treated by many musicians of the present day, and also by philosophers who have had considerable experience of musical education, to these we would refer the more exact student of the subject; we shall only speak of it now after the manner of the legislator, stating the general principles.

We accept the division of melodies proposed by certain philosophers into ethical melodies, melodies of action, and passionate or inspiring melodies, each having, as they say, a mode corresponding to it. But we maintain further that music should be studied, not for the sake of one, but of many benefits, that is to say, with a view to (1) education, (2) purgation (the word 'purgation' we use at present without explanation, but when hereafter we speak of poetry, we will treat the subject with more precision); music may also serve (3) for intellectual enjoyment, for relaxation and for recreation after exertion. It is clear, therefore, that all the modes must be employed by us, but not all of them in the same manner. In education the most ethical modes are to be preferred, but in listening to the performances of others we may admit the modes of action and passion also. For feelings such as pity and fear, or, again, enthusiasm, exist very strongly in some souls, and have more or less influence over all. Some persons fall into a religious frenzy, whom we see as a result of the sacred melodies—when they have used the melodies that excite the soul to mystic frenzy—restored as though they had found healing and purgation. Those who are influenced by pity or fear, and every emotional nature, must have a like experience, and others in so far as each is susceptible to such emotions, and all are in a manner purged and their souls lightened and delighted. The purgative melodies likewise give an innocent pleasure to mankind. Such are the modes and the melodies in which those who perform music at the theatre should be invited to compete. But since the spectators are of two kinds—the one free and educated, and the other a vulgar crowd composed of mechanics, labourers, and the like—there ought to be contests and exhibitions instituted for the relaxation of the second class also. And the music will correspond to their minds; for as their minds are perverted from the natural state, so there are perverted modes and highly strung and unnaturally coloured melodies. A man receives pleasure from what is natural to him, and therefore professional musicians may be allowed to practise this lower sort of music before an audience of a lower type. But, for the purposes of education, as I have already said, those modes and melodies should be employed which are ethical, such as the Dorian, as we said before; though we may include any others which are approved by philosophers who have had a musical education. The Socrates of the *Republic* is wrong in retaining only the Phrygian mode along with the Dorian, and the more so because he rejects the flute: for the Phrygian is to the modes what the flute is to musical instruments—both of them are exciting and emotional. Poetry proves this, for Bacchic frenzy and all similar emotions are most suitably expressed by the flute, and are better set to the Phrygian than to any other mode. The dithyramb, for example, is acknowledged to be Phrygian, a fact of which the connoisseurs of music offer many proofs, saying, among other things, that Philoxenus, having attempted to compose his *Mysians* as a dithyramb in the Dorian mode, found it impossible, and fell back by the very nature of things into the more appropriate Phyrgian. All men agree that the Dorian music is the gravest and manliest. And whereas we say that the extremes should be avoided and the mean followed, and whereas the Dorian is a mean between the other modes, it is evident that our youth should be taught the Dorian music.

Two principles have to be kept in view, what is possible, what is becoming: at these every man ought to aim. But even these are relative to age; the old, who have lost their powers, cannot very well sing the highstrung modes, and nature herself seems to suggest that their songs should be of the more relaxed kind. Wherefore the musicians likewise blame Socrates, and with justice, for rejecting the relaxed modes in education under the idea that they are intoxicating, not in the ordinary sense of intoxication (for wine rather tends to excite men), but because they have no strength in them. And so, with a view also to the time of life when men begin to grow old, they ought to practise the gentler modes and melodies as well as the others, and, further, any mode, such as the Lydian above all others appears to be, which is suited to children of tender age, and possesses the elements both of order and of education. Thus it is clear that education should be based upon three principles—the mean, the possible, the becoming, these three.

52. The Autonomy of Art   Jean-Paul Sartre

Jean-Paul Sartre (1905–   ), French existentialist, former professor of philosophy and World War II Resistance leader, is a successful novelist and playwright, as well as philosopher. In 1964, Sartre refused to accept the Nobel Prize for Literature.

. . . We often hear it said, in fact, that the artist first has an idea in the form of an image which he then *realizes* on canvas. This mistaken notion arises from the fact that the painter can, in fact, begin with a mental image which is, as such, incommunicable, and from the fact that at the end of his labors he presents the public with an object which anyone can observe. This leads us to believe that there occurred a transition from the imaginary to the real. But this is in no way true. That which is real, we must not fail to note, are the results of the brush strokes, the stickiness of the canvas, its grain, the polish spread over the colors. But all this does not constitute the object of esthetic appreciation. What is "beautiful" is something which cannot be experienced as a perception and which, by its very nature, is out of the world. We have just shown that it cannot be *brightened,* for instance, by projecting a light beam on the canvas: it is the canvas that is brightened and not the painting. The fact of the matter is that the painter did not *realize* his mental image at all: he has simply constructed a material analogue of such a kind that everyone can grasp the image provided he looks at the analogue. But the image thus provided with an external analogue remains an image. There is no realization of the imaginary, nor can we speak of its *objectification.* Each stroke of the brush was not made *for itself* nor even for the constructing of a coherent real whole (in the sense in which it can be said that a certain lever in a machine was conceived in the interest of the whole and not for itself). It was given together with an unreal synthetic whole and the aim of the artist was to construct a whole of *real* colors which enable this unreal to manifest itself. The painting should then be conceived as a material thing *visited* from time to time (every time that the spectator assumes the imaginative attitude) by an unreal which is precisely the *painted object.* What deceives us here is the real and sensuous pleasure which certain real colors on the canvas give us. Some reds of Matisse, for instance, produce a sensuous enjoyment in those who see them. But we must understand that this sensuous enjoyment, if thought of in isolation—for instance, if aroused by a color in nature—has nothing of the esthetic. It is purely and simply a pleasure of sense. But when the red of the painting is grasped, it is grasped, in spite of everything, as a part of an unreal whole and it is in this whole that it is beautiful. For instance it is the red of a rug by a table. There is, in fact, no such thing as pure color. Even if the artist is concerned solely with the sensory relationships between forms and colors, he chooses for that very reason a rug in order to increase the sensory value of the red: tactile elements, for instance, must be intended through the red, it is a *fleecy* red, because the rug is of a fleecy material. Without this "fleeciness" of the color something would be lost. And surely the rug is painted there *for the red* it justifies and not the red for the rug. If Matisse chose a rug rather than a sheet of dry and glossy paper it is because of the voluptuous mixture of the color, the density and the tactile quality of the wool. Consequently the red can be truly enjoyed only in grasping it as the *red of the rug,* and therefore unreal. And he would have lost his strongest contrast with the green of the wall if the green were not rigid and cold, because it is the green of a wall tapestry. It is therefore in the unreal that the relationship of colors and forms takes on its real meaning. And even when drawn objects have their usual meaning reduced to a minimum, as in the painting of the cubists, the painting is at least not flat. The forms we see are certainly not the forms of a rug, a table, nor anything else we see in the world. They nevertheless do have a density, a material, a depth, they bear a relationship of perspective towards each other. They are *things.* And it is precisely in the measure in which they are things that they are unreal. Cubism has introduced the fashion of claiming that a painting should not *represent* or *imitate* reality but should constitute an object in itself. As an esthetic doctrine such a program is perfectly defensible and we owe many masterpieces to it. But it needs to be understood. To maintain that the painting, although altogether devoid of meaning, nevertheless is a *real* object, would be a grave mistake. It is certainly not an object of nature. The real object no longer functions as an analogue of a bouquet of flowers or a glade. But when I "contemplate" it, I nevertheless am not in a realistic attitude. The painting is still an *analogue.* Only what manifests itself through it is an unreal collection of *new things,* of objects I have never seen or ever will see, but which are not less unreal because of it, objects which do not exist *in the painting,* nor anywhere in the world, but which manifest themselves by means of the canvas, and which have gotten hold of it by some sort of possession. And it is the configuration of these unreal objects that I designate as *beautiful.* The esthetic enjoyment is real but it is not grasped for itself, as if produced by a real color: it is but a manner of apprehending the unreal object and, far from being directed on the real painting, it serves to constitute the imaginary object through the real canvas. This is the source of the celebrated disinterestedness of esthetic experience. This is why Kant was able to say that it does not matter whether the object of beauty, when experienced as beautiful, is or is not objectively real; why Schopenhauer was able to speak of a sort of suspension of the Will. This does not come from some mysterious way of apprehending the real, which we are able to use occasionally. What happens is that the esthetic object is constituted and apprehended by an imaginative consciousness which posits it as unreal.

What we have just shown regarding painting is readily applied to the art of fiction, poetry and drama, as well. It is self-evident that the novelist, the poet and the dramatist construct an unreal object by means of verbal analogues; it is also self-evident that the actor who plays Hamlet makes use of himself, of his whole body, as an analogue of the imaginary person. Even the famous dispute about the paradox of the comedian is enlightened by the view here presented. It is well known that certain amateurs proclaim that the actor *does not believe* in the character he portrays. Others, leaning on many witnesses, claim that the actor becomes identified in some way with the character he is enacting. To us these two views are not exclusive of each other; if by "belief" is meant actually real it is obvious that the actor does not actually consider himself to be Hamlet. But this does not mean that he does not "mobilize" all his powers to make Hamlet real. He uses all his feelings, all his strength, all his gestures as analogues of the feelings and conduct of Hamlet. But by this very fact he takes the reality away from them. *He lives completely in an unreal way.* and it matters little that he is *actually* weeping in enacting the role. These tears, . . . he himself experiences—and so does the audience—as the tears of Hamlet, that is as the analogue of unreal tears. The transformation that occurs here is like that we discussed in the dream: the actor is completely caught up, inspired, by the unreal. It is not the character who becomes real in the actor, it is the actor who *becomes unreal* in his character.[1]

But are there not some arts whose object seem to escape unreality by their very nature? A melody, for instance, refers to nothing but itself. Is a cathedral anything more than a mass of *real* stone which dominates the surrounding house tops? But let us look at this matter more closely. I listen to a symphony orchestra, for instance, playing the Beethoven Seventh Symphony. Let us disregard exceptional cases—which are besides on the margin of esthetic contemplation—as when I go mainly "to hear Toscanini" interpret Beethoven in his own way. As a general rule what draws me to the concert is the desire "to hear the Seventh Symphony." Of course I have some objection to hearing an amateur orchestra, and prefer this or that well-known musical organization. But this is due to my desire to hear the symphony "played perfectly," because the symphony will then be *perfectly itself.* The shortcomings of a poor orchestra which plays "too fast" or "too slow," "in the wrong tempo," etc., seem to me to rob, "betray" the work it is playing. At most the orchestra effaces itself before the work it performs, and, provided I have reasons to trust the performers and

---

[1]It is in this sense that a beginner in the theatre can say that stage-fright served her to represent the timidity of Ophelia. If it did so, it is because she suddenly turned it into an unreality, that is, that she ceased to apprehend it for itself and that she grasped it as *analogue* for the timidity of Ophelia.

their conductor, I am confronted by the symphony itself. This everyone will grant me. But now, what is the Seventh Symphony itself? Obviously it is a *thing*, that is something which is before me, which endures, which lasts. Naturally there is no need to show that that thing is a synthetic whole, which does not consist of tones but of a thematic configuration. But is that "thing" real or unreal? Let us first bear in mind that I am listening to the Seventh Symphony. For me that "Seventh Symphony" does not exist in time, I do not grasp it as a dated event, as an artistic manifestation which is unrolling itself in the Châtelet auditorium on the 17th of November, 1938. If I hear Furtwaengler tomorrow or eight days later conduct another orchestra performing the same symphony, I am in the presence of the same symphony once more. Only it is being played either better or worse. Let us now see *how* I hear the symphony: Some persons shut their eyes. In this case they detach themselves from the *visual* and dated event of this particular interpretation: they give themselves up to the pure sounds. Others watch the orchestra or the back of the conductor. But they do not see what they are looking at. This is what Revault d'Allonnes calls reflection with auxiliary fascination. The auditorium, the conductor and even the orchestra have disappeared. I am therefore confronted by the Seventh Symphony, but on the express condition of understanding *nothing about it,* that I do not think of the event as an actuality and dated, and on condition that I listen to the succession of themes as an absolute succession and not as a real succession which is unfolding itself, for instance, on the occasion when Peter paid a visit to this or that friend. In the degree to which I hear the symphony it is *not here,* between these walls, at the tip of the violin bows. Nor is it "in the past" as if I thought: this is the work that matured in the mind of Beethoven on such a date. It is completely beyond the real. It has its own time, that is, it possesses an inner time, which runs from the first tone of the allegro to the last tone of the finale, but this time is not a succession of a preceding time which it continues and which happened "before" the beginning of the allegro; nor is it followed by a time which will come "after" the finale. The Seventh Symphony is in no way *in time.* It is therefore in no way real. It occurs *by itself,* but as absent, as being out of reach. I cannot act upon it, change a single note of it, or slow down its movement. But it depends on the real for its appearance: that the conductor does not faint away, that a fire in the hall does not put an end to the performance. From this we cannot conclude that *the* Seventh Symphony has come to an end. No, we only think that the *performance* of the symphony has ceased. Does this not show clearly that the performance of the symphony is its *analogue?* It can manifest itself only through analogues which are dated and which unroll in our time. But to experience it on these analogues the imaginative reduction must be functioning, that is, the real sounds must be apprehended as analogues. It therefore occurs as a perpetual elsewhere, a perpetual absence. We must not picture it (as does Spandrell in *Point Counterpoint* by Huxley—as so many platonisms) as existing in another world, in an intelligible heaven. It is not only outside of time and space—as are essences, for instance—it is outside of the real, outside of existence. I do not hear it actually, I listen to it in the imaginary. Here we find the explanation for the considerable difficulty we always experience in passing from the world of the theatre or of music into that of our daily affairs. There is in fact no passing from one world into the other, but only a passing from the imaginative attitude to that of reality. Esthetic contemplation is an induced dream and the passing into the real is an actual waking up. We often speak of the "deception" experienced on returning to reality. But this does not explain that this discomfort also exists, for instance, after having witnessed a realistic and cruel play, in which case reality should be experienced as comforting. This discomfort is simply that of the dreamer on awakening; an entranced consciousness, engulfed in the imaginary, is suddenly freed by the sudden ending of the play, of the symphony, and comes suddenly in contact with existence. Nothing more is needed to arouse the nauseating disgust that characterizes the consciousness of reality.

From these few observations we can already conclude that the real is never beautiful. Beauty is a value applicable only to the imaginary and which means the negation of the world in its essential structure. This is why it is stupid to confuse the moral with the esthetic. The values of the Good presume being-in-the-world, they concern action in the real and are subject from the outset to the basic absurdity of existence. To say that we "assume" an esthetic attitude to life is to constantly confuse the real and the imaginary. It does happen, however, that we do assume the attitude of esthetic contemplation towards real events or objects. But in such cases every one of us can feel in himself a sort of recoil in relation to the object contemplated which slips into nothingness so that, from this moment on, it is no longer *perceived;* it functions as an *analogue* of itself, that is, that an unreal image of what it is appears to us through its actual presence. This image can be purely and simply the object "itself" neutralized, annihilated, as when I contemplate a beautiful woman or death at a bull fight; it can also be the imperfect and confused appearance of *what it could be* through what it is, as when the painter grasps the harmony of two colors as being greater, more vivid, *through* the real blots he finds on a wall. The object at once appears to be *in back of* itself, becomes *untouchable,* it is beyond our reach; and hence arises a sort of sad disinterest in it. It is in this sense that we may say that great beauty in a woman kills the desire for her. In fact we cannot at the same time place ourselves on the plane of the esthetic when this unreal "herself" which we admire appears and on the realistic plane of physical possession. To desire her we must forget she is beautiful, because desire is a plunge into the heart of existence, into what is most contingent and most absurd. Esthetic contemplation of *real* objects is of the same structure as paramnesia, in which the real object functions as analogue of itself in the past. But in one of the cases there is a negating and in the other a placing a thing in the past. Paramnesia differs from the esthetic attitude as memory differs from imagination.

53. Art in Life and Artists in Society   D. W. Prall

David Wight Prall (1886–1940) was an American professor of philosophy whose work in aesthetics has stimulated artists and critics, as well as philosophers.

. . . But what . . . is this mature and lasting good that art brings into life? The answer is too simple and too obvious to be at all convincing, for all that art brings to life may be put in one word; if it is successful, what art furnishes men's world with is beauty, which a serious-minded people may think of at the best as a pleasant luxury instead of a necessity, an expense, not an investment, if we must put it in our most vulgar terms. This is like condemning art as legislatures condemn universities, whose presidents in answer use the same vulgar terms. Even in these terms it is not hard to make out our case for art. We may do so merely by remarking the traditional and common application of great wealth to the acquiring of works of art, as all that wealth in the end can be spent upon, all that it is good for, if it is to buy immediately and intrinsically valuable objects instead of mere means to further wealth, or more indirect means to the welfare of others, or those expensive evidences of itself that capture the attention of men and give it prestige and power in their eyes. But we may do much better not to rely on such arguments but to seek the evidence of clear thinking, to meditate upon the true satisfactions of life, that is, until beauty comes into its own proper place in our estimation. Persuasion is not the province of aesthetics, and the question here is in any case one of value in general and of relative values in society, not a question of aesthetic theory only. . . . Aesthetic considerations are considerations as to the immediate and often ultimate nature of the actual qualitative world in which we live. When this quality is at its most satisfactory, the world is beautiful; and since the creation of beauty is the aim of art, and since the achievement of artists is the beauty of their works, there is some ground at least for admitting the great actual value of both artists and their works to all men everywhere.

Another consideration enforces this point and carries it much further. It is after all aesthetic criteria that are final in judging the values of all things, including even that of social usages and laws, and of forms of society in general. And it is direct aesthetic attention that most realistically and surely discerns the features of society as it is. The artist as artist is innocent of ulterior purposes and looks upon the world to see it as it actually appears. And such judgments as he gives us as a critic, as well as such accounts of it as his own artistic medium may express and present to us, are likely to upset our habitual notions of its character, constituted as these notions so largely are of social and religious prejudices, pseudoscience, personal inclinations, and dogmatic conceptions, instilled by conventional education and training. It is the artist's very innocence that is so disconcerting here, like that of a child who fails to see reason in an unreasonable order of things, until he is initiated into the mysteries of adult economic fears, religious dogmas, and social superstitions. So the artist fails to see the ugly aspects of our world and our society as beautiful, or its beautiful ones as ugly. But unlike the child, who is gradually tamed into conformity, he fails here permanently, refusing to falsify his own sure, trained perception to suit such esoteric fancies or palpable delusions as are thrust upon him on all sides, refusing to be initiated into a view of life and the world that denies those very appearances that he apprehends so clearly, in the interest of an abstract and often foolish or imaginatively inadequate construction which purports to account for them as merely superficial, and hence somehow unimportant aspects of a reality handed down by the fathers, or built up by patriotic or industrious and ambitious sons.

Radical reformers themselves also often lack the artist's innocent and direct perception of actual beauty and ugliness for the same reason as conservative businessmen or politicians. For their attention is likely to be focussed less on genuine appearances, which are the sole indications of any possible underlying reality, than on their own theoretical explanation of a state of things that does not even exist, but merely exemplifies their theories, and so in actuality needs no remedy, or upon some one, single, objectionable aspect of civilization which can not sanely be removed, unless it has been fully grasped as one aspect of the form and character and quality of the larger complex whole of which it is an element. When such critics and reformers do turn their attention to the form and features of this whole, they succeed in working it over towards a better one, only so far as they have clearly present to mind the content of that better world, a content viewed in the imagination under a structural form, and with a filling which, so far as it is defined at all, is defined in aesthetic data as the vision of a greater perfection. There are obvious, crying evils which men may mitigate without too long hesitating over the further effects of ulterior transformations involved, but once a critic or a prophet or a reformer turns to the future, his dreams themselves are aesthetic structures, made out of such elements as he may have discovered in his discriminating perception of the aesthetic surface of the actually appearing world.

More than this, the society he dreams of and works towards will not be adequate to any full human living, or rationally to be desired by other men, or a satisfactory consummation if achieved, unless the dreamer has dreamt of beauty in it, and of art and artists, the function of art in life and of artists in society being of prime importance to men's happiness in any circumstances.

When we come to the ethical and social standards themselves by which we attempt to measure the satisfactoriness of a society, actual or imagined, these two, like all standards, turn out to be qualities, or degrees of qualities. Obviously, of good qualities and characteristics, the degree is to be heightened; but what are these qualities and characteristics, and what is our test of their goodness? Aesthetic vision again, direct feeling of their intrinsic satisfactoriness, which is so difficult to distinguish from beauty that the great thinkers have named it always in aesthetic terms, justice itself being only a sort of harmony. And in judging specific details these aesthetic categories are equally important. If the rich were forced to look upon the squalor and suffering of the poor, they could not endure it, as the officials of great corporations can not allow themselves to dwell even in imagination on the actually appearing misery or the sordid ugliness of the surroundings of men at the bottom of the great edifices of industry, and still remain content with the scheme that necessitates such sights. It is in their ultimately felt aesthetic quality that men all find such sights revolting and unendurable, and it is this ugliness that tells us unconditionally that they must be removed if any of us are to live even tolerably free from anguish in the world.

Hence the real strength of the democratic principle, which simply reminds us that we live in a world with other men, but with *all* other men, the various aspects of whose lives and surroundings we can not forever conceal, since in our dependence upon them they must come to our attention and finally be exhibited to us as integral aspects of our own life and world. If we are to be happy in a world as it really lies before us and about us in its actual appearance, that appearance can not remain unsatisfactory to contemplate, that is, aesthetically unsatisfactory,—condemned in the bare honesty of recording aesthetic judgments. If poverty and disease bore a pleasant aspect to discriminating perception, if injustice were aesthetically and directly satisfying to experience, and to dwell upon, what would there be to condemn it in any rational creature's eyes? For it is only in the embodiment in concrete aesthetic data of such abstractions as injustice and suffering and poverty, only their appearing in the world as unmistakably marked for aversion in a direct aesthetic view, that makes them unsatisfactory and ugly and bad. Thus it is finally aesthetic criteria that allow us to make those ethical and moral evaluations that we agree upon sooner or later; and it is aesthetic discernment that is required both to see the evils of the world and to picture a better one from which they can be said to have been removed—not merely changed for other or worse evils—just so far as this new world itself is positively valuable in beauty.

But such criticism or such social constructive thinking and imagining as either condemns or rejects or praises and elevates artists and their function in society, will judge artists not only as the makers of art, but as men. In their sensuous and emotional vitality such men as artists almost inevitably are, may do things in life neither aesthetically nor morally praiseworthy. The criticism that this activity calls down upon their heads, whatever their merits or failures, and whatever the competence of the criticism, is not of course criticism of art, nor even of artists as such, nor has it any place in aesthetic theory, though in much purported art criticism it has been dragged in or substituted for aesthetic judgment itself. It would be an absurd mistake to confuse moral shortcomings with aesthetic ones, even though the ultimate criteria both in morals and in scientific theory are themselves aesthetic standards. Beauty is as such a pure good, whatever it is the beauty of, and whoever may be its author; and beauty transforms the surface of what might be in itself merely unclean or unchaste or unholy, into what may be still unlovely in itself, and yet so hold our eyes to its beautiful surface that it seems purified of its evil, as actually happens in a work of art, where it is just this surface that specifies the whole beauty and significance of the object.

The authors of artistic beauty, being men, may also of course be bad men, except in just this authorship, in so much of their activity, that is, as satisfactorily fulfills their artist's function. And what they do here is so absolutely valuable, their function as artists is so precious, that society may perhaps wisely forgive them for their aesthetically irrelevant sins, especially since what we think of as sins in such men are so much oftener the natural and innocent expression of that vitality and power that makes them artists of significance. In a fully civilized society which allowed free rein to the expression of natural human instincts, or at least tried to provide for such expression as the basis of its polity, these so-called sins might turn out to be childlike innocence, or inventive gaiety. Artists need not be allowed to steal or murder; but these are not the crimes of which they are likely to be accused as characteristic failings. In a world where we are just discovering how antiquated and inhuman most of our social institutions are, and how discordant with the necessary or even possible nature of men, and hence how inimical to their happiness, we can afford to be indulgent to any one or anything in the world of which in any sure sense we can affirm great positive human value. This we can do in the case of art and artists, and if society must have high priests at all, we might well substitute great artists as at least better candidates for the temple than the philosophers whom Plato would have made kings.

54. Art and Civilization   John Dewey

... The moral office and human function of art can be intelligently discussed only in the context of culture. A particular work of art may have a definite effect upon a particular person or upon a number of persons. The social effect of the novels of Dickens or of Sinclair Lewis is far from negligible. But a less conscious and more massed constant adjustment of experience proceeds from the total environment that is created by the collective art of a time. Just as physical life cannot exist without the support of a physical environment, so moral life cannot go on without the support of a moral environment. Even technological arts, in their sum total, do something more than provide a number of separate conveniences and facilities. They shape collective occupations and thus determine direction of interest and attention, and hence affect desire and purpose.

The noblest man living in a desert absorbs something of its harshness and sterility, while the nostalgia of the mountain-bred man when cut off from his surroundings is proof how deeply environment has become part of his being. Neither the savage nor the civilized man is what he is by native constitution but by the culture in which he participates. The final measure of the quality of that culture is the arts which flourish. Compared with their influence things directly taught by word and precept are pale and ineffectual. Shelley did not exaggerate when he said that moral science only "arranges the elements that poetry has created," if we extend "poetry" to include all products of imaginative experience. The sum total of the effect of all reflective treatises on morals is insignificant in comparison with the influence when "intellectual" products formulate the tendencies of these arts and provide them with an intellectual base. An "inner" rational check is a sign of withdrawal from reality unless it is a reflection of substantial environing forces. The political and economic arts that may furnish security and competency are no warrants of a rich and abundant human life save as they are attended by the flourishing of the arts that determine culture.

Words furnish a record of what has happened and give direction by request and command to particular future actions. Literature conveys the meaning of the past that is significant in present experience and is prophetic of the larger movement of the future. Only imaginative vision elicits the possibilities that are interwoven within the texture of the actual. The first stirrings of dissatisfaction and the first intimations of a better future are always found in works of art. The impregnation of the characteristically new art of a period with a sense of different values than those that prevail is the reason why the conservative finds such art to be immoral and sordid, and is the reason why he resorts to the products of the past for esthetic satisfaction. Factual science may collect statistics and make charts. But its predictions are, as has been well said, but past history reversed. Change in the climate of the imagination is the precursor of the changes that affect more than the details of life.

The theories that attribute direct moral effect and intent to art fail because they do not take account of the collective civilization that is the context in which works of art are produced and enjoyed. I would not say that they tend to treat works of art as a kind of sublimated Aesop's fables. But they all tend to extract particular works, regarded as especially edifying, from their milieu and to think of the moral function of art in terms of a strictly personal relation between the selected works and a particular individual. Their whole conception of morals is so individualistic that they miss a sense of the *way* in which art exercises its humane function.

Matthew Arnold's dictum that "poetry is criticism of life" is a case in point. It suggests to the reader a moral intent on the part of the poet and a moral judgment on the part of the reader. It fails to see or at all events to state *how* poetry is a criticism of life; namely, not directly, but by disclosure, through imaginative vision addressed to imaginative experience (not to set judgment) of possibilities that contrast with actual conditions. A sense of possibilities that are unrealized and that might be realized are when they are put in contrast with actual conditions, the most penetrating "criticism" of the latter that can be made. It is by a sense of possibilities opening before us that we become aware of constrictions that hem us in and of burdens that oppress.

Mr. Garrod, a follower of Matthew Arnold in more senses than one, has wittily said that what we resent in didactic poetry is not that it teaches, but that it does not teach, its incompetency. He added words to the effect that poetry teaches as friends and life teach, by being, and not by express intent. He says in another place, "Potential values are, after all, values in a human life. You cannot mark them off from other values, as though the nature of man were built in bulkheads." I do not think that what Keats has said in one of his letters can be surpassed as to the way in which poetry acts. He asks what would be the result if every man spun from his imaginative experience "an airy citadel" like the web the spider spins, "filling the air with a beautiful circuiting." For, he says, "man should not dispute or assert, but whisper results to his neighbor, and thus, by every germ of spirit sucking the sap from mold ethereal, every human being might become great, and Humanity instead of being a wide heath of Furze and briars with here and there a remote Pine or Oak, would become a grand democracy of Forest Trees!"

It is by way of communication that art becomes the incomparable organ of instruction, but the way is so remote from that usually associated with the idea of education, it is a way that lifts art so far above what we are accustomed to think of as instruction, that we are repelled by any suggestion of teaching and learning in connection with art. But our revolt is in fact a reflection upon education that proceeds by methods so literal as to exclude the imagination and one not touching the desires and emotions of men. Shelley said, "The imagination is the great instrument of moral good, and poetry administers to the effect by acting upon the causes." Hence it is, he goes on to say, "a poet would do ill to embody his own conceptions of right and wrong, which are usually those of his own time and place, in his poetical creations. . . . By the assumption of this inferior office . . . he would resign participation in the cause"—the imagination. It is the lesser poets who "have frequently affected a moral aim, and the effect of their poetry is diminished in exact proportion as they compel us to advert to this purpose." But the power of imaginative projection is so great that he calls poets "the founders of civil society."

The problem of the relation of art and morals is too often treated as if the problem existed only on the side of art. It is virtually assumed that morals are satisfactory in idea if not in fact, and that the only question is whether and in what ways art should conform to a moral system already developed. But Shelley's statement goes to the heart of the matter. Imagination is the chief instrument of the good. It is more or less a commonplace to say that a person's ideas and treatment of his fellows are dependent upon his power to put himself imaginatively in their place. But the primacy of the imagination extends far beyond the scope of direct personal relationships. Except where "ideal" is used in conventional deference or as a name for a sentimental reverie, the ideal factors in every moral outlook and human loyalty are imaginative. The historic alliance of religion and art has its roots in this common quality. Hence it is that art is more moral than moralities. For the latter either are, or tend to become, consecrations of the *status quo,* reflections of custom, reënforcements of the established order. The moral prophets of humanity have always been poets even though they spoke in free verse or by parable. Uniformly, however, their vision of possibilities has soon been converted into a proclamation of facts that already exist and hardened into semipolitical institutions. Their imaginative presentation of ideals that should command thought and desire have been treated as rules of policy. Art has been the means of keeping alive the sense of purposes that outrun evidence and of meanings that transcend indurated habit.

Morals are assigned a special compartment in theory and practice because they reflect the divisions embodied in economic and political institutions. Wherever social divisions and barriers exist, practices and ideas that correspond to them fix metes and bounds, so that liberal action is placed under restraint. Creative intelligence is looked upon with distrust; the innovations that are the essence of individuality are feared, and generous impulse is put under bonds not to disturb the peace. Were art an acknowledged power in human association and not treated as the pleasuring of an idle moment or as a means of ostentatious display, and were morals understood to be identical with every aspect of value that is shared in experience, the "problem" of the relation of art and morals would not exist.

The idea and the practice of morality are saturated with conceptions that stem from praise and blame, reward and punishment. Mankind is divided into sheep and goats, the vicious and virtuous, the law-abiding and criminal, the good and bad. To be beyond good and evil is an impossibility for man, and yet as long as the good signifies only that which is lauded and rewarded, and the evil that which is currently condemned or outlawed, the ideal factors of morality are always and everywhere beyond good and evil. Because art is wholly innocent of ideas derived from praise and blame, it is looked upon with the eye of suspicion by the guardians of custom, or only the art that is itself so old and "classic" as to receive conventional praise is grudgingly admitted, provided as with, say, the case of Shakespeare, signs of regard for conventional morality can be ingeniously extracted from his work. Yet this indifference to praise and blame because of preoccupation with imaginative experience constitutes the heart of the moral potency of art. From it proceeds the liberating and uniting power of art.

Shelley said, "The great secret of morals is love, or *a going out of our nature* and the identification of ourselves with the beautiful which exists in thought, action, or person, not our own. A man to be greatly good must imagine intensely and comprehensively." What is true of the individual is true of the whole system of morals in thought and action. While perception of the union of the possible with the actual in a work of art is itself a great good, the good does not terminate with the immediate and particular occasion in which it is had. The union that is presented in perception persists in the remaking of impulsion and thought. The first intimations of wide and large redirections of desire and purpose are of necessity imaginative. Art is a mode of prediction not found in charts and statistics, and it insinuates possibilities of human relations not to be found in rule and precept, admonition and administration. . . .

55. Art and Censorship: A Critical Survey of the Issues
F. E. Sparshott

Francis Edward Sparshott (1926–) is professor of philosophy at the University of Toronto, Toronto, Ontario, Canada. Besides his writings in technical philosophy, he has published a number of poems. Indeed, he has declared that he has always thought of himself as "primarily a poet."

Censors operate in terms of morality, not in terms of general welfare. Some hold that the prohibition of morally offensive artefacts is wrong in principle, as though there were no circumstances in which the institution could be desirable. This position is scarcely tenable. Morality's entrenched position in our scheme of values reflects the recognition that if a social system is to cohere and continue there must be some actions that are forbidden to its members. If an artefact moved its public to commit those actions, contact between artefact and public must therefore be prevented. If it were proved that everyone who saw a certain statue committed thereafter a burglary or murder that he would not otherwise have committed no one would deny that it should be removed from public exhibition; and if it were shown to have that effect on all or most people of a certain kind, no one would deny that it must be prevented from coming into contact with people of that kind. But to admit this is to admit the principle of censorship, for it is precisely in order to defend the entrenched standards of morality that censorships are established.

Why, then, is censorship a controversial institution? First, because the claim for morality has been put too strongly. It is not true that all actions that can be described as breaches of the moral code are disastrous. A total neglect of the moral law would indeed constitute a breakdown of social relations; but one cannot assume *a priori* that no breach of the moral law could be justified unless one interprets morality so widely as to take in all values, including aesthetic ones. The second reason for doubting the propriety of censorship is a stronger one, that the principle does not justify the practice. "No girl was ever raped by a book": causal connections between specific crimes and exposure to specific artefacts have often been alleged but never demonstrated. People argue rather that works of certain kinds *must be* harmful, or *must have* contributed to certain results. There are indeed some works which do plainly offend because the works themselves constitute the offences: specifically, libellous works and publications prejudicial to fair trial. For the rest, controversy turns, not on the principle, but on the estimated probability of an undemonstrated connection and on the propriety of basing decisive action on such a contestable guess.

It should be noted that the actions whose production I envisaged as justifying censorship were not just immoral acts but crimes, actions themselves forbidden and penalized by law. It is reasonable that the law should

Reprinted from *The Structure of Aesthetics,* by F. E. Sparshott, by permission of University of Toronto Press. ©University of Toronto Press 1963.

prohibit whatever gives rise to actions that are themselves prohibited, such as treason, rape or arson. But if an action (such as fornication or adultery) is not itself forbidden by law it would be strange to make the fact that an object impelled its public to commit such an act a sufficient reason for taking legal action to remove it from circulation. If the law allows me to be depraved and corrupt, why should it forbid me access to books that will deprave and corrupt me? The justification could only be that the book has a secret power that I cannot detect and from which I need to be protected, as from a food containing hidden poison. But that an artefact could have a moral power that was both so strong and indiscernible is hard to believe.

Granted that works may have such compelling power to corrupt, two arguments for censorship are possible. One is, that there exist men of superior moral insight able to detect a moral poison hidden from others less gifted or worse taught. This argument is sometimes put forward by clergy to justify ecclesiastical censorship. Just as children playing near a cliff, they say, can play more safely and happily if a thoughtful adult has set a fence between them and it, so the rest of us can take our aesthetic recreations more safely and happily if a responsible cleric has put a wall between us and perdition. So the analogy is: child is to adult as adult is to censor. Adults, however, are not children: it is just because children are not adults that they are supposed unable to exercise prudence in their own affairs. Let it be supposed, though, that prudence is not enough, that adults stand in need of a super-prudence that censors have. The censors must be thus endowed either *de facto* or *de jure*. If they are super-prudent *de facto*, this should appear in the wisdom of their decisions: the imprudent can usually recognize prudence in others. Whether censorships for whom this justification is offered do thus recommend themselves is a question I need not presume to answer. But their super-prudence may be *de jure*: they may be hierarchically charged with the duty of taking moral decisions for their flocks. The justification of such a structure of authority is a task for moral theology. I will only say that it is disingenuous to recommend such a system for its supposed results unless it is thought that persons thus charged do in fact decide wisely. If the fence is in the wrong place it will not save us from falling but only cramp us.

The other argument for censorship holds even if no one has super-prudence, but our censors must be people no better than ourselves. Of course, one argues, a community of free men may delegate one of their number to inspect their amusements, just as they appoint inspectors of weights and measures, just to save themselves the trouble of checking everything for themselves. Indeed, if artefacts had such compelling power as we are supposing, we should be well advised to appoint such persons and should doubtless do so, making sure that they were themselves either liberally dosed with some spiritual antidote or else kept locked up. But, it is time we reminded ourselves, no work is known to have such powers.

It is less often argued that certain works cause crimes than that works of certain kinds tend to promote crimes, to make people more likely to commit them. And if even this could be shown most people would admit that censorship was desirable if practicable.[1] But not even such a connection has been established. "I saw it on television" is a self-exculpation more hopeful than realistic. Does a literature of violence encourage violent action, or does a propensity to violent action give rise to a literature of violence? Presumably such a literature gives expression to violent tendencies that already exist; but does it, by giving them voice, encourage them? Or does it rather, by providing a safety-valve, prevent them from issuing in action? Perhaps the same work might prove to some people an incentive to crime, to others a harmless substitute for it. Or perhaps works take effect only in the realm of fantasy, in a context so different from that of action as neither to affect nor be affected by it. All these possibilities are canvassed, with much confident opinion but little reliable evidence.

Some hold that, since works of art demand contemplation and one cannot be both active and contemplative at the same time, art in general inhibits action.[2] And certainly, whatever the effects of a literature of brutality may be, at least while one is engrossed in it one is neither committing nor planning brutalities. Such inhibition would be a good thing if the action inhibited were evil, a bad thing if the action were laudable.[3] In either case the argument suggests that we should distinguish between art on the one hand and propaganda and pornography on the other. Works of pornography and propaganda are designed to inflame desire or stimulate action, works of art are designed as objects of contemplation.[4] If there is to be censorship, different actions and attitudes will be appropriate to the two classes of object. But it is not always easy to decide to which class a work belongs, though sometimes it is very easy. In order to provide a basis for such decisions, one might wish to distinguish between the proper effect of a work and its side effects. These may be distinguished in terms of the relation between representation and referent, or of the relative transparency of the medium. A book or picture may be so composed

[1]The proviso of practicability is important. Uncontrolled administrative action, which many dislike, can be avoided only by legally defining what is to be condemned. But precise definitions can be evaded by the astute, while they catch the harmless but unwary; and vague definitions give the censor no guidance.

[2]Parker argues (1920, 334) that since art is concerned with the imagination rather than with the will, and "is an appeal to mind as well as to sympathetic feeling," it cannot be inflammatory. Similarly, Keats wrote to Richard Woodhouse in 1818: "What shocks the virtuous philosopher, delights the camelion Poet. It does no harm from its relish of the dark side of things any more than from its taste for the bright one; because they both end in speculation." (Keats 1956, 166.)

[3]Marxists condemn bourgeois art just because it inhibits moral (i.e. revolutionary) action. Thus Mr. Harap writes (1949, 115) that sophisticated art-forms by their reactionary content "influence social attitudes and consequently social action—often by promoting social inaction"; whereas "popular" art is "actually a form of narcosis which induces delusions of the acceptability of capitalism." He could, but does not, extend his strictures from the content of art to the concept of aesthetic "distance" itself.

[4]The contrast between inflammation and contemplation is Platonic, and is most readily stated in archaic terms: works are condemned in so far as they make for disorder in the mind or the city, producing lust (pornography) or violence (horror comics, etc.) or rebelliousness (sedition) or irreligion (blasphemy); they are praised in so far as every work of art is orderly and makes for order (pp. 329 ff.). One could say that the imaginative disorder was an inoculation against real disorder and therefore hygienic. Otherwise the worth of a work will depend on whether it is a greater force for order or for disorder.

and worked that the appropriate reaction is to the scene or action shown or described and not to the work as artefact; or it may have its own value as composition. A work of pure pornography would be one that it would be pointless to study if not for the sake of the erotic stimulation it gave. But there are other works in which an erotic stimulus may be sought but which are more apt to provide a complex aesthetic satisfaction (intended presumably by the author and found there by its likely public) from which the erotic aspect could not readily be detached. People do act in strange ways, and some may pore panting over the pages of *Ulysses* while others savour the style of *Fanny Hill;* but surely it is legitimate to judge a work by its proper use and not by its abuse. It may be said that, on the contrary, one must not distinguish between the designed and the accidental effects of public actions: if measures intended to prevent goitre should prove to cause cancer, it would be irrelevant that the latter result was not meant. Unfortunately, even if the principle of distinction between what is art and what is not be accepted, it will not be easy to apply. Recent controversies over censorship have concerned works whose status and intentions are equivocal in that they lend themselves with equal facility to different attitudes.

If nothing is to be forbidden that does not certainly promote crime, it should by now be clear that censorship cannot in fact be justified. If it is immorality rather than illegality that is to serve as basis the same difficulties arise and are compounded by the possible impropriety of forbidding the promotion of what is not forbidden. If there are censors, apparently, they are going to make lots of mistakes; and why should any citizen prefer another's errors to his own?

There are still two arguments in favour of censorship, one weak and the other strong. The weak one rests on a possibility we have ignored, that it is not our attitudes to wickedness but our knowledge of it that is affected. If there were some obscure but horrid misdeed whose very possibility the unperverted mind would not suspect, would it not be reasonable to prohibit anyone who stumbled upon it from divulging its nature? More realistically, since there are unlikely to be any new sins, but heresies are always cropping up, might it not be proper to forbid the publication of dangerous beliefs and discoveries, obscure truths or subtle errors subversive of the established order? Perhaps so. But the propriety holds only for an established authoritarian order in which both moral and intellectual truth are supposed immutably and infallibly secure. Otherwise one might say that perhaps the convincing error convinces because it is no error; that what the truth subverts is well subverted; and that perhaps if the recondite sin became less recondite it would be seen to be no sin. Within such an established order, on the other hand, the moral censor already has *de jure* super-prudence and needs no further justification for the exercise of his office.

The strong argument that remains to justify censorship is that it should be based neither on illegality nor on immorality, but on impropriety: that what should be excluded is not what harms, but what shocks. The two are often confused. Attorneys, required to show that a work is degrading, will argue that it is disgusting. But the difference is important.

Morality requires justification, propriety does not; morality is supposed to be based on invariant principles, propriety changes from time to time and place to place and is determined solely by what is felt fitting for a context. It used to be improper to print what everyone said; now it is improper to say what everyone prints. What is decent in the *Partisan Review* would be indecent in the *Saturday Evening Post*.

We have then to ask: do people have the right not to be shocked? Perhaps it does them no harm, but if they dislike it why should they have to endure it? If there are standards of what is done and not done, why should they not be enforced? Here at least the problem of evidence, that so severely limited the justification of a censorship based on illegality and immorality, does not apply: a man who claims to be shocked is surely entitled to be believed. What better authority could there be?

No one has an absolute right not to be shocked. In the first place, anyone may be shocked or disgusted by anything. In the second place, being shocked is partly voluntary: one who says "I'm shocked" or "You disgust me" is not simply describing what is happening to him but is expressing an attitude, taking up a social position, whose relation to his feelings may be tenuous (Sparshott 1961b).[5] If there is a right at all, it is a right to have public standards observed. Unfortunately, as I have said, these vary subtly, and it is not easy to keep censors accurately informed of what standards are current in various social contexts. It is easy to apply standards of impropriety, for one has only to consult the feelings of the appropriate persons. What is hard is to determine which standards are the right ones. Moral standards, on the other hand, are as we have seen harder to apply than to determine.

Since propriety varies with social context, people unwilling to be shocked should stay away from contexts where they risk offence. Nuns are expected not to eavesdrop on barrack-rooms. If, then, there is to be censorship for impropriety, it should impinge differently on different arts. What is imposed on the public ear and eye, as by poster or public broadcast, may be expected to conform to standards more rigid than what none need see or hear unless they wish, such as books or private exhibitions. Indeed, one does not see how a case could be made out for condemning any such object for impropriety. For whose susceptibilities are to be considered? The maiden with blushing cheeks may put the book down;[6] those for whom it is intended will not be shocked by it, for their disgust would itself show that they were not its proper public.

If a work shocked everyone it would have no proper public. And that might lead one to think that there was never any need for a censorship based on impropriety. The social penalties of giving offence are direct. If a cinema poster really shocked the public, no one would go to the film; if a book disgusted everyone no one would read it. In fact, as we know, one can be sure of selling many copies of a book that is publicly proclaimed obscene, for the standards of propriety officially upheld do not prevail

[5]It is this that justifies, if anything can, the laughable pretence of middle-aged lawyers to be disgusted by books whose publishers they are prosecuting.

[6]Bernard Mandeville remarked (1914, 65–6) that the maiden's cheek is likely to blush only if she is *found* reading something improper.

throughout the community. A great many people not only rejoice in pornography, but see no reason why they should not. It is because it seems grotesque to denounce as disgusting what gives most people no offence that attacks on impropriety are often disguised as attacks on immorality.

At this point I may be expected to denounce the hypocrisy of the age. I shall not do so. The concept of hypocrisy applies to morals: a man should be good and not merely seem so, and a bad man is little mended by his pretence of goodness. But propriety is altogether a matter of how actions appear, so that the concept of hypocrisy does not apply. If a man seems to give no offence, he gives no offence. Why, then, should a society not have public standards of propriety different from those applied by each citizen to his own private conduct? It would be no more absurd to advertise filthy movies by decorous posters than it is to advertise decorous movies by filthy posters; and if a society in which everyone avidly read pornography were to forbid its public sale, that would mean only that it combined a taste for such reading with a taste for decorum.

Though it may seem hard to defend a public check on private improprieties, it is not absurd to demand the public observance of standards of decorum that are shown by the very need of enforcement to differ from those held by most private persons. But is such a control desirable? Perhaps it is good for shockable people to be shocked: their readiness to be disgusted may be a sign of a moral complacency that is itself harmful. But one might argue on the other side that it is the best and most sensitive people who are most easily disgusted, and that it is immoral as well as improper to surround such people with what they think coarse and low. Not only does it distress them, and to distress a person without cause is no virtuous act, but so far from stimulating them into awareness it depresses them and resigns them to evil. What harm may a person not take from being perpetually deluged with what he is convinced is foul and shoddy? One could argue, too, that even the circulation of improper material among those who welcome it should be hindered, on the ground that public consumption is no proof of public taste: most people can distinguish their higher from their lower impulses, and while they will indulge the latter if they can they will at heart be glad to be forbidden this indulgence. The censor of propriety stands to his public not as parent to children but as representative of each man's "real" self to his "lower" or "natural" self. That is not an absurd argument, though it is not fashionable, but it assumes that standards of propriety differ only as being looser or more stringent, and that the most stringent set is the best. And both these assumptions are questionable.

If the standards of propriety that censorships enforce are not actually those accepted even for public observance by most people, and are not demonstrably those of the morally best people, whose are they? And why are they enforced? I suspect that they are the standards of wowsers, and are enforced because wowsers must be placated. A "wowser" is a person with a passion for saving people from themselves by taking their moral and prudential decisions for them. Wowsers tend to be morally obtuse, since the basis of their activity is a failure to respect the moral status of other persons; and they tend not to distinguish between immorality and impropriety, for the same reason: they use their own susceptibilities as sole criterion of good and bad. Such persons are abundant and active in our society and are much given to forming committees and writing to government officials. It is possible that some government censorships exist not to protect the public but to keep the wowsers quiet. Fortunately there are some artefacts, such as filthy postcards, which are easily recognized, unlikely to become respectable, and devoid of aesthetic pretension. Such material might as well circulate surreptitiously as openly—indeed, overt suppression might be welcomed by distributors as keeping prices up; and a carefully chosen censor might serve a useful purpose by diverting the energies of wowsers against these cultural scapegoats. It could be held, however, that it is wrong to encourage wowsers in their form of moral depravity.

Contemporary Issue

Art and Pornography

56. Beyond the (Garbage) Pale: The Case for Censorship Walter Berns

Walter Fred Berns (1919–) is professor of political science, University of Toronto, Ontario, Canada. He has written a number of articles for legal and political science journals.

The case for censorship is at least as old as the case against it, and, contrary to what is usually thought today, has been made under decent and democratic auspices and by intelligent men. To the extent to which it is known today, however, it is thought to be pernicious or, at best, irrelevant to the enlightened conditions of the twentieth century. It begins from the premise that the laws cannot remain indifferent to the manner in which men amuse themselves, or to the kinds of amusement offered them. "The object of art," as Lessing put the case, "is pleasure, and pleasure is not indispensable. What kind and what degree of pleasure shall be permitted may justly depend on the law-giver."[1] Such a view, especially in this uncompromising form, appears excessively Spartan and illiberal to us; yet Lessing was one of the greatest lovers of art who ever lived and wrote.

We turn to the arts—to literature, films and the theatre, as well as to the graphic arts which were the special concern of Lessing—for the pleasure to be derived from them, and pleasure has the capacity to form our tastes and thereby to affect our lives, and the kind of people we become, and the lives of those with whom and among whom we live. Is it politically uninteresting whether men and women derive pleasure from performing their duties as citizens, parents, and spouses or, on the other hand, from watching their laws and customs and institutions ridiculed on the stage? Whether the passions are excited by, and the affections drawn to, what is noble or what is base? Whether the relations between men and women are depicted in terms of an eroticism wholly divorced from love and calculated to destroy the capacity for love and the institutions, such as the family, that depend on love? Whether a dramatist uses pleasure to attach man to what is beautiful or to what is ugly? We may not be accustomed to thinking of these things in this manner, but it is not strange that so much of the obscenity from which so many of us derive our pleasure today has an avowed political purpose.[2] It would seem that these pornographers know intuitively what liberals—for example, Morris Ernst—have forgot-

From *Censorship and Freedom of Expression: Essays on Obscenity and the Law* (Rand McNally: 1971), Harry M. Clor, Editor.

[1] *Laocoön* (New York: Noonday Press), ch. 1, p. 10.
[2] *Che!* and *Hair*, for example, are political plays. See also note 3, this chapter.

ten, namely, that there is indeed a "causal relationship . . . between word or pictures and human behavior." At least they are not waiting for behavioral science to discover this fact.

The purpose is sometimes directly political and sometimes political in the sense that it will have political consequences intended or not. This latter purpose is to make us shameless, and it seems to be succeeding with astonishing speed. Activities that were once confined to the private scene—to the "ob-scene," to make an etymological assumption—are now presented for our delectation and emulation in center stage. Nothing that is appropriate to one place is inappropriate to any other place. No act, we are to infer, no human possibility, no possible physical combination or connection, is shameful. Even our lawmakers now so declare. "However plebian my tastes may be," Justice Douglas asked somewhat disingenuously in the *Ginzburg* case, "who am I to say that others' tastes must be so limited and that others' tastes have no 'social importance'?" Nothing prevents a dog from enjoying sexual intercourse in the marketplace, and it is unnatural to deprive man of the same pleasure, either actively or as voyeurs in the theatre. Shame itself is unnatural, a convention devised by hypocrites to inhibit the pleasures of the body. We must get rid of our "hangups."

But what if, contrary to Freud and to what is generally assumed, shame is natural to man in the sense of being an original feature of human existence, and shamelessness unnatural in the sense of having to be acquired? What if the beauty that we are capable of knowing and achieving in our lives with each other derives from the fact that man is naturally a "blushing creature," the only creature capable of blushing? Consider the case of voyeurism, a case that, under the circumstances, comes quickly to mind. Some of us—I have even known students to confess to it—experience discomfort watching others on the stage or screen performing sexual acts, or even the acts preparatory to sexual acts, such as the disrobing of a woman by a man. This discomfort is caused by shame or is akin to shame. True, it could derive from the fear of being discovered enjoying what society still sees as a forbidden game. The voyeur who experiences shame in this sense is judging himself by the conventions of his society and, according to the usual modern account, the greater the distance separating him from his society in space or time, the less he will experience this kind of shame. This shame, which may be denoted as concealing shame, is a function of the fear of discovery by one's own group. The group may have its reasons for forbidding a particular act, and thereby leading those who engage in it to conceal it—to be ashamed of it—but these reasons have nothing to do with the nature of man. Voyeurism, according to this account, is a perversion only because society says it is, and a man guided only by nature would not be ashamed of it.

According to another view, however, not to be ashamed—to be a shameless voyeur—is more likely to require explanation, for voyeurism is by nature a perversion.

> Anyone who draws his sexual gratification from looking at another lives continuously at a distance. If it is normal to approach and unite with the partner, then it is precisely characteristic of the voyeur that he remains

alone, without a partner, an outsider who acts in a stealthy and furtive manner. To keep his distance when it is essential to draw near is one of the paradoxes of his perversion. The looking of the voyeur is of course also a looking at and, as such, is as different from the looks exchanged by lovers as medical palpation from the gentle caress of the hand.[3]

From this point of view, voyeurism is perversion not merely because it is contrary to convention, but because it is contrary to nature. Convention here follows nature. Whereas sexual attraction brings man and woman together seeking a unity that culminates in the living being they together create, the voyeur maintains a distance; and because he maintains a distance he looks at, he does not communicate; and because he looks at he objectifies, he makes an object of that with which it is natural to join. Objectifying, he is incapable of uniting and therefore of love. The need to conceal voyeurism—the concealing shame—is a corollary of the protective shame, the shame that impels lovers to search for privacy and for an experience protected from the profane and the eyes of the stranger. The stranger is "at odds with the shared unity of the [erotic couple], and his mere presence tends to introduce some objectification into every immediate relationship."[4] Shame, both concealing and protective, protects lovers and therefore love. And a polity without love—without the tenderness and the charming sentiments and the poetry and the beauty and the uniquely human things that depend on it and derive from it—a polity without love would be an unnatural monstrosity.[5]

To speak in a manner that is more obviously political, such a polity may even be impossible, except in a form unacceptable to free men. There is a connection between self-restraint and shame, and therefore a connection between shame and self-government or democracy. There is therefore a danger in promoting shamelessness and the fullest self-expression or indulgence. To live together requires rules and a governing of the passions, and those who are without shame will be unruly and unrulable; having lost the ability to restrain themselves by observing the rules they collectively give themselves, they will have to be ruled by others. Tyranny

---

[3]Erwin W. Straus, *Phenomenological Psychology* (Basic Books, New York, 1966), p. 219. I have no doubt that it is possible to want to observe sexual acts for reasons unrelated to voyeurism. Just as a physician has a clinical interest in the parts of the body, philosophers will have an interest in the parts of the body and soul, or in the varieties of human things which are manifestations of the body and soul. Such a "looking" would not be voyeurism and would be unaccompanied by shame; or the desire to see and to understand would require the "seer" to overcome shame. (Plato, *Republic*, 439e) In any event, the case of the philosopher is politically irrelevant, and aesthetically irrelevant as well.

[4]*Straus*, p. 221.

[5]It is easy to prove that shamefulness is not the only principle governing the question of what may properly be presented on the stage; shamefulness would not, for example, govern the case of a scene showing the copulating of a married couple who love each other very much. That is not intrinsically shameful—on the contrary—yet it ought not to be shown. The principle here is, I think, an aesthetic one: such a scene is dramatically weak because the response of the audience would be characterized by prurience and not by a sympathy with what the scene is intended to portray, a beautiful love. This statement can be tested by joining a collegetown movie audience; it is confirmed unintentionally by a defender of nudity on the stage; see note 12, this chapter.

is the mode of government for the shameless and self-indulgent who have carried liberty beyond any restraint, natural and conventional.

Such was the argument made prior to the twentieth century, when it was generally understood that democracy, more than any other form of government, required self-restraint, which it would inculcate through moral education and impose on itself through laws, including laws governing the manner of public amusements. It was the tyrant who could usually allow the people to indulge themselves. Indulgence of the sort we are not witnessing did not threaten his rule, because his rule did not depend on a citizenry of good character. Anyone can be ruled by a tyrant, and the more debased his subjects the safer his rule. A case can be made for complete freedom of the arts among such people, whose pleasures are derived from activities divorced from their labors and any duties associated with citizenship. Among them a theatre, for example, can serve to divert the search for pleasure from what the tyrant regards as more dangerous or pernicious pursuits.[6]

Such an argument was not unknown among thoughtful men at the time modern democracies were being constituted. It is to be found in Jean-Jacques Rousseau's *Letter to M. d'Alembert on the Theatre*. Its principles were known by Washington and Jefferson, to say nothing of the antifederalists, and later on by Lincoln, all of whom insisted that democracy would not work without citizens of good character; and until recently no justice of the Supreme Court and no man in public life doubted the necessity for the law to make at least a modest effort to promote that good character, if only by protecting the effort of other institutions, such as the church and the family, to promote and maintain it. The case for censorship, at first glance, was made wholly with a view to the political good, and it had as its premise that what was good for the arts and sciences was *not* necessarily good for the polity.

There was no illusion that censorship laws would be easy to administer, and there was a recognition of the danger they represented. One obvious danger was that the lawmakers will demand too much, that the Anthony Comstocks who are always present will become the agents of the law and demand not merely decency but sanctity. Macaulay stated the problem in his essay on Restoration Comedy (mild fare compared to that regularly exhibited in our day):

> It must, indeed, be acknowledged, in justice to the writers of whom we have spoken thus severely, that they were to a great extent the creatures of their age. And if it be asked why that age encouraged immorality which no

[6]The modern tyrant does not encourage passivity among his subjects; on the contrary, they are expected by him to be public-spirited: to work for the State, to exceed production schedules, to be citizen soldiers in the huge armies, and to love Big Brother. Indeed, in Nazi Germany and the Soviet Union alike, the private life was and is discouraged, and with it erotic love and the private attachments it fosters. Censorship in a modern tyrannical state is designed to abolish the private life to the extent that this is possible. George Orwell understood this perfectly. This severe censorship that characterizes modern tyranny, and distinguishes it sharply from premodern tyranny, derives from the basis of modern tyrannical rule: both Nazism and Communism have roots in theory, and more precisely, a kind of utopian theory. The modern tyrant parades as a political philosopher, the heir of Nietzsche or Marx, with a historical mission to perform. He cannot leave his subjects alone.

other age would have tolerated, we have no hesitation in answering that this great depravation of the national taste was the effect of the prevalence of Puritanism under the Commonwealth.

To punish public outrages on morals and religion is unquestionably within the competence of rulers. But when a government, not content with requiring decency, requires sanctity, it oversteps the bounds which mark its proper functions. And it may be laid down as a universal rule that a government which attempts more than it ought will perform less. . . . And so a government which, not content with repressing scandalous excesses, demands from its subjects fervent and austere piety, will soon discover that, while attempting to render an impossible service to the cause of virtue, it has in truth only promoted vice.

The truth of this was amply demonstrated in the United States in the Prohibition era, when the attempt was made to enforce abstemiousness and not, labels to the contrary, temperance. In a word, the principle should be not to attempt to eradicate vice—the means by which that might conceivably be accomplished are incompatible with free government—but to make it difficult, knowing that while it will continue to flourish covertly, it will not be openly exhibited. And that was thought to be important.

It ought to be clear that this old and largely forgotten case for censorship was made by men who were not insensitive to the beauty of the arts and the noble role they can play in the lives of men. Rousseau admitted that he never willingly missed a performance of any of Molière's plays, and did so in the very context of arguing that all theatrical productions should be banned in the decent and self-governing polity. Like Plato he would banish the poets, yet he was himself a poet—a musician, opera composer, and novelist—and demonstrated his love for and knowledge of poetry, or as we would say, the arts, in his works and in his life. But he was above all a thinker of the highest rank, and as such he knew that the basic premise of the later liberalism is false. A century later John Stuart Mill could no longer conceive of a conflict between the intrinsic and therefore legitimate demands of the polity; whereas Rousseau had argued that the "restoration" of the arts and sciences did not tend to purify morals, but that, on the contrary, their restoration and popularization would be destructive of the possibility of a good civil society. His contemporaries were shocked and angered by this teaching and excluded Rousseau from their society; if we were taught by them and more directly by Mill and his followers—Justice Douglas, for example—we might tend to dismiss it as the teaching of a madman or fool. Are we, however, still prepared to stand with Mill and his predecessors against Rousseau to argue that what is good for science is necessarily good for civil society? Or have certain terrible events and conditions prepared us to reconsider that issue? If so, and especially in the light of certain literary and theatrical events, we might be prepared to reconsider the issue of whether what is good for the arts is necessarily good for civil society.

In practice censors have acted out of an unsophisticated concern for public morality, with no concern for the arts and with no appreciation of what would be sacrificed if their policy were to be adopted. Their opponents have resisted them out of a sophisticated concern for the freedom of expression, but with no concern for the effect of this on public morality. It would appear that concern for public morality requires censorship and that concern for the arts requires the abolition of censorship. The law developed by our courts is an attempt to avoid this dilemma by denying that it exists. But with what results? Rousseau predicted there would be not only a corruption of public morality but a degradation of the arts. His case for censorship appears only at first glance to be made wholly with a view to protecting the simple and decent political order from corruption at the hands of literature and the theatre; it was in fact also a case made with a view to preventing the corruption of the arts themselves. Their popularization would be their degradation. To deny the tension between politics and the arts is to assume that the subject requires no governing, that what is produced by writers and dramatists may be ignored by the law in the same manner that the production of economic goods and services was once said to be of no legitimate concern of the law. The free market will be permitted to operate, with the result that what appears in print and on the stage will be determined by the tastes operating in that market, which in a democracy will be a mass market. The law will no longer attempt to influence this market; having denied the distinction between the nonobscene and the obscene, it will in fact come to deny the distinction between art and trash. This is what has happened. Justice Douglas, who told us that the "ideal of the Free Society written into our Constitution . . . is that people are mature enough . . . to recognize trash when they see it," also denies that anyone, mature or immature, can define the difference between art and trash. "Some like Chopin, others like 'rock and roll.' Some are 'normal,' some are masochistic, some deviant in other respects. . . . But why is freedom of the press and expression denied them? When the Court today speaks of 'social value' does it mean a 'value' to the majority? . . . If a publication caters to the idiosyncracies of a minority, why does it not have 'social importance'?[7] To him, whether a publication has "social value" is answered by whether anyone wants to read it, which is to say that any publication may have "social value." It is all a question of idiosyncratic taste: some like Chopin, some like rock and roll; some are normal—or as he writes it, "normal"—and some masochistic or deviant—or, as he ought to have written it, "deviant." These statements of course make nonsense of his business of ascending "from plateau to plateau and finally reach[ing] the world of enduring ideas"; because if everything has value, and if there is no standard by which to judge among them, then there is no upward or downward, no "plateau" higher than another "plateau," no art or trash, and, of course, no problem. Art is now defined as the "socially important," and this, in turn, is defined by Douglas as anything anyone has a taste for.

It is true that Douglas is uniquely vulgar for a Supreme Court justice, but his colleagues have not been far behind him on the substantive issue. In principle they acknowledge the category of socially "important" publications and productions, but they do not depend on an educated critical judgment to define it. They simply accept the judgment of any literary hack willing to testify, which amounts to transferring the mass market to

[7]*Ginzburg v. United States,* 383 U.S. 463, 489–490 (1966). Dissenting opinion.

the courtroom. It was solemnly said in testimony that *Fanny Hill* is a work of social importance, which was then elaborated as "literary merit" and "historical value," just the sort of thing to be taught in the classroom (and, as Douglas argued, in sermons from the pulpit). Another "expert witness" described it as a work of art that "asks for and receives a literary response." Its style was said to be "literary" and its central character, in addition to being a whore, an "intellectual," which is probably understood to be the highest praise within the power of these experts to bestow. An intellectual, the court was then told, is one who is "extremely curious about life and who seeks . . . to record with accuracy the details of the external world"—in Fanny's case, such "external details" as her "physical sensations."

Censorship, undertaken in the name of the public necessity to maintain the distinction between the nonobscene and the obscene, has the secondary effect of lending some support to the distinction between art and trash. At a minimum it requires a judgment of what is proper and what is improper, which is to say a judgment of what is worthy of being enjoyed and what is unworthy, and this has the effect of at least supporting the idea that there is a distinction to be made and that the distinction is important. Our law as announced by the judges of our highest court now denies this, explicitly in the case of Douglas and implicitly in the case of his colleagues making up the rest of the Court's majority. The law has resigned in favor of the free mass market, and it has done so not because the free market is seen as a mechanism best calculated to bring about a particular result (for example, the material wealth desired by the *laissez-faire* economists) but because it attaches no significance to the decisions the market will make. The popularization of the arts will not lead to their degradation because there is no such thing as degradation.

The New York Times does not agree with this when it calls for "sophisticated critical judgment" to save us from the pile of muck that now passes for art. But the "sophisticated critical judgment" of its own drama and book pages praised the very works condemned in the editorial; besides, much of this market is impervious to "sophisticated critical judgment." This is confirmed in the *Times* itself in a piece printed a few months later on the first page of the Sunday drama section: "Nobody yet knows how to control the effect of nudity for a production's purposes, but producers encourage it anyhow. Why? The explanation, I should think, is obvious: sex, as always, is good box office."[8] Exactly. It was the law, not the critics, that kept the strip tease and the "skin flick" confined to the illegitimate theatre, and it is foolish to think, or to have thought, that the critics alone will be able to keep them there, or, in fact, from flourishing in the legitimate theatre. That game is caught, as Lincoln would have put it. What remains at large, unanswered, is whether "sophisticated critical judgment" can preserve artistic tastes in another part of the same theatre, or whether

[8]*The New York Times,* January 18, 1970. The author of this piece, Martin Gottfried, a man of "sophisticated critical judgment" presumably—after all, the *Times* printed him— defends *Che!* and the others, and ends up with a very sophisticated defense of a homosexual rape scene from a production entitled *Fortune and Men's Eyes,* done, of course, in the nude and apparently leaving nothing to the imagination. His principle is that "no climactic scene, in any play, should happen offstage. . . ."

there will be any "sophisticated critical judgment." To ask this is to wonder whether the public taste—or at least a part of the public taste—can be educated, and educated with no assistance from the law. This is an old question; to ask it is to return to Rousseau's quarrel with Voltaire and the Enlightenment, and to Tocqueville and John Stuart Mill—in short, to the beginnings of modern democracy where, in political philosophy, the question received thematic treatment.

The principle of modern democracy is the natural equality of all men, and the problem was to find some way of preventing this principle from becoming all-pervasive, and especially from invading the arts and sciences themselves. Stated otherwise, the problem was to find a substitute for the aristocratic class which had formerly sustained the arts and sciences, some basis on which, or some citadel from which, the arts and sciences could resist public opinion. The constitutional principle of freedom of speech and press would, perhaps, protect them from hostile political passions, but this institutional device would not protect them from the much more subtle danger, corruption by public opinion, of coming to share the public's taste and of doing the public's work according to the public's standards. One solution, it was hoped by some, would be the modern university, which, as Allan Bloom has recently written, was to be "a center for reflection and education independent of the regime and the pervasive influence of its principles, free of the overwhelming effect of public opinion in its crude and subtle forms, devoted to the dispassionate quest for the important and comprehensive truths."[9] Tenure and academic freedom would protect the professors of the arts and sciences, and thereby protect the arts and sciences themselves, and the students would be educated in the principles of the arts and sciences and their tastes formed accordingly. The education of the public's taste in the arts, which will prevent the popularization of the arts from becoming the cause of their degradation, must take place in the universities if it is to take place at all.

But the so-called expert witnesses who testified in the obscenity cases came from the universities. *Fanny Hill's* champions were university professors, and not, by any means, in minor institutions. To rely on the professors to provide the "sophisticated critical judgment" or to educate the tastes of the mass market, or of any part of it, is to ignore what is going on in the universities. Several years ago Cornell paid $800 to a man to conduct (lead? orchestrate? create?) a "happening" on campus as part of a Festival of Contemporary Art. This happening consisted of the following: a group of students was led to the city dump where they selected the charred remains of an old automobile, spread it with several hundred pounds of strawberry jam, removed their shirts and blouses, and then danced around it, stopping occasionally to lick the jam. By 1970 standards this is not especially offensive; it is silly, as so many "college boy" antics have been silly. What distinguishes it from goldfish swallowing and panty raids is that it was conducted under official university auspices and with the support and participation of professors.

The call for a "sophisticated critical judgment" is merely a variety of

---

[9]"The Democratization of the University," in Robert A. Goldwin (ed.), *How Democratic Is America?* (Chicago, Rand McNally, 1971).

the general call for education, which libertarians have customarily offered as an alternative to the policy of forbidding or punishing speech. It is an attractive alternative, attractive for its consistency with liberal principles as well as for its avoidance of the difficulties accompanying a policy of censorship; unfortunately, in the present intellectual climate, education in this area is almost impossible. Consider the case of the parent who wants to convince his children of the impropriety of the use of the four-letter verb meaning to copulate. At the present time the task confronting him is only slightly less formidable than that faced by the parent who would teach his children that the world is flat. Just as the latter will have to overcome a body of scientific evidence to the contrary, the former will have to overcome the power of common usage and the idea of propriety it implies. Until recently propriety required the use of the verb "to make love,"[10] and this delicacy was not without purpose. It was meant to remind us—to *teach* us, or at least to allow us to be taught—that, whereas human copulation can be indistinguishable from animal copulation generally, it ought to be marked by the presence of a passion of which other animals are incapable. Now, to a quickly increasing extent, the four-letter verb— more "honest" in the opinion of its devotees—is being used openly and therefore without impropriety. The parent will fail in his effort to educate because he will be on his own, trying to teach a lesson his society no longer wants taught—by the law, by the language, or by the schools. Especially by the schools. When in 1964 the University of California at Berkeley could not find a reason to censure the students for whom "free speech" meant the brandishing of the four-letter verb on placards, it not only made legitimate what had been illegitimate, but announced that from that time forward it would not attempt to teach its students anything contrary to their passions—sexual, political, or, with reference to drug use, physiological. What became true then at Berkeley is now true generally. The professors have nothing to teach their students. The younger ones have joined the students and have come to share their tastes and their political passions; the older ones are silent, and together they are in the process of abdicating to the students their authority to govern the universities, to enforce parietals, to prescribe the curriculum, and even their right to teach them. Critical judgment is being replaced by "doing your own thing," which is what Justice Douglas was talking about, and this being so, it is doubtful, to say the least, whether the universities will be able to educate the tastes of anyone. And if this is not done in the universities, where can it be done?[11] Where in the midst of all the vulgarity and this incessant

[10]That this is not merely the product of English or American "puritanism" is proved by, for example, the French *faire l'amour* and the Italian *fare-all'amore*, as well as the fastidious German *mit einem liebeln.*

[11]In a number of universities, students are permitted to receive course credit for "courses" taught by themselves to themselves. Not surprisingly, it was left to Cornell to carry this to its absurd extreme. In May, 1970, the Educational Policy Committee of the College of Arts and Sciences voted 5–2 to grant "three credit hours to ten students who had 'taught' themselves a course in children's literature"—including not only *Alice in Wonderland,* but *Pinocchio, Where the Wild Things Are,* and *Now We Are Six.* "The students claimed that they had not read the books before taking their course." This implies that it is one of the jobs of a university to remedy deficiencies in kindergarten education. In any case, as one of the two dissenters later reported to the full faculty, "whether the books had ever been read to them remains unclear." Cornell *Chronicle,* June 4, 1970.

clamor for doing one's own thing can be found a refuge for the arts? There can be no "sophisticated critical judgment" without it.

One who undertakes to defend censorship in the name of the arts is obliged to acknowledge that he has not exhausted his subject when he has completed that defense. What is missing is a defense of obscenity. What is missing is a defense of the obscenity employed by the greatest of our poets—Aristophanes and Chaucer, Shakespeare and Swift—because it is impossible to believe, it is unreasonable to believe, that what they did is indefensible; and what they did, among other things, was to write a good deal of obscenity. Unfortunately, it would require a talent I do not possess to give a sufficient account of it.

They seemed to employ it mainly in comedy, but their purpose was not simply to make us laugh. Comedy, according to Aristotle,[12] makes us laugh at what is ludicrous in ugliness, and its purpose is to teach, just as tragedy teaches by making us cry before what is destructive in nobility. The latter imitates what is higher, the former what is lower, but they are equally serious; Aristotle discussed both, and Shakespeare, for example, was a comic as well as a tragic poet.

Those aspects of his soul that make man truly human and distinguish him from all other beings—higher or lower in the natural order of things—require political life. And no great poet ever denied this. Man's very virtues, as well as their counterparts, his vices, require him to be governed and to govern; they initiate demands that can be met only in political life, but the poet knows with Rousseau that the demands of human virtue cannot be fully met in political life because they transcend political life. The poet knows the beauty of that order beyond the polity; he reminds us that there is an order outside the conventional and that we are part of that natural order, as well as of the conventional. Shakespeare knows with Rousseau that there is a tension between this natural order and the conventional or legal order, and his purpose is to resolve it, at least for some men, at the highest possible level. They must first be shown that the conventional world is not the only world—that beyond Venice there is Belmont[13]—and here is where obscenity may play a part. It can be used to ridicule the conventional. But it is used in the name of the natural, that order outside the conventional according to which the conventional may be criticized and perhaps, if only to an extent, reformed. Obscenity in the hands of such a poet can serve to *elevate* men, elevate them, the few of them, above the conventional order in which all of us are forced to live our mundane lives. Its purpose is to teach what is truly beautiful—not what convention holds to be beautiful—and to do so by means of pleasure, for obscenity can be pleasurable.

Shakespeare expresses this conflict between nature and law in Edmund's soliloquy at the beginning of Act I, Scene 2, of *King Lear:*

> Thou, Nature, art my goddess; to the law
> My services are bound. Wherefore should I

[12]*Poetics, 1449a–35.*
[13]See the chapter on "The Merchant of Venice" in Allan Bloom with Harry V. Jaffa, *Shakespeare's Politics* (New York: Basic Books, 1964).

Stand in the plague of custom, and permit
The curiosity of nations to deprive me,
For that I am some twelve or fourteen moonshines
Lag of a brother? Why bastard? wherefore base?
When my dimensions are as well compact,
My mind as generous, and my shape as true,
As honest madam's issue? Why brand they us
With base? with baseness? bastardy? base, base?
Who, in the lusty stealth of nature, take
More composition and fierce quality
Than doth, within a dull, stale, tired bed,
Go to th' creating a whole tribe of fops,
Got 'tween asleep and wake?—Well, then,
Legitimate Edgar, I must have your land:
Our father's love is to the bastard Edmund
As to th' legitimate: fine word,—*legitimate!*
Well, my legitimate, if this letter speed,
And my invention thrive, Edmund the base
Shall top th' legitimate. I grow; I prosper:—
Now, gods, stand up for bastards!

This serves to illustrate a theme to which great poets address themselves—what is right by law and what is right by nature—and in the development of which the obscenity in comedy has a legitimate and perhaps
even noble role to play. When it is so used it is fully justified, especially
because great poetry even when it is obscene is of interest only to a few—
those who read it primarily for what is beyond its obscenity, that towards
which obscenity points. But when obscenity is employed as it is today,
merely in an effort to capture an audience or to shock without elevating,
or in the effort to set loose idiosyncratic "selfs" doing their own things, or
to bring down the constitutional order, it is not justified, for it lacks the
ground on which to claim exemption from the law. The modern advocates of obscenity do not seem to be aware of this consequence of their
advocacy. They have obliterated the distinction between art and trash,
and in so doing they have deprived themselves of the ground on which
they might protect the law. What possible argument could have been used
against the police had they decided to arrest the participants in the Cornell "happening" for indecent exposure, or against a law forbidding these
festivals of contemporary "art"? In this generous world the police must be
accorded a right to do their "own thing" too, and they would probably be
able to do it with the support of the majority and therefore of the law. In
a world of everyone doing his own thing, the majority not only rules but
can do no wrong, because there is no standard of right and wrong. Justice
Douglas sees his job as protecting the right of these contemporary "artists"
to do their own thing, but a thoughtful judge is likely to ask how an artistic
judgment that is wholly idiosyncratic can be capable of supporting an
objection to the law. The objection, "*I* like it," is sufficiently rebutted by
the response, "*we* don't."

How to express in a rule of law this distinction between the justified
and the unjustified employment of obscenity is no simple task. That I
have argued and that I willingly concede. I have also argued that it cannot

be done at all on the premise from which our law has proceeded. I have, finally, tried to indicate the consequences of a failure to maintain the distinction in the law: not only will we no longer be able to teach the distinction between the proper and the improper, but we will no longer be able to teach—and will therefore come to forget—the distinction between art and trash. Stated otherwise, censorship, because it inhibits self-indulgence and supports the idea of propriety and impropriety, protects political democracy; paradoxically, when it faces the problem of the justified and unjustified use of obscenity, censorship also serves to maintain the distinction between art and trash and, therefore, to protect art and, thereby, to enhance the quality of this democracy. We forgot this. We began with a proper distrust of the capacities of juries and judges to make sound judgments in an area that lies outside their professional competence; but led by the Supreme Court we went on improperly to conclude that the judgments should not be made because they cannot be made, that there is nothing for anyone to judge. No doubt the law used to err on occasion; but democracy can live without *Mrs. Warren's Profession,* if it must, as well as without *Fanny Hill*—or to speak more precisely, it can live with the error that consigns *Mrs. Warren's Profession* to under-the-counter custom along with *Fanny Hill.* It remains to be seen whether the true friend of democracy will want to live in the world without under-the-counter custom, the world that does not know the difference between *Mrs. Warren's Profession* and *Fanny Hill.*

57. The Case Against Censorship   Marshall Cohen

Marshall Stephen Cohen (1929–   ) is an American philosopher who has written articles for journals on subjects in social and political philosophy. He is editor of the journal *Philosophy and Public Affairs.*

For classical liberalism, and for contemporary constitutional theory, freedom of speech and the press require far more than a mere absence of censorship. Contrary to Walter Berns' suggestion, the claims of liberalism in the last century went well beyond the Blackstonian conception and required freedom not only from prior restraint but from subsequent punishment, not only from governmental interference but from social pressure as well. Mill certainly did not suppose, as Berns characterizes him as supposing, that truth would inevitably prevail against the winds of doctrine. This is one reason why the protections he urged for speech and the press go well beyond Milton's call for an end to licensing.

If Mill did not think the triumph of truth inevitable he did think that truth was, in general, a boon to mankind, and that society should adopt

From "Concurring and Dissenting Opinions," *The Public Interest,* No. 22 (Winter 1971), 38–44. Copyright ©by National Affairs, Inc., 1971.

those principles most congenial to its discovery, appreciation, and dissemination. Mill therefore urged that mature civilizations adopt the principles of free speech and discussion and it is clear that these principles are more crucial still where democratic regimes are in question. Nothing in his argument suggests that particular instances of speech may not be harmful (or that artistic expressions inevitably benefit society) but only that, in the case of speech, society's best interests are served by leaving it free. It is better to suffer the harms this policy permits than to compromise the principle and prohibit various, often vaguely specified, types of speech. This is precisely what Justice Black has in mind when he says that the Constitution does all the balancing that is necessary in the First Amendment area. And the wisdom of this approach is made abundantly clear by the history of Justice Black's First Amendment opinions.

Despite this fact, arguments of the sort Mill and Black make are not inevitably persuasive. If particular instances of speech do, in fact, cause harm, it may be possible to specify kinds of speech that could profitably be prohibited. In fact, of course, Mill himself excludes speech that incites violence in volatile circumstances, and the Supreme Court is willing to prohibit, at very least, speech that constitutes a "clear and present danger" of certain kinds of evils. And these are by no means the only candidates for exclusion. Mill's discussion conspicuously lacks any consideration of speech that interferes with privacy or with a fair trial; we hear nothing of the solicitation of crimes or of complicity by encouragement; no mention is made of perjury, misrepresentation, false advertising, or of libel which, in some of its forms, few besides Justice Black think protected by the First Amendment. In all these cases it is possible to mention a harm that is often enough, or inevitably, the consequence of the type of speech in question and it is reasonable to argue that we may enjoy the benefits free speech is intended to secure without enduring these evils. In the case of obscenity, however, I do not think that this kind of argument is persuasive. The concept of obscenity is a dangerously vague one to play so important a role in criminal legislation; the attempt to control pornography and obscenity, in addition to requiring an indeterminate sacrifice of general principle, endows the criminal authorities with an undesirable degree of discretion, especially unfortunate in so sensitive an area; and it does all this to protect us from harms that are generally exaggerated and often simply fabricated.

Why, then, are these harms? I confess that I find little merit in Berns' specific suggestions; indeed, they are among the most implausible known to me. For there is little reason to believe that pornographic literature rouses men to such transports of lust that they will fling themselves upon the body politic. (Is Denmark a case in point?) In general, I am impressed by the argument of Tocqueville and Mill that modern democracies are biddable and conformist, and am skeptical of the classical argument that democracies are by nature unruly and self-indulgent. Insofar as pornographic literature and sexual permissiveness have any effect, it seems as likely to be of the kind that Marcuse detects—an increased willingness to accept "the system"—as it is to be of the kind that Berns fears—the rape of republican institutions. The harms Berns has in mind are too remote and implausible to provide a reasonable ground for restraining speech, and it is worth remembering that Berns is interested in restraining not only obscenity but, like Marcuse, vicious speech quite generally. Neither of these extravagant men provides the kind of guidance we need in the delicate area of First Amendment freedoms.

If the argument from sexual permissiveness to political debauchery is unpersuasive, so is the far more plausible argument that finds some connection between pornographic representations and various other kinds of undesirable, and even criminal, behavior. It is not enough to say as some say, on principle, that we should content ourselves with punishing criminal acts and not try to reach the states, conditions, and actions that give rise to them. There is nothing in principle objectionable about a prohibition on drunken driving. But the analogy between drunken driving and randy reading is tenuous indeed. Self-abuse is not to be compared to death on the highways and it is questionable whether the frequency of sex crimes is significantly increased by the availability of pornography (recent Danish experience suggests the opposite). This is not to say that in particular cases some connection cannot be established. We know what Paolo and Francesca were reading when they decided to read no more that day. But it is possible to believe that in such cases some other stimulus would have produced the same result and to doubt, in any case, whether preventing the evils in question justifies the restraints that would be required to do so. The case may be different when we consider the pornography of violence. For it has been claimed that Suetonius and Sade are responsible for the murder of children (and if recent reports from the White House are correct, John Wayne movies may have to be added to the list). If literature is a crucial factor here, and if significant connections between the circulation of violent representations and violent crimes can be established, a case might be made for restraint in this area. After all, what we need is less killing, not less masturbating and fornicating. In the end, I am inclined to think it is the moral atmosphere it creates, not the criminal actions it causes, that explains the animus against pornography and obscenity.

Lord Devlin has suggested that morality is so intimately connected with society that a threat to a society's morality constitutes a threat to its survival, a threat against which it must obviously protect itself. Even if one does not make so extreme a claim as this, however, it is plausible to argue that society has a right to protect its moral environment, and the institutions that embody its moral principles, against destruction, and to use the techniques of the criminal law to do so. There is much truth in these claims, which are too complex to discuss on this occasion. But some caveats must be entered, especially as they bear on the immediate issue. For the attempt to encourage sexual purity by controlling sexual thoughts and fantasies (even when they are consummated by a honeymoon in the hand) does constitute an attempt at thought control; and the attempt to preserve the institutions of marriage and the family by controlling pornographic publications does constitute an attempt to control freedom of speech and the press. It is not at all clear what considerations are supposed to exempt these thoughts from the protections, and these institutions from the irreverence and criticism, that are expected in other cases. The attempt to escape the burden of specifying these considerations by arguing that obscene speech and pornographic publications are "without redeeming social value" is unacceptable. The President may find the term 'smut' adequate to his purposes but the fact is that there are many kinds of speech and writing covered even by the more precise terms, 'obscene' and 'pornographic.' 'Pornography' denotes, among other things, a literary genre that needn't employ obscene language (such abstinence is crucial to the artistic effect of Musset's *Gamiani* and of Cleland's *Fanny Hill*) and it is a genre that can claim distinctive and impressive artistic achievements. Besides, as Berns himself notices, pornography is not only sexually arousing it is morally and politically tendentious. (Pornography is "kinetic" on both of Stephen Dedalus' criteria, which contrary to Stephen and the entire tradition going back to Kant and Schopenhauer, does not render its nature "improper" or unartistic.) It is no accident that the earliest examples of the genre take dialogue form, and it has been well observed that Sade may be read as a reply to Dante, *Fanny Hill* as a reply to *Pamela*. The genre itself makes a moral point, and as David Foxon has indicated, specific works have exposed the hypocrisy of society and the falsity of appearances, even as they have attacked romantic love, the family, the clergy, repressive morality and religion itself. No doubt this is precisely why some may wish to suppress them but it is one of our guiding principles, and a sound one, that these institutions, though they may be protected in various ways, are not to be immune from the effects of moral criticism and artistic interpretation. If our moral principles, or the institutions they embody, cannot survive this kind of criticism and awareness, then they should not survive. For in that case we are faced not with unacceptable injury, but with justifiable change.

Of course, all pornography and obscenity does not consititue an artistic achievement or amount to "the advocacy of an idea." It may have no "redeeming social importance." The Supreme Court has held that, when it does not, such speech and writing qualifies as legally obscene, and it is not afforded constitutional protection. The Supreme Court's attempt to devise legally manageable standards to distinguish what is ordinarily taken to be obscene from what is obscene in the legal sense has been woefully inadequate. And Justice Stewart's Augustinian admission that although he knows hard-core pornography when he sees it, he cannot define it, though ingratiating, does not provide a satisfactory guide to the law of the land. If the Court cannot devise adequate legal standards in this area, and it seems unlikely that it can, I believe that it ought to take the liberal course. Certainly the feeble arguments it offers for the view that obscene speech is not speech in the constitutional sense provide no serious obstacle to such a solution.

It does not follow from what I have urged that no concessions can be made to the section of the public that finds pornographic representations disgusting and offensive, and here I think that Richard Kuh in *Foolish Figleaves?* makes some sensible suggestions. Indeed, two of his proposed statutes are, I think, substantially acceptable on liberal principles and to Court opinion as well. For it is one thing to say that the publication or sale of obscene materials ought to be free and another to say that these materials may be forced upon people. In *Redrup v. New York* the Court indicates that it will not protect "an assault on individual privacy by a publication in a manner so offensive as to make it impossible for unwilling individuals to avoid exposure to it." The Court rests the argument on the proper ground, the invasion of privacy, and the control of public nuisances, insofar as the notion of a public nuisance is understood to require such an invasion of privacy, is perfectly acceptable. Such an approach would permit the prevention of "offensive public displays" of the kind that Kuh seeks to control. Times Square can go. It is possible, too, that some proper constitutional ground can be found for prohibiting sales to minors. In his statement rejecting the report of the Commission on Obscenity and Pornography, President Nixon suggested a return to the view that pornography must be denied to adults because leaving it free will have indirect effects on minors. But this approach is of dubious constitutionality *(Butler v. Michigan)* and despite the obscurities that attend the notion of obscenity we should be able to manage in the case of pornography the kind of prohibitions that we are able to manage, tolerably well, in the case of intoxicating liquors.

Kuh seems to feel less confident about his call for a third type of statute and I think that this lack of confidence is well merited. For he proposes a complete ban on nudity and obscenity in live performances and films—no experiments by the Netherlands Dance Theater, no *Flaming Creatures,* and no Lenny Bruce (whose moral psychology and phenomenology of shame seem to me far more penetrating and sweet-tempered than that of Berns). This extreme limitation on freedom, which I find unsupported by any clear showing of harm, and without any sound constitutional basis, is relaxed for the case of printed matter, on which I shall concentrate.

In the case of printed matter Kuh proposes that the intention "to exploit commercially a morbid interest" in sexual and other lurid detail shall constitute a criminal offense. What then, will be accomplished by punishing, not only public nuisances, but also any attempt to exploit pornography commercially? Because this part of Kuh's proposed statute imposes no restrictions on the private possession of pornography, or on sales to adults where those sales do not involve "commercial exploitation," the harm to be eliminated will be the increase in distribution accomplished by commercial exploitation, as opposed to that which would be achieved by—well, what? Orthodox capitalistic sales techniques? If, as a matter of constitutional right, pornographic materials may be bought and sold, it is difficult to see what constitutional principle permits the government to abridge this right where "commercial exploitation" is involved. Besides, to gain this advantage, it is necessary to become involved once again, not only in drawing the distinction between a "morbid" and a normal or healthy interest in sex, but also in making the distinction between "commercial exploitation" and normal or healthy sales techniques. All this raises, most acutely, difficulties about unconstitutional vagueness, and invites the most extreme exercise (and abuse) of discretion on the part of the criminal authorities. On balance, the advantage, dubious in itself, seems hardly worth the risks involved.

Of course, one may feel, as I expect that Berns does, that a central, perhaps that the most important, function of the criminal law is to express the community's judgment about various kinds of conduct and to condemn those it deplores. It would, therefore, be surprising if someone with principles like Berns' were willing to endorse Kuh's proposals in this area. For they acquiesce in the circulation of pornography among adults (if it is sold in a seemly fashion) and thereby, in addition to permitting a possibly fatal self-indulgence, fail to denounce the evil to which Berns and others object. They settle for an indirect and probably fruitless attempt to contain that evil and denounce, if they denounce anything at all, a mode of commerce to which the community does not, in general, take exception. Far from it.

I would confine myself to prohibiting public nuisances by law and hope that other institutions could raise the level of literary taste. Surely a liberal society is capable of distinguishing between art and trash (and, I should think, of seeing that this is not the distinction between *Mrs. Warren's Profession* and *Fanny Hill*). The circulation of pornography, even of hard-core pornography, does not undermine this distinction or anything else that is fundamental to our social arrangements. The same cannot be said for the interpretation of the First Amendment that Berns has been circulating for some years now. If widely accepted, it would constitute a far greater threat to the Republic than all the pornography now in print, here and in Denmark.

Suggestions for Further Reading

Anthologies

Ellmann, Richard and Feidelson, Jr., Charles (eds.). *The Modern Tradition: Backgrounds of Modern Literature.* New York: Oxford U.P., 1965. Although this hefty volume contains numerous selections from philosophers, it is particularly rich in selections from artists revealing the attitudes and ideas so influential in the development of modern art. The relationships of the artist to morality and to society constitute pervasive themes of this anthology.

Girvetz, Harry and Ross, Ralph (eds.). *Literature and the Arts: The Moral Issues.* Belmont, Calif.: Wadsworth, 1971. Selections by aestheticians, artists, and critics on such subjects as aestheticism, art and politics, art and sex, and art and alienation.

Hofstadter, Albert and Kuhns, Richard (eds.). *Philosophies of Art and Beauty.* Chicago: University of Chicago Press, 1976. A collection of lengthy selections from comprehensive and systematic philosophies of art and beauty ranging from Plato to Heidegger.

Kennick, W. E. (Ed.). *Art and Philosophy: Readings in Aesthetics,* 2nd ed. New York: St. Martin's, 1979. A new edition of a well-known anthology containing some of the most recent and influential writings in aesthetics.

Rader, Melvin (ed.). *A Modern Book of Esthetics,* 5th ed. New York: Holt, 1979. A recent American textbook in aesthetics with an unusually large and valuable bibliography. Particular attention is called to the bibliographic sections "Ecology and Environmental Design" and "Art and the Social Order."

Individual Works

Barrett, William. *Time of Need: Forms of Imagination in the Twentieth Century.* New York: Harper, 1972. A lucidly written study of contemporary art and Nihilism by an American philosopher strongly influenced by Martin Heidegger. Although painting and sculpture are discussed, the main emphasis falls on literature.

Beardsley, Monroe C. *Aesthetics.* New York: Harcourt, 1958. A clear, stimulating, and critical discussion of various subjects in the field of aesthetics. Chapter XII, "The Arts in the Life of Man," deals with such topics as art for art's sake and art and obscenity. The close of each chapter is followed by a large and annotated bibliography.

Bell, Clive. *Art.* New York: Capricorn, 1958. A famous and relatively recent statement of a nearly pure Aestheticist view of art as form and only form.

Dickie, George. *Aesthetics: An Introduction.* Indianapolis: Pegasus, 1971. A concise but informative introductory exposition of the history and problems of aesthetics written from the contemporary analytic point of view in philosophy. Particular attention is called to Chapter 11: "Art As a Social Institution."

Gotshalk, D. W. *Art and the Social Order,* 2nd ed. New York: Dover, 1962. A lively, easily read book, in which the author develops his own theory of art and emphasizes the relations of art and society. A good example of recent American philosophical thinking on the social context of art.

Holbrook, David (ed.). *The Case Against Pornography.* New York: Library P., 1973. A large collection of recent essays attacking pornography by philosophers, novelists, psychologists, literary critics, sociologists, psychiatrists, journalists, and others.

Hughes, Douglas A. (ed.). *Perspectives on Pornography.* New York: St. Martin's, 1970. A collection of recent pro and con essays on the artistic status of pornography and the desirability of censorship.

Maritain, Jacques. *The Responsibility of the Artist.* New York: Scribner's, 1960. A succinct discussion of the interrelations of the contemporary artist with morality and society by one of the outstanding Neo-Scholastic philosophers of the twentieth century. Maritain's reflections were nourished by an extensive knowledge of the various arts and personal acquaintance with individual artists.

Osborne, Harold. *Aesthetics and Art Theory: An Historical Introduction.* New York: Dutton Paperback Original, 1970. A philosophically informed account in nontechnical language of theories about the fine arts with particular emphasis on their social functions, purposes, and values from ancient Greece to the present. This richly illustrated book includes a discussion of Chinese and Indian aesthetic thought. The author is the editor of *The British Journal of Aesthetics.*

The Report of the Commission on Obscenity and Pornography. Introduction by Clive Barnes. New York: A New York Times Book, Bantam Books, 1970. (Hardback edition published by Random House.) The highly controversial report of the commission established by President Lyndon Baines Johnson. Also contains separate statements by the Commission members dissenting from the majority report.

Santayana, George. *Reason in Art.* (*The Life of Reason,* Vol. IV.) New York: Scribner's, 1933. A classic work on the role of art in human life and human life as an art by a great American philosopher and poet.

Tolstoy, Leo N. *What Is Art?* Translated by Almyer Maude. Indianapolis: Bobbs, The Library of Liberal Arts, 1960. A great artist's defense of the subordination of art to morality and religion.

Williams, Duncan. *Trousered Apes.* New Rochelle, N.Y.: Arlington, 1972. The author vigorously argues and copiously illustrates his thesis that modern literature assaults all those characteristics and standards distinguishing man from the animals.

Dictionary of the History of Ideas: Studies of Selected Pivotal Ideas. Philip P. Wiener, editor-in-chief. New York: Scribner's, 1973. Substantial and clearly written essays emphasizing the historical development of topics discussed in this part. Designed to inform the nonspecialist, each essay concludes with a select bibliography.

Encyclopedia of Philosophy. Paul Edwards, editor-in-chief. New York: Macmillan, 1967. The beginning student will find many worthwhile articles on the subjects treated in this part, and excellent bibliographies.

Epilogue

In 1918, Clarence Darrow delivered a high school commencement address remarkable for its brevity and Socratic wisdom. While waiting to speak, Darrow suffered through a verbose and preposterously flattering introduction depicting him as a perfect model whom young people should emulate. Finally the introductory speech came to an end, and Darrow ambled to the lectern, smiled, and gave probably one of the shortest commencement addresses ever given.

> That was as fine a lot of bunk as I ever heard in my life and I know darned well you youngsters didn't believe a word of it. You're no more fit to go forth and serve than the man in the moon. You're just a bunch of ignorant kids, full of the devil, and you've learned practically nothing to show for the years you spent here. You can't fool me, for I once spent four years in such a place.

If, after reading this book and reflecting on what he has read, the student now knows he is ignorant, he will be a true friend of Socrates.